Ride the Rai

with Rail Pass D and experience Thrill of a Lifetime

Rail Pass Direct - your one stop shop for Australian Rail Passes

- The Austrail Pass allows you either 14, 21 or 30 consecutive days of travel on the main rail network, giving you the freedom to explore Australia at your own pace.
- Austrail Flexipass - is a more versatile option and allows you to travel any 8, 15, 22 or 29 days on the main Rail Australia network within any 6-month period.

For more information call us on

01733 502808

or email:railpassdirect@thomascook.com

Rail Pass Direct specialises in the sale of rail passes only and no other form of rail tickets. ABTA No.20606

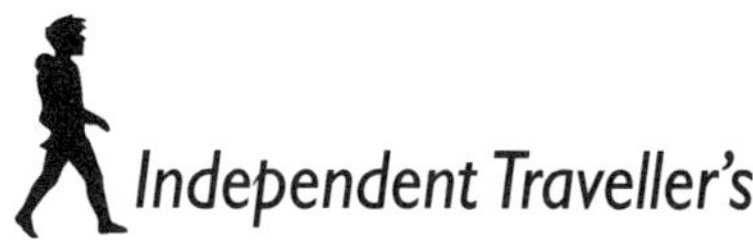

AUSTRALIA 2000

Other titles in this series include:

Independent Traveller's Europe 2000
The Inter-Railer's and Eurailer's Guide

Independent Traveller's USA 2000
The Budget Travel Guide

Independent Traveller's New Zealand 2000
The Budget Travel Guide

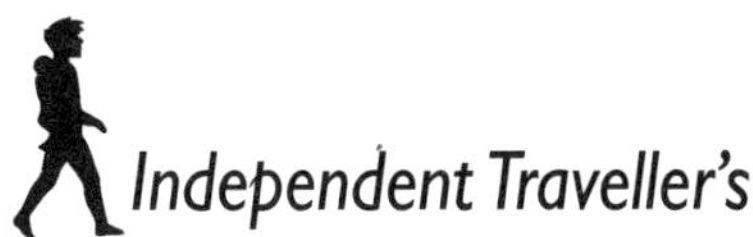

AUSTRALIA 2000

THE BUDGET TRAVEL GUIDE

Gareth Powell

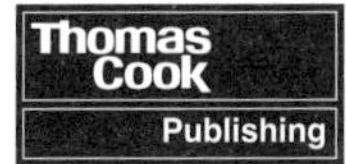

Published by Thomas Cook Publishing
The Thomas Cook Group Ltd
PO Box 227
Thorpe Wood
Peterborough PE3 6PU
United Kingdom

Telephone: 01733 503571
email: books@thomascook.com

ISBN 1 900341 72 7

Publisher: Stephen York
Commissioning Editor: Deborah Parker
Map Editor: Bernard Horton
Text Design: Tina West

Cover Design by Pumpkin House
Copy-editors: Katy Carter, Karen Kemp
Proofreader: Linda Bass
Maps supplied by: Polly Senior Cartography

Text typeset in Book Antiqua and Gill Sans using QuarkXPress
Layout and imagesetting:
PDQ Reprographics, Bungay
Printed in Spain by GraphyCems, Navarra

Written and researched by:
Gareth Powell

Transport Information:
Peter Bass, Assistant Editor,
Thomas Cook Overseas Timetable

Book Editor:
Caroline Ball

The Author

Gareth Powell was born in Wales and started his career working in circuses. After a spell in the regular British army he moved into journalism and publishing. In England he started Mayflower Books and was the publisher of *Fanny Hill* which resulted in a charge under the Obscene Publication Act. He emigrated to Australia where he started, among other magazines, *Pol.* In Hong Kong he started **Discovery** for Cathay Pacific which he published for ten years.

He is the author of several books including *The Practical Traveller, My Friend Arnold's Guide to Personal Computers, My Friend Arnold's Guide to Camcorders* (all Allen and Unwin), *The Book of Fax* (Philips) and *Touring Australia* and *Signpost New Zealand* (Thomas Cook) He has been a journalist most of his working life and is currently associated with an Asian daily newspaper as well as being a columnist for several magazines.

Gareth Powell has a house in Sussex and in Sydney and spends much of his time travelling. Either in aircraft and by train or electronically on the Internet.

Gareth would like to thank Tom,'who taught me much about Australia'.

Photographs

The following are thanked for supplying the photographs (and who hold the copyright):

Colour section p. 32–33 (i) & (ii) Ethel Davies (iii) Elizabeth Ryder (iv) Blue Mountains: Elizabeth Ryder; Skiing: Tourism NSW

pp. 128–129 all Ethel Davies except (iv) Hervey Bay: Bruce Postle.

pp. 224–225 all Ethel Davies except (ii) Snorkelling: Tourism office, Tourism Queensland, (iv) Sealion, south Australian.

pp. 320–321 all Ethel Davies except (i)Wolf Creek, Photo index Photo Library (ii) Olgas & Uluru: David Hancock. (iiii) Rick Eaves.

Thomas Cook Publishing wishes to thank Sue Neales for additional picture research.

Help improve this guide

This guide will be updated each year. The information given in it may change during the lifetime of this edition and we would welcome reports and comments from our readers. Similarly we want to make this guide as practical and useful as possible and are grateful for any comments, criticisms and suggestions for improving future editions.

A free copy of this guide will be sent to all readers whose information or ideas are incorporated in the next edition. Please send all contributions to the Editor, Independent Traveller's Australia, Thomas Cook Publishing at: PO Box 227, Thorpe Wood, Peterborough, PE3 6PU, UK, or email books@thomascook.com

CONTENTS

GENERAL INFORMATION

ROUTES & CITIES

Routes are shown in one direction only but can, of course, be travelled in the opposite direction. See pp.14–15 for a diagrammatical presentation of the routes.

REFERENCE SECTION

The price of getting to Australia has dropped dramatically over the past few years, so that you no longer have to take out a mortgage on your house to be able to afford to visit. But, yes, it is a long way away, and from Europe you will be enjoying – if that is the right word – some of the longest flights in the world. Is it worth it? Certainly. That is why visitors keep coming back again and again.

This book is not a comprehensive guide to Australia. It is a guide to Australia for 'soft backpackers' - that is, travellers who would like to see as much of the country as cheaply as possible – but still with some style and comfort.

When talking to travellers, however long they have been exploring the country, you find that there are parts of Australia that none of them – not one – has ever seen. But neither is any one of them dismayed at the fact. There is only so much of Australia that the traveller can see at one time, and you have to be selective. And so is this book. Thus, Fraser Island is in because almost every traveller coming to Australia is hell-bent on visiting that magical island. On the other hand, you will find little about Lithgow or Wangaratta or a hundred other towns because, in the main, the traveller goes through without stopping or bypasses these places.

From looking at the destinations provided by Greyhound Pioneer and McCafferty's, and from my own travelling experience, the following routes seem to be the most popular:

Sydney – Brisbane (including Newcastle, Coffs Harbour, Byron Bay, Surfer's Paradise)
Brisbane – Cairns (including Fraser Island, Airlie Beach, Magnetic Island, Barrier Reef)
Cairns – Alice Springs via Townsville and Tennants Creek (Including Uluru)
Alice Springs – Darwin via Tennants Creek (including Katherine, Kakadu tours)
Alice Springs – Adelaide
Adelaide – Melbourne via the Great Ocean Road (including Apollo Bay)

ROUTE DETAIL

Once out of Sydney the freeway climbs Mt Colah and Mt Ku-Ring-Gai, past Bobbin Head and Berowra and through Cowan, then drops down to cross the Hawkesbury River at Mooney Mooney. The road then climbs out of the valley with Brisbane Water on the right and continues to the turn-off for Gosford (85 km). Beyond Gosford; Hwy 1 takes the inland route to Newcastle (156 km from Sydney).

ROAD DETAILS
Route details and approximate cumulative mileages given.

PRICES

The price indications given below have been used througout this book. Please bear in mind that prices do fluctuate – these symbols have been given for guidance. Occasionally we do mention accommodation, food and highlights that are very expensive (shown $$$$+) but these are included in this budget guide if the attraction is an unmissable one or in case you want to splash out on a special treat.

Accommodation

$	=	under $30
$$	=	$30–50
$$$	=	$50–80
$$$$	=	over $80

Based on standard double room, no meals but including all taxes.

Food

$	=	under $7
$$	=	$7–12
$$$	=	$12–20
$$$$	=	over $20

Based on the price of a mid-range main course.

Highlights

If an admission charge is made:

$	=	under $6
$$	=	$6–$12
$$$	=	over $12

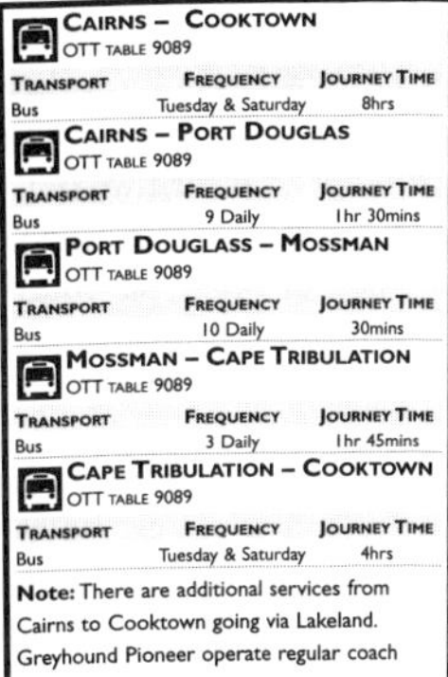

CAIRNS – COOKTOWN
OTT TABLE 9089

TRANSPORT	FREQUENCY	JOURNEY TIME
Bus	Tuesday & Saturday	8hrs

CAIRNS – PORT DOUGLAS
OTT TABLE 9089

TRANSPORT	FREQUENCY	JOURNEY TIME
Bus	9 Daily	1hr 30mins

PORT DOUGLASS – MOSSMAN
OTT TABLE 9089

TRANSPORT	FREQUENCY	JOURNEY TIME
Bus	10 Daily	30mins

MOSSMAN – CAPE TRIBULATION
OTT TABLE 9089

TRANSPORT	FREQUENCY	JOURNEY TIME
Bus	3 Daily	1hr 45mins

CAPE TRIBULATION – COOKTOWN
OTT TABLE 9089

TRANSPORT	FREQUENCY	JOURNEY TIME
Bus	Tuesday & Saturday	4hrs

Note: There are additional services from Cairns to Cooktown going via Lakeland. Greyhound Pioneer operate regular coach

PUBLIC TRANSPORT DETAILS

Mode of travel, journey time, frequency of service and *OTT* table numbers are given.

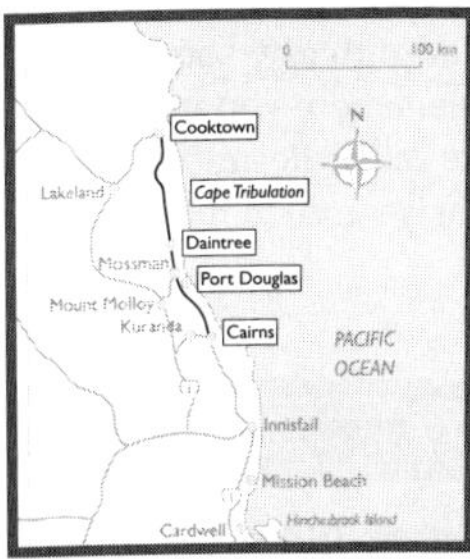

KEY TO ICONS

- Rail
- Bus
- Car
- Ferry Services
- Information
- Accommodation
- Food

Melbourne – Sydney via Canberra
Adelaide – Perth (including Albany)
Darwin – Perth (including Monkey Mia, Broome, Carnarvon)
Tasmania.

Even those driving around Australia - as opposed to taking a bus - seem to stick to the basic bus routes that backpackers follow. There are stops and areas on these bus routes that may not be interesting to everyone. For example, towns such as Gympie, Childers and Bowen on the east coast are just fruit-picking towns and would not interest anyone who isn't on a working holiday.

TRAVELLING ON A BUDGET

Australia loves travellers on a budget. You could even say Australia adores them: it is almost as if the whole country was set up specially for those happy wanderers who need to watch their pennies. There are three main reasons for this.

Australia has a long and honoured tradition of people travelling light. In the early days they were called — and in some places they still are — swaggies. That is because they carried their baggage in a blanket roll across their shoulders and this was called the swag (possibly derived from thief's cant in England). These swaggies were not tramps in the English tradition. They were itinerant workers, with perhaps the nearest equivalent being a hobo in the United States. They travelled from town to town following seasonal work. They were utterly independent and the relationship with the boss was ever a meeting of equals. If the boss wanted to fire a swaggie — downsize in the modern parlance — the phrase, 'It's a nice day for travelling, but', would be used and there would be little embarrassment on either side. (That 'but' on the end means nothing. It is a sort of sentence ending. Strangely enough you also find it in Canada.) So the tradition of travelling light and inexpensively is an old and honourable one.

WEBWISE
When collecting information on Australia, you may want to bypass the tourist offices unless you can conveniently call in, and go straight to the huge amount of facts and advice on the Internet.

Then there is the odd circumstance of the country pub. In Australia the word pub means both a bar – quality varying wildly – and hotel. It was the law in Australia for nearly a century that every pub had to offer inexpensive accommodation. Would you want to stay there? Probably not, unless you like the idea of being serenaded to sleep by slightly tipsy Crocodile Dundees each blessed with a tin ear and brass lungs. But that idea of inexpensive accommodation in every town has been passed down directly to the motels of Australia. They are one of the glories of the country.

Another strand that makes Australia so attractive for the money-wise (that sounds so much better than budget) traveller is that a few years ago the country suddenly found that it could make money out of the intelligent traveller working within a tight budget. Indeed, it is one of the major sources of tourist revenue. The backpacking boom in Australia has been something to watch over the past ten years. Suddenly every state government and many business people realised that here was a seriously viable business. In the beginning there were, admittedly, some rough edges. There were backpacker hostels in Sydney, for example, where you would not house your dog. But competition and some legislation drove the undesirables out of the business. Now backpacker hostels are very, very inexpensive and, in many cases, more than acceptable to the soft backpacker.

WHEN TO GO

Whatever budget you are travelling on, there is one firm rule – try to avoid travelling to Australia over Christmas, the New Year, the whole of January and much of February, unless you will be staying with relatives and the accommodation is free. And even then it might not be such a good idea.

The main school holidays in Australia are in January and most Australians think that it is a great idea to let Christmas slide into the New Year and then have their annual holiday in January. Universities stay out an extra month. This is also the hottest part of the year, which can make some places pretty uncomfortable.

Plainly there are still lots of Australians left in, say, Sydney, but many hotel and motel rooms around the country will be fully booked with holidaying Australians and, as always in times of scarcity, prices go up. From Christmas to 1 February it can be totally impossible to find accommodation at the last moment. Anyone, for example, who would like to spend that period in Lorne in Victoria had better start thinking a year ahead. At any other time of the year, with minor exceptions, you will never have any problems booking accommodation as you go.

HOW TO USE THIS BOOK

Independent Traveller's Australia provides you with expert advice and details on 60 different routes, regions, towns and cities, each in its own chapter. Reflecting the tremendous variety of the country, as well as its almost daunting size, these chapters vary in their approach, each featuring the best way to see and enjoy that part of the country.

Because Sydney is the most popular arrival point, that is where this book also starts. It then journeys south to explore the cities and countryside of New South Wales, ACT, South Australia and Victoria before embarking on the long route up the coast to Brisbane and Queensland. A further route sets off inland for Alice Springs and Uluru (Ayers Rock). Perth, the main city on the west coast, is the starting point for discovering the vastness of Western Australia, with routes south to dairy country and the national parks of the south-west coast, and inland to Kalgoorlie and the goldfields. Another major route takes you north towards the Great Sandy Desert, beyond which lie Broome, Darwin and the true outback.

Each chapter is accompanied by a map, showing the route or city and the stops described in the text. For driving routes the exact route is detailed, town by town, with stopovers and the most important attractions, together with price ranges, opening hours and other details. Cities or attractions which are worth longer stops each include detailed information on how to get there and get around, and how to make the most of your time. All chapters give suggestions for budget-friendly lodgings and places to eat, as well as how to find local entertainment highlights. Throughout the book you will see notes and tips in the margins. These provide added information, suggest places to stop en route or day trips from the main destination, tell you about interesting facts, or recommend an onward route connecting this with other chapters.

Melville Island
DARWIN
0
500 km
N
Jabiru
340
Katherine
Mataranka
Wyndham
405
Daly Waters
340
Newcastle Waters
Derby
Broome
Halls Creek
NORTHERN TERRITORY
Margaret River
405
Tennant Creek
Port Hedland
Dampier
313
Newman
405
Alice Springs
Mount Olga
Ayers Rock
Carnarvon
Shark Bay
WESTERN AUSTRALIA
407
SOUTH AUSTRALIA
Geraldton
Kalgoorlie
Coolgardie
407
PERTH
Northam
Fremantle
381
Bunbury
Esperance
Pemberton
381
Albany
AUSTRALIA ROUTES
149 page number
INDIAN OCEAN

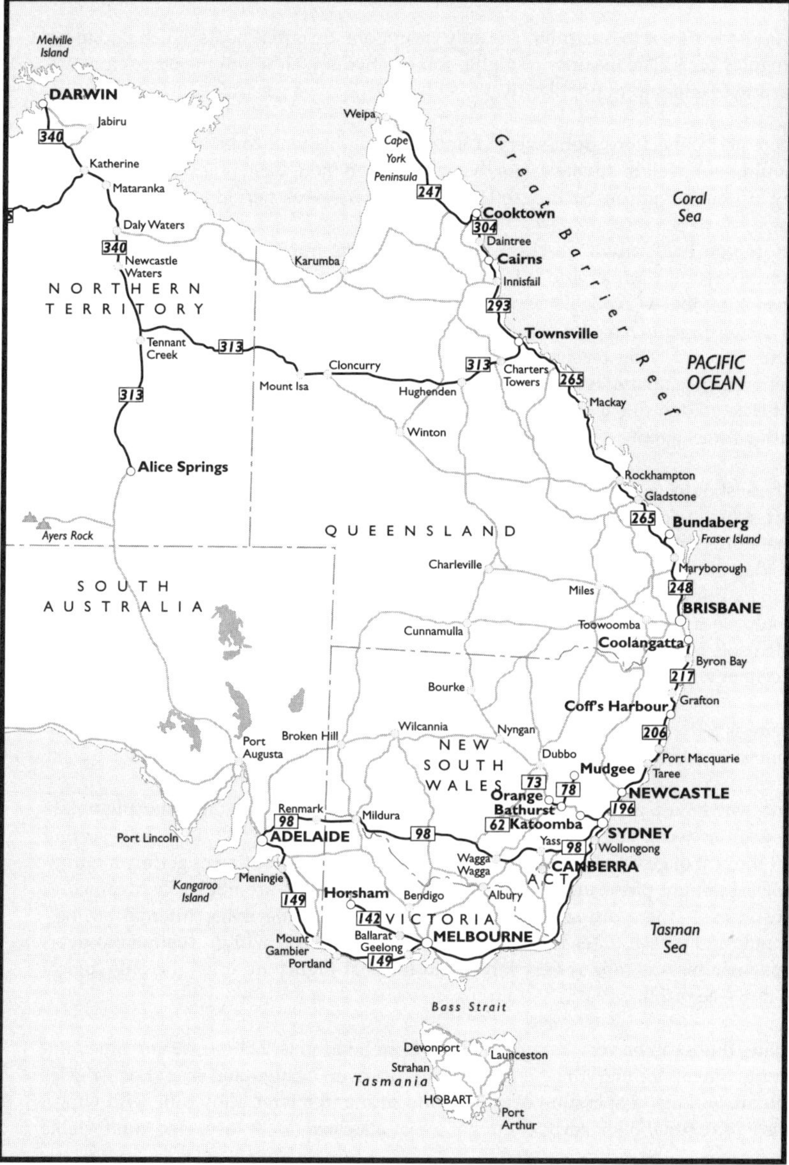
Melville Island
DARWIN
Jabiru
340
Katherine
Mataranka
Daly Waters
340
Newcastle Waters
NORTHERN TERRITORY
Tennant Creek
313
313
Alice Springs
Ayers Rock
SOUTH AUSTRALIA
Weipa
Cape York Peninsula
247
Cooktown
304
Daintree
Cairns
Innisfail
293
Townsville
Great Barrier Reef
Coral Sea
PACIFIC OCEAN
Karumba
Mount Isa
Cloncurry
313
Hughenden
Charters Towers
265
Mackay
Winton
Rockhampton
Gladstone
265
Bundaberg
Fraser Island
Maryborough
248
BRISBANE
QUEENSLAND
Charleville
Miles
Toowoomba
Cunnamulla
Coolangatta
Byron Bay
217
Grafton
Bourke
Coff's Harbour
206
Port Macquarie
Taree
Wilcannia
Nyngan
Broken Hill
Port Augusta
NEW SOUTH WALES
Dubbo
Mudgee
73
78
Orange
Bathurst
NEWCASTLE
196
62
Katoomba
SYDNEY
Renmark
98
Mildura
98
ADELAIDE
Port Lincoln
Yass
98
Wollongong
Wagga Wagga
CANBERRA
ACT
Kangaroo Island
Meningie
149
Horsham
Bendigo
Albury
142
VICTORIA
MELBOURNE
Ballarat
Geelong
Mount Gambier
Portland
149
Tasman Sea
Bass Strait
Devonport
Launceston
Strahan
Tasmania
HOBART
Port Arthur

Reaching Australia

Everybody flies into Australia. The only exceptions are cruise boats which pop in on a regular basis. The majority of flights come to Sydney, although the other cities are starting to edge up in popularity.

There are connections from every country, but flights tend to be very full and you should book well in advance. (As this was written there were no economy seats on any airline flying from Sydney to London for a two-week period.)

Before you book anything, check the Internet. The number of special bargains is almost beyond number and it is impossible for your normal travel agent to know everything that is available, especially as the situation changes almost from day to day. A few agents have 'sweetheart' deals with specific airlines which give them an extra discount. That means the agent will perhaps steer you towards an arrangement which is not necessarily the best available. On the Internet, you can check it all out. The golden rule is to be fairly sure what you want before you start negotiating with a travel agent.

Where should you start? An Australian site, **www.travel.com.au**, contains a database which is constantly being updated and shows what is available ex-Australia. These prices may not be available from your starting point, but the site will give you an idea of the range of options and which airlines offer the best bargains. You can then look at what is being offered in your country. In Britain the way to go about that would be to use either Teletext or the Internet; in the United States, the Internet. Microsoft Network's Expedia site is becoming extremely useful and it is another excellent way of checking prices.

There is a departure tax on international flights but this is included in the cost of your airline ticket and taken care of by your travel agent.

Once you have a grasp of the prices you may find that if you change your flight date by just one week you can often save a quarter of the airfare. While you are sorting out the cost of getting there and back, look carefully at the option of getting a round-Australia flight pass built into the ticket. Typically, these are not easily obtained in Australia – there are some exceptions – but both the major internal airlines, Qantas and Ansett, offer multiple-flight tickets for travel within Australia to overseas visitors. Australia is very large, and internal flights are often the only logical option (see p. 22).

Flying times can be very long. To Sydney from London is 22 hours flying time minimum. Singapore to Sydney is something just over 7 hours and from Los Angeles you are looking at spending over 13 hours sitting in a large alloy tube with wings. It is a long time. Book early, try to get a seat allocated, wear loose and comfortable

KEEPING THE COSTS DOWN

The cost of travelling breaks down into three areas: those totally outside your control, those you can partly control and those where you make decisions.

Costs outside your control include, for example, flying around Australia. Although there are different categories of fares they are fixed.

Costs you can partly control include those incurred in hotels. The published rate for a room, called the rack rate in the trade, is the opening stage in the bargaining process. Unless the hotel is booked solid, rack rates can normally be negotiated. They are discounted as a matter of course for corporate accounts, tour packagers and members of certain travel clubs.

The same applies to hire car rates. There is a fixed basic rate and then a raft of special offers floating somewhere below. Getting those discounts may only require that you be a member of a frequent flyer club.

You will often find that costs included in a package beat anything you can arrange yourself. A good example is flight stopovers. Many airlines offer a deal with a hotel room thrown in for a few nights. There is no way you could match that price by booking each part separately.

Costs you can completely control. There are very few cities in Australia where any form of locomotion can beat walking. In Sydney, for example, walking is often faster than any other means of getting around. Plan all your activities so that you can walk to where you want to go. It is healthy, you meet a better class of person, and you save a lot of money. Your only investment will be a small map which you get at the tourist information office whenever you arrive at a destination. Mostly these maps are free.

If you cannot walk to your destination, because of distance or weather, use public transport.

Do not make interstate or international telephone calls from a motel or hotel telephone until you have ascertained the charges.

clothes, take two books you have been dying to read and the time will pass.

If you are travelling from Europe, try to build in a stopover on the way out. A 25-hour flight is no way to set you up to enjoy your holiday in Australia. (Strangely the reverse does not seem to apply. When people get home they manage to adjust back to the old, familiar timetable very quickly.) From Europe the possibilities of a stopover are many, with Thailand, Malaysia, Singapore and Hong Kong making the front running. Of those, Thailand is by far the cheapest, and a good choice for your outward stopover if you are travelling on a budget.

Most airports have trolleys, which are free of charge for inbound flights, but there is a small hire charge for outbound passengers. Airport porters are alleged to exist. This may well be the case, but they are an endangered species and possibly only nocturnal; I have never seen one.

PAINLESS AIR TRAVEL One way of making your travel easier is to use a series of checklists to make sure you have covered the essentials.

● *Which airline are you flying with and where is it going?*
This is more important than you might imagine. Airlines have a cosy arrangement called code share. You are flying, say, to Sydney and you are booked on Virgin. The problem is that, no matter what the ticket says, Virgin does not, as yet, fly to Sydney. What it does is code share with Malaysian Airlines System. There is nothing at all wrong with MAS, but it is a little disconcerting if your ticket says Virgin, the flight code is Virgin and yet you find yourself on an MAS aircraft. This is an example you could live with, but some of the other code-sharing arrangements are between very disparate airlines. There are some airlines one would not wish to fly with even at half price.

So before you finally make the booking cross-examine the agent to make sure that you will actually fly with the airline that you are supposed to be booked on, or at least an acceptable substitute.

● *Are there any stops?*
If you are flying a long distance you certainly do not want to be hanging around airports more than you need. Nothing is more irritating than thinking you are going directly to Sydney only to find you are going to Melbourne first. There you will spend well over an hour in a waiting room at Melbourne airport when you have better things to do with your life.

Airlines, for obvious reasons, do not make much of the fact that a flight is not direct. They do not advertise it in large letters. You need to check carefully. Watch out for anything that is called a technical stop. This is precisely the same as a normal stop in that it extends your journey by at least an hour. The airlines believe that because no passengers are getting on and off the technical stop makes little difference. It does – to the passenger. An hour added to your journey on the homeward run stretches into infinity.

● *Can you rearrange the trip to be cheaper/more convenient/more desirable?*
It is tempting to take the first itinerary or fare offered. It is more intelligent to shop around or change your itinerary to take advantage of reduced-fare offers. The Internet is superb in helping you do this. You can spend a happy hour juggling around possibilities to see which is the best mix of convenience and low cost.

● *Can seats on the aircraft be booked ahead?*
Some of us prefer an aisle seat, some a seat by the window. Getting that sorted out before you even get to the airport is a great relief.

● *Have you let the carrier know your meal requests?*
Meal requests are useful. I, for example, am a flying vegetarian, because experience has shown that on some airlines vegetarian meals are fresher and better presented than normal meals.

● *Is your passport up to date?*
Airlines will not carry you unless your passport is valid, because in most countries, by law, they then have to fly you back at their own expense. To avoid a last-minute panic, allow plenty of time to send off for a new passport if necessary – holiday times, computer glitches and work-to-rule by passport office staff are causes of delay.

● *Do you have enough nostrums and medicaments to keep you healthy on your travels?*
Injections and vaccinations are not needed for travel to Australia. Medicines are not universally the same, so if you are taking any prescription medicines, try to take enough for the whole of your trip. Take the prescription along in case.

● *A final travel checklist*
About three days before you leave, do a final check

- Money – small cash, some travellers' cheques
- Tickets
- Credit cards in credit
- Confirm bookings
- Check suitcase is not broken
- Clothes clean and ready to pack
- Sufficient film for camera and check all batteries.

When travelling, at every port of call, at every check-in and check-out, I recite a magic mantra: 'pamcam'. It is not Sanskrit. It is an acronym for 'passport, airline tickets, money, credit cards, address book and medicines'. Keep getting 'pamcam' right and you will have no problems.

ENTRY FORMALITIES Most visitors need a visa but in some cases this is an automatic extension of the airline ticket and not a major problem. A visa will normally allow you to stay for a maximum of six months in any one 12-month period. You cannot work or take up formal study but you can take up non-formal study for up to three months.

INSURANCE

You can insure against almost any mishap that can happen on your travels — including loss of cash up to $500. Travel insurance should include provision for cancelled or delayed flights and weather problems, as well as immediate evacuation home in the case of medical emergency. If you are ill in Australia you will have the very best of medical care, but it can be expensive if your holiday is disrupted and you need special treatment. The only way to get over that worry is to have medical cover. Thomas Cook and other travel agencies offer comprehensive policies. Insurance for drivers is covered in more detail under Travelling by Car, p. 24.

Temporary working visas can usually be obtained by people sponsored by companies or an employer in Australia. There is also a youth employment visa which allows those who are students and under 25 to work during a long stay.

Permanent entry is very difficult. You need to be sponsored as a spouse, fiancé(e) or dependent child. It is worked on a points system and the Department of Immigration takes a fairly firm line on the subject.

Vaccinations are not required unless you have come from or visited a yellow fever infected country or zone within six days prior to arrival, which is unlikely. No other health certificates are needed to enter Australia.

You can tell people until you are blue in the face how big Australia is, and they still do not believe you. They ask if they can go on an afternoon's trip to Ayers Rock from Sydney. They decide it would be a good idea to drive across the whole country to Perth. They take the bus from Darwin to Cairns to catch a flight and wonder why they walk funnily for days afterwards.

This is a big country. It is as big as the continental United States minus Alaska, and 50 per cent bigger than Europe without counting the old USSR. She's a beaut country, as they say, but she is a hell of a size. To give you some exact figures: from the most northerly point, Cape York, to Wilson's Promontory in Victoria is 3,690 km. Measured from east to west, Australia is somewhere around 4,000 km.

Australia is also very empty. Sydney to Perth is roughly the distance from Finland to Greece, and there is not an awful lot in between. In fact, the only towns you pass through worth seriously talking about are Broken Hill and Port Augusta – unless you are willing to think of Iron Knob as an important destination. There are 4,768 towns which are gazetted in Australia. But by applying a 'sacred and profane test' – that is, if a town does not have a church and a pub and, say, 500 people, it does not count – there are fewer than 850 towns in the whole of Australia. The most densely populated states – New South Wales, Victoria, Queensland, Tasmania and the Australian Capital Territory (ACT) – cover not much more than one-third (36 per cent) of the land area, but have over 80 per cent of the population. The only two cities in Australia that even know what a traffic jam is are Melbourne and Sydney. Traffic jams do not exist elsewhere.

Getting from one place to another therefore requires some thought. If you have all the time in the world, the easiest way to see a lot of the country is to buy or hire a car and drive everywhere. Some of the drives will be long and boring, but petrol is relatively inexpensive and you can set your own timetable.

Without the luxury of limitless time, the best bet for seeing the most of Australia is to hire cars from the second echelon firms (see below) on an as-needed basis, and to use either the internal airlines or the buses to connect the major destinations. That way you have the best of both worlds. The easiest way to operate is to let someone else – a pilot or a bus driver – do the driving while you sit back and have a snooze.

TRAVELLING BY AIR

No matter what decision you make about how to get around the country, it is worth noting that for Australians flying is the only way to go between cities if any distance is involved, and in Australia that is almost every time. An amazing 80 per cent of

TIME ZONES

There are three time zones in Australia:

Eastern Standard Time (for which the acronym used by the government is, confusingly, WEST). This covers New South Wales, Australian Capital Territory, Victoria, Tasmania and Queensland.

Central Standard Time (unromantically called CYST). This covers South Australia and Northern Territory.

WAST covers Western Australia.

This all becomes confused in the summer months because the Northern Territory, Western Australia and Queensland have opted not to have daylight saving, so the time differentials between the areas vary with the time of the year.

long-distance trips by public transport are made by air with either Qantas, Ansett or one of the feeder airlines.

You can fly almost anywhere within Australia, not just between the major cities but out to Uluru (Ayers Rock) and even to the Great Barrier Reef. Flights connecting small country towns tend to be expensive because they serve a captive market. Often, it can work out cheaper to fly to the nearest large town and pick up a car. To reach Byron Bay, for example, it is possible to fly Air NSW from Sydney up to nearby Casino or Ballina. This is very costly. Much less expensive is to fly that bit further, to the Gold Coast airport at Coolangatta, and then hire a car to drive back through Tweed Heads and over the border between Queensland and New South Wales to Byron Bay.

AIRLINE PASSES

Airline passes are not great bargains. They are not sold on any major basis by either Qantas or Ansett who, bluntly, do not want to discuss them. Ansett has the Kangaroo Air Pass which allows you 6000 km with a minimum of two stop-overs and a maximum of three stop-overs for $A949 with large amount of restrictions on where you can use them.

However, you may do better using specials and holiday packages and whatever. The Qantas Boomerang Pass (originality was never a feature of airline marketing departments) is a book of flight coupons with a minimum of two and a maximum of eight. These must be purchased outside Australia and for shorter flights. It is about $250 and for longer flights nearly double that. Again, restrictions apply. Ansett also has the G'Day Australia and Qantas the Discover Australia Pass both of which you can get in Australia gives you roughly a 25 percent discount on any domestic flight although you have to show your international flight ticket. Is it worth it? Nothing there to make a great fuss over. The point is that Qantas and Ansett have the place sewn up and you are simply not going to get any decent deals because there is no competition. The best bet is to get a Qantas Discover Australia Pass when you get to Australia and then see whether there is any way to can top that discount with a stand-by ticket, a student's ticket or whatever.

TRAVELLING BY BUS AND RAIL

Within cities, most public transport is fine. Melbourne has its trams. Sydney has an excellent bus system interconnecting with the ferries and the railways. Most of them run pretty much on time. In Sydney, for example, the figure for buses being on time is around 97 per cent and for ferries it is better than 98 per cent. Almost every city in Australia has an Explorer bus that follows a circular route: visitors can get on and off as they wish at points of interest.

The rail system connecting the cities of Australia, however, is fairly awful. It cannot be recommended as the best way of travelling from one place to another, even if you are on the most desperately tight of budgets, as trains can be quite an expensive way to travel. They may start off clean but no attempt appears to be made to clean them and they arrive at their destinations like travelling garbage heaps. They tend to be crowded with pensioners taking advantage of concessionary travel. One simple solution would be to ban all concessionary travel for pensioners. It would be a brave government that tried to do that in Australia.

Rail and bus passes

If you do decide to travel by train, rail passes are available. The Ausrail Pass allows unlimited economy-class travel over 14, 21 or 30 consecutive days. Prices range from £235 to £370, with 7-day extensions available at £125. The Ausrail Flexipass allows economy-class travel over 15, 21 or 29 days within a 6-month period. An 8-day pass is available, but it isn't valid on all routes. These must be purchased before travelling to Australia, and are not available to Australian residents; in the UK they are available through Rail Pass Direct; tel: 01733 503596. Other passes allow travel on more restricted areas of the rail network. Westrail's Southern Pass allows 28 days of travel on Westrail (tel: 8 9326 2244) trains and buses south of Perth and Kalgoorlie for $119. The Sunshine Rail pass offered by Queensland Rail (tel: 61 7 3235 2222) has options for 14, 21 or 30 days' travel and ranges in price from $267 to $388 for economy-class travel. The Road Rail pass from Queensland Rail is valid on long-distance Traveltrain services and McCafferty's Express Coach Services througout Queensland; 10 days for $269, 20 days for $349.

Greyhound Pioneer offer a wide range of bus passes. For information, tel: 7 3258 1600, fax: 7 3258 1910, www.greyhound.com.au, or email your request to passinfo@greyhound.com.au. Discounts are given to students and seniors. Their passes can be purchased in Australia as well as before you arrive. The Aussie Kilometric pass allows travel by distance, in blocks of 1000 km, from 2000 km to 20,000 km. Prices start at $215 for 2000 km. The Aussie Day Pass for 7, 10, 15 (valid over 30 days) or 21 days travel (valid over 90 days) on the Greyhound Pioneer network. McCafferty's Express coaches Day Passes (which can only be purchased outside Australia) allow between 7 and 90 days worth of travel, with prices ranging from $495 to $2445. Discounts are offered to students and seniors, and McCafferty's Travel Australia passes cover pre-determined routes with unlimited stops. For details tel: 61 7 4690 9809; fax: 61 7 4638 3815; www.mccaffertys.com.au or email: infomcc@mccaffertys.com.au.

Coaches or long-distance buses – which are less expensive than the train and widely available – are by far the better option. But a long bus journey is only for the young. If you are past the age when you find nine hours bus travel exciting, then explore flying to your destinations or break the journey up into easy sections.

One of the most popular routes for tourists, for example, is Sydney to Cairns. It's a long way (nearly 3,000 km), and the bus journey takes 46 hours. But a bus pass which allows unlimited stops, enabling you to do the journey in several short hops, will give you the opportunity to spend time at places on the way up. The bus companies offer a variety of special fares and passes such as Apex and Aussie Pass. One with a validity of three months with unlimited stops would cost under $200 if you are a member of the YHA or some similar organisation.

HIKING

Hiking - bushwalking - is a wonderful way to see the countryside and is perfectly safe, providing you follow some basic rules. The biggest danger comes not from getting lost, but from fire. The best way to be safe is to avoid dense scrub and heavy vegetation during periods of high bushfire danger. Observe all fire bans religiously. Every park has indicators at the entrance and they are also to be seen along most main roads. Warnings are also given in newspapers and on the radio. When the indicator tells you that there is high or extreme fire risk, consider some other activity. If you are in a car and you get caught in a bush fire, the most sensible thing to do is to wind up all the windows and stay there until the fire passes. Petrol tanks rarely explode.

When walking in the bush, dress correctly. You may think that shorts would be cooler, but lightweight, full-length trousers will protect you from bites and scratches. You need solid footwear - not thongs and sandals - and you should wear a shirt with long sleeves that can be rolled down when needed.

If you are not an experienced bushwalker stick to the trails and marked paths. The National Parks and Wildlife Service has laid out an immense network of trails covering every national park in Australia and you will never be bored. And if you stick to the paths, you will never be lost.

HITCH-HIKING

Do not even think of doing it. In all parts of the world this is a most dangerous way of getting around, and Australia is no exception. No matter what your sex and no matter what your belief in your invulnerability, you are putting yourself at serious risk hitch-hiking. The converse holds true — never pick up hitch-hikers on the road.

TRAVELLING BY CAR

Australians always harp on about the need for a serious new road-building programme. In the main this is clever PR by the road hauliers who have managed to get the government to abandon the railways so that most freight goes by road. Having achieved that, they start another campaign to say that the roads are not good enough for the traffic they carry.

Almost any visitor over 21 can drive in Australia on his or her own national driver's licence for the same class of vehicle. You are told that you must carry your licence and your passport when driving, but the police are not stuffy about the last provided you have sufficient identification. On the Internet there are several sites offering an International Driver's Permit for a silly amount of money. Do not be conned. They are not accepted in Australia as being sufficient and as you still need an ordinary licence there is not much point.

HIRING A CAR

The big operators such as Hertz and Avis are present at every airport of any size in Australia. Second-echelon hire car companies exist in every big city but never have offices at the airport. This requires some explanation.

Business travellers come off the aircraft, walk up with their folding suit bag over their arm and ask for their pre-booked car. Within minutes, they are handed an envelope with the keys to the car and the insurance documentation and are directed out to the car park where a clean, new, air-conditioned saloon with automatic gearbox and full petrol tank awaits them.

Unfortunately this is not the cheapest way of hiring a car. The company is paying serious money for the airport concession, and if you hire from the airport you are paying for a car that will be very new and meticulously maintained.

There are many advantages in hiring through a second-echelon car company. First, the car will be far less expensive. It will invariably be on a flat rate with no mileage charge. The downside is that the car will be somewhat older and will have covered a fair distance. But it will typically have air-conditioning, an automatic gearbox and power steering and, most important, it is very unlikely to break down. You could arrange to have your car delivered to the airport, but it is better to take the airport bus – not a taxi – into town, check into your motel and collect the car later. This way, you do not have to worry about the drive in from the airport, which can be difficult especially after a long flight.

There are many places you may want to drive where 4-wheel drive is an attractive option – or even a necessity. The lower age limit is usually 25 for hiring a 4-wheel drive vehicle, although it is only 21 on Fraser Island.

GENERAL TIPS FOR CAR HIRE

- An automatic gearbox will make life much easier.
- You must have your licence with you and present it when you pick up the car.
- If you have a companion who is going to drive, make sure both names are listed on the hire form, otherwise the insurance cover will not be valid.
- Before you drive off, find out who to call if the car should break down. Breakdowns, although rare, do happen.
- Get the hire company to provide you with any maps that are available.

When you hire a car you are given a form full of small print which you are asked, nay instructed, to sign on the spot. General legal opinion appears to be that much, if not most, of the contract is unenforceable, because (a) the clauses are in a typeface that is something less than easily legible; (b) the implications of the clauses are not verbally explained; and (c) pressure is applied to make you sign the form on the spot and not give careful consideration to its contents.

None of this matters very much providing you take full collision insurance. While the company is almost certainly making a profit on this extra insurance, the peace of mind from knowing that you are fully covered outweighs the extra cost. If you do not take out the extra insurance, you are totally responsible for the car and you must make quite sure that all defects – especially in the bodywork – are listed on the form and accepted by the renter. This, in theory, can be done. In practice, all you want to do is to get away, so the best bet is always to take the extra insurance.

Important note Many hire cars in Australia are not insured if you go on an unmade road. You need to check this very carefully indeed if you intend to explore in any serious way.

BUYING A BANGER

In most major cities there are companies that specialise in the sale of cars for the budget traveller. Sometimes these can be a great bargain, sometimes not.

Buying such an old banger is only seriously an option for the young and desperate. For most, car hire is the only realistic option.

FUEL

Although not as cheap as in the United States, the price of petrol is less than two-thirds that of Britain. That makes a big difference if you are driving around

Australia. And the fact that speed limits, very low speed limits, are strictly enforced, means you get better consumption.

Leaded petrol has almost totally been banned and all hire cars use unleaded grades. Prices are by the litre. Australia has more petrol stations than it needs – there has been a recent culling – and they all accept credit cards. Some of them offer forecourt service which is a pleasant change. Almost all of them also run a store as part of the complex offering everything from milk to magazines.

Tolls

Most roads and highways in Australia are free, with the exception of a few, recently built roads and bridges that have been privately funded or financed by tolls. Important tolls to remember are the $2 charge for crossing Sydney Harbour Bridge or going through the Harbour tunnel (only imposed in one direction), the Gateway bridge linking Brisbane airport with the Gold Coast, and the new private CityLink tollway system in Melbourne which affects almost all major highways around the city. This CityLink system has its fees charged electronically and invisibly, which means that every car must carry a special card on its dashboard with credit registered on it, to be able to use these roads. Hire car companies in Melbourne will sell you day passes to enable you to use the network, or they can be bought from booths by the side of the tollway near Tullamarine airport.

Rules of the road

When you drive in Australia, slip your brain into a lower gear. There are no superhighways and many of the main roads of Australia are two-lane highways with passing places – that is, you drive single file until you come to a passing place which may well be 20 km away. In these circumstances a tranquil approach and an understanding of the virtues of meditation comes in particularly useful.

This lack of multi-lane race tracks has a plus side. The accident rate in Australia is relatively low and generally is falling. In 1972 there were 26.59 fatalities per 100,000 of the population. By 1995 that had dropped to 11. The figures have been dropping fairly steadily with some occasional blips in the wrong direction.

The reasons for the improvement in the figures are many. Random breath testing is carried out all the time and if you have been drinking you will eventually be caught. Visitors to the country imagine it is a law that is sketchily enforced. Not a bit of it. There are regular campaigns throughout Australia and on a long trip you can expect to be stopped and have your breath checked at least once or twice.

The speed limit is generally 100 kph on the open road and 50 kph in town (about 60 mph and 30 mph). There are some carriageways where you can speed up to 110 kph

TAXIS

There are always taxis for hire and they are inexpensive and well regulated.

Sydney uses cabs far more than any other city — twice as much as Melbourne. The waiting times for cabs called over the telephone are accepted as being some of the best in the world. Eighty-five per cent of passengers are collected within ten minutes of making the call. There is a slight problem at around 1500 which is changeover time for drivers, but it is never great.

Although cab drivers do not pass the stringent locality tests of, say, London cab drivers they are tested and can find most places. They are also very strictly regulated as to dress and manners. The suggestion that you are even thinking of filing a complaint will sort out any problem immediately. I have never had a problem of any sort in any cab in Australia — and that is in a long career as a journalist where a cab is a tool of the trade.

(just under 70 mph) – and that is it. (The Northern Territory has its own rules, which is why it has the worst accident rate in Australia – see p. 338) There is very little tolerance regarding speed limits. They are regarded as absolutes – speed and you will be nicked. It is illegal to have a radar detector of any kind, and the police use plain cars, spotter planes, speed cameras and radar guns which can read forward or back.

At the same time as the authorities have been getting tougher, cars are becoming safer and drivers more safety conscious. So driving in Australia is pretty safe provided, if you are a European, you adjust to the different speed and, if you are almost any nationality other than British, you get used to being on the wrong side of the road.

Seat belts must be worn by all passengers at all times in all cars, with the single exception of taxis, and that will probably change in the near future. Infants must be in approved infant carriers. Up to the age of four, children are allowed to travel in a properly fitted child car seat and after that they must wear seat belts. All new buses must be fitted with seat belts and where available these must be worn.

Most of the road signs follow international practice and most of the rules are those you have been used to. There is only one exception and that is in Melbourne. At some intersections where there are tramlines as well as a two-way road system, to turn right you move to the left-hand lane first. Melburnians are happy to sit down and explain to you the mad logic of this system, which is called the hook turn. It can lead to exciting moments for the novice driver and much enjoyment for the Melburnian spectators.

In short:

- Never drive when you are tired. It is difficult enough to adjust to a new car and a new landscape without adding this extra burden.

- Do not speed.
- Do not drive if you have had more than a glass of wine or so.
- Work on the basis that all other drivers are as mad as cut snakes. This is undoubtedly true in the Northern Territory outside the few major towns.

OUTBACK DRIVING

If you are driving in the Northern Territory and parts of Queensland you will come across road trains - trucks with three or four trailers. In dry weather they leave a cloud of dust behind them which can reduce your visibility to almost zero.**Overtaking** them is not easy and you need a long clear stretch of road before you should even think of doing so. It is better to stop, take a rest and then drive on. Driving across the Nullabor Desert towards Perth you may be dazzled by the lights of an oncoming truck. Get used to it: the road is so straight that it sometimes takes five or ten minutes to meet and pass.

The most dangerous times for hitting **animals** are dawn and dusk. Keep a special look out for them and reduce your speed. Hitting a full-grown kangaroo at speed is a very serious accident and roo bars are worse than useless.

Make sure you know the route and that you have discussed it with locals. The police are, as always, a mine of useful information. If you are seriously 'going outback' on unmade roads into the desert, you must carry essential supplies, especially water and fuel. You simply cannot have too much water: 20 litres a head is a good rule as this could easily last you a week with care. The heat of the day in Australia will mean that you will be running with the air-conditioner set on high most of the time. Although this technology has improved tremendously in the past few years, it still means that your fuel consumption will be relatively high, so when in doubt, fill your tank. If you break down, stay with your vehicle. It provides shade and is a good target for a search party.

All of this sounds somewhat forbidding, though this is not the intention. Australia is a very easy country to drive around and the locals think nothing of covering very long distances in a day - 1,000 km being not uncommon.

BACKPACKERS

A number of travel companies provide services aimed at backpackers and other independent travellers, offering accommodation and travel packages (usually involving HI or other similar networks of hostels) plus bus, rail or air passes. And they often give discounts on these services – surf the net to see what is available. In the UK, the Travellers Contact Point (tel: 0181 994 2247; www.travellers.com.au) sells travel passes, and offer message holding and email address services – useful if you are planning a longer stay.

If you look at a map you will see a road that runs right around the whole of mainland Australia. This is Highway 1. It is known as the Pacific Highway in parts and in some stages along its route is given other names by the locals.

If you leave Sydney and head north, you immediately find yourself on Highway 1 which will take you to Newcastle then up the coast – Port Macquarie, Coffs Harbour, Byron Bay – and then Tweed Heads. You are now moving out of New South Wales into Queensland, still on Highway 1.

From there it goes up the coast through Surfers Paradise to Brisbane, then on from that delightful city through Bundaberg and Rockhampton where it crosses the Tropic of Capricorn. Now the Great Barrier Reef is about 100 km out to sea on your right-hand side and seems to follow the contours of the highway as it heads north.

You go on through Townsville to Cairns. Then Highway 1, unable to tackle the Daintree River, sharply turns to the west and nips across the Gregory Range to Normanton and the Gulf Country. It runs along the Gulf of Carpentaria and through places like Borroloola which are unknown to anyone except outback Australian travellers, and then follows through to Daly Waters which takes you down through Mataranka to Katherine. There are those who would argue that the stretch from Normanton to Katherine is not truly Highway 1. As roads go it has its deficiencies. Indeed, in most countries it would not be considered a country road. But this is Australia and it is Highway 1.

From Katherine, once again certain of its identity, Highway 1 zooms over to Willeroo and Timber Creek and just bypasses Wyndham. (If you have never heard of these towns, don't let it worry you: they are not major centres of civilisation.)

Then the road jinks south and goes through Turkey Creek and over Mount Lush until it reaches Halls Creek, where it heads out to the west coast of Australia at a magical place called Broome. Then it runs along the Eighty Mile Beach and skirts the Great Sandy Desert on its way to Port Hedland.

From there to Dampier and through two totally forgettable towns (Minilya and Boologooro) to Carnarvon, Highway 1 then heads dead south as it makes its way through Geraldton and, with a sigh of relief, drops down to Perth. It has come right around the top end of Australia from the east coast to the west.

From Perth it swings down to the bottom of Western Australia and then to Esperance where it kinks back inland to Norseman. Now it takes a deep breath and hurtles across the Nullarbor Plain - a Latin name meaning no trees - until it is in South Australia where the first serious sign of civilisation is Ceduna. From there it continues east to Port Augusta before turning south to the wonderful city of Adelaide and then along the coast past Kingston SE – the odd initials to differentiate it from another Kingston – to Melbourne. From this queen of a city the road hugs the coast as it goes through Bairnsdale and Orbost to reach Eden, which is in New South Wales and is a very fair name for a most pleasant spot. Then it is a gentle stroll north again through Narooma, Berry, Wollongong and ... what is that on the horizon? Sydney yet again.

That gives you the basic infrastructure of the road system – a not very well drawn lasso around the main island of Australia called Highway 1. Along the way its quality varies widely. There are much quicker ways to do some of the component parts of the journey — no one would ever drive from Melbourne to Sydney on Highway 1, for instance, unless they had plenty of time to spare. But it does go right the way around Australia, with the sole exception of Tasmania – which has a wonderful road system (lots of scenery, few cars) of its own.

Right down the centre a road that bisects the oval of Highway 1, from Darwin at the centre top end through Alice Springs to Adelaide at the centre bottom is Highway 87. It has been around in one form or another for some time but as a sealed road it has only been operating in the last 15 years or so. (Nearly the same can be said about Highway 1.)

Where do all the other main roads run? The answer is that there are not that many. Within Victoria and, to a lesser extent, New South Wales, there is a network of interlinked roads. But Victoria is, relatively, a small state and New South Wales, although much larger, is not in the size race with Western Australia. Even in New South Wales, once you get past Orange the roads are few and far between. There are, indeed, different ways of running inland to get from, say, Sydney to Cairns. One way is to take Highway 71 from Dubbo through to Bourke. After that you are 'back of Bourke', which is the Australian way of saying that a place is seriously deep in the wild country. The road then crosses the border into Queensland and goes through Cunnamulla, Charleville, then down to Torrens Creek and on to Cairns. Highway 39 does the same sort of thing but runs closer to the sea, going through Narrabri on the New South Wales side and then over to Queensland and Goondiwindi, then towards Gladstone where it peters out when it hits Highway 1.

The point here is that, once you are outside urban areas, you simply do not have the choice of roads you get when you drive in, say, Europe or New England. If you want to get from Newcastle to Port Macquarie you have one road that you can take, unless you want to cut inland on country roads and substantially extend your journey. In any move from one major place to another your choice will have been made for you by the fact that there is only one logical route.

Cross-Country Routes

ACCOMMODATION

MOTELS In Australia motels are less expensive and more salubrious than those of the United States. Typically they provide inexpensive, squeaky clean, plainly designed accommodation designed for Australia on the move.

There is no town, no matter how mean or humble, no matter how far beyond the Black Stump - that means serious bush country - that does not have a motel. And all the motels are immensely affordable. During the holiday season, which lasts from the week before Christmas to 1 February, you will find motel rooms in popular places to be very expensive - but only by Australian standards.

Every motel provides you with equipment to make tea and instant coffee — other hotels around the world please copy. Without exception they are air-conditioned. Without exception they supply you with a tablet of soap that would not work up sufficient lather for a well-endowed ant — carry your own. Without exception they will serve breakfast to your room if you ask. Do yourself a favour, however, and do not ask: motel breakfasts are not the glory of Australia. Otherwise motels in Australia are, by and large, pretty marvellous.

They are also almost all the same. They are constructed from brick or breeze block, and typically are single- or at most two-storey. The manager is normally the owner, frequently a couple. The motel may say it is, for example, Golden Chain, but that is merely a group-selling organisation; most are individually owned with the owners on the premises.

Although almost all motel owners have plenty of local knowledge, you should take their advice on routes and sightseeing but not on restaurants. The restaurants you will be guided to are never the least expensive and rarely the best. As far as laundry is concerned you will find that almost all motels will offer laundry and ironing facilities, possibly at a small charge. Do not bother to ask, however, whether there is such thing as a laundry service, as this only exists in the top hotels.

BACKPACKER HOSTELS AND YOUTH HOSTELS The backpacker hostels and the Youth Hostel Association (YHA) have both found that there is a major market for people who would like a clean double room with air-conditioning and en suite facilities — a loo and shower — at a reasonable price. So the name 'hostel' can be misleading. They are hardly hostels any longer, but still very good value.

Colour Section

(i) Sydney (see pp. 49–70): Sydney Harbour; the Queen Victoria Building; Darling Harbour monorail

(ii) Sydney Opera House

(iii) Beside Lake Burley, Canberra (p. 88); Didgeridoo player, Blue Mountains (pp. 71–72); Canberra Parliament House (p. 81)

(iv) The Blue Mountains (pp. 71–72); skiing in the Snowy Mountains (pp. 78–81)

Canon

THE STUDIO

FIRE BANS AND BUSHFIRES

In some areas of Australia, open camp fires are banned because of the risk of bushfires, a serious threat particularly during the summer months. Fire ban warnings are issued through newspapers, radio and television and by signs along the roads. During a total fire ban no fires may be lit in the open. Campers are always advised to carry portable stoves. It is a serious offence to light a fire on a day of total fire ban, as well as posing a grave risk to land, wildlife, property and lives.

It is an interesting sidelight on Australian behaviour that to get in to some of these backpacking hostels you need your passport to show you are not Australian. Most backpacking establishments (apart from the YHA) do not welcome Australians. Indeed, they bar them. It is, perhaps, as well not to enquire too closely into the reasons. (Incidentally, each time this has been written there have been anguished squeals from assorted Australian tourist authorities suggesting that it is not the case. As one said, off the record, 'It may be true but it does no good to talk about it.' So we won't.)

CAMPING, CARAVANS AND CAMPER VANS (RVS) There are campsites throughout Australia and, almost without exception, in all the national parks. In some cases the only way to see a national park is to hike in, camp and explore from there. Camping outside designated sites may be forbidden; when in doubt check with a ranger as you enter the park. Camping gear can be hired from the YHA and several camping stores. For some of the more popular sites such as Kakadu and Wilsons Promontory it is necessary to book in advance.

RVs are not as popular in Australia as they are in other countries. They can be hired but most travellers tend to use motels. However, there are plenty of caravan and trailer parks, frequently supplied with power points, shower and toilet facilities. Parking an RV by the side of the road for an overnight stay is frowned upon and not recommended.

FOOD AND DRINK

In the 1960s the food in Australia, despite the quality of the produce, ranged from dire to dreadful. A balanced diet was a meat pie in each hand.

Now it has been improved beyond measure by the influx of other nationalities. The country is positively alive with restaurants of every background and cuisine. Thai is probably currently leading the charge, with Vietnamese and Korean restaurants galloping up on the inside rail. But there is everything including what can only be referred to as Pacific cuisine, the style of cooking incorporating Asian ingredients which is so popular in California, Australia and, to a slightly lesser extent, New Zealand.

The food in Australia is not just totally marvellous but it is immensely affordable, say half of that in a smoky pub with a surly waitress in England. You can still get a bad meal. I was recently served in country Victoria a delicate dish of fresh scallops on a bed of lightly steamed spinach, rice and chips. Some old habits die hard. There is also a terrible tendency to make puns on restaurant names. We can cope with Thaitanic but we must draw the line at a restaurant in Perth called Thai Me Kangaroo Down Sport.

Not only is there a plethora of superb and affordable restaurants, there is also a wondrous range of fruit. As you drive around the country you will see roadside stalls selling fruit at derisory prices. In truth, Australian apples are not in the race with British apples and some of the oranges are big on size and low on flavour, but overall there is a magnificent range and you can load up for very little expenditure. Driving around Australia with a sack of fruit on the back seat makes for very inexpensive dining.

VEGETARIAN FOOD Despite the image of steak-eating, beer-drinking macho Australians, the country is in fact becoming slowly more and more vegetarian; or to be more precise,it is consuming less meat. Because of the plentiful supply of a wide range of fresh fruit and vegetables, being a vegetarian at any level - from vegan to occasional practitioner - is very easy in Australia. Most restaurants offer vegetarian dishes and most Asian restaurants have several vegetarian specialities. The way things are moving it will not be that long before vegetarian dishes offered on the menu outweigh meat dishes. This is of great concern to Australia's farmers but is welcomed by the health authorities.

BYO, PUBS AND LICENSING LAWS Many, but by no means all, restaurants outside the big cities are BYO, which means bring your own wine, and very few restaurants — some exceptions in Sydney and Melbourne — mind if you bring your own bottle of wine although, understandably, they charge corkage.

Where you choose to drink is invariably in a pub, whether it's the only bar in a one-dog outback town or the Hilton Hotel in Sydney — in Australia 'pub' is an all-embracing term. Drinking pubs can be open for almost any 12 hours in 24; most are open until 2300 Mon—Fri, midnight on Sat and 2200 on Sun. Wine bars exist, but are still quite scarce in many of the big cities, because of determined efforts by the major hotel chains to prevent them from getting a licence. Licensed premises cannot serve liquor to anyone under the age of 18, and this rule is strictly enforced.

AUSTRALIAN WINE

The wine in Australia is marvellous and relatively inexpensive. Every bar will have a bottle shop attached, stocking a range of wines which will be quite remarkable, and at reasonable prices. If you want a red which is softer on the palate, look for wines which have Merlot grape incorporated. Most of the whites will be Chardonnay but if you see a straight Semillon go for that. It will be a remarkable experience. I might argue that the Semillon produced by Peter Lehmann is the best Australia has to offer — but there are many contestants for that title.

If you are interested in wines you will find that Australia is a wine lover's paradise. Its only weakness is in sparkling white, which it used to call champagne until the French, rightly, complained. Although it may look the same and the bottle will have a splendid label it will not taste the same. If you want champagne, buy the genuine article. The problem with the Australian equivalent is that the vintners appear to eat the grapes first.

MEALS

Typically, breakfast is a substantial meal taken early, mainly because of the coming heat of the day. As almost everywhere, the move is towards lighter, healthier breakfasts but the croissant and coffee continental breakfast has not, as yet, found much favour.

Dinner, rather than lunch, is the main meal of the day, and is generally served early – perhaps a relic of when pubs used to close at 1800. There is a move in the cities to later dining but booking a table after, say, 2100 in a restaurant would be a rarity in Sydney and Melbourne and unheard of elsewhere.

'Tea' might mean a cup of tea and a cake, but you will also hear it to describe the main evening meal.

SMOKING

Smoking is now banned in all public buildings, airports, taxis, railway trains, buses, at least some sections of restaurants, almost all offices, and all aircraft flying to, from and within Australia.

Cigarette advertising is banned, cigarette sponsorship is being banned, and cigarette vending machines are in the process of being totally banned. As a rough rule of thumb you can take it that, unless you are outdoors or in an area where there are signs specifically permitting you to smoke, you can't. There is even a serious movement to ban smoking in bars and in nightclubs.

TIPPING

The dreaded tipping disease only exists in international hotels where it has been brought in by Americans who know no better. You do not tip cab drivers. Indeed, you will find cab drivers who tip you. If the meter says $10.50 they will say, 'Make it ten bucks, mate.' That does not happen a lot in Manhattan.

In the service industries the unions have ensured that all employees are paid decent, living wages. They do not need, and mostly do not expect, tips as a supplement to their income. Strangely, people in the service industry are totally unimpressed by big tippers. They feel that the tippers have something to prove and are trying to make themselves look superior.

If you must tip make it small — $5 is splashing out big time. Forget 15 per cent of the bill. Just leave some small change for good service. (In Europe, Australian waiters hate to wait on Australians and New Zealanders. They know the pickings will be pitiful.)

SAFETY

CRIME Considering its convict heritage Australia is remarkably crime free. Take the worst crime — murder. If you take murder and manslaughter together throughout the whole of Australia it works out at roughly one a day. And violence is at a similar low rate. But for visitors the average is much lower. The vast majority of assaults happen at pubs at closing time. Avoid pubs at closing time and you will avoid almost any chance of violence.

To all intents and purposes Australia is a gun-free country — and becoming more so. Handguns are almost unheard of and it is difficult, although not impossible, for the average citizen to acquire any firearm unless working on the land or a member of a gun club.

There are petty crimes against property which are committed, in the main, by drug addicts. Australia, like every other country, has a drug addiction problem, but if you take elementary precautions it is almost certain you will not be bothered. I have travelled the length and breadth of Australia many, many times and have yet to see a crime committed or to be a victim of one.

WILDLIFE The chances of **shark** attack are remote. It rarely happens: there has been less than one a year since records were kept. Most of the sharks in Australian waters will not attack. The exception is the white pointer, but even this is not something to be over-concerned about. The white pointer is now so rare that it has been made a protected species, so if one attacks you must not fight back and harm it in any way. That is illegal.

Crocodiles are another matter. If there is a sign up saying that you should not swim because of crocodiles then take great heed. No one knows why they prefer tourists – sweeter meat? – but this appears to be the case. Paddling in shallow water is no safeguard. They can come and get paddlers.

There are over 4,000 species of **snakes**, spiders and other rotten things that can bite you and make you very ill, but they need not truly worry you. Just take normal precautions and the worst thing that will ever bother you is a **leech**. No one dies from leech sucks.

The two most common dangerous **spiders** are the redback and the funnel-web. On ABC radio some years ago, a commentator delighted audiences by saying: 'A lady on the North Shore has been bitten on her funnel by a finger-web spider.' Sunburn (see p. 38) is a far, far greater danger.

Flies are much less of a problem than they were some years ago. The introduction of a beetle that eats cow dung has cut down on the number of flies. But in the wrong season some places, Uluru (Ayers Rock) for example, have enough flies for them to be seriously annoying. In theory, insect repellent will keep them away, but after you have been sweating for a short while it loses its efficiency. Some people in the outback go to the extent of wearing veils but this is only for those who are seriously affected. However, it would be wrong not to mention that the flies are there and can be a nuisance. Always carry insect repellent.

WEATHER

Mainly the weather is beaut so you do not need extra clothes. It is relatively dry, with 80 per cent of the country having a mean annual rainfall of less than 600 mm. The terrible twins, El Niño and La Niña, can cause unexpected extremes: With El Niño you get drought, and the reverse for his sister.

In the centre the weather does get extremely hot, with places like Marble Bar sometimes averaging 41°C, which is pretty unbearable. In the summer you can usually expect something around 28°C in most places, dropping to freezing in the alpine region in the winter. Apart from the high country, it never gets seriously cold so you don't need an overcoat. The biggest problem is the sun.

SUN Forget all other dangers. The sun, shining through very clear air, can create all of the problems. It is not quite the same spectrum as Europe or most parts of the United States, and it is interesting that film manufacturers often have different formulations to deal with the different light in Australia.

Australians, for reasons which are hidden deep within the collective psyche, equate suntans with physical and mental health, which is why Australia has the highest skin cancer rates in the world. The effect the sun has on skin depends upon heredity, the length of time of exposure, and the strength of the sun's rays. It is worth remembering that sunburn is exactly that - a burning of the skin. The Anti-Cancer Council of Victoria has started a campaign with the catchy slogan 'Slip, Slop, Slap', to remind you to slip on a shirt, slop on some suncream and slap on a hat.

You need to wear **suncream** with a high protection factor whenever you are outdoors. Choose a suncream factor that suits the sensitivity of your skin – total block if necessary. Reapply after you go swimming or every two hours. Remember that you can burn under a cloudy sky, and that both sea and snow make reflective surfaces which can intensify the rays of the sun, as does water on the body.

You should never go out in the sun without a **hat**. Ever. It should shade the peaks of your ears which tend to be easily caught by the sun. Gentlemen who are thinning on top will find that sunburn of the bald bits is particularly nasty. School kids wear floppy hats with flaps over the neck. They look like miniature Foreign Legionnaires but it is a good idea. You must cover up.

Sunglasses are an absolute must. The stronger the sun, the darker the lenses should be. They not only stop you from squinting into the glare, they protect the tender skin around your eyes from sunburn.

If you must build up a tan, do it in the morning before the sun has built up its full power. It is better to remain pale and interesting.

HEALTH AND MEDICINE

Not all chemists will accept all **prescriptions** issued overseas. You may need to have another issued by an Australian-registered doctor. There are 24-hour medical centres in all the major cities where this can be arranged very quickly for a very small fee. Note that not all prescription drugs are available in Australia.

DRUGS

The most dangerous drug in Australia, as in almost every other country, is alcohol. In the last year with up-to-date records 85 per cent of all arrests were connected with marijuana — cannabis. Almost all of those arrests were connected with dealing. The police tend not to take action against a user with a very small supply. The next highest category was Ecstasy, and heroin arrests came in at 5.5 per cent. There is, indeed, a drug problem in Australia but it is probable that you will never see evidence of it. As you enter Australia your bags will be checked by sniffer dogs. Do not carry drugs. The sentences are very severe for anyone caught importing.

Always take special precautions when travelling with **contact lenses**. It is usually best to remove them before you fly, especially if it is going to be a long journey, if you have been wearing them excessively, or if you intend to sleep on the plane. The pressurised air of the plane has an extremely destructive drying effect on contact lenses, and the circumstances are not ideal for taking them out halfway through the flight.

When you arrive, restrict your wearing times to allow your contact lens tolerance to be re-established, as jetlag can often cause sore eyes when coupled with excessive contact lens wear. Remember to take your contact lens prescription and, if possible, a spare pair.

DISABLED TRAVELLERS

In the past, facilities for disabled travellers around Australia have been shameful, but now a serious effort has been made to remedy this. Most national parks and wildlife reserves have paid special attention to this problem and many cities have taxis specially equipped for wheelchairs, which charge normal rates. Many restaurant guides now list whether restaurants have wheelchair access or not. Having said that, there is much still to be done, but it is a problem of which everyone is conscious and all new facilities are, almost without exception, equipped so that they can easily be accessed by disabled people.

For advice and information in the UK, RADAR, 12 City Forum, 250 City Rd, London EC1V 8AF; tel: (0207) 250 3222. In the USA, contact SATH, 347 5th Ave, Suite 610, New York, NY 10016; tel: (212) 447 7284.

There are several organisations in Australia that provide information and guides for disabled people. On the Internet there is **Easy Access Australia** – http://www.vicnet.net.au/~brucean – which also publishes a book of that name, a complete guide to access throughout the country. The book can be obtained for $19.95 plus $4.90 p.

& p. from PO Box 218, Kew 3101, Victoria; tel: (03) 9853 9000. The book's author has a complete C5/6 spinal injury and other contributions are by wheelchair users.

Other contact addresses: **ACROD**, 55 Charles St, Ryde, NSW 2112; tel: (02) 9809 4488; **ACROD**, 33 Thesiger Court, Deakin, ACT; **Brisbane City Council**, Disability Services Centre, GPO Box 1434, Brisbane 4001; tel: (07) 3391 2044; **Disabled Persons Information Bureau**, Ground floor, 555 Collins St, Melbourne 3000; tel: (03) 9616 7704; fax: (03) 9616 8142; **Darwin City Council**, Civic Centre, Harry Chan Ave, Darwin; tel: (08) 8982 2511; **Disability Information and Resource Centre**, 195 Gillies St, Adelaide; tel: (08) 8223 7522; **ACROD**, PO Box 8136, Perth Business Centre; tel: (09) 221 9066; **Tasmania Paraplegic Quadriplegic Association**, tel: (002) 381 874.

MONEY AND BANKS

The way in which you take care of your money can make a big difference if you are budget conscious.

There are several ways of taking your money with you. First, you can pay for as much as possible in advance. Secondly, to travel around Australia you need at least one good credit card. Before you leave make sure that bills will be settled monthly or that you have a reasonable credit limit. Unlike some other countries there are very few establishments in Australia which will not accept a credit card. The most widely accepted in Australia is Visa, with MasterCard following close behind. American Express has no credit limit, but you will find that many of the less expensive motels do not accept Amex.

You can also use Visa and MasterCard for drawing cash almost anywhere in Australia. ATMs are everywhere and ATM cards can be used in Australia so long as they have been enabled for international access. Your ATM card must carry either the CIRRUS, PLUS or STAR international ATM mark or the Interlink or Maestro POS mark. Contact your bank at home for information on availability and service charges. Any financial organisation which has a sign in its window for either card issuer will normally advance money against the card.

Travellers' cheques are safe and can be easily replaced if you mislay them, provided you have the list of numbers kept safely somewhere else. Photocopy the list and keep it separately in your suitcase; leave the original list in your passport. If anything should happen, you can rattle off the numbers and easily get a replacement. Most shops will accept travellers' cheques in payment of goods, but the rates you get will not be favourable.

In Australia it is perfectly safe to carry reasonably large amounts of **cash**. Many Australian banknotes are made of plastic and are shiny and slippery; they are not loved by most Australians.

Banks are generally open 0830–1600 Mon-Thur, 0930–1700 Fri. In some states selected banking facilities are available on Saturday morning. All will handle cash advances against the right credit card.

WHAT TO PACK

Because Australians are informal to a fault – Crocodile Dundee was not a caricature – wearing formal clothes becomes a nonsense. Ross Gittins, who is perhaps the best Australian writer on economics, was forced to wear a dinner jacket at a vice-regal dinner. With it he wore a pair of white trainers. He was congratulated on this stylish note by many present. In Darwin formal attire is called tropical rig and for men means shorts and long white socks. That pretty much sums up the attitude towards formality.

So coming to Australia you need to pack your jeans, your cossie – swimming costume – some underwear and a few T-shirts. And that's your lot.

LUGGAGE DOS AND DON'TS

- Do not bring expensive brand name luggage. They are called 'steal-me' cases — if you can afford a genuine Louis Vuitton suitcase you can afford to pack valuables inside. Bring something anonymous, easily cleaned and light.

- Do not buy any luggage which has built-in or hang-on gimmicks. They invariably fail, as do combination locks.

- A suitcase with wheels is not a bad idea. Some are easy to manoeuvre, some aren't. Test before you buy. Better yet is a folding trolley which most aircrew members use. Oil the wheels before you leave, otherwise you will squeak, squeak, squeak your way around the world.

- Clearly identify your luggage with labels and tags, preferably plastic. Paste your name, address and telephone number into the inside lid. Buy a strap-around belt in a bright colour with a difficult buckle.

- Pack with care. The experts – frequent travellers, airline cabin staff, and butlers and valets – all come up with the same advice: fold it carefully, pad it well, pack it tight.

Sightseeing

Nothing in Australia is old; or rather, nothing Europeans had anything to do with is old. Visitors from Europe will laugh at the thought that a hundred years is considered seriously old, but that is the case. As a result there is little of the great architectural heritage of other countries. Yes, there is the Opera House in Sydney, which is more wonderful than you would believe and, yes, Canberra (designed by an American) is not so shabby. Many of the buildings in Australia, however, are (to use a local phrase) as ugly as a bucketful of bum-holes. In the main, nature makes the beauty and architects do their best to defile it.

There is some sort of town planning and there is also some protection for places of historic importance. Having said that, the local council wanted to destroy The Rocks, perhaps historically the most important centre of Sydney, and replace it with high-rise office blocks – and still defends that decision with great vigour. The project was only stopped by the unions, led by Jack Mundey, who will be remembered in history as one of the great Australians. (This is not just an Australian problem. Lord Curzon, when Viceroy of India, was actively engaged in a plan to knock down the Taj Mahal and sell it as marble scrap. Let he who is without sin cast the first stone.)

This odd attitude towards style and design is best shown by the Big syndrome. Many places in Australia have a Big –. It will be considered a major local attraction and it will be ugly to a degree that passes description. One example will do. Coffs Harbour has a strange, monstrous edifice just outside the town. It is the Big Banana. The town's website states: 'Coffs Harbour's and indeed Australia's most famous icon would have to be THE BIG BANANA. This 33 year old giant structure modelled on a prize-winning banana is probably the most photographed object in Australia. It is 11 metres long, 5 metres high, and 2.4 metres wide. The Big Banana is always a favourite stopping place with people of all ages and has been for over 30 years.'

The idea that anyone should consider this Australia's 'most famous icon' gives one pause for thought. It puts Uluru (Ayers Rock) and Sydney Harbour Bridge, not to mention the Opera House and the Great Barrier Reef, firmly in their place. The idea that this immensely ugly representation of a banana should be the most photographed object in Australia is monumental farce. But there are dozens of these Bigs dotted around the country and you will find driving past with the eyes momentarily averted is the only way to deal with the problem.

By and large you come to Australia to see the natural attractions rather than to wonder at what man hath wrought. Australia did not have the first national park – that was Yosemite in the United States – but it was very close behind and is still declaring new parks every year. Within spitting distance of every city there are large and numerous national parks run intelligently with a view to both preservation and access. You will find the park information offices treasure troves of useful information. And with a very few exceptions, access to all national parks is free.

The park rangers are all willing to have a yarn and tell you what to look for and what to avoid. You could spend three years just looking at national parks and you would still not have covered half of them. As well as the parks there are forestry reserves, which are similar but easier to drive through. And throughout Australia there is more wild country than you could ever explore in one lifetime.

Some of the national parks are wild and free and therefore hold dangers for the inexperienced traveller. The simple and absolute rule is – when in doubt ask a ranger. They will always err on the side of caution and safety but they will never let you stray into danger.

CLASSLESSNESS AND EGALITARIANISM

There are serious attempts to gloss over Australia's convict heritage. It is claimed that those sent to Australia were deported for stealing a silk handkerchief or, at worst, a sheep. This simply is not true. Australia received hardened criminals who had committed crimes that would, even to this day, give you pause when you read about them. And the soldiers sent to guard the prisoners were not, in truth, much better. The officers were not from good regiments and were not averse to criminal endeavour to line their own pockets. This encouraged an attitude which exists to this day.

The police are not popular. (A recent royal commission showed that the police of New South Wales were corrupt beyond belief. No Australian was in the slightest surprised at this revelation.) Strangely, the result has not been a large amount of crime, but simply a culture that has no time for class distinctions. Being rich is fine. Being up yourself – full of your own importance – is totally unacceptable.

When I originally heard the following I put it down to urban myth, but have since been able to confirm it in every detail. A bishop was paying a visit to a vicar in a small Queensland town. The bishop was dressed for the part with a hard collar and the scarlet shirt which is the mark of his rank. The vicar was in his usual open neck shirt and blue jeans. He took the bishop for lunch to his normal café. The waitress said to the vicar, 'G'day. Bert, the usual?' The vicar nodded assent. Then she turned to the bishop and said, 'And what will little Robin Redbreast be having?'

You should not expect servility at any level in Australia. When Bob Hawke was prime minister of Australia – and for much of that time the most popular prime minister the country has ever known – you called him Bob. Everyone called him Bob. Is there another country in the world where the head of state is called familiarly by his first name?

In international hotels you will sometimes find the level of service which you find in, say, a European grand hotel. The person offering that will not have been resident in Australia for very long.

Most visitors find Australians' instant friendliness endearing, although it can take you aback to begin with. Mateship is a vital part of the Australian character and, in a sense, it is what makes economical travelling around Australia so pleasant. There is simply no social cachet in staying at a very upmarket hotel – Australians will still call it a pub no matter how many stars it boasts.

If you are a single passenger and you are male, when you hail a cab you sit in the front seat next to the driver so that he can bore you to death with his views on everything from cricket to politics. Typically in politics he will be somewhat to the right of the late, lamented Genghis Khan and, even more typically, he will have no interest in your views. That is taking egalitarianism too far.

SEXUAL AND RACIAL TOLERANCE

There is no serious intolerance regarding homosexuality in Australia. The Mardi Gras parade in Sydney is held every January and brings crowds from all over the world. The banks and building societies sponsor floats, as do the police. It is a major attraction for what is predominantly a heterosexual crowd. It is possible that among older Australians you will still meet with intolerance, but it is rapidly disappearing. Recently a High Court judge announced that he was gay and named his long time partner in *Who's Who*. It was hardly worth a story in the newspapers.

Sadly, Australia has a long history of ethnic prejudice. The treatment of the Aboriginal peoples of Australia by the governments and the people of Australia has been a disgrace beyond measure and it is a shame that all thinking Australians feel most keenly. It is seldom discussed in social situations and you should not bring it up as a topic of conversation unless you want to start a very heated argument. Even now, with all the goodwill in the world, the situation is appalling. In the 1996 census 350,000 people identified themselves as being indigenous, so they are a sizeable proportion of the population.

KEEPING IN TOUCH WITH THE WORLD

Commercial **radio** in Australia is as bad as anything you will hear overseas. Yet it boasts the highest paid radio personality in John Laws, who is compulsive listening and is totally willing to go against the mainstream. He sets his own agenda and any visitor should listen to at least one broadcast to see how professional talk-back radio can be when it tries. The government, in the form of the ABC, runs several excellent radio stations although, in the name of economy, it is cutting back.

Television is also woeful but, again, Australia has a lively export market for such programmes as *Neigbours* and *Home and Away*. When travelling around the country you will find in many motels that you only have two television channels to choose from. They will both be dire. Make sure you have reading material.

Newspapers tend to be very provincial. There are two national newspapers — *The Australian* and *The Australian Financial Review*. All the rest devote much space to local happenings, especially sport, and can be quickly scanned.

If you want to know what is happening in the world, head for an Internet café. You will find that almost every daily newspaper in the world has its own website so keeping in touch with the news at home is remarkably easy. If you cannot find an Internet café — and almost every town now has one — head for the local library which will probably offer Internet access. Again, this is a growing trend. While you are on the Internet you can check your email.

The health of Aborigines is worrying. Alcohol is a major problem. Aboriginal and Torres Strait Islanders suffer blindness ten times more frequently than other Australians. In many communities 8–13 per cent of the people are affected by diabetes. The life expectancy for men is about 57 and for women 64. More than 20 per cent of Aboriginal children under ten years of age in rural areas have follicular trachoma. All the figures are horrifying. Everyone agrees that the situation is dreadful, though improving – but there is little agreement on how to tackle the problem.

Until about 1960 *The Bulletin*, a sort of Australian *Time* magazine, ran a line under its banner that read: 'For a White Australia'. In 1947 the Minister for Immigration, Arthur Caldwell, said, 'Two Wongs don't make a white.' As recently as 1967 the right wing of the Liberal Party prepared a poster which showed a white man pulling a rickshaw over the Harbour Bridge. Riding in the rickshaw was a blonde young lady with dishevelled clothes fending off the advances of a Chinese commissar.

All that has now virtually disappeared. The White Australia policy died in the 1970s. There was no big announcement – it just went away. The immigration figure now stands at around 250,000 a year, the numbers depending on the level of employment on the one hand and the needs of refugees on the other. The biggest group comes from New Zealand at about 12 per cent – the same is true in the reverse direction – followed by the British at about 11 per cent and Asians only very slightly less. About one-quarter of the current Australian population was born overseas.

There is very little racial tension between the various groups. This is partly because there has been so much intermarriage and partly because Australians have found out that immigrants brought charm, culture and excellent food. "Ethnics' is a non-pejorative term used by Australians to describe those peoples who have brought colour and life to this large, brown country.

USEFUL READING

Referred to throughout this guide as the OTT, the *Thomas Cook Overseas Timetable* is published every two months, price £8.99 per issue. Indispensable for independent travellers using public transport in Australia, it contains timetables for all the main rail, bus and ferry services, plus details of local and suburban services. It is available from UK branches of Thomas Cook or by mail order, phoning (01733) 503571/2 in the UK. In North America, contact Forsyth Travel Library Inc., 226 Westchester Ave, White Plains, New York 10604; tel: (800) 367 7984 (toll-free). A special edition of the Overseas Timetable is available from bookshops and from the outlets given above – the *Thomas Cook World Timetable Independent Traveller's Edition* include bus, rail and ferry timetables, plus additional information useful for travellers.

Please note that the OTT table numbers very occasionally change – but services may easily be located by checking the index at the front of the *Overseas Timetable.*

New South Wales

New South Wales has dusty outback, rainforests, snow-covered mountains (in season), vineyards, historic towns, some of the best beaches in Australia, and weather which, for the most part, encourages a hedonistic outdoor lifestyle.

The Great Dividing Range that runs down the eastern side of Australia rears up in the south of the state from a few insignificant hills to a series of mountains culminating in Mount Kosciusko, at 2,228 m the highest mountain in Australia. It is here that the people of New South Wales — a million or more each year — come to ski each winter.

The beaches, which stretch from near-tropical Tweed Heads in the north to Eden in the south, form an amazing 1,900 km crescent of white sand, blue sky and Pacific Ocean. Yet, to the people of New South Wales, they are merely an integral part of their lives. On any weekday in summer you can drive the short distance from Sydney along the coast to Wollongong and pass at least 30 long beaches, each more perfect than the last. And most of them will be deserted. With nearly one-third of Australia's population, New South Wales may be the most populated state, but there is still room enough to spare for everyone.

The story of European settlement of the continent started in New South Wales, when in January 1788 just over 1,000 people, three-quarters of them convicts, arrived on the alien shore of Port Phillip, soon to be Sydney Town. The people of Sydney do not always like to be reminded of this: 'We Australians often display a certain queasiness in recalling our founding fathers', wrote Russell Ward in *The Australian Legend* in 1958. Transportation ended in 1840, but the effect of those early convict settlers is still to be felt. The use of cockney rhyming slang from London convicts is still prevalent in the Australian language, and an uneasy relationship between the population and the police lingers on from those days.

Those early settlers faced an uncertain future in an unexplored land, but the infant colony expanded and grew, at first along the farmlands of the Parramatta River and the flats around Windsor and Richmond. Ahead lay the seemingly insuperable barrier of the Blue Mountains. Of course, the Aboriginal people had been crossing them for centuries, but no European settler thought of asking them if they knew the way across.

However, once the first party saw, in 1813, the vision of sunlit plains on the far side it was only a very short time before settlement followed: the fertile plains of Bathurst and the Central West were ripe for agricultural development.

A dozen years later the gold rushes began. The influence of gold on the formation of Australia cannot be overemphasised, as wave upon wave of free settlers created makeshift, tented towns overnight, which rapidly increased in size and then just as quickly died. But this influx of optimistic prospectors made Sydney rich and filled the coffers of the New South Wales government.

After gold came coal, and later metal ores, but agriculture has remained one of the major props of the New South Wales economy. In a good year the gentle slopes and broad plains west of the Great Dividing Range can produce one-third of Australia's total wheat crop, and flood-prone land to the south-west has been transformed into lush pastures that produce almost all of the nation's rice, 80 per cent of the wine grapes and huge quantities of fruit and vegetables.

FEDERATION AND THE SHAPING OF NEW SOUTH WALES

The original state effectively covered half of Australia and, indeed, it has been argued, extended as far as Fiji. In 1856, when it was granted self-government, New South Wales was already the founding state of Australia and its destiny was clear. The northern half of the state gained its independence as Queensland in 1859 (see p. 232) but all the fledgling states were still separate parts of a British colony (there were even customs posts between New South Wales and Victoria). Then came Federation. In Sydney's Centennial Park on a very hot, windy 1 Jan 1901, Lord Hopetoun, representing Her Majesty's government, and the leaders of the States of Australia, signed the document that made Australia one nation and the states one federation.

Sydney and Melbourne, capital of Victoria, constantly vied for the leadership of the new country. Eventually a special area — the Australian Capital Territory — was set up as near equidistant as possible between the rival cities, and Canberra was declared the nation's capital (see p. 82). But New South Wales became the premier state of Australia, with Sydney the favoured entry point for the majority of tourists who started arriving from overseas. And so it remains.

Beyond all this abundant agriculture are the dry and dusty plains of the outback, where nothing grows except stunted scrub and desert grass. The only town of great significance is Broken Hill, the city in the desert that has provided enormous wealth in minerals from the largest single body of silver-lead-zinc ore in the world. Here the land is so flat that you can see the curvature of the Earth.

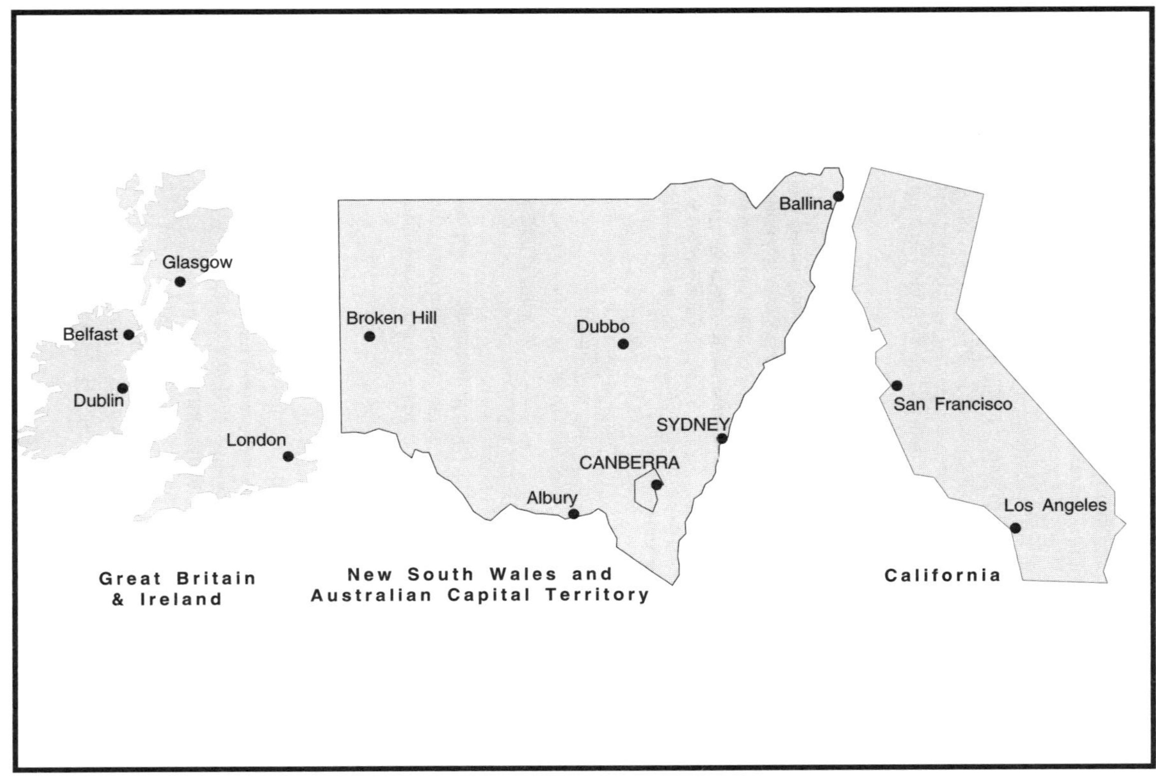
Glasgow
Belfast
Dublin
London
Broken Hill
Dubbo
Ballina
SYDNEY
CANBERRA
Albury
San Francisco
Los Angeles
Great Britain
& Ireland
New South Wales and
Australian Capital Territory
California

SYDNEY

Sydney is often criticised for being a raucous, bustling town with the rough edges showing and frequent clear reminders of its convict past. It pleads guilty to all this, as this is what accounts for much of the city's attraction. And though Sydney can at times be honky-tonk vulgar, it is never less than beautiful. For Sydney is blessed with a position on one of the great natural harbours of the world and is, for its inhabitants, the only place on earth to live. An airline advertisement in 1980 got it nearly right: 'It's part San Francisco. A bit of England. The flavour of New York.'

Sydney was, at the beginning, mainly a convict town, although from quite early days the word was considered distasteful and many more elegant euphemisms were used. By 1815, the town had a population of 5,500 (out of a total white population of Australia of about 13,000), and the new governor, Lachlan Macquarie, had expansive ideas. He engaged the services of the counter-feiter-turned-architect Francis Greenway, who was pardoned by Macquarie on the understanding that he would design great buildings. This Greenway did, and many of his creations, including Hyde Park Barracks and St James's Church, still stand.

SYDNEY'S LOCATION

The location of Sydney was arrived at almost by mistake. When Captain Arthur Phillip and the First Fleet arrived in Australia they were, as in the words of the song, bound for Botany Bay. Captain Cook had landed here in 1770 and his appeared a good example to follow. But Botany Bay is shallow: when the fleet arrived on 18 Jan 1788 Captain Phillip thought it unsuitable and cruised along to what Cook had called Port Jackson. Four days later, on 26 Jan 1788, an official ceremony was held in Sydney Cove.

The new town and the new country galloped along in a period of commercial expansion fired by the pastoral boom and waves of prospectors on their way to – or from – the goldfields. By 1850 Sydney had 50,000 inhabitants and in that year the New South Wales Legislative Council decided that it should have a university. This, perhaps more than anything else, set the seal of respectability on the colony.

The city's past is now being recognised and preserved – at least quite a bit of it – but it also has outstanding modern landmarks. Darling Harbour has been developed into one of the world's great convention centres, and the Opera House has reached its majority in all glory. But Sydney remains the supreme harbour city, and the harbour, so felicitously discovered by Captain Phillip, is one of the natural wonders of the world.

ARRIVAL AND DEPARTURE

Kingsford Smith airport (known as Mascot, after the suburb where it lies) is probably the most centrally placed international airport in the world. It is about 9 km south of the city centre and there are shuttle links between the international and domestic terminals and between the airport and the city. By taxi the journey takes about 35 mins and costs about three–four times a shuttle fare.

There are three main routes into Sydney, each comprehensively signposted. From the south, Hwy 1 comes in from Botany Bay and alongside the aiport, where it turns into a freeway called Southern Cross Drive that comes to a confused stop at South Dowling St. The approach through the northern suburbs brings you to the Harbour Bridge or the Harbour Tunnel (both have a $2 toll entering the city, but are free on leaving). From the west, the Blue Mountains and Melbourne the Western Motorway enters the city as Broadway and, as it passes the Central Railway, becomes George St, which runs through the heart of the city. A car is not necessarily the best way of getting around Sydney (see p. 57).

All long-distance buses come into the Sydney Coach Terminal, on the corner of Eddy Ave and Pitt St; tel: 9281 9366.

INFORMATION

TOURIST OFFICES **Sydney Convention and Visitors Bureau**, 80 William St; tel: 9331 4045.

The Rocks Visitors' Centre, 106 George St; tel: 9255 1788. A cut above most visitor centres, with very knowledgeable staff. It has a large range of free brochures and magazines and also hands out a useful free map of the area. Open daily from 0900.

NSW Travel Centre, 19 Castlereagh St; tel: 9231 4444. The range of magazines, newspapers and pamphlets — almost all of them free — will give you a complete perspective on what is what and where in Sydney.

Darling Harbour Visitors' Centre, between Cockle Bay and Tumbalong Park; tel: 9286 0111.

INTERNET ACCESS You can get Internet access at almost every inexpensive hotel and hostel and there are several cybercafés as well. The two listed have ISDN connections which are much faster.

SYDNEY

Well Connected Café 35 Glebe Point Rd, Glebe; tel: 9566 2655.

digi.kaf, 174 St Johns Rd, Glebe; tel: 9660 3509.

INTERNET SITES According to Yahoo there are 1,700 sites — and that is listed sites — that deal with Sydney. The ones that follow are probably the best starting points. Yahoo rates Sydney Online as the best of the bunch. I think **Walkabout by Fairfax** at http://www.walkabout.fairfax.com.au/fairfax/locations/NSWSydney.shtml is somewhat superior. Almost all of them are designed for visitors on unlimited budgets, so the restaurants listed in these sites, for example, provide wonderful food but, almost without exception, fall in the $$$$ bracket.

Attractions of Sydney http://www.sydney.net/sydsyd/links.html

Australian & Sydney Travel Guide http://www.sydney-australia.net/tourism/sydney/ozinfo.html

City of Sydney http://www.sydneycity.nsw.gov.au

Hyperdome http://www.geocities.com/SunsetStrip/Alley/1355/

Kings Cross, Sydney http://www.kingscross.nsw.gov.au

Open World City Guides: Sydney
http://www.worldexecutive.com/cityguides/sydney/index.html

Sydney — All day long, all night long http://www.sofcom.com.au/sydney/

Sydney 2000 http://www.sydney.auscape.net/

Sydney Australia http://www.australiavideo.com/sydney/index.htm

Sydney Australia Travel Guide http://www.ozemail.com.au/~bunton/sydney.html

Sydney City http://www.ozemail.com.au/~hloh/sydney/

Sydney City — What's On http://www.sydneycity.net/whatson.htm

Sydney City Net http://www.sydneycity.net

Sydney in Profile http://www.sydneyinprofile.au.com

Sydney Interactive Visitors Guide http://www.sydney-australia.net

Sydney Links Page http://www.magna.com.au/~rhap/sydney.html

Sydney Online http://www.sydney.com.au/

Sydney Sidewalk http://www.sydney.sidewalk.com.au/

Sydney Sights Day & Night http://www.sydneysights.com.au

Sydney Sites http://www.trailerpark.com/siesta/sydney/index.htm

Sydney Visitors Guide http://www.sydney-australia.net

Sydney Web Guide http://www.sydneywebguide.com

Sydney! http://www.sydney.simplenet.com

Sydney: The Best Address On Earth
http://www.ourworld.compuserve.com/homepages/deckard97

SydScene http://www.geocities.com/SunsetStrip/Venue/5556/

MONEY Thomas Cook has several foreign exchange offices which are open outside normal banking hours. In Central Sydney these are at: Shop 509, Kingsgate Shopping Centre, Kings Cross, Sydney 2011; tel: 9356 22311; and at Shop 22, Lower Ground Floor, Queen Victoria Bldg, George St, Sydney 2000; tel: 9264 1133; and 210 George St; tel: 9251 9063. There are four locations within the international airport, tel: 9317 2100.

POST AND PHONES Unlike most large cities around the world, Sydney has no central post office. Branches are continually being closed down or opened up within shopping centres. They will keep usual shopping hours.

The telephone code for Sydney is 02.

ACCOMMODATION

Staying in the city centre has its advantages, but hotels a little further out are cheaper and often the better option. Glebe is coming up fast behind Paddington in the gentrification stakes but still has much of the alternative lifestyle about it. Staying in Manly and using a travel pass can save a lot of money and you have the bonus of a

VERY CHEAP LODGINGS

To stay at the YHA you need to be a member. This can be arranged at the hostel but is cheaper to arrange in your home country.

Billabong Gardens Motel/Hostel $ 5–11 Egan St, Glebe; tel: 9550 3236.

CB Hotel $ 417 Pitt St; tel: 9211 5115. Right in the heart of the city. Airport pick-up and luggage storage.

Harbour City Hotel $ 50 Sir John Young Crescent, Wolloomooloo; tel: 9380 2922; email HarbourCityHotel@Bigpond.com.

Kirketon Hotel $ 229 Darlinghurst Rd, Kings Cross; tel: 9360 4333. 63 rooms and licensed restaurant. All rooms have phones, fridge, TV and coffee- and tea-making facilities.

Manly Beach Resort $ 6 Carlton St; tel: 9977 4188. Ferry ride from the city. Twin, double and family rooms with en suite and new bathrooms.

Nomads Clovelly Beach Backpackers $ 381 Clovelly Rd, Clovelly; tel: 9665 1214. 5 km from city. All rooms have private bathrooms, with communal cooking facilities available.

Nomads Forest Lodge $ 117 Arundle St, Glebe; tel: 224 0919. 3 km from the city but in the heart of the alternative action and strolling distance from the street life and cafés of Newtown.

Olympic Hotel $ 308 Moore Park Rd, Paddington; tel: 9361 6315; email olympicHotel@msn.com.

Sydney Central YHA $ Cnr Pitt St and Rawson Ave; tel: 9565 1699. Was the biggest in the world until New York found out and added enough rooms just to be bigger. Twin, double and en suite options.

Sydney Glebe Point YHA $ 262–4 Glebe Point Rd; tel: 9565 1699. Rooms are non-smoking twin/double and family or shared/group accommodation.

harbour crossing to start your day. Even if you miss the last ferry back the taxi fare for the 11 km from the city is quite affordable.

It is also worth checking out the major hotel chains, which are all represented in the city. They sometimes offer special deals, especially at the weekend.

CENTRAL SYDNEY

All Seasons Park Regis $$ 27 Park St; tel: 9267 6511.

Castlereagh Inn $$ 169 Castlereagh St; tel: 9264 2281.

Central Railway Motel/Hotel $$ 240 Chalmers St; tel: 9319 7800.

Golden Gate Hotel $$ 179 Thomas St; tel: 9281 6888.

Grand Hotel $$ 30 Hunter St; tel: 9232 3755.

Hyde Park Inn $$ 271 Elizabeth St; tel: 9264 6001.

Hyde Park Plaza Hotel $$ 38 College St; tel: 9331 6933.

Mercantile Hotel (The Rocks) $$ 25 George St. Note this is a pub and can be noisy; tel: 9247 3570.

Oxford Koala Hotel & Apartments $$ Cnr Oxford & Pelican Sts; tel: 9269 0645. email: oxfordkoala@oxfordkoala.com.au.

Royal Garden International $$ 431 Pitt St; tel: 9281 6999.

Sydney Park Inn $$ 2-6 Francis St; tel: 9360 5988.

Travelodge Hotels $$ 7 York St; tel: 9299 3000.

Westend Hotel $$ 412 Pitt St; tel: 9211 4822.

GLEBE AND NEWTOWN

Australian Youth Hotel $$ 63 Bay St; tel: 9692 0414.

Haven Inn $$ 196 Glebe Point Rd; tel: 9660 6655.

Hereford Lodge $$ 51 Hereford St; tel: 9660 5577.

Rooftop Motel $$ 148 Glebe Point Rd; tel: 9660 7777.

MANLY

Manly Beach Resort $$ 6 Carlton St; tel: 9977 4188.

Manly Ocean Waves Motel/Guest House $$ 35 Pine St; tel: 9977 6426.

Manly Pacific Parkroyal $$ 55 North Steyne; tel: 9977 7666.

Manly Paradise Motel & Apartments $$ 54 North Steyne; tel: 9977 5799.

Manly Seaview Motel $$ Malvern Ave. Cnr Pacific St; tel: 9977 1774.

Manly Windsor Plaza Hotel $$ 95 West Esplanade; tel: 9907 0688.

Radisson Hotels International $$ 8 South Steyne; tel: 9977 8866.

FOOD AND DRINK

In the past 20 years the Sydney restaurant scene has transformed itself. Greeks, Italians and, more recently, Thais, Japanese and Indonesians have ensured that the choice of cuisine is eclectic, interesting and reasonably priced. With the advantage of a wealth of fresh ingredients and such a mix of culinary traditions, the Pacific Rim style is, at its best, an exciting fusion of colours, aromas and tastes.

CIRCULAR QUAY

Restaurants overlooking the harbour are not the cheapest in town, but the price is worth it for that wonderful view of the harbour, and you can linger over lunch and watch the comings and goings of the craft on the water. Also worth watching out for is the *Sydney Showboat* when it docks; aboard is a smashing lady jazz trumpeter who blows her heart out. The following are all cheek by jowl on Circular Quay West and open 7 days a week: $$.

Waterfront Restaurant. In a recovered warehouse, with an outside dining area with canvas sails as shelter. In the cool of the evening this area is heated. A very large restaurant, yet the service is personal and the food superb.

Wolfies Grill. Next door and under the same management; specialises in Australian prime grain-fed beef.

Italian Village. At the end of the block; three levels decorated with Italian decor and artefacts.

CENTRAL SYDNEY

Bodhi $ 187 Hay St. Open 7 days. Vegetarian.

Buon Gusto $$ 368 Abercrombie St, Chippendale. Not quite central, but close enough. Amazing servings. Always busy, always noisy and vibrant; tel: 9319 4798.

Centennial Park Cafe $$ cnr Parks Dr and Grand Dr, in Centennial Park. Less than half a km from where this book is being written. Marvellous for lunch in the sun. A little way out of town but worth the journey; tel: 9360 3355.

Hard Rock Cafe $$ 121 Crown St, Darlinghurst; tel: 9331 1116.

Lantern Restaurant $ 515 Kent St. All you can eat Chinese buffet. Lunch 1130-1500. Dinner 1700-2100; tel: 9277 1153.

Malaya $$ 761 George St. One of the best-known Asian restaurants in Sydney. Inexpensive, Malay/Chinese food. Try the laksa which is brilliant. Always room at lunch time; book for dinner; tel: 9211 0946.

Planet Hollywood $$ 600 George St; tel: 9267 7827.

Soup Plus $ 383 George St. Live jazz while you eat. Open Mon-Sat 1200 until late; tel: 9358 7728.

See also Pubs in the Rocks, p. 62.

GLEBE AND NEWTOWN

Newtown, which has one of the more interesting high streets in the suburbs, is a low-rent area and the restaurants and cafes reflect this. You will find inexpensive eating and shopping and some amazing bargains.

Bali Indonesian $$ 135 King St. BYO restaurant which tends to be full in the evenings. Book; tel: 9557 3441.

Happy Chef $ 264 King St. Chinese dishes and soups which make a full meal; tel: 9550 3423.

Prego Restaurant $ Cnr Missendon and King St. Italian pasta until you cannot move; tel: 9519 7673.

Tamanas North Indian $ 236 King St. Very large serves; tel: 9550 8557.

Thai Pothong $$ 298 King St, Newtown; tel: 9550 4572. Traditional Thai food, wine at bottle shop prices.

YUM CHA RESTAURANTS

Although not as inexpensive as you might think but still remarkable value for money are the yum cha restaurants clustered around the Haymarket in Chinatown. Literally the name means to drink tea but it normally involves choosing the dishes you want from series of circulating trolleys or trays. The quality is as good as Hong Kong or Taiwan; in the case of the Marigold, perhaps better.

East Ocean $$ 421-429 Sussex St. One of the best. No reservations required unless you are in a large party; tel: 9212 4198.

Golden Harbour $$ 31-33 Dixon St; tel: 9211 5160.

Kam Fook Sharks Fin Seafood Restaurant $$ Shop 3.06, 3rd Floor Market City; tel: 9211 8988.

Marigold $$ 683 George St; tel: 9281 3388.

Nine Dragons $$ 39 Dixon St; tel: 9211 3661.

GETTING AROUND

For almost all visitors the answer is the **SydneyPass**, which gives unlimited travel for either three, five or seven days on all the city's buses, ferries, central CityRail services, the jetcat to Manly and the high-speed RiverCat to Parramatta. It also includes Airport Express transfers, with the return journey to the airport valid for two months. The only services SydneyPass does not include are Monorail services, private bus and ferry services, and train trips beyond the Red Travel Pass zone; tel: 131 500. Using the pass you can enjoy a series of ferry cruises on the harbour and explore all the sights of Sydney without ever thinking of using a car.

Driving in Sydney is nowhere near as efficient as using public transport. Because of the many harbour inlets the roads tend to be narrow and parking is at a premium. All the major hire car companies are, of course, present at the airport. Cheaper, off-airport companies include:

Ascot Car and Ute Rentals, 113 William St. (Ute, short for utility, means a small truck.) Tel: 13 24 94. http://www.ascotcarrental.com.au.

Advantage Car Rentals 12 Princes Highway, Arncliffe; tel: 9599 3000. http://car-rentals.net.au/.

HIGHLIGHTS

The best way to orient yourself is to first take one of the **Explorer Buses** which circulate around the city and stop at twenty of the top tourist attractions. They even go through the Harbour Tunnel on their continuous 18 km loop around the city. Passengers may join and leave at any of the specially marked Explorer stops, and, using the booklet provided, wander between stops and then rejoin the bus. Sydney Explorer buses leaves Circular Quay at 15-minute intervals from 0840 with the last round trip service departing at 1725.

Having obtained an overview, start walking. Sydney is a city made for walkers, with lots of shelter from the sun and the rain provided by the awnings that line most of the streets.

AROUND SYDNEY COVE

Sydney's two great man-made landmarks are the Harbour Bridge and the Opera House. The water between them, an inlet of the greater Harbour, is Sydney Cove. Circular Quay, at its southern end is, of course, not circular, but the original name has stuck.

Nowadays, the **Opera House** is such a part of Sydney that it is difficult to remember the anguish that surrounded its creation. A rough sketch of the possibilities of such a building by the architectural genius Joern Utzon, submitted to an international competition in 1956, was initially almost ignored, but was eventually selected as the plan most suited to the site's unique position on Bennelong Point.

The technology for much of what Utzon designed did not exist and had to be invented as the job went along. As a result there were staggering cost escalations, met by the Opera House lottery, and a final bill of over $100 million. In the end Utzon resigned – driven out by government philistines is a widely accepted theory but there are two sides to every argument – and the great building was completed by others. It opened in 1973 to a fanfare of trumpets.

Today the cost is forgotten, the greatness remains. It is one of the major architectural achievements of the world. Technically, though, it is not an opera house – you cannot hold major productions there as the stages and backstage areas are too small. Billy Wentworth, Sydney MP and minister, said that the Sydney Opera House was the greatest public-relations building since the pyramids. He may well be right. You can go on a guided tour of the Opera House ($$). These run right through the day from 0900 to 1600 and last up to one hour; tel 9250 7111.

Next to the Opera House there has been constructed a block of apartments which intrudes on the view of the Opera House, a controversial move deplored by most residents of Sydney.

The **Harbour Bridge** is, for the people of Sydney, a reality that they know is there but hardly ever think about. The **Pylon Lookout** inside the Bridge's south-east pylon is open every day and from it you have marvellous views of Sydney Harbour.

For a different perspective on the city and the harbour, you can climb to the top of the bridge – with a guide and a lot of safety equipment. You cannot take pictures but pictures will be taken of you. You make your way over 1,500 m of steel as you venture across catwalks, steep ladders and arches until you reach the top 134 m above sea level. It is a climb of a lifetime, but does come fairly expensive, about $100. The climb operates every day at ten-minute intervals from 0745 weekends and 0805 weekdays. There are night climbs from 0655 on selected days of the week; tel: 9252 0077. Email admin@bridgeclimb.com

A Remarkable Prediction

In 1789 Erasmus Darwin, grandfather of Charles Darwin, wrote an epigraph to the official volume *The Voyage of Governor Phillip to Botany Bay*. At the end he makes a remarkable prediction:

There the proud arch, Colossus-like, bestride

on glittering streams, and bound the chafing tide . . .

a description that uncannily fits Sydney Harbour Bridge but written 143 years before the bridge was opened.

The busy ferry terminals are on the west side of Sydney Cove and the Overseas

Passenger Terminal, opened in 1961, is regularly used by the largest liners that enter Sydney. The first wharf in Australia was built here by Robert Campbell in 1800, and his warehousing is now transmogrified into a trio of delightful restaurants. The old **Customs House** is currently being renovated. At a nearby jetty is a replica of the ***Bounty*** and a splendid assortment of other vessels. This is also where the two **Sydney Showboat** paddle wheelers dock.

Although the **Museum of Contemporary Art** is officially in George St its front entrance is on Circular Quay, on the site of a government commissariat store built in 1812. The MCA is home to over 5,000 artworks acquired since the 1960s through the JW Power Bequest. Extensive Aboriginal collections are also held in trust. The Museum has an active programme of changing international exhibitions. $. Open daily 1100–1800.

THE ROCKS

The area rising up to the west of Sydney Cove, loosely defined by Grosvenor St and a loop of George St to the south and the road that crosses Sydney Harbour Bridge to the west, is known as The Rocks. It was allegedly named by working parties of convicts who landed with the First Fleet and is the oldest area of Sydney.

By 1970 The Rocks away from the waterfront was in sad disarray and developers were ready to rebuild the area as high-rise collections of offices and apartments. Jack Mundey and the Builders Labourers Federation instituted a series of "green bans" during the 70s to stop this havoc. If he had not done so The Rocks as we know it today would have totally disappeared. Intelligent redevelopment and restoration has created what is now one of the most interesting and attractive areas of Sydney.

There are those who would say that The Rocks has become yuppified and made into a tourist shopping area. If there is some truth in that statement, it has been executed in a style that is immensely attractive and the standard of shopping is very high. The Rocks is strong enough in both buildings and personality to survive any such minor onslaughts. For it has survived almost everything else (see box).

George Street, now the central street of Sydney, began as a track connecting the hospital (more a collection of unsanitary huts) with the main settlement. Once you pass the Regent Hotel in George St everything to the left is The Rocks. There were stocks in George St but they were later removed because they caused an obstruction. For even in those days there were traffic problems: the narrow alleys and steps were barely wide enough for two people to pass side by side. Argyle Street, which visitors now saunter up with pleasure, was a foot track too steep for wheeled vehicles, and the Argyle Steps were hewn to make passage easier. In 1843 it was decided to make a deep cutting underneath The Rocks. The Argyle Cut was the last major work started by convicts (it was finished by labourers and the use of explosives). It is still

THE ROCKS IN THE EARLY DAYS

The Rocks was indeed the birthplace of Australia but for many years it was a prison camp where deported criminals were guarded by soldiers who were, in truth, not much better. There were problems with drainage, with corrupt officials, with transportation. Later, it became the refuge of prostitutes, drunks, sailors and criminals.

In The Rocks were built the first observatory in Australia, the first warehouses, the first flour mill and bakery, the first military camp, the first cemetery. Flogging was common and the hangman was often at work.

The forerunner of the formal police force began here as twelve watchmen appointed by the governor. They later covered the waterfront to prevent the escape of prisoners and the smuggling of rum. In 1817 the service came under the control of John Cadman and the watchmen were renamed constables. They were relatively disciplined and well-organised but hardly had a chance against convicts in the maze of narrow alleys and with easy access to the sea.

The Rocks became notorious for gangs of criminals — in Australia called a push — who fought with cut-throat razors and struck terror into the hearts of the general public. The Push gangs all had colourful names — the Cabbage Tree Mob, the Orange and the Green — and they defended their territories ferociously. The standard dress was tight trousers with bell-bottoms and a slouch hat set at the back of the head. (The term Push came into popularity again after the Second World War to describe some of the literary and Bohemian sets of Sydney; the dress was not that dissimilar.)

What stopped the gangs was not the police but bubonic plague, which struck at the end of the 19th century. In an effort to contain the plague great tracts of The Rocks were burned or demolished. Much more then disappeared in the building of Sydney Harbour Bridge, which effectively split The Rocks from Millers Point, and in the construction of the Cahill Expressway.

the main east-west thoroughfare through The Rocks and an impressive engineering feat.

Although The Rocks does not cover a very large area, it is a maze of very small nooks and crannies, and a map can be most useful. The visitor centre in George St (see p. 51) can supply one and also publishes a wonderful booklet called *The Rocks Self-Guided Tour,* which pinpoints 31 places of historical interest as part of a local **heritage walk**.

Just down from the visitors centre is **Cadman's Cottage**, which was built in 1816 and is the oldest house in Sydney. It was nearly destroyed when they built the passenger terminal in 1960, but was reprieved by the Maritime Services Board. This four-room stone cottage was living quarters for the coxswain and crew of the governor's gig. At the time the back door of the cottage was less than two metres from the water's edge. The original cottage had a thatched – or perhaps tiled – roof and the galvanized roof was put on in the 1890s. Cadman the coxswain, who had been sentenced to transportation for the term of his natural life, was later pardoned, but preferred to remain in Australia. He lived in the cottage for 29 years, ending up as Superintendent of Government Boats and died in 1848.

Susannah Place, 58-64 Gloucester Street, is a museum in a working-class terrace of four brick houses built in 1844 and now incorporates a turn of the century corner shop. Open 1000-1700 weekends.

The Merchant's House at 43 George Street was built in 1848. It now houses a Museum for Children, open Wednesday to Sunday 1000-1600. It contains the National Trust's Australian Childhood Collection which has a wide range of books,

Pubs in the Rocks

In 1810 the Judge Advocate listed some 50 licensed taverns in the Sydney area, and most of them were in The Rocks. They had splendid names — The Sheer Hulk, The Labor in Vain, The Hit or Miss, The Lord Nelson (which still exists), The Rose of Australia, The World Turned Upside Down, and The Erin Go Bragh. The drink of the time was rum — the only beer available was called Stringy Bark and was not considered a gourmet's tipple.

Here, in strict alphabetical order so that we cannot be accused of favouritism, are some of the present day pubs of The Rocks. All of them serve, at the very least, counter meals. Eating in this way tends to be relatively inexpensive and the surroundings are always fascinating. When you are exploring Sydney Cove and Circular Quay and the Opera House these are all within walking distance.

The Australian Hotel, 100 Cumberland St. Has its own brewery on the premises, brewing German style beers.; **The Brooklyn Hotel**, 225 George Street.; **Fortune of War**, 137 George St. Another old pub with great traditions.; Glenmore Hotel, 96 Cumberland Street.; **Hero of Waterloo**, 81 Lower Fort Street. One of the oldest pubs in the area.; **Lord Nelson**, 19 Kent St, has its own brewery on the premises and makes an excellent wheat beer which is highly spoken of by connoisseurs.; **Mercantile Hotel**, 25 George St. An Irish pub which frequently has Irish bands. Built in 1914.; The **Observer Hotel**, 69 George St. Bistro on the premises.; **Orient Hotel**, 89 George St. Perhaps the pub most frequented by tourists. Has a first-rate restaurant.; Phillip's Foote, 101 George St. Serves barbecues in the garden.

prints and toys from 1850 to the present.

George St does a left turn under the Bradfield Hwy to join Lower Fort St which leads up to Observatory Hill. Fort St was the route the troops took between the fort and the garrison church in Argyle Place. From the hilltop are views down over Millers Point and the harbour. Before radio broadcasting The Observatory used to have a time ball signal which gave ships in the harbour the exact time every day at noon. Since 1982 it has been a museum of astronomy, open Mon–Fri 1400–1700, Sat 1000–1700. In addition, every evening except Wednesday there is a two-hour tour which includes a short lecture and a chance to view the sky through telescopes and learn about astronomy. Free daytime admission.

Waterside Walk

Walk along the western side of Sydney Cove until you come to the Overseas Passenger Terminal, then take an escalator to the top level and enjoy the elevated views. There are stairs down at the end or you can walk down the short street until you are back at water level. If you continue on, past the elegantly designed Park Hyatt, Hickson Rd will take you past Dawes Point and then hook smartly under Sydney Harbour Bridge and back on the other side of the peninsula, to Walsh Bay and its piers.

Millers Point and Walsh Bay

In the 1820s some of the more respectable and richer citizens started to build large houses on the heights above The Rocks. The two most fashionable streets were Cumberland and Prince's, and some examples of these houses can be found around Argyle Place in the **Millers Point** area. The old cobbled streets remain and most of the colonial buildings have been restored to their former beauty. The Point is thought to have got its name from John Leighton, known as Jack the Miller, who ran three windmills here from 1795 to 1800. Billy Blue, a Negro boatman, ran his ferry service from here across the harbour to what is now known as Blue's Point on the northern shore.

The old piers and warehouses of Walsh Bay, between Millers Point and Dawes Point, have been given a new lease of life. **Pier One** is a converted wharf containing a series of shops which are more tourist oriented than, perhaps, the rest of The Rocks area. Further down is the Wharf Theatre, which also has a fine restaurant which is hardly known, yet affords superb views and excellent food and wine.

Central Sydney: The Rest

South of Circular Quay, between George St and Macquarie St, lies the heart of central Sydney. Several of the streets are pedestrian malls. Down past Market St is the Town Hall which is not, in truth, an architectural inspiration. Part of it, the **Queen Victoria Building**, was, a century ago, the fruit and vegetable market of Sydney but has now been restored and contains nearly 200 shops. The statue of Queen Victoria that sits outside was the result of a worldwide search – it was eventually found in Ireland.

Heading uphill to the east will bring you to **Hyde Park**, which is, as you would imagine, named after London's Hyde Park. It is one of the green lungs of Sydney and daft notions by the city council to lease out part of the park to commercial interests have been scotched. **Hyde Park Barracks** are further up Macquarie St next door to the Mint Museum. These barracks were designed by Francis Greenway (see p. 47) and built to house convicts but, beautifully restored, they are now a museum of social history with many convict relics. $. Open daily 0930–1700.

The **Australian Museum** alongside the park, on the corner of Park and College Sts, tries very hard to be accessible, friendly and welcoming. It has Australia's largest natural history collection and is continually putting on themed displays. The frequent special exhibitions are worth visiting. Free. Open daily 0930–1700.

The chain of parks continues northwards with the Domain, which stretches out in front of Parliament House. Just beyond Parliament House, a little further along Macquarie St, is the **State Library of New South Wales.** This is an exemplar of what a library should be: modern, inviting and efficient. The library contains Australia's finest collection of Australian history and a superb reference library.

On the eastern flank of the Domain is the **Art Gallery of New South Wales**. The gallery is housed in a spectacular building and consistently puts on brilliant displays of its vast contemporary collection of Australian, European, Asian and Aboriginal art. The problem is that it has nowhere near enough space to display its treasures. What it really needs is another major gallery. Free. Open 0900–1700 Mon–Fri, 1100–1700 Sat and Sun.

From the art gallery you can gently stroll back to Macquarie Street and make your way downhill towards the Opera House and the harbour. Near the Opera House are the **Royal Botanic Gardens**, another of the green lungs of Sydney. The gardens are situated on the edge of Farm Cove and have

The Aquarium is remarkably good. Indeed, it is one of the best of its type in the world and well worth visiting. There is a walkthrough tunnnel which magnifies the size of the fish and when a white pointer shark comes towards you with malice in its heart you are right to be afeared. The Aquarium, which is right on Darling Harbour, is open from 0930–2100 every day; $$. The Maritime Museum, across the harbour from the Aquarium, gets better by the month. It already has a wide range of artefacts on display but bit by bit to this it is adding historic vessels. It is open 1000–1700 every day, and a 'Big Ticket' which covers everything, including inspecting the historic ships, costs $15 for adults.

the sea on one side and Macquarie St on the other. Among its attractions are three special places to visit: the field of wildflowers; the tropical glasshouse and the walk along the harbour's edge, with some of the finest views of the harbour and, of course, the Opera House. Free. Open daily 1000–1700.

DARLING HARBOUR AND CHINATOWN

West of the central business district, Darling Harbour has undergone a multi-million dollar redevelopment and contains what is almost certainly the best convention centre in the southern hemisphere. **The Harbourside Festival Marketplace** has 200 speciality shops, eight waterfront restaurants and terrace cafes and more than 30 food outlets. Apart from the convention centre, Darling Harbour contains **Sydney Aquarium** and the **Maritime Museum**.

The **Powerhouse Museum**, an easy stroll from Darling Harbour, has modern and exciting displays of the decorative arts, science, technology and social history.

It is easy to walk to **Chinatown** from Darling Harbour or from George Street a block away. The main street is Dixon and has colourful arches at the entrance. Chinatown is full of good, some great, Chinese restaurants.

BEACHES

One of the joys of Sydney is that you are never far from a beach. While there are some complaints of pollution on some of the beaches they are magnetic attractions in the summer.

The most famous beach is **Bondi**, 8 km from the city. It is, strangely, not one of the great Sydney beaches, but it has the name, is on a pleasant part of the coast and the main street fronting the beach has some splendid cafes.

Two beaches to the north of Sydney have a fanatical following and, indeed, there are those who have built their lives around them – **Whale Beach** and **Palm Beach**. Whale Beach attracts the surfers; and Palm Beach attracts the beautiful people.

SHOPPING

At the weekend the north end of George Street is closed to cars and covered with awnings, to become **The Rocks market.** Its 150-plus stalls are open from 10am to 6pm in summer, and until 5pm during the cooler months. Almost everything of a craft nature is on sale here – jewellery, hand- blown glass, tie-dyed fabrics, amazing pictures - and the standard is extremely high. And it is not just the stalls that are

THE SYDNEY OLYMPICS

The Sydney 2000 Olympic Games will be held from Friday, 15 September to Sunday, 1 October, 2000. Sydney has prepared for these games perhaps better than any other city has before this. The buildings have been completed well ahead of target, the new roadways sorted out, the rail system checked. There have been several dry runs with the usual problems – but that it what dry runs are for.

A totally new site, Homebush, (about 12 km west of the Harbour bridge) has been built. This was, true, the rough end of Sydney. Now it is a jewel. The pavilions have been erected, the communications are in place, the transport system seems set to cope with the situation. .

The easiest way to get there is by jet-cat from Circular Quay to Homebush Bay Wharf, up the Parramatta River. Check with Infoline (tel: 13 1500) for ferry times. Buses meet the ferry and will deliver you to the visitors centre (open 0900–1700) where you can take a self-guided tour or join a guide ($) at 1100 and 1200 daily. There is also an Olympic Explorer Bus ($) which departs every 20 minutes and takes in the Olympic venues including the Athletic Centre, Aquatic Centre, Tennis Centre, Stadium Australia and Bicentennial Park.

Responsibility for the 2000 Games rests with the Sydney Organising Committee for the Olympic Games which is called SOCOG. Every politician in Australia was trying to take responsibility, in one way or another, for the smooth functioning of the games. Up until the fateful day when the ticket scandal exploded.

What happened was not, in truth, that bad. SOCOG, in order to make a profit – or at least less of a loss – had decided to sell tickets at a premium to high rollers. And little would have been said but they kept it secret, then told lies and then were caught with their pants down. The Prime Minister of Australia led the charge when it came to criticism but, in truth, the Australian public was outraged and heads rolled. None of which in any way changes the fact that these will be the best housed and best organised games of all time

What then can go wrong?
The weather.

Friday, 15 September to Sunday, 1 October may not be the depth of winter in Sydney but it is certainly in the very variable period which is the New South Wales spring. In 1999 during that period it was cold and wet and chilly and there were hailstorms. The deadly weather twins, La Nina and El Nino, where playing silly games – possibly in unison.

If the weather is right these will be a totally and utterly brilliant Olympic Games. The numbers involved are staggering. There will be over 10,200 athletes and about 5,100 officials – nobody has ever explained why you need one official to every two athletes – from 200 countries taking part in 28 sports. There will be joined by 15,000 reptiles of the media and

THE SYDNEY OLYMPICS (CONT)

the world audience should be well over 3 billion. And the budget, for the record is well over two billion Australian dollars. Probably worth every cent. Australians are sports mad and, for a small nation of 18 million people, have the happy knack of winning in most sports which they enter. At the moment Australian teams are world champions in rugby union, rugby league and cricket. Australians hope that there will be a swag of medals in this for Australia but expectations are fairly realistic. But Australians are also totally dedicated to the idea of seeing that any visitor who comes to Australia to see the Games – in Australia it now takes a capital letter – leave with a positive impression of the sunburnt country.

More information is available by calling (02) 9297 2000 or calling up its official website: HYPERLINK http://www.sydney.olympics.org www.sydney.olympics.org

the attraction – the market is alive with buskers, music groups, clowns and street entertainment of all sorts. Many of the local shopowners started as traders in the market.

EVENTS

The **Festival of Sydney and Carnival** is held every year in Jan and Feb. It hosts a number of popular events and performances, including the much-loved Domain outdoor concert series where classical, opera, jazz, blues and country music are performed to huge crowds. There is also a high-quality theatre and music programme, featuring the best of Australian and overseas artists.

The **gay Mardi Gras** each Feb/Mar is quite the most tremendous celebration that any city in the world celebrates, supported by institutions as straight as the police, the government and various banks.

NIGHTLIFE

The best guide to shows is in Friday's *Metro* supplement of the *Sydney Morning Herald*; this gives details of every show, gig and happening.

The theatre in Sydney is good in parts. No one can accurately count how many theatres there are in Sydney because it depends on your definition. But it is somewhere between ten and twenty.

The **Sydney Opera House** (tel: 9250 7777) may not be able to stage full-scale opera but it does have a live theatre which works well enough. Major international stars touring Australia perform at the **Sydney Entertainment Centre** in Harbour St, Haymarket (tel: 9266 4800 for bookings; 9320 4200 for enquiries).

The **Sydney Theatre Company** at the Wharf Theatre is a true repertory company (tel: 9250 1700) with an excellent restaurant. The **Ensemble Theatre** on the other side of the harbour also has a good restaurant and every now and again stages a production which astounds with its excellence. It is at 78 McDougall St, Milsons Point; tel 9929 8877.

Her Majesty's (107 Quay St, tel: 9212 3411) plays it safe with shows where you come out humming the scenery. They are the same shows that have run forever in London and New York and pretty much everywhere else. The **Theatre Royal** at the MLC Centre in King St has its moments and is always worth checking (tel: 9320 9191). The **Seymour** is part of Sydney University at Chippendale (cnr City Rd and Cleveland St) and has theatre in the round and sometimes productions that electrify.

The Basement, 29 Reiby St, Circular Quay, runs jazz evenings at which you can have a late supper and listen to some of the great jazz players of our time. It tends to be crowded late in the evening so check before turning up.

There are several major venues for comedy, including: **Harold Park Hotel**, 115 Wiggin St, Glebe; tel 9682 0564; **Comedy Store**, 450 Parramatta Rd, Peterhsam; tel: 9564 3900 and the **Double Bay Comedy Club**, 16 Cross St, Double Bay; tel: 9327 6560.

Sydney's pop music scene is very large, with never less than seventy gigs playing at the weekends: check for bands and venues in *Metro*.

Sydney's sin centre is **Kings Cross** and, yes, you can walk around there without being mugged. However, possibly the most attractive sight in Kings Cross is the illuminated Coke sign seen through the rear window of a cab as you leave.

Much more entertaining is **Oxford Street** as it rolls on from Hyde Park to Paddington. This is a centre for homosexuals – Sydney has sometimes been called the homosexual capital of the world – and it is cheerful and stylish, and heterosexuals are quite welcome. There are cafes, bars and little restaurants galore and, very much later in the evening, shows to which you should not take Aunt Ethel.

DAY TRIPS

If you visit the harbour via the bridge or the tunnel the first thing to greet you on the north shore is office blocks. Instead, take one of the many ferries from Circular Quay so that you can enjoy something of the harbour and its views, and visit some of the myriad coves, headlands and small resorts. **Manly**, a half-hour ferry ride away, has always been a holiday suburb for Sydney – reminiscent of many English seaside towns but with more charm and much more sunshine. There is a pedestrian mall, the Corso, which has restaurants and shops.

Watsons Bay, at the furthermost end of the harbour, just before the open ocean, has stunning views, pleasant small beaches and some pretty houses. But you can find those in many other places in Sydney. What you cannot find elsewhere is **Doyle's on the Beach** ($$$), the perfect place to be on a sunny day with a bottle of chilled white wine and a feast of the best seafood Australia has to offer.

The **Hawkesbury River** is a couple of hours' drive to the north of Sydney. A cruise up that most lovely river, with national parkland on both sides, takes you further away from city life than you would believe possible.

The Blue Mountains offer another exhilarating day trip from Sydney (see p. 71).

Mark Twain said of the Blue Mountains: 'It was a stunning colour, that blue. Deep, strong, rich, exquisite; towering and majestic masses of blue — a softly luminous blue, a smouldering blue, as if vaguely lit by fires within. It extinguished the blue of the sky'. More prosaically, the blue haze that gives the mountains their name is caused by vaporised gases released by the gum trees.

The Blue Mountains became a major resort for Sydney at the end of the 19th century when the opening of the railway line made it feasible to visit the area over a long weekend — or even on a day trip. Before the trains, it was an exclusive haunt for the well-to-do. The heat of the Sydney summer was quite unbearable in the thick clothes of the late Victorian era and the cool of the mountains offered a pleasant respite. Fresh mountain air was also the only known cure at the time for the killer disease tuberculosis, and sanatoriums sprang up all over the Blue Mountains. Many of them are still there.

As a holiday destination, the area lost favour after World War II to Bali and Queensland, but in the past few years, the Blue Mountains have been rejoicing in a comeback. The scenery is breathtaking.

GETTING THERE

The main Western Hwy runs straight through the mountains to Katoomba, on its way to Lithgow 146 km away. En route are many look-outs and small detours, such as **Govettís Leap** and **Bridal Veil Fall**s.

An interesting alternative drive from Sydney is to head for Windsor along Rte 40 and then join the Bell's Line of Road — such a splendid name — which you will find on the road to Kurrajong. This will take you through orchards to the Mt Tomah Botanical Gardens and then Mt Banks. After that, circle around via Bell and Mt Victoria so that you come back through Katoomba. The round trip is about 250 km.

Blue Mountains Information Centre, Echo Point, Katoomba; tel: (02) 4739 6266.

The Blue Mountains are an easy day-trip from Sydney, but there are plenty of places to stay overnight in Katoomba.

Try also Leura, Blackheath and Mt Victoria, all along the main highway, for places to eat.

HIGHLIGHTS

The largest place in the mountains is **Katoomba**. On one side of Katoomba is a vertical drop into the Jamison Valley and on the other side is the Grose Valley. The best way to see the town is to follow Cliff Drive, which is well signposted and starts at the railway station, goes along Lurline and Merriwa Sts and then follows around the Jamison and Megalong Valleys.

THE THREE SISTERS

The rock formation of the Three Sisters – Mennhi, Wimlah and Gunnedoo – is very important in Aboriginal legend. This does not stop rock climbers from clambering all over it, although the sandstone is well weathered and crumbly and accidents are not that infrequent.

Not far away is the popular lookout of **Echo Point**, which has a glorious view across to the **Three Sisters**, the **Ruined Castle** and **Mt Solitary**. It is possible to pick out many animal shapes on the mountains on the other side of the Grose valley. This is one lookout where a pair of binoculars is invaluable.

For the energetic and those who do not have heart problems the **Giant Stairway** of nearly 1,000 steps leads down to the floor of the Jamison Valley. An easier route, the **Prince Henry Cliff Walk**, leads left towards Leura or right towards the Scenic Railway complex. The **Scenic Skyway** was originally part of a mine and the ride down to the Jamison Valley is reputed to be one of the steepest in the world, although the idea that it is not for the faint-hearted seems more publicity hype than reality.

EXPLORER'S TREE

This tree, on the highway 2 km west of Katoomba, commemorates the first Europeans – Blaxland, Wentworth and Lawson – to cross the Blue Mountains in 1813.

Leura is, perhaps, a little more upmarket than, say, Katoomba. It has **Leuralla**, a historic art deco mansion containing a collection of 19th-century Australian art and a memorial museum to Dr H. V. Evatt. There is also a toy and railway museum. Nearby **Sublime Point** gives more views of the Three Sisters and the Jamison Valley, and **Gordons Falls Reserve** is a pleasant picnic area with toilets a gentle walk away from the **Pool of Siloam** and **Lyrebird Dell**. A number of bushwalks start from Leura. The **Everglades** is one of the great gardens of Australia, with unique sandstone terraces, mature trees, native flora and a grotto pool.

WHERE NEXT?

Instead of treating the Blue Mountains as a round trip, they could be a first point on the route to the inland destinations of Orange and Mudgee (see pp. 75 and 80).

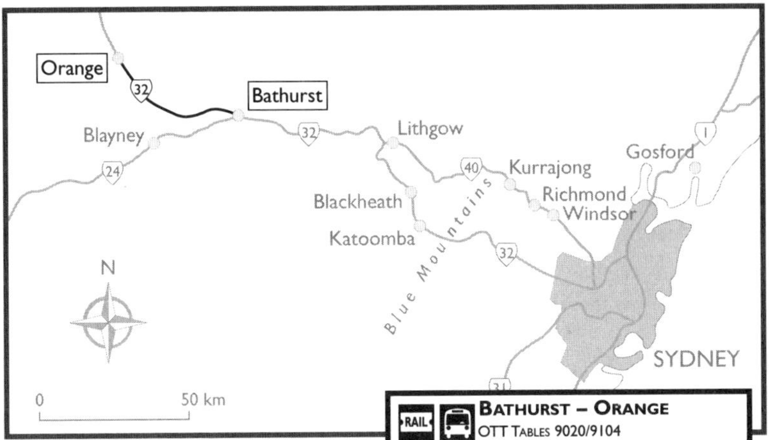

Orange
Bathurst
32
Blayney
24
Lithgow
Kurrajong
40
Gosford
1
Richmond
Windsor
Blackheath
Katoomba
Blue Mountains
32
N
SYDNEY
31
0 50 km

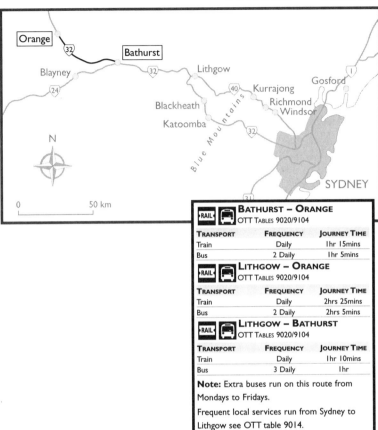

BATHURST – ORANGE
OTT TABLES 9020/9104

TRANSPORT	FREQUENCY	JOURNEY TIME
Train	Daily	1hr 15mins
Bus	2 Daily	1hr 5mins

LITHGOW – ORANGE
OTT TABLES 9020/9104

TRANSPORT	FREQUENCY	JOURNEY TIME
Train	Daily	2hrs 25mins
Bus	2 Daily	2hrs 5mins

LITHGOW – BATHURST
OTT TABLES 9020/9104

TRANSPORT	FREQUENCY	JOURNEY TIME
Train	Daily	1hr 10mins
Bus	3 Daily	1hr

Note: Extra buses run on this route from Mondays to Fridays.

Frequent local services run from Sydney to Lithgow see OTT table 9014.

ROUTE DETAIL

The route over the Blue Mountains can either be straight up along the Western Hwy via Katoomba or along Bell's Line of Road (see p. 71 for both). After Lithgow the road is flat — although it passes through interesting cultivated scenery — right through to Orange (267 km).

Bathurst – Orange

Beyond the Blue Mountains

Orange is one of the most pleasant towns of inland New South Wales. It is not that large but it has immense charm; the phrase to describe it is country civilised. It is the hub of a major farming area – fruit, cattle, sheep, wheat and pigs all prosper on the red volcanic soil and vineyards are the fastest growth industry. Banjo 'Once a jolly swagman' Paterson was born in Orange (where an obelisk commemorates the fact) and you can see exactly what he meant by 'the vision splendid, of the sunlit plains extended' as you make the steep descent from the mountains to industrial Lithgow. The road across these sunlit plains runs through the surprisingly interesting town of Bathurst.

BATHURST

As the road zigzags through Bathurst, the only place of note you see is Bathurst Prison, which is not its most appealing feature. In fact, Bathurst deserves far better treatment, for it is a fascinating town. Founded in 1815, it is Australia's oldest inland city, and possesses some superb colonial architecture in the grand style dating from the gold rush and before. It is sometimes referred to as the City of the Plains.

The finest of the buildings in Bathurst is the Victorian Renaissance-style **courthouse** in Russell St. It has a double-storey portico, a large octagonal central dome and two wings. The wing with verandahs was built as a telegraph office; the other houses the local museum.

In the market place is a **statue to George Evans** who was probably – there is some considerable argument – the first white person to arrive in the district. The **Boer War Memorial** has on it the name of Lt Peter Handcock, who was hanged with Breaker Morant for murdering Boer prisoners. (The story that in 1910 Lord Kitchener, a man who went in for butchery on a larger scale, refused to unveil the memorial is, sadly, a myth.)

Bathurst has associations with other historic names. A plaque in Machattie Park shows that Charles Darwin visited in 1836, and **Ben Chifley's Cottage** in Busby St is the birthplace of a former prime minister. Less edifyingly, **Ribbon Gang Lane** is named after a gang of bushrangers who wore ribbons in their hats and were hanged here.

Mt Panorama, on the edge of town, is home to koalas, a small **motor racing**

museum ($; open daily 0900–1630) and an epic road race. At Easter every year the place attracts hordes of racing enthusiasts and the night is noisy with revved engines. The race actually takes place on the public road up Mt Panorama and you can motor along it sedately in your hired car if you wish.

Worth visiting here is the Sir Joseph Banks Nature Reserve, which has koalas, kangaroos and wallabies in a 41 ha park.

GOLD TOWN

Bathurst grew rich from provisioning and accommodating would-be millionaires who came to make their fortune in the New South Wales gold rush of the 1850s: see Where Next? below.

The **Bathurst Sheep and Cattle Drome** in Kelso, a short drive from town, allows townies to see how the country folk live. Visitors can try to milk a cow, which is harder than you would imagine, or sit back in air-conditioned comfort and enjoy an hour-long show of sheep shearing and wool classing. If the weather is clement you can see sheepdogs in action.

Holy Trinity Church in Kelso was completed in 1835, which makes it the oldest consecrated Anglican church in Australia. Australia's old churches go through wondrous contortions to claim to be the oldest in one sense or another, but in a country where anything built by Europeans before 1850 is very old, this is perhaps understandable.

i **Information Centre,** William St; tel: (02) 6332 1444.

ORANGE

On reaching Orange you have arrived in a true Australian countryside town which has grown and prospered with the area. The houses on the tree-lined western approach to the town are examples of Australian country architecture at its very best.

i **Orange Visitors Centre,** Civic Gardens, Byng St; tel: (02) 6361 5226.

Downtown Motel $ 243 Summer St; tel: (02) 6362 2877.
Central Caleula Motor Lodge $$ 60 Summer St; tel: (02) 6362 7699.
Mid-City Motor Lodge $$ 243 Lords Pl; tel: (02) 6362 1600.

Occidental Hotel Motel $ 174 Lords Pl; tel: (02) 6362 4833.
Orange Motor Lodge $$ 110 Bathurst Rd; tel: (02) 6362 4600.
Oriana Motor Inn $$ Woodward St; tel: (02) 6362 3066.
Templers Mill Motel $$ 241 Anson St; tel: (02) 6362 5611.

There appear to be more Chinese restaurants in Orange per head of population than anywhere else in Australia.
Alfio's Pizzeria $ 193 Lords Pl; tel: (02) 6362 6720.
Canton Chinese Restaurant $$ 84 Summer St (opposite fire station); tel: (02) 6362 6906. Fully licensed.
Golden Bowl Chinese Restaurant $$ Warrendine St; tel: (02) 6362 0144.
Gumbos Restaurant 297 Summer St; tel: (02) 6362 3118.
Hong Kong Chinese Restaurant $$ 199 Lords Pl; tel: (02) 6363 1646.
Loc Sing Chinese Restaurant $$ 293 Summer St; tel: (02) 6362 4663.
Man Kee Chinese Restaurant $ Summer St; tel: (02) 6362 0885.
Phoenix Chinese Restaurant $ 296 Summer St; tel: (02) 6362 8011.
The Keg $$ Bathurst Rd; tel: (02) 6363 1580.
Welcome Inn French Restaurant $$ 87 March St; tel: (02) 6362 4103.

HIGHLIGHTS

The local historical society has put together a brochure (available from the information centre) which describes a **walk** that takes you past over 40 places of interest. The walk takes about 1½ –2 hrs.

The **Orange Regional Gallery** was opened in April 1986 and is one of the better regional art museums in Australia. It is set in landscaped gardens in the middle of the Civic Square, and was awarded the Sulman Prize for Architectural Merit. The gallery collects Australian contemporary paintings and prints, but specialises in jewellery, ceramics and art clothes.It holds up to 30 exhibitions annually. Open Tues–Sat 1100–1700, Sun 1400–1700. Visits outside these hours can be arranged; tel: (02) 6361 5136.

From Orange you can drive up to **Mt Canobolas** (a long-extinct volcano just south-west of the town) and then explore along the marked nature trails. There is also a large bird and animal sanctuary. **Lake Canobolas** – a separate park – is a recreation park built around the lake with a deer park and camping area with hot showers.

The **Nangar National Park** is in the Nangar-Murga Range some 50 km west of Orange. It is an important wildlife refuge of forests and scrub in an area which has been mostly cleared.

Orange's prosperity was not just built on farming. About 30 km north lie the **Ophir goldfields** – named after the goldfields in South Africa – where the first payable gold was discovered in Australia by Edward Hargreaves in 1851. This was the first gold from which anyone could make money. On the outskirts of town is the **Gallery of Minerals**, one of the finest private mineral collections in the country. Ophir is now a flora and fauna reserve.

WHERE NEXT?

For more old gold fever ghost towns, see p. 402, or a take trip up into the Blue Mountains (p. 71).

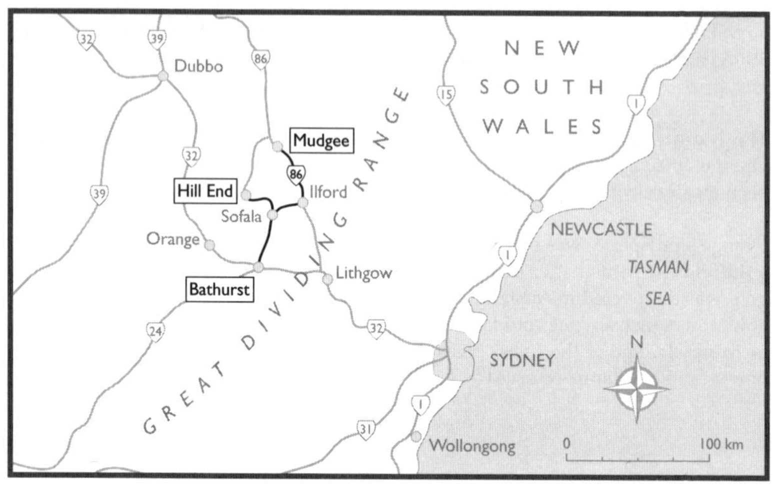

ROUTE DETAIL

Hill End is about 80 km from Bathurst, the last 30–40 km on unmade roads (make sure your insurance covers this; see p. 81).

You can either drive via Sofala or via Turondale or along the old bridle track. This can be driven in a normal 2-wheel-drive car and is very scenic but it is a bone-shaking journey — in the Wet the river of water running down leaves immense potholes. Most of Hill End to Mudgee is again on unsealed roads; alternatively there is a fast direct road, Rte 86, from Sydney.

THE GHOSTS OF THE GOLDFIELDS

The Free Press in Bathurst, 16 July 1851, exclaimed: 'Gold! Bathurst is mad again! The delirium of golden fever has returned with fever increased intensity. Men meet together, stare stupidly at each other, talk incoherent nonsense and wonder what will happen next.' What happened next, usually, was that the gold ran out, the miners would depart, and most of the bustling settlements became ghost towns.

EN ROUTE

Sofala gets its name from a mining town in Africa, and is much as it was in the 1860s, except that its population is only a fraction of the 40,000 who lived here in the gold rush years.

You can still hire panning equipment and try your luck for gold, but the most you can expect are a few traces in the pan. There is no Lasseter's Reef to be found hereabouts. Today's gold comes from film sets in Hill End and wine in Mudgee.

HILL END

You can argue over whether Hill End qualifies as a ghost town, but it was once a major town and is now a backwater. The village is all common land so you might find the access road blocked by wandering cows. In 1967 Hill End was declared a historic site and is administered by the Parks and Wildlife Service. It is often used as a backdrop for period movies.

In 1873 Hill End had 53 hotels and 'a mile of shops': the gold discovered in 1851 made this one of the most profitable places in Australia. It was, at the time, the largest inland centre in New South Wales and, with its sister town of Tambaroora, had a population of 20,000.

All the mining done here was alluvial because the rights had been allocated to a single company which used Cornish miners to hammer away at the reef. The Holtermann nugget was found here on 19 Oct 1872. It was 1.5 m high by 50 cm wide and weighed 236 kg. Its gold content was estimated as in excess of 3,000 oz. But as is often the case, the discovery of that immense nugget marked the beginning of the end, because by 1875 miners had started to drift away.

Markers on the empty sites tell you what once stood where. One church, St Paul's, is still used but St Andrew's is now rubble. The Royal Hotel, which dates from 1872, still operates and is much frequented by the locals. It sells an exquisitely cold drop of beer, but the food is not so good. The hospital, built at the same date as the Royal

Hotel, houses a small museum and information centre. A few shops have been restored and several of the houses are still lived in, but the old glory days have long departed.

National Parks and Wildlife Service Information Centre, Old Hospital Building, Bathurst Rd; tel: (02) 6337 8206. Open 0930–1630 on a fairly casual basis.

MUDGEE

James Blackman was, arguably, the first European to reach the area, when in 1821 he crossed the Cudgegong River. By 1837 he had built a house, of sorts, where the town now stands. Within a few years there were 36 dwellings, including the essential three hotels, to cater for a resident population of fewer than 200 people.

With the gold rush Mudgee became important as a trading and supply centre and by 1861 there were some 1500 people living there. Today Mudgee is becoming increasingly well known for its wine.

Mudgee Visitors' Centre, 84 Market St; tel: (02) 6372 5875. Open 0900–1700 weekdays, 0900–1400 weekends.

Horatio Motor Inn $$ 15 Horatio St; tel: (02) 6372 7727; email: motorinn@lisp.com.au. Mudgee's newest motel. Pool.
Central Motel $ 120 Church St; tel: (02) 6372 2268.
Motel Cudgegong Valley $$ 212 Market St; tel: (02) 6372 4322.
Motel Winning Post Motor Inn $$ 101 Church St; tel: (02) 6372 3333.
Mudgee Motor Inn $ Sydney Rd; tel: (02) 6372 1122.

Augustine Wines & Vineyard Restaurant $$ George Campbell Dr.; tel: (02) 6372 3880.
Craigmoors Restaurant $$ Craigmoor Rd; tel: (02) 6372 4320.
Golden Dragon Chinese Restaurant 78 Church St; tel: (02) 6372 1882.
Jumbucks Restaurant $$ 67 Market St; tel: (02) 6372 3159.
Louisa's Restaurant $$ Market St; tel: (02) 6372 6222.

Rafters Seafood Restaurant $ Church St; tel: (02) 6372 4288. BYO.
Rajarani Indian Restaurant Church St, corner of Gladstone St; tel: (02) 6372 3968.

HIGHLIGHTS

Many of Mudgeeís historic buildings survive, some of which are floodlit at night.The oldest is the **Catholic Presbytery** which was built in 1852. **St Mary's Church** was started in 1857 and has interesting stencilled decorations. The **Colonial Inn Museum** on Market St is open at weekends and public holidays and a **craft centre** has been built into the now non-operative railway station.

DAYS OF WINE AND ROSES

Mudgee is also becoming famous for its rose gardens and now it has a **Days of Wine and Roses Festival** in Sept/Oct every year.

Mudgee is known for its **honey** - you can watch honey processing at two factories - and it is perhaps even better known for its wine. This used to be disparagingly known as Mudgee mud, because it was on the thickish side – it would come out of the bottle, but not quickly. All that has changed and now Mudgee wines are much sought after. There are well over a dozen wineries in the area, all of which welcome visitors for tastings and cellar sales. One produces wine without using any chemicals or fertilisers – the vineyard has the splendid notice: 'Trespassers will be composted.'

The Australian poet Henry Lawson (1867–1922) lived as a child in **Gulgong**, north of Mudgee, where there is a **Henry Lawson trail**. Apart from being a fine poet and short story writer, Henry Lawson was a heroic alcoholic – claims that tales of his alcoholism are exaggerated are misguided.

WHERE NEXT?

Ophir, another gold ghost town, is north of Orange (see p. 77) and to the east of Mudgee lies the scenic Wollemi National Park, an extension of the Blue Mountains (see p. 71).

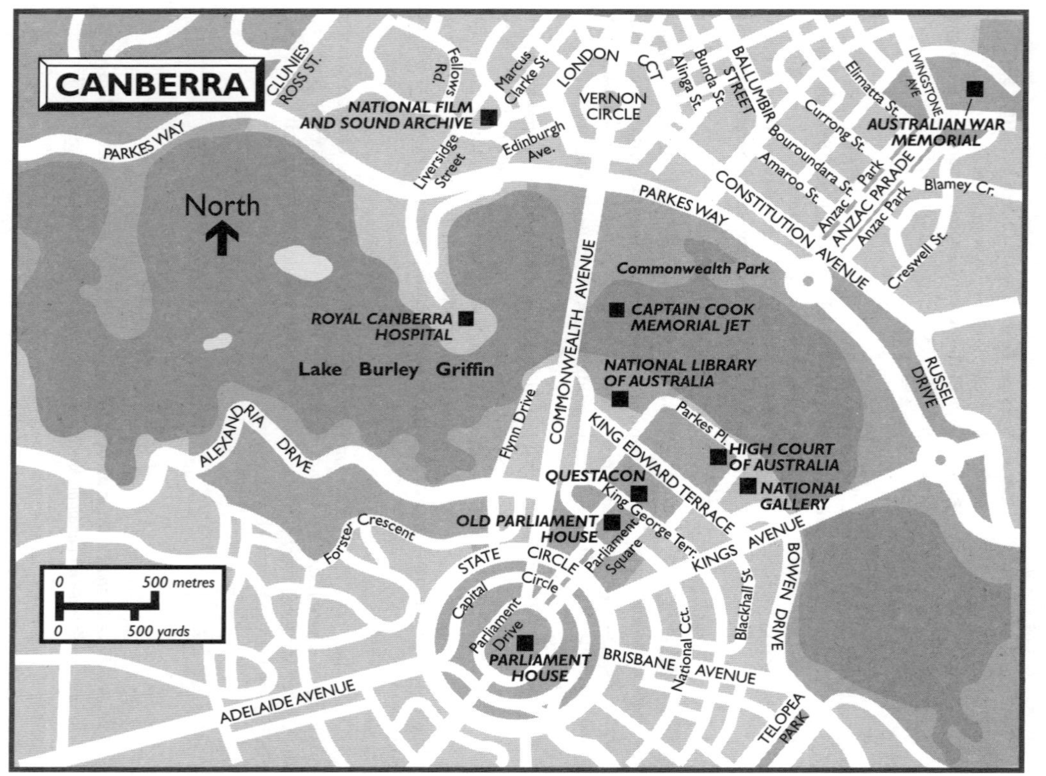
CANBERRA
CLUNIES ROSS ST.
Fellows Rd.
Marcus Clarke St
LONDON CCT
VERNON CIRCLE
Alinga St.
Bunda St.
BALLUMBIR STREET
Elimatta St.
LIVINGSTONE AVE
Currong St.
AUSTRALIAN WAR MEMORIAL
NATIONAL FILM AND SOUND ARCHIVE
Bouroundara St.
Amaroo St.
Anzac Park
ANZAC PARADE
Anzac Park
Blamey Cr.
PARKES WAY
Liversidge Street
Edinburgh Ave.
PARKES WAY
CONSTITUTION AVENUE
Creswell St.
North
Commonwealth Park
COMMONWEALTH AVENUE
CAPTAIN COOK MEMORIAL JET
ROYAL CANBERRA HOSPITAL
Lake Burley Griffin
NATIONAL LIBRARY OF AUSTRALIA
RUSSEL DRIVE
Parkes Pl.
Flynn Drive
KING EDWARD TERRACE
ALEXANDRIA DRIVE
HIGH COURT OF AUSTRALIA
QUESTACON
NATIONAL GALLERY
King George Terr.
OLD PARLIAMENT HOUSE
Forster Crescent
Parliament Square
KINGS AVENUE
STATE CIRCLE
Capital Circle
BOWEN DRIVE
Blackhall St.
0 500 metres
0 500 yards
Parliament Drive
PARLIAMENT HOUSE
National Cct.
BRISBANE AVENUE
ADELAIDE AVENUE
TELOPEA PARK

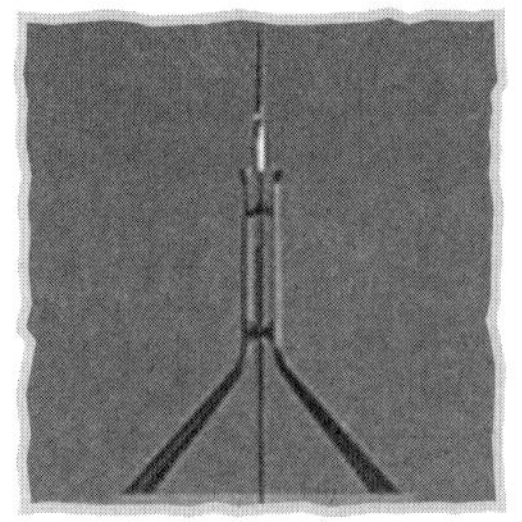

Australia's capital lies within its own enclave, the Australian Capital Territory (ACT), in the mountainous country of south-eastern New South Wales. Canberra is a new city, expressly located and designed to house the nation's government, and it arouses much contradictory opinion. Many Australians outside the ACT dislike it intensely, seeing it as soulless, and politicians, who are forced to stay, are perhaps the most critical. But most of the other residents think it a delightful place to live.

Because it is the seat of government everything works very well (the politicians, after all, have to live here), the entertainment available is always world-class and it is fairly rural — not too far a drive from the sea or to the mountains for skiing in winter. For the visitor, its openness and orderliness have an appeal and every important collection of almost anything is represented in the city — if it carries the weight of being 'national', the reasoning goes, it belongs in Canberra.

The city rejoices in amazingly clear skies most of the year. It has even been remarked that the sky seems larger over Canberra. It does get cold in winter but for some that is part of the charm of the place.

Canberra as a capital city was not even conceived until the beginning of the 20th century, but Aboriginal people, most recently the Wiradjuri, had occupied the region for possibly 21,000 years before that. The first European explorer to arrive here, in 1821, was Charles Throsby and he called the area Limestone Plains. Three years later the first land grant, at the foot of Black Mountain, was bought and by 1845 there was a small town with St John's Church and a school.

When the Australian colonies united as a federation in 1901, one of the basic understandings was that there would be a national capital. The rivalry between Melbourne and Sydney was such that to have chosen either would have been impossible, although as an interim measure many departments were based in Melbourne. (The splendidly named King O'Malley, a politician whose heart was in Sydney, managed to ramrod through two amendments: first, that the new capital would be within 100 miles of

Sydney, and second that it would have sea access. The fact that this was nigh on impossible did not stop him for a moment.)

Eventually, in 1908, a compromise was reached and the Australian Capital Territory was created between Sydney and Melbourne but with an exclave on the sea in Jervis Bay, still used by the Royal Australian Navy for its Naval Training College. But the states never totally relinquished their autonomy, so each state also has two houses of parliament, making Australia the nation most over-provided with politicians on earth. The only exception used to be the ACT itself. Even though the people of Canberra showed in a referendum that they were quite happy to fall under the jurisdiction of the federal government, bills passed in 1988 made the territory self-governing.

WHAT'S IN A NAME

The official story is that Canberra was named in 1913 from an Aboriginal term meaning 'meeting place'. This is very unlikely. No one knows what the Aboriginal term was precisely or how it translates, but 'hatchet to back of knee' is more probable than 'meeting place' – and, considering the usual state of Australian politics, more appropriate.

Parliament was first convened in the capital in 1927 but it was 30 years before the government of Australia seriously started to move to Canberra. The city sprung up through the 1960s, with suburbs and satellite towns to house the civil servants.

ARRIVAL AND DEPARTURE

For international flights, Canberra uses Sydney (see p. 50) or Melbourne (see p. 171) -- Sydney is closer. There is a domestic airport 7 km east with a shuttle link to the city centre.

Canberra is 300 km from Sydney (it is 650 km from Melbourne). The quickest and easiest way from Sydney to Canberra is to take Hwy 31, turning on to Hwy 23 at Goulburn. The road is undoubtedly the best in Australia. It is also perhaps the most heavily patrolled of all main highways — speed at your peril. Long-distance buses make the journey in about 4½ hrs and come in to the Jolimont Centre, in the middle of Civic. Canberra's railway station is in Kingston, on the south side of the lake.

INFORMATION

TOURIST OFFICES **Canberra Visitors' Centre**, Northbourne Ave; tel: 6205 0044.

Travellers Maps and Guides, Jolimont Tourist Centre, Northbourne Ave; tel: 6249 6006.

INTERNET SITES www.canberratourism.com.au

Almost every national gallery and exhibition has a website.

POST AND PHONES The telephone code for Canberra is 02.

ACCOMMODATION

Prices in Canberra tend to fluctuate somewhat depending on whether or not parliament is sitting.

Blue and White Lodge $$ 524 Northbourne Ave, Downer. Price includes breakfast. 4 km from CBD; tel: 6248 0498.

Canberra Carotel Motel $$ Federal Highway, Watson. Set in 22 acres of tranquil bushland just minutes from the city centre; tel: 6241 1377. email carotel@spirit.com.au.

Canberra YHA $ 191 Dryandra St. O'Connor. In a tranquil bush setting; tel: 6248 9155. email canberra@yhansw.org.au.

Diplomat Boutique Hotel $$ Cnr Canberra Ave & Hely St, Griffith. Close to Parliament House and the National Gallery of Australia, Freecall 1800 026 367. email phg@dynamite.com.au.

Garden City Premier Inn $$ Jerrabomberra Ave. Narrabundab. Swimming pool and garden. Freecall 1800 675 622. email gdncity@dynamitc.com.au.

Kythera Motel $$ 98-100 Northbourne Ave. Braddon. 10 minutes walk to the city shops. We have both Italian and Chinese restaurants on the premises; tel: 6248 7611.

Last Stop Ambledown Brook $$ 198 Brooklands Rd via Hall. 20 minutes from Canberra City. Stay in renovated 1929 Melbourne Tram or 1935 Sydney Train Carriage. Breakfast included; tel: 6230 2280.

National Capital Village Motel $$ Antill St. Watson. Rural bush setting but close to city attractions. Award winner; tel: 6241 3188. email ncv@dynamite.com.au.

Northbourne Lodge $$ 522 Northbourne Ave. Downer. Breakfast included; tel: 6257 2599.

Pasmore Cottage Bed & Breakfast $$ 3 Lilley St, O'Connor. 3 km from CBD. Renovated early Canberra cottage; tel: 6247 4528.

Ursula College $ The Australian National University, Cnr Daley & Dickson Rds Acton. The price includes breakfast. Landscaped grounds and courtyard; tel: 6279 4300. email Principal.Ursula@anu.edu.au.

White Ibis Holiday Park $$ 1520 Bidges Rd, off Federal Highway, Sutton. On 20 acres of rural setting. Ten minutes north of Canberra; tel: 6230 3433.

Zimmermann's Apartments $$ 5 Gooreen St. Reid. Two and three bedroom apartments; tel: 6247 7132.

FOOD AND DRINK

The food in Canberra is brilliant, possibly because politicians are fussy eaters.

Asian Cafe $$ Quest Canberra Apartments, West Row, Melbourne Building. Chinese and Malaysian cuisine. Courtyard seating with electronically controlled roof shutters. Licensed. Open 1130-2230 seven days; tel: 6262 6233.

Cafe Fontaine $ Shop CF03, Canberra Centre, Ainslie Ave. Cafe food and great coffee. Open 0800-1730 weekdays, Sat 0800-1600, Sun 1130-1500; tel: 6257 6978.

Charcoal Restaurant $$ 61 London Circuit. Lunch Mon-Fri. Dinner Mon–Sat. Licensed. Opened in 1962. Great Australian wine list; tel: 6248 8015.

Fig Cafe $$ Shop 2/4 Barker St, Griffith Shops. Tue to Sat 1000–2200. Award winning restaurant. Shaded courtyard; tel: 6295 6915.

Foreign Affair $$$ Upstairs, 8 Franklin St, Manuka. Modern Italian. Licensed. Upmarket. Highly regarded. Closed Sun. No lunch Mon; tel: 6239 5060.

Greater Indian & International Restaurant $$ Curtin Shopping Centre, Curtin Place, Curtin. Lunch Mon to Fri. Dinner seven nights; tel: 6285 3679.

Greek Symposion Restaurant $ Capitol Theatre Centre, Franklin St, Manuka. Traditional Greek food and wines. Seven days 1200 till late. Licensed; tel: 6295 7068.

Gus' Cafe $ Shop 8, Garema Arcade, Bunda St. Canberra's first outdoor cafe. Serves a breakfast until 1300 in the old English good-pull-up-for-truck-drivers tradition. 0730 till late, seven days. Licensed; tel: 6248 8118.

Hudson's in the Garden $ Australian National Botanic Gardens, Clunies Ross St. Morning teas, light lunches and afternoon teas. 0900–1600 seven days; tel: 6248 9680.

Lemon Grass Thai $$ 71 London Circuit, Melbourne Building. Authentic Thai but calmed down a little. Lunch Mon-Fri 1200-1500. Dinner Mon–Sat 1800–late; tel: 6247 2779.

Red Belly Black Cafe $$ Stromlo Exploratory Building, Mt Stromlo Rd. Best views, light meals. Open weekdays 0930 to sunset. Weekends 0830 to late. BYO; tel: 6287 1518.

Rincon Latino $$ 5 Garema Place. Peruvian and Chilean cuisine. Mon-Sat 1000-late; tel: 6248 0840.

Rose Cottage Restaurant $$ Cnr Isabella Drive & Monaro Highway, Gilmore. Open Wed 1000–1600, Thu, Fri and Sat 1000–2200, Sun 1100–2100; tel: 6260 1314.

Superior Peking Chinese Restaurant $$ Kythera Motel, 100 Northbourne Avenue, Braddon. Seafood with buffet Friday night. Licensed. Open seven days. Lunch 1200–1430, dinner 1530–2230; tel: 6257 4308.

Terra Ferma Restaurant $$ Shop 4, Campbell Shops, Blamey Place, Campbell. Five minutes from city centre. Open dinner seven days. Open lunch 1200–1400 Mon–Fri. Licensed; tel: 6249 6889.

Tosolini's $$ Cnr of Franklin and Furneaux Sts. Manuka. Lunch Tue to Sun. Italian. Dinner seven days. Licensed; tel: 6232 6600.

Woodstock Steak and Pizza House $ 185 City Walk. Licensed; tel: 6249 7969.

GETTING AROUND

Public transport in Canberra means the Action bus – the Australian Capital Territory Internal Omnibus Network. However, on Sundays it seems to disappear. It is far better to hire a bike (there are lots of cycle paths) or, best of all, walk. There are also plenty of taxis — the city boasts over 200.

A valid criticism of Canberra is that it is somewhat difficult to navigate. T A G Hungerford in *A Knockabout with a Slouch Hat* put it quite well when he wrote:

Bicycle Museum

Canberra is very keen on bikes. There is a bicycle museum inside the Canberra Tradesman's Union Club, where about 700 ancient bikes are held in storage. You can see some 60 of them on display, including a penny-farthing. The club is at 2 Badham St, Dickson and is open 24 hrs a day, seven days a week (but as it is a club it is not suitable for children in the late evening). Check by calling 6248 0999 or look at the website — www.ctuc.asn.au/bicycle/.

'The mad-woman's knitting of roads connecting and slicing through the enclaves was so circuitous, so confusing, that they'd become the basis of a local joke that the half of the population not employed in the Government offices consisted of touring motorists who'd despaired of ever finding their way out' Having said that, Canberra has the best maintained roads in the country and parking is fairly easy.

HIGHLIGHTS

An international competition to design the nation's new capital was won in 1912 by an inspired American architect, Walter Burley Griffin. He designed Canberra from scratch and did a magnificent job. His wife, Marion Mahoney Griffin, who was also an architect, was totally involved in the project and she well deserves joint billing. Yet, despite its splendour, Canberra still has its critics – who say that its rectangles, ellipses and circles render it a city laid out by geometry rather than the natural development that most towns undergo. But it is easy to argue that it is much better for this.

Lake Excursion

It is very pleasant to cruise Lake Burley Griffin with Australian Capital Cruises. The boats leave from the Acton Ferry Terminal at 1030 or 1230 and you sail on the *Lake Explorer*. The lower deck is fully enclosed and centrally heated — Canberra can have chilly winters. For information tel: 6284 7160 or email auscc@dynamite.com.au.

To get an understanding of the way Canberra is laid out, start with the artificial but splendidly positioned Lake Burley Griffin. On the northern side of the lake is Civic, with shops, businesses, university and suburbs such as Reid, Braddon, Turner and Acton. To the south of the lake is parliament and other important buildings and, further out, the suburbs of Parkes, Barton, Forrest, Deakin and Yarralumla. This last is home to the prime minister and Governor-General.

Exploring Canberra is a pleasure because you can walk to most places. The main attraction south of the lake must be the newish **Parliament House**. It was opened in

1988 and sits at the top of the Parliamentary Triangle. It is actually built into the hill, and the roof has been covered with lawn so that it blends in. It is very common for Australians to make sneering remarks about this building but it is immensely impressive. And, according to the politicians who are there at least part of the year, it is a fine place to work.

NATIONAL DISPLAYS

Carrying the label 'National' has led to something of a competition between the various venues and as a result the quality of the many exhibitions is astonishingly high. You may not be enthralled by everything but you will not find any of the assorted National displays dull in any way. As a bonus, with a very few exceptions, you can visit everywhere for free.

On the inside it is light and airy and full of artworks by Australian artists – it is claimed that there are 3,000 works on display. If the houses are not sitting there are free guided tours. When the house is in session you can still wander around the public areas or sit in and listen to the House of Representatives and the Senate.

Visitors to Australia should not judge the country by the standard of political debate in the two chambers. It may well sound like an ill-informed rabble engaged in shouting each other down using terms you would not hear at Sunday school. But these are carefully selected political leaders who have dedicated their lives to finding better ways of serving the people of Australia – so if they sound like an ill-informed rabble it must be something to do with the acoustics!

Old Parliament House was used until 1988 and has now been adapted for other uses. There are guided tours through the building but you may find it more relaxing to wander around on your own. Canberra is a city of gardens, and the one at Old Parliament House is all roses which are in full bloom throughout the summer – Oct to April. $$ King George Ter; tel: 6270 8222; open every day except Christmas, 0900–1600.

Also at Old Parliament House is the **National Portrait Gallery** which has just been totally overhauled (free). The problem is that many portraits – especially portraits of the colonial period – are stiff and uninspiring, but the gallery does its best with what it has.

The **National Gallery of Australia** in Parkes Place was opened in 1982 and has a remarkable collection of indigenous Australian culture. It also has *Blue Poles* by Jackson Pollock, which created a sensation when it was bought. A pleasing addition is the outdoor sculpture garden, with 24 sculptures by Australian and overseas artists in a native garden setting. Free Open daily 0900–1700; tel: 6240 6502; website: www.nga.gov.au.

The **National Library of Australia**, also in Parkes Place, has some 200 km of shelving and everything that has anything to do with Australia is probably here. There is a very informative visitors' centre which gives you a splendid idea what it is all about. What's more, you can sip excellent coffee while looking out on what are reputed to be Canberra's best views of Lake Burley Griffin. Check on what is available at the website – www.nla.gov.au; tel: 6262 1111.

OLD BUS DEPOT MARKETS
Every weekend in the Old Bus Depot in Wentworth Ave on Kingston Foreshore they hold the Old Bus Depot Markets, which are mainly craft-orientated. To check times, tel: 6292 8391.

The **National Capital Exhibition** is just across the lake, at Regatta Point in Commonwealth Park. It tells the story of Canberra and has on show some of the original competition designs. Look carefully and you will understand why Walter Burley Griffin got the nod. There are some superb audio-visuals and many hands-on exhibits. Open daily 0900–1700; tel: 6257 1068.

Anzac Parade provides a fitting approach to the **Australian War Memorial**. This was opened in 1941 and is far from morbid. Moving, yes. Morbid, no. It comprises an amazing collection of pictures and artefacts, including a series of miniature battle scenes done in exquisite detail. There are guided tours, although many people find it an emotional place to visit that needs to be taken in at a personal pace. Open daily 0900—1600; tel: 6243 4211.

The **National Film and Sound Archive** on the McCoy Circuit in Acton alone justifies a visit to Canberra. It is housed in a splendid art deco building but is unfortunately very tight for space - only a small fraction of the treasures are on display. But within what space is available they have created miracles. It is almost as if there were a series of small interlocking cinemas which let you see the long, long history of film in Australia. Fragments of documentaries go back to the 1880s. Most fascinating is a pre-20th-century Melbourne Cup and the signing of Federation in 1901. The Salvation Army was one of the first film-makers (although its *Soldiers of the Cross*, on all the evidence available, was a collection of slides inter-cut with movies). This is a magical place if you are at all interested in movies. Open daily 0900–1700; tel: 6209 3111; website: www.nfsa.gov.au.

EVENTS
Canberra celebrates the start of spring every year with Floriade, in which the most astounding exhibition of flowers and plants seems to spread right across the city. Learn more on the website at www.anbt.gov.au/anbg.

The archive lies on the edge of the university grounds, beyond which are the **Australian National Botanic Gardens** in Clunies Ross St. It is boasted that the gardens contain the world's finest living collection of Australian plants, but in truth they are not as good as those of Melbourne. Open daily 0900–1700 with regular guided walks; tel: 6250 9540.

Rising up from the gardens is Black Mountain, and the best views of Canberra are from the 195 m high **Telstra Tower** on the mountain. This has both open and enclosed viewing galleries (the latter because in winter it can be bitterly cold up there). $ Open daily 0900–2200; tel: 6248 1911. The Telstra Tower also contains Canberra's only revolving restaurant. It is open daily for lunch and dinner and the food is neither better nor worse than in any other revolving restaurant in the world. Reservations tel: 6248 6162.

OUTSIDE THE CENTRE

In the south-western suburb of Deakin is the **Royal Australian Mint**. The visitors' gallery lets you see some of the collector's coins, medals, medallions and tokens for Australia and for a number of overseas countries that are made at the mint. The gallery also provides excellent views of the minting process and you can make your own special $1 coin on the public coining presses. This is not an approved activity outside the mint. Denison St; tel: 6202 6999; open Mon–Fri 0900–1600, Sat–Sun 1000–1500.

Ginninderra is very much a question of personal taste. It is 11 km north-west of the city and has a collection of colonial-era buildings which have been turned into something resembling an English tea house. Next door is Cockington Green, a miniaturised version of an English village. Open daily 0930–1700 with the last entry at 1630; tel: 6230 2273. It is difficult to know what all this has to do with Canberra but it appeals to children.

Just outside the village (in Gold Creek Village, at the corner of Gold Creek Rd and Barton Hwy) is what is called the **National Dinosaur Museum**. This is in fact a private collection with replica skeletons of dinosaurs plus some real bones, including the 150-million-year-old shin bone of an apatosaurus. Open daily 1000–1700.

North of Canberra there is an active gold mine. **Bywong Town Gold Mining Village** is 28 km from the city; follow the signs off Federal Hwy to Millyn Rd, Geary's Gap. Open daily 1000–1600; guided tours at 1030, 1230 and 1400; tel: 6236 9183.

Canberra is an ideal place to find out about the stars. **Stromlo Exploratory** has a giant telescope and within the astronomy hall you can see spectacular images of the solar system. The views of the surrounding area and the Brindabella Ranges from the Red Belly Black Café are wonderful. The centre is 15 mins from Canberra off Cotter Rd in Weston Creek; open daily 0930–1630 with stargazing sessions every Wed night, for which you have to book: tel; 6249 0232.

NIGHTLIFE

Each Thur the *Canberra Times* lists every concert and gig in the area. There is also the quarterly *Canberra What's On*, but its details are not always up to date.

As throughout Australia, rock bands mainly play the pubs. Performances of classical music are held at the **Canberra Theatre Centre** (Civic Sq; tel: 6257 1077) and the **Canberra School of Music** (Llewellyn Hall; tel: 6249 5700). The Theatre Centre also puts on plays and other performance arts.

DAY TRIPS

The Australian Capital Territory measures 80 km from north to south and is about 30 km wide. Canberra takes up a good deal of it and what is left over is mostly the **Namadgi National Park** which, in part, borders the mountainous Kosciuszko National Park in the Snowy Mountains (see p. 93). There are seven peaks over 1,600 m which can make bushwalking challenging. You get to the park on the road south from Tharwa to Adaminaby.

Beside the river near Tharwa, about 30 km south of the city, is **Lanyon Homestead** which has been beautifully restored. An early stone cottage on the site was built by convicts, but the surviving grand homestead was completed in 1859. This is a National Trust building, worth visiting just to see the collection of Sydney Nolan paintings. $ Open Tues–Sun; 0800–1600.

The Tidbinbilla Nature Reserve is 45 km southwest of the city. The kangaroos here are semi-tame, as are the emus. In theory there are koalas but they are very shy and difficult to spot. The reserve is criss-crossed with walking tracks. Open daily; 0900–1800.

On the way to the nature reserve is the **Tidbinbilla Tracking Station** or, more formally, the Canberra Deep Space Communication Complex. This is a joint US–Australian venture and it has a visitors' centre with displays of spacecraft and tracking technology. Paddy's River Rd, Tourist Route 5, Tidbinbilla; website: www.cdscc.nasa.gov. Open daily 0900–1700.

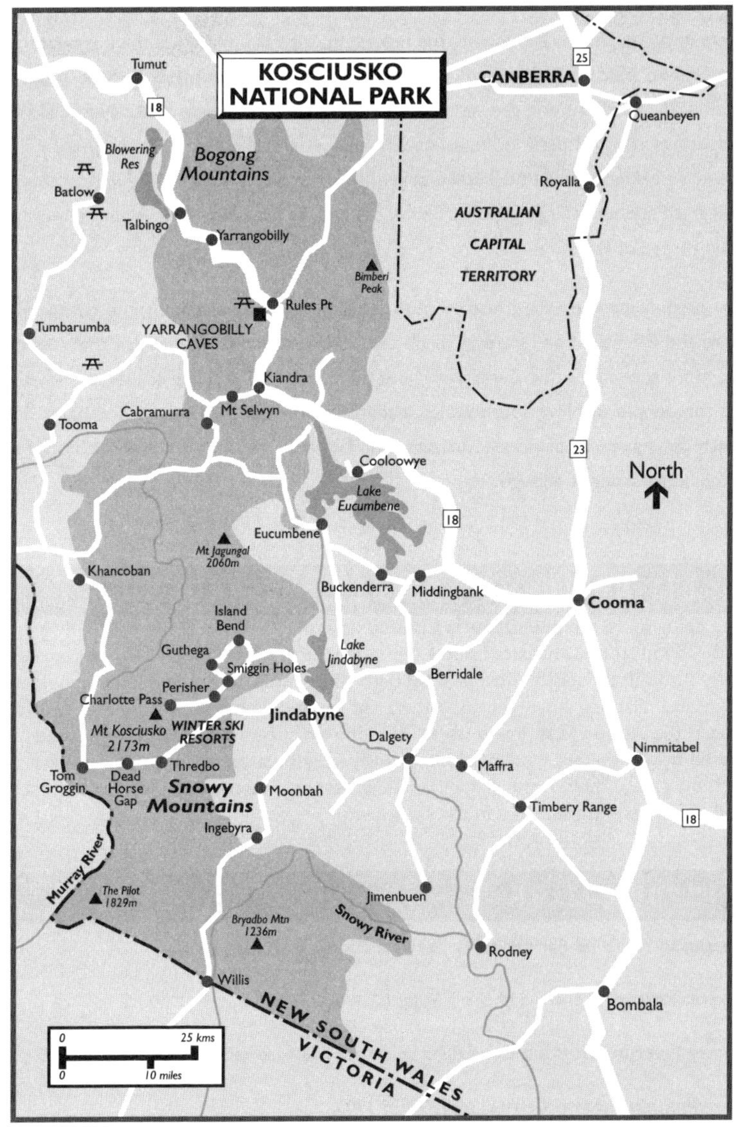
KOSCIUSKO NATIONAL PARK
Tumut
18
Blowering Res
Bogong Mountains
Batlow
Talbingo
Yarrangobilly
Bimberi Peak
Rules Pt
Tumbarumba
YARRANGOBILLY CAVES
Kiandra
Cabramurra
Mt Selwyn
Tooma
CANBERRA
25
Queanbeyen
Royalla
AUSTRALIAN CAPITAL TERRITORY
23
North
Cooloowye
Lake Eucumbene
18
Eucumbene
Mt Jagungal 2060m
Khancoban
Buckenderra
Middingbank
Cooma
Island Bend
Guthega
Smiggin Holes
Lake Jindabyne
Berridale
Perisher
Charlotte Pass
Jindabyne
Mt Kosciusko 2173m
WINTER SKI RESORTS
Dalgety
Nimmitabel
Tom Groggin
Dead Horse Gap
Thredbo
Maffra
Snowy Mountains
Moonbah
Timbery Range
18
Ingebyra
Murray River
The Pilot 1829m
Jimenbuen
Bryadbo Mtn 1236m
Snowy River
Rodney
Willis
Bombala
NEW SOUTH WALES
VICTORIA
0
25 kms
0
10 miles

The Snowy Mountains

South of Canberra the Great Dividing Range that runs down Australia's eastern side rears up as the Snowy Mountains, the highest in Australia. Here are the headwaters of the Snowy, Murrumbidgee and Murray Rivers and the country's highest peak, Mt Kosciusko (2,228 m), and the whole area is protected within Kosciusko National Park, the largest national park in New South Wales. The park contains much breathtaking scenery in all seasons but is known primarily for its skiing. During the winter there is skiing at Perisher, Smiggins Holes, Blue Cow and, further down the Alpine Way, at the main resort of Thredbo.

Although skiing has a long history in Australia it has two problems: the changing climate and the height and general shape of the mountains. You can argue that Australia has more snowfields than Switzerland, but the quality of the skiing is uneven. However, for the people of New South Wales it matters not that the Snowy Mountains don't reach the standards of Vail or Klosters. The fact that they can drive to the slopes and catch some skiing is enough.

GETTING THERE AND GETTING AROUND

The gateway to the mountains is Cooma, on Hwy 23; it is 420 km south of Sydney and 115 km from Canberra. From Cooma the Snowy Mountain Hwy snakes diagonally through the mountains, past Mt Selwyn towards Tumut and Gundagai (see p. 98). Most visitors, however, take the road to Jindabyne, 40 km further on, from which the Alpine Way leads up to Thredbo and the snowfields. Some roads are closed in winter, and you should be equipped with snow chains between May and Oct. Buses run daily from Sydney and Canberra to Cooma and sometimes beyond, and there are extra services in the ski season.

INFORMATION

Kosciusko National Park Wildlife Service, Cooma; tel: (064) 65 2102.

Cooma Visitors' Centre, 119 Sharp St; tel: (064) 50 1742.

Snowy River Information Centre, Petamin Plaza, Jindabyne; tel: (064) 56 2444.

Thredbo Information Centre; tel: (064) 59 1400.

COOMA

Cooma is at the crossing of the Monaro and Snowy Mountain Highways, and it would be fair to call it the capital of the Snowy Mountains. The odd name comes from an Aboriginal word that has been interpreted as either lake or swamp. This is appropriate because Cooma was the centre of the Snowy Mountain Scheme. To celebrate this multinational endeavour Cooma has the **International Avenue of Flags** which contains the flags of 27 nations representing all of those who worked on the scheme.

THE SNOWY MOUNTAIN HYDROELECTRIC SCHEME

This was the largest civil engineering project that Australia has ever seen. The scheme took 25 years and more than $800 million to complete and at the height of construction – the 1950s and 1960s – there were around 10,000 workers billeted in the area. The scheme transformed the region in several ways. First, it supplies 'clean' electricity to the ACT and huge areas of New South Wales and Victoria. Secondly, because the scheme was mainly built by migrants, many of them Europeans made homeless by World War II, they brought their individual cultures to what had been a country based on British food, British style and British sense of dress.

To see the scheme close up and to visit one of the power stations, contact the Snowy Scheme's Information Centre in Cooma (tel: 1800 623 776).

In the winter the population of Cooma varies wildly from day to day as skiers pour through on their way to the ski fields. At 810 m above sea level it can be chilly even in the summer, with temperatures ranging from 26°C down to 11°C. In the winter, of course, the weather is decidedly chilly and the thermometer often drops to 1°C.

Lambie St, which is pretty much unspoilt Victorian design, has been declared a historic precinct, with each of the 21 buildings marked with a plaque. The **Royal Hotel** was opened in 1858, and **The Lord Raglan**, once also a hotel, is now an art gallery. A memorial to aviation pioneers contains remnants of the *Southern Cloud*, an airliner that crashed in the mountains in 1931. This was Australia's first airline disaster and the wreckage was not recovered from this largely unexplored region until some 27 years after the event.

JINDABYNE

The original township of Jindabyne was beside the Snowy River, but with damming for the hydroelectric scheme it was moved piece by piece up the mountain. The original site disappeared under the water on 22 Apr 1967 and now Jindabyne is said to

SKIING IN THE SNOWY MOUNTAINS

There was skiing in Australia even in the 19th century. Reports of skiing appeared in the pages of the *Sydney Morning Herald* as early as 1861 and in the 1920s there was a social skiing scene around the slopes of Mt Kosciuszko — indeed it is claimed, on little evidence, that the Alpine Ski Club in Kiandra was the first in the world.

Although Australia may have more snow-covered mountains than Switzerland, not all of them are suitable for skiing and so downhill skiing has developed only in a few well-publicised resorts. Skiing as a seriously commercial venture did not start until 1956 when Tony Sponar, a Czech ski instructor working as a hydrographer on the Snowy Mountains Project, came to Thredbo and realised that the side of the steep valley would be an ideal ski resort, especially as the Snowy Mountain Authority was building a road, now the Alpine Way, to the door. In 1957 the NSW state government granted a lease over Thredbo village with a view to developing a year-round alpine resort development.

Snow and skiing conditions reports in Australia have the same credibility as sightings of the Easter Bunny. To get around this, Thredbo and most other skiing resorts have installed snowcams so that it is possible actually to see the conditions on the slopes.

be on Lake Jindabyne not on the Snowy River. Jindabyne is the closest centre to the ski fields and comes alive during the skiing season.

THREDBO

This is the closest ski resort to Sydney and the one that is perhaps the most professionally run. It has the highest skiing and longest runs anywhere in Australia, 5 km from the top of Karels lift to Friday Flat, with a total vertical drop of 672 m. A must for all skiers is to ski the 3.7 km Crackenback Supertrail, starting at the highest lifted point in Australia. There are 12 lifts including four quad chairlifts, and a purpose-built beginners' area at Friday Flat has an easy quad chairlift operating on a gentle slope of only 12° inclination. There are also over 380 snow gun outlets spread over 25 km of underground tubing throughout the mountain.

Thredbo has developed into a full-blooded ski resort and the apres-ski nightlife is, in a word, awesome.

By far the best bet is to go on a package tour, which every travel agent in Sydney will be delighted to sell you. This will include transport and lift passes and will work out cheaper than booking each item individually.

Bursills Mountain Lodge Restaurant $$ Alpine Way, bar, pool; tel: 6457 6222.

Bernti's $$ Mowamba Pl; tel: 6457 6091.

House of Ullr $$ Diggins Ter; tel: 6457 6210.

Lantern Lodge $$ Banjo Dr; tel: 6457 6215.

Pender Lea Chalets $$ Alpine Way; tel: 6456 2088.

THE MOUNTAINS IN OTHER SEASONS

During spring, summer and autumn there are walks throughout Kosciusko National Park, ranging from mild to extremely strenuous. The weather is ideal for walking and in summer the carpets of wildflowers are stunning. In areas of heavy traffic, walkways have been laid down. During the summer you can drive on past Thredbo to Charlotte Pass, from where a series of walks begins, some extending up to Mt Kosciusko. At Thredbo, the ski chairlift operates right around the year, allowing you the luxury of downhill only walks in the mountains. Or you can get to the track of steel mesh (to stop serious erosion) that has been laid to the peak of Mt Kosciusko.

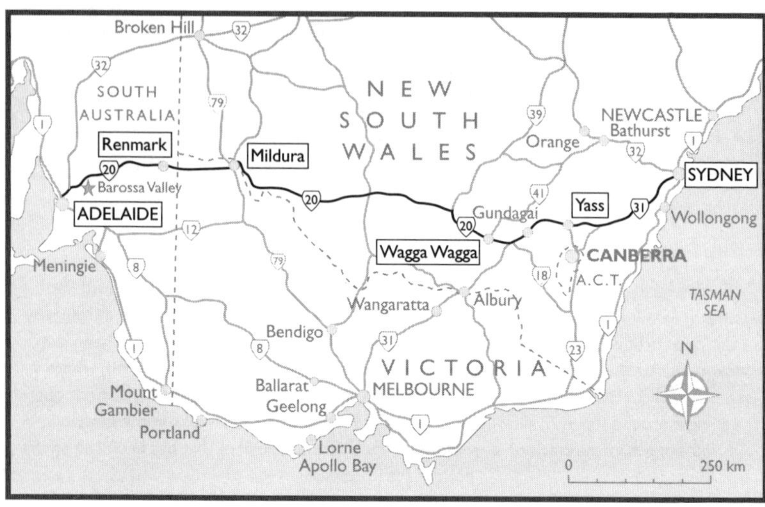

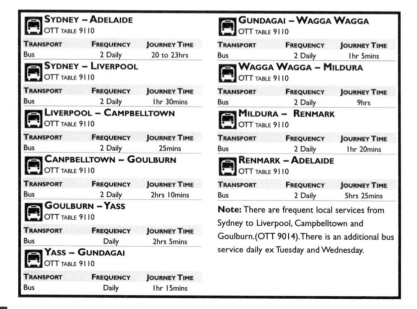

SYDNEY – ADELAIDE
OTT TABLE 9110

TRANSPORT	FREQUENCY	JOURNEY TIME
Bus	2 Daily	20 to 23hrs

SYDNEY – LIVERPOOL
OTT TABLE 9110

TRANSPORT	FREQUENCY	JOURNEY TIME
Bus	2 Daily	1hr 30mins

LIVERPOOL – CAMPBELLTOWN
OTT TABLE 9110

TRANSPORT	FREQUENCY	JOURNEY TIME
Bus	2 Daily	25mins

CANPBELLTOWN – GOULBURN
OTT TABLE 9110

TRANSPORT	FREQUENCY	JOURNEY TIME
Bus	2 Daily	2hrs 10mins

GOULBURN – YASS
OTT TABLE 9110

TRANSPORT	FREQUENCY	JOURNEY TIME
Bus	Daily	2hrs 5mins

YASS – GUNDAGAI
OTT TABLE 9110

TRANSPORT	FREQUENCY	JOURNEY TIME
Bus	Daily	1hr 15mins

GUNDAGAI – WAGGA WAGGA
OTT TABLE 9110

TRANSPORT	FREQUENCY	JOURNEY TIME
Bus	2 Daily	1hr 5mins

WAGGA WAGGA – MILDURA
OTT TABLE 9110

TRANSPORT	FREQUENCY	JOURNEY TIME
Bus	2 Daily	9hrs

MILDURA – RENMARK
OTT TABLE 9110

TRANSPORT	FREQUENCY	JOURNEY TIME
Bus	2 Daily	1hr 20mins

RENMARK – ADELAIDE
OTT TABLE 9110

TRANSPORT	FREQUENCY	JOURNEY TIME
Bus	2 Daily	5hrs 25mins

Note: There are frequent local services from Sydney to Liverpool, Campbelltown and Goulburn.(OTT 9014).There is an additional bus service daily ex Tuesday and Wednesday.

FROM SEA TO SHINING SEA

This is just one possible route between Sydney and Adelaide — and to have a choice is an unusual situation in Australia. The journey of nearly 1,500 km crosses three states and takes you from the shores of the Pacific to the Southern Ocean. Much of the western half of the route is through land that has been transformed from desert to fruitfulness by irrigation schemes.

YASS

At one time, because of its situation in fertile country on the Yass River, Yass was considered as a site for the federal capital. The Hume Hwy once ran through the centre of town, creating massive traffic jams in the summer, but now there is a bypass.

The district of Yass was undiscovered by Europeans for over 30 years after the first convicts arrived, but by the 1830s settlers were arriving in a flood. Wheat production was established, then cattle raising, but it was sheep that dominated the economy, and Yass 'rode to prosperity on the sheep's back'. Its superfine wool is world famous and most of the world-record prices have been set by the Yass clip. The favourable soil and climate have also made this a major wine region.

ROUTE DETAIL

Hwy 31, the Hume Highway, is a real superhighway from Liverpool through Campbelltown to Goulburn and then north of Canberra to Yass (280 km). It is tempting to speed along it, but beware: this is one of the most closely patrolled roads in the country.

Gundagai is 105 km further on, and about 40 km past Gundagai turn right on the Sturt Hwy, Hwy 20, for Wagga Wagga (45 km). From here Hwy 20 runs clear across the state 560 km to Mildura, on the border between New South Wales and Victoria. (See p. 109 for a circular detour route to Broken Hill.)

Hwy 20 shadows the northern edge of Victoria to Renmark (140 km), then crosses the border into South Australia and reaches Adelaide after 255 km. The total journey is about 1,425 km.

Yass Tourist Information Centre, Coronation Park, Comur St; tel: (02) 6226 2557.

Australian Hotel-Motel $ 180 Comur St; tel: (02) 6226 1744.

Colonial Lodge Motor Inn $$ Hume Hwy, Cnr McDonald St; tel: (02) 6226 2211.

Hamilton Hume Motor Inn $$ Hume Hwy; tel: (02) 6226 1722.

Hi Way Motor Inn $ Hume Hwy; tel: (02) 6226 1300.

Swaggers Motor Inn $$ Hume Hwy; tel: (02) 6226 3188.

Thunderbird Motel $$ Hume Hwy; tel: (02) 6226 1088.

Yass Caravan Park $ Hume Hwy; tel: (02) 6226 1173.

Yass Motel $$ 38 Laidlaw St; tel: (02) 6226 1055.

Anna Lee's Restaurant $ 73 Comur St; tel: (02) 6226 2196.
Aussie Bistro $ 180 Comur St; tel: (02) 6226 3966.
Fook Lee Loy Chinese Restaurant $ 58 Comur St; tel: (02) 6226 1896.
Harlequin Restaurant $ Hume Hwy; tel: (02) 6226 2488.
Jolly Jumbuck Bistro $$ Comur St; tel: (02) 6226 3272.
Lien's Vietnamese Chinese Restaurant $ 164 Comur St; tel: (02) 6226 2595.
Mario's Pizzeria $ Pollux St; tel: (02) 6226 3144.

HIGHLIGHTS

Many handsome buildings line the wide central road of Yass and some still have their hitching rails for horses. The ornate ironwork clearly shows the prosperity of this area in the 19th century.

The Hamilton Hume Museum in Comur St next to the TIC relates local history and development. A simulation shearing stand occupies the rear of the museum, along with details of Sir Walter Merriman, founder of Fine Wool in the Yass district.

The tramway that opened in 1892 became a railway line in 1917 until it closed in 1988. The station has the shortest platform in Australia. Now it is a **railway museum**, in Lead St, only open Sun 1200–1600.

Several places within a 30-km radius of Yass are worth taking time to explore. The lake of the vast **Burrinjuck Dam** snakes around west of Yass. Its 645 km of foreshore are a delight, although in summer it attracts many water-skiers, making it somewhat noisy. **Wee Jasper Valley** at the lake's southern end is an idyllic little village with views of dramatic mountain ranges, magnificent caves, flowing clear streams and the lake.

HAMILTON HUME

Hamilton Hume was born in Australia in 1797 and could therefore be thought of as one of the first true Australians. By 1818 he had already discovered Lake Bathurst and the Goulburn Plains, and three years later he crossed the Yass Plains and discovered the Yass River. Later he led an expedition to the Murray River and accompanied Charles Sturt on his 1828 expedition into the bush. He settled in Yass, becoming a magistrate, and lived most of the time in **Cooma Cottage** (built about 1835), 4 km from the centre on the Yass Valley Way. The cottage is listed by the National Trust and is open every day except Tues. Before Hume died he supervised the building of his own tomb which can still be seen in the Yass graveyard. In 1860 he was elected a fellow of the Royal Geographical Society. He died in 1873.

BANJO PATERSON (1864–1941)

Banjo Paterson was one of Australia's first great literary figures and will be remembered forever if only for writing the words of 'Waltzing Matilda'. He grew up in the Yass region and later owned a station in the Wee Jasper area. After working as a correspondent for Australian newspapers during the Boer War he returned to Sydney to become editor of the *Evening News* from 1903 to 1908. He joined the army in 1915, rising to the rank of major, but after the war resumed his career as a sports editor, journalist and freelance writer. He had begun to write verses and ballads as early as 1885, heavily influenced by his childhood years in Yass, and adopted the pen name 'Banjo' from the name of a family racehorse. Best-known among his other works are *The Man from Snowy River* and *Clancy of the Overflow*.

EN ROUTE

Gundagai is a name known to every Australian because of the lines in a folk song: 'And the dog sat on the tuckerbox/Five miles from Gundagai'. In fact, 'sat' is a politely altered version to allow schoolchildren to sing it. A statue of the dog, decorously sitting on the tuckerbox, is to be found at Five Mile Creek, just off the highway.

Murrumbateman, to the south, is the centre of the fast-growing wine industry. There are wine tastings in many of the numerous vineyards in the area.

Binalong to the north-west is famous because A. B. 'Banjo' Paterson is buried there. Binalong is also associated with the 'gentleman' bushranger Johnny Gilbert, known for the gallantry he displayed to his lady victims before he killed them. Legend tells that he was betrayed by his own grandfather. Visitors can see Gilbert's grave and the site where he was shot. **The Southern Cross Glass Studio** is worth visiting to observe the skill of the glass blowers and cutters.

WAGGA WAGGA

The largest inland city in Australia is most commonly just called Wagga, pronounced something like 'wohguh'. In the Wiradjuri language wagga (or wahga or wahgam) means 'crow', and wagga wagga means 'crows'. The tourist office would prefer that Wagga be known as the Garden Town of the South. And, indeed, it is renowned for its gardens and parks.

Among the first European explorers was Captain Charles Sturt, on a voyage of discovery down the Murrumbidgee River in 1829. Wagga quickly developed because it was where the north–south track between NSW and Victoria crossed the river. By 1847 the village had been laid out, and the police station and court of petty sessions established. The first river steamer to reach here was Francis Cadell's *Albury* in 1858. This was the start of a very brief period when the paddleboats navigating the inland

BUSHRANGERS BOLD AND NOTORIOUS

The area around Wagga was a haven for bushrangers. Mad Dan Morgan terrorised the area from 1863 to 1867, shooting the police magistrate. Although there was a reward on his head Morgan is said to have sat near the police magistrate at the Wagga Christmas races without being caught. He was eventually gunned down in an ambush.

In 1877 James Kelly, younger brother of the more famous Ned, was sentenced to ten years' gaol at Wagga courthouse for horse stealing. When released he dissociated himself from his family and led a respectable life, dying in 1946 aged nearly 90.

Captain Moonlite, whose real name was Andrew Scott, was the bushranger who brought most fame to Wagga. He had plenty of style and committed at least one robbery while acting as a lay preacher. His downfall came at Wantabadgery Station, east of Wagga, where he and his gang of five had taken 39 people hostage. Reports of the time are colourful in the extreme, but it is certain that he and his gang did not kill anyone. A hostage escaped and called the police, and in the ensuing shoot-out a trooper and two bushrangers (one of whom was only 15) were killed. The gang surrendered and Captain Moonlite and one accomplice were later hanged.

waterways of Australia were an important form of transport. The last steamer to visit Wagga was in 1905, which means that, glorious though they were to look at, the paddle steamers were commercially important for less than 50 years.

Water, however, is still an essential part of Wagga. The city is the centre of the Riverina, an agricultural district dependent on irrigation. The Murrumbidgee runs right through the town. It even has a beach, which allows the town to boast of having Australia's only inland life-saving club patrol. Lake Albert, formed by diverting water from Crooked and Stringybark Creeks into a swamp, now has sailing, fishing, canoeing and water-skiing.

i **Tourism Wagga Wagga**, Tarcutta St; tel: (02) 6923 5499/5402 or Free Call (1800) 68 1141.
Wagga Wagga City Library, 40 Gurwood St; open weekdays 1000–1900, Sat 1000–1700.

There are two main areas for motel accommodation: along the Sturt Hwy and Tarcutta St.
Ashmont Inn Hotel Motel $$ Tobruk St; tel: 6931 1899.
Boulevard Motor Inn $$ 305 Edward St; tel: 6925 5388.
Caravan Park Carinya $ Pine Gully Rd; tel: 6933 1256.
Club Motel $$ 73 Morgan St; tel: 6921 6966.

Crepe Myrtle B&B $$ 102 Kincaide St; tel: (02) 6921 4757. Email jbarter@dragnet.com.au
Old Wagga Inn $$ Tarcutta St, cnr Morgan St; tel: 6921 6444.
Red Steer Hotel Motel $ Olympic Way; tel: 6921 1344.
Riverview Caravan Park $ 93 Hammond Ave; tel: 6921 4287.
Squatters Own Motor Inn $ 60 Tarcutta St; tel: 6921 5400.
The Manor $ 38 Morrow St; tel: 6921 5962.
Wagga Tourist Caravan Park $ 2 Johnston St; tel: 6921 2540.

Most of the restaurants can be found on and around Baylis St and the Baylis Centre. This is a good place to taste the local wines. In Australia it is said that the irrigation wines of the Riverina have a salty taste which makes them instantly detectable.
Choices Restaurant $$ 55 Baylis St; tel: 6921 2208.
Ii Corso Pizza Restaurant $ 21 Baylis St; tel: 6921 9133.
Jasmin Village Chinese Restaurant $$ 35 Kincaid St; tel: 6921 3300.
Kebab Place Restaurant $ 152 Fitzmaurice St. Authentic Lebanese food; tel: 6921 6307.
Montezuma's Mexican Restaurant $$ 85 Baylis St; tel: 6921 4428.
Tokyo Teppanyaki Japanese Restaurant $$ 146 Fitzmaurice St; tel: 6921 9211.
Wagga Thai Restaurant $ 229 Baylis St; tel: 6921 5252.
Wagga Wagga Eating House $ 46 Baylis St; tel: 6921 3748.
Zester's Restaurant $$ 81 Peter St; tel: 6921 5897.

HIGHLIGHTS

The **Wagga Wagga and District Historical Museum** includes a selection of photographs and documents detailing Wagga's colourful local history. It also has a blacksmith's shop, a collection of historical engines and vehicles and a range of period clothing, as well as a bullet fired by Dan Morgan. The museum is on Lord Baden Powell Dr in the Yallowin Hut (which dates from 1834) and, like most country town museums in Australia, is open limited hours. Usually this is 1400–1700 weekends, Tues and Wed but this may be extended – check at the TIC.

The highlights among Wagga's many gardens and parks range from the **Botanic Gardens and Zoo** (about 1.5 km south of the station) to the formal **Shakespearean Garden** and **Apex Park** on the shores of Lake Albert. **Collins Park** is the oldest and

WALKING AND DRIVING TOURS

There are three historic walks through the city for which you can get maps and directions at the TIC. These take you past many of Wagga's historic buildings and start from the visitors centre. Two are very serious walks: the Wollundry Loop (10 km) circumnavigates the lagoon or, for the ultimate challenge, there is the 32 km Wiradjuri Walking Track. There is also a self-drive Red Arrow 28 km motor tour that takes in 31 of Wagga's main attractions.

features the South African War Memorial and a great array of colour provided by hydrangeas, azaleas and rhododendrons. An **Outdoor Entertainment Centre and Music Bowl** can accommodate a symphony orchestra and has seating for 3,000 people.

Charles Sturt University, which does much work on soil conservation, is unique in having its own **winery**. Other universities go quite green with jealousy at the thought. It is in Coolamon Rd, 9 km north of the city centre, and is an extension of Australia's leading wine science school, which focuses on combining traditional winemaking methods with state-of-the-art technology. It produces an excellent university-label wine and is open daily 1000–1600 for wine tastings and cellar door sales. There is also the **Wagga Wagga Winery** at 427 Oura Rd, open daily 1100–1800.

The **Murray Cod Hatcheries and Fauna Park** are on the Sturt Hwy 8 km out of town. Here you can discover the life story of Australia's majestic Murray cod from hatchery to pond. You can also see Big Murray – a cod believed to be over 100 years old, weighing in at 52 kg and 1.37 m long. There is also an indoor multi-aquarium complex displaying a wide selection of live native fish and crustaceans.

At **Junee**, 40 km north, is what is left of the railway system of New South Wales. The line runs through the centre of the town and the railway station, built in 1883, has immense presence and dignity. The Monte Cristo Homestead on a hill overlooking Junee is a two-storey Georgian mansion completed in 1884; $$ open daily 1000–1600.

MILDURA

Mildura is at the point where Victoria, New South Wales and South Australia meet, but what defines it is the Murray River.

The first white squatter arrived in 1846, and just nine years later came the epic event that was to change the fate of Mildura. In 1855 Alfred Deakin, who was later to become prime minister of Australia, managed to talk the Canadian irrigation experts, George and William Chaffey, into coming to Australia. The Chaffey brothers saw that exotic fruits would flourish in the red soil of the Mildura area,

THE TICHBORNE CLAIMANT

Improbably, Wagga is involved in the story of the Tichborne Claimant. Arthur Orton was a butcher and a small-time sheep stealer. He arrived in the town in 1864 claiming to be Roger Charles Doughty Tichborne, the heir to a Hampshire baronetcy who was believed drowned when the ship in which he was travelling disappeared off South America. Orton was fat and almost illiterate. The man he impersonated was slim and fairly well educated. Yet Orton went to England and was able to persuade Lady Tichborne that he was her son.

The trustees of the Tichborne estate were not so gullible. They rejected his claim and the ensuing legal action by Orton still holds the record for being the longest in English legal history. Eventually, in 1874 Orton was sentenced to 14 years in gaol for perjury. On his deathbed he still swore he was Tichborne.

The Tichborne Claimant was one of the great melodramas of Victorian times and made Wagga so notorious that Mark Twain, on his visit to Australia, made a special detour to see the place.

provided there was water. Accordingly, the Chaffey Agreement set aside 250,000 acres at Mildura, on which the brothers promised to spend £300,000 developing an irrigation system, using the Murray as the source. Following numerous setbacks, during which George returned home and Chaffey Bros Ltd went into liquidation, the plan became profitable after the turn of the century. William, who had stayed on, established a winery, White Cliffs (now Mildara Blass) and became mayor of the town in 1920.

Now Mildura is at the centre of the great Sunraysia district, the largest producer of dried vine fruits such as raisins, currants and sultanas in Australia. Around 80 per cent of Australia's total production of fruit is grown in the district as well as a range of stone fruits and vegetables.

EN ROUTE

The Clydesdale Stud and Pioneer Farm, towards Narrandera, has antique machinery, a pioneer's hut and demonstrations of Clydesdale horses in action. Open daily except Thur.

Mildura Tourist Information Centre, corner of Deakin Ave and Twelfth St. The centre has an interpretative display on the main attractions and history of the region, and also a small theatre and licensed restaurant; tel: (03) 5021 4424.
Department of Natural Resources and Environment, corner of Eleventh St and Langtree Pde, for information on national and state parks; tel: (03) 5022 3000.

Most of the motels are on Deakin Ave – all 12 km of it. You will have no trouble finding accommodation at almost any time of the year. Most of the restaurants are in the same avenue.

Apex Caravan Park $ Cureton Ave; tel: 3523 2309.
Chaffey International Motor Inn $$ 244 Deakin Ave; tel: 3523 5833.
Commodore Motel $ Deakin Ave, cnr Seventh St; tel: 3523 0241.
Cottonwood Motel $$ 326 Deakin Ave; tel: 3523 5166.
Deakin Motor Inn $ 413 Deakin Ave; tel: 3523 0218.
Early Australian Motor Inn $$ 453 Deakin Ave; tel: 3521 1011.
Kar Rama Motor Inn $ 153 Deakin Ave; tel: 3523 4221.
Mildura Park Motel $ Eighth St; tel: 3523 0479.
Motel Sunraysia $ Deakin Ave; tel: 3523 0137.
Murray View Motel $ San Mateo Ave, cnr Seventh St; tel: 3521 1200.
Northaven Motor Inn $ 138 Deakin Ave; tel: 3523 0521.
Plantation Motel $ 145 Deakin Ave; tel: 3523 0317.
River City Motel $ San Mateo Ave, cnr Fifteenth St; tel: 3523 5177.
Riviera Motel $ 157 Seventh St; tel: 3523 3696.
Rosemont Holiday Guest House $ 154 Madden Ave; tel: 3523 1535.
Sandor's Motor Inn $$ 179 Deakin Ave; tel: 3523 0047.
Seventh Street Motel $ 153 Seventh St; tel: 3523 1796.
Three States Motel $ 847 Fifteenth St; tel: 3523 3735.
Vineland Motel $ 363 Deakin Ave; tel: 3523 4036.
Wheatlands Motel $ 433 Deakin Ave; tel: 3523 3834.

Barnacle Bill Seafood $$ 360 Deakin Ave; tel: 5021 2166.
Chaffey Restaurant $$ 244 Deakin Ave; tel: 5023 5833.
Dragon Tower Chinese Restaurant $ 29 Langtree Ave; tel: 5023 1925.
Indian Tandoori Oven $ 27 Deakin Ave; tel: 5023 6255.
Jessica's Restaurant $$ 232 Deakin Ave; tel: 5022 1466.
Kings Palace Chinese Restaurant $ 98 Madden Ave; tel: 5023 0994.
Lauretz of Langtree $$ 19 Langtree Ave; tel: 5022 1722.
Lee's Garden Restaurant $$ 117 Eighth St; tel: 5023 2772.
Our Shenanigans $$ 70a Langtree Ave; tel: 5023 5279.
Regal Chinese Restaurant $ 224 Deakin Ave; tel: 5021 3688.
Rendezvous Restaurant & Bistro $$ 34 Langtree Ave; tel: 5023 1571.

Retreat Restaurant $$ 413 Deakin Ave; tel: 5023 0218.
Simpson's Restaurant $$ 153 Deakin Ave; tel: 5023 4221.
Steak Cave Restaurant $$ 29 Deakin Ave; tel: 5022 2223.
Sunny's $ 66 Lime Ave; tel: 5021 2439.
Vegetarian Restaurant $ Chaffey Ave, cnr Seventh St; tel: 5023 4542.

HIGHLIGHTS

Mildura owes much to the irrigation pioneers George and William Chaffey. The brothers were also responsible for the design of the town, which is why, following the North American pattern, avenues run north–south and have names, while streets run east–west and have numbers. The main thoroughfare is named after Alfred Deakin and runs for 12 km – the longest straight main road in Australia. Originally, the Chaffeys intended that the town would be served with trams so the central avenue is very wide to allow for this. Mildura's many gum and palm trees were planted by William Chaffey, and the town remembers him with a statue in Deakin Ave, erected in 1929.

William's home, **Rio Vista**, is open to the public. It demonstrates the Victorian way of announcing success. It has German lead lighting, hand-painted windows imported from England, Italian floor tiles and beautifully crafted red gum fittings. Displays upstairs relate to colonial and Aboriginal history, including furniture, photographs, period costumes, letters and other memorabilia. Rio Vista was completed in 1892 and is now part of the **Mildura Arts Centre** which is on the corner of Chaffey and Cureton Aves. Nearby is the replica of the red gum slab homestead which was the first home in the district. Other buildings in the complex include a woolshed and stables, and there are exhibitions relating to irrigation and the town's riverboat past. $. Open Mon–Fri 0900–1700 and weekends 1300–1700. **Rio Vista Park**, opposite, contains a number of outdoors sculptures and an amphitheatre.

THE SNAKE RIVER

The Murray River flows for 2,530 km, which makes it one of the longest navigable rivers in the world; its catchment area covers about 14 per cent of Australia.

The Aboriginal people have a fable to account for the presence of the river. The area was without water and had little vegetation. One day Biami, one of the most powerful ancestral beings of the Yorta Yorta community, sent a woman to dig for roots in the dry ground. As protection, he sent with her a giant snake. The snake faithfully stayed with the woman, following the line of her digging stick in the dry dusty land. Then Biami shouted out to the skies in his voice of thunder. Lightning flashed and the rain fell. The rain traced the snake's movements and developed the great, winding river we now call the Murray.

EN ROUTE

At **Lake Cullulleraine**, 58 km west of Mildura, there is boating and swimming and a track runs for 10 km around the lake.

MILDURA WINES

Some of Victoria's finest wineries are to found in the Mildura district. Apart from **Lindemans**, the largest winery in the southern hemisphere, some local wineries include:

Mildara Blass: on the white cliffs overlooking the Murray. First established (as White Cliffs) in 1888 by William Chaffey. Open Mon–Fri 0900–1700, Sat–Sun 1000–1600.

Capogreco Winery: a small family winery in Mildura itself (Riverside Ave, between 17th and 18th Sts); produces wines in the Italian style. Open Mon—Sat 1000–1800 for tastings and cellar door sales.

Allambie Wines: south of Irymple; wine-tasting Mon–Fri 1000–1630.

The **Mildura Regional Art Gallery** has a substantial collection of traditional Australian paintings as well as one of the the largest collections of contemporary sculpture in Australia.

Woodsie's Gem Shop, on the corner of Morpung and Cureton Aves, is not a promising name but this is one of Australia's largest gemstone cutting and jewellery manufacturing complexes. Open daily 0900–1730 with demonstrations of gem cutting at 1100 and 1430. On display are gems from around the world including a private collection which is quite rightly called Aladdin's Cave. Outside, a garden is set up to keep children amused and there is a small cafeteria.

The **Murray River**, of course, is an attraction in itself. There are cruises along the river and cycle paths which follow its course. **Paddle steamers** leave from Mildura Wharf at the end of Madden Ave for trips on both the Murray and Darling rivers. One of the boats, **PS *Melbourne***, is still steam-driven, making it probably one of the only two passenger ships in the world still running on coal-fired boilers (the other is the TSS *Earnslaw* in Queenstown, New Zealand). To book, tel: (03) 5023 3300. On the other side of the river, the **Buronga Boatman** hires out powerboats, canoes and kayaks which can be used to explore the river; tel: (03) 5023 5874.

The **Golden River Zoo** is 4 km from town along River Rd, but you can also reach it by cruise boat. There is a large aviary and a good selection of wombats and kangaroos, some of which can be patted and fed. $. Open daily 0900–1700.

BROKEN HILL: THE SILVER CITY

Broken Hill, 300 km north of Mildura, is an artificial oasis built in the arid wastelands of the Barrier Ranges. The reason for its existence is that it stands on the richest silver-lead-zinc deposit ever discovered. The mine has so far provided minerals worth almost $2 billion and more than one-third of the silver in the world.

There were gold prospectors in the area by 1867, but it wasn't until 1883 that Charles Rasp, a watchful boundary rider at Mount Gipps station, discovered what he thought were tin deposits at the 'broken hill'. A syndicate of seven was set up to purchase the surrounding land to prevent a rush from other miners. In January 1885 they hit what turned out to be a body of silver-lead-zinc lodes in a continuous arch 7 km long and 220 m wide. The syndicate's Broken Hill Proprietary Company (BHP) is now Australia's largest company. (A station hand who won a one-fourteenth share from his boss in a card game found that three years later it was worth £1,250,000.)

Charles Rasp was not just a knockabout boundary rider who got lucky. He was born Hieronymous Salvator Lopez von Pereira in Saxony, a scion of the Portuguese aristocracy. He appears to have abandoned his army career during the Franco-Prussian War – an astute move – and headed for Australia.

Within eight years of the first find Broken Hill was a major town with a population of 20,000. More than 4,000 people now work directly for the mining company. What the town will do when the ore runs out or when silver is no longer needed for photography is the subject of much debate.

Broken Hill Tourists' and Travellers' Centre, corner of Blende and Bromide Sts; tel: (08) 8087 6077.

Broken Hill Caravan Park $ Rakow St; tel: (08) 8087 3841.
Day Dream Motel $$ 77 Argent St; tel: (08) 8088 3033.
Hill Top Motor Inn $$ 271 Kaolin St; tel: (08) 8088 2999.
Lakeview Caravan Park $ 1 Mann St; tel: (08) 8088 2250.
Lodge Outback Motel $ 252 Mica St; tel: (08) 8088 2722.
Mario's Hotel Motel $ 172 Beryl St; tel: (08) 8088 5944.
Miners Lamp Motor Inn $$ 357 Cobalt St; tel: (08) 8088 4122.
Motel Broken Hill Overlander $$ 142 Iodide St; tel: (08) 8088 2566.
Motor Inn Silverhaven $$ 577 Argent St; tel: (08) 8087 2218.
Mulberry Vale Cabins $ Menindee Rd; tel: (08) 8088 1597.
Old Willyama Motor Inn $$ 30 Iodide St; tel: (08) 8088 3355.
Susan Spicer's Holiday Cottages $$ Beautifully decorated. 143 Knox St; tel: (08) 8087 8488.

Broken Hill Musician's Club Bistro $$ 279 Crystal St; tel: (08) 8087 5428.
Golden Lotus Room $ 328 Crystal St; tel: (08) 8087 2656.
Old Capri Pizza & Pasta $ 415 Argent St; tel: (08) 8088 2804.
Pagoda Restaurant $ 357 Cobalt St; tel: (08) 8087 3679.
Paragon Restaurant $$ 181 Argent St; tel: (08) 8088 5101.
Silver City Restaurant $$ 1 Oxide St; tel: (08) 8088 5860.
Swagman's Restaurant $$ 182 Ryan St; tel: (08) 8087 8184.
Victoria's $$ Oxide St., cnr Argent St; tel: (08) 8087 2895.

HIGHLIGHTS

It is a surprise to find Broken Hill a green and pleasant town. A local naturalist, Albert Morris, who worked with the Zinc Corporation in 1936, experimented with the regeneration of vegetation, and a green belt now separates Broken Hill from its dry and inhospitable surroundings.

Broken Hill is very much a union city – possibly the most unionised in the world – and the**Trades Hall** which was built at the turn of the century was the first building in Australia to be owned by a trade union. The city also has a **mosque** which was built in 1891 by and for the Afghan camel drivers who made the development of much of the outback possible.

An ideal way to get the feel of the town is to go on one of the walking tours. These start on Mon, Wed, Fri and Sat at 1000 outside the visitors' centre. **Argent St** (all the main streets are named after chemicals) has been classified by the National Trust and includes the post office, the town hall facade, the police station, technical college and courthouse.

The **Gladstone Mining Museum** displays life-size replicas of current and old-time mining procedures. Wearing a miner's hat, boots and overall, you can tour **Delprat's Mine**, descending in a miner's cage to 122 m under the ground. $$. The tour price may seem expensive but half goes in insurance. The 2-hr tours start 1030 Mon–Fri.

You may recognise **Silverton**, 25 km northwest of Broken Hill, from *Mad Max 2* or *Razorback* or any of the many other films which have been made here. Silverton was the largest town in the Barrier Ranges before the discovery of Broken Hill, but the development of Broken Hill coincided with the exhaustion of its own deposits, and by 1907 it ceased to be a municipality. Today, Silverton is a ghost town that is sort of coming to life. The gaol has been converted into a small museum (open daily 0930–1630) and there are half a dozen private art galleries. The population is at least 60.

A further 10 km out of Silverton is the **Mundi Mundi Lookout** which offers exceptional views of the plains.

BRUSHMEN OF THE BUSH

Although very much a mining city, Broken Hill has produced a remarkable number of artists, collectively known as Brushmen of the Bush. There are at least 20 art galleries in the city.

Lying 195 km east of Broken Hill, **Wilcannia** was the boom town of the 1870s. Gold, copper, silver and opals drew prospectors from far and wide, and its location on the Darling made it the third largest inland port in the country – the entire wool clip of north-west New South Wales was loaded here. By 1920 it was all over and the Queen City of the West quietly went to sleep.

If you stroll around the town you can still see its past glory in the fine old buildings, most of which have been recognised by the National Trust as buildings of historic importance. A Wilcannia shower, by the way, is a dust storm.

RENMARK

Renmark is, in a sense, a sister city to Mildura. The town is in the heart of the Chaffey brothers' irrigation scheme (see p. 107), and is Australia's oldest irrigation settlement, begun by the brothers after they were granted 100 ha on which to test their project. The town was named by George Chaffey in 1887 and may come from an Aboriginal word said to mean 'red mud'.

The irrigation scheme still operates; it covers nearly 7,000 ha of land along the Murray and the land around Renmark produces wine and table grapes, citrus, stone and dried fruits, and vegetables for local and export markets. Renmark is a provincial centre on a beautiful bend of the river with tourism added to wheat, wool, fruit, wine and brandy production as a source of income. It is also a retirement home for some of the old paddle wheelers which ran the river trade until the railways came in and showed they could do the same thing faster and cheaper.

i **Renmark Information Centre,** Murray Ave; tel: (08) 8586 6704.

Citrus Valley $$ 210 Renmark Ave; tel: 8586 6717.
Grays Caravan Park $ 27 Pyap St; tel: 8586 6522.
Motel Ventura $ 234 Renmark Ave; tel: 8586 6841.
Renmark Country Club Motel $$ Sturt Hwy; tel: 8595 1401.
Renmark Hotel Motel $ Murray Ave. Bistro, outdoor swimming pool and spa; tel: 8586 6755.

Renmark Riverfront Caravan Park $ Patey Dr. Cabins and on the river; tel: 8586 6315.
Renmark YHA $16th St; tel: 8586 6937.
Riverbend Caravan Park of Renmark $ Sturt Hwy. Cabins but not on the river; tel: 8595 5131.

Ashley's Restaurant $$ 210 Renmark Ave; tel: (08) 8586 6717.
Ginger Mick's Pizza $ 124 Murray St; tel: (08) 8586 4066. Open until late every night except Sun.
Riverland Golden Palace Chinese Restaurant $ 114 Renmark Ave; tel: (08) 8586 6065. Licensed.
Sophia's Restaurant $ 202 Renmark Ave; tel: (08) 8586 5316. Greek food. Actually in the Caltex service station.

HIGHLIGHTS

Next door to the TIC, an **Interpretive Centre** tells the full story of the Murray – its history from ancient times, its geology, the story of the local Aboriginal inhabitants, the irrigation scheme and the boats that plied its waters. Open Mon–Fri 0900–1700, Sat 0900–1600, Sun 1200–1600.

For 50 years riverboats were the easiest way of moving people and goods around much of Australia. Captain Charles Sturt travelled by whale boat down the Murrumbidgee in late 1829, joining the Murray and passing the present site of Renmark in late Jan 1830. But although the potential of this inland waterway had been recognised quite early on, its use for transportation did not become a reality until the port of Goolwa was established at the river's mouth. Then, for the 20 years between 1880 and 1900, over 200 paddle boats and barges operated from Goolwa right up to the Victorian goldfields.

The **PS** *Industry* was built in Goolwa in 1911 for the Engineering and Water Supply Department. Its job was to go up and down the river removing snags that were a danger to navigation. Now it has been fully restored to working order and turned into a museum - one that can and does still regularly steam up and down river, an impressive sight as its two massive paddle-wheels churn along. Open Mon–Fri 0900–1630, Sat 0900–1530, Sun 1200–1530. The tourist office has information about cruise times and prices.

The **PS *Murray Princess***, the largest stern-paddle steamer in the southern hemisphere, takes five-day cruises out of Renmark. This old-style vessel has all modern conveniences – spa, sauna and even an electric lift.

As they did in Mildura, the Chaffey brothers had the streets of Renmark numbered in the North American style, and **Olivewood**, in 21st St, is a log cabin built in 1887 for George Chaffey. The design undoubtedly reflects the brothers' Canadian origins, but with adaptations, such as broad verandahs, made to suit its Australian location. The interior has period furniture and the house now operates as a museum telling the story of Renmark's pioneering days. The orchard has been well maintained with orange, lemon, olive and grapefruit trees. $. Open Thur–Mon 1000–1600, Tues 1400–1600.

Community Hotel

What is reputed to be the first community hotel in the British Empire was set up here in 1897; the Renmark Hotel is still run by an elected board of management, with the profits going to community improvements. This system exists in many towns in the area. It means they have one huge pub which makes the community a profit, but it does not lead to interesting and exciting venues.

Ruston's Rose Garden on Moorna St, off 23rd St, is home to 40,000 rose bushes, with over 3,500 different varieties. Planting started back in 1924. The roses are at their best in the second part of Oct and remain in bloom through the summer and autumn. Open daily 15 Sept – 1 July, 0900–1800.

Bredl's Wonder World of Wildlife on the corner of Sturt Hwy and 28th St is one of the largest private zoos in Australia. It reportedly has the biggest collection of reptiles, with over 200 species on display as well as crocodiles and other animals and birds. Open daily 0900–1800. There is snake handling daily at 1100 and 1400, and you can see the snakes being fed every Sun 1400–1500.

There are several major vineyards in the area. **Renmano** was established in 1914, starting life as a co-operative until it became a private company and eventually merged with Thomas Hardy. Open Mon–Fri 0900–1700, Sat 0900–1600 and Sun 1000–1400. **Angove's** was the first vineyard on the river, having started in 1886. Open Mon–Fri 0900–1700.

Renmark is surrounded by national parks and reserves, of which the most accessible is the **Murray River National Park**. It has four separate areas – Katarapko Creek, Lyrup Flats, Bulyong Island and Eckert Creek. The nearest to Renmark is Bulyong Island, which you reach by way of Renmark North. Towards Berri, southwest of Renmark, is Lyrup Flats, and beyond Berri, hanging down in a great loop towards Loxton, is Katarapko. Lyrup Flats and Eckert Creek starkly reveal the potential problems of irrigation – most of the trees have been killed either by salt or high flood levels. This is a bleak landscape but an amazing breeding and feeding ground for wild birds. Nearly 150 different species have been recorded in the park's quiet backwaters and horseshoe lagoons.

Danggali Conservation Park, 90 km north of Renmark, was created by putting together four major sheep stations. The vegetation here varies from mallee woodland to blue bush shrubland and is home to both red and grey kangaroos.

Some 50 km east of Renmark are the flood plains and wetlands of **Chowilla Game Reserve**, accessible from either Wentworth Rd or Murtho Rd. All of these form part of the **Bookmark Biosphere Reserve**; for information, tel: (08) 8595 8010. This is rugged country with no facilities whatsoever, and should only be approached in serious expedition mode.

WHERE NEXT?

An unmissable detour before reaching Adelaide is the Barossa Valley (see p. 127), one of Australia's premier wine regions.

Adelaide is a dignified city, a place with much style and sensibility. There is none of the rivalry between Adelaide and the other cities of Australia that so adversely affects the reputations of Melbourne and Sydney: it stands alone, serene and slightly aloof, although it is far from being a stuffy city. Adelaide has an almost European style and many Australians consider it the premier city of Australia.

The city was founded in 1836 and named after Queen Adelaide, wife of King William IV. Her portrait is well known in Australia, as it appears on every bottle of Queen Adelaide wine. It is called the City of Light, partly because of its airiness and spaciousness, and punningly because much of it was designed by that remarkable pioneer, William Light. The original European explorer of the area was Captain Collett Barker in 1831, but it was Colonel Light who laid out the plan of Adelaide, 10 km inland from its port. It is impossible to overestimate Light's influence on the future style of the city, for despite huge expansion, his original plan, which reserved large areas for parkland, has been maintained.

In 1842, settlers were moved to the present city from what is now Glenelg, and in 1841, only four years after Colonel Light presented his city plan, the town fathers had formed a council to run Adelaide's affairs. In 1838 the first school in South Australia was opened here, and in 1842 the discovery of copper at Kapunda, followed by the Burra find in 1845, speeded up the growth of Adelaide and pushed its expansion into the outer suburbs.

Colonel Light (1786–1839)

During the Napoleonic Wars, William Light had fought as a volunteer at Corunna, where he was severely wounded, and interned by Napoleon at Verdun. He arrived in South Australia in 1836 as its first Surveyor-General, and began his plans for Adelaide in Jan 1837. Perhaps town planning was in his blood: his father was responsible for the layout of Georgetown on Penang, and Adelaide is now twinned with it. He resigned the post in 1838 and died from tuberculosis on 6 Oct 1839. A memorial in the form of a marble column marks his grave in Light Square, and his statue overlooks Adelaide from Montefiore Hill, but his true memorial is the City of Light itself.

The feeling prevalent in

other Australian cities, that Adelaide is perhaps a little slow, a little stick-in-the-mud and overly conservative, is simply not correct. In many ways Adelaide has led the country. The University of Adelaide, which opened in 1882, admitted women as well as men from its inception, and Adelaide can claim several firsts: the Chamber of Commerce (1839) and the Chamber of Manufactures (1869) were the first institutions of their kind in the colonies; in 1856 the first state-owned steam railway in the British Empire was opened between Adelaide and Port Adelaide; and Adelaide was, with the completion of the Overland Telegraph to Darwin in 1872, the first major Australian settlement to have a telegraph-cable link with London.

In the last three decades Adelaide has become a cultural city, a dining-out city, a sophisticated city. And yet it has managed to do this without losing any of its country town charm.

ARRIVAL AND DEPARTURE

Adelaide's airport, for both international and domestic flights, is just 6 km west, between the centre and the sea. There is an airport bus (tel: 8381 5311) to city hotels and some hostels, which runs every 30 mins or so Mon–Fri 0700–2130 and hourly on Sat and Sun; this takes about 30 mins to Victoria Square. Hostels will pick you up or drop you off if you are staying there.

Hwy 1 passes through Adelaide on its trip around Australia's perimeter and other highways end (or begin) here: the Stuart Hwy (Rte 87), which crosses the Red Centre, and the Barrier and Sturt Hwys (Rtes 32 and 20) which link Adelaide and Sydney. Buses run directly between Adelaide and most other cities: Melbourne is about 11–12 hrs, Sydney 20–26 hrs depending on the route and Alice Springs about 25 hrs. The central bus station used by most carriers is at 101–11 Franklin St.

INFORMATION

TOURIST OFFICE

South Australian Travel Centre, corner of North Ter and King William St; tel: 8212 1505.

Port Adelaide Visitor Information Centre, corner Commercial Rd and St Vincent St, Port Adelaide; tel: 8447 4788.

INTERNET ACCESS The impressive **State Library of South Australia**, North Ter, is open Mon–Fri 0930–2000 and weekends 1200–1700.

INTERNET SITE http://www.acta.com.au/ shows the way it should be done.

MONEY Thomas Cook has foreign exchange office at 4 Rundle Mall; tel: 8231 6977; and at the international airport, James Schofield Dr; tel: 8234 3320.

POST AND PHONES The main post office is cnr King St and Franklin St. The phone code is 08.

ACCOMMODATION

Adelaide Backpacker's Hostel $ 263 and 253 Gilles St. Has double rooms; tel: 8223 5680.

Adelaide Backpackers Inn $ 112 Carrington St. Singles and doubles in annexe; tel: 8223 6635.

Adelaide City Central Motel $ 23 Hindley St; tel: 8231 4049.

Adelaide City Parklands Motel $ 471 Pulteney St; tel: 8223 1444.

Adelaide Meridien $$ 21 Melbourne St. North Adelaide. Bit expensive but sauna, spa and outdoor pool; tel: 8267 3033.

Adelaide Paringa Motel $$ 15 Hindley St. Heart of the CBD walking distance to Casino, Mall; tel: 8231 1000.

Adelaide Travelodge $$ 208 South Ter; tel: 8223 2744.

Albert Hall $ 16 South Esplanade, Glenelg. Opposite the sea; tel: 8376 0488.

Ambassadors' Hotel $$ 107 King William St. En suite. Tea making; tel: 8231 4331.

Austral Hotel $ 205 Rundle St. Basic rooms in music pub so check for noise; tel: 8223 4660.

Backpack Oz $ 144 Wakefield St, corner of Pulteney St. Single and double rooms; tel: 8223 3551.

Backpackers Glenelg Beach Headquarters $ Near beach with doubles and singles. 7 Moseley St, Glenelg; tel: 8376 0007.

Barron Townhouse $$ 164 Hindley St. Central location; tel: 8211 8255.

City Central Motel $ 23 Hindley St. Centrally located budget motel; tel: 8231 4049.

Clarice Hotel Motel $ 220 Hutt St. En suite. Car park; tel: 8223 3560.

Colley Motel Apartments $$ 22 Colley Ter, Glenelg. Opposite beach. Self-contained affordable apartments; tel: 8295 7535.

Crown and Sceptre $ 308 King William St. Centrally located budget – very inexpensive – hostel; tel: 8212 4159.

Director's Studios & Suites $$ 259 Gouger St. Self-catering apartments. Close to Chinatown and the Central Market. Very affordable; tel: 8231 3572.

East Park Lodge $ 341 Angas St. Single and double rooms; tel: 8223 1228.

Festival Lodge Motel $$ 140 North Ter. Restaurant; tel: 8212 7877.

Flagstaff Hotel $ 233 Franklin St; tel: 8231 4380.

Georgia Mews $$ 31-33 Wakefield St, Kent Town. Walk to city across park. One-bedroomed apartments; tel: 8362 0600.

Glenelg Seaway Apartments $$ 18 Durham St, Glenelg. Inexpensive apartments; tel: 8295 8503.

Greenways Apartments $$ 41 King William Rd, North Adelaide. Self-catering units; tel: 8267 5903.

Grosvenor Vista $$ 125 North Ter. Dates from 1918 with spacious rooms, gym and sauna. Price includes breakfast; tel: 8407 8888.

Kent Town Lodge Motel $$ 22 Wakefield St., Kent Town. Pool, sauna; tel: 8332 7571.

Kiwi Lodge Motel $$ 266 Hindley St; tel: 8231 2671.

Meledon Villa $ 268 Seaview Rd, Henley Beach. Seafront B and B; tel: 8235 0577.

Metropolitan Hotel $ 46 Grote St. Old, basic but very affordable rooms; tel: 8231 5471.

New World International Youth Hostel $ 29 Compton St; tel: 8212 6888.

Princes Arcade Motel $$ 262-266 Hindley St. Car park. Room service; tel: 82319524.

Princes Lodge Motel $ 73 Lefevre Ter, North Adelaide. En suite. Tea making; tel: 8267 5566.

Richmond Hotel On The Mall $$ 128 Rundle Mall. Restaurant, pool, spa, sauna, room service; tel: 8223 4044.

Riviera Motor Inn $$ 34 North Ter; tel: 8231 8000.

Strathmore Hotel $$ 129 North Ter. Restaurant, car park, room service; tel: 8212 6911.

Taft Motor Inn $$ 18 Moseley St, Glenelg. Self-catering motel near the beach; tel: 8376 1233.

Wests Private Hotel $ 110b Hindley St. Very budget accommodation; tel: 8231 7575.

Wilpena Pound Motel $ 219 East Terrace; tel: 8232 5454.

FOOD AND DRINK

Adelaide claims one eatery to every 32 citizens. It seems a ridiculous ratio, but in North Adelaide O'Connell St alone has over 40 restaurants, cafés and wine bars and several pubs that sell wine by the glass. Gouger St has almost as many, possibly reflecting its nearness to Central Market and its fresh produce. Nearby is Adelaide's Chinatown area.

Hutt St is said to be where modern Australian cuisine was born. In truth, it grew organically in a number of places from a number of sources, but Hutt St is a pleasant place to eat and watch the world go buy under the shade of the old broad verandahs.

Rundle St, especially the eastern end, is a lively place for street dining, and Melbourne St gives you choices from Mexican and Japanese to Cajun, Mediterranean and Asian. Hindley St, once rather sleazy and downmarket, has lifted its game and has some splendid ethnic restaurants as well as a range of nightclubs.

Al Fresco Gelateria & Pasticceria $, 260 Rundle St. 0630-very late. The place to be seen and drink superb coffee.

Amadora $$ 18 Leigh St. Italian flavour. Open lunch Mon-Fri, dinner Mon-Sat. Licensed; tel: 8231 7611.

Aroma $$ 108 Jetty Rd, Glenelg. Italian. Wood-fired pizza. Pasta. Seven days 1800-2230. Licensed; tel: 8376 9222.

Bacall's $$ 149 Melbourne St, North. Adelaide. Licensed. Open dinner Mon-Sat; tel: 8267 2035.

Brasserie Irodori $$ 291 Rundle St. Japanese bistro which you may not have thought existed. Licensed; tel: 8232 6799.

Buongiorno Caffe $, 145 The Parade, Norwood. Large, always lively café which reaches a crowded and noisy crescendo on Sunday night. Serves a wide variety of Italian food and drink. Daily 8am-1am or later.

Cactus Mexican Café, 236 Rundle St; tel: 8224 0631. Licensed. Open lunch, dinner Tue-Sun.

THE ADELAIDE PIE CARTS

For all Adelaide's trendy and cosmopolitan restaurant scene, its pie carts have remained very special. You can see them most easily at North Terrace but they appear in several places. The best known is Cowley's Pie Cart, which takes up its position each night at 1800 outside the post office on Franklin St and stays there until 0100 (0330 Fri and Sat). These carts have been around since 1915 and are something of an institution. The *specialité de la maison* is the floater. This is a hot meat pie with tomato sauce, sitting in a bowl of steaming green pea soup. Don't knock it until you've tried it.

Cafe De L'Orient $$ Moseley Sq, Glenelg. Asian food in the broadest sense. Lunch, dinner Mon-Sat. Licensed; tel: 8376 1222.

Cafe Miramare $$ 10 Jetty Rd, Glenelg. Wood-oven pizzas. Seven days, 0800-late. Licensed. Tel: 8295 6060.

Café Paradiso $ 150 King William Rd, Hyde Park. Long-established favourite; great coffee and real Italian alfresco dining, from pasta to osso buco. Licensed. Daily 0830–2200.

Café Piccante $$ 128 King William Rd, Goodwood. Gourmet pizzas. Wine by the glass. Daily 1100-late; tel: 8232 3213.

Capriccio Restaurant $$ 10 Sussex St, Glenelg. Traditional Italian. Licensed. Dinner 7 nights 1800-2300. Lunch Mon-Fri; tel: 8295 6453.

Ceylon Hut $ 27 Bank St. Carefully specify the level of heat. Licensed. Open lunch Mon-Fri, dinner Mon-Sat; tel: 8231 2034.

Chop Sticks in the City $ 9 Field St. Fast, inexpensive. Also takeaway; tel: 8231 3883.

Cork & Cleaver at the Bay $$ 712 Anzac Hwy, Glenelg. Steak house. Lunch Tue- Fri. Dinner Tue-Sun. Licensed.Tel: 8376 1066.

Embers Grill Restaurant $168 Gouger St. Barbecued beef; tel: 8410 0399.

Eros Ouzeri $$ 275-277 Rundle St. Licensed. Open lunch Sun-Fri, dinner 7 days. Greek meze. Sit outside at the attached café for Greek pastries and coffee. Licensed; tel: 8223 4022.

Gaucho's Argentinian Restaurant $$ 91 Gouger St. Not for vegetarians; tel: 8231 2299

Glutton's Corner Restaurant $ 237 Rundle St. Asian in a general sense; tel: 8232 1836

Hawkers Corner $, corner of Wright St and West Ter. Chinese, Thai, Malaysian and North Indian stalls. Tue-Sat 1700-2030, Sun 1130-2030.

Jerusalem Sheshkebab House $, 131A-131B Hindley St. Lebanese for Middle Eastern dishes. Mon–Sat noon until late, Sun noon–1600. BYO.

Jimmy Watson's Restaurant $$ 92 Pirie St.Reflecting the most famous name in Australian wine; tel: 8232 2644.

Magill Estate Restaurant $$, 78 Penfold Rd, Magill. 8 km out of town on the Magill Estate Vineyard. Great food but greater wines.

Marcellina Pizza Bar $ 273 Hindley St. At the quieter western end. All-night pizza, steak and pasta bar. Daily 1100-0500; tel: 8211 7560.

Ozone Fish Cafe $ 45 Commercial St, Port Adelaide. Possibly the oldest chippie in Australia having been there since 1884. Current owner has been there since 1955 and it is the only Australian fish and chip shop under Royal patronage. Queen Elizabeth and the Duke of Edinburgh dropped in during a royal visit in 1977.

Petaluma's Bridgewater Mill $$ Mt Barker Rd, Bridgewater. 17 km from the city in the vineyard. The food is great but Brian Croser's Petaluma and Bridgewater Mill wines are totally wonderful.

Rakuba African $ 33a O'Connell St, North Adelaide; tel: :8267 3227.

Red Ochre Grill $$ 129 Gouger St. Licensed. Lunch Mon-Fri, dinner 7 days; tel: 8212 7266.

Rising Sun Inn $$ 60 Bridge St, Kensington. 4 km out of town. Has won all sorts of awards. Licensed. Open lunch, dinner Mon-Sat; te:l 8333 0721.

Ruby's Café $ 255b Rundle St. This market caff has been there since the fifties but is now coming up to date. Open evenings 1830-late and Sunday breakfast.

The Mt Lofty Summit Café Bistro $ Summit Rd, Crafers. 12 km from town on Adelaide's highest peak with views over Adelaide, the Hills, and coast. Everything from a cappuccino to a three-course meal. Open seven days lunch and dinner.

Vego and Lovin' It $ 1st Floor, 240 Rundle St. Vegan café done with some style and very affordable.

Zuma Café $ 56 Gouger St. Near Central Market. Quiche is superb. Mon–Thu 0700–1800, Fri 0700–2100, Sat 0700–late.

GETTING AROUND

Getting around Adelaide is easy: it is a delightful city in which to walk, and the integrated public transport system is excellent. It is run by TransAdelaide, which has an information bureau on the corner of King William St and Currie St; tel: 8210 1000.

The TransAdelaide Busway, the **O-Bahn**, provides the world's fastest suburban bus ride. The track runs between the city centre and Tea Tree Plaza, one of Adelaide's largest undercover shopping malls. The buses leave Currie and Grenfell Sts in the city at about 15-min intervals during the week and at regular intervals on weekends.

The **Bee Line Free Bus Service** runs from Victoria Square via King William St into North Terrace and round in a loop. The buses run about every 10 mins 0800–1800 from bus stops on the route which have a bee symbol.

HIGHLIGHTS

Adelaide is Australia's fifth largest city, with a population of more than one million and a metropolitan area that stretches from Gawler in the north to Willunga in the south.

The best place to get an overall view of the city is **Light's Vision** on Montefiore Hill in North Adelaide. The statue of Colonel Light, a fine piece of sculpture, points across the parklands and the Torrens to the city and the Adelaide Hills which lie beyond.

For reasons which are not that easy to explain, Adelaide has always been something of the cultural centre of Australia. This is reflected in the **Art Gallery of South Australia**, which is on North Terrace. It has been in operation since 1881, only 45 years after the first European settlers arrived, and its collection of Australian colonial art is arguably the most comprehensive in Australia. Well worth searching out is the collection of Aboriginal Western Desert paintings, which are just stunning. It has its own website on www.artgallery.sa.gov.au. Open daily 1000–1700.

The **Performing Arts Collection of South Australia** is in the Southern Plaza basement of the Adelaide Festival Centre in King William St. More than 40,000 acquisitions – of which only a percentage are on display – trace the growth of the performing arts in the state and reflect some of the passion that the people of Adelaide have always had for the performing arts. Open Mon–Fri 0900–1700.

CRICKET'S HERO

Sir Donald Bradman is the greatest batsman in the history of cricket, an Australian legend and international hero. When Bob Hawke was prime minister of Australia he was asked if there was anyone he would prefer to be. He answered, without hesitation, Don Bradman. Bradman's record shows that he was at least twice as good as any other cricketer that ever lived. There is a priceless personal collection of cricket memorabilia covering 1927–77, much of it provided by the great Don, housed in a wonderful 19th-century building, the Institute on North Terrace. You can worship at the shrine Mon–Fri 1000–1700, weekends 1200–1700.

Performing arts of another sort are on show at

Parliament House, on the corner of North Terrace and King William St. On days when parliament is not sitting there are tours between 1000 and 1400. When parliament is sitting entry is permitted after 1400 to watch proceedings. The parliament was built in two stages, with half a century between them, but it now forms a very impressive exterior. This is the staid place of government where the then premier of the state, Don Dunstan, turned up in a pair of shocking-pink shorts. The place has never been the same since.

The **Jam Factory Craft and Design Centre** is at the corner of North Terrace and Morphett St. Despite the name, this is not amateur arts and crafts with thick pottery ill-decorated with glaze – the quality is very high. Open Mon–Fri 0900–1730, Sat–Sun 1000–1700.

Within Adelaide University on North Terrace is the **Tate Museum**, where the collection of rocks and fossils includes many from the Antarctic expeditions of Sir Douglas Mawson. The museum is in the Geology Department on the ground level: open Mon–Fri 0900–1700; website: www.geology.adelaide.edu.au/.

Australia is a country of grateful migrants – although of course, in the early days some of them may not have been as wholeheartedly keen on the move as later arrivals. The **Migration Museum** at 82 Kintore Ave (originally the Destitute Asylum) tells the story of the migrants, both convicts and free settlers. The museum is open Mon–Fri 1000–1700 and weekends 1200–1700.

The National Aboriginal Cultural Institute - **Tandanya** – in Grenfell St is the first of its size and scope in Australia. It is a multi-arts complex and includes galleries, workshops and performing areas. Tandanya is the Kaurna name for the Adelaide area. Here you can hear the didgeridoo being blown: the performers manage to keep a long continuous note by breathing in and blowing out simultaneously, which is not easy to do, as you will find out if you try. But this rotary breathing has been taken up by many other wind instrument performers, notably clarinettists, to allow the playing of far longer notes. Open daily 1000–1700.

The foundation stone for **Holy Trinity Anglican Church** in North Terrace was laid in 1838, and Adelaide is, indeed, a city of churches: Christ Church was built in 1848–9, **St Francis Xavier's Roman Catholic Cathedral** near Victoria Square was begun in 1856 and St Peter's Anglican Cathedral was started in 1869. A mosque, finished in 1890, was paid for by the Afghans who were running camel trains into the interior. These men were absolutely vital to the building and maintenance of the Overland Telegraph from Adelaide to Darwin.

Adelaide is also a city of parks and open spaces. **Elder Park**, between the Festival

Centre and south bank of the Torrens Lake, has a rotunda dating from 1882, which is one of the most identifiable sights of Adelaide. You can move elegantly and romantically along the River Torrens in a real Venetian gondola - available most days outside Gekkos, Elder Park near the Hyatt Regency. **Bonython Park**, off Port Rd, has a lake with paddle boats for hire, a playground and model-boat pond. The **Adelaide Himeji Garden**, on the corner of South Terrace and Glen Osmond Rd, is a traditional Japanese garden with a temple gate, lanterns, bridge and small lake marking a sister city link. There are many more. Like every other city in Australia Adelaide has magnificent botanic gardens. The **Adelaide Botanic Gardens and Bicentennial Conservatory**, begun in 1855, feature the oldest glasshouse in Australia, and the conservatory contains a complete tropical rainforest. Off North Terrace; open Mon–Fri 0800–1830, weekends 0900–1830; conservatory open 1000–1600.

Adelaide Zoo, one of the oldest zoos in Australia, is in shady parklands off Frome Rd, only a short stroll from the city centre. Like all intelligent zoos it is moving away from the caged exhibit. Open daily 0930–1700.

EVENTS

South Australia enjoys two of the country's major festivals: the **Barossa Valley Vintage Festival** on odd-numbered years (see p. 127) and the **Adelaide Arts Festival** in Feb–Mar of even-numbered years. For three weeks the Arts Festival is celebrated across the city, embracing theatres, clubs and open spaces, with its epicentre the Adelaide Festival Centre in King William St, on the banks of the River Torrens. Book well in advance (tel: 8216 8600).

NIGHTLIFE

Adelaide has a reputation for being dead after 2000 in the evening. A browse through *The Guide* in the Thur edition of the *Adelaide Advertiser*, or *Rip It Up* (for gigs) or the *Adelaide Review* will prove otherwise.

The **Festival Centre** (details above) has three major auditoriums and on Sun there is a free concert in the foyer 1400–1600.

The **Theatre Bar** at the Lion Arts Centre, on the corner of North Terrace and Morphett St (tel: 8231 7760) has an irregular repertoire (the tourist office should have details of what's coming up); and **Theatre 62** at 145 Burbridge Rd, Hilton (tel: 8234 0838) has two theatres, one small and experimental, the other tending towards musi-

THE FLEURIEU PENINSULA

A gentle drive down the Fleurieu Peninsula will take you to Cape Jervis and the Southern Ocean.

South of Glenelg the coast road runs along the shore to Marion, right on the edge of the Sturt Gorge Recreation Park, and then to Old Noarlunga. Turning inland here will bring you shortly to McLaren Vale.

McLaren Vale is 39 km south of Adelaide and the centre of the Southern Vales wine-growing district. Farmers grew vines here from the 1850s, mainly for their own use, but winemaking seriously began in 1873 when Thomas Hardy moved into the area. Hardy had come out on the barque *British Empire* in 1850, and drove cattle to the Victoria goldfields to make himself enough money to buy a property near Adelaide and to marry. In 1853 he grew his first crop of Shiraz and Grenache grapes. His winery increased and, in a bold stroke, in 1873 he bought the Tintara Winery in McLaren Vale for a modest sum – he was the only bidder. Today the company is one of the biggest in Australia.

Hardy's Tintara is one of 46 wineries in the area, many of which are open for tastings and cellar door sales. Most also offer snacks and some have high quality restaurants; usual opening hours are 1000–1700 daily. The tourist association has a free publication *South Australian Wine and Food Guide* which is comprehensive and intelligently written.

The inland road crosses over the South Mount Lofty Ranges and reaches, 30 km further on, **Victor Harbor**, which faces the Southern Ocean and is spelled in the American way.

From there you can cut back again over the peninsula to the Gulf of St Vincent at Normanville. As the land narrows you pass through the tiny hamlet of **Second Valley**, of which Colonel Light said: 'I have hardly seen a place I like better.' The road ends at **Cape Jervis** at the very tip of the Fleurieu Peninsula, 110 km from Adelaide. Ferries cross from here to Kangaroo Island (see p. 137) and **Deep Creek Conservation Park** is just to the east.

The world's longest footpath, the Heysen Trail, begins near Cape Jervis and ends 1500 km north in the Flinders Ranges. The trail is marked with orange triangles but parts of it require bushwalking skills. Information from Recreation SA; tel: 8226 7301.

cals and pantomime. At the **Old Lion Hotel**, 165 Melbourne St, North Adelaide (tel: 8267 3766) you can drink real ale and watch pretty high standard cabaret.

There are dance clubs at the **Big Ticket** (tel: 410 0109) on Fri and Sat nights, and jazz and soul and the **Cargo Club** (tel: 231 2327). Both are in Hindley St. At the **Synagogue** (yes, it is a converted temple) in 9 Synagogue Pl. off Rundle St (tel: 8422 3433) the music is very loud and you either love it or stay away.

Adelaide

Almost every casino in Australia looks as if it were designed to dazzle rather than entertain. They all lack style, most are noisy and all the players seem never to smile. The one exception is the **Adelaide Casino** on North Terrace, in what was the old railway station. Open Sun–Thur 1000–0400, Fri–Sat 1000–0600.

DAY-TRIPS

Port Adelaide Adelaide's port is about 20 mins from Victoria Square by tram and is on the Port River, a wide inlet from Gulf St Vincent. It was a serious working port in the 1880s and this has left a heritage of splendid buildings. The best way to follow how it developed is to visit the **South Australian Maritime Museum** in Lipson St; open daily 1000–1700. The museum extends over several sites: an 1850s bond store, the 1869 lighthouse, the wharf and the vessels tied alongside.

Even though you are still very close to the city you can often see dolphins here, and take a trip into a mangrove wilderness.

Glenelg Glenelg is Adelaide's seaside suburb. The tourist office likes to boast that Adelaide has the closest beaches to a city in Australia. Although this is not really true, it can boast long sweeps of magnificent beach from Semaphore past North Haven, West Lakes, Grange, Henley Beach, Glenelg, Brighton, Seacliff, Hallet Cove and southwards to the Fleurieu Peninsula.

Getting to Glenelg is easy and very pleasant if you travel on the historic tram. Itruns the 10 km from Victoria Square in the heart of the city to the seaside in about half an hour.

At Patawalonga Boat Haven on Adelphi Terrace is **HMS *Buffalo***, a replica of the vessel which brought the first European settlers to South Australia. It has a restaurant as well as a small museum. $. Open Mon–Sat 0630–2100, Sun 1200–1400.

WHERE NEXT?

Adelaide was the start of the Overland Telegraph and towns born along the line can be found all the way north to Darwin, the most famous of which is Alice Springs (see p. 322. South Australia's great wine-producing region is the Barossa Valley (see p. 127) and a spectacular coastal route runs along the shore of the Southern Ocean from Adelaide to Melbourne (see p. 142).

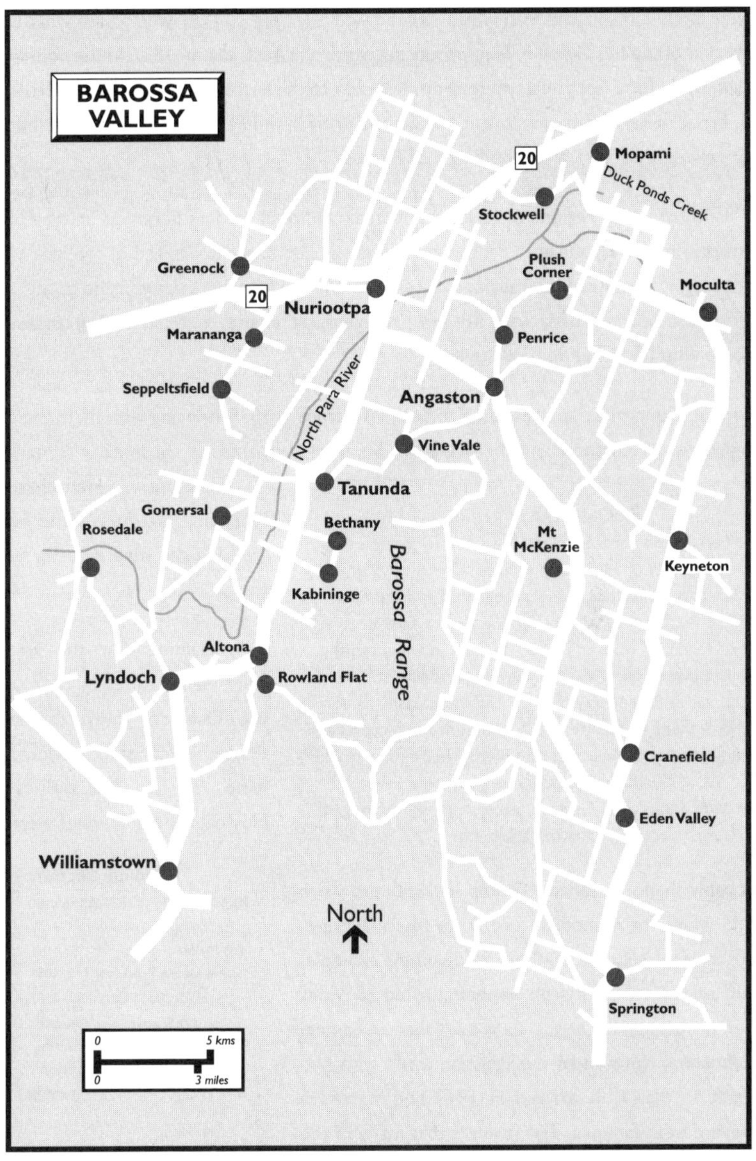
BAROSSA VALLEY
20
Mopami
Duck Ponds Creek
Stockwell
Greenock
20
Nuriootpa
Plush Corner
Moculta
Marananga
Penrice
Seppeltsfield
North Para River
Angaston
Vine Vale
Tanunda
Gomersal
Bethany
Rosedale
Mt McKenzie
Keyneton
Barossa Range
Kabininge
Altona
Lyndoch
Rowland Flat
Cranefield
Eden Valley
Williamstown
North
Springton
0
5 kms
0
3 miles

It was Colonel Light, the man who designed Adelaide (see p. 115), who found what is now one of the best-known wine-producing regions in Australia. In 1837, in the course of surveying for a north-east route from Adelaide to the eastern states, he came across this broad valley and, having fought Napoleon's army in the Peninsula Wars, named (but misspelled) it Barossa after the Battle of Barrosa.

Unlike most other regions of Australia, the main influx of settlers here was neither of convicts nor of hopeful gold prospectors. George Fife Angas conceived of the idea of encouraging settlement by religious dissenters. The God-fearing Lutherans he brought in from Silesia and Prussia were not poor refugees; rather, they were successful tradespeople who had fallen foul of the Kaiser.

The first group of 25 families came to South Australia in 1838, bringing with them their language, their customs and their religion. Some of the names of those early settlers – Seppelt, Henschke, Hoffmann, Gramp – are to be found in the wine industry of today.

Barossa Valley Villages

Early settlements followed the German pattern of Strassendorf or Hufendorf villages. Owing to original language difficulties, these stayed small and self-contained, with households producing almost all their own food including smoked meats, cheese and wine, and the cellars and smokehouses of the village houses still recall this self-sufficient way of life. Villages such as Krondorf and Bethany, and some of the cemeteries and churches, retain traces of their German origins, but during World War I German as a spoken language was severely frowned upon and German placenames were changed by act of parliament.

It is claimed that the first vines were planted in 1847 at the Orlando vineyards, an estate which still produces wine in large quantities. However, the first wines were probably made by Johann Gramp in 1850 and were table wines for immediate use, from his small vineyard at Jacob's Creek. Others followed his example: snuff manufacturer Joseph Seppelt turned to vines after unsuccessfully trying to grow tobacco; Samuel Hoffmann, a veteran of the Prussian army who had fought at Waterloo, arrived in 1847 and started a vineyard near Tanunda. The result is that many of the

Colour Section

(i) Adelaide (pp. 115–126); Seppelt Winery, Barossa Valley (p. 133)

(ii) Melbourne (pp. 170–183); the Great Ocean Road (pp. 149–169)

(iii) Surfers Paradise (p. 230)

(iv) Brisbane (pp.234–243); a humpback whale in Hervey Bay (p. 253); A Kuranda rail station (p. 303)

AUSTRAL
FARES
B. SEPPELT & SONS LTD.

traffic info.
Trains & trams for no G.P. traffic
FLINDERS STREET STATION
Is your face stopping you from getting ahead?

WOOLG

PLATFORM 2

wineries scattered around the Barossa Valley have a very distinct European style, a matured German manner.

Today, the Barossa produces a very wide range of wines. It could be argued that its strength is in the dry whites and dry reds, leaving the seriously heavy reds to the Hunter Valley in New South Wales (see p. 203), but this is a generalisation with many exceptions. Although many wines on offer might be described as German-style, the closest resemblance to the soil and weather conditions of the Barossa can be found in Portugal rather than Germany. The Barossa crushes, but does not necessarily grow, about a quarter of the Australian vintage — a substantial percentage of the grapes processed here are in fact grown elsewhere.

The Barossa Valley is not geographically distinct — it is too broad and flat for that — but this is a disappointment only if you are expecting spectacular scenery. There are about 50 wineries in the region and most welcome visitors for cellar door tastings, guided tours and cellar sales. Most of them offer light refreshments as well. The wineries are mainly between Nuriootpa and Lyndoch, which are about 20 km apart. Seppeltsfield is perhaps the most visually interesting, but all are worth a visit. Details of just a small selection are given here, but more information can be had from the information centres.

INFORMATION

The telephone code for the area is 08.

TOURIST OFFICE **Barossa Information Centre,** 66 Murray St, Tanunda; tel: 8562 1866 or Free call (1800) 812 662. Open daily 1000–1600. There is a clever use of cylinders to tie in the history of the area with the history of Australia and, indeed, the world, and lots of information on wine and wine tasting.

Kies Estate, a small-scale winery on Barossa Valley Way, acts as a tourist information office as well as offering wine tastings. Open daily 1000–1600; tel: 8524 4110.

INTERNET SITES **Barossa Valley** www.southaustralia.com/tourism/barossa.htm

Wine News Magazine — The Barossa Valley www.thewinenews.com/febmar99/barossa.html

Accommodation

Angaston

Barossa Brauhaus Hotel $ 41 Murray St; tel: 8564 2014. Basic accommodation in a pub first licensed in 1849. Central location, breakfast available.

Collingrove Homestead $$$ Eden Valley Rd, 6 km from Angaston; tel: 8564 2061. National Trust-listed B&B accommodation in what was once the servants' quarters of the Angas home.

Vineyards Motel $$ corner of Stockwell and Nuriootpa Rds; tel: 8564 2404. Near Saltram vinery. Solar-heated swimming pool and spa.

Lyndoch

Chateau Yaldara Estate Motor Inn $$ Barossa Valley Hwy; tel: 8524 4268.

Nuriootpa

Barossa Gateway Motel & Hostel $ Kalimna Rd, Nuriootpa 5355; tel: 8562 1033.

Barossa House $$ Barossa Valley Way, between Tanunda and Nuriootpa; tel: 8562 4022. B&B with en suite rooms.

Bunkhaus Travellers Hostel and Cottage $ Barossa Valley Way; tel: 8562 2260. Hostel in the vineyards. Self-contained cottage available.

Hotel/Motel Vine Inn $$ 14 Murray St; tel: 8562 2133.

Seppeltsfield Holiday Units $$ Seppeltsfield Rd, nr Nuriootpa; tel: 8562 8240. Log cabins overlooking the winery.

Top of the Valley Tourist Motel $$ 49 Murray St; tel: 8562 2111.

Vine Inn Hotel Motel $$ 14 Murray St; tel: 8562 2133. Modern motel. Spa and heated pool.

Tanunda

Barossa Junction Resort $$ Barossa Valley Way; tel: 8563 3400.

Langmeil Cottages $$ Langmeil Rd; tel: 8563 2987. Stone cottage with cooking facilities. Heated pool.

Langmeil Rd Caravan Park $ 70 Langmeil Rd; tel: 8563 0095.

Lawley Farm $$ Krondorf Rd; tel: 8563 2141. Restored stone cottages. Spa. Breakfast.

Tanunda Caravan & Tourist Park $ Barossa Valley Way; tel: 8563 2784. Parkland setting with cabins.

Tanunda Hotel $$ 51 Murray St; tel: 8563 2030. Dates from 1845. Some rooms en suite.

Wycombe Lodge $$ High Wycombe Winery, Bethany Rd. Tanunda; tel: 8563 2776.

FOOD AND DRINK

Vineyards and wineries always attract good restaurants and the Barossa is no exception. Standards are remarkably high and you should make your own discoveries. However, do not miss out on tea at the Zinfandel Tea Rooms in Tanunda where, after the cakes and strudel, you will not be able to eat dinner.

ANGASTON

Barossa Bistro $ 37 Murray St; tel: 8564 2361. Lunch and dinner daily. Has kangaroo on the menu. Licensed.

Barossa Brauhaus, 42 Murray St; tel: 8564 2014. Open for lunch daily, dinner Tues–Sun. First licensed in 1849.

Saltram Wine Estate Bistro $$ Nuriootpa Rd; tel: 8564 3355. Bistro attached to a 19th-century winery. Meals lunchtime only.

Vintners Bar and Grill $$ corner of Stockwell and Nuriootpa Rds; tel: 8564 2488. Impressive wine list; vine-covered courtyard. Tues–Sun lunch, Wed–Sat dinner.

LYNDOCH

Errigo's Cellar Restaurant $ 23 Barossa Valley Way; tel: 8524 4015. Licensed. Open daily for lunch.

NURIOOTPA

Chinese Dragon Restaurant $ 9 Gawler St; tel: 8562 2797. Licensed. Cantonese.

Kaesler Restaurant $$ Barossa Valley Way; tel 8562 2711. Open daily for lunch and dinner. Licensed. Part of the Kaesler Estate.

Nuriootpa Vine Inn $ 14 Murray St; tel: 8562 2133. Licensed. Open daily for lunch and dinner.

Shangri-la Thai Restaurant $ 31 Murray St; tel: 8562 3559. Licensed.

Wild Olive Restaurant $$$ Pheasant Farm Rd; tel: 8562 1286. French chef has a seasonal regional menu. Crayfish caught in a lake on the grounds. Licensed or BYO.Open for lunch Wed–Sun, dinner Thur–Sat.

TANUNDA

1918 Bistro and Grill $, 94 Murray St; tel: 8563 3408. Open daily for lunch and dinner. Licensed. Garden setting with dining on the verandah. BYO or local wines.

Bergman's $$ 66 Murray St; tel: 8563 2788.

Cafe Lanzerac $ Main St. Trendy café. Barossa wine sold by the glass. Blackboard menu. Open daily from breakfast to dinner.

Fortune Garden $ 46 Murray St; tel: 8563 0099. Asian.

La Buona Vita $ 89a Murray St; tel: 8563 2527. Licensed. Lunch and dinner daily.

Tanunda Hotel $ 51 Murray St; tel: 8563 2030. Good range of vegetarian dishes.

Park Restaurant/Café $ 2a Murray St; tel: 8563 3500. 1840s stone villa set in a park. South-east Asian cuisine.

Zinfandel Tea Rooms $ 58 Murray St; tel: 8563 1822. Lunch and tea daily. Unbeatable strudels and cakes, not for the calorie conscious. Open daily 0830–1800.

GETTING THERE AND GETTING AROUND

There are two sub-regions in this area: the Barossa Valley itself which includes Nuriootpa, Tanunda and Lyndoch, and the Barossa Hills with the towns of Eden Valley, Springton and Angaston.

There are several ways of exploring. State Rail has several packaged holidays; you could take a coach tour; or it is a pleasant drive, about 60 km, from Adelaide. The route through Elizabeth and Gawler to Lyndoch at the south end of the valley can have a fair amount of traffic and is, perhaps, a less than interesting drive. The other and more scenic way is to come in from the other end, through Angaston and Nuriootpa.

ANGASTON

Angaston, at the eastern end of the valley, is set in the highest reaches of the Barossa (which is not that high at 361 m above sea level). The town is named after George Fife Angas, sponsor of many of the valley's early German settlers.

A 2.5 km **Heritage Walk** will take you around the town. Angaston has two beautiful parks, a small creek flowing through its centre and good examples of colonial architecture. It boasts two of the Barossa's oldest wineries, and a dried fruit outlet.

Worth seeing in the area is the **Collingrove Homestead**, 6 km from town on Eden Valley Rd (open Mon–Fri 1300–1630, Sat–Sun 1100–1630; tel: 8564 2061). It was built in 1856 as a home for the second son of George Fife Angas and remained in possession of the family until 1976 when it was given to the National Trust. It still contains many of the original furnishings and is surrounded by lush gardens. Angas also lived at nearby Lindsay Park which is now the Lindsay Park Stud, Australia's leading racehorse breeding and training complex.

NURIOOTPA

This is the commercial centre of the Barossa Valley, and its largest and busiest town. Nuriootpa is possibly the most consistently mispronounced and misspelled town name in Australia – everyone bar its inhabitants tends to pronounce it incorrectly. Say 'nurreuutpa'.

In 1843 William Coulthard opened a hotel – a flattering term – called the Red Lion, to serve bullock drivers en route from Adelaide to Kapunda and Burra. This was not what you would call an upmarket trade. It is now the community-owned Vine Inn. William Coulthard's house, now a National Trust museum, was built in 1855 on the corner of Murray and Penrice Sts. It is built from local bluestone and is of an elegant Victorian design and superb workmanship. Coulthard is said to have died of thirst in 1858 while looking for new land to the north of the town.

Nuriootpa has a number of famous wineries: **Penfolds**, **Wolf Blass**, **Eldetron**, and **Old Stockwell**.

Meandering through the town is the North Para River which, with the open spaces, interesting old buildings, parks and picnic spots makes Nuriootpa a pleasant enough town to visit, although the Penfolds winery gives it something of an industrial feel.

LIGHT PASS

In this small village near Nuriootpa are two Lutheran churches and a cairn that marks the place where Colonel Light met Captain Sturt. Nearby is **Luhr's Cottage**, which was built in 1848 by the Barossa's first German schoolteacher, J. H. Luhrs. The house has been restored and furnished in the authentic German style. Open daily 1000–1600.

MARANANGA AND SEPPELTSFIELD

Originally called Gnadenfrei – which roughly translates as 'freed by the Grace of God', the name of this tiny settlement was changed in World War I to an Aboriginal word which can be translated as 'my hands'. Marananga is minute but has a wonderful church, restored barns and cottages and its own brass band.

From Marananga, an imposing avenue of date palms lines the route to **Seppeltsfield**, a mini-village of I9th-century stone winery buildings, the focus of the large winemaking operations of B Seppelt & Sons. Joseph Ernest Seppelt had run a liquor and snuff company in Silesia until, like other dissenting Lutherans, he was driven out by the religious intolerance of the Prussian emperor. He arrived in Australia in 1849 with his family and 13 employees and their families.

The Seppeltsfield complex offers tasting, picnicking spots and touring, while the old Seppelts' family home has been restored and is available as accommodation. The beautifully maintained gardens add to the impressive buildings to make it one of the showplaces of the Barossa. The Seppelt family mausoleum sits on a hilltop which provides wonderful views over Seppeltsfield. Open Mon–Fri 0900–1700, Sat 1030–1630, Sun 1100–1600.

TANUNDA

Tanunda is one of the oldest towns in the Barossa Valley and is the heartland of German culture in South Australia.

The town was originally known as Langmeil when the first vines were planted in 1847. Two years later they built the Tabor Lutheran Church. In Tanunda, as in the rest of the Barossa, Lutheran churches are in the majority – the town has four. Pastor Auricht, who had come from Silesia with the immigrants, started a German newspaper for the town in 1855 and a printing office was built in that year. The Chateau Tanunda winery was founded in 1889, and was later bought by the Seppelt family.

Tanunda is now very much a tourist town, which you sense as soon as you enter through the Orlando archway that spans Murray St, the main street. As you wander along you will hear German music – the town got its first brass band in 1860, with a Lieder-tafel (singing society) in the year following – but you will get a better feel for the place in the smaller streets on the western side of town, towards the river. Here Goat Square is classified by the National Trust and is surrounded by century-old cottages.

The **Barossa Valley Historical Museum**, in Murray St, is housed in Tanunda's 1865 post and telegraph buildings. It specialises in Barossa German heritage, with a collection that includes wedding gowns, artefacts, books and photographs. One room has an altar and church furniture with German inscriptions. Usually open daily, but opening hours may vary; tel: 8566 0212 for current times.

Barossa Kiddypark, on the corner of Magnolia St and Menge Rd, is a truly woeful name for a splendid and well-equipped fun park which includes activities such as electric cars, dodgem cars, train rides, merry-go-round and super slide. A wildlife section has wallabies, kangaroos, emus, wombats, ponies and native birds.

The **Keg Factory** (St Hallett Rd; tel: 8563 3012; open daily) makes kegs, wine racks, barrel furniture – almost any application of the craft of coopering.

A little way out of town, on the Barossa Way at Dorien, is the Kev Rohrlach

Museum. It is built on the site of the former Siegersdorf – later Hardy's – Winery and has over 3,000 exhibits in an esoteric and eclectic private collection that includes everything from space rockets to a 1902 electric car, old clothes, a Canberra bomber and a rare 19th-century maharajah's carriage used by the Duke of Edinburgh; tel: 8563 3407 for opening times.

VALLEY PANORAMA

Mengler's Hill Lookout on Mengler's Hill Rd to the east of Tanunda has panoramic views of the valley. There is a sculpture garden on the slopes below, and at night you can see the lights of Adelaide.

BETHANY

This is the valley's oldest German settlement, founded in 1842 by a group of Lutheran families – the biblical name is an indication of their devotion. They mapped out their village along Prussian lines and the cottages facing the road replicate those the settlers lived in before coming to Australia. The bell of **Herberge Christi Church** still rings each Sat at dusk to mark the working-week's end. Several houses have been restored and are open to the public as craft shops and art galleries. The village reserve where the cows used to graze is great for picnics.

LYNDOCH

Lyndoch is the southern gateway to the Barossa Valley and one of the oldest towns in South Australia. Colonel Light named it (but again misspelled it) after his friend Lord Lynedoch, who led his men to victory at the Battle of Barrosa. On seeing the site for the first time, Light reported: 'A beautiful place, good land, plenty of grass and its general appearance open with some patches of wood and many kangaroos.'

The village that began to develop in 1847 was flooded in 1854 and the move made to higher ground. The first winery did not come here until 1896 – the focus in the early days was the watermill driven by the Para River, which was used for grinding corn. Now there are many wineries in the area, ranging from small family operations to major ones: they include **Wards**, **Yaldara**, **Cimicky**, **Burge**, **Kellermeister** and **Redgum Cellars**.

Fine examples of early dwellings survive. The **Mechanical Music Museum** has a range of 19th-century clockwork musical boxes, Edison wax cylinder machines and Berliner phonographs. Open daily 0900–1700.

Rosedale, a short distance from Lyndoch, has a quaint cemetery and an interesting herb farm.

The retaining wall of the Barossa Reservoir, 7 km south-east of Lyndoch off Yettie Rd, is known as the **Whispering Wall**. Its shape enables a whispered message at one end to be heard 140 m away at the other. It also provides excellent scenic views of the reservoir and barbecue and picnic facilities.

Wineries

Angaston	**Henschke**, Moculta Rd, Keyneton, south-east of Angaston, has been making wine for five generations. Open Mon–Fri 0900–1630, Sat 0900–1200.
Tanunda	**Yalumba Wines**, Eden Valley Rd, was established in 1849 and has lovely building and gardens. Open Mon–Sat 1000–1700, Sun 1200–1700.
	Grant Burge Wines, Barossa Valley Way, Jacob's Creek. New winery on an old site. Open daily 1000–1700.
	Charles Melton, Krondorf Rd. Full-bodied reds. Tasting in a wooden shed. Open daily 1300–1700.
	Krondorf Wines, Krondorf Rd. 1860s winery and vineyard which has been updated. Open daily 1000–1700.
	Langmeil Winery, Langmeil Rd. Built in the 1840s.Three reds, three whites and a tawny port. Open daily 1000–1700.
	Peter Lehmann, Para Rd. Homestead with vine-entwined verandahs. The Sémillon Blanc is inexpensive but possibly the best of its type in Australia. The wine labels feature South Australian artists, whose original paintings are on display. Open Mon–Fri 0930–1700, Sat–Sun 1030–1600.
	Rockford Wines, Krondorf Rd. Big, traditional wines. Tasting in an old stone barn. Open daily 1100–1700.
	St Hallett Winery, Krondorf Rd. Medium-sized quality producer. Open daily 1100–1700.
Bethany	**Bethany Wines.** The Schrapels have grown grapes here for five generations. Open Mon–Sat 1000–1700, Sun 1300–1700.

Many visitors are surprised at the size of Kangaroo Island – at 155 km long and up to 55 km wide it is the third largest island off the coast of Australia. It sits at the mouth of Gulf St Vincent, on which Adelaide lies, and is almost totally undeveloped.

In the early 20th century evidence of stone tools and Aboriginal campsites was discovered. Subsequent dating of charcoal campfire remains indicate that Aboriginal people were living on the island at least 10,000 years ago. Why or when they abandoned Kangaroo Island is not known. The first white people to live here were sealers, escaped convicts and runaway sailors seeking refuge in the early 19th century. They lived on kangaroos and other wildlife and traded salt plus seal, kangaroo and wallaby skins for spirits and tobacco.

The lighthouses at Cape Willoughby and Cape Borda, erected in the 1850s, were desperately needed. Kangaroo Island was a serious hazard to shipping and there are over 40 wrecks in the seas around. The lighthouse keepers and their families were the first of the legitimate European population which was later swelled by sheep farmers and, after World War II, ex-soldiers sent as part of a war service land settlement scheme. But even to this day, the population is fairly small.

Kangaroo Island is treasured for its wildlife. More than half the island has never been cleared of vegetation, and numerous reserves and conservation parks, including five significant Wilderness Protection Areas, guarantee that it will remain wild and spectacular. These measures and the absence of foxes and rabbits combine to provide safe habitats for an extraordinary variety of wildlife, some of which have disappeared from the mainland.

ARRIVAL AND DEPARTURE

The island is a 30-min flight from Adelaide. The airport is 13 km from Kingscote, the island's principal town – transport is available, but arrangements should be made at the time of booking.

Ferries operate from Cape Jervis on the tip of the Fleurieu Peninsula to Penneshaw, on the island's eastern tip. There are coach connections between Adelaide and Cape Jervis, and between Penneshaw and Kingscote..

INFORMATION

Tourist Offices **Kingscote Tourist Information Centre**, National Parks and Wildlife, 37 Dauncey St, Kingscote; tel: (08) 8482 2381. **Penneshaw Tourist Information Centre**, Howard Dr.; tel: (08) 8553 1185.

Internet Sites **Kangaroo Island** http://www.tea-net.com/kangaroo-island

Kangaroo Island Visitors' Guide http://www.tourkangarooisland.com.au/

ACCOMMODATION

American River Resort Motel $$ 2 Wattle Terrace, American River; tel: (08) 8553 7044.

Chapman's Gum Valley Resort $$ North West Corner, Parndana; tel: (08) 8559 3207.

Ellson's Seaview Motel $$ Chapman Ter., Kingscote. Courtesy transport, licensed restaurant; tel: (08) 8482 2030.

Graydon Holiday Lodge $$ 16 Buller St, Kingscote. Fully equipped kitchen and fridge; tel: (08) 8482 2713.

Island Resort Motel $$ 4 Telegraph Rd, Kingscote. Licensed restaurant. Swimming pool; tel: (08) 8482 2100.

Kangaroo Island Holiday Village $$ 9 Dauncey St. Fully equipped kitchen and fridge; tel: (08) 8482 2225.

Kohinoor Holiday Units $$ 16 Buller St., Kingscote; tel: (08) 8553 2657.

Matthew Flinders Terraces $$ American River; tel: (08) 8553 7100.

Ozone Seafront Hotel $$ Foreshore, Kingscote. Licensed restaurant. Sauna, spa, swimming pool; tel: (08) 8482 2011.

Penguin Walk Hostel $ 33 Middle Ter, Penneshaw; tel: (08) 8553 1233.

Penneshaw Youth Hostel $ 43 North Ter, Penneshaw; tel: (08) 8553 1284.

Queenscliffe Family Hotel $$ Dauncey St, Kingscote. Coffee shop/snack bar; tel: (08) 8482 2254.

Sorrento Resort Motel $$ Esplanade, Penneshaw; tel: (08) 8553 1028.

Wanderers Rest Of Kangaroo Island $$ Bayview Rd, American River; tel: (08) 8553 7140.

Wisteria Lodge $$ 7 Cygnet Rd. Kingscote. Licensed restaurant, spa, swimming pool; tel: (08) 8482 2707.

FOOD AND DRINK

Beachcomber Restaurant $$ 7 Cygnet Rd, Penneshaw; tel: (08) 8553 2707.

Blue Gum Cafe $$ Dauncey St, Kingscote; tel: (08) 8553 2089.

Cape Willoughby Cafe $ adjacent to lighthouse; tel: (08) 8553 1333.

Crafty Fisherman $$ Tangara Dr, American River; tel: (08) 8553 7102.

Cygnet Cafe $ Playford Highway, Cygnet River; tel: (08) 8552 9187.

D'Estrees Bay Cafe $ D'Estrees Bay Rd, D'Estrees Bay; tel: (08) 8553 8234.

Dolphin Rock Cafe $$ 43 North Ter. Penneshaw; tel: (08) 8553 1284.

Ellsons Seaview Seafront Restaurant $$ Chapman Ter. Penneshaw; tel: (08) 8553 2030.

Emu's Nest $$ The Esplanade, Emu Bay; tel: (08) 8553 5384.

Mulberry Tree $$ Foreshore, Penneshaw; tel: (08) 8553 2866.

Old Post Office Restaurant $$ North Ter, Penneshaw; tel: (08) 8553 1063.

Ozone Family Bistro $$ The Foreshore, Penneshaw; tel: (08) 8553 2011.

Palms Seafood Platter Restaurant $$ Telegraph Rd, Penneshaw; tel: (08) 8553 2100.

Pelican Pete's $ Dauncey St, Kingscote; tel: (08) 8553 2138.

Ricks Seaview Takeaway $ 3 Kingscote Ter, Kingscote; tel: (08) 8553 2585.

Rockpool Cafe $$ North Coast Rd, Stokes Bay; tel: (08) 8559 2277.

Sorrento Restaurant $$ 49 North Ter, Penneshaw; tel: (08) 8553 1028.

GETTING THERE AND GETTING AROUND

There is little public transport on the island, but there are bicycles, scooters and cars for hire. If you are thinking of cycling, bear in mind that the island is 155 km long. You can bring your vehicle from the mainland or hire cars are available from: **Budget**, tel: (08) 8553 3133; **Caudell's Thrifty**, tel: (08) 1800 552 008; **Hertz**, tel: (1800) 088 296; **KI Camper Trailer**, tel: (1800) 088 296; **Koala**, tel: (08) 8553 2399; and

ROAD CONDITIONS

The major roads between Penneshaw, American River, Kingscote and Parndana are sealed, as is the road to Seal Bay and Vivonne Bay. Other roads are being upgraded but many are unsealed, and require reduced speed and caution. The road surface is ironstone, a loose floating material that tends to build up on corners, requiring careful steering and braking. Make sure that the insurance on your hire car covers you for driving on unsealed roads.

Fuel is available at Kingscote, American River, Island Beach, Penneshaw, Parndana, Vivonne Bay and Tandanya so you should never run out.

Penneshaw Car Rentals, tel: (08) 8553 1284. Four-wheel drive vehicles are not necessary as long as you drive with care.

If you prefer someone else to do the driving, there are coach tours, or more personalised 4-wheel drive tours can be arranged. Most tours will pick up from your accommodation or the airport.

HIGHLIGHTS

Kingscote is the arrival and departure point for visitors to Kangaroo Island, and also the largest town. This was the first settled part of the island and makes a good base for exploration. Nearby **Brownlow Beach** has good swimming and sailing as well as fishing from the jetty. In **Hope Cottage** the National Trust has established an excellent display of photographs, family histories, china and early newspapers. Open daily 1000–1200 and 1400–1600.

One of Kangaroo Island's main tourist resorts, **American River**, is a sheltered tidal estuary between Kingscote and Penneshaw. It takes its name from the American sealers who built two 35-tonne schooners here in 1803–4. The town is on a small peninsula and shelters an inner bay, the bird sanctuary of **Pelican Lagoon**.

The island's plant catalogue lists over 850 native species, as well as approximately 250 which have been introduced from other parts of the world. The flowers are at their best in the spring months of Sept and Oct, but winter is the best time to see the wildlife. Most of the mammals are nocturnal and easily frightened. They are most successfully observed and least stressed from a distance.

The Kangaroo Island kangaroo, a sub-species of the Western grey, is smaller, darker and has longer fur than the mainland species. It shelters in the bush during the day, coming out to graze at dusk. Areas where bush and pasture adjoin make ideal places to observe them.

Tammar wallabies, with smaller and finer features than the kangaroo, are abundant on the island, whereas mainland populations are almost extinct. Wallabies are frequently seen at night along the roads, where they are easily confused by vehicle lights – drive cautiously to prevent damage to either animals or vehicles.

Of the numerous reserves and conservation areas, **Flinders Chase National Park** is the largest. It covers the western end of the island from Sanderson Bay in the south to Cape Borda in the north and has some of the most amazing proliferation of animal and plant life in Australia. There are well-marked trails throughout the park and in the centre is a substantial clearing which is home for a large number of kangaroos and also Cape Barren geese. A few extremely docile kangaroos can usually be seen around the park headquarters, even though feeding is no longer allowed. **Cape du Couedic** in the south-west is a haven for about 6,000 New Zealand fur seals. They breed in summer and can be seen energetically interacting in and around the natural formation of Admiral's Arch.

The other major park on the island is Cape Gantheaume Conservation Park along the rugged southern coast, which extends as far inland as Murray Lagoon. No vehicles are allowed but the park has much wildlife especially around the lagoon, which when full after rain can cover 2,000 ha and is home to more than 200 species of bird.

Italian Bees

In 1881 August Freibig brought 12 hives of bees from the province of Liguria in Italy, and established an apiary near Penneshaw. Since then no other breeds of bee have been introduced and all present-day honey bees on the island are descendants of those 12 hives. They are pure Ligurian and unique in the world.

Although Seal Bay Conservation Park on the south coast is relatively small, it is home to about 500 Australian sealions, probably about 10 per cent of the world's population. These sealions spend as much time on land as at sea. They can seem tame and accepting of visitors, but every now and again they get irritable and charge at humans, so the number of visitors is restricted. An Interpretative Centre, tel: (08) 8489 4207, explains the life cycle of the sea-lion. The bay is an aquatic reserve and swimming and fishing are prohibited.

Other animals native to the island include the brushtail possum, short-beaked echidna, southern brown bandicoot, western and little pygmy possum, endemic sooty dunnart, bush and swamp rat, six bat species, six frog species, Rosenberg's sand goanna, black tiger snake and the pygmy copperhead. Koalas, platypuses and ring-tailed possums were introduced and still survive here.

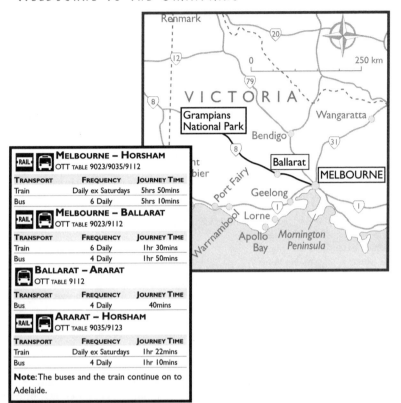

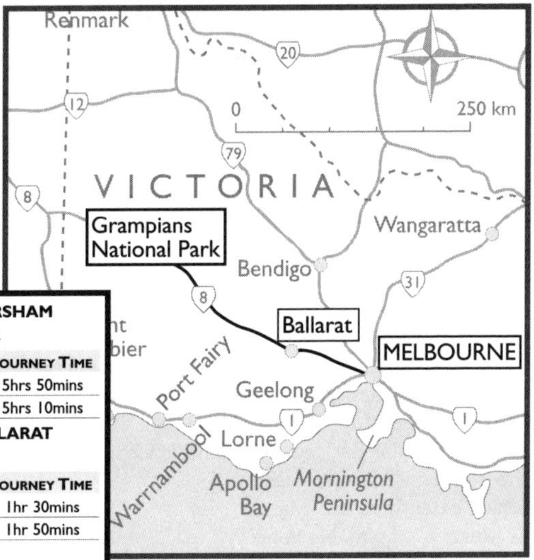

MELBOURNE – HORSHAM
OTT TABLE 9023/9035/9112

TRANSPORT	FREQUENCY	JOURNEY TIME
Train	Daily ex Saturdays	5hrs 50mins
Bus	6 Daily	5hrs 10mins

MELBOURNE – BALLARAT
OTT TABLE 9023/9112

TRANSPORT	FREQUENCY	JOURNEY TIME
Train	6 Daily	1hr 30mins
Bus	4 Daily	1hr 50mins

BALLARAT – ARARAT
OTT TABLE 9112

TRANSPORT	FREQUENCY	JOURNEY TIME
Bus	4 Daily	40mins

ARARAT – HORSHAM
OTT TABLE 9035/9123

TRANSPORT	FREQUENCY	JOURNEY TIME
Train	Daily ex Saturdays	1hr 22mins
Bus	4 Daily	1hr 10mins

Note: The buses and the train continue on to Adelaide.

ROUTE DETAIL

Ballarat (112 km) is the first large town and the meeting place of the Midlands Hwy from Geelong (see p. 166) and the Glenelg Hwy from Mt Gambier. From Ararat (138 km) the direct road to Horsham is 95 km, but turn onto Rte 124 for Halls Gap and the Grampians. Total journey approx. 300 km.

The Melbourne–Perth express buses running along Rte 8 reach Adelaide in about 8½ hrs but make few if any interim stops. Stopping buses take 1½–2½ hrs from Melbourne to Ballarat, with Stawell a further 1–1½ hrs.

ALONG THE WESTERN HIGHWAY

Although the Western Highway (Rte 8) is the 'fast' inland route to Adelaide, as opposed to the scenic but much longer route via the Great Ocean Rd (see p. 132), the only quick way between the two cities is to fly. The pleasures of this route lie in exploring the successful gold town of Ballarat – the place where independence and democracy in Australia might be said to have been born – and the rugged ranges of the Grampians, with their prolific wildlife and annual explosion of spring flowers.

BALLARAT

Ballarat - a town that was made by the gold rush – has played an important part in Australia's history.

In 1851 gold was found at Poverty Point and for the next 50 years the Ballarat fields produced more than a quarter of all Victoria's gold. At its peak it was probably the richest alluvial goldfield in the world. In 1897 Mark Twain wrote in *Following the Equator* : 'Forty five years ago the site now occupied by the City of Ballarat was a sylvan solitude as quiet as Eden and as lovely. Nobody had ever heard of it. On the 25th of August, 1851, the first great gold-strike made in Australia was made there The news of the strike spread everywhere in a sort of instantaneous way. A celebrity so prompt and so universal has hardly been paralleled in history, perhaps.'

The mining and processing needed heavy equipment, which meant the growth in local industries like Cowley's Eureka Iron Works and The Phoenix, companies that created the ballast of wealth on which Ballarat was built.

But it was the political action of the miners of Ballarat that made history – their armed civil uprising against the government (see p. 146) has been the only one in Australia's history.

EN ROUTE

Just before Ballarat is the **Great Southern Woolshed**. Here you can see sheep shearing – 100 sheep are shorn every day — a working dog display and have morning tea or lunch in the country cookhouse. Open daily 0930–1700.

Ballarat Visitor Information Centre, 39 Sturt St; tel: 5332 2694. The area code is 03.

Official Visitors' Guide to Ballarat
http://www.ballarat.com/

Alfred Motor Inn $ 1843 Sturt St; tel: 5334 1607.
Ansonia $$ 32 Lydiard Sth St. In restored Victorian building in town centre; tel: 5332 4678.

MELBOURNE TO THE GRAMPIANS

Arch Motel $ 1853 Sturt St; tel: 5334 1464.
Avenue Motel $$ 1813 Sturt St, Ave of Honour; tel: 5334 1303.
Ballarat Caravan Park $ 263 Scott Pde; tel: 5332 6818.
Ballarat Colony Motor Inn $$ Melbourne Rd; tel: 5334 7788.
Ballarat Miners Retreat Motel $ 602 Eureka St; tel: 5331 6900.
Cardigan Lodge Motel, Ave of Honour. 27 larger than average rooms all at ground floor level; tel: 5344 8302.
Central City Motor Inn $$ 16 Victoria St; tel: 5333 1775.
Craigs Royal Hotel $$ 10 Lydiard South St. Both Mark Twain and Prince Alfred once slept here; tel: 5331 1377.
Eureka Lodge Motel $ 119 Stawell South St. Garden setting; tel: 53311900.
George Hotel $ 27 Lydiard North St; tel: 5333 4866.
Gold Sovereign Motor Inn $$ Learmonth Rd, cnr Waltham Dr. Minutes from City Centre. Own restaurant; tel: 5339 3161.
Lake Terrace Motel Apartments $$ 20 Wendouree Pde; tel: 5332 1812.
Main Lead Motor Inn $$ 312 Main Rd; tel: 5331 7533.
Motel Ballarat $ Melbourne Rd; tel: 5334 7234.
Quest Colony Motor Inn $$ 674 Melbourne Rd. Set in landscaped garden. Heated indoor swimming pool; tel: 5334 7788.
Sovereign Park Motor Inn $$ 221 Main Rd. Between Sovereign Hill and the City. Has bar and bistro; tel: 5331 3955.
Tawana Lodge Complex $ 128 Lydiard North St; tel: 5331 3461.

Sturt Street is full of restaurants of every style, shape and price. The Lydiard Street historic quarter has almost as many.
Assunta's $$ 34 Sturt St; tel: 5331 6327.
Beijing City Chinese Restaurant $ 1607a Sturt St; tel: 5334 2455.
Cafe Pazani $ 102 Sturt St; tel: 5331 7100.
Caffe Bar Restaurant $ 417 Sturt St. Bustling, stylish cafe, bar and restaurant with great atmosphere coming partly from music. Open weekdays breakfast, lunch. Open Thu-Sat dinner. Licensed; tel: 5333 1789.
Camp Hotel & Restaurant $ 38 Sturt St; tel: 5331 4091.

Conders Restaurant $ 12 Sturt St. Open Tue-Fri for dinner. BYO. Middle Eastern food; tel: 5331 7570.
Emcee's Restaurant $$ 18 Doveton St, North Ballarat. Open dinner Mon-Sat. Licensed; tel: 5331 1222.
Eureka Pizza Parlour $ 316 Sturt St; tel: 5331 3682.
Frangali's Kafeeneo $ 313 Sturt St; tel: 5331 1312.
George Restaurant $$ 27 Lydiard North St; tel: 5333 4866.
Jasmine Thai Restaurant $ 213 Sturt St; tel: 5333 2148.
Mee Hing Chinese Restaurant $$ 739 Sturt St; tel: 5331 3891.
Memories On Lydiard $$ 120 Lydiard North St; tel: 5333 1166.
Mimosa Park $$ 1821 Sturt St; tel: 5334 1123.
Peals Restaurant $$, 1845 Sturt St. Licensed. Open Mon-Sat for dinner; tel: 5334 1600.
Priscilla's Cottage $$ 109 Eureka St. Licensed. Lunch daily. Dinner Saturday. An 1860 miner's cottage transformed into a restaurant, tea rooms and art gallery; tel: 5331 5705.
Singapore Kitchen $ 1005 Sturt St; tel: 5333 3611.
Spot Restaurant $ 5 Sturt St; tel: 5331 1053.
Tokyo Grill House $$ 109 Bridge Mall. Licensed, dinner 7 days; tel: 5333 3945.

HIGHLIGHTS

Sovereign Hill, located on the site of the former Sovereign Quartz Mining Company, is a superb reconstruction of life on the goldfields, with shops and mines being run by people in period costume. There are guided tours underground using the original tramway. This is not for the claustrophobic. Bradshaw St; open daily 0930–1700. **Blood on the Southern Cross**, a re-enactment of the battle for the Eureka Stockade, is held here four times every evening, Mon–Sat, with each show lasting about an hour ($$$).

Opposite Sovereign Hill is the **Gold Museum** on Bradshaw St, which has a series of galleries devoted to the lure, mining and refining of gold. Open daily 0930–1730.

Montrose Cottage in Eureka St is the last miners' bluestone cottage in Ballarat and has a collection of memorabilia from the Eureka Stockade. Open daily 0930–1700.

The **Ballarat Fine Art Gallery** in the Lydiard St Historic Precinct – a place of beautiful Victorian buildings – houses what is almost certainly the original Eureka Flag, and was donated by a policeman's widow. Also in the gallery are a number of works

THE EUREKA STOCKADE

In 1854 the miners of Ballarat rose up against the authorities that ruled them. What were their grievances? All gold miners in Victoria had to pay for a licence. This entitled the holder to work a single 12 ft (3.6 m) square claim and cost 30 shillings a month, regardless of the amount of gold recovered. Procedures for settlement of the many claim disputes were inadequate, there were frequent licence hunts and sly grog raids, and policing was arbitrary and often brutal.

Exercising absolute authority over the diggings and the 25,000 miners was the government-appointed Resident Gold Commissioner, Robert Rede, backed by a large contingent of police and a military garrison. On Sunday 22 October, some 10,000 miners assembled and formed the Ballarat Reform League. Their attempts to negotiate with Commissioner Rede got nowhere.

At a mass meeting on Wednesday 29 November, the blue Southern Cross flag flew for the first time. The miners rallied around the old slogan 'no taxation without representation' and the meeting voted in favour of burning licences. Commissioner Rede replied the next day with yet another licence hunt. The miners, led by Peter Lalor, seized the moment. Licences were burned and the rebel flag unfurled. The next day the miners started constructing a defensive fortification at the Eureka mine. At 3 am on Sunday 3 December, 276 police and military support approached the Eureka Stockade. Which side opened fire first is uncertain.

Those behind the stockade, probably outnumbered and certainly outgunned, were quickly routed. Peter Lalor later estimated that 22 miners died and a further 12 were wounded. On the government side were 4 dead and 12 wounded. Martial law was declared.

The groundswell of public indignation extended to Melbourne. When 13 of the rebels were tried for treason early in 1855, all were acquitted. An official inquiry was scathingly critical of the handling of the affair. The licence system was replaced by an export duty on gold and a Miner's Right, which cost a small annual fee.

Within a year, rebel leader Peter Lalor was representing Ballarat in the Legislative Council; he went on to become Speaker of the Legislative Assembly. The Southern Cross is still flown in Australia to this day. The battle of the Eureka Stockade lasted 15 minutes but saw the birth of democracy in Australia.

by Australian artists, including Sidney Nolan, who chronicled the history of early Ballarat and Australia. $?? Open daily 1030–1700.

The oldest theatre in Australia, **Her Majesty's**, is also in Lydiard St and has, in its time, starred Harry Lauder and Dame Nellie Melba.

EN ROUTE

Ararat is named after its neighbouring mountain, which in turn is named after the mountain in modern-day Turkey. In 1840 the first of Victoria's squatters, Horatio S. Wills, rested here on his journey from New South Wales. He reached the top of the 600-m high hill and wrote: 'This is Mount Ararat, for, like the Ark, we rested here.' One of the best views of the Grampians can be found at **Carrolls Cutting** which is 8 km out on the road from Ararat to Moyston.

The **Botanic Gardens** on the shores of man-made Lake Wendouree are magnificent. A fine collection of classical statues includes the Prime Ministers' Ave, updated with a new bust to record each incumbent. Many of the trees in the gardens are over 120 years old and feature on the National Trust's Register of Significant Trees. The **Ballarat Vintage Tramway** runs at weekends and during school holidays on 1.3 km of original track along the lake shore.

WINERIES OF SOUTHERN VICTORIA

There are several wineries in the area, producing mainly cool climate table wines. **Cathcart Ridge Estate Winery** is on the Halls Gap Rd and is open daily 1000–1700. **Montara Winery** is on Chalambar Rd 3 km to the south and is open Mon–Sat 0930–1700, Sun 1300–1700. **Mt Langi Ghiran Vineyard**, Warrak Rd, Buangor, off the Western Hwy has the same opening hours.

Five minutes from Sovereign Hill, on the corner of Fussel and York Sts, is the **Ballarat Wildlife Park**. Its wide range of wildlife includes koalas and Tasmanian devils, with kangaroos, wallabies and emus ranging freely. Open daily 0900–1730 with guided tours at 1100.

THE GRAMPIANS

The park is renowned for its rugged mountain scenery and wildflower displays. Access from Hwy 8 is via either Ararat or Stawell to Halls Gap.

i **Stawell and Grampians Information Centre**, Western Hwy, Stawell; tel: (03) 5356 4381. The main information centre for the Grampians.

Grampians National Park Visitor Centre, 2.5 km south of Halls Gap on Grampians Rd; tel: (03) 5358 2823.

Halls Gap, the only town within the park, has several places to stay, including a YHA hostel.

Grampians Motel $$, Dunkeld Rd; tel; (03) 5356 4248.

Grand Canyon Motel $$, Grampians Rd; tel: (03) 5356

There are a number of restaurants on Dunkeld Rd $$.

HIGHLIGHTS

There are over 900 different plant species in the park, but it is the wildflowers, coming into glorious bloom every spring, that attract the most attention. The prime time is Aug–Nov.

The park also has a great variety of birdlife – over 200 species have been recorded – and there are also kangaroos, gliders, echidnas and koalas.

Most parts of the park are accessible by car. Halls Gap has a circular road going up into the **Wonderland Range**. This road also connects with Mt Victory Rd, which leads to points of interest in the northern section of the park: **Boroka Lookout**, **McKenzie Falls**, **Lake Wartook** and **Zumstein**. Zumstein has kangaroos in abundance (look but don't feed).

Running south from Halls Gap is the road to Dunkeld, which passes through the Serra Range and **Mt Abrupt**. All these roads are sealed and can be used in all weathers. The park also has a wealth of secondary roads. These only become a problem after heavy rain, when they may become impassable - the rangers erect warning notices.

Also in the park are more than 160 km of marked footpaths, which range from easy strolls from the visitors' centre to serious bushwalking with overnight stays. It is important to keep to the tracts to minimise soil erosion.

WHERE NEXT?

Hwy 8 continues west across the border to South Australia and Adelaide (see p. 115). From Horsham the Henty Hwy (Rte 107) runs south along the western edge of the Grampians to Hamilton and the Southern Ocean at Portland (see pp. 149–169) or north to Sunraysia and Mildura (see p. 105).

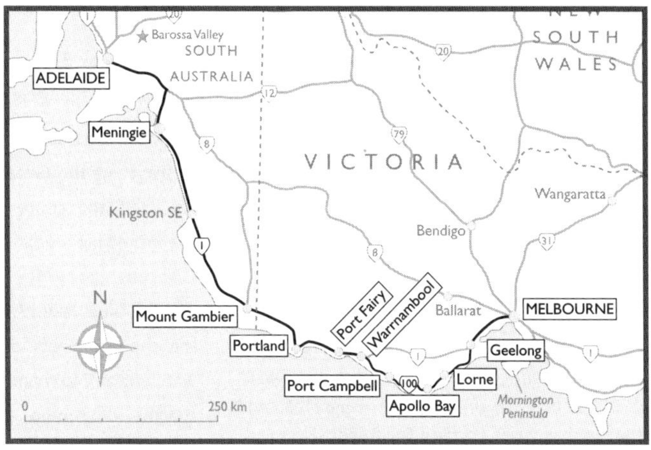

ADELAIDE – MELBOURNE
OTT TABLE 9027/9121/23

Transport	Frequency	Journey Time
Bus& Train	Fridays	17hrs 40mins

ADELAIDE – TAILEM BEND
OTT TABLE 9123

Transport	Frequency	Journey Time
Bus	Daily ex Saturday	1hr 25mins

TAILEM BEND – MENINGIE
OTT TABLE 9123

Transport	Frequency	Journey Time
Bus	Daily ex Saturday	35mins

MENINGIE – KINGSTON SE
OTT TABLE 9123

Transport	Frequency	Journey Time
Bus	Daily ex Saturdays	1hr 30mins

KINGSTON SE – MOUNT GAMBIER
OTT TABLE 9123

Transport	Frequency	Journey Time
Bus	Daily ex Saturdays	2hrs 1mins

MOUNT GAMBIER – PORTLAND
OTT TABLE 9121

Transport	Frequency	Journey Time
Bus	Daily	2hrs 5mins

PORTLAND – PORT FAIRY
OTT TABLE 9121

Transport	Frequency	Journey Time
Bus	Daily	1hr

PORT FAIRY – WARRNAMBOOL
OTT TABLE 9121

Transport	Frequency	Journey Time
Bus	Daily	40mins

WARRNAMBOOL – PORT CAMPBELL
OTT TABLE 9135A

Transport	Frequency	Journey Time
Bus	Fridays	1hr 30mins

PORT CAMPBELL – APOLLO BAY
OTT TABLE 9135A

Transport	Frequency	Journey Time
Bus	Fridays	1hr 45mins

APOLLO BAY – LORNE
OTT TABLE 9135A

Transport	Frequency	Journey Time
Bus	2 Daily	1hr

LORNE – GEELONG
OTT TABLE 9135A

Transport	Frequency	Journey Time
Bus	2 Daily	1hr 30mins

GEELONG – MELBOURNE
OTT TABLE 9027

Transport	Frequency	Journey Time
Train	2 Daily	56mins

Note: As the services do not connect to do this route by public transport involves lengthy stops or overnights at Mount Gambier and Warrnambool

THE GREAT OCEAN ROAD

The direct route between Adelaide and Melbourne is along Highway 8 (see p. 142), but if you can possibly squeeze in the time, the coastal route is full of magical delights.

There are a great many coastal drives in Australia, but this one exercises a total fascination on everyone who has ever travelled it. Even before reaching the Great Ocean Rd itself, the route includes the incredible wetlands of the Coorong, and Mt Gambier and its blue lake. After that are the prospects of whale-watching at Warrnambool, the charms of Apollo Bay, and Lorne, the preferred holiday spot for the rich of Melbourne. And the views are breathtaking – which creates a problem for the driver, because this road requires full concentration. Pull over at as many viewing stations and parking bays as you can along the way, so you don't miss out.

ROUTE DETAIL

Take Hwy 1, here called the Princes Highway, from Adelaide to Tailem Bend and stay on it as it swings south for Meningie (153 km) and the sea. The highway shadows the coast for the next 145 km and then at Kingston SE draws back from the shore as it runs to Mt Gambier (157 km). Continue on to Portland (115 km) and the sea, then round Portland Bay to Port Fairy and Warrnambool (100 km). Hwy 1 heads inland direct for Geelong, but Warrnambool is where the Great Ocean Rd now begins, winding along the coast for 300 km to Torquay. From Torquay Geelong is just 21 km inland, from where you pick up Hwy 1 for the final 74 km into Melbourne. Total journey: 1,065 km.

Buses do not follow this route – they take Highway 8 (see p. 142). The inland route from Adelaide to Melbourne via Horsham takes from 9hrs 30 mins by bus and 11 hrs 30 mins by train. See OTT tables 9035 and 9112.

MENINGIE AND THE COORONG

Meningie is on the shores of Lake Albert; the name is said to come from an Aboriginal word for mud. At the end of the 19th century travellers from Adelaide to Melbourne would have had to cross Lake Alexandrina and its smaller offshoot, Lake Albert, by paddle steamer before taking a coach south, and Meningie was a terminus for the steamers. In those days, Meningie, like other river towns, was ministered by clergy who travelled up and down the river on the boat *Etona*.

Meningie is now very much a fishing town (there are 40 professional anglers here), favoured for its position at the northern end of one of Australia's greatest surviving tracts of wetlands: the Coorong.

EN ROUTE

This is the route taken by the Chinese diggers as they travelled from South Australia to Victoria in search of gold, and about 15 km past the entrance to Coorong National Park, you pass **Chinaman Well**, now restored.

Meningie Tourist Information Centre, Coorong Cottage Industries and Melaleuca Centre, 76 Princes Hwy; tel: 8575 1698. Open daily. As well as information, the centre has a great selection of crafts and a large nursery.
The telephone code is 08.

Lake Albert Motel $ 38 Princes Hwy; tel: 8575 1077.
Meningie Lake Albert Caravan Park $ Narrung Rd; tel: 8575 1411.
Meningie's Waterfront Motel $$ Princes Hwy; tel: 8575 1152.
Mill Park $ Yumali Rd; tel: 8575 6033.

HIGHLIGHTS

The **Coorong** is a special place. The name comes from an Aboriginal word meaning 'long neck of water', an accurate description of the Coorong, which is only 2 km wide but stretches for over 100 km. The Coorong is basically a series of lagoons created by the estuary of the Murray River. As it approaches the sea the river appears to lose all its power and the flow is so depleted that bulldozers have to be used to effect an exit to the sea. Its silted waters spread slowly to Lakes Alexandrina and Albert and along the Coorong. Although in theory this is freshwater, the Coorong gets progressively saltier. The shallow lagoons are sheltered from the Southern Ocean by the Younghusband Peninsula, which is mainly sandhills occasionally bound by coastal mallee gums and bushes of golden wattle.

The **Coorong National Park** covers the Coorong along with the associated Lakes Albert and Alexandrina and has some of the most prolific birdlife in Australia. At any given time there are as many as 240 species of native birds here, some of which migrate annually to Siberia, Japan and China. Literally millions of them feed on the lagoons and fish in the Southern Ocean. This was the setting for Cohn Thiele's children's novel *Storm Boy* , which tells of a boy's friendship with a pelican; it was later made into a movie. As well as the giant pelicans, wild duck, shags, ibis, cormorants, spoonbills, black swans, gannets, plovers and terns all breed here.

The park headquarters is near Salt Creek about 64 km from Meningie along the Princes Hwy, just opposite the Messent Conservation Area. A nature trail here explains the formation of the sand dunes and the assorted vegetation within the park.

There is car access off Princes Hwy and two crossings which span the Coorong to the ocean. **42 Mile Crossing** is accessible throughout the year, while **Tea Tree Crossing** is a summer crossing only – at other times it can be flooded up to half a metre deep.

Just 12 km to the south of Meningie is **Camp Coorong**, an Aboriginal museum and cultural centre run by the Ngarrindjeri Lands and Progress Association – tel: 8575 1557. Aboriginal guides are available to take visitors on day walks to ancient Aboriginal fish traps and introduce them to plants and shrubs which the Ngarrindjeri used as medicine.

Although Coorong is the draw, there are several other attractions around Meningie. There is windsurfing, water-skiing or boating on Lake Albert. **Poltalloch Station**, along the shores of Lake Alexandrina, was established in 1836 and its 1870s homestead is a superb example of a beautifully crafted Victorian building. Buggies and carriages are kept in the barn; the shearing shed used to be the workplace of up to 22 shearers, and the old store, carpenter's shop and blacksmiths' have been converted into cottages and outbuildings. There is a 2-hr talk and tour about the station and its history. Portalloch is 34 km from Meningie; tours by appointment, tel: 8574 0013.

MOUNT GAMBIER

Mount Gambier is a modern city built on the slopes of an extinct volcano that bears the same name, in the middle of some of the largest softwood plantations in Australia. The volcano was last active approximately 5,000 years ago, and was first climbed by Europeans in 1839. Mount Gambier is sometimes referred to as the Blue Lake City, after the crater lake that is its greatest natural attraction. The ballet dancer, choreographer and actor Robert Helpmann was born here in 1909.

i **Lady Nelson Information and Interpretive Centre,** Jubilee Hwy East; tel: 8724 9750; free call (1800) 087 187. The **Interpretative Centre** includes a full-size replica of the *Lady Nelson*, the brig which made the first eastward passage along the southern coast of Australia. Aboard was Lt Grant, who first saw and named Mt Gambier. Also in the centre are a time walk, cave walk, geology and wetlands exhibitions. Open daily 0900–1700.

The telephone code is 08.

Avalon Motel $ 93 Gray St; tel: 8725 7200.
Blue Lake City Caravan Park $ Park Bay Rd; tel: 8725 9856.

EN ROUTE

Piccaninnie Ponds Conservation Park is a very large reed swamp with scenic beach areas and good bushwalking. The park is well known for its cave diving. Special diving equipment is required and permits for qualified divers are available from the Department of Environment and Natural Resources in Mount Gambier.

Blue Lake Motel $ 1 Kennedy Ave; tel: 8725 5211.
Gambier Lodge Inn $ 92 Penola Rd; tel: 8725 1579.
Jens Hotel $ 40 Commercial (east) St; tel: 8725 0188.
Jubilee Motor Inn $ Jubilee Hwy (east); tel: 8725 7444.
Le Cavalier Court Motel $ 37 Bay Rd; tel: 8725 9077.
Mac's Hotel $ 21 Bay Rd; tel: 8725 2402.
Motel Mount Gambier $ 115 Penola Rd; tel: 8725 5800.
Mount Gambier Central Caravan $ 6 Krummel St; tel: 8725 4427.
Willow Vale Camping Park $ Princes Hwy (east); tel: 8725 3631.

Domenica's Restaurant $$ 175 Commercial (east) St; tel: 8723 1175.
Fasta Pasta $ 102 Commercial (west) St; tel: 8723 0011.
Golden Chopsticks Restaurant $ 95 Commercial (east) St; tel: 8725 3935.
Nooky's Restaurant $$ Jubilee Hwy (east); tel: 8725 5122.
Oriental Restaurant $ 43 Commercial (east) St; tel: 8725 9762.
Ric's Pizza & Pasta Bar $ 109 Commercial (east) St; tel: 8725 5044.
Roma Pizza Bar $ 91 Commercial (west) St; tel: 8725 5332.
Sirroco's Restaurant $$ 118 Crouch (north) St; tel: 8723 1288.
Wing Wah Chinese Restaurant $ 222 Commercial (east) St; tel: 8725 0136.

HIGHLIGHTS

The mountain of Mt Gambier has four craters, of which the principal one contains the197-m deep **Blue Lake**. About Nov each year, the lake turns from grey-green to an intense cobalt blue, remaining this colour until late Mar. It has been suggested that the onset of warm weather precipitates countless particles of calcite, which absorb all visible light except blue. When the water cools in autumn, the particles dissolve once more and the water goes back to grey-green. The lake is over 3 km in circumference and some of the cliffs which surround it are 70 m high. The lookout points give spectacular vistas of both the lake and surrounding area. The town's domestic water supply is drawn from the lake so you can go on a tour of the pumping station.

In the **Mount Gambier Courthouse**, which was in operation from 1865 to 1975, the jury box, judge's chamber and cells are open to the public, along with an exhibition

POET'S LEAP

At the top of Mt Gambier an obelisk commemorates a mad act by a poet, Adam Lindsay Gordon, who served with the mounted police in the town from 1853 to 1855. Gordon, an exceptional horseman, took his horse to the summit and then raced it towards a post-and-rail fence, beyond which was a ledge 2 m wide and then a drop of 60 m to the rocks bordering the Blue Lake. The horse cleared the fence, turned in mid-air and landed on the very edge of the drop. It has been suggested that Gordon was world-weary and did not care whether he survived; this one jump brought him contemporary fame in Australia that he never achieved with his poetry.

of local history. Bay Rd; open daily 1200–1600.

One of the distinguishing features of the town is the use of local white coralline limestone for building, and there are several limestone caves. The **Cave Gardens** incorporate an open cave in the midst of rose gardens, while the **Umpherston Cave** has outside barbecue facilities and terraced gardens. The **Engelbrecht Cave** actually runs under part of the city and was used in the 19th century as a dump by a whisky distiller. This cave sometimes floods with water – as do many of the caves to be found in the area – but much of the time it is open to visitors. The tourist office has details.

PORTLAND

The first settlers here were sealers and whalers. A minimal shore-based whaling hut had been established in 1829 but the settlement grew rapidly as Portland Bay proved one of the best whale-catching areas in the world. Each year hundreds of whales were caught.

It was the arrival of the Henty family, of whom the first was Edward in 1834, that marked the beginning of serious settlement of Victoria. Ploughing started almost immediately, with the first piece of soil being turned on 6 Dec 1834 in what is now known as the Ploughed Field. The first Henty home, a hut, was somewhere in the area of the present-day Richmond Henty Hotel Motel.

The Henty clan spread inland to establish various stations; by 1839 they already owned 30,000 sheep and 500 head of cattle. When the township was surveyed and the first town lots went on sale in 1840 they commanded high prices, as Portland was in competition with Melbourne to be the premier settlement of the southern region. The major building boom that followed absorbed all available labour: by 1842 four hotels were opened, as well as four churches, and the first trading bank appeared in 1846. What finished the contest was the injection of wealth Melbourne received in the Victorian gold rush.

Having lost the contest - although the people of Portland compare their lot with those of Melbourne and are sure they won – Portland continued to develop. There are now over 200 heritage buildings in the city.

Portland Tourist Information Centre, Cliff St; tel: 5523 2671; free call (1800) 035 567. It is housed in the gaol which dates back to the 1850s.
The telephone code for Portland is 03.

Admella Motel $ 5 Otway St; tel: 5523 3347.
Burswood Homestead Bed & Breakfast $$ 15 Cape Nelson Rd; tel: 5523 4686.
Caravan Park Centenary $ 184 Bentinck St; tel: 5523 1487.
Claremont Holiday Village $ 61 Julia St; tel: 5521 7567.
Dutton Way Caravan Park $ 50 Dutton Way Rd; tel: 5523 1904.
Grosvenor Motel $ 206 Hurd St. Quiet off-highway location, all ground floor units; tel: 5523 2888.
Melaleuca Motel $ 25 Bentinck St; tel: 5523 3397.
Motel William Dutton $ 141 Percy St; tel: 5523 4222.
Siesta Motel $ 66 Julia St; tel: 5523 1300.

Canton Palace Restaurant $ 7 Julia St; tel: 5523 3677.
Le Capitaines Old Bond Store Seafood Restaurant $$ 6 Julia St; tel: 5523 3845.
Pilipino Kamayan Restaurant $ Gore Pl; tel: 5523 4424.
Pino's Pizza House $ 8 Julia St; tel: 5521 7388.
Portland's Top Of The Town Restaurant $$ 41 Percy St; tel: 5521 7469.
Ric's Pizza Bar $ 21 Henty St; tel: 5523 5699.
Settlers Kitchen $ 71 Bentinck St; tel: 5523 5972.

HIGHLIGHTS

Portland is the only deep-water port between Melbourne and Adelaide and its port development is huge, with much of the city's revenue deriving from the aluminium smelter. This does not detract from the charms of Portland; indeed, it is one of the few places where visitors can drive or walk into the heart of the wharf area. For those with an interest in the sea and sea trade, the wharf is the opportunity to take a close look at a range of vessels, from small coastal fishing boats to 80,000 d.w.t. bulk carriers.

With a self-guide map from the tourist centre you can see some of the oldest buildings in Victoria. Among them are the **Customs House** and **courthouse** in Cliff St, several old inns, Edward Henty's bluestone residence at **Burswood** on Cape Nelson Rd with its sweeping 19th-century tree-lined drive, and his brother Francis Henty's home at **Claremont**. The **Old Town Hall History House Museum and Research Centre** in Charles St is open daily 1000–1200, 1300–1600. The **RSL Memorial Lookout Tower** in Wade St has great 360° views of Portland and the surrounding districts; open daily 1000–1600.

SMELTER TOURS

The **Portland Aluminium Smelter** is claimed to be Australia's single biggest export earner and is one of the most modern ever built. There are guided tours on Tues mornings for which you need to book (tel: 5523 2671). The smelter's tree-planting programme will see over one million trees planted in and around the smelter over five years.

The original inhabitants of the area were the Kerrup-Tjmara people. There are still signs of Aboriginal presence in the area, and the **Lake Condah Mission** displays examples of their lifestyle.

Nearby there are some excellent beaches, good surfing and outstanding coastal and forest scenery. The circular track of the 250-km **Great South-West Walk** begins and ends at Portland and winds its way through national parks and state forests to Discovery Bay and Cape Nelson. There are 17 sections of varying lengths, and 16 campsites supplied with fresh water, wood barbecues, cleared tent space and bush toilets.

PORT FAIRY

There is considerable debate as to who was the first European to visit Port Fairy and when, with claims varying from 1810 to 1828. One candidate for the first landing is Captain James Wishart, and there is no argument that the town was named in honour of Wishart's ship, the cutter *Fairy*.

By 1828, the region from Port Fairy to Portland was well known to sealers and whalers, and over the next few years buildings were established and the whalers started to settle in permanent homes. Around 1839 John Cox set up a small store on the riverbank; Cox St marks its approximate location. In the same year a Mr McNeill established an inn he called the Merrijig, which still stands today.

At one time Port Fairy was set to become a major port in Australia. What stopped it was the start of the gold rush in the mid-19th century. There are still a number of unfinished buildings which show the suddenness with which workers simply downed tools and left for the goldfields. Now over 50 of Port Fairy's small cottages and bluestone buildings have been classified by the National Trust.

Port Fairy Visitor Information Centre, 22 Bank St; tel: 5568 2682.
The telephone code is 03.
Backpackers Guide to Port Fairy
http://www.greatoceanrd.org.au/backpackers/pfairy.html

Affordable Bed & Breakfast $ 21 Bank St; tel: 5568 1143.
Caledonian Inn Hotel Motel $ 41 Bank St. Victoria's oldest continually licensed hotel circa 1844. Motel accommodation in adjacent units; tel: 5568 1044.
Celtic Cottage and Garden House $$ 198 Princes Hwy. 1850s Port Fairy cottage. Secluded gardens; tel: 5568 2478.
Cherry Plum Cottage $ Albert Rd; tel: 5568 2433.
Hanley House $ 14 Sackville St; tel: 5568 2709.
Merrijig Inn $$ 1 Campbell St. The oldest hotel in town; tel: 5568 2324.
Port Fairy YHA Hostel $ 8 Cox St. En suite and double rooms. Built in the 1840s by the merchant king of Port Fairy, William Rutledge. Tel: 9670 3802.
Royal Oak Hotel $ 9 Bank St. Built around 1857. Double rooms with shared facilities; tel: 5568 1018.
Seacombe House Motor Inn $$ Cnr Cox & Sackville Sts. In a National Trust building in the centre of town; tel: 5568 1082.
Southcombe Park Caravan Park $ James St; tel: 5568 2677.
The Boathouse $ 19 Gipps St; tel: 5568 2608.

Caledonian Inn $$ 41 Bank St; tel: 5568 1044. Victoria's oldest continually licensed hotel, built about 1844. Bistro with an extensive seafood and steak menu; dinner and lunch 7 days a week.
Full House Chinese Restaurant $ 79 Gipps St; tel: 5568 1889. Cantonese. Licensed.
Lady Julia Percy Restaurant $$ 54 Sackville St; tel: 5568 1800.
Lunch on Bank Café $$ 20 Bank St; tel: 5568 2642. Modern Australian cuisine. Open from 0830 Wed–Sun for breakfast and lunch; dinner Fri–Sun. Licensed.

Highlights

Port Fairy marks one end of the Shipwreck Coast, which stretches east to Cape Otway. One of its attractions is the **Moyne River** which provides safe anchorage for large fishing vessels and pleasure craft. When the fleet returns with the day's catch visitors can buy fresh fish and crays from the wharf. **Pea Soup Beach** and **East Beach** are popular spots for pleasure and relaxation; East Beach runs parallel with the Moyne River and is accessible by footbridge and roadway.

Return of the Mutton Birds

One of Port Fairy's most spectacular sights is the return of the mutton birds to Griffiths Island. Within three days of 22 Sept each year tens of thousands of these birds arrive after a 15,000-km flight across the Pacific Ocean. Each bird returns to the same nesting burrow every year and usually maintains the same mate for life. They all fly out to sea during the day and return again each evening. A viewing platform and walking trails on Griffiths Island, which is connected to the town by a causeway, enable visitors to observe the birds and their young, though extreme care has to be taken not to leave the set paths.

There are many spectacular walks to be enjoyed in Port Fairy including the walk along Fisherman's Wharf, the Lighthouse Walk and the 22-km Mahogany Walking Track to Warrnambool. The tourist information centre has brochures.

The **Port Fairy History Centre** in the old 1859 courthouse gives a good idea of the history of the whole area within an hour or so's visit. Gipps St; open Wed and weekends 1400–1600, daily during school holidays. **Emoh** at 8 Cox St is a fine example of a rich merchant's home. It was built around 1847 by William Rutledge, the Merchant King of Port Fairy and was a centre for convivial hospitality until Rutledge's firm crashed in 1862. Now it is a youth hostel.

The Crags, 12 km west of Port Fairy, has windswept sand dunes and panoramic views of **Lady Julia Percy Island** and the coastline. The public is not allowed on the island, 17 km from Port Fairy, but its colony of fur seals can easily be seen at close quarters from a cruise boat. (Trips are arranged in good weather; the tourist centre will advise you.) The island is also home to rookeries of mutton-birds, kestrels, swamp harriers, sooty oystercatchers and blue penguins.

WARRNAMBOOL

When this town was surveyed by Lt Pickering in 1856 he gave it an Aboriginal name taken from a hill by the Hopkins River which has been variously translated as 'place of plenty', 'place between two waters' and 'running swamps'. You can take your pick.

Warrnambool was a whaling and sealing port in the early 1830s and was first permanently settled in 1839, but it may have been discovered by Europeans much earlier. In 1836 two shipwrecked sealers discovered an ancient wreck in the sand dunes. Called the **Mahogany Ship** because of the dark timbers used in its construction, it was last seen some time in the 1880s; it is presumed to have been buried by drifting dunes. Old Portuguese charts have since been discovered showing Australia's southern coastline as far as Armstrong's Bay, just 6 km west of Warrnambool. These suggest a Portuguese ship sailed off the coast of Australia in 1522, and some historians believe that the Mahogany Ship was a Portuguese caravel captained by Cristovão Mendonça, which was lost in the early 16th century. This theory, if proven, would rewrite the history of European discovery of Australia. Numerous searches and a reward of $250,000 offered by the government in 1992 have so far failed to solve the mystery. The 22-km **Mahogany Walking Track** runs from Warrnambool to Port Fairy, past the possible site of the mystery ship.

These were always dangerous waters and between 1836 and 1908 28 ships were wrecked here. Today, the shore is best known for the whales that come each winter to calve.

Tourist Information, 600 Raglan Pde; tel: 5564 7837. The telephone code is 03.
Warrnambool http://www.warrnambool.com

Colonial Village Motel $ 31 Mortlake Rd; tel: 5562 1455.
Downtown Motel $ 620 Raglan Pde; tel: 5562 1277.
Elm Tree Lodge Motel $ 179 Kepler St; tel: 5562 4133.
Flagstaff Hill Motel $ 762 Raglan Pde; tel: 5562 1166.
Kareja Apartments $$ 698 Raglan Pde. Quiet central location; tel: 5562 4244.
Mahogany Motel $ 463 Raglan Pde; tel: 5562 5722.
Norfolk Lodge Motel $ 692 Raglan Pde; tel: 5562 6455.
Warrnambool Beach Backpackers $ 17 Stanley St. Between the beach and the river. Has double rooms; tel: 5562 4874.
Western Hotel-Motel $ 45 Kepler St; tel: 5562 2011.
Whale Beach B & B $$ 234 Hopkins Point Rd. 2 km east of the Southern Right Whale nursery; tel: 5562 0577.

Balena's $$ Brasserie. Australian with European and Asian influences. Timor St; tel: 5562 8391.

Beach Babylon $$ 72 Liebig St. Open 7 Days a week from 1800 until late. Wed to Sun 1200-1430. Licensed and BYO; tel: 5562 3714.

Dino's Pizza Parlour $ 76 Liebig St; tel: 5562 0099.

Eighty-eight Chinese Restaurant $ 60 Liebig St; tel: 5562 1661.

Mahogany Ship $$ Flagstaff Hill Maritime Village. Open daily. Licensed; tel: 5561 1833.

Merihop Café $$ 78 Liebig St. Open dinner Tue-Sat. Licensed. Mediterranean and Asian influenced menu; tel: 5561 3188.

Proudfoots Boathouse $$ 2 Simpson St. National Trust Classified building on the Hopkins River. Open 7 days lunch and dinner. Licensed; tel: 5561 5055.

Restaurant Malaysia $ 69 Liebig St; tel: 5562 2051.

Warrnambool Dragon Inn Restaurant $188 Liebig St; tel: 5562 1517.

Whalers Inn $$ Cnr Liebig and Timor Sts. Lunch. Live music at dinner time; tel: 5562 8391.

HIGHLIGHTS

Warrnambool is spoken of as Victoria's southern right whale nursery. Every year between May and October, southern right whale cows return to the waters of Warrnambool to calve and prepare their young for the return trip to Antarctic waters. The whales often swim within 100 m of the shore: Logan's Beach, only minutes from the town centre, is one of Australia's most popular land-based whale-viewing sites. You can watch from the beach or from a special viewing platform in the dunes, which allows a far better view.

THE SOUTHERN RIGHT WHALE

Once hunted nearly to extinction, the southern right was one of the first whale species granted protection by an international agreement signed in 1935. Although it is relatively rare, with only a few thousand known, its numbers are slowly growing. The southern right has been sighted regularly along the southern coastline since 1970, with sightings and visits becoming more frequent in recent years.

One of the other major attractions of the town is the **Flagstaff Hill Maritime Museum** in Merri St. This is a life-size recreated village to give visitors a feeling of the port in the 19th century. In addition to the original lighthouse and lighthouse-keeper's cottage, there are replicas of many buildings of the time, including a sailmaker's loft, bank, town hall and chapel. The museum also tells the story of the *Loch Ard* wreck and displays the fortunate peacock (see p. 163). $$. Open daily 0900–1700.

The town's **Botanic Gardens**, on the corner of Queen St and Botanic Rd, had the same great designer as the Melbourne Botanic Gardens. There is a bandstand rotunda, a fernery, and winding shaded walkways.

The **Aquarium** on the breakwater has a display of many fish from local waters as well as a large collection of seashells. Open daily 0900–1700.

The **Wollaston Bridge** is an early example of a suspension bridge, erected in 1890 for noted district pastoralist Sir Walter Manifold, to provide easy access to the Wollaston Estate. The cables used in its construction came from Melbourne's early cable trams.

Granny's Grave is a monument to Mrs James Raddleston, the first white woman to be buried in the Warrnambool area. She died in 1848, and the monument was erected in 1904. It is off Hickford Pde, by way of the sand dunes.

A popular picnic area is **Cannon Hill**, off Artillery Crescent, which has panoramic views of Lake Pertrobe and Lady Bay. It contains a marble marker which just possibly might have links with 17th-century Portuguese explorers.

At low tide you can wade across to **Middle Island** at the mouth of the Merri River; part of the Thunder Point Coastal Reserve, it has a fairy penguin colony. There are tracks laid down so that visitors do not disturb the birds.

THE GREAT OCEAN ROAD

The Great Ocean Rd runs for about 300 km between Warrnambool and Torquay. Although it is famed for its scenery, the road was built for purely practical purposes. Until it was opened there was no connection between the isolated communities along the coast of Victoria, which were cut off from the rest of the world by the Otway Range. Its construction, which began at the end of World War I, was also a form of job creation for returning servicemen and at the same time it was thought that the road would provide a fitting memorial to all those Australians who had fallen in the war. Using, in the main, manual labour, squads of men cut the road out of the mountainsides that swept down to the sea. The road was completed in 1932.

Along the Princes Hwy and 12 km west of Warrnambool is the **Tower Hill Game Reserve**. Tower Hill is believed to have been formed some 25,000 years ago in a volcanic eruption. The blast created the funnel-shaped crater, later filled by a lake, and the islands. Noted Victorian artist Eugene von Guerard painted an exceptionally detailed picture of Tower Hill in 1855 and a revegetation programme based on species identified from the painting began in the late 1950s. The revegetation has provided new habitats for many animals – the koalas have succeeded so well that population control is being tried including feeding them a contraceptive pill. There are boardwalks, nesting boxes and a bird hide to let you get close. There is open access to the reserve at all times and the natural history centre is open daily 0900–1630.

PORT CAMPBELL

Port Campbell National Park is famous for its striking cliffs and rock formations – London Bridge, the Twelve Apostles, Loch Arch Gorge and the Arch. The **Twelve Apostles** are rock stacks which have been isolated from the coast by the sea and have become one of the most photographed natural features in Australia.

This is the centre of the notorious Shipwreck Coast, where the slightest swell results in treacherous surf and billowing spray. One of the best-known tragedies was the wreck of the *Loch Ard* in 1878. There were only two survivors and 52 lives were lost; four of the victims were buried on the cliff top in what is now called the Loch Ard Cemetery. A sign at the top of the gorge steps tells the story. Also aboard was a priceless Minton statue of a peacock, being transported to Melbourne in 1878 for display at the 1880 International Exhibition. It was washed ashore in its packing case, in perfect condition save for a small chip in its beak. It is on display in the maritime museum in Warrnambool (see p. 144).

i Port Campbell National Park Information Centre, Morris St, Port Campbell; tel: (03) 5598 6382.

APOLLO BAY

One of the most appealing features of the Great Ocean Rd is that as it winds its elegant way around the coast it passes through a series of small townships, each of which is attractive in its own right. Apollo Bay is one of them. It was once described by Rudyard Kipling as 'paradise', a fair summing up of a town which stands among cool fern gullies, rushing streams, magnificent waterfalls and rainforests, with calm waters and ocean views.

First among the Europeans were the whalers who worked in small boats from the shore. A whaling station was established in 1840 and stood where the golf club is

EN ROUTE

Otway National Park stretches from Cape Otway almost to Apollo Bay and contains varied birdlife as well as swamp wallabies and ring-tailed possums.

Cape Otway was first discovered by Europeans in 1802 by Matthew Flinders, but this was ever a dangerous coast and it was not until the lighthouse was built in 1848 that it seriously attracted settlers. After World War II there was a timber boom for houses and the national park was created to protect the coast above Cape Otway and Blanket Bay.

The Great Ocean Rd runs right through the park, with Lighthouse Rd – unsealed but very well maintained – running down from the centre to the coast. You can easily explore it from Maits Rest, where there is a boardwalk. You can also visit the lighthouse (usually open Tues and Thur, 1000–1130, 1400–1530; tel: 03 5237 9240 to check). You can get information at the Otway National Park offices in Cartwright St, Apollo Bay; tel: (03) 5237 6889.

today. After the whalers came the timber cutters, who arrived in the 1850s, and Apollo Bay was born.

The town depended almost totally on the sea for connection with civilisation until the Great Ocean Rd was completed in 1932. In that year the bay was the scene of a major Australian shipping disaster: as the coastal steamer Casino was coming into the jetty a series of freak waves turned it over and it sank. Ten lives were lost. The anchor of the ship is now outside the Apollo Bay Post Office.

Today Apollo Bay is a major tourist destination, but it is also a fishing port supporting a large fleet. Much of the action is centred on the jetty, and there are local markets on the foreshore on Sat.

The **Old Cable Station Museum** displays a photographic record of the history of the area, with some interesting artefacts. The original cable station was set up to achieve telecommunications between Tasmania and the mainland. (Nowadays communication is by microwave and satellite, since there are no longer any cable-laying ships in the southern hemisphere and if something should go wrong Tasmania could be cut off for months.) The museum is open daily 1400–1700 during the summer holidays but otherwise only at weekends.

The town is surrounded by interesting lookout and picnic spots including the **Barham Paradise Scenic Reserve**, the exceptionally beautiful **Barham River Valley, Grey River Scenic Reserve and Walk** (23 km east of Apollo Bay), **Elliot River** (10 km south-west) and the picturesque **Carisbrook Falls**. The **Marriners Falls** are on Barham River Rd, with a 2-km track running through lush forested areas. Access to **Marriners Lookout** is by a steep, narrow road, worth the effort for the superb views.

i Apollo Bay Great Ocean Rd Information Centre, Apollo Bay Foreshore; tel: 5237 6529. Open daily 0900–1700. The telephone code is 03.

EN ROUTE

Cape Patton, Kennett River and Wye River are all charming villages at which to pause and be bowled over by the stunning ocean views.

For the Christmas period, say, 15 Dec–1 Feb, every room will have been booked some time before and the prices adjusted upwards. Only go out of season.

Apollo Bay Beachfront Motel $$ 163 Great Ocean Rd; tel: 5237 6437.

Bay Pines Motel & Guest House $ 1 Murray St; tel: 5237 6732.

Coastal Motel $$ 171 Great Ocean Rd. Modern units opposite beach 150 m to shops; tel: 5237 6681.

Iluka Motel $$ 65 Great Ocean Rd. Has its own restaurant; tel: 5237 6531.

Kooringal Tourist Van Park $ 27 Cawood St. This is probably the least expensive place to stay in town. Tel: 5237 7111.

Pisces Caravan Resort $ Great Ocean Rd; tel: 5237 6749.

Waratah Caravan Park $ 7 Noel St; tel: 5237 6562.

Choose the locally caught fresh fish.

Beacon Point Restaurant $$ Skenes Creek Rd. Just out of town. Famous for its seafood; tel: 5237 6411.

Bernie's Restaurant $$, 13 km east of Apollo Bay, Great Ocean Rd. Open lunch Sun. Dinner daily. Licensed. Fish specialities; tel: 5237 0228.

Buffs Bistro $$ 51 Great Ocean Rd. Open daily spring-autumn. Thu-Mon winter. Licensed. Rambling café; tel: 5237 6403.

Chris's Beacon Point Restaurant $$ Skenes Creek Rd, Skenes Creek. Open daily lunch and dinner. Licensed. Greek-style cooking; tel: 5237 6411.

Otway Restaurant $$ 275 Great Ocean Rd; tel: 5237 6215.

Whitecrest Resort $ Great Ocean Rd; tel: 5237 0228.

LORNE

This is one of the preferred haunts of the golden people of Melbourne: over the extended Christmas holiday period you could not force yourself in with a shoehorn. As an idea of how full this little village can become, the field for its famous **Pier to Pub Swim** has to be restricted to 2,500 entries. At that time of the year it will be expensive as well, so go on a weekday outside the holiday period.

The town grew around a site from which timber was shipped and until 1869 was called Loutit Bay. It became popular with pastoralists from inland areas and developed rather in the style of an English seaside resort. For years the only easy access to Lorne was by sea, but when the Great Ocean Rd opened in 1932 Lorne immediately became Melbourne's favourite playground.

EN ROUTE

Torquay, 45 km from Lorne, marks the eastern end of the Great Ocean Rd. It rejoices in the fact that it has two of the world's great surfing beaches — Bells and Jan Juc.

Surfcoast Tourist Information Centre, 144 Mountjoy Pde; tel: 5289 1152. Telephone code 03.

Anchorage Motel $$ 32 Mountjoy Pde; tel: 5289 1891.
Babington Family Park $$ 19 Deans Marsh Rd; tel: 5289 1760.
Coachman Inn Motel $$ 1 Deans Marsh Rd; tel: 5289 2244.
Great Ocean Rd Backpackers $ 11 Erskine Ave; tel: 5289 1809.
Lorne Hotel Motel $ Mountjoy Pde; tel: 5289 1409.
Motel Kalimna $$ Mountjoy Pde; tel: 5289 1407.
Ocean Lodge Motel $$ 6 Armytage St. Tel: 5289 1330.
Pacific Motel $$ 268 Mountjoy Pde; tel: 5289 1609.
Sandridge Motel $$ 128 Mountjoy Pde; tel: 5289 2180.

Arab Expresso Bar $ Mountjoy Pde. Open lunch and dinner until late. BYO; tel: 5289 1435.
Chris's Restaurant $$ Cumberland Resort; tel: 5289 2455.
Kosta's, 48 Mountjoy Pde. Open daily 0900-0100. Licensed. Greek influenced cuisine; tel: 5289 1883.
Mark's, 124 Mountjoy Pde. Open 7 days lunch and dinner. Licensed; tel: 5289 2787.
Normandy Fare Cafe $ Grove Rd; tel: 5289 1004.
Pier Restaurant $$ Pier Head; tel: 5289 1119.
Rancheros Mexican Foods $ 55a Mountjoy Pde; tel: 5289 2523.
Reif's Restaurant $$ 84 Mountjoy Pde. Open seven days, lunch and dinner. Licensed; tel: 5289 2366.
Seaside Palace Chinese Restaurant $$ 114 Mountjoy Pde; tel: 5289 2330.
Torrens Motel & Restaurant $$ 124 Mountjoy Pde; tel: 5289 1307.

HIGHLIGHTS

Lorne was the first town in Victoria to be declared by the state government as being of special significance and natural beauty. It is an appropriate choice. The approaches to Lorne along the Great Ocean Rd, whether from east or west, are quite spectacular, and the town is surrounded by beach, forests and the beautiful Otway Range. It has a year-round mild climate.

Two headlands sweep down to the sea either side of the white beach. The beach is patrolled and very safe, and is ideal for kids – the foreshore reserve has a children's playground, pool, amusement centre, trampolines and picnic ground. Pedal boats can be hired.

The town itself has remained relatively unspoiled. The **Shell Shop and Museum** in William St is open daily 0900–1630. The **Lorne Historical Society** has a collection of photographs and memorabilia on the town at 59 Mountjoy Pde; open weekends only 1300–1600.

The entrance to the **Angahook-Lorne State Park** is about a 30-min walk – go up Bay St and turn left on George St. The park stretches from Aireys Inlet to Kennett River and in just the Lorne section there are more than 50 km of maintained walking tracks through a variety of habitats with extensive birdlife. Some of the trails are the old timber tramways and bushwalking tracks built in the 19th century. The **Erskine Falls** are along the park's Erskine River Track, a magnificent 8-km drive or 3-hr walk among scenic forested hills. The falls, set among lush tree ferns and bush, drop 30 m. There are stunning views from **Teddy's Lookout**. Maps and information from the Angahook-Lorne State Park office; tel: 5289 1732.

GEELONG

In a sense Geelong has it all. It is Victoria's second largest city, a thriving commercial centre and a quite remarkably elegant town. The surrounding countryside around Corio Bay is a paradise for walkers and nature lovers and within the city are superb recreational areas. It emanates a feeling of metropolitan sophistication overlaid by a provincial charm.

Geelong is one of Victoria's most historically significant cities. It is in an area which was one of the first parts of Victoria discovered by Europeans; possibly the first was Lt John Murray in 1802. The land was ripe for pastoral development, and by 1841 the town had a post office and what is claimed to be Australia's oldest morning newspaper, the *Geelong Advertiser*.

Almost from the start Geelong was prosperous as a major port for wool and grain. Then, as for so many Australian cities, came gold. Geelong was a crucial link to the Ballarat goldfields (see p. 143) and as the gold passed through some of the money stuck. The goldfields enticed many citizens to try their luck at the diggings but many others stayed to take advantage of the trade it brought. It is interesting that almost without exception towns that had a strong agricultural economy benefited greatly from the trade brought about by gold, while those which only grew with gold tended to die with it.

The Aboriginals called the bay Jillong and the surrounding land Corayo but over time the names have reversed and the bay is now Corio and the town Geelong. Jillong is said to mean either "place of the cliff' or 'white seabird".

Geelong Otway Tourism, National Wool Centre, 26 Moorabool St; tel: 5223 2900.
Geelong Net http://www.geelong.net.au/

Admiralty Motor Inn $$ 66 McKillop St; tel: 5221 4288.
Bay City Geelong Motel $$ 231 Malop St; tel: 5221 1933.
Bayview Hotel $ 2 Mercer St; tel: 5229 2164.
Colonial Lodge Motel $ 57 Fyans St; tel: 5223 2266.
Eastern Sands Motel $$ 1 Bellarine St; tel: 5221 5577.
Geelong Motor Inn & Serviced Apartments $$ Kooyong Rd, cnr Princes Hwy; tel: 5222 4777.
Innkeepers Motor Inn $$ 9 Aberdeen St; tel: 5221 2177.
Kangaroo Motel $ 16 The Esplanade; tel: 5221 4022.
Rippleside Motel $ 67 Melbourne Rd; tel: 5278 2017.
Shannon Motor Inn $ 285 Shannon Ave; tel: 5222 4355.

Chantra Thai & Laos Restaurant $ 138 Pakington St; tel: 5229 4348.
Elephant and Castle Pub Restaurant $ 158 McKillop St. Open daily for lunch; dinner Tue-Sat. English pub food; tel: 5221 3707.
Empire Grill $$ 66 McKillop St. Open lunch Mon-Fri. Dinner Mon-Sat . Licensed. Imaginative menu; tel: 5223 2132.
Fishermen's Pier $$ Yarra St. Open daily lunch and dinner. Licensed; tel: 5222 4100.
Karuna Thai Restaurant $$ 22 Pakington St. Seven nights. Modified Thai. BYO; tel: 5223 2832.
Lamby's Restaurant $$ National Wool Museum, Moorabool St. Terrible name. Open 7 days lunch and dinner. In the basement of the 1872 Bluestone Building. Licensed. Medium price; tel: 5223 2392.
Le Parisien $$ 16 The Esplanade. Open lunch Mon-Fri, dinner Mon-Sat. Licensed. French cooking; tel: 5229 3110
Lord of the Isles Bistro $ 3 West Fyans St. Open seven days a week for lunch and dinner. Licensed and BYO. Why the title? In 1884 the landlord liked Sir Walter Scott's poem of the same name; tel: 5221 8424.

EN ROUTE

A short drive north of Geelong **Serendip Sanctuary** in Lara is home to over 150 species of native birds as well as koalas and wallabies. The birds include threatened species such as brolgas and Australian bustards. The **You Yangs Recreational Park** has granite peaks towering above the Western Plains. They are easy to walk up, with no serious climbing involved, and from the top there are great 360° views.

Mexican Graffiti $ 43 Yarra St. Californian-style Mexican cuisine. Open 7 days. Licensed. Totally smoke-free; tel: 5222 2036.
Portico Restaurant $$ All Seasons Ambassador Hotel, Gheeringhap St. Open for dinner seven nights. Licensed; tel: 5221 6844.
Savvas Restaurant $$ 51 Moorabool St. Opposite the National Wool Centre. Medium price. Open lunch and dinner Mon–Sat; tel: 5229 3703.
Sawyers Arms Tavern $$ 2 Noble St, Newtown. Lunch Mon–Fri. Dinner Mon–Sat. Licensed; tel: 5223 1244.

HIGHLIGHTS

With over 200 classified Victorian buildings in its well-laid out streets, and over 14 per cent of its area reserved for parks and sports grounds, it is difficult to remember that Geelong's principal trade is crude and refined petroleum products.

The easiest way to see how Geelong developed is to take the **Heritage Trail Walk** which starts in Moorabool St outside the Wool Museum which holds the tourist centre. The walk, which takes about an hour, lets you see most of the major sights of Geelong.

Geelong's character is defined by its remarkable historical buildings and its magnificent parks and gardens. The buildings include **Merchiston Hall** (Garden St, East Geelong), an eight-roomed stone house built in 1856 for an early settler and **Osborne House** (Swinburne St, North Geelong), a bluestone mansion built in 1858. Within **Osborne House** is the comprehensive memorabilia of Geelong's **Naval Museum.** Two houses in Newtown are now open to the public. **The Heights**, in Aphrasia St, is a 14-roomed prefabricated timber mansion built in 1855, and **Barwon Grange** in Fernleigh St, built in the same year, is a well-maintained homestead on the banks of the Barwon River. All the rooms are furnished in the style of the times. Barwon Grange is open Wed; tel: (03) 5221 3906, and The Heights is open Wed–Sun 1100–1630.

The old Denys Lascelles Woolstore, built in stages from 1872 on the corner of Moorabool and Brougham Sts, houses the **National Wool Centre**. Three galleries record in splendid detail Australia's wool heritage, and it has graphic sculptured displays, relics, models, photographic records, magnificent wool murals and a range of video and audio presentations.

The **Geelong Art Gallery** in Little Malop St has a splendid collection of over 3,000 works, mainly Australian, including 'Bush Burial' by Frederick McCubbins and

Eugene von Guerard's 'View of Geelong', on loan from Sir Andrew Lloyd Webber. Johnstone Park, in which the gallery is set, also includes the war memorial, library, city hall, and historical records centre.

EVENTS AND ENTERTAINMENT

The impressive **Performing Arts Centre** in Little Malop St offers some of the best theatre and opera from around the world. The **Geelong Racing Carnival** (tel: 5229 4414 for information) is held at the end of October, neatly tying in with the Melbourne Cup (see p. 442).

The recently restored historic semi-circular promenade overlooking Corio Bay has added to the popularity of **Eastern Beach**. The beautiful **Corio Villa**, a prefabricated iron house built in 1856, is near the Eastern Beach swimming enclosure and the entrance to **Geelong Botanic Gardens**. The gardens, which include an annexe of botanical woodlands overlooking Corio Bay, were established in 1850 and show the far-sighted thinking of the pioneer fathers of the city. They are open daily from dawn until dusk.

Buckley Falls Park, on the western outskirts of Geelong, straddles the Barwon River, which tumbles over rocks and rapids before it joins with the Moorabool River.

In the **Geelong wine district** there are properties that date back to when grapes were first planted in the area 150 years ago by Swiss immigrants. Part of Geelong's prosperity came from wool and **Barrunah Plains**, once the largest sheep station in Victoria, is still in operation and visitors are welcome. This 150 year old estate includes a historic grazier's mansion with blue-stone out-buildings and shearers quarters. Open by appointment; tel: 5287 1234.

The **Twin Lakes**, a fauna sanctuary 19 km from Geelong, is a breeding haven for kangaroos, emus, koalas and wildfowl.

WHERE NEXT?

Melbourne (see p. 170) is about an hour away, or the Midland Hwy (Rte 149) will take you past the nature reserves and old gold towns of the Brisbane Ranges to Ballarat (see p. 143).

Melbourne

Victoria has the pleasure of having as its capital city Melbourne, the most civilised city in Australia. Here are the best restaurants, the best theatre, the best art galleries and the best shopping. It has been called in more than one survey the World's Most Livable City. Melbourne is a delight.

The city was named in 1837 after the British prime minister, Lord Melbourne, which may not seem much of a name but is better than Bearbrass, Dutigalla and Glenelg, which were the original names of the settlement. One of the key figures in the city's history is John Batman, who in 1835 'bought' 243,000 ha on the western shore of Port Phillip from the local Aboriginal people for a few trinkets (Peter Menhuit made the same sort of deal when he bought Manhattan). On the land he had swindled, John Batman chose a site for a village which within a year had started to develop into the township that was to be Melbourne.

All of this had been done with the strong disapproval of the authorities in New South Wales, and eventually notice had to be taken of this illegal upstart. In 1837 the township was surveyed, the regular rectangular street grid laid out and a magistrate sent from Sydney to maintain law and order. Two years later Charles La Trobe was appointed Superintendent of the Port Phillip District and established a separate police force and a customs office. It was the start of the break between Melbourne and Sydney.

The first building in the town was, following the Australian sense of priorities, John Pascoe Fawkner's grog shop. Through the 1840s the town grew to respectable proportions. Then came the gold rush. It is difficult to imagine the impact today, but the population left almost en masse for the tented fields of Warrandyte and Ballarat, leaving behind them a ghost town that, in 1851, was named the capital of the new colony of Victoria.

The wealth the gold rush brought can be seen in the style, architecture and presence of Melbourne to this day. Money poured in from the goldfields and started an era of major civic construction — the post office, the public library, Parliament House and the Treasury were all erected in an imposing style which gave Melbourne much of its character. Over 1,000 buildings were erected in 1853 alone. Melbourne Cricket Ground, a sure and certain sign of civilisation, was established that year. The first Melbourne Cup was run in 1861, and instantly became a national institution (see p. 180). The first airmail service to Sydney began in 1914 and Essendon Airport was established in 1921.

MELBOURNE V. SYDNEY

It would be wrong to make too much of the rivalry between Sydney and Melbourne, but it would be wrong as well to underestimate its strength. Journalists in Sydney have been forbidden to refer to Melbourne as Bleak City; in Melbourne they have been asked not to refer to Sydney as being built of plastic. Elspeth Huxley in *Their Shining Eldorado* wrote: 'One of the stock Sydney jokes is of the census-taker who enquired; "How many children have you, ma'am?" "Two living and three in Melbourne".' That was written in 1967 and the same joke is still told.

Sydney began life nearly 50 years ahead of Melbourne — but Sydney began as a penal colony, Melbourne did not. For a while in the 19th century Melbourne was the larger and more exciting city and was known as 'Marvellous Melbourne'. Sydney now appears to have pulled ahead, in size if nothing else. Melbourne can, at times, make Sydney look like a vulgar yahoo which has just come into money.

When seeking a capital for the new Federation of Australia, the rivalry between the two cities made the choice of either impossible, and Canberra was created (see p. 82).

The Age newspaper was founded in 1854 and became one of the bastions of civilisation. It is interesting that in the matter of the Eureka Stockade at Ballarat *The Age* sided with Peter Lalor and the miners, while *The Sydney Morning Herald* sided with the government. The two newspapers are now owned by the same company but still offer very divergent views of the world.

The ethnic mix of Melbourne's population has always been an important influence on the city's character. Chinese and Irish diggers were attracted by gold in the 19th century and a large Chinatown grew up in the 1850s, a small area of which remains in Little Bourke St. The postwar arrival of refugees and migrants from all over Europe (particularly Greece, Italy, Yugoslavia, Turkey and Poland) and more recently from Vietnam and Cambodia, have all contributed elements of their cultures to what could otherwise have been a conservative, passionless English society. As a direct result of these waves of migrants, eating out in Melbourne is a gourmet's dream. Name the culinary style and Melbourne has it — one restaurant even offers Jamaican cuisine.

Melbourne

The weather in Melbourne is a constant topic of conversation and the subject of many jokes and jibes. Statistically, the climate of Melbourne is mild and sunny, but the city lies in a west to east air stream and the weather is, to put it politely, changeable and not easy to predict. It can change so rapidly it is possible to have all four seasons in one day – temperature changes in just a few hours can defy belief. Summers are fairly short, with really hot days confined mostly to Jan and Feb, and winters are cloudy, chilly and often windy. Melburnians dress for the weather, and do so very stylishly. You will see more elegantly dressed people in Melbourne in half an hour than you would see in Sydney in a week.

ARRIVAL AND DEPARTURE

Tullamarine is Melbourne's international and domestic airport and is 22 km north-east of the city centre. When it was opened the airport was a delight but it is now showing signs of fraying at the edges. The domestic terminals work very well but the international side seems somewhat sub-standard. The Tullamarine freeway makes it a fairly quick and painless trip except in the morning and evening rush hour. A Skybus shuttle service runs every half hour between the airport and the central Franklin St depot – much cheaper and just as convenient as taking a cab all the way to the airport.

Trains come in to Flinders St station, right in the heart of the city. The station, with its attractive dome and feeling of presence, was completed in 1899 and is a traditional meeting place for the people of Melbourne.

Greyhound Pioneer buses arrive at Melbourne Bus Terminal, Franklin St; other lines use Spencer St Bus Terminal.

INFORMATION

Tourist Office **Victoria Visitor Information Centre,** Melbourne Town Hall, corner of Little Collins St and Swanston St; tel: 9790 2121. There is a wide range of free brochures available, covering every aspect of life in Melbourne. The staff can also book you a room within your budget. The earlier in the day you make your request the likelier it is that you will get exactly what you want.

INTERNET SITES **Australia Magazine** http://www.ozramp.net.au/~senani/melb.htm

Chinatown Melbourne http://www.melbourne.citysearch.com.au/chinatown/
CitySearch Melbourne http://www.melbourne.citysearch.com.au/
Living in Melbourne Australia http://www.home.vicnet.net.au/~gnaust/vic7/indexreload.html
Melbourne http://www.members.ocean.com.au/conwaywn/
Melbourne Australia http://www.melbourne.org
Melbourne Hotel Discounts and City Guide
http://www.worldexecutive.com/cityguides/melbourne/index.html
Melbourne Information http://www.infoline.com.au
Melbourne Online http://www.melbourne.com.au
Melbourne Sidewalk http://www.melbourne.sidewalk.com.au
Melbourne Visitors Guide http://www.Melbourne.8m.com/
Melbourne Webspot http://www.webspot.com.au/

INTERNET ACCESS **Binary Bar**, 243 Brunswick Street, Fitzroy. Open: seven days, 1100–1700.

Central Internet, Level 2, Melbourne Central, 300 Lonsdale St. Open: seven days, 1100–late.

MONEY Thomas Cook foreign exchange offices are at Shop 5, 253–67 Bourke St, Melbourne 3000; tel: 9654 4222; and at the airport, tel: 9335 5455.

POST AND PHONES The main post office is in Elizabeth St, on the corner with Bourke St. The area code for Melbourne is 03.

ACCOMMODATION

In the 1830s accommodation in Melbourne was not of the best and landlords were not popular. A letter written to the lieutenant-governor reads, in part: 'Of all the impositions inflicted on mankind an inn in the district is the most dreadful abomination. It appears to me the licensee considers only one duty, that is, to persecute and victimize the traveller.' Things have improved since then.

This list is of affordable accommodation in the centre of the city; all the major hotel chains are, of course, also here. In the suburbs of Melbourne there are motels aplenty well within the reach of the budget conscious.

Astoria City Travel Inn $$ 288 Spencer St; tel: 9670 6801.
Batmans Hill Hotel $$ 66 Spencer St; tel: 9614 6344.
City Limits Motel $$ 20 Little Bourke St; tel: 9662 2544.
City Square Inn $$ 67 Swanston St; tel: 9654 7011.
Duke of Wellington $ 146 Flinders St; tel: 9650 4984.
Gordon Place $$ 24 Little Bourke St; tel: 9663 2888.
Hollyford Hotel $ 650 Elizabeth St; tel: 9347 8558.

Hotel Enterprize $ 44 Spencer St; tel: 9629 6991.

Ibis Hotel Melbourne $$ 15 Therry St; tel: 9639 2399.

Kingsgate Budget Hotel $ 131 King St; tel: 9629 3049.

New Chateau Hotel $$ 131 Lonsadale St; tel: 9663 3161.

Palm Lake Motel $$ 52 Queens Rd; tel: 9243 9999.

Savoy Park Plaza International $$ 630 Little Collins St; tel: 9622 8888.

Sheraton Hotel $ 13 Spring St; tel: 9650 5000.

Victoria Holdings Four Seasons $ 215 Little Collins St; tel: 9653 0441.

YWCA Melbourne $ 489 Elizabeth St; tel: 9329 5188.

FOOD AND DRINK

CENTRAL

Café d'Orsay $$ 184 Collins St; tel: 9654 6498. Forget the French name, this is an Italian restaurant with French flavours. There are sidewalk tables where you can watch the rest of the world. Why is outside dining not as popular in Australia as in Europe? No one knows. Perhaps Australians are shy.

Café La $$ Hotel Sofitel, 25 Collins St; tel: 9653 0000. Only go for the views.

Grossi Florentino $$$ 80 Bourke St; tel: 9662 1811. The restaurant where the great and grand of Melbourne often dine. European service of a quality you will see nowhere else in Australia. Ultra-expensive, but take heart: the cellar restaurant is much, much cheaper.

Hairy Canary $$ 212 Little Collins St, nr Swanston St; tel: 9654 2471. Currently one of the cool spots to be seen, although by the time you read this it may well have changed (people are fickle).

Il Solito Posto $$ 113 Collins St; tel: 9654 4466. Italian-style food modified with Asian and Australian influences. Always busy. Fast service.

Kappo Okita $ 17 Liverpool St, nr Bourke St; tel: 9662 2206. Very affordable, minute restaurant serving bento boxes which will give you a full meal.

Kenzan $$ Collins St. Japanese restaurants are also very popular and this is one of the favourites.

Pellegrini's $ 66 Bourke St; tel: 9662 1885. You can either sit at the long bar or round the big wooden table in the kitchen. Basic Italian cuisine, great fun and great value.

MEALS ON WHEELS

If you insist on a totally unusual experience have dinner on the Colonial Tramcar Restaurant. It runs daily offering lunch and dinner with two sittings for dinner. You eat and drink as the tram glides its way through Melbourne. $$ Tel: 9696 4000.

Porta Via $ 277 Little Collins St; tel: 9654 3100. Italian espresso bar with excellent coffee and focaccia which makes a magnificent meal.

Punch Lane $ 43 Little Bourke St; tel: 9639 4944. Experimental cooking mixing assorted cuisines.

CHINATOWN

Chinese restaurants are to be found all over Melbourne, but some of the best in Australia are around Little Bourke St. It is almost impossible to get a bad Chinese meal in Chinatown.

Banana Palm Curry House $ 195 Little Bourke St; tel: 9639 2680. Malaysian food. Excellent satay.

Camy Shanghai $ 23 Tattersalls Lane; tel: 9663 8555. Not true Shanghai food – more general northern cuisine but fantastic value for money.

Shanghai Provincial Kitchen $$ 113 Little Bourke St; tel: 9663 1811. Open daily for lunch and dinner. Licensed. Northern Chinese if not true Shanghainese cooking.

Shark Fin House $$ 131–5 Little Bourke St; tel: 9663 1555. Great Cantonese seafood plus yum cha service.

FITZROY

There are many ethnic restaurants and coffee shops in Brunswick and Smith Sts, mostly very affordable.

CARLTON

Lygon St is best known for Italian food and there is a raft of restaurants all serving a multitudinous array of pastas.

Ajays $$ 555 Nicholson St, Carlton North; tel: 9380 5555. Open lunch Fri, dinner Tues–Sat. The best of the BYO restaurants.

Casa Malaya $$ 118 Lygon St; tel: 9663 7068. Widely considered to produce the best laksa in Melbourne. BYO. Closed Sun and lunch Sat.

Jamaica House $$ 106 Lygon St; tel: 9663 5715. Almost certainly the only Jamaican restaurant in Australia.

Jimmy's the Original $$ 130 Lygon St; tel: 9663 5138. Seafood/meat on charcoal. BYO. Dinner only; closed Mon.

Lemongrass $$ 189 Lygon St; tel: 9347 5204. Arguably the best Thai restaurant in the city. BYO.

Nyonya $$ 191 Lygon St. Straits Malay cooking normally only available in Singapore, and there with difficulty.

Shakahari $$ 329 Lygon St; tel: 9347 3848. Vegetarian; intelligent and well-assorted menu.

Toto's Peza House $ 101 Lygon St; said to be the first pizzeria in Australia.

RICHMOND

Swan St has mainly Greek food — this is one of the great Greek cities — which is filling and inexpensive. Victoria St is very strong on Vietnamese restaurants, most at budget prices.

SOUTH YARRA

Toorak Rd and Chapel St are fairly upmarket with fine dining and prices to match.

Caffe Grossi $$ 199 Toorak Rd; tel: 9827 6076. Consistently gets rave reviews in a town where good Italian restaurants abound.

Saigon Rose $$ 206 Chapel St, Prahran; tel: 9510 9651. Great Vietnamese food even though the name of the restaurant seems distinctly odd to Vietnam war veterans.

ST KILDA

Fitzroy St has a strong Italian influence, cheap bistros and bars. There are more along the beachfront.

SOUTH MELBOURNE

Blue Train $$ Southgate Shopping Centre; tel: 9696 0111. Wood-fired pizza. Great views. Open for breakfast, lunch and dinner.

OTHERS

Café Segovia $ 33 Block Pl; tel: 9650 2373. Noisy. Mixed ethnic food. Live music on weekend nights. The staff are friendly in the Australian tradition.

Chez Bob $$ 22 Beatty Ave, Armadale; tel: 9824 8022. Open Mon–Sat. French bistro style. Licensed.

Kao Thip $$ 36 Jackson Crt, Doncaster East; tel: 9848 1181. Open daily for dinner. Licensed. Consistent high quality Thai.

Langton's Restaurant and Wine Bar $$ Sargood House, 61 Flinders Lane; tel: 9663 0222. Simple French bistro food. Dining room and wine bar with counter food service.

Syracuse Wine Bar & Restaurant $$ 23 Bank Pl; tel: 9670 1777. This is the sort of restaurant that Melbourne does superbly. There is a sort of opulent decadence about the place. The food is Pacific Rim with Asian influences plus some Middle Eastern dishes. Very Melbourne.

GETTING AROUND

Walking is the best way to see this city. It is laid out on a logical grid of broad boulevards, which makes it difficult to get lost, but lest this gets boring these are interspersed with narrow streets, alleys and lanes which create an interesting maze of thoroughfares, adding humanity to town planning.

Public transport is an integrated system, bringing together bus, suburban railway and the trams. Horse trams started in 1873 and the current trams, such a feature of the Melbourne scene, are their lineal descendants. The trams are the basis on which the public transport system works. They are easy to use and the routes are clearly

TOP TOQUES

The very upmarket restaurants are seriously expensive, but they are the best in Australia.

Jacques Reymond Restaurant $$$ 78 Williams Rd, Windsor; tel: 9525 2178. Open lunch Tues–Fri, dinner Tues–Sat. Widely considered the best restaurant in Australia. The only restaurant given five chef's hats in *The Age* Guide.

Flower Drum $$$ 17 Market Lane; tel: 9662 3655. Open lunch Mon–Sat, dinner seven days. Four chef's hats and widely accepted as Australia's finest Asian restaurant. Better Peking duck than you will ever get in Beijing.

Mask of China $$ 115 Little Bourke St; tel: 9662 2116. Open daily. Four chef's hats and seen as the contender for the same title.

Paul Bocuse Restaurant $$$ Daimaru Level 4, Melbourne Central, La Trobe St; tel: 9660 6600. Four stars. Better than his original establishment near Lyon.

Stephanie's $$$ 405 Tooronga Rd, Hawthorn East; tel: 9822 8944. Open Tues–Fri and Sun for lunch, Tues–Sat dinner. Four chef's hats. Run by the great chef Stephanie Alexander. $130 for two plus drinks. Formal elegant dining at its very best.

marked. There is also a City Circle Tram that runs around the central business district every 10 mins. It is free and you can easily recognise it because it is painted cream and burgundy. The service runs 1000–1800 seven days a week.

The trams add to the Melbourne style but they also give visiting car drivers some surprises. At certain intersections in the city where trams take up the centre of the road, you have to get in the left-hand lane in order to turn right. This is called a hook turn. It may seem mad, illogical and dangerous but Melburnians will explain its virtues to you at great length. No one from anywhere else in Australia has ever understood it.

Taxis are ubiquitous and can either be phoned for or picked up at one of the many ranks. They are not easily hailed in the streets.

HIGHLIGHTS

The main streets within the central 'golden mile' are Collins and Bourke which run south-west—north-east and are crossed by Swanston and Elizabeth Sts. This is where Melbourne goes to shop. **Collins St** has solid Victorian business architecture

— we've made a fortune and we will show it — and modern skyscrapers which manage not to be obstructive. The eastern end is called the Parisian end and the trees make it possible, if only just, to see the resemblance. It is stylish without being snobbish. At the other end of the street lies the business centre of the city. North, the centre drifts via Flagstaff Gardens and the Queen Victoria Market to Carlton and North Melbourne. The southern border is the Yarra River.

Beside the river is the ornate **Flinders St Station**, a railway station in the grand tradition. It is the only railway station left in Australia that engenders the sense of excitement, a feeling of departing on great missions, that once all railway stations had.

A well-known attraction of Melbourne — **Young and Jackson's** — is one of the world's great pubs and a place of pilgrimage. It is famed mainly for the painting of a young nude, *Chloe,* hanging in the upstairs bar. The painting, by Chevalier Jules Lefebvre in 1875, was brought to Melbourne for the Great Exhibition of 1880 where it was judged to be indecent, and its fame was established. Morton O'Keefe in the *Australasian Post* in March 1950 wrote what might be thought of as a love letter to this painting: 'Sydney, for a brief time, used to boast proudly of "our Bridge, our Harbour, and our Bradman". The triumvirate broke up somewhat when the only mobile member of it moved to South Australia. Now it's just "our Bridge and our Harbour". But here in Melbourne it's definitely "our Chloe". We may not rhapsodise about our Yarra (and there's one very good reason — the Yarra — why we shouldn't). But over Chloe we do go into raptures. Most of us, anyway.'

Melbourne: a city of discreet raptures and quiet passions.

THE TRAGEDY OF CHLOE

Legend has it that Lefebvre used as his model a beautiful Parisienne named Marie. One evening she gathered her friends about her, and gave them a dinner of startling magnificence. When the last of her guests had gone, she spent her remaining sou on a box of matches, boiled the heads, and drank the poisonous water.

The building of **St Paul's Cathedral**, across Swanston St from Young and Jackson's, started in 1880 and continued until 1933. It is rigidly Anglican and Gothic. Representing, as it were, the opposition, **St Patrick's Cathedral** on the corner of Cathedral Pl. and Gisborne St is Gothic Revival architecture but, for once, done with restraint. It was designed by William Wilkinson Wardell.

At the other end of Swanston St is the **Victoria Museum and State Library**. The museum has a notable collection of Aboriginal artefacts — probably the finest in Australia. The library, opened in 1856, has an octagonal reading room which is interesting, attractive and unusual. Its dome was added in 1911 and was believed then to be the largest concrete dome in the world. Open Mon 1300–2100, Tues, Thurs, Sun 1000–2100.

Flagstaff Gardens are in the north-west corner of the central business district. This was Melbourne's first cemetery although burials ceased in 1838. Here, on 11 Nov 1850, the news was received that Victoria had been granted its independence from New South Wales. Thirty years later it was decided to turn Flagstaff Hill into gardens, and a lake and children's playground were installed.

The nearby **Queen Victoria Market** dates back to 1857 and many of the buildings in the market complex are now classified by the National Trust. This started off as a fruit and veg market but has now expanded to sell almost anything, including an enormous array of clothing.

To the north of the city are the **Royal Melbourne Zoological Gardens**, which try very hard to house the animals humanely. It is perhaps the only zoo in the world where the public is caged and the lions roam outside. $$$ Open daily 0900–1700.

Melbourne is a city of gardens, and it is possible to wander through large areas of seemingly European gardens laid out in the romantic tradition. This adds much to the charm of the city and accounts, in part, for its unique atmosphere. It is not generally realised how important gardens were to the early settlers. It seems that the first thing that colonists did after settling in was to create botanical gardens and a series of green spaces. Fitzroy and the adjoining Treasury Gardens, for example, were opened in 1857, very early in the history of Australia.

Fitzroy Gardens were the work of a Scottish landscape gardener, James Sinclair. As one of his previous clients was Czar Nicholas of All the Russias, he came well recommended. The magnificent conservatory was added in 1928. In 1934, when Melbourne celebrated its centenary, **Cook's Cottage** was installed in the gardens – it was moved in 253 crates, brick by brick, from Great Ayrton in Yorkshire. To make sure it was completely authentic they even shipped a cutting from the ivy which had grown on the original building. The cutting took root and today the house looks as though it has been there for centuries. Unfortunately, it wasn't the house of Captain Cook; it was the house of his parents. $ Open daily 0900–1700.

Across the Yarra lie Melbourne's most splendid gardens.

SOUTH OF THE YARRA

Elspeth Huxley wrote: 'The Yarra Melburnians will tell you is the only river in the world that runs upside down – it looks so brown and muddy.' Despite this, the **Yarra** is one of the great attractions of Melbourne. The banks of the river have been carefully landscaped for leisure activities, with barbecues and picnic grounds, and bicycles, canoes, kayaks and rowing boats for hire. Or you can take one of the river tour boats from Princes Walk beside Princes Bridge. There are some beautiful old bridges across the Yarra and to look down the river from one of them at night is always a magical delight.

The south bank of the Yarra, not unlike London's South Bank, has been the focus of a political drive to make it work. Along with political intent has gone a large amount of money and, eventually, it has worked. The modern architecture of the **Victorian Arts Centre** theatre complex – what might be called modern Eiffel Tower style – is now well on the way to becoming a major landmark for Melbourne which, in truth, sorely needs one.

To service this the **Southgate complex** contains shops, wine bars, snack stalls and restaurants running along the bank of the Yarra.

Running alongside the Yarra are the **King's Domain Gardens** which are open Mon and Wed 1000–1600 and weekends 1100–1600. Within the gardens is **La Trobe's Cottage**, originally the home of Charles La Trobe, the first Governor of Victoria. This was built in England, dismantled, shipped to Melbourne and assembled on the site in 1839. Open daily except Tues and Thur, 1100–1630.

Adjoining the King's Domain are Melbourne's famed **Botanic Gardens**. These were the brainchild of the government botanist Dr Ferdinand Mueller, who aimed to have a specimen garden so that it could be studied by botany students. This first garden had a sort of Prussian military flavour to it. It was later softened and modified by curator William Guilfoyle who turned the 40 ha into a series of lovely interlinked gardens with lawns, lakes, trees, flowerbeds and a permanent colony of birds. Open daily from sunrise to sunset.

EVENTS

The **Melbourne Cup** is one of the world's great horse races. It is run at the Flemington Racecourse on the first Tues in Nov. The race is over 3.2 km and the horses are handicapped, so this race is more of a gamble than normal; no even remotely scientific approach is possible. This matters not in the least for this is an event, a social occasion, a time when the beautiful people of Australia emerge in all their finery and have a great day out. Everyone in Australia has a bet - frequently through an office sweep – and while it is running the whole country comes to a standstill. About 100,000 spectators attend the race itself and an estimate (improbably high) of 350 million watch the race in some way or another.

All the horses that have won the Melbourne Cup are revered as true heroes. Perhaps the two most famous are Carbine, who won despite a handicap of a staggering 145 lb, and Phar Lap, Australia's greatest racehorse.

The Melbourne Cup is the highlight of a week-long array of entertainment that is Melbourne's **Spring Carnival**.

NIGHTLIFE

Melbourne has traditionally been the financial capital of Australia and the headquarters of giant industrial and mining companies, although that is gradually changing with some of the focus moving to Sydney. But it still has what is called old money and, perhaps because of this, the city seriously patronises fine arts, music and the ballet. A substantial percentage of the internal tourism of Australia is created by Australians from other cities, including Sydney, coming to Melbourne for a particuar show that cannot be held anywhere else.

The **Sidney Myer Music Bowl** in the King's Domain Gardens is Melbourne's main outdoor concert area. The auditorium has seating for 2000 and room for another 20,000 on the sloping lawn; tel: 9281 8000.

The other principal performing arts venues are across St Kilda Rd in the Victoria Arts Centre (tel: 9281 8000). The **State Theatre** holds over 2,000 people on three levels and is decorated with the grand golds and reds of traditional theatre. The smaller **Playhouse** in the centre seats 880 and is used for drama, mainly by the Melbourne Theatre Company. The **Melbourne Concert Hall** is a large circular theatre which also houses the **Performing Arts Museum**.

The unutterable vulgarity of the **Crown Casino**, west along the river bank, proves, once again, that nothing exceeds like excess.

DAY TRIPS

The **Bellarine Peninsula** forms the western side of Port Phillip Bay. The traditional seaside resort of Queenscliff is now being restored to something of its former glory. Fort Queenscliff is a splendid example of military madness, built in the 1880s to protect Melbourne when a Russian invasion was feared.

AUSTRALIAN RULES FOOTBALL

When the first official Australian Rules football match was played in 1858 a new religion was born. It is impossible to visit Melbourne, especially in the winter, without getting involved in the mania for Australian Rules football which grips the city. At the first recorded game, in 1858, Scotch College played Melbourne Grammar School and each side had 40 players. T W Wills, the umpire, made the rules restricting each side to a more manageable 20 players.

To get the full, fine flavour of this frenzy, here is Edward Kinglake writing in 1891: 'The colony of Victoria has a game of its own. It is supposed to be an improvement on all other species in the matter of eradicating brutality. Whether it is so is a very open question. There have been more brutal fights in Melbourne over football matches than in any other colony it is even contended that the fact that it raises such enthusiasm, even to the point of broken heads and bloody noses, is a conclusive argument that it is the best of all games.'

Nothing has changed since he wrote those words.

The **Yarra Valley**, on Melbourne's northeast outskirts, is one of Australia's greatest wine-growing regions. It has more than 30 wineries producing great wines, of which Yarra Yering is undoubtedly the most glorious. Several are open daily, and many others welcome visitors at weekends. (see p. 183)

From Aug to Nov the **Brisbane Ranges National Park**, about 50 km west of Melbourne, is carpeted with wildflowers. There are also 170 bird species inhabiting the park. **Steiglitz**, now a historic park within the ranges, was once a booming gold-mining township: now all that remains are remnants of several mines and buildings and a courthouse built in 1875. Many of the relics of the area have been assembled in the courthouse. There are guided tours of the area as well as fossicking and gold panning, carried out in exactly the same way as it was in the mid-19th century.

Bendigo, 150 km north of Melbourne, had the greatest goldfield in Australia. It extended over 360 square km and had about 35 gold-bearing reefs with a total output of more than 22 million ounces. The gold brought solid wealth to the town, and Bendigo is often regarded as the best-preserved example of Victorian architecture in Victoria, possibly Australia.

Bendigo has several reminders of the large community of Chinese miners who helped make Bendigo – and Melbourne – rich.. The **Golden Dragon Museum** in Bridge St contains Chinese ceremonial regalia and a brilliant red Chinese joss house. It also includes the dragons Loong and Sun Loong, who are carried in the Easter Monday Chinese Procession. Open daily.

YARRA WINERIES

There is a constant argument in Australia as to the quality of wines from the Yarra region. Yarra has many admirers who believe that red wines from the Yarra are superior to those from the Hunter Valley (see p. 203). There is a very distinctive Australian taste and within that range there is a very distinctive Yarra flavour which is powerful and lingers. It is well worth experimenting with in depth.

Amond the many wineries in this area offering cellar door sales are:

Allinda Winery, Dixons Creek, Tel: (03) 5965 2450.

Oakridge Estate, Seville, Tel: (03) 5964 3379.

Yarra Ridge Vineyard, Yarra Glen, Tel: (03) 9730 1022.

Yarra Yering Vineyard, Gruyere, Tel: (03) 5964 9267.

Yarra Burn Winery, Local Cuisine Restaurant Yarra Junction, Tel: (03) 5967 1428.

Right in the heart of Bendigo is the **Central Deborah Mineshaft** which passes through 17 levels to a depth of almost 400 m. This was the last deep-reef mine in the area to close. Now it has been fully restored and is a working exhibit for the public. $$ Violet St; open daiily.

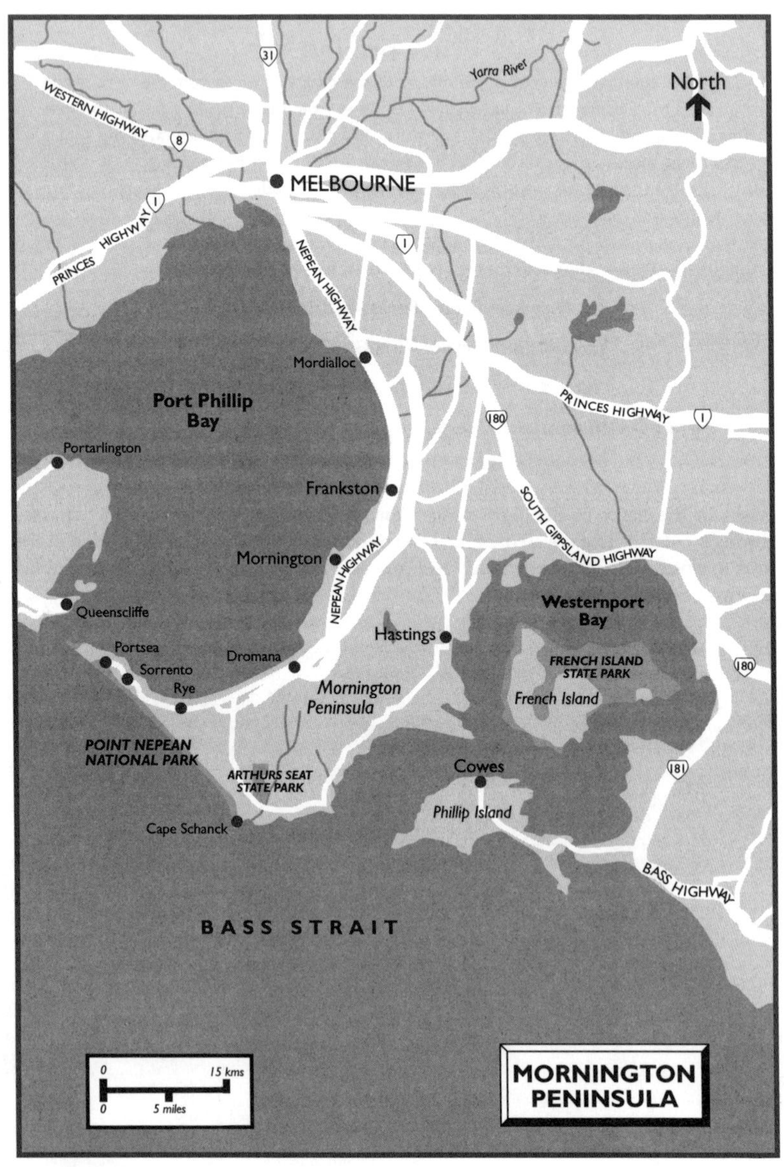

Yarra River
North
31
WESTERN HIGHWAY
8
MELBOURNE
1
PRINCES HIGHWAY
NEPEAN HIGHWAY
1
Mordialloc
Port Phillip Bay
PRINCES HIGHWAY
1
180
Portarlington
Frankston
SOUTH GIPPSLAND HIGHWAY
Mornington
NEPEAN HIGHWAY
Westernport Bay
Queenscliffe
Hastings
Portsea
FRENCH ISLAND STATE PARK
180
Sorrento
Dromana
Rye
Mornington Peninsula
French Island
POINT NEPEAN NATIONAL PARK
Cowes
181
ARTHURS SEAT STATE PARK
Phillip Island
Cape Schanck
BASS HIGHWAY
BASS STRAIT
0
15 kms
0
5 miles
MORNINGTON PENINSULA

The Mornington Peninsula hangs like a hook of Italy to the south of Melbourne and is, for the inhabitants of that city, a favoured weekend retreat. The peninsula has 190 km of coastline. The beaches on Port Phillip Bay are known as front beaches and those facing out to the open sea, with rougher water, are the back beaches. Swimming is excellent (and at Sorrento you can swim with seals and dolphins), but take notice of life-saver instructions: this is where a serving Australian prime minister, Harold Holt, was drowned.

GETTING THERE AND GETTING AROUND

The Nepean Hwy follows the coast of Port Phillip Bay from Mordialloc, in the southern fringes of Melbourne, through a series of almost interlinked small towns – Edithvale, Chelsea, Carrum, Seaford – to Frankston. Technically, you are still in the Melbourne greater metropolitan area but you are also at the start of the Mornington Peninsula. From here a network of roads crosses to Westernport Bay and Phillip Island on the peninsula's eastern side and reaches down to its 'toe' at Portsea.

INTERNET SITES **Mornington Peninsula** http://www.aussie.net.au/pl/atc?273929:32:16514.

Victorian Wineries — Mornington Peninsula
http://www.wineries.tourism.net.au/index1.html

MORNINGTON

Mornington is just off the highway at Snapper Point. Once a remote seaside village, it is now a thriving bayside area that has managed to retain its country atmosphere. Settlement began in 1840 around the harbour, its industries mainly fishing and timber. Later Mornington became a market town with a fine array of colonial buildings along the main street. Many of these now have a new lease of life as restaurants and boutiques. Mornington's **racecourse market** operates on the second Sun of each month throughout the year.

The **Old Post Office**, built in 1863, is in elegant premises near the Esplanade and Main St. It is now a museum run by the local historical society and houses local historic pieces and old telecommunications equipment. The problem is its restricted hours – a practice that seems to have infected many local museums on the peninsula and beyond. This one is only open Sun 1400–1700 and is closed mid-June–early Sept, which makes it very difficult to visit unless you are a local.

Studio City, on the other hand, is open daily 1000–1700. It contains a large amount of television memorabilia and a fully equipped studio and control room which are available to visitors. You can check what you would have looked like on Blind Date. It is at 1140 Nepean Hwy on the road to Mt Eliza.

The **Mornington Peninsula Gallery** on the corner of Dunns and Tyabb Rds has an extensive collection of drawings, lithographs and posters as well as housing travelling exhibitions. Open Tues–Fri 1000–1630.

i **Mornington Information Centre,** corner of Main and Elizabeth Sts; tel: 5975 1644. The area code is 03 for the whole peninsula.

Brooklands Motor Inn $ 101 Tanti Ave; tel: 5975 1166.
Mornington Caravan Park $ 98 Bungower Rd; tel: 5975 7373.
Mornington Motel $$ 334 Main St; tel: 5975 3711.
Ranch Motel $$ cnr Nepean Hwy and Bentons Rd; tel: 5975 4022.
Royal Hotel $$ 770 Esplanade; tel: 5975 5466.

Backyard Seafood Restaurant $$ 37 Main St; tel: 5975 7500. Licensed and BYO.
Chopsticks Inn $ 95 Beleura Hill Rd; tel: 5975 4400.
Costaverde Restaurant $$ 39 Main St; tel: 5975 8900.
Dragon Town Chinese Restaurant $ 7 Main St; tel: 5975 2926. Cantonese, licensed.
Julius Caesar Restaurant $$ 1002 Nepean Hwy; tel: 5975 3987. Italian. Licensed and BYO.
La Colombe $$ Vale St; tel: 5975 5155.
Polly Flinders Cottage $$ 84 Main St; tel: 5975 2966.
Satay 'n Spice $ Main St; tel: 5975 5154. Open for dinner Wed–Sun. BYO. Malaysian Indian food of a high quality.
Silver Palace $$ 205 Main St; tel: 5975 2488.
Tai Pak Chinese Restaurant $ 177 Main St; tel: 5975 6600.
Tarts Restaurant $$ 176 Main St; tel: 5975 7559. BYO.

DROMANA

One of the great experiences on the peninsula is to ride the chairlift from Dromana up to the summit of **Arthur's Seat** (305 m) for its panoramic views over the peninsula. There is a scenic road you can drive up, but gliding at treetop level is much more fun. This is the largest chairlift in Victoria and it is a 20-min ride. It runs daily 1000–1700 Sept–May, weekends and public holidays the rest of the year.

Once you reach the top you will find lots of wildlife, including koalas and echidnas. The Old Viewing Tower has been renovated and is open dawn to dusk.

Dromana itself is a popular bayside beach resort. The **Dromana and District Historical Society** has its museum at the Old Shire Offices, 359a Point Nepean Rd. Some excellent model ships are on display, but it is only open 1400–1600 Sun and 1000–1600 first and third Tues each month. In the peak holiday period of Jan, when you do not want to visit, it is open every day.

On the slopes of Arthur's Seat is one of the oldest houses on the peninsula, the McCrae Homestead (11 Beverley Rd, McCrae). It was built in 1844 and is one of the few remaining examples of drop-slab construction; it is now a National Trust property.

Dromana Tourist Information Centre, Point Nepean Rd; tel: 5987 3078.

Acacia Park $$ Tonkin St; tel: 5987 2007.
Bayview House $$ 215 Palmerston Ave; tel: 5987 1444.
Blue Dolphin Motor Lodge $$ 86 Nepean Hwy; tel: 5987 2311.
Dromana Beach Motel $$ 91 Nepean Hwy; tel: 5987 1837.
Dromana Caravan Park $ Nepean Hwy; tel: 5981 0333.
Kangerong Caravan Park $ 105 Nepean Hwy; tel: 5987 2080.
Ponderosa Caravan Park $ 10 Ponderosa Pl; tel: 5987 2095.

Arthurs $$$ Arthurs Scenic Rd; tel: 5981 4444. Open Easter–Christmas, lunch Fri–Sun, dinner Thur–Sat. Licensed. Very superior French cooking by Hermann Schneider who is accepted as one of the great chefs of Australia. Wine bar.

SORRENTO

It is not often that you come across a seaside resort which has been designed as one from the start. In the 1870s, entrepreneur George Coppin realised the holiday potential of the site and envisaged it as an ideal resort for Melburnians to escape the heat of summer in an idyllic seaside setting. He started a paddle steamer company to bring holidaymakers from Melbourne to Sorrento pier and a steam train company to take them over to the rugged back beach. He also built rotundas, walkways and lookouts. And he did it without stinting, so that it was a success almost from the beginning.

HORSE POWER

Sorrento is small enough that everywhere is within walking distance, but a delightful old form of travel has been resurrected. The original Sorrento Tramway was designed in 1889 and originally consisted of a light carriage drawn by two horses. This has been recreated as the Sorrento Portsea Horse-Drawn Tram Company, which has excursions every Sun and during the school holidays.

Some of the original structures he created remain among the attractions of Sorrento. Fine Victorian buildings built from the local limestone give it considerable style, and the impressive hotels, excellent restaurants, open-air cafes, boutiques, galleries and other delights keep the people of Melbourne returning to the town. Sorrento has some of the most expensive real estate in Victoria outside the Melbourne central business district. This is where the rich come for the holiday season, and from Christmas through until Easter it is both crowded and expensive.

One of the big attractions of the area is **swimming with dolphins and seals**. This has become so popular that a code of practice has been put in place to make sure the animals are not frightened off. Two operators are Polperro Dolphin Swims (tel: 5988 8437) and Moonraker (tel: 5984 4211). There are two trips a day during the season which runs, roughly, Oct–May.

Bell's Sorrento Backpacker Hostel $ 5 Miranda St; tel: 5984 4323.
Carmel Bed & Breakfast $$ 142 Ocean Beach Rd; tel: 5984 3512. Limestone house with period dining room. In main street.
Midway Caravan Park $ 86 St Pauls Rd; tel: 5984 2419.
Motel Saltair $ 780 Melbourne Rd; tel: 5984 1356.
Rose Caravan Park $ 791 Melbourne Rd; tel: 5984 2745.
Sorrento on the Park $$ 7 Hotham Rd; tel: 5984 4777.
Tamasha House $$ 699 Melbourne Rd; tel: 5984 2413. En suite. Home-made food.
Whitehall $$ 231 Ocean Beach Rd; tel: 5984 4166.

Big Joe's No 1 Pizza & Bistro $ 77 Ocean Beach Rd; tel: 5984 3633.
Fresco's $ 3293 Nepean Hwy; tel: 5984 4255.

Palms Tea Rooms & Brasserie $$ 154 Ocean Beach Rd; tel: 5984 1057. Inventive modern cuisine. Open daily lunch and dinner. BYO.
Sarchi's Restaurant $$ 145 Hotham Rd; tel: 5984 1472. BYO.
Smokehouse 182 Ocean Beach Rd; tel: 5984 1246. Gourmet pizzas.
Tham Dynasty Chinese Restaurant $ 113 Ocean Beach Rd; tel: 5984 3177.

SULLIVAN BAY

Sullivan Bay, 3 km south-east of Sorrento, was the site of the first white attempt to settle what was to become Victoria. Lt Governor David Collins established a camp here in 1803, consisting of 299 convicts, some free settlers, 50 royal marines, a chaplain and civil officers – in all 460 men, women and children. They tried for seven months before giving up and moving to Van Diemen's Land (now Tasmania). A stone memorial marks the site of this short-lived settlement, and a display centre (open Sun 1300–1600) tells more of its story.

With this abortive expedition was the infamous convict William Buckley, who did a runner. He was adopted by the local Aborigines and lived with them for 32 years. When the 'wild white man' was seen again by settlers he could scarcely remember how to speak English.

PORTSEA

Sorrento is for the rich, but Portsea is for the very rich of Melbourne. Their playgrounds are **Portsea Front Beach**, on the bay by the pier, and **Shelley Beach**, which has dolphins. Portsea is more a place where you own a weekend home rather than somewhere to come and stay. Despite this, it is also one of the best skin-diving spots in the area, with excellent dives of up to 40 m off Port Phillip Heads. It is essentially a quiet seaside resort with mainly private houses and just one important hotel. The Portsea Hotel has extensive lawns which overlook the beach and are packed on summer weekends.

Although it has some impressive back beaches, your best bet is to stay with the front beach. The ocean beach can be dangerous and you should only swim where indicated by the life-savers.

Delgany Country House Hotel $$$ tel: 5984 4000.
Portsea Caravan Park $ Back Beach Rd; tel: 5984 2725.

Two Faces $$$ Delgany Country House Hotel; tel: 5984 4166. One of the major restaurants of Australia. Extensive wine list.
Manuka's Café 3756 Nepean Hwy; tel: 5984 1811.

MORNINGTON PENINSULA NATIONAL PARK

When this park was created in 1988 it opened up the tip of the peninsula, with its fortifications, quarantine station and army base which had been banned to the public for a century. The park is open daily 0900–1700, but visitor numbers are limited so that you need to book ahead (tel: 5984 4276). An open-topped transporter runs hourly the 7 km to the fortifications at the point, as cars are not allowed into this part of the park.

THE OCEAN SHORE

Back-tracking from Portsea, the road passes through Rye, with a side road down to Rye Ocean Beach in the Port Nepean National Park. A road looping round from Rosebud on Port Phillip Bay gives access to Cape Schanck with its lighthouse, Angel Cave, neighbouring Bushranger Bay and Flinders on West Head. From here the road goes up the Westernport Bay side of the peninsula to Hastings.

PHILLIP ISLAND

At the mouth of Westernport Bay is the small, fish-shaped Phillip Island. The only land access is from the far side of Westernport Bay, across a bridge from San Remo, but from the Mornington Peninsula you can take a boat from Stony Pt, just south-east of Hastings.

The island is rugged and windswept, with several small resorts, plenty of beaches and a fascinating collection of wildlife. One of the major attractions is at **Summerland Beach**, where every evening little penguins emerge from the sea and waddle up the beach to their nests. In the southwest of the island are **Seal Rocks**, which are inhabited by Australia's largest colony of fur seals.

There is an information centre in Newhaven (near the San Remo crossing), tel: 5956 7447.

The Victorian Alps are to the east and northeast of Melbourne. They are much lower than alpine ranges in other parts of the world and do not have sheer escarpments and jagged peaks. They are not high enough to have a permanent cover of snow but during the winter months they can provide excellent skiing.

The snowfields of Australia may lack the regular and inevitable snow of the best European resorts. But Victoria's snow resorts are equipped with the latest lifting and snow-making equipment, they have luxurious and affordable accommodation, and they are all within relatively easy reach of Melbourne. Finally, unlike their great rivals in New Zealand, all of these snowfields have ski-in ski-out access so that there is no long drive to and from the snow each day. The skiing season officially opens on the Queen's Birthday long weekend each June and closes in Oct but the weather and location controls exactly how long the season lasts.

Arrival and Departure

Victoria has nine ski resorts, all within easy reach of Melbourne (Falls Creek, the furthest, is about a 5-hr drive). The three big ones are Mount Buller, Mount Hotham and Falls Creek, all reached via the Hume Hwy (Rte 31). Come prepared with snow chains. In the ski season buses from Melbourne run to the main resorts, some with a very early start to enable you to ski and return the same day.

Costs

There is a range of accommodation in each of the large resorts, but booking, naturally, is necessary in the high season. In every case a package tour of the snowfields will be less expensive than buying the components separately. Check on what prices include, because they can be better value than they at first appear. Breakfast, dinner and use of such facilities as spa and sauna for just over $100 a night

Snow-making

All resorts make extensive use of snow-making machines. Falls Creek, for example, has 100 ha covered by snow-making machines, giving the certainty of snow within a defined area. The snow makers begin their task of making a good snow cover using high-tech snow guns in late May. This freezes into an excellent base which means subsequent snowfalls remain intact, creating a good early snow base which gets deeper as the season progresses.

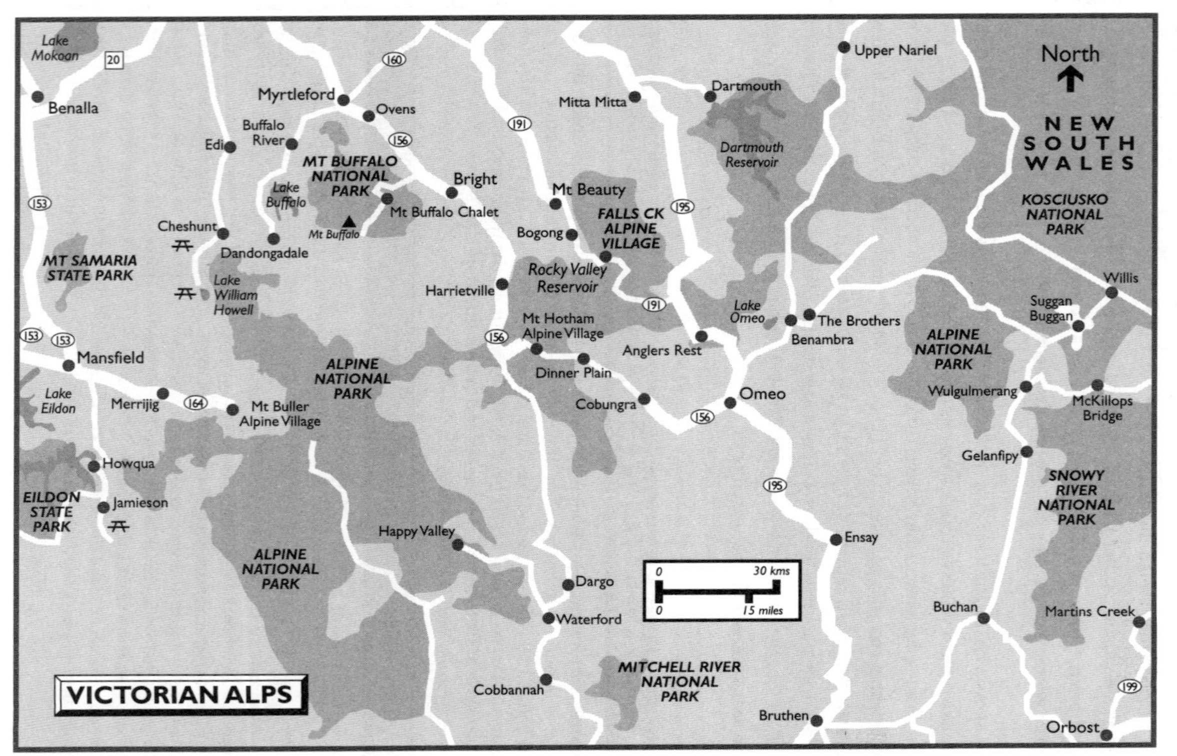
North
NEW SOUTH WALES
KOSCIUSKO NATIONAL PARK
Upper Nariel
Dartmouth
Dartmouth Reservoir
Mitta Mitta
Lake Mokoan
Benalla
Myrtleford
Ovens
Buffalo River
Edi
MT BUFFALO NATIONAL PARK
Lake Buffalo
Mt Buffalo
Mt Buffalo Chalet
Bright
Mt Beauty
FALLS CK ALPINE VILLAGE
Bogong
Cheshunt
Dandongadale
MT SAMARIA STATE PARK
Lake William Howell
Harrietville
Rocky Valley Reservoir
Lake Omeo
The Brothers
Benambra
Willis
Suggan Buggan
Mt Hotham Alpine Village
Anglers Rest
Dinner Plain
Cobungra
Omeo
Mansfield
Lake Eildon
Merrijig
Mt Buller Alpine Village
ALPINE NATIONAL PARK
Wulgulmerang
McKillops Bridge
Gelanfipy
SNOWY RIVER NATIONAL PARK
Howqua
Jamieson
EILDON STATE PARK
Happy Valley
Ensay
Dargo
Waterford
0
30 kms
0
15 miles
Buchan
Martins Creek
Cobbannah
MITCHELL RIVER NATIONAL PARK
Bruthen
Orbost
VICTORIAN ALPS
20
160
191
156
195
153
164
199

appears to be very reasonable. A few examples are given here, but the ARC can give you details of many more.

Information

Alpine Resorts Commission (ARC); tel: (03) 9895 6900.

Mount Buller

Mount Buller, 241 km from Melbourne via Mansfield, caters for all levels, from beginners to advanced skiers; ski hire and instruction are available. At nearby **Mount Stirling** there is cross-country skiing. Most trails start at Telephone Box Junction, which has a visitor centre with public shelter, ski hire and trail maps.

Accommodation

YHA Youth Hostel $ tel: 5777 6181. Very inexpensive, but gets booked up quickly. The best budget snowfield accommodation.

Arlberg Hotel $ Tel: (03) 5777 6260.

Mt Buller Chalet. **$$** Widely accepted as one of the finest alpine lodgings in Australia — advance bookings essential, tel: (1800) 810 200. The chalet has massage, a beauty therapist, indoor swimming pool, spa, sauna, steam rooms and a first-class restaurant, the Cockatoo. And it is still affordable.

Mount Hotham

The 'powder snow capital' of Australia is 367 km from Melbourne via Wangaratta. Ski hire and instruction are available, but the resort attracts experienced downhill skiers; there is also unlimited cross-country skiing. **Mt Buffalo**, on the way to Mt Hotham, is geared to beginners, families and cross-country skiers; features include Dingo Dell and Cresta. Dinner Plain, a new resort, is a 10-min ski-shuttle ride away from Mt Hotham.

Falls Creek

Falls Creek, 379 km from Melbourne via Wangaratta and Wodonga, has protected ski-runs for novices, intermediate and advanced skiers; good cross-country skiing. There is ski hire and instruction, and a wide range of resort facilities.

ACCOMMODATION

Nelse Lodge $$$ is operated by the Ski Club of Victoria but membership is not required. Prices include breakfast and a three course dinner. Book well ahead; tel: 9826 0428.

Woodsmoke Apartments $$$ sheer luxury but book early; tel: (1800) 062 822.

If you are willing to stay off the mountain and forego the delights of ski-in ski-out there are several places where the price drops to around half. **Mount Beauty**, 32 km from Falls Creek, has several lodges and bed-and-breakfast establishments offering budget accommodation.

Alpha Ski Lodge $ 5 Parallel St, Falls Creek. Tel: (03) 5758 488. Self catering.

OTHER RESORTS

Mount Donna Buang, just 95 km from Melbourne via Warburton, and **Lake Mountain**, 109 km via Healesville, both have novice skiing and wonderful sight-seeing. **Mount Baw Baw**, 177 km due east of Melbourne via Drouin, caters for beginners and has good cross-country skiing.

LONG-DISTANCE ROUTE

This is one of the most common travel routes used by Sydneysiders going on holiday. To put it in its simplest form, you head north out of Sydney. This is Hwy 1 (see p. 197), but it goes under a number of different names: Route National 1, Route 85, Pacific Hwy .... There is an abundance of petrol stations along the way – never more than 50 km apart. All have small shops, most sell snack food, some sell full meals. Part of Hwy 1 is multi-lane freeway, but in other places it is an ordinary two-lane highway. Even on the fast stretches, however, speed limits are rigorously enforced. Once you get free of Sydney, for instance, the speed limit increases for a while to 110 kph (although there is a strong movement to bring it down to 100 kph). Unlike other countries, no leeway is given and if you exceed that speed limit by any margin eventually you will be stopped and fined by the police. Many, perhaps most, Australian drivers who cover long distances have cruise controls fitted to their cars which they set at 3 kph above the speed limit to make sure that they are not stopped and seriously fined.

Bus companies have several buses a day doing the Sydney–Brisbane run in either direction; the journey takes about 16 hours, although Greyhound Pioneer have a super express which runs through the night in just over 12 hours. Usually, the buses make many stops and it makes sense to break the journey or just use the bus for one leg. Sydney to Newcastle, for example, takes around 3 hours.

In the pages that follow, three routes combine to cover the 1,000 km: Sydney to Newcastle, Newcastle to Coff's Harbour and Coff's Harbour to the Gold Coast.

RAIL **SYDNEY – BRISBANE**
OTT TABLES 9017/9090

TRANSPORT	FREQUENCY	JOURNEY TIME
Train	Daily	13hrs 36mins
Bus	10 Daily	12hrs 16mins

Note: Regular buses operate from Sydney to Brisbane via Tamworth see OTT table 9074.

There is a daily train from Sydney to Murwillumbah with a bus connection to Brisbane.

Sydney – Newcastle

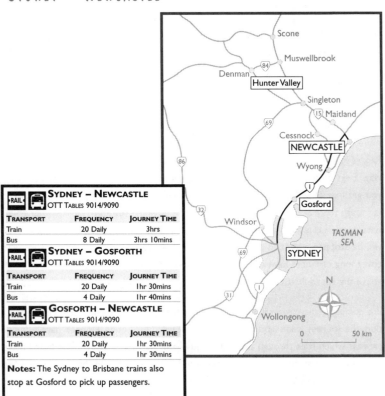

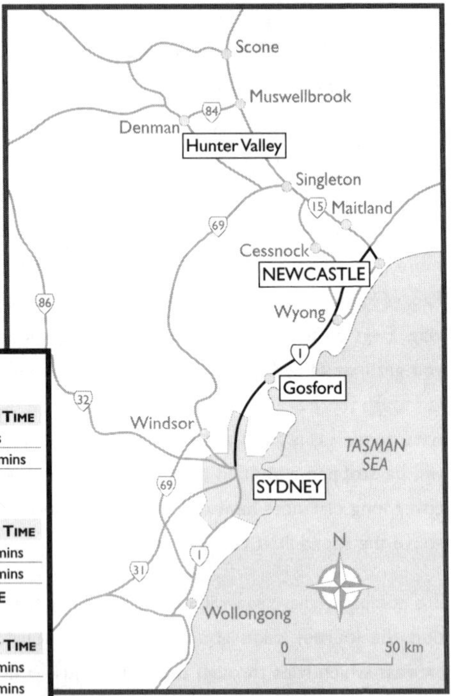

Sydney – Newcastle
OTT Tables 9014/9090

Transport	Frequency	Journey Time
Train	20 Daily	3hrs
Bus	8 Daily	3hrs 10mins

Sydney – Gosforth
OTT Tables 9014/9090

Transport	Frequency	Journey Time
Train	20 Daily	1hr 30mins
Bus	4 Daily	1hr 40mins

Gosforth – Newcastle
OTT Tables 9014/9090

Transport	Frequency	Journey Time
Train	20 Daily	1hr 30mins
Bus	4 Daily	1hr 30mins

Notes: The Sydney to Brisbane trains also stop at Gosford to pick up passengers.

Route Detail

Once out of Sydney the freeway climbs Mt Colah and Mt Ku-Ring-Gai, past Bobbin Head and Berowra and through Cowan, then drops down to cross the Hawkesbury River at Mooney Mooney. The road then climbs out of the valley with Brisbane Water on the right and continues to the turn-off for Gosford (85 km). Beyond Gosford; Hwy 1 takes the inland route to Newcastle (156 km from Sydney).

The Central Coast

Newcastle is an industrial city, but it also has more than its fair share of magnificent beaches with superb surfing. It is the entrance to the Hunter Valley, Australia's premier wine-growing area, where the vineyards are interspersed with coal mines which, luckily, are not overly obtrusive. The direct drive to Newcastle takes about 1½ hours and on the way there are national parks, waterways and seaside attractions worth a detour.

Getting out of Sydney

Cross the Harbour Bridge or drive through the harbour tunnel and follow the signs to Chatswood. This is a motorway with an 80-kph limit and you need to keep in one of the right three lanes. The motorway will eventually narrow down to two lanes each way; keep in the left lane for the turning to Chatswood. This brings you out onto the Pacific Hwy. This is Hwy 1 (or Route National 1 or Route 85). Drive for 13 km through suburb after suburb – Chatswood, Roseville, Gordon, Turramurra – until, at the beginning of Hornsby, you come to the Sydney–Newcastle Freeway, a turning on the right clearly marked to Newcastle.

GOSFORD

Gosford is worth a small diversion. It is a dormitory town for Sydney, set at the head of Brisbane Water and with a range of resorts running along the coast on both sides. Sydneysiders nearly all have an ambition to own a small seaside cottage or bungalow in this area – a weekender is the local phrase – and this is very much part of the coast that is focused on family holidays.

The most highly populated areas are Gosford/Narara Valley, Woy Woy Peninsula – comedian Spike Milligan is the most famous export – and the coastal strip along Forresters Beach to MacMasters Beach.

In the pioneering period, the attractions of the Brisbane Water area were its proximity to Sydney and its wealth of timber resources. The shores of the waterways were occupied by settlers – including ex-convicts – while the timbered country on Erina and Narara Creeks was dominated by the gentry. The grave and cottage of Frederick Hely, Superintendent of Convicts in NSW, can still be seen there, beside the Pacific Hwy.

En Route

The freeway swoops through **Ku-ring-gai Chase National Park**. This park provides a real challenge to the bush-walker and yet it is only 22 km from the centre of Sydney, demonstrating how close the real bush is to the heart of the city. As you drive towards Gosford you pass **Old Sydney Town** (open Wed–Sat and all school holidays 1000–1600), a re-creation of Sydney prior to 1810. Serious attempts have been made to keep it.

En route (cont.)
authentic although some of the dramatic re-enactments of life in the convict days – the floggings, the duel, colonial justice – have a large component of ham much appreciated by children. To keep it in perspective you need to realise that Disney in Anaheim or Florida would spend on a single ride more money than can be invested in such an operation in Australia. Within those constraints it works very well. Near to Old Sydney Town is **Somersby Falls**, a pleasant spot for a picnic, and close by is a **Wildflower Farm** which is open to visitors.

Henry Kendall's cottage, 27 Henry Kendall St, is where the Australian poet lived for two years from 1874. It was built as an inn in 1838 and has been restored with elegant grounds where you can picnic. Open Wed, Sat and Sun and all holidays 1000–1600.

Just outside Gosford, 15 minutes by road, are the **Glenworth Valley Stables** (open daily 1000–1700; tel: 4375 1222). They offer free-range or guided rides with 200 horses to choose from and nearly 1,000 ha to ride in.

The **Australian Reptile Park and Wildlife Sanctuary** has one of the world's largest crocodiles in captivity. His name is Eric and he is fed every Sun. There are twice-daily reptile shows and in the park are friendly kangaroos, emus, koalas, wombats and dingoes. Open daily 0900–1700. From the F3 take the Gosford Exit to the Pacific Hwy at Somerby.

Brisbane Waters National Park, off the Pacific Highway just south of Gosford, covers 11,372 ha and borders the Hawkesbury River. It is especially rich in Aboriginal art. There are several walks laid out through open woodlands with occasional pockets of rainforest. Panoramic views spread from 100-m-high cliffs overlooking the Hawkesbury River at Warrah Trig and Staples Lookouts. Aboriginal art may be seen on the sandstone landscape with engravings at Bulgandry on Woy Woy Road. Displays of Christmas bells and scarlet waratah are stunning during November and December.

Gosford Tourist Information Office, Rotary Park, Terrigal Dr.; tel: 4385 4430.
Gosford City Council www.gosford.nsw.gov.au/

With all motels on the Pacific Highway always check for noise levels before booking in.
Bermuda Motel $ Henry Parry Dr., Cnr Pacific Hwy; tel: 4324 4366.
Elanora Hotel Motel $ 41 Victoria St; tel: 4325 2026.
Galaxy Motel $ 26 Pacific Hwy; tel: 4323 1711.
Gosford Motor Inn $$ 23 Pacific Hwy; tel: 4323 1333.
Metro Inn Gosford $$ 512 Pacific Hwy; tel: 4328 4666.
Villa Sorgenti $$ Kowara Rd; tel: 4340 1205.

EN ROUTE

Instead of heading straight back for the freeway, you can drive to the lovely seaside town of **Terrigal** – a very popular spot with excellent surfing – and then follow the coastline north past **Wyrrabalong National Park** and through seaside resorts to The Entrance, which is one of the pincers that enclose the expanse of Tuggerah Lake. Among the many attractions is the **pelican feeding** that takes place at 1530 every day on the shores of Memorial Park. Take the narrow causeway between Tuggerah Lake and the sea through Norah Head and Budgewoi and then rejoin the freeway.

Andale Mexican Restaurant $$ Pacific Hwy; tel: 4324 2828.

Crowne Plaza $$ Pine Tree Lane in nearby Terrigal; tel: 4384 9111. Has the upmarket La Mer and a more relaxed Norfolk Brasserie.

Enthaising Chatthipha Restaurant $$ 26 Adelaide St; tel: 4324 5959. The practice of making truly awful puns for Thai restaurants has spread right across Australia. BYO.

Gee Kwong Restaurant $$ 197 Mann St; tel: 4325 2489. Cantonese.

Gosford Shoreline Restaurant $$ Masons Pde; tel: 4325 0644.

Joel's Restaurant $$ On Avoca beach; tel: 4382 3666. Has won several awards for its Euro-Australian menu with Asian influences.

Jun Bo Chinese Restaurant $ 78 Mann St; tel: 4325 7488. Cantonese.

Oscar's Cafe & Restaurant $ 105 Marketplace St; tel: 4325 7947.

Peking Garden Chinese Restaurant $$ Dane Dr., tel: 4324 3788.

Willows Restaurant in the Metro Inn $$ 512 Pacific Hwy; tel: 4328 4666. Has a fixed-price menu.

NEWCASTLE

Newcastle has a population of half a million and is the biggest industrial city in Australia, the second largest city in NSW and the sixth largest city in Australia. The site was discovered when Lt Shortland was searching for convict escapees in 1879 and discovered coal. This, together with steel, dominated life in Newcastle until the mid-1960s, and the city previously had the unenviable reputation of being one of the dirtiest, grimiest, most polluted cities in Australia. Dymphna Cusack, in her novel *Southern Steel*, describes the city during and after World War II with its 'innumerable factory chimneys' and 'the smokestacks of Southern Steel and Broken Hill Proprietary under their perpetual silver-black clouds.'

That was then. These days Newcastle is a pleasant city with some fine surfing beaches and extensive inland waterways. If you had to put a date to the time that Newcastle started to get its act together, it was 18 Dec, 1989. On that day it was hit by a major earthquake a great loss of life and many buildings destroyed. Some of the city had to be rebuilt and it was done with some style - Newcastle moved from being a place of dark, satanic mills to being an industrial town, but with a lovely seafront showing some intelligent modernisation, excellent accommodation and restaurants. On top of this it is the entry point to the Hunter Valley, the greatest wine-growing area in Australia. (Please do not say that when you are in the Barossa or at Margaret River or you will find yourself in the centre of a very heated discussion.)

Newcastle Tourism, 92 Scott St; tel: 4929 9299. Open Mon–Fri 0900–1700, weekends 1000–1530.
Newcastle–Hunter Regional Tourism Organisation, 2/11 Watt St; tel: 4927 0755; email: bookings@huntertourismaccom.com.au
Newcastle City Centre – Online www.newcastlecitycentre.com/
Newcastle Coffee Houses cust.idl.com.au/mgw/coffee/index.html
Newcastle Visitor Information newcastle.infohunt.nsw.gov.au/visitor/index.html

Bimet Lodge $$ 121 Union St; tel: 4929 6677.
Esplanade Newcastle Beach $$ Shortland Esplanade; tel: 4929 5576.
Harbourside Motel $ 107 Scott St; tel: 4926 3244.
Jacks on King $ 471 Hunter St; tel: 4929 2274.
Newcastle Star Motel $ 410 King St; tel: 4926 1466.
Noah's on the Beach $$ Zaara St, Cnr Shortland Esp; tel: 4929 5181.
Radisson Hotel Newcastle $$ Steel St, Cnr King St; tel: 4926 3777.

Big Al's Family Restaurant $$ Brown St, Cnr King St; tel: 4929 2717. Part of a chain based on Al Capone. Reliable if predictable food.
Brewery Brasserie $$ 150 Wharf Rd; tel: 4929 5792. On the ground floor of the Queens Wharf Brewery on the harbour front. Always fairly busy which is a good sign. Happy hour daily 1700–1900.
Cafe Plumes $$ Cnr Hunter and Wolfe Sts, Hunter Mall; tel: 4929 7333. Voted best café and restaurant in 1998. Open Mon–Fri 0800–1800, Sat–Sun 0900–1700.
Eliza's Café Brasserie $$ The Esplanade; tel: 4929 5576.

Newcastle has many safe beaches, one of which is in the city. These include Newcastle, Nobbys, Horseshoe, Stockton, Bar, Susan Gilmore, Merewether, Dixon Park Beach, Burwood and Dudley.

Informal venue for light meals. In the Holiday Inn. Daily 0630 till late.

Istana Malaysia $ 31 Marketown Shopping Centre; tel: 4929 3522. Try the laksa and the rendang. Licensed and BYO.

Paymaster's Cafe $$ 18 Bond St, Newcastle; tel: 4925 2600. On what was once the site of the government employees pay office which opened in 1879. Features art works from local artists. Lunch and dinner weekdays. Plus brunch at weekends.

Scott Street Cafe $$ 19 Scott St; tel: 4927 0107. Knock-out vegetarian dishes. BYO. Mon–Sat dinner from 1800. Non-smoking.

Scratchley's $$ Hunter St; tel: 4929 1111. Has won best BYO for several years. Absolute waterfront, open daily.

Squid's Ink $$ 690 Pacific Highway, Belmont; tel: 4947 7223. Has won several awards for its seafood. Open daily from 0700.

Thara Thong Thai Restaurant $ 541 Hunter St; tel: 4929 6722. Authentic Thai food.

Highlights

The easiest way to see the city is on board the **Newcastle Tram** which leaves the railway station on the hour 1000–1500, daily. It is not a true tram, rather a bus decked up to look like a tram, but the seating is comfortable, the view excellent and the driver gives an informative running commentary. A Free Settler Class ticket allows you to break your journey as you go around and effectively hop on and off as the mood takes you.

The city also has many historic 19th-century buildings, some of which have been recently restored to their former glory. The information centre offers an excellent free map of a town walk which takes in most of the sights, including the **Newcastle Police Station Museum** at 90 Hunter St, open Mon–Fri 0900–1300 and Sat, Sun 1100–1600. **Newcastle Regional Museum**, 787 Hunter St, is a leading Australian museum and contains Supernova, Newcastle's Science and Technology Fun Centre. Children are encouraged to touch and use the displays. Open Tues–Sun 1000–1700 (daily in school hols).

The trees planted at the eastern and western edges of the large **Civic Park**, opposite City Hall, were gifts from Newcastle's sister city, Ube in Japan. The Captain Cook Memorial Fountain forms a backdrop and is illuminated at night.

On the waterfront, **Queen's Wharf** has been redeveloped into a modern, even trendy area with shops, restaurants, one of Australia's many mini-breweries and a watchtower. It is a very pleasant place to walk and watch the sunset. *The William the*

Fourth anchored here was the first coastal steamship built in Australia; it offers historical cruises around the harbour.

THE FORT THAT WENT TO WAR

Fort Scratchley on Nobbys Head, about 30 m above the entrance to the port, claims to be Australia's only fort that went to war. It was originally built in the 1880s to repel a possible Russian invasion very near the spot where Lt Shortland first landed on his search for the missing convicts. In June 1942, it was attacked by a Japanese submarine. The guns of the fort returned fire. This is almost certainly the only time in Australian history that the heavy guns of the coastal defences have been fired in deadly earnest. The fort now houses the Newcastle Region Maritime Museum.

Christ Church Cathedral, overlooking the city, was not completed until 1979, although it was dedicated in 1902. It replaced Newcastle's first cathedral, which now serves as the Cathedral Hall opposite. Up the hill to the south is the **Obelisk** which marks the site of Newcastle's first windmill. The mill, which lasted from 1820 to 1874, became a navigation mark for ships approaching the port.

LAKE MACQUARIE

The Pacific Hwy passes through the city and if you follow it south you will come to the great expanse of Lake Macquarie. It is the largest seaboard lake in Australia and contains about four times as much water as Sydney Harbour, with 175 km of eucalyptus-lined foreshore. It opens out into the ocean at Swansea.

Lake Macquarie is a superb sailing area and the MV *Wangi Queen* cruises the lake on Wed and Sun.

On the eastern shore of the lake is **Belmont**. On the high ground in the town is what may have been an Aboriginal mission opened by Rev L E Threlkeld, who also opened the first coal mine. The all-timber parish hall was built at the turn of the 20th century.

In nearby Wangi Wangi is **Dobell House**, a modest place where Sir William Dobell lived and worked; it is open to the public and contains a collection of his work and memorabilia.

WHERE NEXT?

The trail continues north towards Brisbane, but don't leave Newcastle without a taste of the wine-famous Hunter Valley.

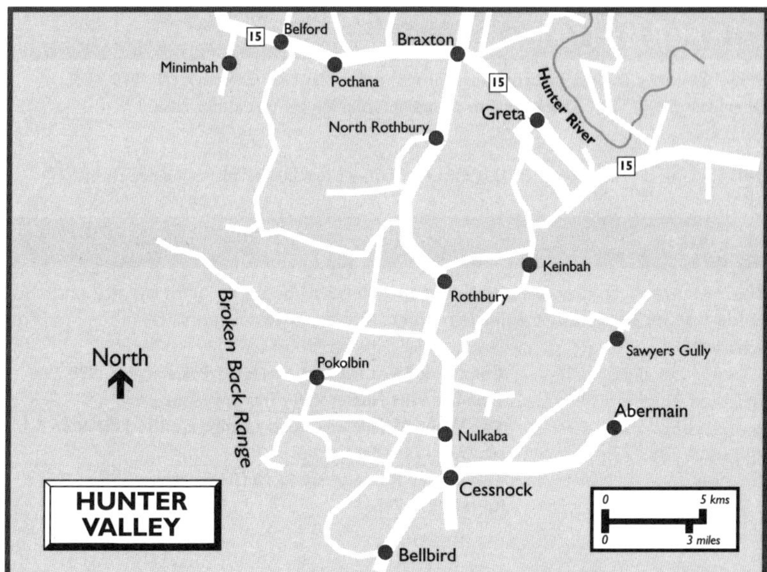

Back in the 1960s, wine from the Hunter came in bottles with hand-typed labels and was thick and strong, full of flavour and unbelievably inexpensive. Gradually the world caught on to the fact that some of the best red wines came from the red earth of the Hunter and thus vineyards and coal mines were developed in curious juxtaposition. Most, but not all, of the mines in the Hunter Valley no longer operate while the vineyards expand and prosper.

The valley lies an hour and a half's drive northwest of Newcastle. The New England Hwy (Rte 15) will take you through Hexham, Maitland, Branxton and Singleton to Muswellbrook. To the left of Branxton, running around Cessnock and down to Wollombi, is the main wine country. To the left of Muswellbrook, down and round to Denham, are the Upper Hunter wineries. Alternatively, the Hunter Vineyard Tour is one of several coach tours that visits some of the vineyards and wineries with cellar door tastings included. Vintage time is normally around February when the vignerons will be at their busiest bringing in the crop.

HUNTER VALLEY WINE TOUR

INFORMATION

Wine Country Tourist Information, Turner Pk, Aberdare Rd, Cessnock; tel: 4990 4477. Open daily 0900–1700. There are also several information centres in the valley.

INTERNET SITES **Welcome to the Hunter Valley** users.hunterlink.net.au/index.html

FOOD

The restaurants in any wine-growing area tend to be superior in quality and this holds true for the Hunter, where several of the better restaurants are, in fact, part of a winery.

Chez Pok $$ At Peppers, Ekerts Rd, Pokolbin; tel: 4998 7596. Won the 1994 Hunter Valley Tourism Award.

The Vines $$ Hunter Country Lodge, Cessnock-Braxton Rd; tel: 4938 1744. BYO.

The Cellar Restaurant $$ McGuigan Hunter Village, Broke Rd; tel: 4998 7466.

This is a suggested drive that will take in most of the major vineyards. On this short-ish trip – an easy half-day's drive which could take you two weeks if you were seriously sampling wines – you come within hailing distance of over 40 vineyards, most of which encourage visits and cellar door sales.

At Cessnock take the Allandale Rd (Rte 82). When you pass the airstrip, on the left is Broke Rd where you will find **Lake's Folly** (tel: 4998 7507), a vineyard started by a Sydney surgeon, Max Lake. Further along and again on the left is Palmers Lane, which has four small vineyards. Left off Palmers Lane is the **Rothbury Estate** (tel: 98 7555), started by a syndicate led by Australia's great wine celebrity, Len Evans.

Allandale Rd now continues north through Rothbury. On the left is the extension of Deasys Rd which leads to three more vineyards. Soon Allandale Rd reaches the

There are 50 wineries that you can visit and all offer cellar-door sales. There is no suggestion of being compelled to buy wine at every vineyard you visit or that a tasting puts any sort of obligation on the taster. On the other hand, look at it from the perspective of the vintner for a moment. A bus pulls up. Fifty people get off and taste a generous sample. One buys a single bottle and the bus moves off. If you intend to visit the vineyards try to work in the purchase of a couple of bottles of wine and/or dine at one of the many vineyard restaurants.

New England Hwy (Rte 15) at Branxton. A quick detour right leads to the **Wyndham Estate** winery (tel: 38 3444), which is open daily. Left is Belford and Hermitage Rd. There is an information tourist centre here, and it is also the start of horseback and horse carriage vineyard tours run by **Somerset Carriages**.

Hermitage Rd passes the **Hunter Estate** winery (tel: 4998 7777), which has visits every day by appointment, and the other end of Deasys Rd. Continue past the **Casuarina Restaurant and Country Inn** (tel: 4998 7888) to Broke Rd, which leads back to Cessnock.

Alternatively, a detour along Broke Rd in the other direction, away from Cessnock, leads to the **Hungerford Hill Wine Village** (tel: 4998 7666), which has gone flat out to cater for the tourist with wine tastings, wine sales, an excellent restaurant and a motel. Further on is the **Tyrrell Winery** (tel: 4998 7509), which is run by the Tyrrell family and is a splendid example of a mid-sized winery.

The return journey along Broke Rd passes a dozen vineyards and restaurants, all well signposted. One – McGuigan's (tel: 98 7402) – has become a resort and leisure centre.

Broke Rd ends at a crossroads where there are three information centres. Turn right and you will find yourself driving towards the Pokolbin Mountain Range. In this area there are another dozen of some of the greatest vineyards in Australia. Turn back onto Broke Rd and you swing back past Lake's Folly to Cessnock.

WHERE NEXT?

To complete the circuit, continue on Rte 15 through Singleton and up to Muswellbrook and the seven vineyards of the **Upper Hunter Valley**. A short drive from there you are right on the edge of the 488,060-ha **Wollemi National Park**. This is the largest wilderness area in New South Wales, extending from the Hunter River to the Blue Mountains National Park.

NEWCASTLE – COFFS HARBOUR
OTT TABLES 9017/9090

TRANSPORT	FREQUENCY	JOURNEY TIME
Bus	7 Daily	6hrs 45mins

NEWCASTLE – TAREE
OTT TABLE 9090

TRANSPORT	FREQUENCY	JOURNEY TIME
Bus	6 Daily	2hrs 55mins

TAREE – PORT MACQUARIE
OTT TABLE 9090

TRANSPORT	FREQUENCY	JOURNEY TIME
Bus	6 Daily	1hr 10mins

PORT MACQUARIE – KEMPSEY
OTT TABLE 9090

TRANSPORT	FREQUENCY	JOURNEY TIME
Bus	7	40mins

TAREE – KEMPSEY
OTT TABLES 9017/909

TRANSPORT	FREQUENCY	JOURNEY TIME
Train	3 Daily	1hr 41mins
Bus	10 Daily	1hr 25mins

KEMPSEY – COFFS HARBOUR
OTT TABLES 9017/909

TRANSPORT	FREQUENCY	JOURNEY TIME
Train	3 Daily	1hr 32mins
Bus	11 Daily	2hrs

Notes: The Sydney to Brisbane train does not go through Newcastle, connections are available from Taree.

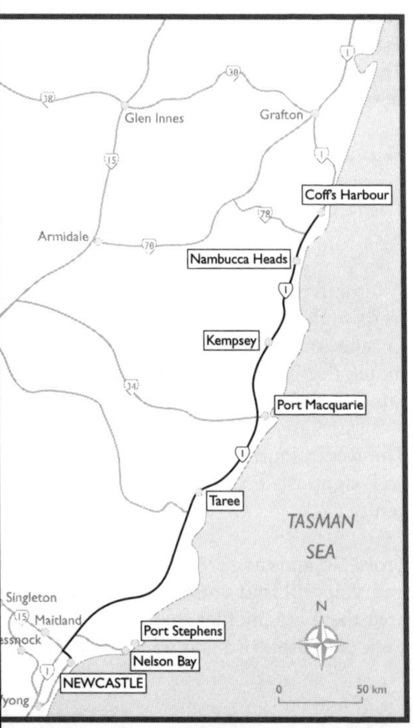

ROUTE DETAIL

Beyond Newcastle, the Pacific Hwy hardly lives up to the promise of its name, as it becomes a three-lane, sometimes a two-lane road, with overtaking impossible except at designated places spaced perhaps 3–5 km apart and normally on hills.

Turn off at Raymond Terrace for Nelson Bay and the Tomaree National Park (you will have to backtrack to rejoin the highway).

From Newcastle to Taree is 150 km, and the turn-off for Port Macquarie a further 73 km. After Macksville the highway moves very close to the sea until it comes to the outskirts of Coffs Harbour, about 370 km from Newcastle without detours.

All along this stretch of coastline are tourist resorts, peaceful national parks and diverting attractions, from 'the pub with no beer' to Australia's first koala hospital.

Inland, north of Port Macquarie, on the lower slopes of the Great Dividing Range are the Werrikimbe and the Oxley Wild Rivers National Parks which lead up to the heights of Armidale, where every winter it snows. In Australia, that seems an unnatural act. Around here begins what is called the Holiday Coast. This is one of the many efforts of tourist boards around Australia to try and identify their area with a name such as Sunshine Coast, Holiday Coast, Paradise Coast and so on. By and large the locals totally ignore these appellations.

NELSON BAY AND PORT STEPHENS

Despite the closeness to Newcastle, and indeed to Sydney, Port Stephens has a totally different look and feel. The white beaches of volcanic sand contrasting with dazzling blue waters make this look like tropical Australia. The area is almost totally a holiday destination and has relatively little industry – the beaches lead back to bush with fine displays of wildflowers in the spring. The waters of the bay are home all year to bottlenose dolphins.

On the south side of the Port Stephens inlet are dozens of marinas, all offering boats for hire ranging from powerboats to houseboats. At the d'Albora Marina – one of the best known – **Pro Dive** offers scuba and snorkelling lessons in the clear waters of Port Stephens (tel: 81 4331). **Big-game fishing** takes place beyond the heads, where the waters – as in Sydney Harbour outside the heads – can be dangerous for an inexperienced sailor. The area is excellent for surfing and there are ocean beaches on each side which, when the wind and tides are right, produce surfing conditions the equal of anywhere in the world.

Oakvale Farm and Fauna World, on Nelson Bay Rd at Salt Ash, has animal feeding at 1100 and 1400 each day, and tame kangaroos wandering around the grounds. Open daily 1000–1700.

Sorting out the names

Port Stephens is the deepwater inlet – two and a half times the size of Sydney harbour – that comes in-between Yacaaba and Tomaree Heads. The main anchorage is Nelson Bay and it is here that the fishing fleet ties up in the late afternoon. Thus Port Stephens is the area, Nelson Bay the principal port.

Tomaree National Park stretches along the coast from Shoal Bay to Anna Bay. There is only one sign-

NEWCASTLE – COFFS HARBOUR

EN ROUTE

Just outside Bulahdelah you can divert right on Lakes Way to **Myall Lakes.** Myall Lakes is an immensely popular holiday spot with the people of Sydney, so is a good place to avoid late Dec–Jan and most weekends in the holiday season. But for the rest of the time this immense park, which runs from Hawks Nest north to the favoured holiday spot of Seal Rocks, is peace and solitude.

Most of the activities centre on the water with sailing, windsurfing and water-skiing. Houseboats for getting around and for sleeping are popular: contact Myall Lakes Houseboats (tel: 97 4221) or Luxury Houseboats (tel: 94 4495), both in Bulahdelah.

Inland, a series of walking tracks include the Mungo Brush Rainforest Walk and, for the healthy, a 21-km walk which links Hawks Nest to Mungo Brush.

Continue the detour through **Booti Booti National Park**, between Wallis Lake and the sea, then on to **Forster**, which has golden beaches extending on each side. You then rejoin the Pacific Hwy at Taree.

posted walk but the park has a series of beaches separated by rocky headlands behind which are heaths and forests. Sometimes fairy penguins come to the headlands and dolphins are often seen in the waves.

Tourist Organisation of Port Stephens, Victoria Pde, Nelson Bay; tel: 4981 1579.
Port Stephens www.portstephens.org.au/

Beaches Serviced Apartments $$ 12 Gowrie Ave; tel: 4984 3255. Short walk from Little and Shoal Bay beaches.
Leilani Serviced Apartments $$ Gowrie Ave; tel: 4981 3304. Self-contained accommodation near beach.
On-Water Accommodation $$ d'Albora Marina, Nelson Bay; tel: 4981 0399. A new concept for holiday accommodation. A specially designed, non-motorised vessel to stay in a marina or alongside a private wharf or jetty, with access to water and electricity.
Port Stephens Motor Lodge $ 44 Magnus St; tel: 49841655. Native gardens. Short stroll to Nelson Bay beach and town centre.
Westbury's Marina Resort $$ 33 Magnus St, Nelson Bay; tel: 4981 4400. 250 m from Nelson Bay CBD and Marina. Water views.

Chez Jules $ 9 Cinema Mall Arcade Stockton St; tel: 4981 4500. Restaurant and coffee shop, serving breakfast, lunch, morning and afternoon teas and dinner. Licensed and BYO.
Hogs Breath Café $$ Shop16/ d'Albora Marina, Teramby Rd; tel: 4984 2842. Hogs Breath Blackened Prime Rib is featured on the menu which gives the basic idea. Part of a chain of restaurants.
Ketch's Restaurant $$ 4th Floor Westbury's Marina Resort, 33 Magnus St; tel: 4981 4400. Stunning views.
Merretts $$ Corlette Point Rd, Corlette; tel: 4984 2555. Part of the Anchorage Port Stephens. Fish specialities. Licensed and BYO.
Moffats Oyster Barn $$ On the waterfront at Swan Bay; tel: 4997 5433. Open daily. Absolute water views.
Scales Restaurant $$ 106 Magnus St, Nelson Bay; tel: 4981 3278. Licensed and BYO. Open every night; offers Hunter beef.

TAREE

Its position on the Manning River and the fact that the nearby beaches are said to have the whitest sand in Australia - a claim made by several other places, incidentally - have made Taree a popular holiday spot. The Aboriginal word for a local fig tree is tareebit, which is probably where the name originates.

First, the bad news. Taree has got itself one of the 'Big' thingies as a tourist attraction, despite having some quite lovely buildings and parks. This time it is the seriously hideous **Big Oyster**. In contrast, Albert St has two of Taree's finest buildings. **St Paul's Church** (1869) is the oldest building in Taree; it is Gothic Revival but not as forbidding as many. On the other side of the road is the **Court House**, completed in 1897. It is the sort of judicial building that is so well designed that it would be a pleasure to be charged there.

The **Manning Regional Art Gallery** on the Pacific Hwy is a small gallery with a strong local flavour, featuring paintings mainly from the 1850-60s. Open Thur–Sun 1200-1600; tel: 6551 0961. Free.

Taree is set back a little from the coast, but its beaches have excellent surfing as well as safe places to laze around. Inland, the upland streams are well stocked with rainbow and brown trout.

Ask at the information centre for details of two tours. A **rainforest walk** along the coast takes in two headlands, Black Head and Red Head. **Manning River Cruises** run a cruise boat up and down the river, mainly during the school holidays.

i **Taree Visitor Information Centre**, Pacific Hwy north of the town; tel: 1800 801 522.

Greater Taree City Council /www.gtcc.nsw.gov.au/. One of the best tourist sites on the Internet. Shows how it should be done.

These are all standard Australian motels offering the usual great value for money if, perhaps, lacking in individuality.

Arlite Motor Inn $ 4 Pacific Hwy; tel: 6552 2433.

EN ROUTE

Between Taree and Port Macquarie are several detours that might be treated as excursions from Taree or alternative routes north.

About 22 km north of Taree you can leave the Pacific Hwy for **Coopernook Forest Drive**. Partway along the drive is **Big Nellie Mountain**, a large volcanic plug rising to 560 m above sea-level. From the top are panoramic views of the Comboyne Plateau, Hannam Vale and Landsdowne Valleys. The climb, more a clamber, takes about 20 minutes. Looking at the view takes longer.

On the seaward side of Coopernook is **Harrington**. A breakwater provides excellent fishing and there is safe swimming on sandy beaches inside the river mouth.

Crowdy Head is 4km from Harrington and from the headland there are spectacular views north over

Crowdy Bay National Park and Diamond Head and to the south over the coastline through to Manning Point and Old Bar. The park, which runs between the road and the sea, has rugged, fractured sandstone cliffs with extensive banksia heaths and good coastal walks.

An alternative route is inland along Tourist Route 8. Around 15 km from Taree is **Wingham Brush**, the last remaining 10 ha of subtropical floodplain rain forest in NSW, with Moreton Bay figs and one of Australiaís largest populations of grey headed flying foxes. Follow the route to **Ellenborough Falls** on the Bulga Plateau about 50 km northwest of Taree. This is one of the largest single-drop waterfalls in the southern hemisphere, and no matter how low the rainfall this waterfall continually flows all year. Continue on Tourist Drive 8 through the villages of Lorne and Kendall to rejoin the Pacific Hwy 30 km south of the turn-off for Port Maquarie, or treat it as a circular tour and turn south back towards Taree.

Caravilla Motor Inn $ 33 Victoria St; tel: 6552 1822.
City Centre Motor Inn $$ 4 Crescent Ave; tel: 6552 5244.
Jolly Swagman Motel $ 1 Commerce St; tel: 6552 3511.
Pacific Motel $$ 51 Victoria St; tel: 6552 1977.
Rainbow Gardens Motel $ 28 Crescent Ave; tel: 6552 1312.

Bertie's Italian Restaurant $$ 217 Victoria St; tel: 6552 1034. Licensed and BYO.
Chandelier Restaurant $$ 33 Victoria St; tel: 6552 1822. Licensed and BYO.
East Court Chinese Restaurant $ 73 Victoria St; tel: 6552 2465. Cantonese. BYO.
Walkers Steakhouse $$ Pulteney St. Cnr Albert St; tel: 6552 6566. Licensed and BYO.

PORT MACQUARIE

Port Macquarie can be regarded as three separate destinations all within 20 minutes of each other. To the south lies Camden Haven – seaside, the quiet life, holiday accommodation; to the west and inland is the timber town of Wauchope, alongside the Hastings River. Port Macquarie itself, founded in 1821 and thus one of the oldest towns in the state, is also one of the most important fishing ports on the east coast as well as being very much a holiday town.

Port Macquarie Tourism, Cnr Clarence and Hay Sts; tel: 1800 025 935 or 6583; email: vicpm@midcoast.com.au

These are all pretty standard Australian motels but, as always, will be booked solid over the Christmas period.
Aquatic Motel $$ Hastings River Dr, tel: 6583 7388.
Beachfront Regency Motor Inn $$ 40 William St; tel: 6583 2244.
Bel Air Motel $$ 179 Gordon St; tel: 6583 2177.
Country Comfort Inn $$ Cnr Buller and Hollingsworth Sts; tel: 6583 2955.
Palm Court Motor Inn $$ 138 William St; tel: 6583 5155.
Sandcastle Motel $$ 20 William St; tel: 6583 3522.

Cray's $$ at Fisherman's Wharf; tel: 6587 1321. BYO.
Patsy's Place $ Hay St; tel: 6584 1143. Grills and seafood. BYO.
Riverview Terrace $$ Overlooks the water; tel: 6584 4446. Open lunch and dinner Tues–Sun.
Spinnakers Restaurant at Sails Resort $$ Tel: 6583 3999. Harbour views, open daily, licensed.

HIGHLIGHTS

The town has all of the attributes of the seaside, with camel rides on the beach, a theme park called **Fantasy Glades** and seals, dolphins and sharks at the **King Neptune Marine Park** at the mouth of the river.

Port Macquarie has an extensive series of parallel canals running back from the shore giving houses water access, a big selling point. Next to this canal development is **Settlement City,** a shopping area containing everything, from the up-market Sails Resort (tel: 6583 3999) to McDonald's.

DAY TRIPS

Camden Haven, the second part of the trio that come together to form the Port Macquarie area, is itself formed by three villages – Laurietown, North Haven and Dunbogan. This is an anglers' paradise. Just outside the town, on **North Brother Mountain**, there is a lookout with panoramic views of the area.

The third centre in the Port Macquarie area, **Wauchope**, pronounced 'war hope', was named after Captain Wauch who farmed there from 1841. It was and is a timber town, and 3 km west of the modern town is a reconstructed timber town of 1880, with steam train rides and demonstrations of working timber machinery, bullock teams and horse-drawn wagons. Wauchope also contains one of those Big Australian icons – a massive model of a bull. It is not very well made, it is not accurate, it is ugly and Wauchope is very proud of it. They will tell anyone who is willing to listen that it is the world's largest fibreglass bull.

KOALAS

You can visit koalas at Kingfisher Park, off the Oxley Hwy, and Billabong Koala Park, just past the Pacific Hwy crossover, are both open daily 0830–1730. $$ But the best place is the Koala Hospital in Lord St. This is Australia's first koala hospital, located on the Macquarie Nature Reserve. Koala Hospital is open every day of the year, and visitors can view koalas up close and watch them being fed at 0730 and 1500 by volunteer carers.

Nearby is the **Bellangry State Forest** which has splendid stands of hardwood trees. Route 34 continues inland up the side of the Great Dividing Range to **Walcha**.

KEMPSEY

The Macleay River wends its way down to the sea through beautiful forests and rural land to the coast where it bisects the town of Kempsey. Like almost every similar town in Australia it boasts the best year-round climate in the country, but it is true that it is always singularly pleasant here.

Slim Dusty was born in Kempsey and every September there is a traditional music festival. Kempsey has a strong art scene, both Aboriginal and western, with several galleries. A central part of the town is the **Aboriginal Heritage** and the **Djigay Centre** adjacent to the TAFE college. This has a Traditional Food Tree park through which you can wander with an Aboriginal guide.

EXPLORING THE MACLEAY VALLEY

All along the valley is a series of small villages such as Gladston, recognised as a historically important village, Smithtown, Frederickton, Bellbrook, Willawarrin, Kinchela, Jerseyville and Kundabung. In the valley's hinterland there are over 100,000 ha of state forests, the world heritage Werrikimbe National Park, the Upper Macleay Gorges and the Oxley Wild Rivers National Park.

The **Kempsey Cultural Centre** has been referred to as the 'first Australian building'. This is open to much debate but the architect, Glenn Murcutt, has given it a uniquely Australian feeling and it houses the tourist centre and a settler's cottage. It also has a **museum** tracing the story of the Maitland Valley, including an excellent display of Aboriginal artefacts with a stress on the pre-European history of the area.

There are some splendid vistas along the river in town, and **Riverside Park** is home to a large family of geese. **Rudder Park**, in East Kempsey, is the site of the first settler's home. A lookout here commands a majestic view of the surrounding mountains, the town and the river.

Along the coast the **beaches** are excellent and accessible, with the Arakoon State Recreation Area, the Hat Head National Park, the Goolawah Reserve and the Limeburners Creek Nature Reserve all offering clean beaches, clean water, miles of uninterrupted coast and, when the wind is in the right quarter, magnificent surfing. Crescent Head provides some of the best surfing in Australia and is the site of the annual Malibu Classic.

EN ROUTE

In the 1950s, Gordon Parson wrote a song, 'A Pub with No Beer'. It was recorded by Slim Dusty and became a hit not only in Australia but overseas. Australians doing 'The Trip' to Europe would assemble in the pubs of Earl's Court in London and make the night resound with their caterwauling of this ditty. But the pub with no beer exists (although the beer supplies have been replenished). To reach it turn off the Pacific Hwy at Macksville South and follow the signs for about 20 km to the Taylors Arms.

Do not take it as gospel that this is the pub that was written about – there is much evidence to suggest that the song was taken from a poem about a similar pub in Queensland. Most official histories try to be even-handed as to which should get the honours. This is not a subject that you bring up when drinking in the public bar at the Taylors Arms.

Skin diving is also well catered for and the base for most diving activity is the small resort of **South West Rocks**, 20 km north of Kempsey by way of the Jerseyville Bridge. Because of the nearness of the Continental Shelf there are clean, warm semitropical waters to dive in for most of the year. Fish Rock Dive Centre, 328 Gregory St; tel: 6566 6614, does a daily dive charter and offers full scuba courses, as does South West Rocks Dive Centre, 100 Gregory St; tel: 6566 6474. For deep-sea fishing try Trial Bay Deep Sea Fishing Charters; tel: 015 256 556.

Trial Bay Gaol, open 0900–1700 daily, is in the Arakoon State Recreation Area. The gaol was built in 1886 but has now been transformed into a museum.

Kempsey Tourist Information Centre, South Kempsey Park; tel: 6563 1555. The building that houses this centre is a splendid piece of Australian architecture and is worth visiting on that count alone.

Many of the motels of Kempsey are on the Pacific Hwy leading to and from the town and should always be checked for noise levels. Your best bet is to ask for the unit furthest from the road.

All Nations Hallmark Inn $$ Pacific Hwy; tel: 6562 1284.
Colonial Court Motor Inn $$ 155 Smith St; tel: 6562 6711.
Fairway Lodge Motel $ Pacific Hwy; tel: 6562 7099.
Moon River Motor Inn $$ 157 Smith St; tel: 6562 8077.
Park Drive Motel $$ 161 Pacific Hwy; tel: 6562 1361.
Skyline Motel $ 40 Pacific Hwy; tel: 6562 4888.

As always in small Australian towns, it is the Asian restaurants which offer the best value for money.

Gold & Silver Chinese Restaurant $ 4 Belgrave St; tel: 6562 6578.
Goldlion Chinese Restaurant $ 95 Smith St; tel: 6562 8111.
Lantern Inn $ The Pacific Hwy; tel: 6562 5236.
Kempsey Chinese Restaurant $ 54 Smith St; tel: 6562 5684.
Lou's Cafe Restaurant $ 7 Belgrave St; tel: 6562 4869.

NAMBUCCA HEADS

Most of the attraction of Nambucca Heads is focused on its river. On the north bank is the long run of Forster Beach leading down to Scotts Head. On the seaward side of town Beilbys Beach is patrolled in the season and comes south to Shelly Beach, protected from the sea by Cliffy Point. In the middle of the river is **Stuart Island**, which has the Nambucca Heads Island golf course, claimed, with considerable justification, to be the only golf course in Australia that is totally surrounded by water.

URBAN RAINFOREST

Nambucca Heads boasts a rainforest reserve in the centre, virtually adjacent to the main shopping area. If you walk across Ridge St from the Nambucca Mall, you enter another world. A series of nature walks have been built through the natural bushland reserves extending to the Rotary Lookout, which overlooks the river entrance. There is a dense section of rainforest in Gordon Park.

Like most museums run by keen amateurs the opening hours of Headland Historical Museum, Mainbeach Headland, are somewhat eccentric - Wed, Sat, Sun 1400–1600, but it is well organised and the area has a colourful history to recount. Some of the first European settlers to come to the area (in 1840) were ticket-of-leave men - convicts leased on patrol - to find and log cedar. The logs were originally taken out overland but were later floated down the Nambucca River and then transported by sailing vessels to Sydney.

Captain Cook Lookout provides excellent views of the area. Even more impressive is the view from the **Yarrahapinni Lookout**, where on a clear day you can see forever. Escorted 4-wheel drive tours of the area are available from Nambucca 4WD Tours (tel: 6568 9963).

i **Nambucca Valley Information Centre**, 4 Pacific Hwy; tel: 6568 6954.
Nambucca Community Site
www.communityonline.com.au/Default.htm

Blue Dolphin Motel $$ Fraser St; tel: 6568 6700. Close to the shops, with river and ocean views.
Coolawin Gardens Motel $$ Bellwood Dr, tel: 6568 6304. Older-style motel in beautiful bushland and garden setting.
Destiny Motor Inn $$ Pacific Hwy; tel: 6568 8044. Pool, spa, Turkish steam bath, private courtyards to landscaped gardens.
Max Motel $$ Fraser St; tel: 6568 6138. Close to the shops with river and ocean views.

EN ROUTE

The Nambucca Valley is at the eastern end of the popular Waterfall Way. A drive through Bellingen and up to the New England Plateau puts you in waterfall country which, depending on the season, has many spectacular falls

Motel Miramar $$ Old Pacific Hwy; tel: 6568 7899. Magnificent river and ocean views. Owned by Nambucca Heads RSL Club which is next door.

Nambucca Resort $$ Pacific Hwy; tel: 6568 6899. A 28-unit family motel and licensed restaurant set in 6 ha on the Nambucca River. Salt water pool, children's playground, golf driving range, spa, boat ramp and canoe hire.

Boatshed Brasserie Restaurant $$ 1 Wellington Dr; tel: 6568 9292. Seafood. BYO and licensed.

Gargles $$ 19 Bowra St; tel: 6568 7795.

Ken Leong Singapore & Malaysian Restaurant $ Short St; tel: 6568 7415. Good satay and laksa. BYO.

Kel's Matilda's Australiana Restaurant $$ 6 Wellington Dr; tel: 6568 6024. BYO and licensed.

COFFS HARBOUR

Coffs Harbour was originally named Korff's Harbour after Captain John Korff who sheltered here in 1847 and liked the place so much he opened a store in the main street. It has retained much of that charm although the population is now over 46,000. In the early days the harbour, halfway between Brisbane and Sydney, was considered very dangerous for shipping and was boycotted by ships' captains until the lighthouse was built in 1878.

The major attraction of Coffs Harbour is the wide range of beaches catering for everyone from surfers to kiddies going paddling. There are even some secluded beaches for nude bathing. This is also the centre of a tropical fruit-growing area.

Coffs Harbour Visitor Information Centre, Marcia St; tel: 6652 1522.

Happy Planet, 85 City Central Mall 2nd Floor; tel: 6651 7520. Open weekdays 0900–1700, Sat 0900–1400.

Pretty much all of the accommodation is standard Australian motel with some being slightly more upmarket than others. Most motels are either on Park Beach Rd or Ocean Pde. Finding a vacancy should only be a problem over Christmas/Jan.

Airlie Court Holiday Apartments $$ 20 Boultwood St; tel: 6652 4101.

Coffs Harbour is at the centre of the largest banana-growing area in Australia. There is not just a Big Banana. There is a Big Banana Leisure Park. All of this is some 3 km north of the town, so once you get there you have seen the last of the Big Banana. If you want to learn more, the Historical Museum in the High St, north of the City Centre Mall, tells the story of how the area was developed first for cedar, then for sugar and finally for bananas and tourists.

Australian Safari Motel $$ 29 Grafton St; tel: 6652 1900.
Caribbean Motel $$ 353 High St; tel: 6652 1500.
Holiday Village $$ 97 Park Beach Rd; tel: 6652 2055.
Toreador Motel $$ 31 Grafton St; tel: 6652 3887.
YHA $ 110 Albany St; tel: 6652 6462. Rooms are non-smoking, twin/double or family accommodation.

The two main groupings of restaurants are on the Pacific Hwy and High St with the inexpensive options normally being in the latter.
Avanti Restaurant $ 368 High St; tel: 6652 4818.
Fisherman's Co-op $ End of the Jetty. Fresh fish and chips which are immensely popular and in the summer you will have to wait. Open 1030–1830.
Golden Crown $ 374 High St; tel: 6651 6787.
Iguana Beach Cafe $ Marina Dr; tel: 6652 5725. At the Yacht Club. Superb seafood. Lunch 1200–1530. Dinner 0900 until latish.
Legendz Restaurant $$ Pacific Hwy; tel: 6652 3855.
Tahruah Thai Kitchen $ 366 High St; tel: 6651 5992. Probably the most authentic Thai food in town.
Tequila Mexican Restaurant $ 224 High St; tel: 6652 1279.
Windmill Restaurant $$ Pacific Hwy; tel: 6652 2400.

HIGHLIGHTS

A circular drive is a useful orientation. It starts at the Post Office, goes east to **Beacon Hill Lookout**, down to the harbour area and then to the **Muttonbird Island Nature Walk**. From there you can come back via the **Pet Porpoise Pool** and the **Park Beach Surf Club** development. The **Butterfly House**, open daily, has one of the world's largest displays of live Australian butterflies in a rainforest setting, and also has a built-in maze.

The **South Coast Regional Botanical Garden**, off the High St and part of the Coffs Creek Walkway, was opened in 1988 and is one of the great places to visit in Coffs Harbour. With Coffs Creek on three sides it has, among other attractions, a mangrove boardwalk and a bird hide in the rainforest setting.

WHERE NEXT?

Coffs Harbour is an easy day's drive from Sydney and you are halfway to Brisbane (see p. 234).

COFFS HARBOUR – COOLANGATTA

OTT TABLES 9090

TRANSPORT	FREQUENCY	JOURNEY TIME
Bus	10 Daily	5hrs 20mins

COFFS HARBOUR – GRAFTON

OTT TABLES 9017/9090

TRANSPORT	FREQUENCY	JOURNEY TIME
Train	3 Daily	1hr 12mins
Bus	10 Daily	1hr

GRAFTON – MURWILLUMBAH

OTT TABLES 9017/9090

TRANSPORT	FREQUENCY	JOURNEY TIME
Train	Daily	3hrs 40mins
Bus	8 Daily	4hrs 20mins

GRAFTON – BALLINA

OTT TABLES 9090

TRANSPORT	FREQUENCY	JOURNEY TIME
Bus	10 Daily	2hrs 25mins

BALLINA – BYRON BAY

OTT TABLES 9090

TRANSPORT	FREQUENCY	JOURNEY TIME
Bus	Daily	40min

BALLINA – MURWILLUMBAH

OTT TABLE 9090

TRANSPORT	FREQUENCY	JOURNEY TIME
Bus	9 Daily	1hr 20mins

MURWILLUMBAH – COOLANGATTA

OTT TABLE 9090

TRANSPORT	FREQUENCY	JOURNEY TIME
Bus	5 Daily	35mins

Note: One of the Goffs Harbour - Grafton trains goes on to Brisbane.

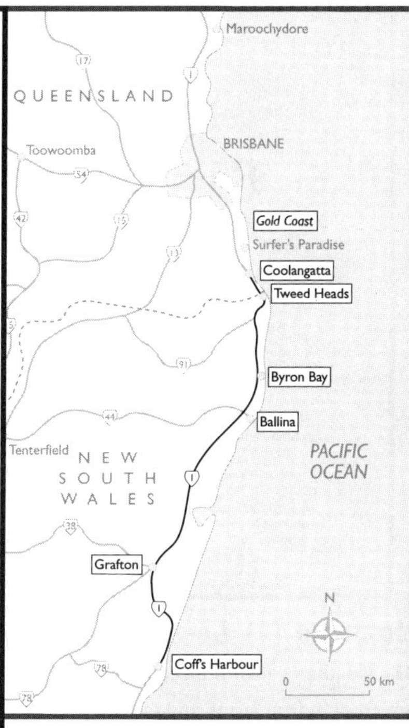

Notes

A regular bus service operates along the Gold Coast between Coolangatta and Brisbane. All services stop at Surfers Paradise and some at the theme parks.

ROUTE DETAIL

The Pacific Hwy – still grandiosely named Rte National 1 – turns inland to Grafton, skirting Yuraygir National Park and Lake Hiawatha. From there the road runs 130 km across the inlet of the Clarence River to Ballina. At Ballina you can stay on the highway or run towards the sea through Lennox Head to Byron Bay and rejoin the highway on the far side of Bangalow. After Brunswick Heads the road kinks slightly inland to Murwillumbah, on the slopes of the long-extinct volcano Mt Warning, before entering Tweed Heads, the last town in New South Wales. Traffic through here can be a problem on summer weekends. Across the Tweed River lies Queensland. The total journey, excluding detours, is about 340 km.

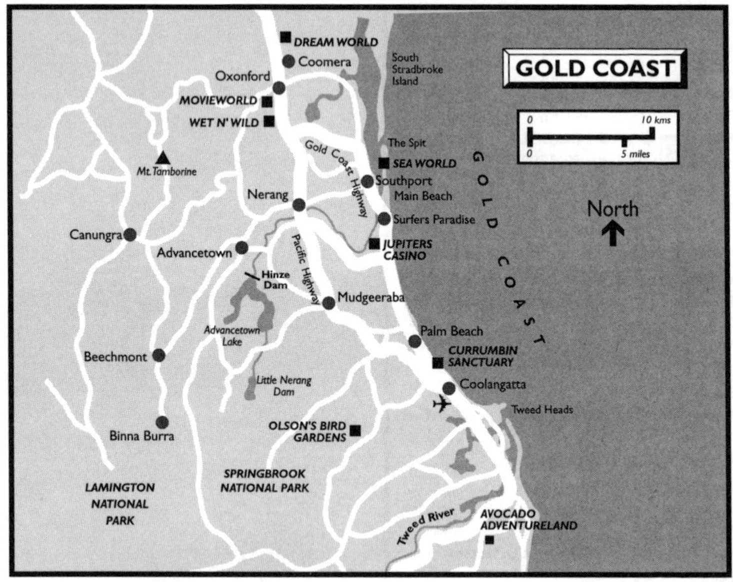

NORTH TO THE GOLD COAST

The weather is now noticeably different as you move into the subtropical zone. There are tropical fruit farms, and many towns in this region were founded on cedar logging, an industry which stripped – literally – the whole of New South Wales of cedar to make Victorian furniture. Much of the coast falls within national parks, and at magical, laid-back Byron Bay whales cruise past in season. No one in Sydney ever has a bad word to say about Byron Bay.

The Gold Coast has been a holiday spot since the turn of the 20th century but has boomed since World War II. The whole strip is the most thoroughly commercialised resort in Australia, with more than 2 million visitors a year.

GRAFTON

Grafton is a pleasant garden town, famous for its trees – the jacarandas are a glorious sight in season. As early as 1866 the council had bye-laws encouraging the planting and preservation of trees. This far-sighted action means that Grafton now has more than 7,000 trees lining the streets and shading the well-maintained parks. A **Jacaranda Festival** has been held every spring - the last Sat in Oct - since 1935.

Many of the buildings in Grafton are classified by the National Trust, including **Christ Church Cathedral**. This was designed by John Horbury Hunt in 1884 in the Gothic Revival style so popular in the Victorian era. Open daily 0700–1730.

Worth seeing is **Schaeffer House Museum**, at 192 Fitzroy St, which was built in 1900 by an architect as an expression of his design philosophy and has now been totally restored. Open Tues–Thur 1300–1600, Sun 1400–1600.

Many of the old homesteads have been preserved, one of which, **Prentice House** at 158 Fitzroy St, now houses the regional art gallery. Open Wed–Sun 1000–1600.

FESTIVAL OF MUSIC

Since 1994, Grafton has hosted the Easter Jazz and Blues Festival. The festival has grown into a very popular event and, now the Festival of Music, is not restricted to jazz and blues. For the best part of a week the streets, the hotels and clubs, and even the riverboats play host to a large number of bands and artists covering a wide range of talents.

A bus tour passes many of the historic buildings and points of interest in the town. Buses leave Market Sq at 20 mins past each hour but do not run on Sun.

Levees, built to protect the town after many floods, now form a riverside walk, which offers a range of water sports. Of the 24 parks within Grafton, perhaps the best positioned is **Memorial Park**, overlooking **Susan Island** and the river. Canoes can be hired to take you across to the island, at one end of which is a rainforest with walking tracks and the largest fruit bat colony in the southern hemisphere. The southern section of the island has a picnic area and toilets.

The original town, simply known as The Settlement, developed as two separate settlements, one each side of the Clarence River, with a rowing boat the only connection. Even after the double-decker bridge (rail and road) was opened in 1932, South Grafton remained a separate community until the 1950s. Today, it is a perfect example of a 19th-century NSW river town.

i **Clarence River Tourist Association**, Pacific Hwy, South Grafton; tel: 6642 4677. There are many special displays including Aboriginal art, National Parks and local products all housed in an excellent purpose-designed building.
Grafton Online www.sfwp.com.au/grafton/index.html

EN ROUTE

Just before you reach Grafton is Merino Mac's Australian Agradome, 25 km south of the town. Here there are trained sheep of different breeds who parade on stage; as well as demonstrations of wool shearing and sheepdogs rounding up herds.

EN ROUTE

Around Grafton is a ring of national parks including, inland along Rte 38, the World Heritage park of **Washpool** and the **Gibraltar Range** and, only 40 km from Grafton, but difficult to access, **Nymboida**. Two smaller parks have combined to form **Yuraygir**, the longest stretch of undeveloped coastline in NSW. The parks comprise long sandy beaches, heathlands, paperbark swamps and lagoons. There is excellent bushwalking, surfing and fishing, as well as canoeing in the lagoons and creeks. **Bundjalung,** immediately to the north, continues the protected coastline. It covers large areas of swamp and heathland, mangrove mudflats, cypress swamps and one of the last wild coastal rivers, the Esk. Attractions include rare rainforests at Woody Head, canoeing on the rivers and lagoons and excellent surfing and fishing. Camping is permitted at Woody Head and Black Rocks.

The motels are clustered along Fitzroy and Prince Sts, which makes it easy to trawl for accommodation that suits you.

Abbey Motor Inn $$ 59 Fitzroy St; tel: 6642 6122.
Big River Motel $ 215 Prince St; tel: 6642 4488.
Clarence Motor Inn $$ 51 Fitzroy St; tel: 6643 3444; email clarinn@nor.com.au; /www.wicinvest.com.au/clarence/. Has its own restaurant – Victoria's – which specialises in prawns and oysters from the river, fish and shellfish from the sea.
Crown Hotel Motel $$ 1 Prince St; tel: 6642 4000.
Fitzroy Motel $ 27 Fitzroy St; tel: 6642 4477.
Grafton Civic Motel $$ 153 Pound St; tel: 6642 4922.
Grafton Hotel $ 97 Fitzroy St; tel: 6642 2000; email gh@wicinvest.com.au; www.wicinvest.com.au/graftonhotel/. Basically for backpackers but it has a pleasant bistro, and there has been a Grafton Hotel in Grafton, but not on this site, since 1853.
Jacaranda Motel $$ Pacific Hwy; tel: 6642 2833.
Keylodge Motel $$ 37 Fitzroy St; tel: 6642 1944; www.tropicalnsw.com.au/accommodation/key-lodge-motel/index.html. Heated spa, indoor pool and large sauna.
Parkview Hotel Motel $$ 93 Prince St; tel: 6642 2375.

The Clarence is one of Australia's biggest seafood harvesting districts and the seafood available in the restaurants of Grafton is outstanding. The best bet is to have it served as simply as possible. The quality of the produce needs no garnishing.

Courtyard Cafe $$ Grafton Regional Gallery, 158 Fitzroy St; tel: 6642 6644.
Daly's Roadhouse Restaurant $ Pacific Hwy; tel: 6643 1990.
Fountain Court $$ 135 Prince St; tel: 6643 1411.
Le Touche Restaurant $$ 139 Fitzroy St; tel: 6643 9011.
New Oriental Chinese Restaurant $ 127 Prince St; tel: 6642 7888.

BALLINA

Ballina is the sort of quiet town where everything moves at a relaxed pace in the pleasantly warm air. It is sited on the mouth of the Richmond River and is divided by The Canal and North Creek, which separate East Ballina from the sea. Ballina has a sizeable fishing fleet and the town is surrounded by beautiful beaches – the coastline heading up to Lennox Heads has some of the best surfing beaches in NSW.

The small **Opal and Gem Museum**, open 0900–1700, has lots of souvenirs for sale made from crystal and gems. Sadly, its address is Shop 8, Big Prawn Complex (yes, Ballina has a Big Prawn). Nearby is **Fenwick House**, now Shaw's Bay Hotel. This is a splendid example of a misplaced Scottish manse, all granite and stained-glass windows and slate roof. Its beautiful red cedar dining-room and staircase were carved in Spain but from local wood. Open 1000–2200.

The lighthouse was built in 1879 to mark the Ballina bar, which has been the doom of many ships. There are tremendous views from the **Lighthouse Hill** look out.

You can go cruising aboard MV *Richmond Princess* (tel: 018 664 784) which has two-hour cruises on Wed, Thur and Sun. The MV *Bennelong* (tel: 018 664 552) also has a variety of cruises up the river, including one to Lismore. Ballina Quay Marina (tel: 6686 4249) has houseboats for rent. Just north of Ballina along the coast road is **Lake Ainsworth**, a freshwater lake which is safe for children.

The whole area inland is one of tropical fruit production.Nearby **Summerland** is an extensive charity-owned fruit farm growing avocados, macadamia nuts, tropical stone fruit, custard apples, lychees and citrus fruits.

The open-air **Lumley Park Pioneer Relics Museum** contains Moreton Bay figs, white booyong, yellow-wood and bumby ash. It was in this environment that the red cedar grew and thrived but was cut down by the early settlers as a cash crop and was, indeed, responsible for much of the European settlement of this area. On display in the park are horse-drawn vehicles and early steam-powered machines. The **Victoria Park Nature Reserve** close by is a remnant of the original scrubland that once covered the whole area.

Broadwater Sugar Mill, 19 km south of Ballina, does tours during the cane-crushing season (Jun–Dec), but this is not an exciting excursion.

i **Ballina Information Centre**, Cnr River St and Las Balsa Plaza; tel: 6686 3484.
Ballina www.ballina.net/ is still in the process of construction but holds considerable promise.

All Seasons Motor Inn $$ 305 Pacific Hwy; tel: 6686 2922; email allsball@fc-hotels.com. Also has spa suites at higher prices.

LAS BALSAS EXPEDITION

An exhibition at the information centre tells the story of the Las Balsas expedition, in which a raft with a four-man crew left Guayaquil in Ecuador in 1973 and came ashore at Ballina 178 days later. The expedition was designed to prove that South Americans could have come to Australia and New Zealand on balsa rafts, a fascinating theory which has attracted much argument over the years. The exhibition would be worth a special detour, but you will probably be going to the information centre anyway. There is also a display recording the maritime history of the Richmond River.

Almare Tourist Motel $ 339 River St; tel: 6686 2833.
Ballina Travellers Lodge Hostel $ 36–8 Tamar St; tel: 6686 6737 email Scarboro@nor.com.au. This is a YHA-affiliated establishment but it has double rooms.
Chaparral Motel $ Pacific Hwy; tel: 6686 3399.
Colonial Motel $$ Skinner St, Cnr Bangalow Rd; tel: 6686 7691; http://www.tropicalnsw.com.au/accommodation/colonial-ballina/index.html. 500 m to waterfront, 5-min drive to the beaches, swimming and surfing.
Palms Motor Inn $$ Owen St, Cnr Bentinck St; tel: 6686 4477.
Travellers Lodge $$ 36–8 Tamar St; tel: 6686 6737; www.tropicalnsw.com.au/accommodation/ballinatravellerslodge/index.html. Central, quiet location.

Many of the restaurants are along River St, which runs beside the Richmond River and heads from Grafton to the beaches.
Australian Hotel $$ 103 River St; tel: 6686 2015. Restaurant, bar, nightspot and accommodation.
Checkers Cafe Brasserie $ Ballina Fair; tel: 6686 8242. BYO.
Mexican Del Rio $$ 196 River St; tel: 6686 2775.
Ping Sun Chinese Restaurant $ 200 River St; tel: 6686 3292. Cantonese. BYO and licensed.
Sabbi's Italian Restaurant $$ 2 Moon St; tel: 6686 7119.
Shelly's On The Beach $$ Shelly Beach Rd; tel: 6686 9844. BYO. Bookings essential. Open daily 0730 onwards for breakfast and lunch.

BYRON BAY

Byron Bay is thought by many people to be the most attractive spot in Australia. Sydneysiders speak of it with awe and affection and many drive or fly up here as often as they can. It is a remarkably charming place and no one ever seems to come away disappointed.

In the 1960s it became a hippie centre and that feeling of an alternative lifestyle is still here in the town, with tarot card readings and iridology and restaurants that specialise in vegetarian food. In theory, the most famous resident is Paul 'Crocodile Dundee' Hogan, although he appears to be rarely there.

Byron Bay is defended from commercialisation by a very active and well organised lobby - all high-rise buildings are banned and Club Med tried in vain for years to open. Despite motels and hotels galore there is no feeling of a tourist trap. Shopping is mostly tie-dyed fabrics, scented candles and handicrafts, but there is a lovely relaxed feel about the place and people smile a lot.

Captain Cook named the town after Sir John Byron, a brave sailor who had circumnavigated the globe in *HMS Dolphin* (1764–6) and thus ventured into the Pacific before Cook himself. He was also the grandfather of the poet Lord Byron.

EN ROUTE

Bangalow, the turn-off from Rte National 1 for Byron Bay, is a small village with a rustic charm of its own, and the art, craft and antiques shops are a foretaste of Byron Bay. The **Byron Creek walking track** goes through rainforest to a picnic area.

Byron Bay Tourist Information Office, 80 Jonson St; tel: 6685 8050.
Global Gossip, 84 Jonson St; tel: 6685 6554. Open daily 0800–2400.
Internet Cafe and Public Telephone Centre, Byron St, Email hellobb@norex.com.au. Open daily 0930–2300.
Koo's Cafe, Marvell St. Only has one computer so you need to time it right. Open Mon–Sat 0730–1730.

Byron Bay is packed to overflowing in Dec and Jan, and prices shoot up accordingly.
**Aquarius Backpackers Resort $$** 16 Lawson St; tel: 6685 7663. The most luxurious backpacker place in Australia? Probably. Split-level rooms. Good café ($). Brilliant beds.
Belongil Beach House $$ Childe Rd; Tel: 6685 7868. Literally on the beach. Balinese-style café.
Blue Iguana Beach House $$ 14 Bay St; tel: 6685 5298. Another backpacker opposite the Surf Club but has double rooms with bath.
Byron Bay Lighthouse $$ Tel: 6685 6222, or ask a tourist office to check availability. Possibly the best accommodation of its kind in Australia, in the keeper's cottages. Quite amazing. The cottages are basic but the walls are massively thick and within there is total silence and, no matter how hot it is outside, it's always cool inside. Advance booking essential (a year in advance during the holiday season);
Cape Byron Hostel $$ Cnr Middleton and Byron; tel: 6685 8788. This is a YHA franchise but has double rooms with bath. Internet access.
Cape Byron Lodge $ 78 Bangalow Rd; tel: 6685 6445. Slightly out from the centre of town. Free bikes and several courtesy buses into town during the day.

GETTING AROUND
Bicycles are widely available for hire and many motels will lend you one for nothing. Earth Car Rentals offers relatively inexpensive car hire and will deliver anywhere within 5 km of Byron Bay. Tel: 6685 7472.

Nomads Main Beach $$ Cnr Lawson and Fletcher Sts; tel: 6685 8695.This is a backpacking hostel but has rooms with bath. Much loved by surfers. Has Internet access.

Jonson St is packed end to end with cafés and restaurants; all of them are affordable and most of them are inexpensive. Many could be thought of as being alternative in the same way that Byron Bay is an alternative resort. This is heaven for vegetarians.

Beach Cafe $ Clarks Beach; tel: 6685 7598. Perfect for breakfast and dinner. Get there early in the morning and you can watch the sun rise over the sea.

Lifestream $$ 46 Jonson St. This is ideal for vegetarians and does knockout things with tofu.

Piggery Supernatural Food $ Skinners Shoot Rd. Large menu but solid vegetarian offerings – that goes for the whole of Byron Bay.

Ringo's Cafe $ Jonson St. Has a second-hand bookshop and there is a desperate danger that someone might start reading poetry. But good food, pleasant service. Open daily 0830–2130.

Thai Lucy $ Bay Lane; tel: 6680 8083 although the telephone is not often answered. Great Thai food at very reasonable prices. Frequently packed. Open Tue–Sun 1200–1500, 1730–2200.

HIGHLIGHTS

The bay is very popular for swimming, body surfing and, a little further out to sea, skin-diving. There is great surfing at **Watego's Beach** on Cape Byron, just below the lighthouse. This is considered to be one of the best surfing beaches on the east coast and the only ocean beach in NSW with a northerly aspect – its long rollers are the delight of surfers. On the beach is a fisherman's hut which can be rented in the same way as the lighthouse keepers' houses (see Accommodation) – ideal if you want to sleep practically on top of the surf.

The **lighthouse**, 2 km south-east of the town, was built in 1901. It is one of the most attractive in Australia and you can drive up there to the car-park near the top. There is a path around the lighthouse and out to the point. The views are stunning and at

Colour Section

(i) Mural at Byron Bay (p. 222); New Queensland beach; Port Douglas Marina (p. 305)

(ii) Cape Tribulation National Park; crossing Mossman River; the mangrove; scuba diving around the Great Barrier Reef (p. 276).

(iii) Billabong in Kakadu (pp. 357–363)

(iv) Australian wildlife: koala; crocodile; kangaroo and sealion

88
WILLOW

the right time of the year it is a good place to spot migrating whales swimming past. On any day you may see dolphins swimming through the totally clear waters. When you see them perhaps you, too, will feel sadness for the dolphins that are kept cooped up in marinas for the entertainment of holidaymakers. The whiff of goat you may detect is from the descendants of the herd the keepers used to maintain for meat and milk.

Running south is **Tallow Beach**, 7 km of golden sand. Except for the summer holidays and weekends it is often totally deserted. This is not the only beach at Byron – there are 37 km of beaches altogether so you are spoiled for choice. From Main Beach at low tide you can see bits of the wreck of the steamer *Wollongbar*, which was wrenched from its mooring by a storm in 1921.

In the bay running north towards Brunswick Heads is the **Julian Rocks Aquatic and Nature Reserve**. It is a 10-minute boat ride from the shore and is Australia's first marine sanctuary and a great place for skin diving. The tropical waters from the Coral Sea stream down to meet with the temperate southern waters and the result, as always, is a wealth of marine life. This is certainly one of the ten best dive sites in Australia and there are several organisations which can handle dives. One is **Byron Bay Dive Centre**, 9 Lawson St; tel: 6685 7149.

Byron Bay is not a scene for formal nightclubs, but at the last count there were seven venues offering live music. These are all in Jonson St, so you can start at the beach and trawl your way inland. The two best-known ones are **The Beach Hotel**, where you can sit in the beer garden and listen to the music at about the right volume and **The Rails**, which is very much a local venue but has music every night.

Within an easy hour's drive from Byron Bay there are eight national parks and 26 nature reserves. One drive worth taking is to **Whian Whian Forest**, **Peates Mountain Lookout** and **Minyon Falls**, 20 km west of Mullumbimby. Or walk through the rainforest at **Broken Head** to the almost total seclusion of King's and Bray's Beaches. The information centre has maps and information on all these places.

TWEED HEADS

For years this town had a substantial source of income simply because poker machines were illegal in Queensland but allowed in New South Wales. The law has now been amended but the clubs linger on – the Twin Towns Services Club has one of the largest arrays of poker machines in Australia.

Tweed Heads is on two major lagoons that stretch inland, one of which, Terranora Lake, offers fishing and boating and is famous for its oysters. The best spot to orientate yourself with views of the area is Razorback Outlet, 3 km out of town.

The coastline around Tweed Heads is, for many visitors, much more pleasant than the hustle and bustle of Surfers Paradise (see p. 229) to the north. In fact, Tweed Heads is an ideal base from which to make forays up the Gold Coast.

Danger Point has the world's first laser beam lighthouse. This was opened in 1970, the bicentenary of the epic voyage undertaken by Captain Cook, to whom there is a memorial, a capstan base made from ballast dumped from the *Endeavour*.

The Minjungbal people once inhabited the lower Tweed Valley, and on Kirkwood Rd, about 5 km south of town is the Minjungbal Aboriginal Culture Museum. It is set in bushland around an old sacred ceremonial bora site and mangrove and nature walks. Open daily 1000–1600 (tel: 5524 2109).

Where the Tweed River joins the Rous lies the small village of Tumbulgum - the name means meeting of the waters - which was the site of a grog shanty (an unlicensed hotel) as early as 1858. The completely restored and renovated Tumbulgum Hotel today dates from 1887 (tel: (02) (not 07) 6676 6202). From here you can explore up the two rivers in a hired boat from Tumbulgum Boat Hire, Riverside Dr; tel: (02) 6676 6240.

i **Tweed Visitors Centre,** Wharf St; tel: (07) 5536 4244. Note: although the town is in New South Wales, Telecom insists it has the Queensland prefix of 07.

These are all very standard Australian motels but the prices tend to be lower than similar seaside resorts.

Blue Pelican Motel $ 115 Pacific Hwy; tel: 5536 1777

Cook's Endeavour Motor Inn $$ 26 Francis St; tel: 5536 5399.

Jack HI Motel $$ 17 Powell St; tel: 5536 1788.

Kennedy Drive Motor Inn $ 203 Kennedy D.; tel: 5536 9288.

Matilda Motel $ 1 Kennedy Dr; tel: 5536 7211.

EN ROUTE

About 17 km north of Byron Bay are the Tweed Valley Tourist Gardens. These contain Australia's largest collection of hippeastrums in a garden which overlooks the valley down to the coast at Kingscliff. Open daily.

Near by is Mount Warning, the first place that the sun hits Australia in the morning. Beyond Mt Warning lies the World Heritage Border Ranges National Park. The park entrance is at Breakfast Creek, 12 km south-west of Murwillumbah off the Kyogle Rd. There are two well-signposted tracks. One is a magnificent if steep walk leading to the summit through a range of vegetation. There are resting points along the way, and the 360-degree view from the summit is truly remarkable. The other, the Lyrebird Trail, only takes 15 mins and leads to an elevated platform within the rainforest.

Tweed Fairways Motel $ Soorley St, Cnr Pacific Hwy; tel: 5524 2111.

First, a most unusual experience. **Mother Nature's Bush Tucker $**, 75 Upper Duroby Creek Rd, North Tumbulgum; tel: 5590 9826. Offers bush food survival kits of 20 local native bush food plants so that you can grow your own. This is, thankfully, followed by morning tea with home-made scones and cream.
Fishermans Cove $$ Coral St; tel: 5536 1646. Ocean views. Dinner daily.
Memory Manor $$ 106 Riverside, Tumbulgum; tel: 6676 6350. Open daily for lunch; dinner Sat.
Outside Inn $ 21 Wharf St, Tweed Heads; tel: 5536 6558.
Tweed Heads Chinese Restaurant $ 103 Wharf St; tel: 5536 5077. Cantonese cuisine.

COOLANGATTA AND THE GOLD COAST

Coolangatta is the gateway to a 35-km strip of seaside gaudiness and gaiety. Surfers Paradise and the Gold Coast are together the Blackpool, the Venice Beach, the Coney Island of Australia. Seaside holiday cottages were already beginning to appear at the end of the 19th century; the railway connection in 1903 gave the place a further boost and interest surged in the 1970s and '80s. If you like your holidays brash and booming this is the place, where the young come to celebrate leaving school and where the elderly come to wallow in the sunshine.

Coolangatta, at the southern end of the strip, is older, quieter, cheaper and less garish. It has not been over-modernised and still retains much of its old charm – more for the family than for ragers and ravers. The town is often promoted as the twin of Tweed Heads across the state border, but both towns have their own style.

There are more beaches here than you could reasonably explore, 14 protected year-round by full-time lifeguards. The Gold Coast City Council patrols more beaches than any other local authority in Australia, using helicopters, boats, jet-skis and watercraft to make the beaches safe for families.

Although Surfers Paradise (see p. 229) is the pulsating heart and unofficial capital of the Gold Coast, there is plenty of activity apart from the sand and surf, including two big theme parks at its north end.

Dreamworld claims the fastest, tallest ride in the world, the Tower of Terror, with other rides to make you scream. It also has a small zoo and an IMAX theatre. Open daily 1000–1700 (Main St, Plaza Restaurant and Koala Country open an hour earlier). Tel: 5588 1111.

Movie World, run by Warner Bros, doesn't operate as a full studio, although some movie-making does go on on there. Instead, it has the country's only suspended looping coaster called ... Lethal Weapon. Open daily 1000–1700; tel: 5573 8485; www.village.com.au.

Nearby **Wet'n'Wild** offers watery excitement, including 1-m waves. There are pleasant grassy areas around the assorted pools where you can picnic and barbecue. Open daily 0900–dusk.

Exploring the country behind the Gold Coast is a delight only half an hour's drive away. Just north of the Gold Coast airport you will find the **Currumbin Sanctuary**. This parkland is full of Australian wildlife and you can explore it by miniature train. Twice a day, when they feed the lorikeets, the birds come down in massive flocks and positively submerge the spectators. Open daily 0800–1700. Along Currumbin Creek Rd are **Olson's Bird Gardens**, set in a subtropical garden. Open daily from 0900–1700. **Mt Cougal National Park**, about another 14 km along the road, contains an old timber mill and walking tracks into the rainforest.

Out past Nerang is the **Advancetown Lake and Hinze Dam**, a swimming spot and a picnic area surrounded by mountains including Springbrook, Binna Burra and Beechmont (open Nov–Mar 0830–1800; rest of year 0730–1700). **Lamington National Park**, a 30-min drive south-west from Surfers Paradise, has 160 km of walking tracks leading through the park which offers some spectacular scenery and views. It is not a tough park to explore and you can select the extent of your exploration to suit your fitness and the time available.

The Gold Coast airport is at Coolangatta, and from here you can enjoy flights over the area.

Coolangatta Tourist Information Office, Beach House Plaza, Marine Pde; tel: 5536 7765.
Gold Coast Bulletin www.gcbulletin.com.au/
About Gold Coast City www.javerang.com.au/aboutgc.htm

The Gold Coast is somewhat different from the rest of Australia. Apartments feature in a major way and are typically taken by families – or groups of young people – by the week. Resorts are not the all-encompassing types found in other countries but do include a swimming pool, restaurants, bars and other facilities within the complex. Prices vary wildly with the season.

Beach House Seaside Resort $$ 52 Marine Pde, Cnr of Marine Pde and Mclean St; tel: 5536 7466. On the beach near to the Coolangatta Surf Lifesaving Club.

Coolangatta YHA Hostel $ 230 Coolangatta Dr; tel: 5536 7644.

Greenmount Beach Resort $$ 3 Hill St; tel: 5536 1222.

Rainbow Place Apartments $$180 Marine Pde; tel: 5536 9144. All units face the water.

St Tropez $$ 27–35 Orchid Ave; tel: 5538 7855. Fully equipped and serviced apartments. Swimming pool, spa, sauna.

Surfers Paradise British Arms International Backpackers Resort $ 70 Seaworld Dr; tel: 5571 1776. Has its own pub on the premises which makes for a lively, and noisy, nightlife.

Victoria Square Apartments $$ 15 Victoria Ave, Broadbeach; tel: 5592 1794; email vicsqr@onthenet.com.au. Luxurious holiday apartments and penthouses. Depending on the time of the year and how many are using the apartments the price can easily fall into the $ bracket.

Acapulco on the Beach Resort $$ 2 Thornton St; tel: 5570 1555; email acapulco@qldnet.com.au. 24-storey high-rise holiday apartments. Resort facilities.

Bahia Beachfront Apartments $ 154 The Esplanade; tel: 5538 3322.

Paradise Inn $ 2826 Gold Coast Hwy; tel: 5592 0585.

Surfers Central Budget $ 40 Whelan St; tel: 5538 4344.

Trickett Gardens Holiday Inn $$ 24 Trickett St; tel: 5539 0988. Air-conditioned, low-rise, self-contained holiday apartments.

SURFER'S PARADISE

Catering for the mass tourist trade does not, by and large, lead to high culinary standards, but you will never starve – and there are dozens of places on practically every street.

Aztec Food Court $ Marine Pde; tel: 5599 2748. Mexican.

Casa Mia Piccola $$ Marine Pde; tel: 5599 2336. Italian. Licensed.

O'Roark's Restaurant & Saloon $ 23 Maclean St; tel: 559 92111.

Orchid Ave and the beach end of Cavill Ave offer a wide range of alfresco cafés, restaurants and snack bars. Broadbeach Mall

WHERE NEXT?

Surfers Paradise is a tiny and unrepresentative corner of Queensland. Beyond Brisbane (see p. 232), Hwy 1 continues up the coast to the wilds of Cape York (see p. 311).

is more upmarket and international, but this is not serious gourmet territory.

Juke Malones $$ Paradise Centre; tel: 5526 7990.

King Arthur's Table $$ Raptis Plaza Cavill Ave; tel: 5526 7855.

La Cucaracha $$ 3022 Gold Coast Hwy; tel: 5526 9199. Mexican.

Ocolini's Restaurant $ 9 Elkhorn Ave; tel: 5526 9455. Italian. Licensed.

Original Restaurant $$ 2995 Gold Coast Hwy; tel: 5531 7979.

You Japanese Restaurant $$ 9 Beach Rd; tel: 5526 7266.

SURFERS PARADISE

Surfers Paradise boasts 300 days of sunshine a year and the sea is never too cold for swimming, the beach never too hot for sunbathing. The first Western residents were probably two loggers, Edmund Harper and William Duncan, who lived in a hut opposite what is now Wharf Rd. Today's population is somewhere around 30,000 – it is increasing at four times the national average – and in holiday times can be unbearably overcrowded. It is brassy, brash, vibrant and, strangely, does not feel at all Australian. Japanese tourists view it with amazement – and have acquired a large percentage of the real estate and hotel rooms. You either love it or hate it: for some Australians it is a place of annual pilgrimage.

The site was known to the Aboriginal people as Kurrungul (after the hardwood used to make boomerangs) and Cascade Gardens is said to have been one of the meeting places for Aborigines from as far away as Maryborough. In 1923, James Cavill of Brisbane paid $80 for land on which he built the Surfers Paradise Hotel, and then years later the area was renamed, mainly through his efforts, Surfers Paradise.

In the 1960s and '70s large residential tracts were developed by what is termed the 'white shoe brigade' – Queensland business people who wear white buckskin slip-ons trendily scuffed with no socks so that you can admire their brown ankles. Their great belief is that every spare piece of land should have a high-rise. Thus we have the remarkable spectacle of the beach at Surfers Paradise, where the high-rises block out the sun during the day.

The high-pressure sales techniques used to sell these developments as summer homes took its toll when the Asian downturn came and apartment blocks were defaulting on their mortgages. Yet there are signs that the tide is turning. Locals are beginning to want to attract up-market overseas visitors and the new message is that Surfers Paradise is more than sun, sand and sex.

Surfers Paradise was well named, and several major international championships are held here. Most years more than 5,000 competitors congregate here to fight for the national surf lifesaving titles.

Learn to surf at the **School of Surfing**, tel: 5535 6978. The school states that if you can swim it can teach you to stand on a surfboard at sea in only two lessons.

One of the main attractions at **Sea World** is a water-ski spectacular claimed to be Australia's longest-running live show. It is quite remarkably well done. On the other hand, Dolphin Cove may be 'the world's most environmentally friendly, natural lagoon habitat' but it doesn't really compare with the experience of seeing dolphins wild and free, as you can in many other places in Australia. In Shark Encounter, divers hand-feeding sharks, rays and giant groupers is pretty exciting and you can get very close to a variety of fish.

The park also contains a scary corkscrew ride and Australia's first monorail system (far better than the one in Sydney). Sea World is out on The Spit and open daily 0930–1700 ($$$$).

A Miscellany of Attractions

Raptis Plaza, Cavill Mall: a celebration of the odd and outlandish. Open daily 0930–2300. **Conrad Jupiter's:** 24-hr casino with free Learn to Play (or Learn to Lose) lessons in blackjack, roulette and craps. Open Tues–Sat 1015. Reach it by monorail from Broadbeach Mall.

Bungee Downunder, Seaworld Dr: a memorable but expensive experience, captured (at further expense) in videos and photos. Open 1000–dusk.

The nightlife, unsurprisingly, tends towards the noisy and unsubtle. There are literally hundreds of nightspots and their popularity changes from month to month. Nightclubs are also located at Main Beach, Coolangatta and Broadbeach, while the Tallebudgera Playroom regularly plays host to leading Australian and international rock bands.

i **Surfers Paradise Tourist Information Office**, The Mall, Cavill Ave; tel: 5538 4419.
Gold Coast Visitors & Convention Centre, Level 2, 64 Ferny Ave; tel: 5592 2699.

QUEENSLAND

Cross the border into Queensland and you could be forgiven for thinking that you were in another country. In *Australian Accent* (1958) John Douglas Pringle wrote: 'Australians themselves have a saying that when a stranger arrives in Perth, the first question he is asked is, "Where do you come from?"; in Adelaide, "What church do you belong to?"; in Melbourne, "What school were you at?"; in Sydney, "How much money have you got?"; while in Brisbane they merely say, "Come and have a drink".'

Flippant, but it contains a basic truth. Brash, self-confident, laid-back are all terms which can be applied to Queensland, but it is a huge region whose contrasts are also huge. Queensland covers more than 20 per cent of Australia and extends from the arid wastes of the Simpson Desert to lush rainforest, and from the coral cays of the Great Barrier Reef to the cosmopolitan and stylish capital, Brisbane.

Almost all the 3 million inhabitants live in the south-east corner, which leaves the rest of the state fairly empty except for the odd farming village and the occasional anomaly like the mining city of Mount Isa. But any population at all to speak of is a recent phenomenon: as late as 1845 the whole region (which was then still an extension of New South Wales) held only 1,599 settlers. What changed this was timber. Sailing ships could berth quite high up the Tweed, Nerang and Coomera rivers (farming has since lowered the levels) to transport the logs of precious cedar that once grew here in abundance. Farmers followed, and Queensland has properties and stations – farms and ranches – bigger than any others in the world. There are farms as big as some European countries.

Queensland's agriculture is based around beef and sugar. The cattle are continually moved around from the dry areas to the green areas, so on country roads you need to keep an eye out for the road trains which come barrelling along at ferocious speeds laden with cattle. Cane fields cover the river flats and take up most of the countryside for 1,400 km from Nambour to Mossman. The sheer extent of the industry is awe-inspiring, the more so when you know that once all this cane was cut by hand.

It is not just agriculture which is on a big scale. The Selwyn Range holds one of the world's richest deposits of silver, copper, lead and zinc. To deal with this, Mount Isa, the city of the outback, was created (see p. 315).

To get Queensland into perspective, think of it as three roughly parallel strips. That great natural wonder, the Great Barrier Reef, shadows the coastline 100 km out to sea; then there is the coastal strip itself, with its endless beaches. Inland, still running roughly parallel, is the Great Dividing Range, and on the other side of the range is the outback. The outback extends forever. In the north, towards the Gulf of Carpentaria, is the Gulf Country. This is good cattle country but in the wet season some of the smaller towns and homesteads are cut off for weeks.

The rugged challenge of the Far North and the phenomenal expanse of the outback are treasured experiences, but in truth, most visitors only make short forays inland, perhaps up to the Atherton Tableland and Kuranda (see p. 303) — the perfect beaches and the Great Barrier Reef beyond (see p. 276) are so utterly seductive.

It would be wrong to introduce Queensland without mentioning the rule of Joh Bjelke-Peterson, which ran from the early 1970s to the late 1980s. It was generally accepted in the rest of Australia that Joh was as mad as a cut snake and somewhat to the right of Genghis Khan. His government disagreed with the rest of Australia on human rights, rainforest conservation, Aboriginal land rights and censorship. Corruption was part and parcel of the regime and several ex-ministers have served time for their sins, but he led the state to great economic success. In 1977 his abolition of death duties led to waves of Australians — probably around a million — moving into Queensland from other states to take advantage of this new law. Queensland land developers mounted a massive campaign for Joh to become premier of Australia. It failed.

Although Joh is in retirement his policies linger on. Queensland is the state of origin of the One Nation party, with policies that make Joh look like a left-wing pinko. It is against immigration, aid for the Aboriginal people and almost anyone who is not white and Australian born. Sadly, to the shame of the state, it has considerable support within Queensland.

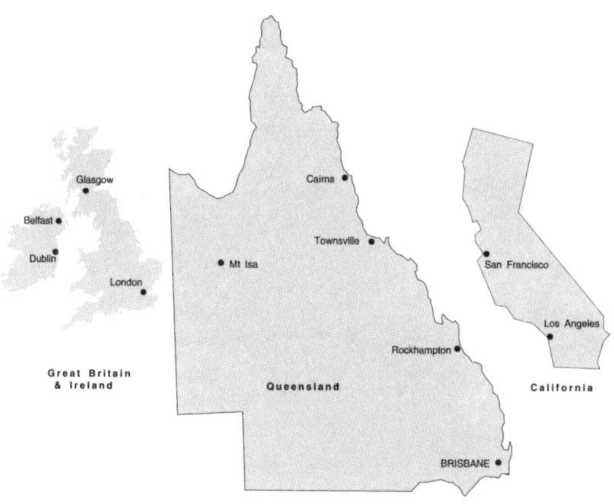

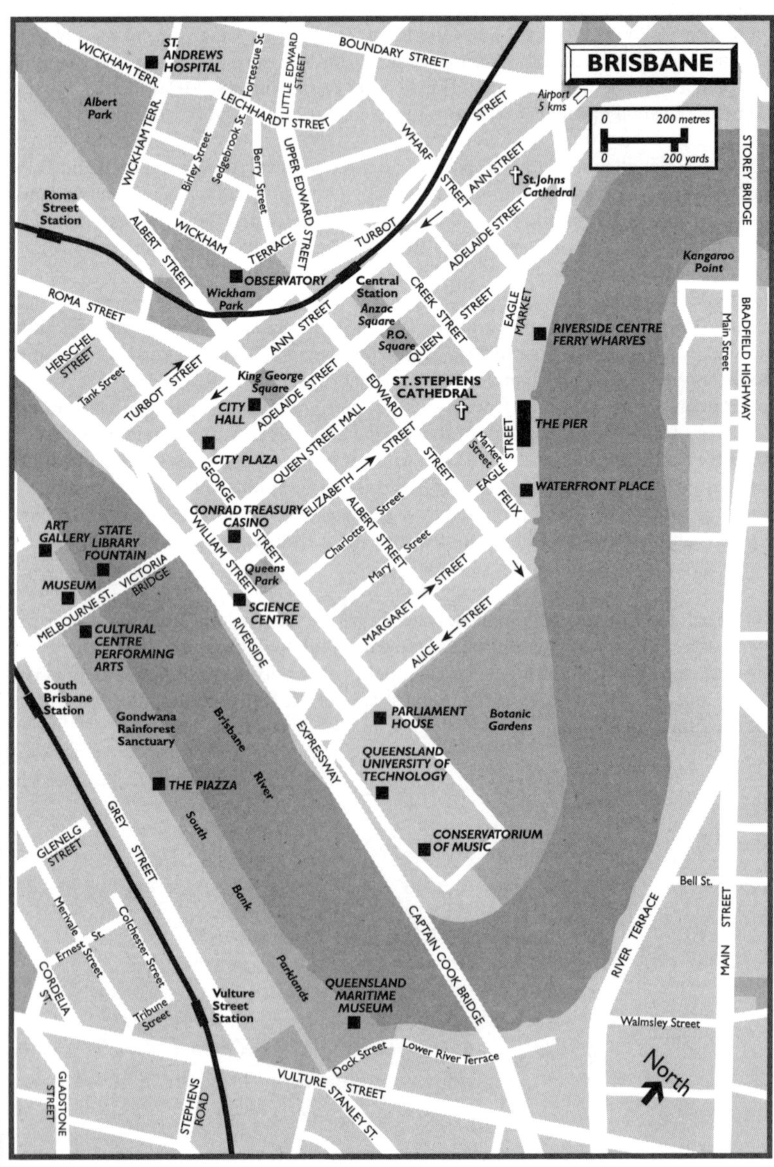
BRISBANE
0 200 metres
0 200 yards
Airport 5 kms
BOUNDARY STREET
WICKHAM TERR.
ST. ANDREWS HOSPITAL
Fortescue St.
LITTLE EDWARD STREET
LEICHHARDT STREET
Albert Park
WICKHAM TERR.
Birley Street
Sedgebrook St.
Berry Street
UPPER EDWARD STREET
WHARF STREET
ANN STREET
St. Johns Cathedral
STOREY BRIDGE
Roma Street Station
ALBERT STREET
WICKHAM TERRACE
TURBOT
ADELAIDE STREET
Kangaroo Point
OBSERVATORY
Wickham Park
Central Station
CREEK STREET
ROMA STREET
Anzac Square
P.O. Square
QUEEN STREET
EAGLE MARKET
RIVERSIDE CENTRE FERRY WHARVES
Main Street
BRADFIELD HIGHWAY
HERSCHEL STREET
Tank Street
TURBOT STREET
ANN STREET
King George Square
CITY HALL
ADELAIDE STREET
EDWARD
ST. STEPHENS CATHEDRAL
THE PIER
CITY PLAZA
QUEEN STREET MALL
STREET
Market Street
EAGLE STREET
GEORGE
ELIZABETH
STREET
WATERFRONT PLACE
FELIX
CONRAD TREASURY CASINO
ALBERT STREET
Charlotte Street
ART GALLERY
STATE LIBRARY
FOUNTAIN
WILLIAM STREET
STREET
Queens Park
Mary Street
MUSEUM
MELBOURNE ST.
VICTORIA BRIDGE
SCIENCE CENTRE
MARGARET STREET
ALICE STREET
CULTURAL CENTRE PERFORMING ARTS
RIVERSIDE
South Brisbane Station
Gondwana Rainforest Sanctuary
Brisbane River
EXPRESSWAY
PARLIAMENT HOUSE
Botanic Gardens
QUEENSLAND UNIVERSITY OF TECHNOLOGY
THE PIAZZA
GREY STREET
South Bank Parklands
CONSERVATORIUM OF MUSIC
GLENELG STREET
Merivale St.
Colchester Street
Ernest Street
CORDELIA ST.
Tribune Street
CAPTAIN COOK BRIDGE
Bell St.
RIVER TERRACE
MAIN STREET
Vulture Street Station
QUEENSLAND MARITIME MUSEUM
Walmsley Street
Dock Street
Lower River Terrace
VULTURE STREET
STANLEY ST.
North
GLADSTONE STREET
STEPHENS ROAD

Brisbane is the third largest city in Australia but it is unlike any other. It is not big as cities go — the population is somewhere over a million – but it has the style, the presence, and the ambience of an international centre. It is possible to date exactly when this happened. Before the 1980s Brisbane was a very pleasant place but it was inward-looking, perhaps a trifle parochial. Then two events changed this for ever and for the better. In 1982 it smartened itself up for the Commonwealth Games, but then came Expo '88, and Brisbane totally reinvented itself. Buildings were refurbished, restaurants opened, and the whole South Bank, which had been an ugly warehouse and industrial area opposite the centre of the city, was brought back to life. Brisbane became one of the most exciting cities in Australia.

Land Rights

As the free settlers spread out into Queensland they took by force and fraud the land belonging to the Aboriginal people. At the time Queensland probably had 100,000 Aboriginal people and they fought fiercely against this white incursion. They lost. By the turn of the century they had been run off their lands, decimated and were made to live in reserves. Only in the past few years have more enlightened policies arisen, with control of the reserves passing to the Aboriginal people. However, the government insists on hanging on to the right of prospecting or mining. The white governments of Australia have much to be ashamed of, and Queensland, perhaps, more than most.

After Expo there was a short period of post coitus tristum but then Brisbane decided to continue and extend the good work. The river banks have been further developed with the Eagle St Complex and the Gateway Marine Centre. More than a decade has passed since that momentous Exposition and the new Brisbane has settled down into its stylish, international and outward-looking mode.

All this, of course, is a far cry from its penal colony beginnings. In 1824 the governor of New South Wales sent Lt Miller to establish a penal settlement up the coast. He set it up originally at Redcliffe Point on Moreton Bay but soon moved it to a more favoured riverside position south of what is now Brisbane's business district. The settlement did not long remain a clutch of convict huts although the convicts were responsible for much of the new building work — the windmill in Wickham Terrace was built in 1828, the commissariat stores in the same year. Despite these civilised additions it was still a convict town and by 1829 it was the largest penal settlement on the Australian mainland, with over 1,000 convicts. Free settlers began to arrive in numbers in 1837 and soon outnumbered the convicts. The penal settlement was abandoned in 1839 and the area was thrown open to free settlers in 1842. As Queensland's huge agricultural and mineral resources were developed, Brisbane grew into a prosperous city; in 1859 the state of Queensland separated from the colony of New South Wales, and Brisbane was declared its capital.

Then everything started to happen in a hurry. In 1865 the present Government House was built and the telegraph to Sydney was connected in 1861. The city had tramways by 1875 and its first railway connection started operating in 1882. A century later the world was its oyster.

ARRIVAL AND DEPARTURE

Brisbane airport is about 15 km north-east of the city, with shuttles running to the transit centre about 500 m west of the city centre. This is also where you will arrive if you're coming by bus or train.

INFORMATION

TOURIST OFFICES **Brisbane City Council Information Booth**, Queen St Mall; tel: 3229 5918.

Brisbane Visitors and Convention Bureau, City Hall, King George Sq.; tel: 3221 8411. Also in Queen St Mall.

Queensland Government Travel Centre, Edward and Adelaide St; tel: 3221 6111.

Queensland Tourist and Travel, 123 Eagle St; tel: 3833 5400.

INTERNET ACCESS **Hub Communications,** The Internet Café, 125 Margaret St; tel: 3229 1119.

Café Kaos, 200 Moggill Rd, Taringa; tel: 3876 7611. Wood-fired pizzas and Internet connections.

INTERNET SITES **Brisbane Stories** http://brisbane-stories.powerup.com.au

Brisbane Central http://www.brisbane-online.com

Brisbane on the Net http://www.brisbaneonthenet.com/

Internet CityWalk Brisbane http://www.citywalk.com.au/

Brisbane: Information for Visitors http://www.dstc.edu.au/brisbane/

Lonely Planet – Destination: Brisbane http://www.lonelyplanet.com/dest/aust/brisbane.htm

Brisbane City Life http://www.maxlink.com.au/bcl/

MONEY Major branches of most banks can be found around Queen and Edward Sts. **Thomas Cook Foreign Exchange** office is at Bowman House, 276 Edward St, Brisbane 4000; tel: 3221 9422.

POST AND PHONES The main post office is at 261 Queen St. The telephone code for Brisbane is 07.

ACCOMMODATION

Astor Motel & Apartments $ 193 Wickham Ter; tel: 3831 9522.

Atoa House $ 95 Annie St, New Farm; tel: 3358 4507.

Aussie Colonial Inn's Tuscany House $ 123 Warry St, Spring Hill; tel: 3257 0799.

Aussie Way $ 34 Cricket St; tel: 3369 0711.

Balmoral House $ 33 Amelia St, Fortitude Valley; tel: 3252 1397.

Brisbane City Travelodge $$ Roma St; tel: 3238 2222.

Brisbane City Youth Hostel $ 392 Upper Roma St; tel: 3236 1004.

Courtney Place $ 50 Geelong St, E. Brisbane; tel: 3891 5166.

Dorchester Inn $$ 484 Upper Edward St; tel: 3831 2967. Self-contained units, walk to city.

Economy Suites $$ 55 Brunswick St; tel: 1800 655 381.

Embassy Hotel $$ Elizabeth St, cnr Edward St; tel: 3221 7616.

Explorers Inn $ 63 Tarbot St; tel: 3311 3485; fax: 3238 2266 SR $110.

Gazebo Hotel $$$ 345 Wickham Ter; tel: 3831 6177.

Metro Inn Tower Mill $$ 239 Wickham Ter; tel: 3832 1421.

FOOD AND DRINK

Bush Tucker Dinner $$ Break O' Day Nature and Heritage Tours take you out of the town for a three course dinner prepared from delicacies such as bunya nuts, wattle seed, crocodile and emu. tel: 3207 5838.

Cafe San Marco $$ South Bank, Mediterranean cuisine with the stunning city skyline across the Brisbane River. Open Mon-Sat 0800–2300. Sun 0700–2230;.tel: 3846 4334.

Capt'n Snapper $ South Bank. Fresh seafood. Licensed. Mon-Thu 1000-2100, Fri-Sun 1100-2200.Tel: 3846 4036.

Casablanca, 52 Petrie Ter, cnr. Caxton St. One km from the city centre. Serves pizza. Licensed. The only restaurant in town which offers Tango and Salsa lessons Sun–Thu. Tel; 3369 6969.

Dashing Food $ 97 Ekibin Rd, Annerley. Monday 0900-1800 Tue-Sun 0900-late. Modern Pacific rim innovative cuisine with a sort of Italian leaning. Good stuff; tel: 3892 5200

Eastern Vegetarian $ 100 Commercial Rd. Just up the road from the old Paddy's Market. Vegetarian. Tel 3852 1033.

Govinda's Vegetarian Restaurant $ 99 Elizabeth St; tel: 3210 0255.

Il Centro $$ 1 Eagle Street Pier. Lunch Sun–Fri. Dinner daily. Licensed. Italian cuisine; tel: 3221 6090.

Io Ti Amo $$ South Bank. Italian cuisine and atmosphere. Seven days 1130-2400; tel: 3846 4599.

Iron Road Restaurant $$. Runs dinner trips according to demand. The dinner trip includes a four-course meal on an old steam locomotive that chugs around Brisbane during the evening. Well worth checking out to see if it is feasible; tel: 3371 4231.

Michael's Riverside $$$ Waterfront Place, 123 Eagle St. Licensed. High quality, perhaps the best in Brisbane; tel: 3832 5522.

Oshin $$ 256 Adelaide St. Lunch Mon–Fri. Dinner Mon–Sat. Licensed. Japanese food; tel: 3229 0410.

Petals At Paddington Natural Cafe $$ 84 Latrobe Ter. Vegetarian; tel: 3367 0717.

Squirrels of Newmarket $$ 184 Enoggera Rd. Vegetarian; tel: 3856 0966.

Wang Dynasty $$ South Bank. Generic Asian fare and panoramic view from the terrace. Mon–Sun 1100–1500, 1700–2230; tel: 3844 8318.

GETTING AROUND

The compact city centre, which focuses on the pedestrianised Queen St, is built along and between the looping meanders of the Brisbane River, so exploring on foot is perfectly practical.

ON YOUR BIKE

One interesting and healthy way of touring the city is by bike. There are 300 km of bike paths in Brisbane and Backpackers Mountain Bike Hire will deliver a bike to your hotel complete with the essential helmet and maps. Tel: (1800) 635 286.

While there are several bridges, a more enjoyable means of getting between banks is by the ferries, which link the city to points such as Kangaroo Point, Dockside and South Bank. You can also catch ferries down the Brisbane River or over to Moreton Bay.

The Day Rover Ticket Unlimited, obtainable at the tourist office, gives one-day travel on buses, ferries and Citycats. The city's fleet of cabs is Black and White taxis, which you can call on 131 008.

HIGHLIGHTS

There are innumerable interesting places to visit in the city, but an integral part of its charm is its brightness, space and sunshine. Brisbane is very much an open, accessible city, partly because of the river, which meanders with a charming lack of logic. Its sinuous curves impart a pleasing shape to the city. Some of Brisbane's individual style also comes from the unique tropical Queensland domestic architecture which still abounds. The traditional bungalow on stilts, with timber walls, lattice screens, shutters and corrugated iron roofing, is eminently functional in a warm, wet climate; it also looks great. For a while it looked as though the developers would knock every single example down and replace them with modern housing, but at last the local authorities and the people of the city have realised how

There is a marked Heritage Trail starting from City Hall, which features colonial landmarks and scenic views. The Visitors' Bureau and most motels and hotels have a booklet.

perfect this architecture is for the climate and the move now is to restoration rather than demolition.

City Hall, overlooking King George Sq, was built in 1931 and contains a circular concert hall with seating for 2,000. Its style is Italian Renaissance modified – that is, Queensland marble, granite and native timbers were used in its construction. Modern skyscrapers now surround it as if to ward off intruders but the observation platform on the clock tower - there is a lift to the top – still has panoramic views of the city and the countryside around. City Hall also houses a museum and art gallery on the ground floor.

The Gothic-style old **St Stephen's** on Elizabeth St was built in 1850 and is the oldest church in Brisbane. Open daily 0800–1800.

Despite its name, you cannot enter **The Observatory** to admire its views, but it has an interesting history, and you can inspect the grounds. It was originally a windmill, built by convict labour in 1828, but due to an error in design (by Captain Patrick Logan, an infamous prison warden who was later murdered but not for this error) it never worked properly. Later it became a punishment centre and convicts were used to make the mill wheels turn. A Quaker mission in 1836 complained of the cruelty of making the prisoners work 14-hour shifts on the mill without rest periods. It was later used as a fire lookout station and a meteorological observatory, and in 1934 it was used for Australia's first experimental TV broadcasts. The Observatory is in Wickham Terrace, just north of the city centre.

The **Commissariat Stores** at 115 William St on North Quay was one of the first permanent buildings in Brisbane. It was built by convicts in 1829 on what was the town's original wharf. Inside are three floors of displays including Aboriginal and convict relics, artefacts, costumes, furniture and paintings. It also houses the offices of the Royal Historical Society of Queensland. Open Tues–Fri 1100–1400, Sun 1100–1600; tel: 3221 4198.

Parliament House, on the corner of George and Alice Sts, was built in 1868 in the style of the French Renaissance. The Public Gallery is open for visitors when parliament is sitting (Tues and Thur 1030–1300, 1430–1800, and from 1930 until House rises; Wed 1430–1800, 1930 until House rises). Guided tours Mon–Fri 1000 and 1400; tel: 3406 7637.

Opposite, in Alice St, are the **Botanic Gardens**, stretching alongside the river. The gardens were designed in 1855 by Walter Hill. There are free tours at 1100 and 1300 Tues–Sun, but the gardens are open from sunrise to sunset if you want to wander around solo.

On the edge of the gardens, **Old Government House** was built in 1862 as the state governor's residence and now houses the headquarters of the National Trust. Queensland's first Government House, built in 1853, is now the deanery for the Anglican cathedral. Open Mon–Fri 0900–1700; tel: 3229 1788.

Across the Victoria Bridge is one of the landmarks of the city. The **Queensland Cultural Centre** covers two blocks on either side of Melbourne St on the south bank of the river, and contains the Queensland Art Gallery, the Queensland Museum, the State Library and a performing arts complex. Each of these is well worth investigating.

The **Queensland Art Gallery** has excellent collections of Australian art, paintings, sculpture, prints and ceramics. It also has some lesser French, European, Asian and English works, antique furniture, silver, glassware and pottery. There are also frequent travelling exhibitions to keep the place on its toes. Open daily 1000–1700, Wed until 2000; tel: 3414 7303.

In the **Queensland Museum** is a vast range of exhibits relating to anthropology, geology, zoology, history and technology. Open daily 0900–1700, Wed until 2000; tel: 3840 7555/7635.

Next to the Cultural Centre and incorporating the old South Brisbane dry dock is the **Queensland Maritime Museum**, which has some exquisitely made models showing the maritime history of the area as well as the steam tug *Forceful*. $ Open 1000–1700; tel: 3844 5361.

The **South Bank Parklands** are 16 ha of landscaped park, rainforest, and a beach facing onto the Brisbane River. The whole area is well served with cafés – well over a dozen – plus a tavern. Within the park, the **Gondwana Rainforest Sanctuary** is a great rainforest experience, with more than 100 species of native Australian wildlife and a pool containing crocodiles. **The South bank Butterfly House**, also in the park, has more than 50 of the world's most deadly giant tarantulas and scorpions. $ Open daily 1000—1800.

OUTSIDE THE CENTRE

Newstead House is Brisbane's oldest surviving residence and is set in parkland on Breakfast Creek, Newstead, on the northern outskirts. The house was built in 1846 for Patrick Leslie with convict labour and has been restored and appropriately furnished. $ Open Mon–Fri 1100–1500, Sun 1400–1700; tel: 3216 1846.

Lone Pine Koala Sanctuary is the oldest, the largest and perhaps the best of the Australian wildlife parks. You can see crocodiles, dingoes, Tasmanian (Tassie) devils, kookaburras, koalas and kangaroos. It is only 11 km from the city on the banks of the Brisbane River at Jesmond Rd, Fig Tree Pocket. $ Open daily 0845–1700; tel: 3222 7278. **Mirimar Cruises** has a vessel going to Lone Pine leaving North Quay daily at 1000; tel: 3221 0300.

MT COOT-THA

Mt Coot-Tha is the best place to get an overall view of the city. It is only 8 km west of the centre but on a clear day you can see across Brisbane to the islands out at sea, and the Glasshouse Mountains which lie to the north. There are well-signposted walks around Mt Coot-Tha and its foothills, and at its foot are Botanic Gardens and the Sir Thomas Brisbane Planetarium, the largest in Australia.

Earlystreet Historical Village is in a reserve of natural forest and includes Queensland heritage buildings, a pub, general store, slab hut and a shipwright's cottage. It is the site of the home of three former Queensland premiers and is in the suburbs at 75 Mcllwraith Ave, Norman Park. $ Open daily 1000–1630; tel: 3398 6866.

SHOPPING

Queen Street Mall runs for two blocks from Edward St to George St and is the main shopping centre of the city, with shops cheaper than those in Melbourne or Sydney.

Brisbane has the climate and the style for markets, of which there are several. Perhaps the best are the arts and crafts **Brunswick Market** in Brunswick St, Fortitude Valley, on Sat morning, and **Riverside Market** in Eagle St which runs all day Sun. The South Bank Market runs Fri night, Sat afternoon and Sun all day.

Cleveland Bayside Markets are open Sun 0900–1500 and are held in Bloomfield St, Cleveland, on the bay. **Paddy's Markets** is across from Kangaroo Point, at the corner of Florence and Macquarie St, and is open daily for extensive undercover shopping from fruit and veg to jewellery, secondhand clothes and books.

NIGHTLIFE

Within the Cultural Centre, the **Queensland Performing Arts Complex** has a concert hall, two theatres and an auditorium which seats 4,700 people; tel: 3840 7190. Concerts are also held at the City Hall (tel: 3403 3038).

The Renaissance-style Treasury Building near Victoria Bridge on the north bank of the river houses Brisbane's 24-hr casino.

DAY TRIPS

The most obvious day trips are out to the islands. At the mouth of the Brisbane River lies Moreton Bay, where there is a plethora of islands. Of these the two most important are Moreton and Stradbroke.

Moreton Island (named after James Douglas, Earl of Morton, but sadly they got his name slightly wrong) is only 40 km from Brisbane. Most of the 19,260 ha of this sand island - beaten only in size by Fraser Island (see p. 261) – is national park, and boasts what is probably the highest sand dune in the world in Mt Tempest (280 m). There is daily access from Holt St Wharf on the *Tangalooma Flyer*. Do not bother taking a car. It is far better to select one of the tours of the island which start and end in Brisbane.

North Stradbroke Island is 20 km off the coast and so about 35 km from Brisbane. It is another sand island, and on weekdays outside the holiday period is very quiet and peaceful. A largely untouched and untouristy nature reserve, it has seven world-class surf beaches, inland lakes, rugged headlands and secluded coves. Point Lookout, at the north-east tip of the island, has some of the best beaches and you can often see dolphins from the headland. Again, although you can take you car it is better to go there on a tour. You can get information from the Stradbroke Island Visitors' Centre which is near the ferry terminal at Dunwich; tel: 3409 9555.

WHERE NEXT?

A short trip inland to Toowoomba (see p. 244) will show you a different side of southern Queensland. North lie miles of beaches and resorts and increasingly tropical towns such as Townsville and Cairns (see pp. 285 and 296), while offshore from Bundaberg is the southern tip of the wondrous Great Barrier Reef (see p. 276).

Toowoomba and the Darling Downs

Most visitors coming to Queensland rarely head into the interior. In doing this they miss much of what Queensland is about. The coast and the Great Barrier Reef are the great tourist attractions but inland lies a great agricultural state with much to offer. On the far side of the Great Dividing Range are the Darling Downs, whose rolling plains are some of the most fertile agricultural land in Australia.

Toowoomba, on the rim of the mountain range, is Queensland's largest inland city and the commercial centre for the Darling Downs. The town has a very full cultural and social life with many galleries and museums. There are also several historical buildings and sites, and the area is full of pleasant scenic drives.

ARRIVAL AND DEPARTURE

You can fly to Toowoomba, but it is only 138 km from Brisbane, about 2½ hrs by car or bus. The town is some 600–800 m above sea level and from Brisbane the route is along the Warrego Highway which makes its way up the escarpment of the Great Dividing Range.

INFORMATION

Toowoomba & Golden West Regional Tourist Association, 4 Little St; tel: (07) 4632 1988.

ACCOMMODATION

Allan Cunningham Motel $ 8 Ruthven St; tel: 4035 5466.

Bridge St. Motor Inn $ 291 Bridge St; tel: 4034 3299.

Burke & Wills Toowoomba Hotel $$ 554 Ruthven St; tel: 4032 2433.

Chalet Motel $ 1 High St; tel: 4035 3422.

Coachman Motel $ 4 Burnage St; tel: 4039 3707.

Downs Motel $ 669 Ruthven St; tel: 4039 3811.

Flying Spur Motel $ 277 Taylor St; tel: 4034 3237.

Garden City Motor Inn $ 718 Ruthven St; tel: 4035 5377.

Gateway Motel $ 41 Margaret St; tel: 4032 2088.

Jacaranda Place Motor Inn $$ 794 Ruthven St; tel: 4035 3111.

Raceview Motor Inn $$ 52 Hursley Rd; tel: 4034 6777.

Ruthven St. Motor Inn $ 786 Ruthven St; tel: 4036 1366.

Toowoomba Motel $$ 2 Burnage St; tel: 4039 3993.

FOOD AND DRINK

Banjo's, The Great Aussie Restaurant $ Ruthven South St, cnr Hanna Crt; tel: 4036 1033.

Casa Mia Pasta $ 205 Margaret St; tel: 4038 5909.

Cobbers Restaurant $$ 26 Russell St. BYO. Tel: 4032 7773.

Colonial Curry House $ 120 Bridge St; tel: 4039 1881.

Da Vinci's Italian Restaurant $$ 22 Hill St. BYO. Tel: 4038 4606.

Golden Dragon Chinese Restaurant $ 250 Margaret St; tel: 4038 1258.

Indira's Indian Restaurant $ Fay Court; tel: 4036 4222.

La Pizzaiola $ 173 Margaret St; tel: 4032 2997.

Mexican Cantina $ 491 Ruthven St; tel: 4038 1888.

Squatters Restaurant $$ 2 Burnage St; tel: 4039 1139.

Thai Cottage $ 160 Margaret St. BYO. Tel: 4032 2194.

HIGHLIGHTS

Toowoomba began life in 1849 as a village near an important staging post for teamsters and travellers. To be technically accurate, the first village was where the suburb of Drayton now exists, and Drayton and Toowoomba were once two separate settlements. Toowoomba was originally known as The Swamp, but the Aboriginals called it t'wamp bah or 'place of large stinging insects', which eventually was anglicised into Toowoomba.

The **town hall**, said to be the first in Queensland, was built in 1862, and because of Toowoomba's position as, effectively, the capital of the Darling Downs area, it quickly became a relatively wealthy city. By the turn of the century this was reflected in the erection of several very solid Victorian buildings and the planting of shade trees in the streets, which are now such a distinguishing mark of the city.

WINDMILLS

A large foundry was established here in 1871, its main successful products being the Southern Cross and Simplex windmills which are such a feature of the landscape. These are not windmills in the old English and Dutch sense, but modern windmills which glisten in the sun and are mainly used to pump up water from underground sources.

At the information office there is a brochure suggesting a self-conducted tour around the remarkably elegant and charming buildings in the centre of the city.

The **Cobb & Co. Museum** traces the history of horse-drawn vehicles in Australia. Although Cobb & Co. was originally an American company it had much to do with the development of Australia, and this museum, part of the Queensland Museum, covers not just the activities of the company but the whole subject of horse-drawn transportation in Australia. Of its kind it is the most comprehensive museum in Australia. 27 Lindsay St; open Mon–Fri 1000–1600, Sat–Sun 1300–1600.

The National Trust now owns the **Royal Bulls Head Inn** in Brisbane St, Drayton. This is appropriate because this well-preserved building was not just a pub; the first religious service on Darling Downs was held here in 1848, when the Revd Benjamin Glennie held a service in one of the rooms. Open Thur–Mon 1000–1600.

ON TO THE DOWNS

There are several scenic drives from Toowoomba, such as the 48 km circuit to Spring Bluff and Murphy's Creek, and the 100 km circuit to Heifer Creek, known as the Valley of the Sun.

On the eastern side of the town is **Picnic Point Lookout** which has a camera obscura. This splendid device – open 1000–1400 – gives you an amazing view of the surrounding country. It was, incidentally, such a device that Canaletto used to help create his marvellous landscapes.

There are over 1,000 ha of parkland within the city. The principal central ones are **Lake Annand, Laurel Bank, Queens** and **Webb Park**. Next to Queens Park are the **Botanical Gardens**, which are well worth visiting.

WHERE NEXT?

If you are travelling north, an interesting but very different foray inland from Cairns up to the Atherton Tablelands is described on *p. 304.*

LONG-DISTANCE ROUTE: BRISBANE TO CAPE YORK

Driving up the east coast of Australia, the great navigator's dictum – keep Australia on your left – springs to mind. The road from Brisbane to Cairns – which is Rte I but also goes by the all-Australian name of the Bruce Hwy – makes you do precisely that. If you deviate to the right you come very quickly to the South Pacific Ocean. If you deviate to the left you will see looming in front of you the Great Dividing Range.

The long distances – 750 km in a day is not considered out of the ordinary – are relatively easy because in most cases the roads are straight and there is little traffic joining the highway. That said, the journey right the way up to the northern tip of Australia is an extremely long one: 2750 km from Brisbane, and without crossing a state border. The following chapters deal with it in several stages, and depending on your schedule, your inclinations and the time of year, it will probably make sense to fly at least certain legs. All the stopping points have airports, and there is even a jet airport out on the Great Barrier Reef, on Hamilton Island.

The first stage north from Brisbane goes to Bundaberg, the ërum capitalí, with Frasier Isand an unmissable detour on the way. The Great Barrier Reef roughly parallels the coast from here right the way up to Cape York and beyond.

Then itís on to Townsville, Australiaís largest tropical city. From Townsville to Cairns, a distance of 350 km, there is not much to detain you on the seaward side apart from access to the reef, but a number of national parks and the Atherton Tableland are worth exploring.

Cairns and beyond is truly the Far North. Across the Daintree River the going gets tough. You can drive, if you have a 4-wheel-drive vehicle and an experienced driver, via the controversial Daintree/Bloomfield Road. On that run, Cairns to Cooktown is about 212 km, but this road creates serious controversy because 32 km of it was slashed virtually parallel to the coast through virgin rainforest from Cape Tribulation to Bloomfield in 1984. The road cuts nearly 200 km off the trip from Cairns to Cooktown but arouses anger among conservationists.

On the other hand, you could try coming up the coastal track which is considered by many to be the worst road in Australia. This is only to be attempted with a 4-wheel-drive vehicle – and then only in the dry.

Cooktown is also served by sea and air, with regular services available from Cairns.

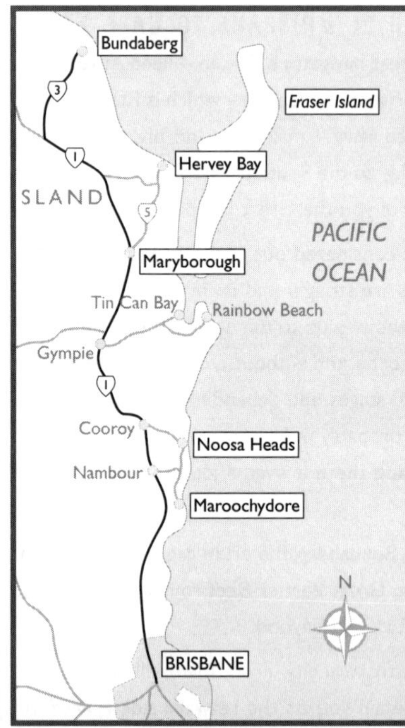

Brisbane – Bundaberg
OTT Tables 9013/9082

Transport	Frequency	Journey Time
Train	Daily see note	5hrs 40mins
Bus	8 Daily	7hrs

Brisbane – Cooroy
OTT Tables 9013/9082

Transport	Frequency	Journey Time
Train	Daily see note	1hr 54mins
Bus	8 Daily	2hrs 10mins

Cooroy – Gympie
OTT Tables 9013/9082

Transport	Frequency	Journey Time
Train	Daily see note	40mins
Bus	8 Daily	1hr 5min

Gympie – Maryborough
OTT Tables 9013/9082

Transport	Frequency	Journey Time
Train	Daily see note	1hr
Bus	8 Daily	1hr 5mins

Note: Train goes to Maryborough West.

Maryborough – Childers
OTT Tables 9082

Transport	Frequency	Journey Time
Bus	10 Daily	1hr 35mins

Maryborough – Bundaberg
OTT Tables 9013

Transport	Frequency	Journey Time
Train	Daily see note	1hr 5mins

Childers – Bundaberg
OTT Tables 9082

Transport	Frequency	Journey Time
Bus	8 Daily	1hr 15mins

Note: There are local bus services from Brisbane to Maroochydore and from Maryborough to Hervey Bay.

Route Detail

Up to Maroochydore the highway runs through an almost totally built-up area – it is only where the highway swings slightly inland at Buderim that you get out of the busiest tourist belt. Maroochydore (100 km from Brisbane) is on a short detour which will carry you on through Bli Bli and Noosa Heads to rejoin the main highway at Cooroy. At Gympie an alternative to the direct road to Maryborough is to detour along the coast to Tin Can Bay and Rainbow Beach. From Maryborough it is a short (21 km) side route to Hervey Bay, the hopping-off point for Fraser Island, or 115 km through Childers to Bundaberg. Total journey approximately 400 km.

Notes

Along with the daily PM train between Brisbane and Rockhampton there are other services that run on various days.

The Sunshine Coast

This is where most of Australia wants to come to retire and a large percentage want to come and spend their holidays. After the high-rise razzmatazz of the Gold Coast, the coastal scene north of Brisbane starts to calm down; by the time you get to Maroochydore things are much more civilised. Beyond the ribbon development, places such as Noosa Heads are all pastel colours and sunshine and trendy cafés, while offshore is Fraser Island, one of Australia's most amazing natural sites. Bundaberg, where Australia's rum comes from, is a lovely city with some considerable presence.

En Route

Bribie Island marks the start of an amazing range of beaches stretching north. Golden Beach has most of the pleasanter water sports while on the foreshore there are shady parks with bunya trees.

In **Caloundra** is a replica of Captain Cook's ship, the ***Endeavou***r. Although built to two-thirds scale, it gives you a very clear idea of the size of the ship in which Cook set off to explore the world. It is on display on Landsborough Parade, open daily 0900–1630. On a rather different level of appeal, Teddy Bear World and Museum at 26 Bowman Rd has over 3,000 teddy bears set up in fantasy scenes. Open daily 1000–1600.

MAROOCHYDORE

Maroochydore caters for tourists in a serious way but the countryside behind, the greenery and the long beaches more than make up for it. Until the tourist boom in the 1960s, Maroochydore was little more than a fly speck where paddle steamers could load up and then head off to Brisbane. A highlight in its history came in 1826 when a convict called John Graham escaped here from Moreton Bay, under the impression, allegedly, that he could row to China. He was adopted by the local Aboriginal people until 1833 when he gave himself up. No more was heard of him on his release four years later, but he had his allotted 15 minutes of fame.

Maroochydore is lucky in its location: between the Maroochy and Mooloolah rivers, with green lushness in the hinterland, the mountains beyond and 25 km of beautiful beaches. The rivers provide safe swimming areas while the beaches can pick up an excellent surf. The **Blackall Range**, only half an hour's drive from the town, is an area full of arts and crafts workers so that every turn of the road seems to bring you to a studio with goods on display and for sale.

The town extends into the Maroochy estuary with Pincushion Island as a pimple off the point. On the right-hand side of the peninsula Maroochydore Beach runs down to Alexandra Headland and **Mooloolaba**, 5 km to the south. The Wharf at Mooloolaba is less of a wharf and more of a shopping and restaurant centre, created in the style of a 19th-century fishing village. **Underwater World** here claims to be the largest tropical oceanarium in the southern hemisphere. There is a 'theatre of the sea', performing seals and a transparent tunnel to enable you to 'walk' among the fish. Open daily 0900–1800. The Mooloolaba Yacht Club hosts a blue-water classic Sydney–Mooloolaba race.

Maroochy River Cruises offers a series of different trips throughout the day. Tel: (018) 71 3275. Or from Mooloolaba there is a wide range of cruises available, nearly all of them leaving from the Wharf. Two are **Gemini Reef Cruises**, tel: 5444 6077 and **Sunshine Coast Ferry**, tel: 5478 0088.

Maroochy Tourist Information Centre, Cnr Sixth Ave and Aerodrome Rd; tel: 5479 1566.

Many of the motels are on Sixth Ave and out of the season you never need to book. There are also several apartment blocks for let on a weekly basis but these tend to be on the expensive side.

Beach Houses $$ Cnr Sixth Ave and Beach Pde; tel: 5443 3049. Self-contained. Beachside. Near restaurants, shops.

Beach Motor Inn $$ 61 Sixth Ave; tel: 5443 7044. Close to surf beach, restaurants and plaza.

Maroochy River Motel $$ 363 Bradman Ave; tel: 5443 3142.

Maroochydore Hotel Motel $ Duporth Ave; tel: 5443 1999.

Wunpalm Motel $ Phillip St. cnr Duporth Ave; tel: 5443 4677.

Maroochydore is an extension of the Gold Coast – you could call it its last gasp of vulgarity – and basically offers resort food, which means it's not a gourmet's heaven. However, the food is piled high and the prices are acceptably low.

BC's Mexican Restaurant $ Aerodrome Rd, cnr Second Ave; tel: 5443 5155.

Bullockies Pioneer Restaurant $$ 80 Sixth Ave; tel: 5443 6665.

Hathi Indian Restaurant $ 14 Aerodrome Rd; tel: 5443 5411. Unusual to find an Indian restaurant in this area. The food is modified for local tastes. BYO.

Santa Lucia Ristorante $$ Aerodrome Rd, cnr Rose Rd; tel: 5443 4530. Traditional Italian.

Signatures Seafood Restaurant $$ 6 Duporth Ave; tel: 5443 6401.

En Route

An appealing detour is to Kenilworth, which can be approached either from Eumundi on the Bruce Hwy or from Nambour via Mapleton through the Obi Obi Valley – either route is picturesque. Activities include bushwalking, gem fossicking and creek fishing for freshwater mullet, bass, perch and cod. The **Ginger Factory** at Yandina is the largest ginger processing factory in the world. You are encouraged to buy samples at the end of your tour.

Thai Garden Restaurant $$ 9 Wirraway St; tTel: 5443 5166. Fairly authentic Thai.

NOOSA HEADS

Noosa is Australia's very own St Tropez. It has international sophistication but with a laid-back, carefree approach to life. Hastings St is a bit like Rodeo Dr in Los Angeles in its number of highly attractive and highly expensive shops. These are interspersed with restaurants, pavement bistros and beachfront apartments.

Europeans first came in 1842. Then, when the surfers discovered its north-facing beach and perfect rollers 120 years later, tourism and the developers followed. But Noosa made a simple rule: no building can be higher than a palm tree. Although the rule has been broken many times the town has avoided all excess and remains charming.

Noosa Heads Tourist Information Centre, Hastings St; tel: 5447 4988.
Noosanetcafe, 2 Palms Arcade, Lanyana Way; tel: 5474 5770; email info@noosanetcafe.com.au.

Noosa Heads vies with Byron Bay (see p. 323) as the most popular resort in Australia. There are some very upmarket places – the golden people of Sydney see it as a second home – but also a lot of affordable accommodation. Much of this is along Noosa Pde and Hastings St.
Hotel Laguna $$ 6 Hastings St; tel: 5447 3077. Motel-style apartments with balconies overlooking the river or Hastings St.
Koala Beach Resort $ 44 Noosa Dr; tel: 5447 3355.
Le Court Villas $$ Key Court, cnr Noosa Pde; tel: 5447 4522.
Maison la Plage $$$ 5 Hastings St; tel: 5447 4400. 23 apartments. Large, heated saltwater pool and spa set in tropical gardens overlooking the sea. Yes, it is expensive, but for a party of four it is manageable.
Noosa Lakes Resort $$ Hilton Ter, Noosaville; tel: 5447 1400. Big resort between the lake and river which specialises in conferences but also individual visitors.
Regatta Holiday Apartments $$ 221–7 Gympie Ter, Noosaville; tel: 5449 0522. Overlooking the Noosa River. Fully

EN ROUTE

One of the pleasanter detours between Noosa and Gympie is to Kin Kin. Head first for Boreen Point, a small town on Lake Cootharaba, then on to Kin Kin and Pomona. Pomona has what is almost certainly the longest-running silent movie theatre, the Majestic Theatre, in the world, complete with a Wurlitzer pipe organ. The cinema operates in a series of festivals (check with the tourist office).

self-contained. Works out very affordable if you are booking as a family outside of the holiday season.

Seahaven Beachfront Resort $$ Hastings St; tel: 5447 3422.

This is probably one of the great dining resorts of Australia. In Noosa Heads itself Hastings St alone has 32 quality cafés and restaurants. And up the road in Noosa Junction is another great selection, which tend to be somewhat less expensive.

Aqua Bar Cafe $$ 10 Hastings St; tel: 5447.

Barry's On The Wharf $$ 279 Quamby Pl; tel: 5447 4277.

China World Chinese Restaurant 1 David Low Way; tel: 5447 4725.

Chinois On Hastings $$ 18 Hastings St; tel: 5449 2200.

Coco's $$ 62 Park Rd; tel: 5447 2440.

Dilozos $$ Hastings St; tel: 5447 2855.

Eduardo's on the Beach $$ 25 Hastings St; tel: 5447 5875. Open daily for breakfast, lunch and dinner. BYO. International cuisine.

Jr's Restaurant Cafe & Bar $$ Sunshine Beach Rd; tel: 5449 2255.

Laguna Bay Beach Club $$ Hastings St; tel: 5449 4793. Ocean views. Greek Italian cuisine. Open daily.

Quarterdeck Restaurant $$ 73 Noosa Dr; tel: 54492851.

Rosers $$ 1 Hastings St; tel: 5447 3880. Open daily for lunch, dinner. Seafood. Licensed.

Saltwater $$ 8 Hastings St; tel: 5447 2234. Open daily for lunch and dinner. Seafood. Licensed.

Tea Tree Cafe $$ Hastings St; tel: 5449,4787.

HIGHLIGHTS

The Noosa Parks Association campaigns actively towards keeping Noosa distinctly different from over-developed resort areas, keeping the river and its lakes the most natural in Queensland, creating a protective green belt around Noosaville and Tewantin and preserving wildlife corridors into the forests. Drive up to **Laguna Lookout** on Noosa Hill and the view will attest to their success: scenes of unspoilt green bushland, rainforest and river. This flora and fauna sanctuary is one of the few places in Australia where it is possible to easily see a koala in the wild.

There are certain walks which have almost become rituals. Stroll along Gympie St and see the sun setting on the other bank of the river among the mangroves. Or take

COOLOOLA NATIONAL PARK

This park, just north of Noosa, protects the largest intact sand dune system in the world. In addition to the coloured sand cliffs it has rainforest, open forest and heathlands, extensive beaches and peaceful lakes. Many tracks within the park are 4-wheel-drive only but there are day tours and safaris available from several sources in Noosa Heads (details from the tourist office). It is possible to take a 4-wheel-drive to the North Shore and then on to Teewah Beach, view the wreck of the Cherry Venture, wrecked here when she was hit by a cyclone in 1973, and eventually end up at Rainbow Beach, gateway to the World Heritage-listed Fraser Island (see p. 261).

a walk along the recently constructed boardwalk from Hastings St to Noosa National Park past peaceful coves, spectacular cliffs and natural heathland to the secluded beaches of Alexandria Bay. (This is Noosa's nudist beach, where every year they hold the Nude Olympics. The mind boggles.) Continue on and make it a half-day stroll right through the park to Sunshine Beach.

Noosa National Park rejoices in the fact that it is the most visited national park in Queensland. The entrance is just a short distance from the town centre and a series of tracks lets you explore rainforest, open eucalypt woodland, scrub and grasslands, and rocky headlands running right to the sea.

A ferry at Tewantin crosses the river for access to **Cooloola National Park** and **Teewah Beach**, famed for its coloured sands (the House of Bottles sells bottles of these as souvenirs). The sandy cliffs, up to 200 m high, contain as many as 72 different coloured sands, produced by combinations of iron oxide and leached vegetable dyes. An Aboriginal legend connects their formation to the destruction of a rainbow by a huge boomerang.

MARYBOROUGH

Maryborough, started as a wool port in 1847, is one of Queensland's oldest cities and in the early days of European settlement it was second only to Sydney as an immigration port for free settlers. In the usual conflict with the local aboriginal people, the actions of the settlers, from exile to wholesale slaughter, were little short of horrific. On Christmas Eve, 1851, many who had been exiled to Fraser Island were driven into the sea to die by native police under the local white commandant, a sad chapter in Australia's history.

The affluence that accompanied the 1867 gold rush, which centred on Gympie, brought major building to the town, and several now have heritage status. One of the most interesting is **Baddow House** at 364 Queen St, which was built in 1883 for

TRAINS PAST AND PRESENT

Maryborough is a train town. Queensland's first steam locomotive, the *Mary Ann*, was built here, as are the latest tilt trains (such as the City of *Maryborough* which runs between Brisbane and Rockhampton). A replica of the *Mary Ann* is being constructed and will run from Wharf St, through Queens Park, to the Central Railway Station in Lennox St, which is being converted into a railway museum; tel: 4723 9261 for an appointment to view.

The historic Mary Valley line is one of the great train rides of Australia. The scenic 40-km journey crosses the Mary River and its major tributaries, passing through small villages with an abundance of curves, gradients and bridges and a tunnel to its final destination, Imbil. It runs each Sun at 1000 from Gympie.

More engineering marvels can be seen at the Olds Engine House and Works at 78 North St, the work of the late William Olds who was a model engineer. Open Thur 0930–1600; tel: 4721 3649.

Edgar Thomas Aldridge, who established trading and wool stores as well as the original Bush Inn (now the Royal Hotel). It has been restored to its full glory and is open daily 1000–1600; tel: 4723 1883.

Brennan and Geraghty's Store in Lennox St, now owned by the National Trust, was run by the same family for over a century and gives a detailed picture of life in the area. Open daily 1000–1500.

Every Thur the two main streets are closed to traffic to make way for the market, selling hand-crafted items, home-made food, or fruit and vegetables. It is a major attraction, full of shoppers from early morning until mid-afternoon. At 1300 on these days the time cannon is fired in the market. This is a replica of the cannon that was originally fired daily when the time signal was received from Brisbane.

Maryborough and District Tourist information centre, 30 Ferry St; tel: 4121 4111.
Maryborough City Life www.dkd.net/maryboro/index.html

Arkana Inn $$ 46 Ferry St; tel: 4121 2261.
Cara Motel $ 196 Walker St; tel: 4122 4288.
Carriers Arms Hotel Motel $ 405 Alice St; tel: 4122 2244.
City Motel $ 138 Ferry St; tel: 4121 2568.
Huntsville Caravan Park $ 23 Gympie Rd; tel: 4121 4075.
Lamington Hotel Motel $ 33 Ferry St; tel: 4121 3295.
Mcnevin's Parkway Motel $ 188 Johns St; tel: 4122 2888.
Royal Hotel Motel $ 340 Kent St; tel: 4121 2241.

FLOOD

In February 1999, the Mary River rose at Maryborough to 8.75 m above its normal level. Such floods are a regular problem: during the worst,

Flood (cont)
in 1893, the river peaked at over 12 m, washing away more than 100 houses, devastating farms and plantations, and destroying the sawmill. Fortunately, Maryborough now gets plenty of warning, enabling precautions to be taken. Many establishments leave their doors and windows open so that the flood water can flow through rather than damage the building.

Spanish Motor Inn $ 499 Alice St, opposite golf course; tel: 4121 2858.
Wattle Grove Motel $$ 65 Derby Rd, 3465; tel: (054) 61 1877.

This is not a gourmet city and the best bet is one of the Chinese restaurants which invariably open daily for lunch and dinner.
Cafe Vita Bella $ 133 Lennox St; tel: 4123 5720.
Colonial Kitchen $$ 115 March St; tel: 4123 2700.
Gardenia Restaurant $$ 193 Adelaide St; tel: 4121 4967.
Lucky Chinese Restaurant $ 302 Kent St; tel: 412 13645.
Mimosa Restaurant $$ 389 Kent St; tel: 41231459.
Restaurant Bali $ March St, Cnr Bowen St; tel: 4121 5211.
Riverview On Wharf Street Restaurant $$ 106 Wharf St; tel: 4123 1000.

HERVEY BAY

The main reason to visit Hervey – pronounced Harvey – Bay is to arrange a trip to Fraser Island (see p. 261) or to go whale watching. Like most resort areas in Australia, Hervey Bay saw rapid growth as a holiday destination in the 1970s and is an agglomeration of what were once separate towns. It was promoted as Australia's family aquatic playground, which, oddly, it is. There is no surf and box jelly fish do not trespass in this area, so swimming is safe even for children. It also rejoices under the title of Caravan Capital of Australia.

Bay Tourist Information Centre, 333 The Esplanade; tel: 4124 6911.
Hervey Bay Central Booking Office, 363 Esplanade; tel: 4124 1300.
Hervey Bay Tourism and Development Bureau, Bideford St, Hervey Bay; tel: 4124 9609.
Hervey Bay Tourist and Visitors' Centre, 63 Old Maryborough Rd; tel: 4124 4050.
Hervey Bay www.hervey.com.au

Bayview Motel $ 399 Esplanade St; tel: 4128 1134.
Beaches Hervey Bay Backpackers $ 195 Torquay Ter; tel: 4124 1322.
Colonial Lodge $$ 94 Cypress St; tel: 4125 1073; email

WHALE WATCHING

Now that whaling is banned by international treaty these splendid creatures are increasing at a rate of over 10 per cent a year and about 3,000 humpback whales now migrate between Antarctica and the Great Barrier Reef. After giving birth in the warm waters of north Queensland, mothers and calves stop in Hervey Bay to rest before completing their journey south. They can start arriving in late July and may be seen until Nov; Aug to mid-Oct is the surest period.

As many as 30 whales come into the bay at the same time. It is not just their size that is so impressive – humpbacks are the most sporting of the species and they leap, roll and breach as if they, too, were on holiday. It is one of the rare and great sights of the world. They also sing and you can hear them from some of the cruise boats equipped with underwater listening devices.

The many operators who offer whale-watching cruises all work within strict restrictions as to how close they can approach. However, the current thought is that the whales have become much more comfortable with cruise vessels and there is little danger of them being frightened off. Tours (half- or full-day) all leave from Urangan boat harbour and operators include:

Islander Whale Watch Cruises, tel: 4125 3399. This runs the largest cruise vessel.

Mimi Macpherson's Whale Watch Expeditions, tel: 4124 7247. The owner is the sister of Elle (which irritates other operators, as this is the one that gets all the publicity. In fact, she has been running these tours since 1989.) Tours depart 1000, return 1630. The boat, *Discovery One*, is a 25-m catamaran.

Whale Watch Safari Mikat, 45 Cunningham St; tel: 4125 1522. Day-cruise with the emphasis on education and explanation. Departs at 0830.

Colonial@Cyberalink.com.au. Self-contained holiday units.
Delfinos Bay Resort $$ 383 The Esplanade; tel: 4124 1666.
Fraser Lodge Carapark $ Fraser St; tel: 4125 1502.
Lisianna Apartments $ 338 Esplanade, Scarness; tel: 4124 2950.
Playa Concha Motor Inn $$ 475 Esplanade St; tel: 4125 1544.
Reef Motel $ 410 Esplanade St; tel: 4125 2744.
Tower Court Motel $ 459 Esplanade St; tel: 4125 1322.

Black Dog Cafe $$ 381 Esplanade, Torquay; tel: 4124 3177. Sushi, teriyaki, salads. Open 1030–1500, 1730–late, but closed for dinner Tues.

Blazing Saddles $$ 140 Freshwater Rd, Torquay; tel: 4125 5466. Steak and seafood. Open weekdays 1100–late, Sat–Sun 1600–late.

Boardwalk Cafe $ Great Sandy Straits Marina Resort, Urangan; tel: 4125 4799. Steak and seafood. Open daily 0700–late.

Brollies Deli Cafe $ 353 Esplanade. Scarness; tel: 4128 1793. Café food. Continental deli breakfast, lunch and dinner. Open Mon–Fri 0800–1700, Sat 0800–1400.

Cassies $ 475 Esplanade, Torquay; tel: 4125 1544. Inexpensive bistro. Open daily 1730–late.

Curried Away $ 174 Boat Harbour Drive Pialba; tel: 4124 1577. Sri Lankan curries. Open daily 1630–late.

Delfinos Restaurant $$ 383 Esplanade, Scarness; tel: 4124 2466. Seafood. Open daily 1800–late.

Dolly's Restaurant $$ 410 Esplanade, Torquay; tel: 4125 5633. Stylish, somewhat upmarket. Open daily 1730–late.

Don Camillo Ristorante Italiano $ 486 Esplanade, Torquay; tel: 4125 1087. The waiting staff did not know it was named after the fictional character created by Giovanni Guareschi. Open daily 1830–late.

Goody's On the Beach $$ 54 Moreton St, Toogoom; tel: 4128 0227. Open Wed–Sun 1000–late for lunch and dinner.

Marina's by the Bay $$ 385 Esplanade, Torquay; tel: 4125 4522. Open daily for breakfast lunch and dinner. International cuisine.

Sails Brasserie and Cafe $$ 433 Esplanade, Torquay; tel: 4125 5170. Modern Australian-European cuisine with Asian flavours. The best restaurant in the area. Closed Sun. Dinners only except Thur–Fri.

Sirens $$ 465 Esplanade, Torquay. Closed Mondays otherwise 0730–late. Steak and seafood. Tel: 4125 6285.

The Deck $$ Hervey Bay Marina, Buccaneer Ave, Urangan; tel: 4125 1155. Light meals intended for healthy eating. Lunch only daily.

BUNDABERG

Bundaberg ranks with Cairns and Coffs Harbour as one of the three principal clearing ports for visiting yachts on the east coast. It is also the southernmost access point to the Great Barrier Reef, so it must be very irritating for the citizens of Bundaberg to know that all other Australians automatically think of rum when the name of the town is mentioned. Sugar growing was established in the 19th century using Pacific Islanders who had been tricked - perhaps kidnapped would be more accurate - into working in the cane fields. The first rum distillery was built in 1888.

But Bundaberg has much more going for it than its rum, however excellent. It is a city of parks and botanical gardens, with wide streets lined with poincianas which give a brilliant display in spring. The Burnett River adds to the charm of the place, with boating and rowing at Sandy Hook and sailing downstream near the port.

i **Bundaberg District Tourism and Development Board,** cnr Mulgrave and Bourbong Sts or PO Box 930; tel: 4152 2333.
Information Centre, cnr of Bourbong St and Tallon Bridge. One of the best of its kind in Queensland. You can get more brochures than you can comfortably carry. Open daily 0900–1700.
Bundaberg sunzine.net/bundaberg/

Motels here are much less expensive than other places in Queensland. The two main motel streets are Bourbong and Takalvan. If you do not have a booking, cruise down these until you find something you like. You will have no problem in finding a place to suit your budget.
Acacia Motor Inn $$ 248 Bourbong St; tel: 4152 3411.
Alexandra Park Motor Inn $ 66 Quay St; tel: 4152 7255.
Bourbong St Motel $ 265 Bourbong St; tel: 4151 3089.
Butterfly Checkmate Motel $ 240 Bourbong St; tel: 4152 2700.
Casper Motel $ 80 Takalvan St; tel: 4153 1100.
Chalet Motor Inn $ 242 Bourbong St; tel: 4152 9922.
Charm City Motel $ 23 Takalvan St; tel: 4152 2284.
Gunnadoo Motel $ 83 Water St; tel: 4151 4346. Quiet, friendly.
Kaula Motel $ 4a Hinkler Ave; tel: 4151 3049.
Oscar Motel $ 252 Bourbong St; tel: 4152 3666.
Reef Gateway Motor Inn $$ 11 Takalvan St; tel: 4153 2255.

Art Gallery Restaurant $$ 73 Takalvan St; tel: 4151 2365.
Bert Hinkler Restaurant $$ Warrell St, cnr Takalvan St; tel: 4152 6400.

De George's Restaurant $$ 238 Bourbong St; tel: 4153 1770.
Eastern Pearl Chinese Restaurant $ 268a Bourbong St; tel: 4151 5145.
Il Gambero Restaurant $$ 57 Targo St; tel: 4152 5342.
Mexican Border Restaurant $$ 27 Elliott Heads Rd; tel: 4152 1675. BYO.
Sizzler Steak $$ 222 Bourbong St; tel: 4153 3210.
Spinnaker Stonegrill $$ On the river front at Quay St; tel: 4152 8033. Jazz at the weekends. Licensed. Open daily lunch and dinner.
Wahdu Restaurant $ 4 Queen St; tel: 4151 3845.

HIGHLIGHTS

The **Bundaberg Rum Distillery** has tours for visitors but, sadly, no free samples. The distillery is off the road to Bargara and there are 1-hr conducted tours at 1000, 1100, 1300, 1400 and 1500.

Bundaberg's parks come in many forms. **Alexandra Park** has a band rotunda dating from 1910 and a free zoo, a great place to take children. **Paradise Park** in Paradise Lane is a private enterprise animal hospital and nursery. Volunteers help care for over a hundred varieties of animals and birds and the park has many kangaroos, wallabies and koalas. Open daily 0900–1700.

Baldwin Swamp environmental park in East Bundaberg is home to many species of birds and wildlife. There are walking tracks including boardwalks which take you around the eucalypt forest. For a retreat from the fast lane stroll through the cool leafy walks of **Avocado Grove**, south of the city on Dr Mays Crossing Rd. It is a large garden with orchids, unusual fruit trees, tropical ferns and some exotic birds. There is a nature walk through a small rainforest, and a restaurant.

In North Bundaberg is the relatively new **Botanical Garden**, on the corner of Mt Perry Rd (Gin Gin Hwy) and Young St. The gardens have a mix of native and exotic plants; the waterlily-filled lagoons are a highlight.

In the centre of the botanical gardens is a curious sight. Bert Hinkler, whose role in early aviation has never been given the credit it was due, was born in Bundaberg. In 1928 he was the first man to fly solo from England to Australia, and died in 1933 in an air crash in Italy while trying for yet another world record. When his house in England, from where he had planned his pioneering flight to Australia, was scheduled for demolition, the people of Bundaberg set up a fund and brought it piece by piece from Southampton and set it up here – and yes, it does look strange to see an

English suburban house translated to the Australian landscape. It is now the **Hinkler Museum**. The museum is a repository of aviation history and especially of the intrepid Hinkler, who is said to have developed his ambition from observing the flights of ibis at the lagoons. His first aircraft, a lightweight glider he flew on Mon Repos Beach, 15 km north-east of town, in 1912, is in the **Hinkler Glider Museum**, on the corner of Mulgrave and Bourbong Sts (open daily 0900–1700).

THE SEA SERPENT MYSTERY

In June 1890, Miss Lovell, a schoolmistress, was taking a stroll along the beach at Sandy Cape when she saw an enormous sea creature lying partly out of the water. At first she thought that it was a giant turtle, but the tail was like the tail of a huge fish. She later wrote: 'When tired of my looking at it, it put its large neck and head into the water and swept round seaward, raising its huge dome-shaped body about five feet out of the water, and put its 12 feet of fish-like tail over the dry shore, elevating it at an angle. Then, giving its tail a half twist, it shot off like a flash of lightning. It had either teeth or serrated jaw bones. ... I think it must be 30 feet in all.' In the early 1930s a book called *The Case for the Sea Serpent* came down on the side of Miss Lovell. But what was it she saw?

Bundaberg is a coastal city even though it is some 15 km from the sea. Within easy reach are over 140 km of unspoilt beaches, frequently deserted out of holiday season. Most important, the waters here are free of stingers, the big jellyfish which can make swimming dangerous in the wrong season as you get further north.

The World Heritage Site of Fraser Island is the largest sand-massed island in the world – 125 km long and an average of 15 km wide – and a special place that imprints itself permanently in the memory of all who visit it.

The island was probably named after Mrs Eliza Fraser who was shipwrecked here when the *Stirling Castle* ran aground in 1836. It was declared a native reserve in 1860 and had an Aboriginal population of between 2,000 and 3,000. After a short-lived mission closed in 1904 the Aboriginal people dispersed to the mainland.

The first mineral sands leases were granted in 1949. When a further application was made in 1971 the nature lobby was up in arms: here was the largest sand island in the world and big business thought the way to deal with it was to mine it. The conservation movement fought long and hard and in 1971 the aptly named watchdog FIDO (Fraser Island Defenders Organisation) was formed. Sand-mining effectively ended in 1976.

Dili Village is the former sand-mining centre, and there is a number of smallish settlements along the coast: Eurong, Happy Valley and Cathedral Beach. The island now gets over 300,000 visitors annually and managing them so that the least damage is done is a major task.

ARRIVAL AND DEPARTURE

There are several ferry routes: Inskip Point, near Rainbow Beach has a 10-minute crossing to Hook Point at the southern end of the island, or from River Heads the *Fraser Venture* makes the journey to Wanggoolba Creek. Booking, especially during holiday periods, is advisable (the tourist offices can do this for you). You need a permit to take across a vehicle; this can be obtained at a nominal price from any Queensland National Park and Wildlife Service office or the Hervey Bay City Council in Torquay.

GETTING AROUND

There are organised bus tours of the island. **Top Tours Ranger Guided Day Tour**, for example, do a full-day tour with buffet lunch. The tour visits Eli Creek, the *Maheno* shipwreck and examples of different habitats in a 4-wheel drive coach. Contact them at Great Sandy Strait Marina, Mainland Terminal; tel: 4125 3933.

The alternatives are to walk, use a trail bike or a 4-wheel drive vehicle. The age limit for hiring 4-wheel drive seems to be only 21 here. One of the problems with such vehicles is that drivers are often inexperienced and not ecologically sensitive, and it is possible that these may one day be totally banned from the island. There are no sealed roads and driving conditions can be tricky, especially after a heavy rain. Bogging down a 4-wheel drive vehicle is distressingly easy as many, many visitors discover each year.

DRIVING TIPS

The speed limit is 35 kph on inland tracks and 60 kph on the beaches. It is desperately important that you keep to the tracks to protect the vegetation and observe vehicle-free areas. Keep 4-wheel-drive constantly engaged to avoid spinning your wheels in the sand. Lowering your tyre pressures to 102–125 Kpa (15-18 psi) will help you maintain traction.

INFORMATION

On the mainland: **Fraser Island Tourist Information Centre**, 8 Rainbow Beach Rd, Rainbow Beach; tel: 4186 3227.

On the island: **Fraser Tourist Information Centre**, Eurong; tel: 4125 0222; Eurong Visitors Centre; tel: 4127 99128.

ACCOMMODATION

Some accommodation, from cabins to motel-style rooms, is available at reasonable cost, mostly on the east coast. There are also designated camping areas, some with showers and facilities. Contact National Parks and Wildlife Camping Areas (tel: 4186 3160) or Cathedral Beach (tel: 4127 9177).

Eurong Beach Resort; tel: 4127 9122.

Fraser Island Retreat Happy Valley; tel: 4127 9144,

Fraser Sands Holiday Apartments Happy Valley; tel: 4127 9147.

Kingfisher Bay Resort and Village North White Cliffs; tel: 4120 3333.

FOOD AND DRINK

Most of the accommodation offers buffet meals, but there are no restaurants as such. If you are camping, bring it all with you. You can buy basic supplies but they are quite expensive.

HIGHLIGHTS

The island stretches along the coast creating a massive bay on its western side, and from some angles it appears to form part of the mainland; Captain Cook certainly thought so when he saw the island in 1770.

The island has an endless variety of landscapes: long surf beaches, cliffs and gorges, dense rainforests, vast, desert-like sandblows, freshwater lakes perched high up in its dunes, winding streams and salt pans with mangrove forests. More than 230 different species of birds make it one of the largest and most varied bird communities in Australia and there are brumbies - Australian wild horses - here, too (in Patrick White's *The Eye of the Storm* the island is fictionalised as Brumby).

The dune systems of the Great Sandy Region, which includes Fraser Island, are the largest and oldest in the world, dating back more than 30,000 years. In **Great Sandy National Park**, the dunes rise to 200 m and the sand comes in at least 72 different colours. The dunes can be seen at their best along a 35 km stretch of ocean beach north of Happy Valley.

Happy Valley lies on Seventy Five Mile Beach, which can at times seem like a city road during rush hour. Low tide is the best time to drive on the beaches, as the sand is flat and hard packed. Drive carefully and enjoy the scenery. When a vehicle is approaching you signal with your indicators on which side you intend to pass. There have been sad collisions between American and Australian drivers each trying to pass on their normal sides.

From Happy Valley two signposted tracks lead inland. One goes to **Lake Garawongera** and the other to **Yidney Scrub** then past a series of lakes until, after 45 km, it returns to the beach. It is water that has given the island the ability to support vast tracts of forest, which survive on nutrients from the breakdown of other plants. Some trees are over a thousand years old, and the variety of vegetation is exceptional, ranging from mangroves to kauri forests and wallum heathlands.

Hundreds of streams flow through the forests and out into the bays. Two are exceptional. **Eli Creek** on the eastern side of the island, is the largest of the freshwater streams flowing into the ocean. At Central Station, **Wanggoolba Creek** flows over white sand along the floor of thick rainforest and the creek-side walkways pass through Angiopteris ferns, an ancient species boasting the largest single fronds in the world. (The many dingoes at Central Station are reputed to be Australia's purest strain; under no circumstances to be fed.)

There are 40 lakes on the island, formed in three ways. Window lakes occur when the ground drops below the water-table and the fine white sandy base acts as a filter, giving the water exceptional clarity. Examples are **Yankee Jack, Ocean Lake** and **Lake Wabby**. Lake Wabby is also termed a barrage lake, which is formed by the damming action of a sandblow blocking the waters of a natural spring. Perched lakes occur above the water-table. The peat-like base generally stains the water the colour of tea. Highest of them is **Lake Bowarrad**y, and further south are **Lake Birrabeen** and the popular **Lake McKenzie**. **Lake Boomanjin** is the world's largest perched dune lake. Swimming in the lakes is a sybaritic delight. Wabby and McKenzie are perhaps two of the most wonderful, but all of them are glorious - much better than the sea, which in many places has a severe undertow.

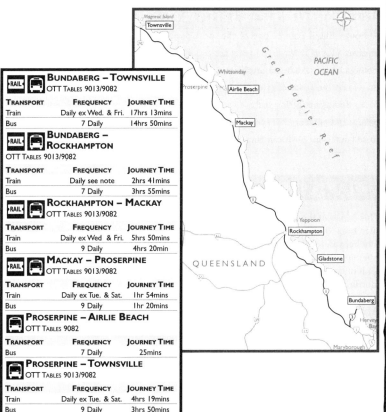

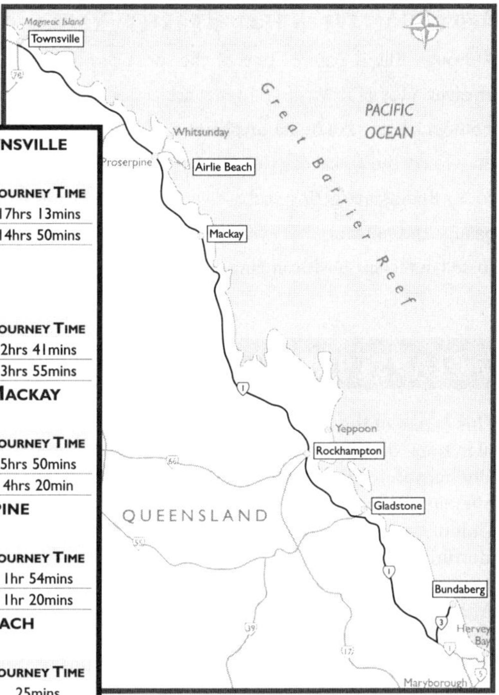

Bundaberg – Townsville
OTT Tables 9013/9082

Transport	Frequency	Journey Time
Train	Daily ex Wed. & Fri.	17hrs 13mins
Bus	7 Daily	14hrs 50mins

Bundaberg – Rockhampton
OTT Tables 9013/9082

Transport	Frequency	Journey Time
Train	Daily see note	2hrs 41mins
Bus	7 Daily	3hrs 55mins

Rockhampton – Mackay
OTT Tables 9013/9082

Transport	Frequency	Journey Time
Train	Daily ex Wed & Fri.	5hrs 50mins
Bus	9 Daily	4hrs 20min

Mackay – Proserpine
OTT Tables 9013/9082

Transport	Frequency	Journey Time
Train	Daily ex Tue. & Sat.	1hr 54mins
Bus	9 Daily	1hr 20mins

Proserpine – Airlie Beach
OTT Tables 9082

Transport	Frequency	Journey Time
Bus	7 Daily	25mins

Proserpine – Townsville
OTT Tables 9013/9082

Transport	Frequency	Journey Time
Train	Daily ex Tue. & Sat.	4hrs 19mins
Bus	9 Daily	3hrs 50mins

Route Detail

The Bruce Highway, aka Route National 1, runs straight through from Gin Gin, just inland from Bundaberg, to Townsville, about 1,000 km, away. From Clairview, about halfway between Rockhampton and Mackay, the road stays pretty close to the coast. Detour right at Proserpine for the complex of Airlie Beach, Shute Harbour and the Whitsunday Islands.

Several buses cruise the Bruce Hwy. Bundaberg to Townsville takes about 15 hrs (but beware, some of the Brisbane buses bypass Bundaberg).

Bundaberg – Townsville

Bundaberg – Townsville

Alongside the Great Barrier Reef

Although this is part of one of the most popular routes for visitors, it nevertheless involves a lot of driving. The great attraction is that there are many stopping-off points from which to take boats or planes to what is probably the greatest natural wonder in the world: the Great Barrier Reef. Along its 2,000 km are perhaps 900 coral cays and rocky islands, attracting scuba-divers, naturalists and tourists to marvel at its complex beauty and extraordinary marine life. There is everything here from exclusive resorts to self-sufficient bush camping.

GLADSTONE

This is one of the busiest ports in Australia and since the 1960s has made a spectacular transition from a quiet coastal town to a major industrial shipping complex. One reason for this growth is the opening-up of the almost inexhaustible coal supplies in the hinterland. Another is that some 4 million tonnes of bauxite from the Gulf of Carpentaria are processed annually here into alumina, the 'half-way stage' of aluminium.

Although Gladstone is a hive of industry, it is also a good base from which to explore the southern section of the Great Barrier Reef for which it has built a splendid marina. The town also has a few attractions of its own.

The **Gladstone Regional Art Gallery** in Goondoon St is housed in a handsome Colonial Georgian-style building constructed as part of an employment programme during the Depression. Three exhibition areas cover touring displays, local arts and crafts, and historical photographs of the region. Open Mon–Fri 1000–1700, Sat 1000–1600.

The **Toondoon Botanical Gardens** in Glenlyon Rd, about 8 km from the centre, are one of Australia's few totally native botanical gardens. Display areas specialise in local plants and those from far north Queensland. There is a signposted 3-km bush walk that takes in two lookouts. Open daily 0900–1730.

Quoin Island has clean beaches, bush walking, and facilities for windsurfing, swimming, fishing and boating.

Most cruises to the Great Barrier Reef leave from the world-class marina. Heron Island is 80 km by launch, catamaran or helicopter. It is a rough stretch of sea and the journey can be a stomach-churning experience.

EN ROUTE

On the Gin Gin Hwy 25 km north of Bundaberg are 27 strange craters. They were discovered in 1971 and are at least 25 million years old, but no one is quite sure how they were caused. Theories range from a meteorite to sea action. An observation platform is open daily 0800–1700.

Gladstone Area Promotion & Development Centre, 56 Goondoon St; tel: 4972 4000.

Ann's Suncourt Motor Inn $ Far St; tel: 4972 2377.
Auckland Caravan Park $ Dawson Hwy; tel: 4978 1419.
Backpackers Hostel $ 12 Rollo St; tel: 4972 5744.
Camelot Motel $$ 19 Agnes St; tel: 4979 1222.
Coconut Court Motel $$ 79 Toolooa St; tel: 4972 2811.
Motel $ 88 Toolooa St; tel: 4972 2144.
Reef Hotel Motel $$ 38 Goondoon St; tel: 4972 1000.
Rusty Anchor Motor Inn $ 169 Goondoon St; tel: 4972 2099.
Young Australian Hotel/Motel 158 Auckland St; tel: 4978 4326.

Amici's Restaurant $$ 111 Toolooa St; tel: 4972 2082.
Basil's Bistro $$ 83 Toolooa St; tel: 49722313. Licensed.
Coconut Court Alfresco Restaurant $$ 83 Toolooa St; tel: 4972 2023. Licensed.
Flinders Seafood Restaurant $$ Flinders Pde; tel: 4972 6666.
Heron Room Restaurant $$ 142 Kinchela St; tel: 02 6567 4944.
Le Beaujolais Restaurant $$ 28 Tank St; tel: 4972 1647.
Marine Cuisine $$ Marine Dr; tel: 4972 6833.
Magzeenz Restaurant $$ 24 Roseberry St; tel: 4972 4711.
Notsos Bistro $$ 124b Goondoon St; tel: 4972 6932. BYO.
Rusty Anchor Restaurant $$ 167 Goondoon St; tel: 4972 2453.
Swaggy's Australian Restaurant $ 56 Goondoon St; tel: 4972 1653.
Village Smorgasbord Restaurant $ Dawson Hwy; tel: 4978 2077.

ROCKHAMPTON

When the cry of 'Gold!' went up at Canoona, 60 km away, Rockhampton grew almost overnight and became known as 'the town of the three S's: sin, sweat and sorrow' The discovery of copper shortly afterwards led to further expansion, then Rocky (everyone in Australia calls it Rocky) became the centre of one of the major beef areas of Australia and still holds that role. Rockhampton is right on the Tropic of Capricorn, and a spire in the Capricorn Information Centre marks the exact spot. It is also one of the access points for the southern islands and resorts of the Great Barrier Reef (see p. 276).

EN ROUTE

Gangalook Heritage Village, on the highway 20 km north of Rockhampton, tries to show exactly how the pioneers of this area once lived. Tours are conducted daily, and on the last Sun of every month the village comes to life with a major fair and market. Open daily 0900–1600.

A couple of km further on, Olsenís Capricorn Caves were probably formed from an ancient coral reef some 300 million years ago. The caves, discovered in 1882, are still privately owned but are open daily 0900–1700; tel: 4934 2883.

Capricorn Information Centre, Curtis Park, Gladstone Rd; tel: 4927 2055.
Rockhampton and District Information Centre, Riverside/Quay St; tel: 4922 5339.
Rockhampton & District Promotion Centre, Bolsover St; tel: 4931 1281.
Rockhampton www.rockhampton.qld.gov.au/

Albert Court Motel $$ Alma St, Ccnr Albert St; tel: 4927 7433.
Bridge Motor Inn $ 31 Bolsover St; tel: 4927 7488.
Central Park Motel $$ 224 Murray St; tel: 4927 2333.
Centre Point Motor Inn $$ 131 George St; tel: 4927 8844.
Citywalk Motor Inn $ Campbell St, cnr William St; tel: 4922 6009.
Fitzroy Motor Inn $ Campbell St, cnr Fitzroy St; tel: 4927 9255.
Golden Fountain Motel $ 166 Gladstone Rd; tel: 4927 1055. Has spacious ground-floor units.
Grosvenor Hotel Motel $ 186 Alma St; tel: 4927 1777.
Mamelon Lodge $$ 329 Hobler Ave; tel: 4922 8484; email joy@intours.com.au. Bed and breakfast.
Motel Lodge $ 100 Gladstone Rd; tel: 4922 5726.
Rockhampton Court Motor Inn $$ 78 George St; tel: 4927 8277.
Rockhampton YHA $ 60 MacFarlane St; tel: 4927 5288.
Simpson's Rockhampton Motel $ 156 George St; tel: 4927 7800.

Albert Court Restaurant $$ Alma St, cnr Albert St; tel: 4927 8261.
Cascades $$ Campbell St, cnr Fitzroy St; tel: 4922 6631.
Eastern Chinese Restaurant $ 54 Denham St; tel: 4927 8887.
Greenhouse Restaurant & Cocktail Bar $$ Gladstone Rd, cnr Larnach St; tel: 4927 8866.

Happy Buddha Chinese Restaurant $ Rockhampton Shopping Fair; tel: 4928 0280.
Hong Kong Seafood Restaurant $ 98a Denham St; tel: 4927 7144.
Italian Graffiti $$ 147 Musgrave St; tel: 4922 6322.
Le Bistro $$ 120 William St; tel: 4922 2019.
Le Jardin Restaurant $$ 24 Up Dawson Rd; tel: 4922 2333.
Malaysia Hut Restaurant $ 7 Wandal Rd; tel: 4927 7511.
Marnies $$ 243 Musgrave St; tel: 4927 5282. Seafood specialities.
Murphy's Irish Bar $ Cnr of Fitzroy and Quay Sts; tel: 4922 1225. Bush Inn steakhouse and beer garden.
Peking Seafood Restaurant $$ 110 Gladstone Rd, cnr Denison St; tel: 4922 6010.
Players Bistro $$ Victoria Pde; tel: 4922 4001.
Troppo's Restaurant $$ Bruce Hwy; tel: 4926 1144.
Whispers Restaurant $$ 116 George St; tel: 4927 7900.
Wintersun Restaurant $$ Bruce Hwy; tel: 4928 8722.

HIGHLIGHTS

The best way to get a feeling for the town is to take the **Heritage Drive** or, for the more energetic, the Heritage Walk, which takes you past most of the grand old buildings which have been lovingly preserved and restored. The visitors' centre has a detailed map.

Dominating the area is the belfry and clock tower of the colonnaded post office on the corner of East St Mall and Denham St. The Quay St historical precinct is particularly noteworthy, and includes the copper-domed **Custom House**. At the Fitzroy Bridge end of Quay St, the **Criterion Hotel**, with its great verandas, was built in 1890 on the site of the first hotel in the town, the 1857 Bush Inn. The Gothic-revival **St Paul's Cathedral**, on the corner of Alma and William Sts (completed 1883), is rivalled by **St Joseph's Catholic Cathedral** along William St, which has twin spires and a vaulted roof.

The list of imposing buildings in Rockhampton goes on and on. It shows how much wealth poured into the town and also reflects the fact that the people of Rockhampton believed that their town, not Brisbane, should be the capital of Queensland and, indeed, were willing to secede from the Federation.

The **Botanical Gardens** to the south of the city are open dawn to dusk. They contain one of the most extensive examples of indigenous flora in Australia, and also **Rockhampton Zoo**. Worth special attention is the Japanese Garden. The whole complex is claimed, with good reason, to be among the finest in tropical Australia.

The **Dreamtime Cultural Centre** is reputed to be Australia's largest Aboriginal cultural centre. It is on the Bruce Hwy, north of Rockhampton, opposite the turning for Yeppoon. The centre highlights the importance of the Aborigine peoples, who have inhabited this land for over 40,000 years, and is built on the site where elders of the Darambal tribe made their campsite and gathered for ancient tribal meetings and burial ceremonies. It is set in natural bushland and has a sandstone cave replica, burial sites, rock art and a timber-lined billabong. Open 1000–1730, with tours at 1100 and 1400.

The Mount Archer Lookout gives the best view of Rockhampton and has bush trails, picnic tables and barbecues. Reach it by way of Lakes Creek Rd along Dean St to Frenchville Rd.

Yeppoon, just up the coast on the shores of Keppel Bay, has developed into a quiet, low-key resort ideal for family holidays. It is wonderfully endowed with beaches and the streets are lined with pines and palms. On a headland overlooking Keppel Bay is an unusual and graceful **'singing ship' memorial** to Captain Cook. It represents a billowing sail, mast and rigging and hidden organ pipes create musical sounds in the breeze which are said to sound like a full-rigged sailing ship at sea. **Rosslyn Bay Boat Harbour** is the hopping-off point for the Keppel Islands and the Great Barrier Reef (see p. 276). **Cooberrie Park**, 15 km north, is a flora and fauna reserve with a variety of animals in bushland and rainforest settings. You can hand-feed kangaroos and wallabies.

Less than an hour's drive – 40 km – south-west of Rockhampton is **Mt Morgan**, which not only has an open-cut gold mine but man-made caves with ceiling formations which are actually 150-million-year-old dinosaur footprints. The museum has an excellent collection of mining memorabilia and tells the fascinating mining history of the area. One man who made his fortune here was William Knox D'Arcy, who went on to make another fortune in Britain financing drilling for oil, thus laying the foundations for British Petroleum.

MACKAY

Mackay (Mac Eye) is often called the sugar capital of Australia – about a quarter of all Australia's sugar is grown in the area. Sugar and coal (Hay Point, to the south of the town, was, for a time, the world's largest coal terminal) have made Mackay prosperous, and the result is a most elegant town in the tropical Queensland style. The streets are broad and well laid out with palm trees and flowering tropical plants, and

PRECIOUS STONES

West of Rockhampton lie Australia's gemfields. All the towns have wonderful names – Emerald, Rubyvale, Sapphire, Anakie. Not many overseas tourists come to these places, but they are well worth visiting.

These are the largest sapphire fields in the southern hemisphere and fossicking licences are available. Do not get excited about making a fortune. The sapphires come out of the ground dark and dingy and are priced by the kilo. It takes a fair amount of alchemy, at which Thai jewellers are experts, to turn them into jewels. It is not generally known that most of the sapphires sold in Thailand come from Australia.

Emerald, Capella and Rubyvale all have early homesteads and mementoes of these pioneering communities. At **Rubyvale's Miners Heritage Walk-in Mine** you can tour one of Australia's largest underground sapphire mines and the splendid **Bobby Dazzler Walk-in Mine** has a museum and gem shop. Springsure's **Old Rainworth Fort** is operated by the descendants of one of the region's oldest families.

Emerald is about 250 km along the Capricorn Hwy, but there are gems closer than this. The **Mt Hay Gemstone Park**, 37 km south of Rockhampton, lets you go digging for your own thundereggs. Each is guaranteed to be 120 million years old and there are guided tours of the diggings and the gemstone processing plant.

the Pioneer River runs through the town. It is also well endowed with shops. The **Botanical Gardens** are the heart of a large recreational area, Queen's Park in Goldsmith St, and are open from 0600–1800. Caneland Park is on the banks of the Pioneer.

There are three **beaches** within the town boundaries: Harbour Beach, which is patrolled and therefore the safest; Town Beach; and, to the south, Illawong Beach. This has the **Illawong Fauna Sanctuary** which is fine for children, especially the crocodile feeding (daily at 1300). Open 0900–1830. If those beaches are not enough there is a run of beaches between Mackay and Sarina, 37 km to the south. In the summer all beaches can have stingers - seriously painful and possibly lethal jellyfish - so check locally before you leap into the water.

Through the suburb of Walkerston, 15 km from Mackay, is the **Greenmount Historic Homestead**. It was built in 1915 and has been renovated, restored and refurbished in the style of the 19th century. It is open Mon–Sat 0930–1230; Sun 1000–1530. The road to Greenmount is clearly signposted from Walkerston, and the old house is 2 km from the highway, set in wonderful gardens on the top of a hill so that it can overlook the surrounding sugar plantations.

EN ROUTE

Eungella National Park is Queensland's largest rainforest national park and contains Mt Dalrymple (1,280 m). This is the home of the Eungella honeyeater, one of only five new bird species discovered in Australia over the past 50 years. The gastric brooding frog and the orange-sided skink also live here, and it is one of the few places in Australia where it is possible, but far from likely, that you will see a duck-billed platypus in its natural environment.

Eungella is rugged and largely inaccessible except to very serious bush walkers. Access to the easiest part is via a bitumen road through the Pioneer Valley to the ranger's offices at Broken River. Walking trails range in length and difficulty from a 1-km rainforest walk at Broken River to 16-km round-trips taking in the best rainforest and mountain views. Rangers are available daily 0700–0800, 1100–1200, 1500–1530, and a display centre (unmanned) is open daily 0700–1700.

Mackay Tourist Information Centre, The Mill, 320 Nebo Rd; tel: 952 2677.
Mackay City www.chalmers.com.au/Mackay/

The vast majority of the motels are in Nebo Rd; prices tend to be acceptably low.
Alara Motor Inn $$ 52 Nebo Rd; tel: 4951 2699.
Boomerang Motor Hotel $ Nebo Rd; tel: 4952 1755.
Central Hospitality Motel $$ 2 Macalister St; tel: 4951 1666.
Cool Palms Motel $ 4 Bruce Hwy, Nebo Rd; tel: 4957 5477.
Country Plaza Motor Inn $ 40 Nebo Rd; tel: 4957 6526.
Four Dice Motel $$ 166 Nebo Rd; tel: 4951 1555.
Golden Reef Motel $ 164 Nebo Rd; tel: 4957 6572.
Hi Way Units Motel $ Webberley St, cnr Nebo Rd; tel: 4952 1800.
Mia Mia Motel $ 191 Nebo Rd; tel: 4952 1466.
Miners Lodge Motor Inn $ 60 Nebo Rd; tel: 4951 1944.
Motel White Lace $$ 73 Nebo Rd; tel: 4951 4466.
Pioneer Villa Motel $ 30 Nebo Rd; tel: 4951 1288.
Star Motel $ 175 Nebo Rd; tel: 4952 2444.
Sugar City Motel $ 66 Nebo Rd; tel: 4951 2877.
White Lace Motor Inn $$ 73 Nebo Rd; tel: 4951 4466; email: reservations@whitelace.com.au.

Courtyard Carvery $$ 45 Wood St; tel: 4957 2249.
Creperie $ 9 Gregory St; tel: 4951 1226.
Golden Reef Seafood Restaurant $$ 164 Nebo Rd; tel: 4957 6572.
Lychee Gardens $ Wellington St, Cnr Victoria St; tel: 4951 3939.
Mariner Restaurant $$ 44 Victoria St; tel: 4957 3279.
Matador Restaurant $$ 158 Nebo Rd, Hwy 1; tel: 4951 1888.
Pipers Restaurant $$ 166 Nebo Rd; tel: 4951 1555.
Pizza Bilities $ 186 Shakespeare St; tel: 4951 4577.
Rialto Restaurant $$ 46 Nebo Rd; tel: 4951 2700.
Sidneys On Sydney St Bar & Grill $$ Shakespeare St, cnr Sydney St; tel: 4951 1119.
Simons Chinese Kitchen $ 330 Shakespeare St; tel: 4957 8296.

Supperhouse Garden Restaurant $$ 136 Wood St; tel: 4957 7266.
Tennysons $$ 40 Tennyson St; tel: 4957 2932.
Toong Tong Thai $ 10 Sydney St; tel: 4957 8051. Open daily. BYO.
Valencia Restaurant $$ 44 Macalister St; tel: 4951 1244.
Waterfront Restaurant $$ 8 River St; tel: 4957 8131. Open daily from 1000. Licensed. The fashionable eating spot in Mackay.

AIRLIE BEACH

Airlie Beach is about the same distance from the equator as Hawaii. It is best to think of it as part of the Whitsunday coast complex rather than as a single town. Both Airlie Beach and Shute Harbour are on the peninsula extending into Repulse Bay, which has developed because of its closeness to the Whitsunday Passage and holiday area. Indeed, the towns have practically merged as the mainland centre for the Whitsundays and Airlie Beach is working hard at having itself called Whitsunday.

The area has a very distinct feeling of being in the South Seas, as well as having a permanent holiday air, and some of the most visited islands of the Great Barrier Reef, the Whitsundays, are at its front door.

i Airlie Beach Tourist Information
Whitsunday District Information Centre, 6 The Esplanade, Airlie Beach; tel: 4946 6673.
In Shute Harbour Road, the main street, are numerous cafés – six of them offering Internet facilities – and information centres.

Most of the motels are on Shute Harbour Rd.
Airlie Beach Hotel-Motel $ The Esplanade; tel: 4946 6233.
Airlie Beach Motor Lodge $$ 6 Lammond St; tel: 4946 6418. Two-bedroom apartments. Easy strolling distance of the centre.
Airlie Cove Resort Van Park $ Shute Harbour Rd; tel: 4946 6727.
Beach House $$ 318 Shute Harbour Rd; tel: 4946 6306.
Beaches $ 362 Shute Harbour Rd; tel: 4946 6244.
Blue Waters Lodge $ 358 Shute Harbour Rd; tel: 4946 6182.
Island Gateway Holiday Resort $$ Shute Harbour Rd; tel:

4946 6228. Swimming pool, spa and lorikeet-feeding every day at 1630.

Reef Oceania Village Resort $$ 147 Shute Harbour Rd; tel: 4946 6137.

Shute Harbour Gardens Caravan $ Shute Harbour Rd; tel: 4946 6483.

Whitsunday on the Beach $$ 269 Shute Harbour Rd; tel: 4946 6359.

Again the action is along Shute Harbour Rd. The leaning is towards budget with quantity rather than high cuisine.

Abel's Restaurant $$ Abel Pt Marina; tel: 4946 4344. Dining overlooking the marina and the Whitsunday Passage.

Airlie Thai $ Beach Plaza, The Esplanade; tel: 4946 4683. Authentic Thai food.

Beaches Backpacker $ Shute Harbour Rd; tel: 4946 6244. Good, cheap meals in pub atmosphere.

Gringos At Airlie $ The Esplanade; tel: 4946 5898. Sort of Mexican food. Licensed.

Hog's Breath Cafe $$ 303 Shute Harbour Rd; Tel: 4946 7894. Part of the chain.

La Perouse Seafood Restaurant $$ 1st Floor Beach Plaza, The Esplanade; tel: 4946 6262.

Palmers Restaurant $ TAFE Cannonvale Campus, Shute Harbour Rd; tel: 4946 8321. This is a school where they are training chefs and you are the guinea pig. The food is never less than brilliant. You must phone for availability and bookings are essential.

Panache On The Beach $$ 263 Shute Harbour Rd; tel: 4946 5600. Balcony dining right on the waterfront overlooking the beach. Italian cuisine.

Shaiz Breakfast Bar & Cafe Beach Plaza $ The Esplanade; tel: 4946 6605. Hot and cold 'all you can eat' buffets. Open for breakfast 0600.

Spice Island Bistro $$ 398 Shute Harbour Rd; tel: 4946 6585.

Whitsunday Sailing Club Restaurant $$ The Galley; tel: 4946 5034.

HIGHLIGHTS

This is an area of beautiful beaches and you are spoiled for choice. Earlando and Dingo beaches are favourites for fishing and beachcombing, while Funnel Bay, 4 km from the village, is one of the most picturesque spots on the coast.

The **Whitsunday Aquarium** has a display of reef fish and turtles as well as a collection of 3,000 shells. It is on Jubilee Pocket Rd and open daily 1030–1630. The **Whitsunday Wildlife Park** is in nearby Cannonvale, about 8 km away with its comprehensive collection of Australian fauna, including kangaroos and wallabies roaming around the grounds. It is in Shute Harbour Rd and open daily 0830–1730.

Conway National Park runs from Proserpine to south-east of Airlie Beach and extends offshore to include many of the Whitsunday Islands. It is wild country - some of the oldest surviving rainforest in the world – and is noted for the famous blue Ulysses butterfly and a wide range of flora and fauna. There are relatively few walking tracks. **Cedar Creek Falls**, set in a beautiful and mountainous region on the edge of the park, tumble 12 m through rainforest into a stream - ideal for swimming if you want to escape the ocean. Reach the park via Cannonvale along Conway Beach Rd.

SAILING IN THE WHITSUNDAYS

The whole point of coming to this area is, if at all possible, to mess around in boats. Bareboat charter is the least expensive choice and it means that you go where you want, when you want. Lack of sailing experience need not be a barrier. This is some of the safest sailing in the world and the people who charter the yachts are adept at giving quick but thorough courses in safe yacht handling.

Sailing in the Whitsundays is as good as it gets. The channels between the islands are deep, which means you are unlikely to get stranded on a reef, and most of the islands are within line of sight of one another so it is almost impossible to get lost. Of the 74 islands, 66 are National Parks so there is always something to explore.

The choice of yachts at the Abel Point Marina at Airlie Beach is unsurpassed. There are also powerboats, but in this area it is a shame not to sail. If you are unsure, you can hire a skipper who will stay on board until no longer needed. There is also reassuring daily radio contact between each of the boats and base. It is all extremely well organised and efficiently run. There are safe, protected anchorages aplenty. Just take note of the marker buoys which warn you against sensitive sites and remember you must not anchor inshore of the buoys.

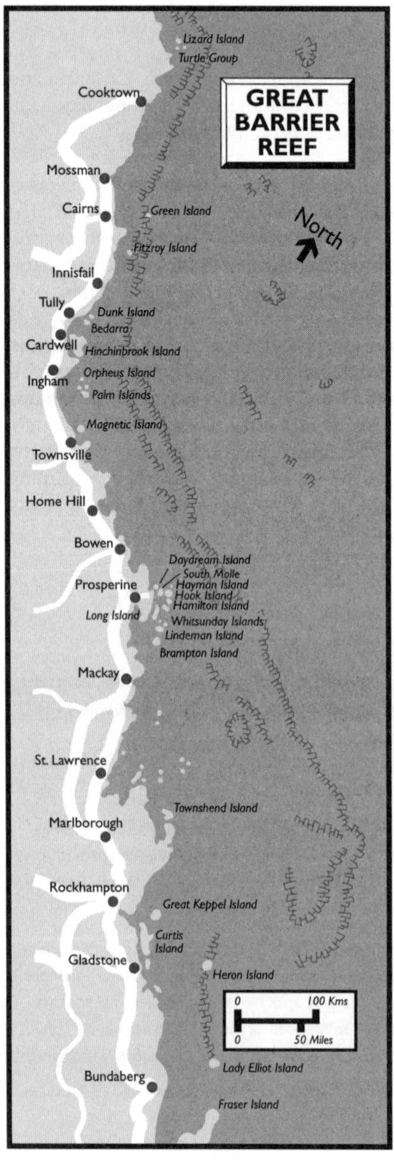

The Barrier Reef is so massive, so astounding, that you just run out of superlatives. It is the most extensive coral reef system in the world and the largest structure made completely by living organisms – its total coverage is greater than the states of Victoria and Tasmania combined. It boasts 1500 types of fish, 4000 types of molluscs, 350 types of echinoderms and 350 types of corals.

The reef, which is not a single reef but features more than 2900 individual reefs and 900 islands, stretches from the Tropic of Capricorn, parallel with Rockhampton, to beyond the tip of Queensland, almost to Papua New Guinea. In the north the reef comes in close to the land – sometimes the greenery of the rainforest actually extends over the coral – while further south it runs parallel to the coast at a distance of about 100 km. In a single visit you will only touch on a few points. To fully explore the reef would take a lifetime.

Average water temperatures on the reef range from around 22°C in July to around 27°C in January, making it perfect for diving all year round. The reef is also the breeding area for a number of rare and endangered species. Humpback whales swim up from the Antarctic to give birth to their young in the warm waters, six of the world's seven species of sea turtle breed here, and dugongs make their home among the sheltered seagrass beds.

One of the problems is keeping the reef in its wondrous natural state, because everyone wants to come and see it. In the 1950s and '60s it used to be the haunt of skin-divers, and even in the 1980s there were only about 150,000 visitors a year on the reef. Now it is approaching 2 million and commercial operators run about 1.3 million scuba-dives per annum. Tourism brings in over $1 billion a year. Most of the reef's tourism is concentrated in two tiny areas – offshore from Cairns and the Whitsundays.

ARRIVAL AND DEPARTURE

Where you arrive on the reef will depend on which part of the mainland you leave from. Main departure points are Rockhampton or Gladstone for the southern islands (see pp. 268 and 266), Airlie Beach for the Whitsundays (see p. 280) and Townsville or Cairns for the northern groups (see pp. 285 and 286). You can fly in and land on the reef itself from any major airport in Australia - there is a full-scale jet airport on Hamilton - or you can helicopter in from almost any Queensland resort.

INFORMATION

Queensland Government Travel Centre, Cnr Adelaide and Edward Sts, Brisbane; tel: 3221 6111.

INTERNET SITES **Great Barrier Reef Discovery** Coast www.barrierreef.net/

Great Barrier Reef in Queensland www.queensland-holidays.com.au/pfm/sites/0001359/body.htm#About
Great Barrier Reef Visitors Bureau www.greatbarrierreef.aus.net/
Great Barrier Reef www.ozramp.net.au/~senani/barrier.htm
Internet North's Globetrotters Travel Guide www.internetnorth.com.au/gt/
Marc's Whitsunday Islands www.geocities.com/TheTropics/Shores/9645/index.htm
Southern Great Barrier Reef Index
www.ozemail.com.au/~unearth/australia/great_barrier_reef/index.html
Whitsunday News www1.tpgi.com.au/users/parrothd/whitnews.html

ACCOMMODATION

A basic problem for any tourist on a budget is that staying at many of the resort islands is totally out of the question - some charge thousands of dollars a week. To preserve their exclusivity they also make it quite difficult to get there unless you have access to a charter boat.

There is justification for the prices charged. Everything, including all rubbish, has to be either shipped or flown in and out. Keeping staff is also a problem. Although it is like living in paradise they are cut off from any serious social life and most last on average three months before heading back to the mainland. There are, however, resorts with budget prices. Especially outside of the holiday season it is well worth enquiring about special rates. Details under individual islands include some expensive resorts, where they are worth the money if you can possibly afford it.

If you are going to camp you need to be totally self-sufficient. Fresh water is almost non-existent and you must bring everything with you. Camping permits are available from the Queensland National Parks and Wildlife Service (tel: 4776 1700), which also provides guidelines to camping on the islands.

THE CORAL

Visitors tend to comment that the coral is not as colourful as they expect from seeing it on television. The problem is that underwater colours are filtered at different depths. Red and yellow disappear first, leaving the reef with a predominantly blue/green appearance which increases with depth. Video taken using lights shows the true colours of the reef. The colours are there - you just need light to see them. To view them at their very best you should try night diving, when the colours are dazzling.

Fishing is not allowed in green national park zones, pink preservation zones and orange scientific zones. In other zones there is a fairly strict set of rules and some animals are, of course, totally protected. Take it that, generally, fishing, and coral and shell collecting are totally barred everywhere on the reef and you will not go far wrong.

The reason why most of the reef is some way off the coast is that coral cannot stand fresh water or the nutrients normally carried in the run-off from the mainland, so the major growth is out at sea away from such conditions. Some corals are more tolerant than others.

Trying to identify particular species of coral is very difficult. Indeed, unless you are a marine biologist, it is almost impossible except by form: plate, branching and so on. Every year over a third of the reef's species of coral reproduce sexually during a mass spawning event. For the majority of inner reefs this is around Nov, with the outer reefs later in Dec. Spawning always takes place at night, any time up to six days after the full moon, when eggs and sperm are released into the water in a massive cloud.

JELLYFISH

When box jellyfish congregate in these coastal waters during the summer (Oct–Mar) you really don't want to go swimming except in protective swimming enclosures or wearing a wet suit. This only applies near the coast – the jellyfish are not found out on the reef – but they can sometimes be found around islands close to the mainland. Other stingers sometimes encountered here include the irukandji and blue bottle. Both can cause a nasty sting. Vinegar can be used on both box jellyfish and irukandji stings but not on blue bottle stings; for these use cold water and ice.

THE REEF ISLANDS

There are islands the length of the Great Barrier Reef, although no one can say precisely how many. Some are small, bare, sand cays, others permanently vegetated cays or continental, ie rock not coral, islands. Wildlife includes goannas, possums, rock wallabies and 156 species of birds. There are vine forests, hoop pines, eucalypts and acacias inland.

THE WHITSUNDAYS

The 70-odd islands of the Whitsunday group, off Airlie Beach, are far and away the most popular part of the Great Barrier Reef, but bear in mind that some of the finest resorts lie elsewhere. Capt Cook, the first European in the area, achieved an amazing feat in navigating the narrow passage though these islands on a Whitsunday - hence the name. All the islands in the group are continental, and most are national parks, with the rules regarding parks strictly imposed.

BRAMPTON Most of this relatively hilly island is forested and was used as a nursery for palm trees. There are clearly marked walking tracks and wildlife on the island includes cockatoos and grey kangaroos.

The only commercial access is via Whitaker Airlines from Mackay Airport, which makes it somewhat exclusive unless you are in a charter boat. This is done mainly to discourage day-trippers. The Brampton Holiday Resort at Sandy Point, opened in 1933, is one of the oldest resorts on the Reef. It is affordable ($$$), low key and has its own train to take guests from the jetty to the resort. Tel: 132 469. At low tide you can walk across to the undeveloped island of Carlisle.

DAYDREAM This is the closest Whitsunday island to the mainland (easily accessible for day-trips) and covers less than 2 sq km. It is covered with dense bush with a beach running the whole of the east side.

The resort ($$$) was closed for a time; now it is thriving once again and is one of the largest in the group. It offers excellent facilities with most normal activities and non-powered water sports free. It is designed for families and has safe beaches and makes a major effort to keep children occupied. Tel: 4948 8488; email: daydream@village.com.au.

HAMILTON ISLAND There are those who consider the development of Hamilton a lesson in how not to develop islands and ecologically sensitive places. It has been called the Gold Coast of the reef islands and is run as a town rather than as a small island resort, with a wide range of accommodation and entertainments not all connected with the Great Barrier Reef (unless you consider a Polynesian floor show an essential part of reef life). Prices tend to be high and it would perhaps be worth considering less obtrusive and pretentious places.

The east side of the island is relatively undeveloped and there is a walk around the coastline at Catseye Beach and up to the summit of Passage Peak, with views north to Whitsunday Island.

HAYMAN ISLAND Hayman is nearer to the outer reef than most other islands in the group. It has bushwalking and snorkelling and is close to good diving sites. It is also one of the most luxurious and expensive resorts. You fly to Hamilton and then take a 55-min boat transfer. The resort ($$$$) has the style of a 5-star international hotel rather than an island resort, which somehow feels out of place in this setting. And men must wear a jacket in the main dining-room in the evening. Tel: 4940 1234.

HOOK ISLAND Hook is a true wilderness island and Hook Peak (459 m) is the highest mountain in the islands. There are few walking tracks but excellent beaches and superb diving. The snorkelling at the north end of the island is some of the finest in the area – the coral is in fair condition, the water is normally very clear and the aquatic life spectacular. Near by is an underwater observatory where you can observe the fish and the coral from 10 m down. Open 1000–1400. There are several campsites, and two fiord-type inlets at the southern end – Nara and Macona – provide safe and scenic anchorage. Ferries run twice daily from Shute Harbour.

LINDEMAN Lindeman was the very first resort island in the Whitsundays. A camp for visitors was established in 1923 and this small beginning grew from strength to strength until, in 1992, the resort was taken over by Club Med. Despite the organisation's reputation of sun, sex and compulsory games, Lindeman Island Club Med ($$$) is ideal for a family holiday in that children are taken care of from dawn to dusk. Everything is included in the price and most packages are for five days. Tel: 3229 3155; email: www.clubmed.com. The excellent beaches are all easily accessible and there are 20 km of marked walking tracks, including a 4-km walk to the top of Mt Oldfield (210 m). Most visitors fly first to Hamilton and then cross by launch on a 30-min trip.

SOUTH MOLLE

This is the largest of the Molle group and to all intents and purposes is joined to Mid Molle and North Molle – no matter what the state of the tide you can paddle to Mid Molle. West Molle is now Daydream (see p. 280).

South Molle is a hilly island with grasslands and patches of rainforest, and is still recovering from overgrazing a century ago. It is 4 km by about 2 km and has 12 km of sand and coral shorelines. Local Aborigines appear to have come here from the mainland to get the hard stone from which they made their weapons. It is ideal for fairly strenuous walking, with well-signposted tracks leading around the island and up Mt Jeffreys.

Getting there takes about 20 mins from Shute Harbour or half an hour from Hamilton Island (see p. 280). The resort is to the north of the island, by the ferry terminus. It has yet to suffer the indignities of massive refurbishment and is eminently affordable, especially for family holidays. ($$ including as-much-as-you-can-eat buffets and most sports.) Tel: 4946 9433.

NORTHERN ISLANDS

DUNK AND BEDARRA ISLANDS

Dunk, part of the Family Group, is 6 km long, 2 km wide and one of only three rainforest islands on the reef, a lush home to native flora and fauna. The island is about 4 km off Mission Beach from which there are regular water taxi services. It also has its own airstrip for access from Cairns or Townsville. There is an area set aside for campers and one resort ($$$), in the northwest of the island overlooking Brammo Bay. Tel: 132 469.

Bedarra, south of Dunk Isand, houses the small, exclusive and expensive 5-star Bedarra Island Resort run by P&O Australian Resorts (16 villas). Most people get there by water taxi from Dunk. The charges are very high ($$$$) but everything is free including the bar and the champagne. Tel: 132 469.

FITZROY ISLAND

Almost ignored and much underrated, Fitzroy is less than an hour by high-speed catamaran from Cairns. It is a true continental island – once part of the mainland – and covered in rainforest surrounding a peak which rises to 271 m. The island is almost completely surrounded by coral reef and has a good safe anchorage. There are excellent tracks, splendid beaches and snorkelling, and affordable accommodation catering for everything from backpackers to families.

Fitzroy Island Resort ($) is one of the few resorts that seriously caters to the economy end of the market. It's a jewel of a place which is often over-looked. Tel: 4051 9588; email: res@fitzroyislandresort.com.au.

FRANKLAND ISLAND This beautiful, uninhabited national park is situated directly off the coast from Russell Heads, 40 km south of Cairns.

GREEN ISLAND Green Island is a true coral cay surrounded by reef, with white sandy beaches and safe swimming. This was where Joe Harman took Jean Paget for an innocent holiday before the romance took a turn for the better in Nevil Shute's novel *A Town Like Alice*.

It is popular for day-trips from Cairns – a fast catamaran takes 50 mins. Serious attempts have been made to maintain as much of the natural charm as possible. The island itself is fairly small –15 ha – and you can stroll around it easily in less than half an hour. The interior is rainforest fringed by a mixture of compacted coral and sandy beaches.

Accommodation in the Japanese-owned resort ($$) has recently gone through a $500 million refurbishment. Tel: 4031 3300.

HINCHINBROOK ISLAND Hinchinbrook is separated from the mainland only by a narrow but deep and mangrove-fringed channel. The main access point is at Cardwell, roughly half-way between Cairns and Townsville.

The island is 52 km long and 10 km wide, with mainly mountainous rainforest soaring on Mount Bowen to 1121 m. Much is barely touched wilderness and the only visitors are experienced bushwalkers. The 3- to 4-day coastal walk along the islandís eastern side is the finest on any of the reef islands. There are some great expanses of beach and wildlife such as wallabies, goannas, echidnas, bats, turtles and interesting birds. The small Hinchinbrook Island Resort ($$$) offers all-inclusive accommodation and is specially suited to serious nature lovers. Tel: 4066 8585. There are also campsites, and bush camping is permitted everywhere except near the resort.

LIZARD ISLAND This national park paradise has abundant wildlife, such as the huge lizards which gave the island its name, five species of snakes, a small colony of bats and more than 40 species of birds. It offers some of the best scuba-diving, snorkelling and game-fishing in the world (it's only 15km from the outer edge of the reef) and you do not need to be able to skin-dive; snorkelling is quite enough.

At times you will have to push the fish to one side to proceed. There are 23 superb beaches and many fine walks. Capt Cook slept at the base of what is now called Cook's Look, climbing before dawn so that he could see clearly at first light a passage through the Barrier Reef.

Lizard is far to the north: 93 km from Cooktown (see p. 309). The Lizard Island Lodge ($$$) is expensive but worth every cent. Tel: 4060 3999; email: lizard@pegasus.com.au; Web site: www.austresorts.com.au/lizard.htm. There is also a research station and a camping site. Campers must be entirely self-sufficient as the resort does not particularly welcome non-tariff-paying visitors. Most visitors fly in to the small airstrip or are divers or anglers on charter boats. There is also a possibility of being dropped off from one of the island cruises out of Cairns.

ORPHEUS ISLAND

Orpheus – just 11 km long and about 1 km wide – is a nature wonderland: 100 species of fish and 340 of the 350 known species of reef coral can be found in the underwater gardens of its sheltered bays. Reefs around the island have been zoned 'A' (limited fishing only) and 'B' (look but don't touch), and the Parks Service go to some trouble to ensure that visitors do not damage the coral in any way.

Orpheus Island Resort ($$$) is one of the few remaining privately owned Australian island resorts, and is the longest established on the Great Barrier Reef. It has only 31 rooms which will handle, at most, 74 guests at a time. They do not welcome day-trippers or cater for under-15s. Tel: 4777 7377; email: orpheus@t140.aone.net.au; Web site: www.orpheus.com.au. There are also little publicised camping sites at Yankee and Pioneer bays.

Orpheus lies 20 km east of Ingham, 80 km northeast of Townsville and 190 km south of Cairns. Most visitors arrive by the Orpheus Seaplane which operates a daily 1-hr flight from Cairns and a twice-daily 30-min service from Townsville. Transport from Taylor's Beach, 25 km from Ingham, may also be possible.

SOUTHERN ISLANDS

GREAT KEPPEL ISLAND

Keppel, only 15 km from the coast and 55 km from Rockhampton is an easy day-trip. You can get there by boat from Rosslyn Bay or fly in from Rockhampton. It has 17 magnificent beaches and despite being some way from the reef there is plenty of coral to explore. Both the diving and snorkelling are good, and there are well-signposted walking trails through the thick forest.

Great Keppel Island Resort ($$) is notorious in Australia for its one-time advertising campaign – 'Get Wrecked on Keppel'. This suggested it was only suitable for young and single people. Since then it has moved somewhat up-market and although it not longer appeals to backpackers and budget travellers with hostel accommodation it is still quite affordable, specially its all-inclusive packages, which cater for families and couples. But it still has a very lively atmosphere. Tel: 4125 6966; email: reservations@greatkeppel.com.au.

HERON ISLAND This tiny coral cay, 100 km from Rockhampton and 72 km out from Gladstone, rises only 3m above sea-level. Its great attraction is the 24 sq km of reef which is all within wading distance – the coral itself is less than stunning but the aquatic life is amazing. It has great diving, which must be done from a boat, not the beach. At the end of each year the Heron Island Underwater Festival attracts divers from all over Australia. Visits can be arranged to the Heron Island Research Centre, which works on numerous reef-related projects.

There has been a resort here since 1932, literally on the edge of a reef. Although many activities are on offer here, the emphasis is on snorkelling and skin-diving. Tel: 4099 4644. (SSS). Camping is not allowed.

LADY ELLIOT ISLAND This small island lies 90 km east of Bundaberg, a 25-min flight. It is very popular with divers because of the numerous shipwrecks in the area – there have probably been more wrecks off Lady Elliot than any other piece of coastline in Australia. Scuba-divers can dive straight off the beach, the underwater visibility is good and the coral is excellent. The island boasts more than 57 varieties of birds – it was originally mined for guano – and more that 200,000 of them nest here in the summer. Sea turtles also nest on Lady Elliott.

Feral goats stripped the island of vegetation before a new owner arrived in 1969. He killed them off to give the vegetation a chance and built an airstrip to take light aircraft. The island still looks comparatively bare, but marine life and the immediate access to the surrounding reef make up for this. The no-frills resort ($$) has safari-style tents with shared facilities or motel-type units. Tel: 4125 5344; mail: ladyelliot@coastnet.net.au.

Most reports in the media of the imminent death of the reef tend to occur when a new area of crown-of-thorns starfish is found. These starfish damage coral, but most scientific evidence suggests that crown-of-thorns outbreaks are a natural phenomenon that may have occurred on the Reef for the last 3000 to 7000 years. According to the Status of the Great Barrier Reef World Heritage Area 1998 report, there is no major widespread decline – we just have to be very careful.

Townsville is Australia's largest tropical city and the business and cultural centre of North Queensland. It is named after Sydney businessman Captain Robert Towns, who was the major financial backer of John Melton Black, the founder of the settlement started in 1864. Towns only visited the place once, but his name lives on.

Townsville was originally used for shipping tallow and it is now a major port for minerals, sugar and meat. World War II saw the region transformed into a garrison for the tens of thousands of American, Australian and other allied service personnel who used it as a forward base for the war in the Pacific. Today it remains strategically important and home to Australia's largest defence establishment.

The people of the town see themselves as being somewhat set apart from the rest of Queensland. The novelist Thea Astley put it neatly when she wrote: 'When I was a teacher in Townsville ... the locals referred to southerners – and they didn't mean the people of New South Wales or Victoria – or even Tasmania (where is it?); they meant Brisbane.'

Townsville is wholly in the tropics. Three-quarters of its annual rainfall comes thundering down between Oct and Mar. Despite this, the area falls into the dry tropics zone, and warm sunny weather is one of Townville's greatest assets, with more sunshine hours than any other North Queensland coastal centre.

Two World Heritage Areas – the Great Barrier Reef and the Wet Tropics World Heritage Area – are within easy reach, and Townsville also boasts one of the best scuba-diving sites in Australia, the *Yongala* wreck.

ARRIVAL AND DEPARTURE

The airport is just to the north-west of the city and for half the price of a taxi you can catch one of the shuttles that meet main flights.

Buses all come into the terminal in Palmer St, from Cairns to the north, Sydney and Brisbane to the south and across the outback from Darwin and Tennant Creek.

Townsville

INFORMATION

Tourist Offices **Flinders Mall Information Centre,** Flinders Mall; tel: 4721 3660.

Highway Information Centre, Bruce Hwy on the southern approach to Townsville; tel: 4778 3555.

Queensland National Parks & Wildlife Service Information Office, Great Barrier Reef Wonderland; tel: 4721 2399.

Internet Sites **City of Townsville** ikarus.jcu.edu.au/Our_Corner/townsville/townsville.html

Townsville www.townsville.com/

ACCOMMODATION

Adobi Motel $ 90 Abbott St; tel: 4778 2533.

Aquarius on the Beach $$ 75 The Strand; tel: 4772 4255.

Beach House Motel $ 66 The Strand; tel: 4721 1333.

Bohlevale Caravan Park $ 910 Ingham Rd; tel: 4774 5101.

Cluden Park Motor Inn $ Flinders Hwy, cnr Bruce Hwy; tel: 4778 4555.

Midtown Hotel Motel $ 718 Sturt St; tel: 4771 5121.

Plaza $$ Stanley St, cnr Flinders Mall; tel: 4772 1888.

Reef Lodge Budget Accommodation $ 4 Wickham St; tel: 4721 1112.

Rex Inn the City $ 143 Wills St; tel: 4771 6048.

Robert Towns Motel $$ 200 m from city; tel: 4771 6908 48 units. Licensed restaurant.

Strand Motel $ 51 The Strand; tel: 4772 1977.

Summit Motel $$ 6 Victoria St; tel: 4721 2122.

The Rocks $$ Cleveland Ter; tel: 4777 7157; email therocks@ultra.net.au. Upmarket bed and breakfast.

Town Lodge Motor Inn $$ 15 Victoria St; tel: 4771 2164.

Walkabout Palms Caravan Park $ 6 University Rd; tel: 4778 2480.

FOOD AND DRINK

Admiral's Seafood Restaurant $$ 300 Sturt St; tel: 47211911.

Covers Restaurant $$ 209 Flinders St; tel: 47214630.

Down Under Restaurant $ 386 Dal Roberts Arcade Flinders St; tel: 4772 3838.

Dynasty Chinese Seafood Restaurant $ 228 Flinders East St; tel: 4772 7099.

Fishermans Wharf $$ Ogden St; tel: 47211838.

Jun Japanese Restaurant $$ 436 Flinders St; tel: 4772 3394. BYO.

Larrikins $$ 95 Denham St; tel: 4772 5900.

Le Boulevard Brasserie Restaurant $$ 215 Flinders East St; tel: 4771 4393.

Omars Restaurant $ 499 Flinders St; tel: 47211377.

Pasini's Restaurant $$ 2 Archer St; tel: 4771 6333.

Pompeii Restaurant $$ 519 Flinders St; tel: 4772 7353.

Sorrento's Restaurant $$ 815 Flinders St; tel: 4772 2288.

Stingers $$ The Strand; tel: 47213033.

Taormina Pizza $ 159 Flinders East St; tel: 4771 3056.

Thai International Restaurant $ 235 Flinders East St; tel: 4771 6242.

Zorba's Restaurant $$ 487 Flinders St; tel: 4771 3211.

HIGHLIGHTS

The easiest way to orientate yourself is to climb **Castle Hill** at Mt Cutheringa. This is a 286-m pink granite monolith that gives a 360-degree panorama and shows the layout of Townsville perfectly. It is possible to drive up, or there is a walking track which starts at the top of Blackwood St. The rock face is floodlit at night and makes orientation very simple.

The city is remarkably easy to get around. At the centre is **Flinders Mall**, a shaded, palm-fringed and tropically landscaped shopping and pedestrian way. Meandering through the town is Ross Creek, an offshoot of Ross River, which is deep enough to provide anchorage for pleasure craft and trawlers. It is from here that fast catamarans run to Magnetic Island (see p. 288), and cruises go to other islands and the Great Barrier Reef (see p. 276).

Flinders St East, with its restored early 20th-century buildings, leads to the **Great Barrier Reef Wonderland** complex. This contains the world's largest living coral reef aquarium and has a walk-through tunnel. All the fish, plants and corals on display come from parts of the Great Barrier Reef. Open daily 0900–1700.

Townsville Museum is at 81–99 Sturt St in what was the Magistrates Court. The museum concentrates on the history of the area, showing how the city has developed since 1865, although it often has displays from other states and overseas. Open Mon–Fri 1000–1500, Sat–Sun 1000–1300.

The **Maritime Museum** in Palmer St displays relics from the *Yongala* which went down with all hands in a cyclone in 1911. There are also items from several other wrecks and the museum covers all of North Queensland Maritime history. Open Mon–Fri 1000–1600, Sat–Sun 1300–1600.

ACCESSIBLE WILDLIFE

The deceptively named **Town Common** is a short 5-min drive from the centre of the city, on the coast at Pallandera. It is in fact a wetland sanctuary fed by the Bohle River and is a remnant of the Townsville-Burdekin wetlands. You may drive through the park on a 7-km-long road and there are bird-hides and walking tracks along the way. The best times to visit are early morning or late afternoon. It is estimated that some 260 different species of birds gather here to nest or stop over on their migratory routes. There are hides near the Pink Lily freshwater lagoon and the Long Swamp, and walking tracks throughout the reserve.

The **Billabong Sanctuary**, 17 km south of the city on the Bruce Hwy, is a native Australian wildlife sanctuary. It has a 2-ha billabong with salt-water crocodiles, cassowary and waterfowl, and in the grounds are koalas, wombats, dingoes and parrots. The daily feeding shows include information about the animals, their habitat and behaviour. Open daily 0900–1700.

NIGHTLIFE

The 1,000-seat **Civic Theatre** and 5,000-seat **Entertainment Centre** bring plays, artists, groups and assorted entertainment to the city every month. The **Sheraton Breakwater Casino-Hotel** on Sir Leslie Thiess Dr is yet another casino designed to make untold fortunes from Asian gamblers. Sadly, the recession in Asia meant that it did not live up to its early promise. It is open 24 hours a day.

MAGNETIC ISLAND

If there was any destination in Australia almost specifically designed for the budget traveller it is **Magnetic Island**. The granite island, only 8 km off the coast, has around 40 km of dramatic coastline, much of it studded with magnificent hoop pines, 23 beaches and endless opportunities for swimming, diving, walking and lotus-eating. Much of it is a national park and its highest point is Mt Cook (497 m).

Captain Cook gave the island its name when the compass aboard his ship, the *Endeavour*, swung wildly as it sailed past the island. No one has ever been able to repeat that anomaly, which still causes much speculation.

The island is partly developed in that there are four settlements and there is vehicular traffic - indeed it has nearly 3,000 permanent residents who commute to Townsville to work. But nearly two-thirds of the island is a National Park, which restricts further development and allows the island to retain its appeal. Getting there is easy: the high-speed catamarans from Townsville take 20 mins and are very inexpensive.

Orientation

The island is a rough triangle with the main centre of **Picnic Bay** at its southern point. This is where the ferries arrive. The right side of the triangle, the east side, is where most of the development has taken place. You first come to **Rocky Bay**, which has an excellent beach, and then **Nelly Bay**. There is a plan to develop Nelly Bay in the canal style which probably started in Florida and is now a serious blight in Queensland. There is a Save Nelly Bay website at enterprise.powerup.com.au/~rod-julie/. Close by is what is left of the Magnetic Quay development, a plan to build a marina and hotel that went bust.

Beyond **Geoffrey Bay** is **Arcadia** and, back from the road, the **Alma Bay Lookout.** The road then splits with the left fork taking you to **Horseshoe Bay** and the right to **Radical Bay Lookout**. **Magnetic Island National Park** fills much of the centre of the island, reaching up to the coast in the north and for a third of the east coast.

Travelling Around

It is possible to ferry a vehicle across but this is expensive and uneconomic for a short stay. Bicycles, motorcycles and cars are available for hire. The amazing Mini Moke is ideal for this island and Moke Magnetic, on the Esplanade at Picnic Bay (tel: 4778 5377) has the largest fleet of Mokes for hire in Australia. The Magnetic Island Bus Service offers 5-day pass tickets and has two guided tours of the island every day.

What to Do

This is a low-pressure sort of place and the weather is ever pleasant: typically 1°

below that of the mainland and in a rain shadow that ensures 320 sunny days a year. Most of the people who come here on holiday are regulars. The only time to avoid is possibly during the Christmas break.

There are things to do. For **bird-watchers** over 100 species of birds have been sighted on the island, including blue-wing kookaburras, sulphur crested cockatoos and black cockatoos. An 8-km walk from Picnic Bay to West Point offers the chance to sight wading birds, mud skippers, fiddler crabs and mangrove snails that inhabit these wetlands, particularly in the Cockle Bay area.

There is plenty of **bushwalking**. An excellent leaflet produced by the National Parks (available at the tourist office) shows all the many walks on the island. These will take you to most places in the national park area, through a variety of flora and fauna. The hillsides are strewn with boulders and covered with mostly open eucalypt woodland of bloodwoods, stringybark and grey ironbarks. There are also small pockets of rainforest in the gullies. You will certainly see rock wallabies and perhaps koalas - this is the most northerly point in Australia to have large free ranging colonies.

For those not willing to make the trek there is the **Koala Park Oasis**. It is always full of visitors being photographed with the koalas, and the kangaroos, lorikeets, wallabies, emus, cockatoos and wombats. The lorikeets come in for a feed at 1130 each day. The sanctuary is on Pacific Dr., Horseshoe Bay and is open daily. Tel: 4778 5260.

WATER SPORTS

The fringing reef is wonderful for snorkelling. Beaches range from the wildly popular to the almost totally deserted. Some, such as **Balding Bay**, are so secluded they can only be reached by walking or by boat. Easier to reach is **Arthur Bay**, which has some of the best snorkelling, as well as interesting caves. The largest, noisiest and busiest bay on the island is **Horseshoe**, where almost every watercraft imaginable is available for hire. There are camel rides along the beach, and if that is too tame for you, try parasailing. Several fishing boats can normally be seen anchored at the eastern end of the bay making ready for their trip out to the Great Barrier Reef.

Pleasure Divers is just metres from some of the best dive sites in Geoffrey and Alma bays. It teaches everything from resort diving to full PADI certification and runs Outer Barrier Reef trips and dive trips to the famous Yongala wreck. Shop 2, Arcadia Resort, Arcadia; tel: 4778 5788; email: pleasure.divers@ultra.net.au

The waters are part of the Great Barrier Reef Marine Park which means that certain activities may be restricted in some zones part of the time. Get details of what is and what is not allowed from the Great Barrier Reef Marine Park Authority or the Department of Environment and Heritage in Townsville.

INFORMATION

Magnetic Island Tourist Information Centre, Esplanade, next to the water taxi pier on Picnic Bay; tel: 4778 5155.

INTERNET SITES **Magnetic Island** www.ozemail.com.au/~magislnd/

ACCOMMODATION

No other island in Australia has such a wide range of affordable accommodation. You can stay within access of a perfect beach probably for less than you can stay anywhere else remotely comparable. The basic idea on Magnetic is to rent an apartment between four people or more, then the prices become very low indeed.

Backpacker's Resort $ 1 The Esplanade, on Picnic Bay; tel: 4778 5166. For backpackers, with three bars and the island's nightclub. Only for the young who don't mind noise and sharing.

Beaches $ 39 Marine Parade; tel: 4778 5303: email: tschaer@tpgi.com.au. Bed and breakfast. Timber cottage on Geoffrey Bay.

Champagne Apartments $$ 21 Marine Pde; tel: 4778 5002. Gently sloping beach of Geoffrey Bay fronts the apartments.

Dandaloo Gardens $ 40 Hayles Ave; tel: 4778 5174. Set among towering paper-bark trees.

Dunoon Beachfront Apartments $ The Esplanade. On the beach at Picnic Bay; tel: 4778 5532. Tropical gardens, two pools, spa.

Hideaway Budget Resort $ 32 Picnic St, on Picnic Bay, 120 m from the Island's ferry arrival and departure point; tel: 4778 5881; email stothart@ultra.net.au. Double and twin rooms.

Island Palms Resort $$ 13 The Esplanade, Nelly Bay; tel: 4778 5571. On the beachfront. A short stroll to shops, restaurants and the supermarket.

Magnetic Haven $$ 7 Rheuben Ter, in Arcadia Bay; tel: 4778 5824; email maghaven@ozemail.com.au.

Magnetic Island Holiday Units $ 16 Yule St; tel: 4778 5246. On Picnic Bay set in tropical gardens with birds, butterflies, possums and rock wallabies. 150 m from beach. 150 m from ferry.

Magnetic Island Tropical Resort $ 26–56 Yates St. Nelly Bay; tel: 4778 5955, email tropres@byte-tsv.net.au. Set in 16 acres, just 200 m from the beach. Winner of 13 major tourism awards.

Magnetic North Apartments $ 2 Endeavour Rd; tel: 4778 5244. Two-bedroom apartments in tropical gardens in Arcadia. A short stroll from Alma Bay beach.

Nautilis House $ 18 West Point Rd; tel: 4778 5802. Bed and breakfast.

Picnic Bay Holiday Hotel $ The Esplanade, beachfront; tel: 4778 5166. Tropical gardens, public and garden bars, bistro.

Ti-Tree Lodge $ 1 Barbarra St; tel: 4778 5499.

FOOD

Most of the restaurants are around Picnic Bay and you can eat there very inexpensively, but this is not the gastronomic destination of Australia.

Crusoe's Magnetic Island Restaurant $ 5a Picnic Bay; tel: 4778 5480. A sort of upmarket fish and chip shop – most of the cafés in Picnic Bay are of that style – but with great views.

The Lattice Winner, Magnetic Island Tropical Resort $ 26–56 Yates St, Nelly Bay; tel: 4778 5955. Winner of many awards. Bistro-style meals at budget prices to à la carte dining.

Magnetic Island Chinese Restaurant 9 The Esplanade, Picnic Bay; tel:4778 5706.

Possum's Cafe $ Nelly Bay Shopping Plaza, Nelly Bay; tel: 4778 5409. Basic, but delicious and inexpensive, grub. Open weekdays 0800–2100, Sat 0800–2000, Sun 0800–1500.

WHERE NEXT?

North lies Cairns, capital of the 'Far North' (see p. 296), or for a very different side of Australia, the Flinders Hwy heads inland for Alice Springs and Uluru (Ayers Rock) (see p. 330).

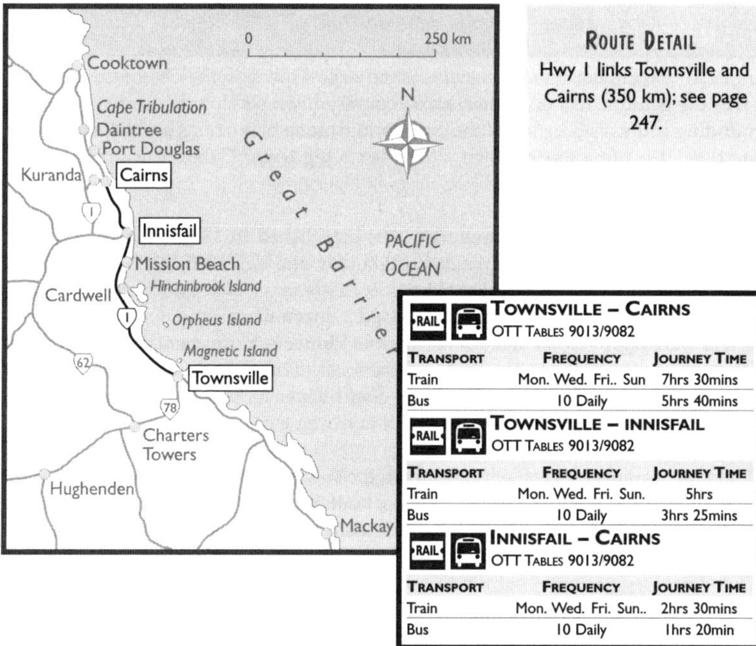

ROUTE DETAIL

Hwy 1 links Townsville and Cairns (350 km); see page 247.

TOWNSVILLE – CAIRNS
OTT TABLES 9013/9082

TRANSPORT	FREQUENCY	JOURNEY TIME
Train	Mon. Wed. Fri.. Sun	7hrs 30mins
Bus	10 Daily	5hrs 40mins

TOWNSVILLE – INNISFAIL
OTT TABLES 9013/9082

TRANSPORT	FREQUENCY	JOURNEY TIME
Train	Mon. Wed. Fri. Sun.	5hrs
Bus	10 Daily	3hrs 25mins

INNISFAIL – CAIRNS
OTT TABLES 9013/9082

TRANSPORT	FREQUENCY	JOURNEY TIME
Train	Mon. Wed. Fri. Sun..	2hrs 30mins
Bus	10 Daily	1hrs 20min

THE CASSOWARY COAST: TOWNSVILLE TO CAIRNS

It was, of course, Captain Cook who, on his momentous voyage in 1770, was the first European to discover what is called the Cassowary Coast region. He did not land as his previous attempts to do so had met with a hostile reception. The first European to actually explore this countryside was Edmund Kennedy, who had undertaken to investigate the country between the coast and the Great Dividing Range up to Cape York. His journey showed that successful settlement of the district's coast would require regular sea communication due to the difficulty and cost of building roads through the dense tropical terrain.

The discovery of rich deposits of gold and other metals on and beyond the Atherton Tableland made the government keen to open up the tropical North Coast. Cardwell was the first settlement, followed by Port Douglas, Cairns and the town of Geraldton – renamed Innisfail in 1910 after a mix-up in a shipping delivery intended for Geraldton, Western Australia.

ROUTE

INNISFAIL

Innisfail, 260 km north of Townsville, is the largest town on the Cassowary Coast. It gives the genuine feel of a Queensland country town serving the needs of the surrounding countryside, mainly the sugar and banana plantations and the small fishing fleet. It is not a tourist town – there is no Big Sugar Cube – but it has a lot of charm.

The town's strong Italian community was established in 1880 when the Catholic Bishop of Brisbane and 11 Carmelite nuns bought and cleared 10,000 ha of jungle for sugar planting. (The nuns probably had very little to do with the transaction, but to acquire such a large tract the bishop needed a dozen names and no doubt the good sisters were happy to volunteer.) The marble **Pioneers Monument** at the end of the main street was given to the town by the local Italians. It shows a cane-cutter at work and reminds everyone that sugar could never have initially been harvested without their unrelenting physical labour in extreme conditions.

Asian immigrants also came here to work the sugar fields and their influence is still very apparent. There is even a **joss house,** built in the 1940s after an earlier one was destroyed in a hurricane. There is also a small **museum**, housed in the old School of Arts building and run by volunteers. Open Mon 1300–1500, Tues–Fri 1000–1200, 1300–1500.

Cassowary Coast Development Bureau, River Dr; tel: 4061 6448.
Queensland National Parks & Wildlife Services, Rising Sun Shopping Centre, Owen St; tel: 4061 4291.
Innisfail www.gspeak.com.au/Innisfail/

On Fitzgerald Esplanade there is a **fish depot** where you can buy seafood fresh from the boats.

Backpackers $ 73 Rankin St; tel: 4061 2284.
Barrier Reef Motel $ Bruce Hwy; tel: 4061 4988. 41 self-contained units.
Black Marlin Motel $ 26 Glady St; tel: 4061 2533. Centrally located.
Carefree Motel $ 14 Owen St; tel: 4061 2266.
Endeavour Hostel $ 31 Glady St; tel: 4061 6610.
Mango Tree Caravan Park $ 26 Couche St; tel: 4061 1656.
Moondarra Motel $ 21 Ernest St; tel: 4061 7077.
Motel Robert Johnstone $$ Grace St, cnr Fitzgerald Esp; tel: 4061 2444.
Motel Walkabout $ 7 Ernest St; tel: 4061 2311.
River Drive Van Park $ Bruce Hwy; tel: 4061 2515.

Downunder Restaurant $ 66 Edith St; tel: 4061 2630.
Flamingo Coffee Lounge $ Rankin St; tel: 40614407.
Gumloon Restaurant $ 96 Edith St; tel: 40611164.
Lee Yick's Joung Var Chinese Restaurant $ 168 Edith St; tel: 4061 1360.
Roscoes Pizza Restaurant $ 166 Edith St; tel: 4061 6888. BYO.
Taste Of The Tropics Restaurant $ Ernest St, cnr Bruce Hwy; tel: 4061 4533.
Underground Restaurant $ 22 Owen St; tel: 4061 1128.
Wai Young Chinese Restaurant $ 156 Edith St; tel: 4061 3309.

NATIONAL PARKS

Between Innisfail and the sea is **Ella Bay National Park**, and next to it the **Eubenangee Swamp National Park**. This preserves the last remaining wetlands between Townsville and Cairns. Car access is off the Bruce Hwy from Miriwinni. There is a long boardwalk to provide access to the interior - you will need insect repellent - which is full of bird life and also has its fair share of crocodiles. Off the boardwalk, vines make the going difficult.

About 30 km west of Innisfail are the **Nerada Tea Gardens and Tourist Centre**. These were started in 1959 and claim to be the only commercially productive tea plantation in Australia. Open daily 0900–1630. The gardens are in the foothills of **Mount Bartle Frere**, Queensland's highest mountain. It lies in the **Bellenden Ker National Park** and if you are following the Bruce Hwy north towards Cairns, the Bellenden Ker range will be there on your left for the rest of the 80-km journey. The park is by and large totally undeveloped and only for experienced bush walkers, but there are picnic areas with low waterfalls and swimming sites near the turn-offs at Babinda, Pawngilly and 5 km south of Gordonvale.

The Palmerston Hwy out of Innisfail cuts through the **Palmerston National Park** which has wonderful rainforest scenery, along with gorges, waterfalls and extremely clear, freshwater swimming holes. Forestry tracks criss-crossing the park can be bumpy going but in the dry season are normally accessible. The North Johnstone River runs through the park, and during and after the wet season provides excellent white-water rafting. At the Tchupala Falls there is a self-guiding trail through the rainforest. Beyond the park the road runs on to the town of Millaa Millaa and the Atherton Tableland (see p. 302).

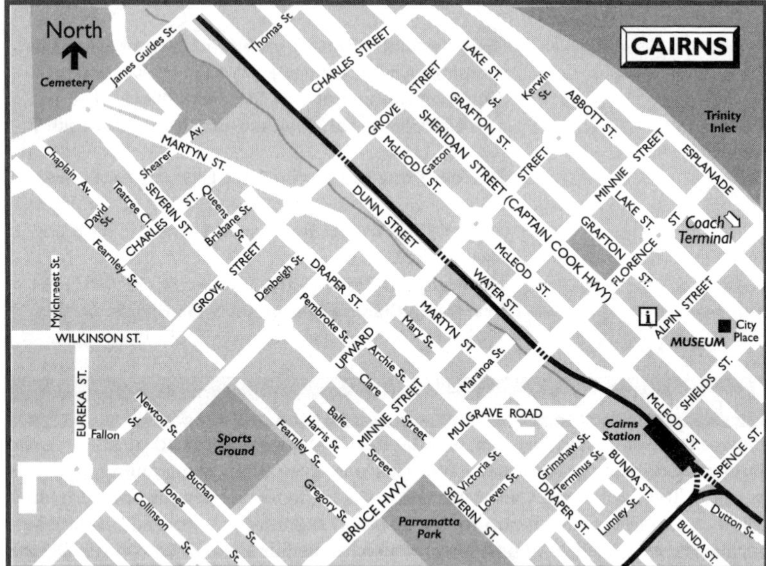

Cairns has a feeling of being planned specifically for the tropics. There is an esplanade running right around the city and the foreshore, parks and gardens appear to be perpetually ablaze with exotic flowers and trees. It is perfectly sited for both relaxing and adventurous exploration, with the Great Barrier Reef to the east, the refreshing green plains of the Atherton Tableland to the west, palm-fringed beaches north and south and, just up the track, the wonders of the Daintree rainforest.

Cairns has a sense that it is just coming into its own, that its prospects are pleasing. Indeed, Cairns is very pleasing, except that it had a distressing tendency until recently to pull down the last beautiful examples of Far North Queensland wooden architecture; only now are the last ones being preserved.

Capt Cook sailed the Endeavour into Trinity Bay on Trinity Sunday 1770, but it was 1873 before the first pioneers came to settle what was then called Thornton. When gold was found in the area it remained a sleepy backwater while Cooktown (see p. 309) boomed. In 1876, the township was renamed in honour of the Governor of

Queensland, Sir William Cairns, and declared the port of entry and customs points. Tremendous trading rivalry arose and continued for many years between Cairns and Port Douglas, just to the north, until the railway line from Brisbane was only extended as far as Cairns and Port Douglas lapsed into tropical somnolence.

Today, tourism is a major factor in the prosperity of Cairns – every day over 600 land, sea and air tours depart from here, taking visitors to experience nearby natural attractions.

ARRIVAL AND DEPARTURE

Cairns has an international airport on the outskirts of the city, with an inexpensive shuttle service into the city centre. Short-hop local flights, such as Cooktown, operate from a separate airport slightly to the north.

Cairns is the end of the line for bus routes up the east coast; the ride from Townsville, 350 km south, takes 4½ to 6 hours depending on the number of stops. The terminus is the central Lake St Transit Centre.

INFORMATION

TOURIST OFFICE **Cairns Tourist Information Office**, Far North Queensland Promotion Bureau, Cnr Grafton and Hartly Sts; tel: 4051 3588.

INTERNET ACCESS **The Call Station**, Pier Market Place, Cairns waterfront. Open daily; tel:4031 4679.

Public Internet Access Shop, 1/343 Sheridan St, North Cairns; tel: 4031 6883.

INTERNET SITE **Cairns Visitor Information**
www.ozemail.com.au/~castaway/cairns/cns.html

ACCOMMODATION

This is very much backpackers' territory. Provided you insist on a room with air-conditioning and your own loo and shower, they are perfectly fine and very inexpensive.

Acacia Court Hotel $$ 223 The Esplanade; tel: 4051 5011.

Adobe Motel $ 191 Sheridan St; tel: 4051 5511.

Bellview $ 83 The Esplanade; tel: 4031 4377.

Cairns Backpackers Inn $ 242 Grafton Rd; tel: 4031 9166.

Cairns Gateway Lodge Motel $ 35 37 Bruce Hwy; tel: 4055 4394. 24 units set amongst mountains but near town.

Cairns Motor Inn $ 187 Sheridan St; tel: 4051 5166.

Caravella Backpackers Hostel $ 149 Esplanade St; tel: 4031 5680. Only a short walk to the city with views to the waterfront.

Coral Tree Inn $$ 166 Grafton St; tel: 4031 3744.

Great Northern Hotel $$ 69 Abbott St; tel: 4051 5966. This 36-room hotel is centrally located and ideal for overnight stays before or after dive trips.

Half Moon Bay Resort $$ 101–3 Wattle St, Yorkeys Knob; tel: 4055 8059; tmail: info@halfmoonbayresort.com.au. Fully self-contained holiday apartments at Half Moon Bay Golf Club on Cairns Northern beaches.

International Hostel $ 67 The Esplanade; tel: 4031 1424.

Leichardt Motel $ 465 Mulgrave Rd; tel: 07 4054 5499: email: wackos@tpgi.com.au.

Mariner Gables Holiday Apartments $$ Trinity Beach; tel: 4057 8417; email: gables@internetnorth.com.au. Two-bed-roomed apartments.

Nutmeg Grove Bed and Breakfast $$ 7 Woodridge Close, Redlynch; tel: 07 40391226; email: ingridd@ozemail.com.au. Set on 3 acres of rainforest

The Flats $ 102 Martyn St; tel: 4031 7123.

Travellers Oasis $ 8 Scott St; tel: 4032 1377.

YHA Esplanade $ 93 The Esplanade; tel: 4031 919.

YHA $ McLeod St. 20-24 McLeod St; tel: 4031 0772.

FOOD

Bangkok Room $ 2 45 Grafton St; tel: 4051 8338. Thai. BYO.

Breezes $$ Wharf Rd; tel: 4052 1599. Overlooks Trinity Wharf. Seafood specialities and the place is as open and airy as the name. Seafood buffet on Fri and Sat from 1800. Open daily. Licensed.

Charlie's 223–7 The Esplanade; tel: 4051 5011. About 2 km from downtown but highly spoken of for its fish dishes. Licensed.

Cock'n'Bull $ Cnr Grove and Digger Sts; tel: 4031 1160. Budget meals and an extensive range of international beers in an English-style pub.

Damari's $$ 171 Lake St; Tel: 4031 2155. Lunch Mon–Fri, dinner nightly. Licensed.

Donnini's $$ Pier Marketplace; tel: 4347 3128. Open daily for lunch and dinner. Licensed. Italian cuisine.

Dundee's $$ 171 Lake St, Cnr Aplin and Sheridan Sts; tel: 4051 0399. Open daily for dinner. Licensed. Australian food crocodile, emu and fresh seafood.

Healthy Life $ 74 Grafton St; tel: 4051 3282. Donít even think about smoking.

Kani's Restaurant $$ 59 The Esplanade; tel: 4051 1550; email: wege@internetnorth.com.au Specialises in seafood and overlooks the Cairns waterfront.

La Fettucine $$ 43 Shields St; tel: 4031 5959. BYO. Italian cuisine. Open daily for dinner.

Red Ochre Grill Restaurant $$ 43 Shields St; tel: 40551010. Sort of modified bush tucker. A new Australian cuisine.

Sawasdee $$ 89 Grafton St; tel: 4031 7993. BYO. Thai cuisine. Open daily lunch and dinner.

Taste of China $$ 36 Abbott St; tel: 4031 3688. Licensed. Open daily for lunch and dinner.

Vegetarian Gardens $ 149 Spence St; tel: 4031 6317.

Vegi Table Grafton St; tel: 4051 0610. Vegetarian and vegan food.

The Woolshed $ 24 Shields St; tel: 4031 6304. Very much for the younger set. Every night until 0300, inexpensive meals, Aussie Woolshed décor, dancing on tables, loud music and outrageous party games.

HIGHLIGHTS

The **Esplanade Walking Trail**, which runs for 3 km along the foreshore, is a chance to get Cairns into perspective. On the walk you will see the wharves around Trinity Inlet, which originally accounted for its prosperity. Hotels and businesses are beginning to appear in this old area, called the Barbary Coast, showing the shift in emphasis within the town. But the character remains.

Almost everything is within easy walking distance, including two big shopping centres, the Pier and Calms Central, catering mainly to the Japanese tourist trade. In fact, shopping is a major part of the city centre attractions.

Wildworld Australia on the Captain Cook Hwy has over 100 freshwater and saltwater crocodiles. Open daily 0900–1700; tel: 4055 3669.

The **House of 10,000 Shells** in Abbott St is basically a shop although it does have an extensive shell collection and a museum with a display of Australiana, souvenirs, semiprecious and coral jewellery. Open Mon–Sat 0900–2200.

The **Cairns Museum and Art Gallery** is housed in what was the school of art at the corner of Lake and Shields Street. Among other delights it has the contents of a joss house which stood until recently in Grafton Street. It also shows the construction of the rail link between Cairns and Kuranda. One major section is devoted to the history of the Aboriginal people in the area - essential if you are to understand how Cairns, a late developer as a town, is the result of a series of conflicting pressures. Open daily 1000–1500.

Boardwalks are very popular in Cairns. There is an **environmental park** with a boardwalk in Anderson Street by which you can walk over a remnant of lowland tea tree swamp. During the Wet this walk shows you the original vegetation of Cairns. **The Jack Barnes Bicentennial Mangrove Boardwalk**, on the road to the airport, is a series of educational walks through the complex ecosystem of a mangrove swamp. Hides let you see the life of the mangrove swamps up close. Spray yourself well with insect repellent before you set out for either.

The **Flecker Botanical Gardens** on Collins Avenue are open daily, 0730–1730 and cover 400 ha up the slopes of Mt Whitfield. Instead of trying to re-create European vegetation, as several parks in the south of Australia do, the plants here reflect the wide range of local coastal wetlands and rainforest - over 10,000 species in all.

At the **Royal Flying Doctor Base**, near the gardens, you can see how this organisation, unique to Australia, has operated in the Outback since 1928. 1 Junction St, Edge Hill. Open daily to the public; tel: 4033 3687.

BEACH AND SEA LIFE

Cairns itself does not have beach but in a 26-km sweep up towards Port Douglas are some of the best in Australia. Closest to the city are **Machans**, **Holloways**, **Yorkey's Knob** and **Trinity Palm Cove**, which is both a beach and a resort. In summer stinger

EXCURSIONS TO THE GREAT BARRIER REEF

Cairns is a good place to take a cruise out to the reef. The boats have to be speedy to get you out and back in a single day and therefore the price of the trip is not inexpensive. See also p. 281.

Seastar Reef Trips Outer Reef. Tel: 4033 0333; 0700–1800.

Sunlovers Reef Cruises Outer edge of the reef and islands full day. Buffet lunch and snacks. Tel: 4031 1033.

You can also sail out to the reef, usually staying out overnight:

Barrier Reef Sailing Company Tel: 4041 1138.

Golden Plover Tel: 4033 2024. Day sailing trips.

Moonlighting II Tel: 4030 0622. Sail, dive, snorkel trips to the outer reef.

Many dive schools and operators rent out scuba gear:

Cairns Dive Centre 121 Abbott St; tel: 1800 642 391.

Deep Sea Divers Den 319 Draper St; tel: 4031 2223.

Down Under Dive 155 Sheridan St; tel: 4031 1288.

Pro Dive 16 Spence St; tel: 4031 3233.

The following are among operators who run 3- to 4-day scuba-diving expeditions:

Reef Encounter Tel: 1800 815 811 or 4050 0688. 2-day/1-night 6 dives.

Santa Maria Tel: 4031 0338. 3 days, 2 nights, food, diving and snorkelling.

Rum Runner Tel: 1800 803 183. 4-day and 3-night trips. Choose Cod Hole and Great Barrier Reef and/or Coral Sea and shark feeding.

jellyfish can inflict a grievous wound, but some of the northern beaches have stinger enclosures, offering safe swimming all year.

Marlin Jetty is where the marlin sports-fishing boats are based, as well as most of the boats that make the run to the islands. One of the more popular short trips is aboard *SS Louisa*, a paddle wheeler which runs a 2½-hr tour around the harbour, up Trinity Inlet and through the Everglades. Tel: 4034 1143.

NIGHTLIFE

Cairns, like every other city in Australia, has a casino. The Reef Hotel Casino in Wharf St is built around and is part of the old Customs House. The casino is topped with a four storey conservatory in a delicate glass dome which is open to the non-gambling public.

DAY TRIPS

One of the great delights of Cairns is its closeness to one of the most pleasant areas of country in Australia. The **Atherton Tableland** stretching out to the west contains rainforest, waterfalls and wonderful wildlife, and has a different style and feel.

Atherton itself is 85 km southwest of Cairns on the Kennedy Hwy and more than 760 m above sea-level. It can be argued that the climate up on the Tableland is the best in Australia. Certainly it seems close to perfect all year - if it is a little too hot and moist for you in Cairns you merely escape by driving up to Atherton.

The Tableland is rich in national parks - seven in all - with lush tropical rainforest, waterfalls and lakes to explore. Many tourists coming through north Queensland skip Atherton and the Tableland thinking, perhaps, that they do not compare with the splendours of the Daintree further north. But the Atherton Tablelands have a quiet, elegant charm all of their own and, if time allows, you should spend at least a day up there looking at the splendid scenery and enjoying the weather.

You can get to **Kuranda**, up on the Tableland, in three different ways. To drive is interesting and pleasant but the alternatives are so much better. The train runs on what is arguably the finest stretch of scenic railway line in Australia. One section actually runs across the face of the Stony Creek Falls and the views are nothing short of amazing.

When the Skyrail to Kuranda was first proposed there was much opposition from environmentalists but it has worked very well, is not intrusive and does not

THE TJAPUKAI ABORIGINAL CULTURAL PARK

This is a rare opportunity to experience Aboriginal culture, in this case the society of the Djabugay and Yirrgandyji peoples. So-called 'cultural shows' are often dreadful. The Tjapukai Aboriginal Theatre is the exception: remarkably entertaining, informative and moving. Each dancer explains a particular aspect of Aboriginal life ranging from the boomerang to the didgeridoo, songsticks, spears and clothing – blended with dancing and singing using quite modern and stunning techniques. The theme which comes across time and time again is 'Proud to be an Aboriginei'. Unmissable.

appear to have damaged the rainforest as was feared. You travel for 7.5 km – perhaps the worldís longest cable-car trip – over rainforest up to the top of the escarpment. It is a most wonderful journey. There are stops at the Barron Falls Station for a staggering view of the Barron Gorge, and at Red Peak Station, where you can inspect the rainforest from a wooden walkway.

Kuranda is pretty, fits neatly into the mountains, and is in a 1960s time warp: in its market you can have your fortune told, buy the right aromatics for what ails you and eat vegetarian food.

There is also Australian Butterfly Sanctuary with up to 2000 butterflies covering 35 indigenous and protected species in a rainforest enclosed by a massive walk-through flight aviary, and the Kuranda Wildlife Noctarium, described as 'the world's best live display of Australian nocturnal animals in a natural rainforest setting.' Both open daily 1000–1600.

WHERE NEXT?

Cairns is the Far North, but the tip of Australia is still over 1000 km away. Take a tour up to Cooktown and the York Peninsula (see pp. 311–12). Or spend time on the Great Barrier Reef (see p. 276).

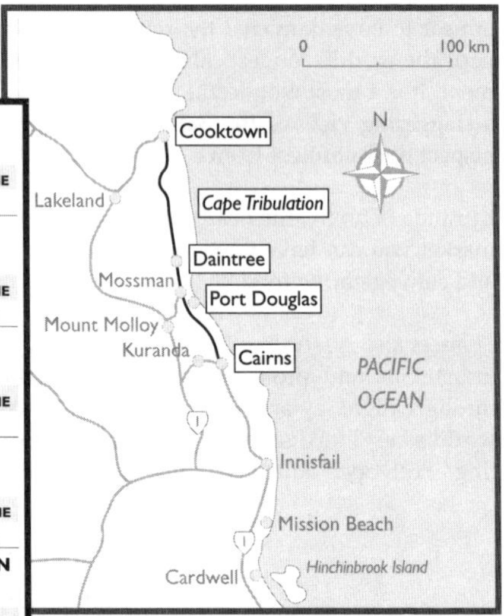

CAIRNS – COOKTOWN
OTT TABLE 9089

TRANSPORT	FREQUENCY	JOURNEY TIME
Bus	Tuesday & Saturday	8hrs

CAIRNS – PORT DOUGLAS
OTT TABLE 9089

TRANSPORT	FREQUENCY	JOURNEY TIME
Bus	9 Daily	1hr 30mins

PORT DOUGLASS – MOSSMAN
OTT TABLE 9089

TRANSPORT	FREQUENCY	JOURNEY TIME
Bus	10 Daily	30mins

MOSSMAN – CAPE TRIBULATION
OTT TABLE 9089

TRANSPORT	FREQUENCY	JOURNEY TIME
Bus	3 Daily	1hr 45mins

CAPE TRIBULATION – COOKTOWN
OTT TABLE 9089

TRANSPORT	FREQUENCY	JOURNEY TIME
Bus	Tuesday & Saturday	4hrs

Note: There are additional services from Cairns to Cooktown going via Lakeland. Greyhound Pioneer operate regular coach tours on these routes but some of their passes are not valid on them.

ROUTE DETAIL

The 53 km north to Port Douglas and Mossman are regular highway. After Mossman it continues in a series of zigzags either north to Daintree or inland to Mount Malloy and then north on the inland road towards Lakeland. But there is a total transformation. Roads which were sealed become intermittently sealed and then just graded dirt. Bulldust, ultra-fine powder, is everywhere choking engine filters which have to be cleaned every day. In the Wet many of the roads to the north, sealed or not, are impassable, in the dry they can be a challenge. With a conventional vehicle you could, in the Dry, drive as far as Cooktown if you head first for Lakeland (220 km from Cairns) and then turn inland for the last 54 km of the journey.

THE COOK HIGHWAY: CAIRNS TO COOKTOWN

Port Douglas, just an hour from Cairns, is a laid-back tropical resort, while Daintree, on the banks of the Daintree River, is the gateway to the Daintree National Park and the starting point for a rough ride up to Cooktown, where the great navigator and 'discoverer' of Australia is commemorated. Driving on the Cape York Peninsula is like embarking on an expedition.

PORT DOUGLAS

Port Douglas is, in some ways, an upmarket extension of Cairns. They are only 70 km apart and the airport services both. The town is all low-rise and possibly the only other two towns in Australia which offer a similarly relaxed yet stylish approach to life are Byron Bay and Noosa Heads.

Port Douglas was first established in 1877 when Christie Palmerston (in full, Cristofero Palmerston Carandini, a remarkable man from a theatrical family but with a great talent for trailblazing) cut a road through the rainforest and down the mountain range. The town rose rapidly with the gold rush, but when Cairns won the battle for major port in the area, Port Douglas went into dormancy.

Then Christopher Skase came along. Skase was one of a handful of over-ambitious entrepreneurs in Australia in the '70s and '80s. He took a total backwater and changed it into an international resort. Then his companies – the lead company was called Quintex – crashed resoundingly. If, in his ambition, he had not tried to buy an American film studio he might have weathered the storm and he would now be praised for his foresight in creating one of Australia's foremost resorts.

i **Port Douglas Tourist Information Centre**, 23 Macrossan St; tel. 4099 5599.
Cyberworld Internet Café, 38 Macrossan St, Port Douglas (at rear of Salsa Bar and Grill). Tel: 4099 3661. Open daily 0900–2200.
Port Douglas Visitors Bureau www.great-barrier-reef.com/vi001.html
Port Douglas Daintree Tourism Association www.ozemail.com.au/~portdoug/dsta1.html

Although Port Douglas does attract the very rich – and some of the prices charged at the top end would choke a

EN ROUTE

During the 1930s, Depression job-creation labourers built a dirt road from Cairns to Port Douglas. A man known as Pop Evans established a roadhouse at Hartley's Creek about halfway between the two towns and to entertain visitors performed shows featuring local wildlife. In 1934 he acquired Charlie the crocodile. Charlie is now estimated to be between 70 and 80 years old and holds the record for the longest held crocodile in captivity. Now **Hartley's Creek Crocodile Farm** (tel: 4055 3576) is not only home to hundreds of crocodiles (both freshwater and salt water), but also koalas, kangaroos, cassowaries, dingoes, snakes and other native animals.

The **Rex Lookout** is also about halfway from Cairns and it is worth pulling over for the view and to watch the hang-gliders soaring like birds.

horse – there is an extensive range of affordable accommodation.

Archipelago $ 72 Macrossan St; tel: 4099 5387. Newly renovated. 50 m from the beach in downtown Port Douglas.

Coconut Grove Motel $ 58 Macrossan St; tel: 4099 5124; email coco@internetnorth.com.au. Very affordable, in the town centre,100 m to the beach.

Garrick House $$ 11–13 Garrick St; tel: 4099 5322; email: garrick@internetnorth.com.au. 200 m from the beach and a 5-min walk from the town centre.

Lychee Tree Holiday Units $$ 95 Davidson St; tel: 4099 5811. 1.5 km from town and 250 m from the beach. Minimum 3-night stay.

Port Douglas Backpackers $ Tel: 4099 4883; email farnorth@ozemail.com.au. Large air-conditioned rooms.

Port Douglas Motel $$ 9 Davidson St; tel: 4099 5248. Slightly out of town but very near the beach.

Port Douglas Queenslander $$ 81 Macrossan St; tel: 4099 5199. 5-min walk from town and beach. Lush tropical gardens and large pool.

Port Douglas Studios $$ 9 Davidson St; tel: 4099 4644; email visitors@greatbarrierreef.aus.net. Long established motel. 2-min walk from main street, Marina Mirage and Four Mile Beach.

Restaurants here tend to be horrendously upmarket and expensive or very noisy. Luckily it is very easy to stroll along Macrossan, Port and Wharf Sts and peer into the many cafés and ethnic restaurants, see if you like the place and then check the menu prices.

Bandito's Mexican Cafe and Expresso Bar $ 38a Macrossan St; tel: 4099 5850. Open daily. Tends to be noisy.

Belmont French Restaurant $$ 30 Macrossan St; tel: 4099 4229.

Catalina $$ Wharf St; tel: 4099 5287. Seafood specialities. Licensed. Open Tues–Sun for lunch and dinner.

Combined Clubs Bistro $$ Ashford Ave; tel: 4099 5553. Super waterfront views.

Courthouse Hotel Bistro $ Corner of Wharf and Macrossan Sts; tel: 4099 5181. Beer-garden setting. Live music.

Danny's $ Wharf St; tel: 4099 5535.

Going Bananas $$ 87 Davidson St; tel: 4099 5340. Very Port

Douglas. Tropical castaway feeling to an upmarket restaurant. Licensed. Open dinner Mon–Sat.

Han Court Chinese Restaurant $$ 85 Davidson St; tel: 4099 5007. Local seafood. Cantonese.

Jade Inn $ 25 Macrossan St; tel: 4099 5974. Cantonese.

La Marina Ristorante Italiano $$ Marina Mirage; tel:4099 5548. Award winner. Dining on the marina boardwalk Port Douglas. Open daily for lunch and dinner.

Marinella On The Waterfront $$ 44 Wharf St; tel: 4099 5081.

Nautilus $$ 17 Murphy St; tel: 4099 5330. Seafood specialities. Open-air setting. Licensed. Open nightly for dinner.

Rusty's Bar and Bistro $ 123 Davidson St; tel: 4099 5266. Noisy. Licensed. Open daily.

Snappers Restaurant $$ Port Douglas Rd; tel:4099 3447. Seafood specialities.

Star Of Siam $ 38 Macrossan St; tel: 4099 4707. Traditional Thai-style seafood.

Taste of Thailand $ Pandanus Plaza; tel: 4099 4384. Authentic Thai.

HIGHLIGHTS

Port Douglas lies on a long low spit of land and one of its charms is that all of the main roads are lined with palm trees.

Rainforest Habitat has won awards galore. You can explore it on your own, but the experience is massively heightened if you go with one of the professional guides. You will see over 60 species of rare birds, koalas, kangaroos and crocodiles in their natural environment, viewing from elevated walkways. You can even have breakfast with the birds. The entrance is on Port Douglas Rd; open daily 0800–1730 (Wildlife Sanctuary gates close at 1630); tel: 4099 3235.

Ben Cropp's Shipwreck Treasure Trove Museum is far better than most in this category (although the signage outside could be toned down). It is at Ben Cropp's Wharf; open daily 0900-1700; tel: 4099 5858.

The activities available in and around Port Douglas are very varied. There are, for example, several world-class golf courses which are also world-class expensive. Much more affordable is the Four Mile Beach, cycling around the town, climbing up Flagstaff Hill or just idling along and enjoying the atmosphere. You can take the **Bally Hooley Railway** from Marina Station for St Crispins (departures on the hour;

LEARN TO SCUBA

The Great Barrier Reef is one place where scuba-diving is not essential – you can see more aquatic life in a day with snorkel and fins then you would see in a lifetime of scuba-diving elsewhere. But because the water is so warm and the scenery so magnificent it is a good place to get at least a resort certificate, which will let you dive with a qualified diver. Many places offer this; in the town itself the **Port Douglas Dive Centre**, Anzac Park (open daily 0845–1730; tel: 4099 5327) probably has the widest range of courses and offers escorted trips out to the reef when you have your resort ticket, which should not take you longer than a day.

check timetable with the tourist office). This open-carriage steam train potters through the interior to a crushing mill for sugar cane. Or the paddle wheeler ***Lady Douglas*** makes her stately way up the Dickson Inlet, with daily departures at 0930, 1025, 1315 and 1425.

Port Douglas is the closest mainland resort to the Great Barrier Reef, but it is never emphasised that the reef is a fair way out and you need to go by very fast boat to get the most out of it. Of the wide range of **cruises** on offer at the Marina the most popular is a super-fast catamaran, *Quicksilver*, which carries 300 passengers and heads out to the Agincourt Reef at 1100. This is an expensive trip but is the easiest way to explore the reef from here. Tel: 4099 5500.

Much closer in are the **coral gardens of the Low Isles**. Visit them aboard the *Shaolin*, a junk of doubtful authenticity.

The **Karnak Playhouse and Rainforest Sanctuary** borders the Daintree National Park under a rocky outcrop called Manjal Jimalji – the Devil's Thumb. It was started by Diane Cilento and her husband as an open-air venue from May to Dec. The voices of Cilento and Anthony Shaffer combine with high-tech laser lights, sound effects and Aboriginal performers in a show that is very much a matter of individual taste. On the other hand it did a magic performance of *A*

STINGERS AND SNAPPERS

In the summer months, Nov–Apr, sea swimming outside swimming enclosures is highly dangerous. **Box jellyfish** or **sea wasps** are active and can seriously zap you. These are not known to inhabit the Outer Reef, and generally only exist within 1–2 km of mainland beaches. Fully protected swimming enclosures are provided at Port Douglas, Palm Cove and Mission Beach.

Crocodiles are a protected species, but the crocodiles do not have a similar ruling for human beings. Both **freshwater** (dangerous) and **salt water crocodiles** (extremely dangerous) live in this area. The warning signs are not some additional tourist attraction – if you swim near a croc warning sign your chances of being attacked are somewhere around 50 per cent. And for reasons not yet fully understood, they prefer the flavour of tourists!

Midsummer Night's Dream and there may be a play on while you are there, in which case do not miss it. $$ Tel: 4098 8144.

DAINTREE

Daintree has a population of less than 250, so it is not a large place. There is a gallery and shop which has a timber workshop with craftsmen turning out turned bowls and other items. On display in a small museum is a large collection of old wood-working tools.

Ranged between the town and the ferry crossing downstream is a series of tour operators offering **cruises** on the Daintree River. Most tours take an hour or so. You will see prolific birdlife and probably, during the winter, crocodiles sunning themselves on the banks of the river, especially at low tide. The Daintree River Ferry runs 0600–2400, but on the other side, the road deteriorates into a mixture of sealed and unsealed and in the Wet can be totally impassable. Far more worryingly, it is used by large trucks driven at a thunderous speed by truckers who believe they own the road. See also p. 304. The **Daintree National Park** is a wonderful piece of rainforest to explore, but the best way is by one of the many tours offered out of Port Douglas. The information office, and every hotel and motel, can load you down with brochures.

CAPE TRIBULATION

Beyond the ferry crossing, the road north leads to Cape Tribulation's beaches and boardwalk and the **Bloomfield Falls**, passing through forest, over tidal rivers and creeks and through small settlements. You are on the Reef and Rainforest Coast. It is here that two World Heritage areas merge as the fringing coral of the Great Barrier Reef is actually overhung in places by the rainforest of the Daintree and Cape Tribulation National Parks.

Cape Tribulation National Park is a World Heritage area of the wet tropics. It has rugged ranges covered with forests and woods and the many tributaries of the Daintree River come tumbling down the slopes in a series of waterfalls. Much of it is only suitable for experienced bush walkers. Right through the park is the deep gorge of the Mossman River with walking tracks leading into the ever-luxuriant rainforest. Animals include tree kangaroos, ringtail possums, golden bower birds and tree frogs.

COOKTOWN

Captain Cook beached the *Endeavour* on the shores of the river here (which he named the Endeavour) in June 1770 to repair the damage created by running onto the reef. Cook and his crew stayed about six weeks, the longest time they spent on land anywhere in Australia, and that, in a sense, was the start of Cooktown.

The convent in Helen St is now the **James Cook Historical Museum and Joseph Bank Gardens**. The story of the fixing of the hole in the *Endeavour* is recorded here, and among many other exhibits are Cook's cannon and anchor, jettisoned in the efforts to get the *Endeavour* off the reef. Open daily 0930–1600.

In the **cemetery** is the grave of the remarkable Mrs Mary Watson. She escaped with a servant and her baby from Lizard Island in 1882 after an attack by Aborigines, but eventually died of thirst. There is also a Chinese shrine dedicated to the 18,000 Chinese who came to the region during the gold rush.

The best view of the town is on **Grassy Hill Lookout** which has an old lighthouse and a memorial to Captain Cook, who used this vantage point to plot a course through the Reef. The **Black Mountains National Park**, 28 km south of Cooktown, gets its name from the massive granite boulders blackened by surface lichen.

Cooktown Tourism Association, Shop 6 Charlotte St; tel: 4069 6100.
Cape York Peninsula Tourist Information, cnr Grafton and Harley Sts, Cairns; tel: 4051 3588.
Port Douglas and Cooktown Tourist Information Centre, 23 Macrossan St, Port Douglas; tel: 4099 5599.

Alamanda Inn $ Hope St; tel: 4069 5203.
Endeavour Falls Tourist Park $ McIvor Rd; tel: 4069 5431.
Golden Orchid Caravan Park $ Charlotte St; tel: 4069 5641.
Hillcrest Guest House $ Hope St; tel: 4069 5305.
River of Gold Motel $ Walker St, cnr Hope St; tel: 4069 5222. Has a restaurant.

Endeavour Inn Restaurant Charlotte St, cnr Furneaux St; tel: 4069 5384. Dinner. Licensed.
Sovereign Hotel Charlotte and Green Sts; tel: 4069 5400. Licensed. Open daily for lunch and dinner.

This northern finger of the continent contains some of the most spectacular and rugged country in Australia and one of the world's last rainforest wildernesses, with thousands of species of tropical birds, beautiful waterfalls and crocodiles. The rainforest near the road which runs up the spine of Cape York often demonstrates a curious phenomenon: it can be thundering down rain on the road but in the rainforest there is just a gentle mist. The tree canopy is so dense that it acts as an effective umbrella.

Safari tours are available from Cairns and take about 10–14 days for a round-trip with visits to Thursday Island off the tip of Cape York. The recommended time for travelling is during the dry season (June–Sept) as the rivers swell during the wet season often closing roads.

In theory, in the Dry, you could drive along the Peninsula Developmental Road as far as Weipa. This is true frontier country. It is best to have a 4-wheel-drive, especially if you intend to explore off the main road, and you must carry enough supplies, especially water and petrol, to get you from place to place with a safe reserve. Having said that, the first vehicle to make the journey all the way to the tip of Cape York was a 1927 Austin 7, and many other 2-wheel-drive vehicles have made the journey in the Dry, although their condition was not enhanced by the journey.

The Quinkan Reserve near Laura contains hundreds of Aboriginal cave paintings and guided tours are available. The reserve is at the southern end of Lakefield National Park, the state's second-largest national park. Lakefield has a wide range of birdlife and other native animals in its rainforest, woodlands, grassy plains and coastal mudflats along Princess Charlotte Bay. On Flinders and Stanley Islands, in Princess Charlotte Bay, are spectacular Aboriginal galleries of marine life – stingrays, crabs, flying fish, turtles and the rare dugongs. Lakefield is a major crocodile habitat, and is for serious bushwalkers only.

Rokeby National Parks and its neighbour, Archer Bend, cover drier woodlands between McIlwraith Range and the Archer River. The Archer and Coen rivers commonly spread over the flood-plains in summer and the lagoons and swamps which remain into the dry season attract an abundance of birdlife. Accessible only in the dry season.

Iron Range National Park is a wilderness area containing the largest remaining tract of lowland rainforest in Australia. It has quite spectacular coastal scenery and unusual wildlife.

In the very north of the peninsula, Jardine River National Park is a tropical wilderness in the catchment of the Jardine River, Queenslandís largest perennial stream. There are swamps and heathlands, with tropical vegetation which includes many varieties of New Guinea origin. Accessible only in the dry season.

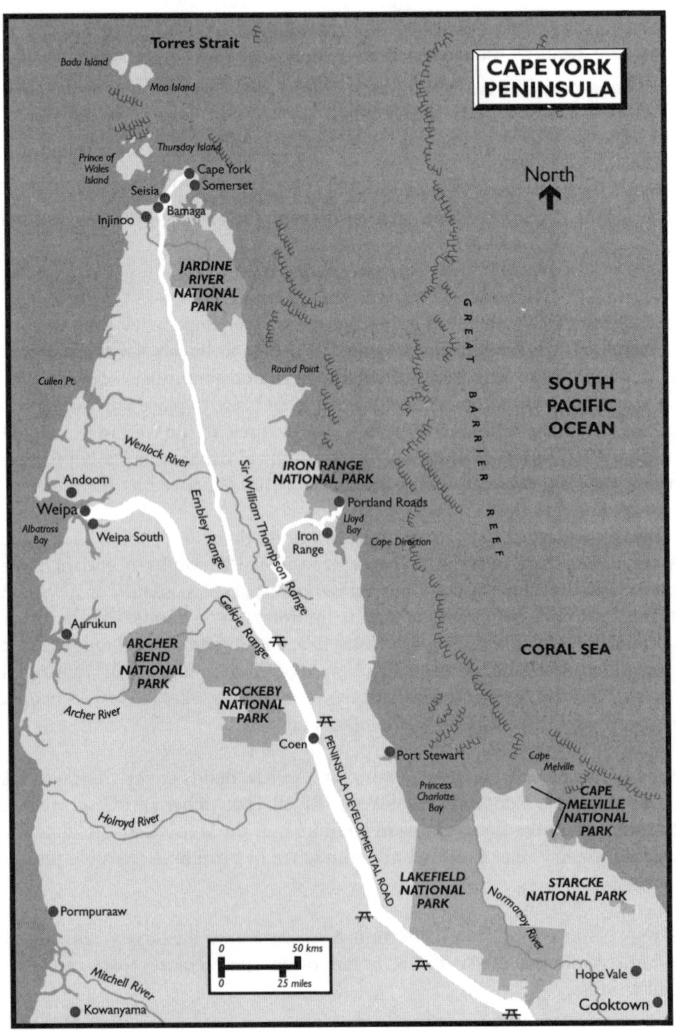

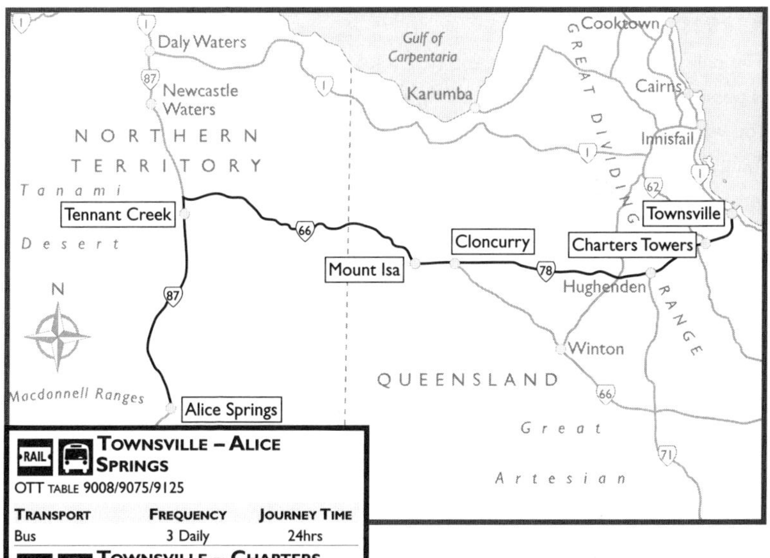

TOWNSVILLE – ALICE SPRINGS

OTT TABLE 9008/9075/9125

TRANSPORT	FREQUENCY	JOURNEY TIME
Bus	3 Daily	24hrs

TOWNSVILLE – CHARTERS TOWERS

OTT TABLE 9008 /9075

TRANSPORT	FREQUENCY	JOURNEY TIME
Train	Wednesday & Sunday	3 hrs 16 mins
Bus	3 Daily	1 hrs 40mins

CHARTERS TOWERS – CLONCURRY

OTT TABLE 9008 /9075

TRANSPORT	FREQUENCY	JOURNEY TIME
Train	Wednesday & Sunday	14 hrs 21 mins
Bus	3 Daily	8 hrs 35mins

CLONCURRY – MOUNT ISA

OTT TABLE 9008 /9075

TRANSPORT	FREQUENCY	JOURNEY TIME
Train	Monday & Thursday	3hrs 48 mins
Bus	3 Daily	1 hrs 25mins

MOUNT ISA – TENNANT CREEK

OTT TABLE 9075

TRANSPORT	FREQUENCY	JOURNEY TIME
Bus	2 Daily	7 hrs 5mins

TENNANT CREEK – ALICE SPRINGS

OTT TABLE 9075

TRANSPORT	FREQUENCY	JOURNEY TIME
Bus	3 Daily	6 hrs

Notes

The connection at Tennant Creek could involve up to a 6hr wait.

If you are intending to travel on a coach pass you should mnake sure that the connecting operator will accept your pass.

ACROSS THE NORTH-EAST

The only way to do this, unless you have a lot of time to spare, is to fly. Of course, it is possible to drive, although it is a long way, just over 2,000 km, but that takes time. If you want to see the wonder of Uluru – Ayers Rock – and you are on a time budget, flying is the only reasonable option. The drive, however long, dry and dusty, is through interesting country, with stops en route at one of the hottest towns in Australia, one of the richest ore deposits in the world and a town which, if legend is to be believed, should never have been built.

ROUTE DETAIL

There's not a lot of tricky navigating to be done, as the Flinders Hwy (Hwy78) runs all the way from Townsville to Mount Isa, from where the Barkly Hwy (Hwy 66) continues through to Tennant Creek to meet the north–south transcontinental Hwy 87, the Stuart Hwy. Be prepared for a lot of long, boring road and take sensible precautions (see p. 247).

The young, impecunious and limber of body can take the bus: they run regularly between Townsville and Tennant Creek, taking about 22 hrs. From there you can pick up the Darwin–Alice bus (a further 5½ hrs).

CHARTERS TOWERS

In this hot, dry region, many consider Charters Towers to be the most attractive town in Queensland. It is to the east of the Great Dividing Range in the gentle undulating country of the Burdekin River Valley. It still has much of the opulence that was given it by the gold rush, although now the main industry in the surrounding country is cattle-raising.

The story, almost certainly apocryphal, is that the first gold here was found by a young Aboriginal boy named Jupiter, who was with a party of prospectors, including Hugh Mosman. Jupiter went out to look for horses that had bolted in a thunderstorm. As he bent down to drink from the local creek he saw gold-bearing quartz below the surface. Mosman registered the claim, was rewarded by the government, adopted Jupiter and brought him up as his son. Statues of Mosman and Jupiter commemorating this event are in Centenary Park.

Charters Towers once had a population of 30,000, more than three times what it is today. In the 40 years from 1871 some 7 million oz of gold were extracted from the region and during the boom there were about 100 gold mines in the area, and possibly even more pubs. In the 1890s the residents called

Charters Towers, with little modesty, The World. It was enough of the world to get Dame Nellie Melba to come there and perform at the Theatre Royal.

To get the town into perspective, **Rotary Lookout** (follow the signs from Mosman St) gives a panoramic view of the town. At ground level you can clearly see the prosperity that came with the gold in the classical Australian Victorian architecture decorated with verandas and lacework. The town has more National Trust properties than any other place in Queensland. Bankers thought the gold would last forever, and many of the most imposing buildings in town were once banks: the **tourist office** is in the old Union Bank; the **library** in Gill St, built in classical revival style in 1880, was the Bank of New South Wales; and the **Civic Theatre** along the street was once the Australian Bank of Commerce, built with no regard to cost by the Australian Joint Stock Bank in 1891. The bank went belly up in 1892. **City Hall** next door was built the same year. The Post Office in Gill St is in the same Victorian we-will-last-forever style and its clock tower acts as a landmark for the whole town.

Charter Towers also boasted Australia's first regional **stock exchange**, opened in 1890. This magnificent heritage building, in Mosman St, has been fully restored and now houses the National Trust and some shops. In 1912, the town started to run downhill quickly as the gold came to an end. By the start of World War I it was pretty much all over and the Exchange closed in 1916.

On the Milchester Rd, about 5 km from the centre, is the old **Venus Gold Battery** (it is well signposted). In 1872 this was the first permanent gold ore battery to be erected in the area and was used commercially for exactly a century. Open daily 0800–1700, with guided tours at 1000 and 1400 which show how it all worked. When running, the noise is beyond belief. At the height of its fortune Charters Towers boasted 29 of these monsters.

Charters Towers & Dalrymple Tourism Association, 74 Mosman St; tel: 4785 2034; email tourinfocentre@httech.com.au

Cattleman's Rest Motor Inn $$ Plant St, Cnr Bridge St; tel: 4787 3555.
Charters Towers Caravan Park $ 37 Mt Leyshon Rd; tel: 4787 7944.
Charters Towers Van Park $ 37 Mt Leyshon Rd; tel: 4787 7944. 2 km from the centre of town.
Dalrymple Caravan Park $ Lynd Hwy; tel: 4787 1121.
Enterprise Hotel Motel $ 217 Gill St; tel: 4787 2404.
Mexican Caravan Park $ Towers St, cnr Church St; tel: 4787 1161.

Park Motel $$ Deane St, cnr Mosman St; tel: 4787 1022.
Powlathanga Cattle Station Homestay tel: 4787 4957; email Margie@t140.aone.net.au. Live the real outback on a 26,000-ha station.
Rix Hotel Motel $ 69 Mosman St; tel: 4787 1605.

Babe's $ 58 Gill St; tel: 4787 3003. BYO
Charmes Restaurant $$ 151 Mosman St; tel: 4787 1391.
Gold City Chinese Restaurant $18 Gill St; tel: 4787 2414.
Gold Mine Chinese Restaurant $ 10 Mosman St; tel: 4787 7609.
Iron Pot Cafe $ 53 Dalrymple Rd; tel: 4787 2200.

CLONCURRY

Cloncurry currently holds the record for the hottest temperature in Australia at 127.5°F or 48.8°C - and is a typical outback Queensland town right in the heart of the Great Northeast. The town was built on its mining riches and it very much looks as if it is being revived through mining. Four major mines - Ernest Henry, Selwyn, Osborne and Cannington - are now in operation and there are other major projects in the pipeline. You can see the style of the original mining in the **Great Australian Mine** and treatment plant 3 km out of town. This was established by the prospector Ernest Henry, who discovered rich deposits of copper in 1867.

Cloncurry/Mary Kathleen Memorial Museum and Park, McIlwraith St; tel: 4742 1251.

Cloncurry Caravan Park Oasis $ McIlwraith St; tel: 4742 1313.
Cloncurry Motel $$ Daintree St, cnr Sheaffe St; tel: 4742 1268.
Gidgee Inn $$ Matilda Hwy; tel: 4742 2429; email: gidgeein@mtisa.topend.com.au. Luxurious outback motel built of rammed red earth with sweeping verandas in traditional colonial style.
Gilbert Park Cabins $ Matilda Hwy; tel: 4742 2300.
Leichhardt Hotel/Motel $ 5 Scarr St; tel: 4742 1389.
Oasis Hotel/Motel $ Ramsay St; tel: 4742 1366.
Wagon Wheel Motel $$ 54 Ramsay St; tel: 4742 1866. The Prince of Wales Inn is part of the premises and these are the oldest remaining licensed premises in North-West Queensland. The licence was granted 119 years ago.

Gidgee Grill $$ Matilda Hwy; tel: 4742 2429. The restaurant is part of the motel which is of quite remarkable and appropriate outback design.
The Prince of Wales Inn $$ 54 Ramsay St; tel: 4742 1866. Now part of a motel but still a part of the history of the town.

HIGHLIGHTS

If you fly into Cloncurry you will see Qantas's original name at the airport – **Queensland and Northern Territory Aerial Service**. The first paying passenger on Qantas was ferried between Charleville and Cloncurry in November 1922. Sadly Qantas no longer flies here, so you will have come in on Flight West Airlines.

In the **cemetery** in Henry St are the graves of what were called Afghan camel drivers – in fact, they were nearly all Pakistanis. Only one is named; the others are just numbers in a foreign land.

Possibly the most comprehensive mineral collection in Australia is in the **Mary Kathleen Memorial Park and Museum** at the eastern entrance to Cloncurry, with more than 18,000 exhibits. The park displays some of the buildings which once stood in the ghost town of Mary Kathleen, dedicated to the mining of uranium. Open weekdays 0700–1600, weekends during the season 0900–1500.

THE FLYING DOCTOR SERVICE

It is difficult to overstate the place that the Flying Doctor Service has in the minds and make-up of Australia. Here is where it all started, pushed along by the sheer guts and energy and vision of Rev. John Flynn. Working with primitive aircraft and small transmitting and receiving sets which, when he conceived of them, were only theoretically possible, he set out to provide the outback with a doctor with wings and wireless communication. In 1927, the *Victory*, a single-engined DH50 aircraft, took off with a doctor on board for its first mission, to Julia Creek.

In the **Flying Doctor Complex** in John Flynn Pl, Daintree St, is a one-third-size model of the *Victory*, together with equipment used in the early days of the service, set into realistic displays. It includes the pedal generator, part of the transceiver equipment which was very important to the early progression of the service, and the first Traegar Pedal Wireless which for many years was the only means of communication for many people living in the outback. The complex also houses the Fred McKay Art Gallery, Alfred Traegar Cultural Centre, the Allan Vickers Outdoor Theatre and the Cloncurry Gardens. Open weekdays 0700–1600, weekends 0900–1500.

MOUNT ISA

Mount Isa exists for the **Mount Isa Mine**, one of the largest mines in the world and the biggest underground mine in Australia. It directly employs about 3,500 people, nearly 20 per cent of the total population, which makes it very much a one-company town. The mine is the world's biggest single producer of silver and lead and is among the top 10 producers of copper and zinc.

EN ROUTE

At the junction of the Barkly and Stuart highways stands a memorial to the famous missionary and pioneer Flying Doctor of the outback, the Rev. John Flynn. Near the remains of the telegraph station at Barrow Creek are the graves of John Franks and James L. Stapleton. The two telegraphers were killed in 1874 by members of the local Kayteje tribe, possibly over an enclosure that denied the Aboriginal people access to a freshwater spring. The telegraphist sent a message for help to the Central Telegraph Office in Adelaide, and as John Stapleton lay mortally wounded he tapped out a last message to his wife: 'God bless you and the children.'

Mount Isa Tourist Information & Riversleigh Fossil Centre, 19 Marion St; tel: 4749 1555; email riversleigh@tpgi.com.au. This is the main tourist information centre.
Outback Queensland Tourist Authority, 11 Barkly Hwy; tel: 4743 7966.

Barkly Hotel Motel $ 55 Barkly Hwy; tel: 4743 2988.
Burke & Wills $$ Mt Isa Motor Inn, Camooweal St, cnr Grace St; tel: 4743 8000.
Carlin Court $$ 11 Boyd Pde; tel: 4743 2019.
Copper City Caravan Park $ 185 West St; tel: 4743 4676.
Fourth Ave Motor Inn $ 20 Fourth Ave; tel: 4743 3477.
Inland Oasis Motel $ 195 Barkly Hwy; tel: 4743 3433.
Moondarra Caravan Park $ Lake Moondarra Rd; tel: 4743 9780.
Mt Isa Caravan Park $ 112 Marian St; tel: 4743 3252.
Mt Isa Outback Motor Inn $$ 45 West St; tel: 4743 2311.
Silver Star Motel $$ Doughan Ter, cnr Marian St; tel: 4743 3466.
Townview Motel $$ 112 Kookaburra St; tel: 4743 3328.
Travellers Haven $$ Pamela St, cnr Spence St; tel: 4743 0313.
Verona Motel $$ Camooweal St, cnr Marian St; tel: 4743 3024.

Casa Della Pasta $ 79 Camooweal St; tel: 4743 7922.
Concordia Restaurant $$ Barkly Hwy; tel: 4743 3899.
David's Restaurant $$ Doughan St, cnr Marian St; tel: 4743 9399.
Los Toros $$ 79 Camooweal St; tel: 4743 7718.
Maxim Chinese Restaurant $ 24 West St; tel: 4743 6567.
Overlander Restaurant $ Marian St; tel: 4743 5011.
Red Lantern Chinese Restaurant $$ 1 Simpson St; tel: 4743 4070.

HIGHLIGHTS

Mount Isa is quite aware of public relations and encourages tours of the mines, but these are very popular and frequently fully booked, so it is important that you give as much advance warning as possible. Either tel: 4749 1555 or write to: IQTDB, PO Box 356, Mount Isa 4825.

In 1927, to accommodate the mineworkers, the company built a low-cost town consisting of 200 tents protected by a permanent roof structure. An example of these unique tent houses is now owned and displayed by the National Trust.

To appreciate the spread and integration of mine and town, climb the **City Lookout** opposite the tourist centre. The view at night is infinitely more attractive as the illumination highlights the good points and darkness disguises the rest, so it is worth visiting the lookout twice.

The **Royal Flying Doctor Service** (open 0900–1500) is still a vital service in this isolated area, as is **Distance Education** (the School of the Air, open 1000–1200 during school term). To check on school terms, tel: 4744 9100. From this centre teachers broadcast to more than 220 children on 150 cattle and sheep properties throughout the north-west every school day.

The World Heritage-listed Riversleigh fossil site does what possibly only a couple of places on the planet can do: it has provided a snapshot of a whole rainforest environment dating back 20 million years. At Riversleigh almost an entire eco-system has been preserved in fossilised form and the **Riversleigh Fossils and Interpretive Centre** in Marian St lets you see in some considerable comfort what all the fuss was about. The centre has re-created limestone caves, a video documentary, palaeontology display and collections of actual fossils from Riversleigh. The fossilised animals bear a slight, but only a slight, resemblance to the animals of today. Open daily 0930–1600.

TENNANT CREEK

If only the story were true, but perhaps it is. A wagon, loaded with beer and building supplies for a hotel to be built at the Overland Telegraph station, broke its axle 10 km short of its destination. In true Australian style the problem was solved by building the hotel were the axle had broken. A town slowly grew around the hotel and before anyone knew it Tennant Creek had been born.

In 1930, gold was discovered in payable quantities, which led two years later to what has been referred to as Australia's 'last genuine gold rush'. More gold was found in 1934 at Noble's Nob. The find – and this is true – was made by one-eyed John Noble and his partner, William Weaber, who was blind. Noble's Nob closed only in 1985 and was beyond doubt Australia's richest goldmine.

Tennant Creek likes to think of itself as being the heart of the Red Centre. It is the largest town between Katherine and Alice Springs.

Tennant Creek Regional Tourism Association, Shop 1, Coach Transit Centre; tel: 8962 3388.

Bluestone Motor Inn $$ Paterson St; tel: 8962 2617. Licensed restaurant.
Desert Sands $ Paterson St; tel: 8962 1346.
Eldorado Motel Lodge $$ Paterson St; tel: 8962 2402. Named after one of the local Tennant Creek mines. Licensed restaurant and pool.
Goldfields Hotel $ 603 Paterson St; tel: 8962 2030. Licensed restaurant.
Safari Lodge Motel $ 12 Davidson St; tel: 8962 2207. Family accommodation in the centre of town.
Tennant Creek Hotel $ 146 Paterson St; tel: 8962 2006.

Eldorado Restaurant $$ Paterson St; tel: 8962 2402.
Margo Miles Restaurant $$ 146 Paterson St; tel: 8962 2227.
Memories Restaurant $$ Memorial Dr; tel: 8962 1166.
Miner's Rights Restaurant $$ Goldfields Hotel, 603 Paterson St; tel: 8962 2555.
Old Dolly Pot Inn $$ Paterson St; tel: 8962 1466.

HIGHLIGHTS

The history of Tennant Creek can be seen in the **Tennant Creek Museum**, Leichhardt St (open daily 1530–1730) and in Schmidt St, where the National Trust Museum has six rooms of local memorabilia and reconstructed mining scenes. The museum itself was a hospital ward until relatively recently. **The Aboriginal Mural** in Paterson St is a community project emphasising Aboriginal mythology in relation to contemporary life.

It is perhaps better to go on a conducted tour of a gold mine than try to find your own way around.

Colour Section

(i) Darwin (pp. 348–356); in the Wet; Wolf Creek Crater (p. 431)

(ii) Uluru (Ayres Rock); The Valley of Winds, Olgas (pp. 330–337); Alice Springs (p. 322–329)

(iii) The market in Freemantle (pp. 376–380); sunset over Margaret River coastline (pp. 381–395)

(iv) Rocky Cape National Park (p. 448); Hobart (p. 437–445)

SNACK·BAR

Johnny
for quality

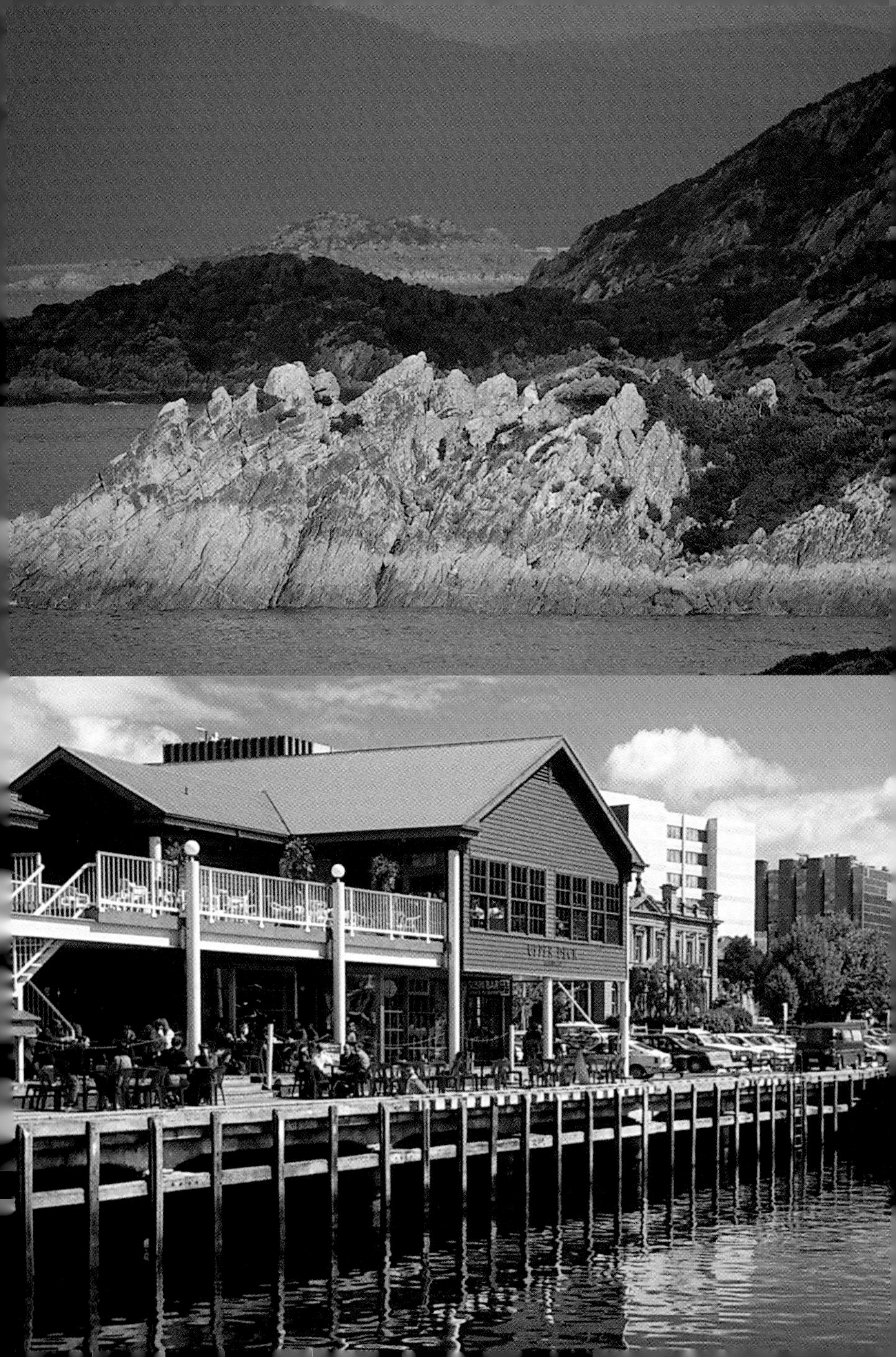

You can organise this through the tourist centre and places you can visit include the **Burnt Shirt Mine** and the **Golden Forty**. You are encouraged to go gold fossicking with all equipment supplied.

EN ROUTE

The massive granite rocks of The Devil's Marbles (not to be confused with the Devil's Pebbles just north of Tennant Creek) can be seen from Hwy 96 to the south of Tennant Creek.

The gold in this area is mainly trapped in quartz – ignore locals who tell you about picking up nuggets the size of your fist – which has to be crushed and treated in a complex process. This is done at the **Government Stamp Battery** on Peko Rd, just east of town. There is a mining museum here, open Mon–Fri 0900–1600, and the battery is operated on demand. There are tours at 0900 and 1600 May–Oct (arranged through the tourist centre).

Just past the Battery is **Bill Allen Lookout**, with plaques showing where the mines were dug and other local points of interest. The **Overland Telegraph Station** was closed down in 1979. It is now a museum but visits can be arranged in advance via the Regional Tourism Association office.

Mary Ann Dam, north of the town off the Stuart Hwy, has facilities for swimming, canoeing and yachting.

The **Devil's Pebbles**, 10 km north-west of town, is a collection of huge boulders stacked up on each other in random fashion. Best time for viewing is at sunset, when they glow in the dying rays of the sun.

WHERE NEXT?

Alice Springs is 500 km south (see p. 322), or Darwin is 1,500 km north (see p. 348).

ALICE SPRINGS

Alice Springs is often thought of as the geographical centre of Australia, which it is not. But for many it is the definitive Outback town, made famous by Nevil Shute's novel *A Town Like Alice* and the subsequent films and television series. The road north, considered a strategic route in World War II, has been sealed since 1943, and in 1987 the old road south to Port Augusta and Adelaide was finally replaced by a new, shorter and fully sealed highway. With these connections both north and south, the influx of tourism has eradicated much of the old Alice Springs and there is little of the noble Outback experience that literature would lead you to expect.

Many visitors find a city that has yet to come completely to terms with tourism; others find it immensely attractive. This is not a new phenomenon. Fred Blakely, who cycled 3500 km through central Australia in 1908, recalled in *Hard Liberty* the intensity of the light and the healthy atmosphere; he called the Alice a perfect winter resort. Winter days are warm but the temperature drops like a stone at sunset. In summer the mercury on occasion climbs to 45°C.

Alice Springs is always spoken of as 'the Alice'. It is not so much a town as a pleasant idea, having a special flavour of its own (and the gender of the idea is feminine). The town is set in the McDonnell Ranges and although the country in the immediate vicinity is not particularly interesting, there is spectacular mountain and desert scenery of great variety within a day's journey.

HOW ALICE GOT HER NAME

The major force driving the construction of the telegraph line, and after whom the river was named, was Sir Charles Todd, the superintendent of telegraphs. There had been great difficulty in finding a way through the McDonnell Ranges, but in 1871 one of the surveyors wrote to Sir Charles Todd that he had discovered a pass which had 'numerous water-holes and springs, the principal of which is the Alice Spring which I had the honour of naming after Mrs Todd.' Despite this, the town was officially named Stuart (after the explorer John McDouall Stuart) when it was surveyed in 1888. But public opinion won out – they insisted on calling it Alice Springs or the Alice, and in 1933 this was formally recognised.

The town grew up around a telegraph repeater station built between 1871 and 1872 at a water-hole in the dry bed of the Todd River. The station was one of a series in the overhead telegraph line

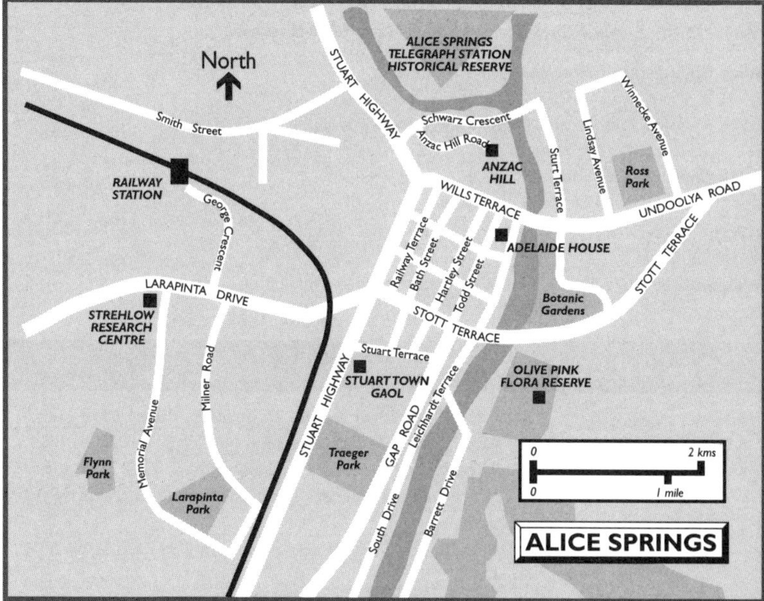

which ran from Adelaide to Darwin, where it connected with the undersea line to Indonesia and put Australia in direct contact with Europe for the first time.

ARRIVAL AND DEPARTURE

The airport is about 15 km south of Alice Springs, with a shuttle bus link to the centre.

Alice Springs is roughly halfway along the Stuart Hwy linking Adelaide and Darwin. The journey from either city takes around 20 hours, although some buses detour to Yulara for Uluru (see p. 330), and not all bus lines run every day.

INFORMATION

Tourist Office **Central Australian Tourism Centre**, Gregory Ter; tel: 8952 5800. **Northern Territory Holiday Centre**, Stuart Hwy North; tel: 8951 8471.

Internet Access **Internet Cafe**, 94 Todd St; tel: 8952 2233; email: melanka@ozemail.com.au

Alice Springs

Internet Sites **Alice Springs** www.taunet.net.au/tuzza/alicewww

Alice Springs Jumpsite www.alice.au.com/alice/

Alice Springs, Movies and More www.ozemail.com.au/~penton/

Alice Springs Town www.alicesprings.net.au/alicemm/.

Northern Territory Holiday Centre www.nttc.com.au

Welcome to Alice Springs www.ozemail.com.au/~kermie/home.htm

ACCOMMODATION

Alice Flag Motor Inn $$ 27 Undoolya Rd; tel: 8952 2322.

Alice Lodge Backpackers $ 4 Mueller St; tel: 8953 7975.

Alice Motor Inn $$ 27 Undoolya Rd; tel: 8952 2322; email: reception@ami.mtx.net. East of the Todd River, a short walk to the town centre.

Alice Springs Backpackers Resort $ 94 Todd St; tel: 8952 4744.

Alice Springs Caravan Park $ Larapinta Dr.; tel: 8952 2547.

Alice Springs Gapview Resort Hotel $$ 115 Gap Rd; tel: 8952 6611.

Alice Springs Heritage Caravan Park $ Ragonesi Rd; tel: 8953 1418.

Alice Sundown Motel $$ 39 Gap Rd; tel: 8952 8422.

Alice Tourist Apartments $$ Gap Rd, Cnr Gnoilya St; tel: 8952 2788.

Desert Palms Resort $$ Tel: 8952 5977. Villa accommodation with private verandas set in garden with palms. 1 km from the centre of town.

Desert Rose Inn $$ 15 Railway Ter; tel: 8952 1411.

Diplomat Motor Inn $$ Gregory Ter, Cnr Hartley St; tel: 8952 8977.

Elkes Backpackers $ 39 Gap; email: elkes@downunder.net.au.

Frontier Oasis Alice Springs $$ 10 Gap Rd; tel: 8952 1444.

Melanka Lodge Motel $ 94 Todd St; tel: 8952 2233.

Midland Motel $ 4 Traeger Ave; tel: 8952 1588.

Outback Motor Lodge $$ South Ter; tel: 8952 3888; email: oml@asaccom.mtx.net.

Pioneer YHA $ Cnr Parsons St and Leichhardt Ter; tel: 8952 8855.

Red Centre Resort $$ North Stuart Hwy; tel: 8952 8955.

Territory Motor Inn $$ Leichhardt Ter; tel: 8952 2066.

FOOD

Alice Springs Bush Restaurant $$ 8 George Cres; tel: 8952 9355.

Bo's Saloon and Restaurant $$ 80 Todd Street; tel: 8952 2873. Serves barramundi, kangaroo, buffalo, territory beef and camel. All of which is better than you think. Open Mon–Sat from 12 for lunch. Dinner daily from 1800.

Camel's Crossing Mexican Restaurant $$ 5 Fan Arcade; tel: 8952 5522. One of the better restaurant names in Australia. BYO.

Daniele's Restaurant $$ Palm Circuit; tel: 8952 4844.

Golden Inn Chinese Restaurant $ 9 Undoolya Rd; tel: 8952 6910.

Golly It's Good $ Springs Plaza; tel: 8952 8388. Included simply because of the name which is not, as it happens, misleading.

La Casalinga $$105 Gregory Ter; tel: 8952 4508.

Number 20 $$ 20 Undoolya Rd; tel: 8952 9400.

Oriental Gourmet $$ 80 Hartley St; tel: 8953 0888.

Palms Restaurant $$ 34 Stott Ter; tel: 8952 6699.

Rocky's Pizza & Pasta & Italian Restaurant $$ Stuart Hwy; tel: 8952 8614.

Romano's Family Bistro $$ 20 Undoolya Rd; tel: 8952 3721.

Vineyard Restaurant $$ Petrick Rd; tel: 89555133.

Zella's Cafe Restaurant $$ 29 Gap Rd; tel: 8952 8101.

HIGHLIGHTS

Alice Springs is easy to get around, as it is basically a square, with the dry Todd River on one side and the Stuart Hwy on the other. Anzac Hill to the north offers good views over the town and at the south end is Stuart Terrace. Most of the shopping, restaurants and many of the hotels are within this rectangle. Todd St for part of its length is a pedestrian precinct and, in truth, it could be anywhere in any tourist resort.

Although the Alice is in a desert area, it does occasionally rain and the normally dry Todd River can flood, cutting off parts of the town.

BOAT RACES

In early Oct Alice Springs holds the Henley-on-Todd regatta when boats are raced along the riverbed despite the fact that there is no water. The boats are all bottomless and the crews run the course.

There is also the peculiar but perfectly genuine anomaly of the Alice Springs Yacht Club of Central Australia. It is the most isolated yacht club in the world and the furthest from the sea. You can join for a small sum and it gives you something to boast about. It was formed in 1993 mainly to enter the Sydney to Hobart Yacht Race (see p. 441). It quickly collected over 200 members and has taken part in most of the races since; in 1996 Alice's *Neata Glass* won division F.

In Todd Street is Adelaide House, which opened in 1926 as Alice Springsí first hospital. It is now the **John Flynn Memorial Museum**. Flynn was the founding flying doctor (see p. 325) and the museum features photographs of the early days in Alice Springs and Outback settlements, and the Radio Hut from which Alfred Traeger and John Flynn made their first field transmission in 1926. Flynn died here in 1951 and his grave is a historical area.

The **Transport, Technology & Communication Museum** in Memorial Dr. is housed in the old hangar of Connellan, the local airline. Displays of historic vehicles include vintage cars, motor cycles and a 60-year-old AEC 8-wheel-drive truck.

LASSETER'S REEF

One day in 1897 Harold Bell Lasseter was found unconscious by an Afghan camel driver. When he recovered he told of a fabulously rich reef of gold which he had discovered out beyond the Petermann Ranges. Lasseter refused to disclose the exact location of the reef. In July 1930, subscribers put up £5000 and an expedition started off from Alice Springs. After incredible hardships the expedition was abandoned but Lasseter went on alone. His body was found by Aboriginal trackers and buried near where he died. In June 1958 he was dug up and reburied in the Alice Springs cemetery. There are still many Australians who believe the reef exists and that one day someone will strike it lucky and find Lasseter's Reef.

The beautifully designed **Strehlow Research Centre** next door has created much controversy. It contains the most comprehensive collection of Aboriginal spirit items in the country, entrusted to Professor Strehlow by the local Aranda Aborigines. There is a computer-controlled display on the work of Strehlow and on the Aranda, but the treasures are only accessible to accredited researchers, who must be male, which disappoints many visitors.

Near by, in the **Old Pioneer Cemetery**, are the graves of the great artist Albert Namatjira and of Harold Lasseter, whose fabled gold reef may or may not have been a figment of his imagination.

The **telegraph station**, just north of town near the original springs, continued in operation until 1932 and is now a museum depicting something of the pioneering lifestyle in Central Australia.

On the Old South Road, just beyond Heavitree Gap, is a **date garden** which, it is claimed, is the only one in Australia. In the same direction, 8 km southeast of Alice Springs on the Ross Hwy, is **Frontier Camel Farm**. Here you can take a short and somewhat rolling ride or go for a three-day trek in the Outback. For many years these camels were the main form of transport in the interior. A museum explains the importance of the camel trains and their 'Afghan' drivers (really Pakistani) in opening up the Outback. Open 0900–1700; tel: 8953 0444.

The Afghans are commemorated in the name of another famous feature of the Outback: the old Ghan Railway. Although you get the idea that the railway had much to do with the opening up of the area, the Ghan did not actually get to Alice Springs until 1929. The roof of the oldest building in the Alice, the **Old Stuart Gaol** in Parsons St, for example, was brought in by camel in 1909 from the railhead at Oodnadatta, some 500 km south. At the **MacDonnell Siding**, off the Stuart Hwy about 10 km south of Alice Springs, local railway enthusiasts have restored a collection of Ghan locomotives and carriages and the station has been made into an information centre. There is a collection of steam and diesel locomotives, carriages and assorted rolling stock, plus a variety of railway paraphernalia and historic photographs.

DAY TRIPS

The number of attractions that can be visited in one or two day trips from Alice Springs can hardly be counted for this is an area full of national parks. Most of the roads are unsealed and a 4-wheel-drive vehicle may be essential depending on the state of the roads. But in the right season some of the countryside around Alice Springs is among the most remarkable in Australia. What follows is a sampling.

SIMPSONS GAP is on the western outskirts of Alice Springs and is an excellent place to gain a brief taste of the MacDonnell Ranges. The MacDonnell Ranges Track from the Cassia Hill car-park leads west for 7 km through shrubland and low hills. The walk takes about five hours and, as it is not over-strenuous, suits beginners to bushwalking. There is always a good display of wildflowers after the winter rains. The eastern wall of Simpson's Gap rises 250 m above the sandy bed of Roe Creek.

ELLERY CREEK BIG HOLE Ellery Creek Big Hole is about 93 km west of Alice Springs, along Namatjira Dr. It is a colourful small gorge with river gums standing out against the dark red rock cliff walls. Depending on the season, there is a large pool in the gorge.

Namatjira Dr. continues as a metalled road as far as Glen Helen, but is unsurfaced from there on. Near Glen Helen and 130 km from Alice Spring is one of Central Australiaís most spectacular canyons, **Ormiston Gorge**. The lower cliffs are deep reds and purples, in the riverbed are white bars of rock, and on the high rim are ridges of quartzite which reflect a dozen different colours. Go down through the gorge and you come to **Ormiston Pound**, a basin valley 10 km across, with a small, episodic stream. Yet it was the power of this river which in ancient times breached the end of the pound and slashed through, leaving the gorge which is the main attraction of the park.

REDBANK NATURE PARK Redbank Nature Park is about 30 km beyond Glen Helen, along an unsealed road. A long narrow cleft carved through the rock by the Redbank Creek has resulted in a series of deep rock pools in a narrow chasm. Swimming can be dangerous, for the water is ice-cold and the handholds are few. The recommended way of progressing through the gorge is on an air mattress.

HERMANNSBURG Hermannsburg is 125 km west of Alice Springs along the largely unsealed Larapinta Dr. Its missionary buildings are up to 100 years old and house a collection of memorabilia of early Lutheran Missionary/Aboriginal contact (the town is named after the place in Germany where the missionaries trained). Lutheran missionaries took nearly two years to make the overland trek with livestock from Bethany, South Australia. The first Aboriginal school was established here in 1879 and a grammar book and dictionary of the Aranda language was compiled in 1891. Freehold title in the land was given to the local Aborigines in 1982, and it is now run as a cattle station.

Hermannsburg is close to **Finke Gorge National Park**. There are walks along the gorge with views of incredible rock formations, which contrast with the greenery and rock pools of nearby **Palm Valley**.

ALBERT NAMATJIRA

The great Aboriginal artist was born here in 1902. He was the first Aboriginal painter to be recognised by Europeans and his memorial here is inscribed: 'This is the landscape which inspired the artist'

Just east of Alice Springs, **Emily and Jessie Gaps Nature Park** encloses two semi-permanent water-holes. Emily Gap – the word gap is used here to mean short gorge – has one wall decorated with Aboriginal paintings with tall caterpillar-like figures. The gaps were created by a tributary of the Todd River flowing south through a jagged ridge of the MacDonnell Ranges. There is sparse vegetation on the ridge, but gums grow along the riverbed, some of them very large. The best time to visit is between June and September when there is often a blaze of wildflowers.

Trephina Gorge, about 70 km further east, was formed in the same way. In places its dark red cliffs are up to 100 m high and along the river bed are many large eucalypts. In the west of Trephina National Park the John Hayes Rock Hole is pleasant and shady. The water is retained in this deep pool well after the summer rains have passed, but sadly it is very attractive to feral cattle and is often polluted.

Close by, near Ross River, is the **N'Dhala Gorge**, which has Aboriginal paintings thought to be 30,000 years old.

At **Arltunga**, 37 km further east, explorer David Lindsay reported the discovery of 'rubies' – they turned out to be garnets – in 1887. The report of rubies drew miners who discovered gold, and mining continued on and off until 1916. The area is now a historical reserve, with a few minersí huts and the ruins of the government battery and police station.

WHERE NEXT?

About 450 km southwest of Alice Springs is perhaps Australiaís most famous natural attraction: Uluru or Ayers Rock (see p. 330). Almost 1500 km north along the Stuart Hwy lies Darwin, capital of the Northern Territory (see p. 348).

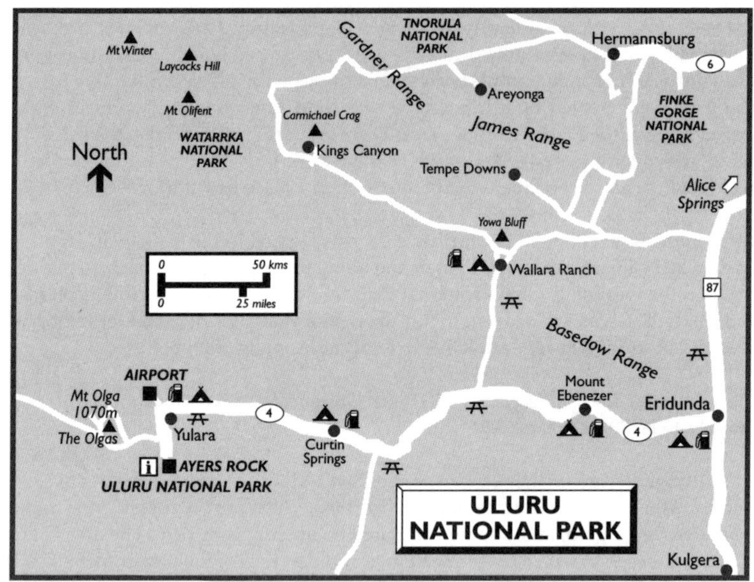

ULURU AND KATA TJUTA (AYERS ROCK AND THE OLGAS)

The great red monolith of Uluru – Ayers Rock – is Australia's most powerful and awesome sight. For millennia it and the neighbouring great rocks of Kata Tjuta have been a place of magic and sanctity for the Aboriginal people, and a visit here can be a deeply moving experience.

It was in 1872 that the first European, the explorer Ernest Giles, set eyes on Uluru. He did not climb it. A year later, on 17 July, 1873, William Gosse, another explorer, climbed this 'immense pebble rising abruptly from the plain' and named it Ayers Rock after his uncle, Sir Henry Ayers, then governor of South Australia.

It was also Ernest Giles who, in October 1872, reached the northern shore of Lake Amadeus and saw, about 80 km to the south, Kata Tjuta rising from the plains. Seeing them as one mountain, he named them Olga after the Grand Duchess of Russia who married the King of Greece. An odd choice.

This was the very start of the white settlement of Australia's Red Centre. With it came the relocation of the traditional owners, the Anangu, from the lands around Uluru, and a severe depletion of the delicate, desert environment by grazing stock. At the time, no one knew any better. Now we do.

More and more these two amazing manifestations of nature are being referred to by their Aboriginal names. As they belong to the local Aboriginal people and we only go there as their guests it seems more appropriate to use the correct name. Uluru and Kata Tjuta also seem names far more in tune with the feeling of the area and the wonder of its sights.

In 1958 the area was declared a National Park and in 1985 control was returned to the original owners, the Anangu. They lease the park back to the Australian Nature Conservation Agency but have kept a strong interest and involvement so that the park has developed without affecting the traditional relationship of the Anangu with their land. Many areas sacred to Pitjantjatjara and Yangkunytjatjara Aboriginal groups and associated with legends of the Dreamtime are closed to the public.

ARRIVAL AND DEPARTURE

From Alice Springs, Yulara is 200 km south along the Stuart Hwy (Hyw 87) to Eridunda, and then west on the Lasseter Hwy for another 250 km. In a reasonable car the journey will take 4 hrs.

There are frequent coaches from Alice Springs, and the major tour companies offer round-trip day tours. These are long and tiring but as you are not driving you may be able to sleep for part of the way.

It is far easier but more expensive to fly. Ansett has direct flights to Yulara from Sydney, Alice Springs, Cairns and Perth, with shuttle coaches to the resort. Often visitors arrive in Sydney with Ayers Rock – they are not quite yet used to using Uluru – pencilled into their itinerary as a day trip. Unless you are chartering a private jet plane that is simply not possible.

INFORMATION

Ayers Rock Resort Visitors and Information Centre, Yulara; tel: 8956 2240. Open daily 0800–2100 with all possible information and informative displays on the geology, nature and

Anangu connections with Uluru. There is also a Park Visitorsí Centre within the park, on the access road to the Rock. Both are staffed by well informed, enthusiastic and helpful people. The rangers within the park are quite willing to give the answer to any question you might care to ask.

INTERNET SITES **Australian Northern Territory Tourist Web** www.world.net/Travel/Australia/NT_info/NTTC/

Australian Travel Guide to the Northern Territory www.webraven.com.au/austrvgd/theguide/nt.cfm

Information on the Northern Territory www.oztourism.com.au/~gdaymate/indexnt.htm

ACCOMMODATION AND FOOD AND DRINK

To see both Uluru and Kata Tjuta you stay at Yulara, on the edge of the park. The resort has a variety of accommodation, places to eat and support services such as a bank and shops.

Outback Pioneer Hotel Yulara Dr.; tel: 8956 2737.

Outback Pioneer Lodge (PO Box 10) Yulara; tel: 8956 2170.

Sails In The Desert Hotel Yulara Dr.; tel: 8956 2200.

Spinifex Lodge Hotel Yulara Dr.; tel: 8956 2131.

For an unforgettable experience, there is the **Sounds of Silence** retaurant (see p. 335).

GETTING AROUND

Uluru is 20 km from Yulara, and Kata Tjuta a further 30 km from Uluru. Excellent roads connect the two and circumnavigate them.

Because of a 'remote surcharge', a saloon car will cost something around 50 per cent more than elsewhere in Australia. As is true in most locations in Australia, you can hire a 4-wheel drive vehicle, but there is an excess charge of $5,000 and as this is an ecologically sensitive area, protecting over 500 species of plants, 24 native mammals and no less than 72 species of reptiles, you are not allowed to drive off the track.

Yulara has a ring road and well-signposted, well-kept roads, although everything within the resort is in walking distance. Special tours out to Uluru and Kata Tjuta include pick-up and drop-off.

ULURU

The largest rock in the world rises 348 m above the flat plain, and its circumference around the base is more than 5 km. The rock moves through an incredible range of colours as you watch, especially at sunrise and sunset, as if it were some sort of supernatural light show.

Uluru is one of the few natural landmarks that lives up, completely, to its prior billing. As you get closer to the Rock there starts a series of magic transformations. People flock to see the rock changing colour at sunset, but it also changes colour during the day. A cloud crosses the sun and the rock changes instantly from red ochre to a deep purple and then back to a complex red. The single shaded colour seen from a distance becomes a subtlety of hues with greys and blacks and reds glinting through the ochre. Right up to the rock and the immensity overwhelms you and the colours change as you move your head. See it a dozen times and you will always find a new view, a new dimension. And is the Rock truly red? Indeed it is. It is not just the reflections from the sun when it is rising and setting. The iron oxide on the rock reacts with the atmosphere and oxidises, producing that deep rusty colour. Underneath, the Rock is a dull grey.

Highlights

Uluru and Kata Tjuta are embraced by the Uluru-Kata Tjuta National Park. The entry fee to the park ($$) lasts for five days and allows unlimited access.

Viewing areas have been set up to take advantage of the sunset and sunrise colours, which can vary from a bright orange/red to the deep brown of the main body of rock to a solid and moody purple. A spectacular sight comes after rain on the rock, when it takes on a silver sheen. At Yulara there is also the Imalung Lookout and, near by, the Observatory, which offers a chance to view the desert stars.

To understand the impact of Uluru you need to get clear in your mind that this is a single piece of rock. It has very few cracks which can be affected by weathering and the hard grain sandstone protects the rock from erosion. In some places, where the surface of the rock has been worn away, it has resulted in caves and spectacular formations such as the fluting effect along the south-east and north-west flanks of the rock. After a storm, waterfalls crash down these flutes for a short but spectacular lifetime.

If you are in a car you can make a slow and careful perambulation of its base – several times. This way you will see the Rock in air-conditioned comfort and, in the summer, without the flies. Or walk around the Rock and feel its solidity with the earth.

Climbing Uluru is not forbidden, but definitely not recommended (see box). You will almost certainly find that a walking tour around its base, with or without a guide, is less physically taxing and also more spiritually rewarding. The 9-km **Base Walk** around the Rock takes about three hours. Take plenty of water with you, for the sun strikes hard and dehydration is ever lurking. There are warning notices to keep you away from the sacred sites. This walk allows you to experience the Rock in a quite remarkable way. Even if there are people around you will feel there are only two spirits in the area: you and the Rock. The feeling is quite eerie but has been experienced by far too many visitors to be written off as pure imagination.

CLIMBING ULURU

Visitors are often tempted to climb Uluru, but most experienced people recommend that you don't, for two reasons. It is an ascent of 1.6 km and very steep in parts, and it is sadly common for elderly visitors to find that it is slightly more than their heart can take, resulting in park rangers having to lower them down with stretchers. There have been deaths on Uluru. In the last year there have been 22 rescues, with climbers suffering from vertigo, torn muscles, broken limbs and worse.

More importantly, the local Pitjantjatjara (see p. 337) have always regarded the Rock as a special place and they find the idea of tourists climbing all over it distasteful. You should not read too much into this. The Rock is not as important a site to the local people as, say, Kata Tjuta, where you are simply not allowed to climb. But the local people do not climb the Rock, they see it as inappropriate, and would prefer it if you didn't. So perhaps you shouldn't, certainly not without giving it much thought and consideration beforehand.

KATA TJUTA

Kata Tjuta – the Olgas – are 50 km from Yulara, and seem at first to be overshadowed by Uluru. This is an illusion. The tallest peak on Kata Tjuta, Mt Olga, is more than 200 m higher than Uluru. The distinctive domes and striated, weathered surfaces of Kata Tjuta match Uluru in colour and some visitors prefer its subtleties and hidden pleasures.

It is probable that Kata Tjuta was originally larger than the Rock, but, whereas Uluru has effectively resisted erosion, Kata Tjuta (meaning 'many heads') has been weathered over the aeons into a group of 36 of what the explorer Giles called 'monstrous domes'.

Climbing the Olgas is forbidden, but there are two exploratory walks. The **Olga Gorge Walk** is an easy stroll through the chasm for about a km. Much more satisfying is the **Valley of the Winds Walk**, which is a 6-km loop that takes about three hours. Dehydration is a serious potential problem and you must take enough water with you. Most people tend to visit Uluru in the morning and Kata Tjuta in the afternoon. Reverse the order and you will be very much on your own.

Typical Central Australian weather has warm to hot days with mild nights in summer and warm days with cool to cold nights in winter. What must be mentioned are the flies. In the summer they are a serious nuisance and you often see people wearing veils to avoid them. An industrial strength insect repellent is an absolute essential.

The **Sounds of Silence** restaurant does not have walls. It is out in the open air, staged in a clearing in the sand dunes a few km from the resort. Over a pre-dinner drink you can watch the setting sun, both reflecting in the western face of Uluru and, to the west, painting the sky over Kata Tjuta a series of vivid colours, for at the Sounds Of Silence you have a 360-degree view and you can get the best of the sunset from any angle.

Tables are lit by gas lantern and the meal is a buffet of Northern Territory specialities such as kangaroo, barramundi and emu from the barbecue, and Australian native fruits and berries. After dinner the lanterns are extinguished and the conversation hushed by the sudden and absolute darkness. For some people, this will be the first time that they have ever truly heard the sound of silence. As eyes become adjusted to the dark, slowly the canopy of stars in all their brilliance is revealed. Because it is in the desert this is one of the clearest skies in the world. An astronomer invites guests to look at some of the better-known planets through a powerful telescope, and tells the tales of ancient mythologies and the Aboriginal stories of creation and how they are played out in the sky. Magic.

YULARA

The Ayers Rock Resort was designed by Philip Cox, who has much to be proud of. It was recognised that a hotel was needed for the park as far back as 1965, but the problems were immense: the inhospitable environment, the huge temperature fluctuations, the lack of any existing infrastructure or services such as power, water or sewage. In addition, the site had to be acceptable to the traditional owners who, after all, have been around for over 22,000 years, and located where it was possible to maintain the environment of the area. Nothing happened for another 20 years.

The resort had to start from base zero, developing its own water and power supplies and bringing in everything from scratch. From the beginning, a concerted effort was made to train all members of staff in environmental awareness and to build up a close and consultative working relationship with the local Aboriginal community and the National Park headquarters and local staff.

The buildings have been positioned and constructed to take advantage of widely varying temperatures. Extensive use has been made of double roofs to provide insulating air space which reduces the need for air-conditioning, and one of the resort's most striking features are the immense white sails which act as air-conditioners. The fabric collects heat and filters out all ultraviolet radiation. Roof-top solar panels provide about 70 per cent of domestic hot water and air-conditioning requirements which reduces the demand on the power station. The resort has its own water treatment plant, which can produce up to 41,000 litres of drinking water an hour as well as 135,000 kg of ice. The water is pumped from underground wells and then purified. Waste treatment plants make sure that as much water as possible is returned to the land.

Running the resort in such an ecologically sensitive area means that if it imports a chocolate bar it has to provide for the silver wrapper to be shipped out afterwards. Not an easy task, so visitors, too, must be eco-sensitive. Leaving litter around in a National Park, especially a National Park such as this, is a serious sin. If you bring it with you, take it back. This is a most remarkable place. Everyone needs to focus most seriously on keeping it that way.

The **Indiginy Amphitheatre** has didgeridoo playing and Northern Territory music under the star-filled skies. You can experience it Mon–Sat at 2030 during summer months, 1930 in the winter.

The **Maruku Arts and Crafts Centre** was established in 1984 to cater for a growing demand for the work of Aboriginal crafts people. It started when nine vehicles containing artists and their work made the journey from Amata, 300 km away. In two weeks they sold more to visitors to Uluru than they did in a whole year in the Amata community. The word quickly spread about the success of this expedition and many communities got together to establish a regional arts centre. Today, in addition to its sales at the centre, Maruku exports more than $500,000 of unique and original arts to international markets. It is based in the Cultural Centre at the foot of Uluru and provides a service to about 800 Aboriginal craftspeople from over 19 communities. Open daily 0830–1200, 1500–1700 (Dec-Apr); 0830–1700 (May–Nov).

The **Cultural Centre** itself has been widely accepted as one of Australia's more remarkable interpretative centres since it opened in late October 1995. The design evolved from sand sketches and paintings by the traditional owners, and the complex comprises two main buildings in the shape of snakes: Kumniya, the female python, and Liru, the poisonous snake. The buildings are constructed with mud-brick walls, with massive timber trunks supporting the roof and the veranda and a roof of copper and shingles which suggest a snake's scales.

The centre offers visitors a basic understanding of Tjukurpa, the creative view of life that forms the foundation of Aboriginal living. The relationship the local people have with the area is relayed through paintings which have been directly applied to the walls, audio recordings of senior members of the Anangu, descriptive panels, displays and videos. Most of the exhibits are interactive so that pushing a button brings the display to life with the words of the people and the distinctive sounds of the desert. The Cultural Centre is on the way to Uluru from the resort and entry is free. Open 0700–1800 (Nov–Mar); 0730–1730 (Apr–Oct).

THE ABORIGINAL PEOPLES AND TJUKURPA

Uluru is in the area that has traditionally been the territory of the Pitjantjatjara and the Yankunytjatjara people. In the 1966 census there appeared to be 948 Aboriginal people living in Pitjantjatjara country, but as they are a very mobile people, this is probably an under-estimation. It is also probable that the population is increasing through improved healthcare.

These are Western Desert peoples and they are all connected, either directly or indirectly, by the religious traditions of the Tjukurpa. Tjukurpa is a most sophisticated and complex relationship between the people and the land. It is, among other things, the law, lore, moral code and religion, defining people's exact relationships and obligations to each other. It includes the code for managing the land and its animals, and it sets out the proper way that things should be done. At Uluru these rules are most often seen in terms of access and appropriate behaviour, such as being quiet in Kantju Gorge or not climbing Uluru. The Tjukurpa is memorised and transmitted by ceremony, its layers or chapters maintained by various members of the community. It is stored in the rituals of dance, and represented in sacred objects that non-Anangu, never mind pirampa – non-indigenous visitors – must never see.

Camels have long been associated with the outback. In the early days they were the only means of getting goods and material around the deserts of the Red Centre, and played an important part in opening up the Australian outback. **Frontier Camel Tours** offer camel tours of the desert (they run a similar and very successful operation in Alice Springs). They neatly avoid the heat of the day by operating very early in the morning and late in the evening, with Take a Camel to Sunrise and Take a Camel to Sunset. Riding a camel is not as difficult as riding a horse as you are securely held in the saddle and the camels do not trot – at least not on these tours. On the other hand, there is a certain amount of lurching around and it is not a recommended experience for someone suffering from a serious hangover.

The Northern Territory

The Northern Territory covers one-sixth of Australia. It is six times the size of Great Britain or twice the size of Texas and has a population of less than 200,000. Alaska has nearly three times as many people.

Until 1911 the whole area was ruled from Adelaide as part of South Australia's Northern Territory. (Adelaide's jurisdiction covered an area larger than any European country.) The Federal Government took over for a while, and then from 1926 to 1931 it was divided into two self-governing districts – Northern Australia centred on Darwin and Central Australia centred on Alice Springs. But this proved costly and inefficient and the Northern Territory again came under Federal control from Canberra. Not until 1978 was the Northern Territory granted self-government.

This is traditionally the province of large-scale pastoralists and miners, although in the 20th century, war and the defence industry have impinged on some areas. As a strategic route north, the Stuart Hwy from Alice Springs was sealed during World War II, and Japanese bombing of Darwin changed both the face and people's perception of this northern city. In 1967 a joint US–Australian defence and space research facility was established at Pine Gap, close to Alice Springs; its exact functions have never been made clear to an apprehensive public.

Its landscape is one of extremes. The Red Centre, around Alice Springs in the south, is a land of sandhills and featureless plains, where the vegetation – acacia scrub, hardy

IN THE WET

The local Aborigines distinguish six seasons throughout the year, but for most visitors it is either the Wet, with up to 1,600 mm of torrential rainfall between Dec and Mar, or the Dry, an almost complete drought. The Northern Territory in the Wet is wonderful; Territorians seem to prefer the Wet. They speak of the tremendous storms with awe and affection. If there is anything in the theory of positive and negative ions it can be easily tested by being at the top end of Australia immediately after a storm. As one Darwinian said, 'That's when you come alive.'

The rain comes down in a Niagara of water, solid beyond comprehension. And such rain. Rain in solid sheets of water. Rain that overwhelms. And then, like a miracle, you are back again in brilliant sunshine and the air is fresh and sparkling and your spirit sings.

semi-desert grasses and stunted eucalypts – has adapted to the aridity and the heat. Northwards, deeply eroded scarps, mountain ranges and broad pastures characterize the high tablelands that fall away to the low-lying coast, washed by the Timor and Arafura seas and the Gulf of Carpentaria. This is Australia's Top End. The contrast between lazing in a flat-bottomed boat as you drift through the Katherine Gorge and the harshness of the land around Alice is immense. But such contrasts are the heart and soul of the Northern Territory.

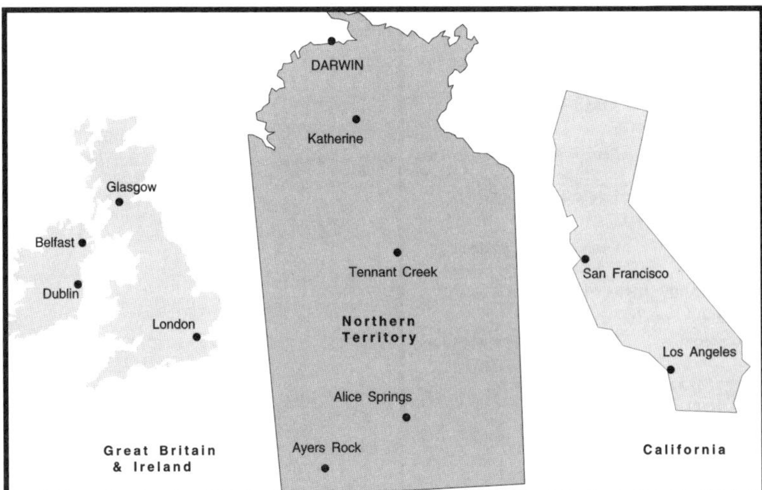

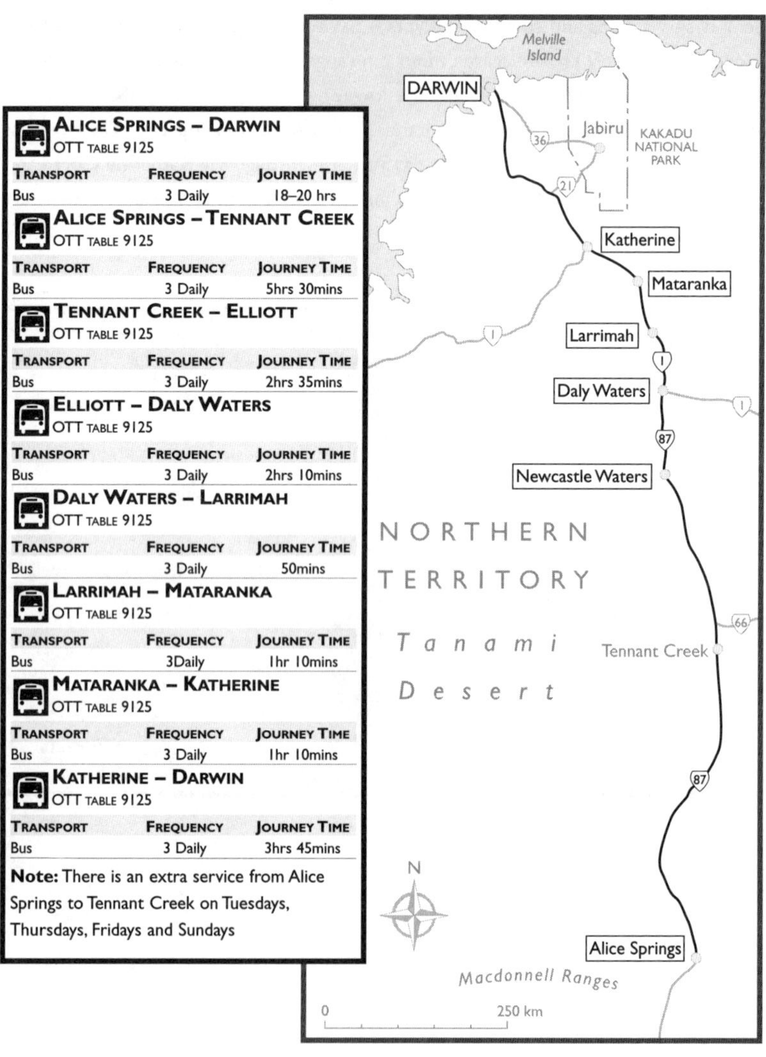

ALICE SPRINGS – DARWIN
OTT TABLE 9125

TRANSPORT	FREQUENCY	JOURNEY TIME
Bus	3 Daily	18–20 hrs

ALICE SPRINGS – TENNANT CREEK
OTT TABLE 9125

TRANSPORT	FREQUENCY	JOURNEY TIME
Bus	3 Daily	5hrs 30mins

TENNANT CREEK – ELLIOTT
OTT TABLE 9125

TRANSPORT	FREQUENCY	JOURNEY TIME
Bus	3 Daily	2hrs 35mins

ELLIOTT – DALY WATERS
OTT TABLE 9125

TRANSPORT	FREQUENCY	JOURNEY TIME
Bus	3 Daily	2hrs 10mins

DALY WATERS – LARRIMAH
OTT TABLE 9125

TRANSPORT	FREQUENCY	JOURNEY TIME
Bus	3 Daily	50mins

LARRIMAH – MATARANKA
OTT TABLE 9125

TRANSPORT	FREQUENCY	JOURNEY TIME
Bus	3Daily	1hr 10mins

MATARANKA – KATHERINE
OTT TABLE 9125

TRANSPORT	FREQUENCY	JOURNEY TIME
Bus	3 Daily	1hr 10mins

KATHERINE – DARWIN
OTT TABLE 9125

TRANSPORT	FREQUENCY	JOURNEY TIME
Bus	3 Daily	3hrs 45mins

Note: There is an extra service from Alice Springs to Tennant Creek on Tuesdays, Thursdays, Fridays and Sundays

CROSSING THE NORTHERN TERRITORY

From the arid scrubland of the Red Centre, this route stretches into the torrid tropic zone, crossing the land of the great cattle drives to reach the frontier city of Darwin. Of course, if time is at a premium you can fly direct from Alice Springs to Darwin but you will be missing much of interest that lies between.

ROUTE DETAIL

It is tough country but there is an excellent sealed highway all the way – although despite its name, the Stuart Hwy is mostly two lanes only. The traffic is light except for the cattle trains – trucks with several trailers – and you would be wise to give them a wide berth. But otherwise this is a perfectly acceptable drive and it takes you to such interesting places. See p. 25 for advice on long-distance driving. By bus the 1,530-km journey takes about 20 hrs.

NEWCASTLE WATERS

Newcastle Waters sits at the intersection of the Barkly and Murranji stock routes. The Murranji, one of the most famous stock routes in the country, was opened in 1886 and cut nearly two-thirds of the distance off the conventional route through Katherine and the Roper River area. The route passed through rich pastoral land owned by some of the wealthiest Territory landowners of the day, and as many as 75,000 cattle travelled along the track annually. Conditions were difficult for the cattle and the drovers, but they endured.

The waterholes were named after the Duke of Newcastle, who was Secretary of State for the Colonies at the time that John McDouall Stuart came upon the area in 1861. (The rough and dangerous wildlife deterred Stuart and his party from persevering in their northward push.)

In the 1920s Newcastle Waters was a depot for construction gangs working on watering facilities for the east–west stock route. When government bores provided reliable water points after 1930, a fledgling township grew up, the stores and a hotel relying almost entirely on the stockmen for its livelihood. As motorised road trains began to replace the stock drives in the early 1960s, alternative transport routes were established, bypassing Newcastle Waters. When the owners of the Newcastle Waters Station found a need for accommodation for

EN ROUTE

On the outskirts of Dunmarra, some 100 km north of Elliott, a roadside marker recalls the spot where the original wires of the Overland Telegraph Line joined more than 120 years ago. Facilities include a shop, a restaurant and bar, and barbecue facilities. Minor mechanical repairs can be handled, and there are camping and caravan park facilities.

ALICE SPRINGS – DARWIN

married workers and their families, the town's deserted buildings were renovated. Today, there is a teacher and basic facilities in the town, catering for the small population. **Jones Store**, known as George Man Fong's house, is one of the oldest buildings, constructed in 1934. It originally sold provisions to drovers and was later used as a butchery, bakery and as a saddlery. The property is managed by the National Trust and has a fine display of memorabilia.

DALY WATERS

Daly Waters is a minute settlement near where the Carpentaria Hwy joins the Stuart Hwy, on an area of land that traditionally belonged to the Jangman people. It has two claims to fame: the oldest pub in the Territory, licensed in 1893; and the first international airfield in Australia.

Daly Waters was chosen as a site for one of the repeater stations of the Overland Telegraph. Like other stations at the time, it was pretty basic, consisting primarily of an office, sleeping quarters and a meat house. Mail and supplies came in once a year, carried by camels and packhorses which had travelled for four or five months. As a result, there was always a chronic shortage of basic necessities. The railway never quite made it from Darwin, but then W T Pearce and his wife arrived to set up a store: the **Daly Waters Pub**. Originally built for the cattle drovers on the months-long overland routes, the low stone building now serves the same need for drivers of the huge road trains conveying cattle to the railheads. It is also a police station, post office, bank and museum, and the main source of employment. There are all sorts of odd paraphernalia on display: saddles, Morse receivers, even a non-operational set of traffic lights.

Daly Waters is also a footnote in aviation history. It was one of the stop-off points in the 1926 London–Sydney air race, and in 1930 Amy Johnson landed nearby on her historic flight from London. In the 1930s it was chosen as a Qantas refuelling stop, and the establishment of the aerodrome created the incentive to expand the pub business to look after the needs of the incoming thirsty and hungry passengers. During World War II, bombers and fighters refuelled here before heading north. Although the airstrip is now closed, the **Daly Waters Hangar** has been restored by the National Trust and is an interesting information source with both text and photos on the history of aviation in the area. Open daily 0800–0900, 1500–1600.

Daly Waters Pub Stuart Hwy; tel: 8975 9927.
Hi-Way Inn $ Stuart Hwy; tel: 8975 9925.

LARRIMAH

The road from Daly Waters is flat but winding, passing through scrub grassland with ghost gums, salmon gums and patches of pink and white hibiscus to Larrimah. Another town that started life mainly because of the Overland Telegraph line, Larrimah later became a railhead on the now-defunct service from Darwin. At one time 3,000 men were stationed here during World War II.

The narrow-gauge line of the North Australia Railway originally ended at Birdum, 8 km south, but was moved closer to the town because of problems with flooding. The train often had trouble pulling her passenger compartments along, and stopped frequently to raise steam or to undergo mechanical adjustments. The train was given the affectionate nickname of 'Leaping Lena' and its slowness was the subject of innumerable outback yarns. But it provided an essential connection with the Top End: in the 1930s passengers could fly from Queensland to Camooweal, connect by air to Daly Waters, continue by pony to Birdum and then take the train to Darwin. All that is left are relics: the Gorrie airstrip a few km out of town, the abandoned railway siding and the building that was the officers' mess and is now the town pub.

MATARANKA

Mataranka is known as the capital of Never Never country. The area came to prominence after the publication of Jeannie Gunn's *We of the Never Never*.

The town was the brainchild of J A Gilruth, who was Administrator in the early part of the 20th century. He believed that there was great potential for the surrounding land; indeed, he was in favour of establishing Mataranka as the Territory's inland capital city, replacing Darwin. Gilruth knew that growth and development meant attracting settlers and investors and he set about trying to prove the quality of the land by establishing the Mataranka Horse and Sheep Experimental Farm in 1913.

In 1928 the railway arrived. There were great expectations for the town, but only 22 out of the 60 blocks offered at auction were actually taken up. A peanut-growing scheme that started in 1930 to help the unemployment situation in Darwin collapsed because of crop failure and a poor market for peanuts and effectively the town was abandoned. Gilruth's plans for Mataranka were finished.

Ranger Station, Mataranka; tel: 8975 4560.

Mataranka Roadhouse $$ Roper Ter; tel: 8975 4571.
Old Elsey Wayside Inn $ 13 Roper Ter; tel: 8975 4512.
Territory Manor Motel $ Martins Rd; tel: 8975 4516.

HIGHLIGHTS

The **Mataranka Homestead**, which dates back to 1916, is where Dr Gilruth set up his experimental station for sheep and horses. The homestead is within **Elsey National Park**, which has numerous walking tracks, waterfalls and rainforest. The park entrance is 10 km east of Mataranka near the junction of the Stuart and Roper highways. The best time to visit is in the dry season (May–Sept). A highlight is the **Mataranka Thermal Springs**, a clear thermal pool surrounded by weeping palms, pandanus, cabbage tree palms, paperbarks and yellow passionfruit in a pocket of rainforest. The waters are guaranteed to cure whatever ails you, but it can get a bit crowded in high season.

Near the springs is the replica of the **Elsey Homestead**, which was built in 1982 for the film of *We of the Never Never*. Inside are various displays relating to the people and early days of the area. Open daily 0700–1500. The site of the original building is near the present-day Elsey Graves, some 20 km south of Mataranka.

WE OF THE NEVER NEVER

Jeannie Taylor Gunn, a teacher, travelled in the region with her husband Aeneas, a Melbourne librarian, whom she had married in 1901. After less than 15 months of marriage he died from malarial dysentery. Jeannie Gunn left the outback but her book, *We of the Never Never*, introduced people for the first to how tough it can be in the outback. The book was rejected by five publishers, but finally published in 1908. It sold nearly one million copies. The story is told that the outback is called the 'never never' because Mrs Gunn wrote that she 'never, never' wanted to leave. This seems doubtful. The grave of Aeneas Gunn is in the Elsey Homestead cemetery. Jeannie Gunn lived to be 91 and is buried in Melbourne.

EN ROUTE

The Cutta Cutta and Tindal Caves are limestone rock formations that lie about 15 m below the surface. There are well-marked and signposted walking tracks, and tours are conducted daily (hourly 0900–1500). Open all year except in the height of the Wet when they can be inundated.

KATHERINE

At Katherine the Stuart Hwy, the Victoria Hwy, the North Australian Railway and the old Overland Telegraph converge, and thus it is a meeting place for the outback. The River Katherine – the locals pronounce it to rhyme with wine – was named in 1862 by John McDouall Stuart after the daughter of one of his sponsors.

The river is important because it is the first permanent water north of Alice Springs. The town is traditionally a cattle centre but adding much to the economy is a local air force base (off limits). The beautiful Katherine Gorge National Park was established in 1963 and has had much effect on the growth of tourism in the town.

Katherine Region Tourist Association, cnr Stuart Hwy and Lindsay St; tel: 8972 2650.

Beagle Motor Inn $ Lindsay St, cnr Fourth St; tel: 8972 3998.
Crossways Hotel Motel $ Katherine Ter; tel: 8972 1022.
Edith Falls Park $ Edith Falls St; tel: 8975 4869.
Hotel Motel Katherine $$ Katherine Ter; tel: 8972 1622.
Knotts Crossing Resort $$ Cameron St, cnr Giles St; tel: 8972 2511.
Kuringgai Motel $$ Giles St; tel: 8971 0266.
Palm Court Motel $$ Third St, cnr Giles St; tel: 8972 2722.
Riverview Motel & Caravan Park $$ Victoria Hwy; tel: 8972 1011.
Victoria Lodge $$ 21 Victoria Hwy; tel: 8972 3464.

While no one would accuse the town of being a gourmet destination the situation has massively improved: just seven years ago there were only four restaurants and two were not the sort of place you would go to. Now at least there is something of a range to chose from.
Alfie's $ 7 Victoria Hwy; tel: 8972 1814.
Annies Family Restaurant $$ 17 First St; tel: 8971 0191.
Buchanan's $$ cnr O'Shea and First Sts; tel: 8972 2644. Part of Paraway Motel. Arguably the best restaurant in town. But now it has competition. Licensed.
Croc Room $$ 2 Fourth St; tel: 8972 3998. In the Beagle Motor Inn. Serves, among other dishes, baked crocodile.
Georgie's Seafood $ Katherine Ter. Good fish and chips and cheap Chinese meals.
Golden Bowl $ Katherine Ter; tel: 8972 1449.
Kirbyí's Restaurant $ Katherine Ter; tel: 8972 1622.
Matilda's $$ Stuart Hwy, 3 km south of town; tel: 8972 1744. Part of the Frontier Motor Inn. Arguably the other best restaurant in town. Licensed.
N & I Pizza & Chicken Palace $ 552 Victoria Hwy; tel: 8972 1814.
Springvale Homestead $$ Shadforth Rd; tel: 8972 1044. Bush kitchen meals are part of a sort of tourist show. Book in advance.

HIGHLIGHTS

What attracts visitors to Katherine is the gorge, but the town itself has a few places worth visiting while you are here.

The easiest way to find out about the history of the area is to go to the **Katherine Museum** in Gorge Rd (open Mon–Fri 1000–1600, Sat 1000–1400, Sun 1400–1700) and the **Katherine Railway Museum and Gallery**, Railway Ter. This old railway station, built in 1926, is now the local headquarters for the National Trust. There is a considerable display of railway memorabilia as well as more information on the history of Katherine. Open Mon–Fri 1300–1500.

EN ROUTE

Pine Creek, 92 km northwest of Katherine, is the gateway to Arnhem Land. The Miners Park tells the history of gold and uranium mining in the area, and old mining machinery is on show. There are still a few buildings left from that time, including a tin pub and a tin lockup, and Ah Toy's General Store is a last reminder of the 2,000 Chinese who worked Pine Creek's goldmines.

The **Katherine School of the Air** claims to be the largest classroom in the world. It broadcasts daily to children over a distance of 800,000 sq. km. During term time you can see it in operation at its headquarters in Giles St and see how the sheer size of the outback has, to a certain extent, been conquered by this early form of distance learning. In term time it is open to the public daily 0900–1200.

Just west of the town is **Katherine Low Level Nature Park**. This park covers the full width of the river valley with paperbarks and pandanus lining the river banks. You can swim there in shallow water during the Dry season but in the Wet the whole area will probably be flooded. Above all Katherine is the gateway to the **Katherine Gorge**, which is 30 km away in the **Nitmiluk National Park**. The Park Visitors' Centre (tel: 8972 1886) is at the end of the sealed road off the highway. The park is rich in Aboriginal art, with rock paintings representing the spiritual 'dreaming' of the Jawoyn people, the traditional owners of the land. More than 100 km of walking tracks meanders through the park, including some that merit serious bushwalking expeditions. It is essential that you register with the park ranger before setting out on any of the major walks. There is a camping area at the entrance to the park and accommodation is available at Katherine.

Near to town are some delightful hot springs. Go along the Victoria Hwy for 3 km, turn off at Riverview Caravan Park and you come to Katherine Hot Springs. While no medicinal benefits are claimed, these hot springs on the banks of the Katherine River make for pleasant swimming.

Springvale Homestead is the oldest homestead still standing in the Territory. It is 8 km from Katherine via Zimmin Dr. or Victoria Hwy, then Shadforth Rd (tel: 8972 1122). It offers tourist version corroboree (jamborees) and crocodile spotting tours. There is a swimming-pool, motel and camping. Free short walking tours daily 1000 and 1430 (Apr–Oct).

KATHERINE GORGE

The name 'gorge' is misleading for this is a series of 13 canyons of stunning beauty, rich in flora and fauna, including crocodiles. It is arguably the most colourful and grandly proportioned river canyon in inland Australia, with walls that tower over the slow-moving water in the dry season and are dotted with Aboriginal murals and paintings.

Formation of the gorges began 23 million years ago as torrents of water poured along tiny cracks in the earth. The Katherine River, which eroded the canyons, rises in Arnhem Land and further downstream becomes the Daly River before it runs into the Timor Sea.

There is a big seasonal difference in the water levels and the behaviour of the river. During the Dry, the gorge and its waters are calm and majestic but in the Wet, between Nov and Mar, the river can storm through the gorge with torrential waters that reach up to 6 m above the normal level.

For most of its length the 12-km-long gorge is filled wall to wall with deep water which reflects the coloured cliffs on either side, and the blue sky above. Experiencing the gorge can be done in several ways. From the Visitors' Centre you can walk about a km to the jetty and go on one of a range of cruises. A two-hour cruise shows you the first two gorges, a four-hour cruise makes it three gorges, and the full-day, nine-hour cruise will take you through five gorges.

If you are fit and adventurous (and it is not the height of the Wet) you can hire a canoe (Kookaburra Canoe Hire; tel: 8872 3604), take your time and explore all the gorges. There are also, for experienced bush walkers, walking tracks that follow the clifftops along the gorge. There is much wildlife, including freshwater crocodiles and rock wallabies.

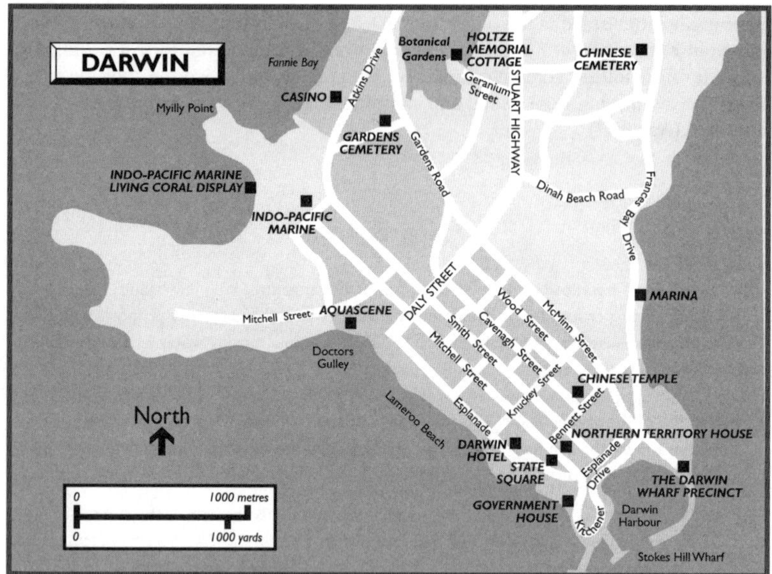

For many tourists the true Australia lies not in Sydney, which is the entry port for the vast majority of tourists, but in Darwin. In the European dream all Australian men are tall, thin, sunburned, laconic, casual, drink ice-cold beer and speak with a strong accent. All Australian women are brave, resourceful, beautiful in an outdoors style and capable of swimming a flooded creek, breaking a recalcitrant horse or fighting bushfires standing alongside their Chips Rafferty-style partner. Darwin is the town that most fits this European dream.

The Northern Territory is a large and empty land and Darwin, its chief city, is a country town with aspirations. This is understandable and not a criticism, but it is important to get into perspective that this is the very small capital city of an immense area of land.

The city was named after Charles Darwin, but not by him. Possibly the first European to visit the area was John Stokes, when he landed in the *Beagle* in 1839. He named the site after the English naturalist who had travelled with him on a previous voyage of discovery on the same ship.

John McDouall Stuart's expedition arrived overland in 1862 and the Northern Territory was made part of South Australia, which was uncertain what to do with its new acquisition. Finally, South Australia's surveyor-general himself visited it, and within a month of his party making camp in the harbour, he reported that he had chosen the principal site for settlement, and a town plan for Palmerston – the original name for Darwin — had already been prepared (basically the design of Adelaide with minor changes).

This was the northern terminus of the Overland Telegraph, so vital to communication across the continent and with Europe, and within five years Palmerston had a population of 600 Europeans and 180 Chinese. There was little in the way of building materials and for the first 20 years of its existence the town had the appearance of a shanty. Administration of the territory passed to Commonwealth control in 1911 and with it came the name change from Palmerston to Darwin.

Cyclone Tracy

Cyclone Tracy hit the city on Christmas Day 1974. It flattened 85 per cent of the city's buildings and left 48 people dead. No one knows exactly what strength the cyclone winds achieved (the anemometer broke after recording a gust of 217 kph) but a guess is that at one point gusts of 270 kph hit the city. Somewhere between $500 million and $1 billion worth of damage was done, making it Australia's most costly natural disaster until it was exceeded by, of all things, a monster hailstorm in Sydney in 1999.

The first Japanese attack on Australia during World War II was a bombing raid on Darwin Harbour on 19 Feb 1942, during which a jetty was destroyed, eight ships sunk and at least 240 people killed. There were 63 air attacks on Darwin through 1942 and 1943. The bombing was to change the relative importance of the city, which was now seen as Australia's northern frontier. In 1951 travel writer Ernestine Hill wrote: 'In its glorious setting Darwin was unloved and unlovely. Apart from a few old faithfuls, there were only two classes – those paid to stay there and those with no money to go.' Times have changed.

GETTING THERE AND GETTING AROUND

Darwin's airport, which serves both international and domestic flights, is close to the city and unless you are travelling alone it may be cheaper to take a taxi into the centre rather than catch the shuttle bus, although some shuttle services are free.

All highways heading north eventually flow into Darwin, but the distances are very great. By bus it's abut 20 hrs from Alice Springs, over 40 hrs from Cairns and nearly 2½ days from Perth.

INFORMATION

The telephone code for Darwin is 08.

TOURIST OFFICE **Darwin Region Tourism Association**, Beagle House cnr Knuckey and Mitchell Sts; tel: 8981 4300; email drtainfo@ozemail.com.au. The people here are informed, friendly, positive and will go to endless lengths to help you enjoy Darwin.

INTERNET SITE **Northern Territory Visitors' Centre** http://www.northernterritory.com

MONEY **Thomas Cook Foreign Exchange** office is at the airport, Henry Wrigley Dr, Darwin; tel: 8945 2966.

ACCOMMODATION

Air Raid City Lodge $$ 35 Cavenagh St. Right in the centre. Communal kitchen and an attached restaurant; tel: 8981 9214.

Asti Motel $$ 7 Packard Pl. Large motel with spa, restaurant and pool; tel: 8981 8200.

Banyan View Lodge $ 119 Mitchell St. Basically for backpackers but twin rooms with fans and fridge; tel: 8981 8644.

Capricornia Motel $$ 44 East Point Rd. Near Fannie Bay, 4 km from the centre; tel: 8981 4055.

City Gardens Apartments $$ 93 Woods St. Family units in a tropical setting. Two minutes from park, five minutes from town; tel: 8941 2888.

CWA Hostel $ 3 Packard Pl. Small, shady house in its own grounds for women, couples and families only; tel: 8941 1536.

Darwin City Lodge $ 151 Mitchell St. Converted house with pool. Rooms $31–45, dorms under $18; tel: 8941 1295.

Elke's $ 112 Mitchell St. Backpackers in restored house with shady pool; tel: 8981 8399.

Fawlty Towers $ 88 Mitchell St. Hostel in an elevated cabin-style building with air-conditioned rooms. Basil is sadly not present; tel: 8981 8363.

Frogshollow Backpackers $ 27 Lindsay St. Attractive tropical building opposite a large park; tel: 8941 2600.

Gecko Lodge $ 146 Mitchell St. Small hostel close to Mindil Beach; tel: 8981 5569.

Globetrotters, 97 Mitchell St. Has just been upgraded. Air-conditioning plus a pool; tel: 8981 5385.

Hotel Darwin $ 10 Herbert St. At one time the only pub in town where you could stay. Still has some of that old charm and there are affordable rooms; tel: 8981 9211.

Melaleuka Lodge $ 52 Mitchell St. Opposite the Transit Centre; tel: 8941 3395.

Seabreeze Motel $$ 60 East Point Rd. In Fannie Bay, 4 km from the centre but close to museum and beaches; tel: 8981 0999.

Top End Hotel $$ corner of Mitchell and Daly St. Attractively designed low-rise with large pool. $95-124; tel: 8981 6511.

Value Inn $$ 50 Mitchell St. No-frills motel but with all the usual facilities; tel: 8981 4733.

YHA $ 69a Mitchell St. Next to the Transit Centre. Pool, good design; tel: 8981 3995.

FOOD

Asian Gateway $ 58 Aralia St. If you are serious about Thai food this is where to go but it is in Nightcliff which is a northern suburb and you will need to take a taxi. Worth it, but tel: 8948 1131.

Charlie's Restaurant $ 29 Knuckey St; tel: 8981 3298.

Christo's on the Wharf $$ Stokes Hill Wharf. Old shed at the end of the wharf. Greek influence. Go with the seafood. Knockout views; tel: 8981 8658.

Corellas Restaurant $$ 100 The Esplanade. Great views; tel: 8941 0755.

Cornucopia $ Museum of Arts and Sciences Complex, Conacher St. Perfect on the terrace at sunset. Australian-Pacific Rim cuisine; tel: 8981 7791.

Holtze Cottage $$ Botanic Gardens. Crocodile, kangaroo and buffalo. Better than you guessed; tel: 8941 1299.

Indonesian Satee House $ West Lane Car Park Arcade. Authentic and as cheap as chips; tel: 8981 4307.

Koh-I-Noor $ Seabreeze Motel, 60 East Point Rd. Indian, Thai and Malaysian cooking. Licensed. Not authentic dishes but lovely tropical outlook; tel: 8981 0999.

Lee Dynasty $ 21 Cavenagh St. Licensed. Cantonese. Fish dishes recommended; tel: 89817808.

Lindsay Street Café $$ 2 Lindsay St. Garden restaurant. Asian influences in cooking. Lunch and dinner; tel: 8981 8631.

Peppi's $$, 84 Mitchell St. French restaurant with some classic dishes; tel: 8981 3762.

Rendezvous $$, Star Village Arcade, Smith St Mall. Malaysian-flavoured cheap and quick lunch.

Rock Oyster $$ 110 Mitchell St. Great fish; tel: 8981 3472.

Somjai's Thai Restaurant $ 21 The Mall. Modified Thai for Australian palates; tel: 8981 9392.

Uncle John's Cabin $$ 6 Gardiner St. Seafood restaurant. Indonesian prau and amazing garden. An event as much as a meal; tel: 8981 3358.

HIGHLIGHTS

The city centre runs south-east from Daly St; the main city centre shopping area, Smith St and its mall, is about 0.5 km further on. It is all within such a small compass that it is very easy to stroll from one end to the other. There is a **historic trail** but as most of the city was flattened by Cyclone Tracy you find yourself often looking at a site where a building used to be, which is less than enthralling.

One building that rode out the cyclone was **Government House** on the Esplanade. It was built in 1883 to replace the timber version of 1870 which had been zapped by ants. There are lovely gardens but you cannot go inside. Just up the road is the **Old Courthouse and Police Station**, built in 1884 and used until Cyclone Tracy. Now the buildings house the offices of the Northern Territory Administrator.

Across Darwin Harbour, the Wharf Precinct has a number of interesting places to visit. The **tunnels** here were constructed for safe oil storage during World War II. One was used as an air-raid shelter and is now a sort of museum which you can tour. $ Open Apr–Oct Mon–Sat 0900–1700; Nov–Mar Tues–Sun 1000–1400. The **Pearling Exhibition** in the precinct records the pearling industry which started in 1884 when the first pearl was found in the Darwin area. The exhibition does not try to gloss over the desperate danger to the pearl divers who often died or got the bends. Open Mon–Fri 1000–1700, Sat–Sun 1000–1800. Tropical fish and living coral reefs can be seen at the **Indo-Pacific Marine** – a great way to find out about the reef. Open daily; tel: 8981 1294 to check times.

TOUR TUB

The easiest way to see Darwin is to take the Tour Tub. It runs from the Mall and passes ten of the city's main attractions, from East Point Reserve and Fannie Bay Gaol to the Aquascene and Botanical Gardens. You can hop on and off all day as you please for a flat, inexpensive fee.

DARWIN'S MARKETS

Darwin is a city with many markets. The **Banyan Junction Market** at the Transit Centre is open every night from about 1900. The **Big Flea Market** is at Rapid Creek every Sun 0800–1400. The **Palmerston Night Market** runs every Fri from about 1730.

More fish can be seen at **Aquascene**, at 28 Doctors Gully Rd. Every day hundreds of fish arrive for hand-feeding sessions, depending on the times of the tides (check timing by phoning 8981 7837). This fish feeding frenzy was started when a well-known diver, Carl Atkinson, started feeding the fish as a hobby and in 1964 had the area declared a Fish Reserve.

The **Fannie Bay Gaol Museum** is at the East Point Reserve (tel: 8981 9702), Fannie Bay. It is full of stories of the desperates who were its past prisoners. It operated as a prison between 1883 and 1979. Also at the East Point Reserve is the **Military Museum**, especially interesting for its thorough coverage of the Japanese bombing of the city in 1942. Open every day 0930–1700.

The **Museum and Art Gallery of the Northern Territory** is on Conacher St in Fannie Bay. Although small, it is wonderfully well laid out, with five permanent galleries and lots of touring exhibitions; the section on Aboriginal art shows how it should be done. Open Mon–Fri 0900–1700, weekends 1000–1700; tel: 8999 8201.

Almost every city in Australia has amazing botanical gardens. **Darwin Botanic Gardens** are no exception: they contain the southern hemisphere's largest array of tropical palms - over 400 species - an orchid farm, a rainforest, waterfalls and wetland flora. The gardens were established in 1879 in Fannie Bay by Dr Maurice Holtze, who had worked in the Imperial Gardens in Russia. He migrated to Australia and with his son Nicholas, who followed him as curator, he started experiments to see what crops would grow in the Northern Territory. In 1866 many of the trees were dug up and moved to their present site; some of these original plantings are now magnificent mature specimens. In the 20th century the gardens have been hit by fire, cyclones and bombs — Cyclone Tracy destroyed some 80 per cent of the buildings, trees and shrubs — but they retain their international importance with regard to tropical flora. Entrance in Geranium St off the Stuart Hwy or Gardens Rd off Gilruth Ave. Open daily 0700–1800.

BOX JELLYFISH

Darwin has plenty of beaches but from Oct to May do not swim because of the box jellyfish. Take local advice on the subject – they are not joking. The sting is dreadful and can be quite dangerous.

Along the Stuart Hwy at Winnellie is Darwin's **Aviation Heritage Centre**. On display is a B52 bomber and the wreckage of a Zero fighter shot down in the first air-raid on Darwin during World War II. You can either wander through the exhibits at your own pace or join a guided tour. Open daily 0930–1700; tel: 8947 2145.

NIGHTLIFE

For an odd night out try the **Deckchair Cinema** at Frances Bay near Stokes Hill Wharf on Darwin Harbour, which during the dry season - it is closed Nov–Mar – shows movies which you never quite got round to seeing. Check what is showing - tel: 8981 0700.

It would be wrong to write about Darwin without mentioning the demon grog. Partly because of the heat and the humidity the people of Darwin can sink more beer than is believable. The last major set of statistics suggests that beer consumption was around 230 litres per year for each head of population. If you take account of children and a few teetotallers, you have a beer consumption that is at least 50 per cent higher than anywhere else in Australia. Realising the health hazard, the government has been pushing the advantages of lite beer, but it is not yet known how effective this campaign will be. Many of the pubs in Darwin have been transformed from swill palaces into slightly more sophisticated bars, but many are still rough as guts and not safe for an unaccompanied woman. There are plenty of bars where you can enjoy a quiet drink, but you need to pick with care.

DAY TRIPS

The **Territory Wildlife Park** is bushland with open-plan natural habitats for the animals and is a great place to visit. It has a walk-through aviary and an excellent aquarium with a walk-through tunnel. There is an astounding display of eagles, hawks and other birds of prey soaring and feeding every day at 1000 and 1500. Finally there is the Nocturnal House where you can see the bilby, water rats, barn owls and ghost bats, none of which you would normally even glimpse. Take the open motorised train or get some exercise and follow the walking trails. $$ On Cox Peninsula Rd, 45 km south of Darwin; open 0830–1800 with last admissions around 1600; tel: 8988 7200.

Noonamah is 44 km from Darwin along the Stuart Hwy. The town developed during World War II as a service depot. Today, Noonamah offers basic facilities – a hotel with a beer garden and a filling station - but its major attraction is the **Crocodile Farm**. There are 8,000 crocodiles and one of them, Goliath, at 5.2 m, is the largest crocodile on display in the Northern Territory. Many of the animals have been relocated here from local rivers and waterways where they have posed a threat to human life. You can try eating farm-raised crocodile meat, which is not bad, and there is a gift shop with a selection of crocodile leather products. There is a guided tour on the hour every hour but the big moment is at 1400, when the big feed takes place and you realise that you never want to swim in crocodile-infested waters; tel: 8988 1491.

At **Howard Springs Nature Park** there is a spring-fed swimming pool surrounded by monsoon rainforest – ideal for swimming and bush walking. A weir crossing the pool was constructed in the 1940s, when World War II troops swelled the local population and Howard Springs was required to supplement Darwin's water supply. The crossing lets you look down on the fish, several of which are large barramundi, although fishing is not permitted. A signposted trail will take you on a 45-min walk through the forest. The park is just off the Stuart Hwy 25 km south of Darwin (sealed roads allow access all year). Open 0800–2000; tel: 8983 1001.

Casuarina Coastal Reserve can be accessed by way of Trower Rd and Lee Point Rd. It has expanses of golden sand stretching from the mouth of Rapid Creek northward to Lee Point. Against a backdrop of cliffs and casuarina trees are pockets of monsoon forest and an attractive picnic area. It also includes a nude bathing beach. Visitors who use the nudist beach must remain within the signposted boundaries and replace their clothing before leaving the area so as not to shock the locals.

The major attraction to the east is Kakadu National Park (see p. 357), which should not be treated as a day trip. However, the drive from Darwin to Kakadu can be an adventure in its own right. Along the way you will pass many attractive places to stop and visit, at which you can either dally en route or treat as trips out from Darwin.

The Arnhem Hwy, which turns east off the Stuart Hwy for Kakadu, is virtually a causeway running through, almost atop, the **Mary River wetlands**. These wetlands are alive with wildlife and driving through you will see more species of birds than anywhere else in Australia outside a zoo. In the Wet this road can be flooded – sometimes for many kilometres at a time - but it is sealed all the way to Kakadu and is hardly ever impassable. Even when it is flooded, if you motor at a steady speed you are unlikely to get into trouble. If your car does break down, do not worry about the lack of garages. The next vehicle along will certainly stop and help you get out of trouble. People in the Northern Territory all appear to belong to a mutual help society.

Humpty Doo, about 11 km after the turning onto the Arnhem Hwy, was the scene of one of the greatest agricultural investment disasters in Australia. This was to be the centre of one of the world's largest rice-growing areas and many millions of dollars were invested before the whole scheme was aborted. At Humpty Doo you will also find **Grahame Gow's Reptile World**, which has a wide range of venomous reptiles on display. Open daily 0830–1730; tel: 8988 1661.

Next comes **Fogg Dam**. This was established in the 1950s as a water source for one of the doomed rice-growing projects, and the surrounding wetlands are now home to spectacular numbers of water birds – pied geese, brolgas, ducks, herons, egrets, ibis, corellas, cockatoos and many, many more. The best time to view the birds is at dawn and dusk but at any time it is worthwhile. You can view them from purpose-built vantage points complete with informative signs along the low dam wall. There is also a signposted 3.5-km walk through the pockets of monsoon rainforest, for which you will need your industrial strength insect repellent. The best time to visit is during the dry season (May–Oct), although the water plants in the dam flower spectacularly in the Wet.

At the **Adelaide River Bridge**, 64 km from Darwin, you will come across a wonderful sight. When you explain it later you will not be believed unless you have photographs to support your claim – and not even then. Cruises on the *Adelaide River Queen* leave here along the river in search of – honestly – leaping crocodiles. There are normally half a dozen cruises a day, but check for times as these vary with the state of the river; tel: 8988 8144. The crew members put out meat bait and the crocodiles leap vertically out of the water as high as 2 m to take it. Sometimes sea eagles swoop in to try and snatch it from their jaws.

Next is the **Leaning Tree Lagoon**, 90 km from Darwin, which is a picnic spot as well as a site for birdwatching. You come off the bitumen and in the Wet it is possible for a 2-wheel drive vehicle to get bogged down, so take care.

Off the highway and 170 km from Darwin are the **Wildman** and **Shady Camp Reserves**, which incorporate a large part of the Mary River flood plain. Within the reserves the Rockhole Billabong and Shady Camp is renowned as the definitive spot to catch the Top End's barramundi. Information can be obtained at the Ranger Information Station at the corner of Point Stuart and the Rockhole Rds.

In 1898 A. B. ('Banjo') Paterson wrote in *Visiting the Park* :'Far in the north of Australia lies a little-known land, a vast half-finished sort of region, wherein Nature has been apparently practising how to make better places. This is the Northern Territory of South Australia.' The decline and fall of the British Empire will date from the day that Britannia starts to monkey with the Northern Territory.' Well, as the Empire has fallen, he might better have forecast some other cataclysmic event, but the general feeling is correct, especially regarding Kakadu National Park.

For many, Kakadu is the prime reason for venturing into the Top End of Australia, and few are disappointed. This huge, untamed wilderness – a world of craggy escarpments, lagoons, billabongs and birdlife – is a most amazing place. It is a UNESCO World Heritage Site and shares with Uluru (Ayers Rock) the title of most visited natural site in Australia. This was where they filmed *Crocodile Dundee*, a movie that helped define Australia colourfully if not accurately. Its history as a park is relatively short. Its history as a homeland of the Aboriginal people stretches back to the Dreamtime. The name Kakadu comes from the Gagudju language group of Aborigines who are among the area's traditional custodians.

About 15 per cent of the world's known reserves of uranium are in this area, and the decision to allow mining, reached in 1978 when the Northern Lands Council agreed to give royalties to the local Aboriginal people, was one of the most contentious issues in Australia. The forces of conservation opposed it absolutely on the grounds that it would irreparably damage one of the last great wildernesses of the world.

In the end the conservationists both lost and won. They lost because the processing plant was built in 1981. They won, because the storm of controversy had much to do with the designation of 6,000 sq. km of the region as a national park in 1979. In 1984 the size of the park was nearly doubled. Its status made the miners very conscious of the cost of putting a foot wrong, and a lot has been done to minimise the effect of the mine on the town of Jabiru and the park. Avoiding the argument about whether uranium mining should be allowed anywhere in the world, let alone in one of the great national parks, the results are, on the evidence available, successful. The Gagudju Association now manages the park in close co-operation with the Australian National Conservation Agency and receives about $10 million a year from the mine.

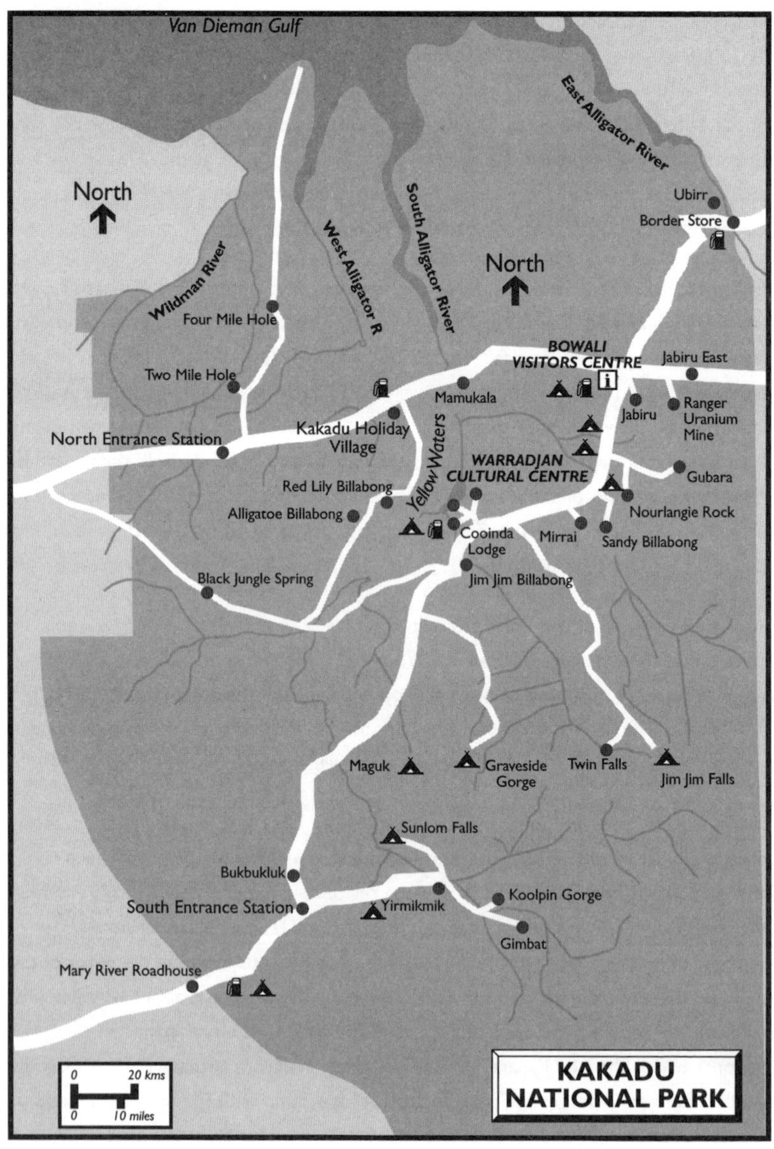
Van Dieman Gulf
North
North
Wildman River
West Alligator R
South Alligator River
East Alligator River
Ubirr
Border Store
Four Mile Hole
Two Mile Hole
BOWALI
VISITORS CENTRE
Jabiru East
Mamukala
Jabiru
Ranger
Uranium
Mine
North Entrance Station
Kakadu Holiday
Village
Yellow Waters
WARRADJAN
CULTURAL CENTRE
Gubara
Red Lily Billabong
Alligatoe Billabong
Nourlangie Rock
Cooinda
Lodge
Mirrai
Sandy Billabong
Black Jungle Spring
Jim Jim Billabong
Maguk
Graveside
Gorge
Twin Falls
Jim Jim Falls
Sunlom Falls
Bukbukluk
Koolpin Gorge
South Entrance Station
Yirmikmik
Gimbat
Mary River Roadhouse
0
20 kms
0
10 miles
KAKADU
NATIONAL PARK

There are many ways of seeing Kakadu. You can roll up in an air-conditioned bus, stay at the air-conditioned Gagudju Crocodile Hotel, see the Aboriginal art at Ubirr and Nouriangle Rock and visit the Jim Jim Falls all in civilised comfort. Or you can go on a 4-wheel drive safari, camp out in the bush, drink tea from a billy, and pretend you are John McDouall Stuart in the year 1862 seeing the wonders of the wild.

In Kakadu, if you travel with care and intelligent forethought and take heed of the advice of the rangers, you will see Kakadu, the soul if not the heart of Australia, at its very best.

GETTING THERE

The route from Darwin is south on the Stuart Hwy, then 10 km after Howard Springs, left along the Arnhem Hwy (Rte 36). The highway enters the park about 40 km after the Bark Hut Inn. Continue for nearly 140 km to the park headquarters near Jabiru. Greyhound Pioneer run daily services to Kakadu from Darwin.

In theory it is possible to visit Kakadu on a day-trip from Darwin, but that is rather like doing Rome on a Tuesday. Kakadu deserves more time.

INFORMATION

TOURIST OFFICE **Jabiru Tourist Centre**, 6 Tasman Plaza; tel: (08) 8979 2548.

Kakadu National Park Bowali Visitor Centre, Kakadu Hwy, Kakadu National Park; tel: (08) 8979 9101. Open daily 0800–1700.

Make sure you get a copy of the *Visitor Guide to Kakadu National Park*, which neatly spells out all the options. Also get a copy of the schedule of ranger-guided walks and talks. Time spent with a tour guide or ranger means that while exploring art sites you learn about Aboriginal Dreamtime and culture. When you are taken on a bush walk your enjoyment is enhanced by the expert commentary and observations of the guides.

INTERNET SITES **Friends of Kakadu** http://home.vicnet.net.au/~kakadu/

Heritage Mission to Kakadu National Park
http://www.biodiversity.environment.gov.au/whats/kakadu/media.html

Kakadu

Kakadu National Park http://www.green.net.au/twswa/kakadu.html; http://www.atn.com.au/nt/north/kakadu.htm; http://www.ozemail.com.au/~eparker/kakadu/kakadu.html

Kakadu National Park Management Plan http://www.environment.gov.au/portfolio/anca/manplans/kakadu/contents.html

ACCOMMODATION

All Seasons Frontier Kakadu Village $$ Jabiru Dr, Arnhem Hwy, 2.5 km west of South Alligator Bridge; tel: (08) 8979 0166. Resort with café and restaurant but slightly isolated if you do not have your own transport.

Bark Hut Inn and Caravan Park $ Arnhem Hwy, Annaburoo; tel: (08) 8978 8988.

Frontier Kakadu Lodge $ Close to the Park HQ, Jabiru; tel: (08) 8979 2422. Caravan park, camping and plain, backpacker four-bed, air-conditioned rooms with shared facilities.

Gagudju Crocodile Hotel $$ Jabiru; tel: (08) 8979 2800. The crocodile-shaped hotel. International standards.

Gagudju Lodge, Cooinda Cabins $. Motel units $$; near Yellow Waters and Warradjan Cultural Centre; tel: (08) 8979 0145. Air-conditioned cabins adequate rather than great; motel units are standard Australian quality.

Kakadu Hostel $ Near Ubirr; tel: (08) 8979 2232. Past its use-by date but inexpensive and open all year if the roads are not flooded.

Point Stuart Wilderness Lodge $$ Point Stuart Rd via Arnhem Hwy; tel: (08) 8978 8914.

Wildman River Wilderness Lodge $ Off Point Stuart Rd, Wildman River; tel: (08) 8978 8912.

Cooinda Lodge $$ Flinders St, Jabiru; tel: (08) 8979 2800.

FOOD AND DRINK

Almost all the eating places are in the motels, hotels and lodges listed above. In Jabiru there is also:

Jabiru Restaurant Leichhardt St; tel: (08) 8979 2600. Licensed.

ABOUT THE PARK

To get Kakadu into perspective you need to accept that it will not be what you expect. The film *Crocodile Dundee* has raised expectations of a green paradise with rocky outcrops and billabongs where the sheila can appear in a thong bikini and get attacked by a croc. It isn't quite like that. In the Dry it is large tracts of undifferentiated flat terrain with scrubby vegetation. There will be green spots and swamps but they are not the majority of the park. In the Wet it is somewhat different but then progress becomes somewhat more difficult.

Kakadu divides into five distinct regions: the sandstone plateau of Arnhem Land and the escarpment walls (which extend for 600 km) so well shown in *Crocodile Dundee*; the vast lowland plain; the flood plain north of the plateau, which in the Wet is almost a lake and in the Dry a series of billabongs; the tidal flats, which are mangrove wastelands because the salt water allows little else to grow; and finally the hills and basins in the southernmost part of the park near Fisher Creek.

You will not be able to explore all of the park on a single visit. At any season access to the various parts of the park are limited. There is also a danger from crocodiles, which keeps you away from some of the wetlands. Some parts of the park are sacred Aboriginal sites where you are not welcome. Finally, this is rough country and getting around the harsh terrain is not that easy. Put it all together and you realise that Kakadu can only be properly seen with a series of visits. Depending on the length of your visit and the time of the year, you need to sort out your priorities. For a short visit, top of the list would probably be Ubirr and the Nourlangie Rock. You should also take a cruise at Yellow Waters.

WHEN TO GO

Most visitors go in the Dry when the humidity and temperatures are down. But a strong case can be made for visiting the park at other times of the year. Kakadu in the Dry is wonderful; in the Wet it is magnificent, a sublime experience. When the rains come the flood plains become inland seas. Some, but never all, of the attractions of Kakadu may be closed, but this seems to many to be a small trade-off for the extra wildlife that can be seen at that time.

In the Wet the road to Kakadu runs like a gangplank across flooded water plains. On both sides the view extends forever with birdlife you would never see at other times of the year, or in any other place on earth. The vegetation is a verdant green, the countryside alive.

JABIRU

Jabiru is both a mining town and the base for travellers to Kakadu. It has a small supermarket (open Mon–Fri 0900–1730, Sat 0900–1300 and Sun 1000–1200), a take-away, bakery, post office and Westpac bank in the shopping plaza. There is also a health and dental clinic, an Olympic-sized swimming pool, an artificial lake and the international-class Gagudju Hotel, in the shape of a crocodile - a design approved by the Gagudju tribe, whose totem is the crocodile. The hotel is owned and run — most successfully — by the tribe.

You can go on a tour of the mine although it is, in the main, a public relations exercise to let you know that uranium is good for you.A walk-through exhibition takes you through a condensed version of Kakadu which sort of sets you up for the coming experience.

HIGHLIGHTS

Almost everywhere you want to go can be reached from the Kakadu Hwy, which runs south-west from Jabiru out of the park. Most attractions within the park are accessible by sealed roads. The exceptions are Jim Jim, Twin Falls and Maguk, which are accessible only by 4-wheel drive. One way to deal with this is to use a 2-wheel drive conventional vehicle to get to the park, then, if you want to venture into 4-wheel drive territory, take a guided tour and let someone else do the driving. Getting stuck is horribly easy.

Nourlangie Rock is far and away the most visited site in the park, mainly because it is so easily accessible, 31 km south of the park headquarters. It contains an amazing collection of Aboriginal rock paintings. These have been repainted within recent history, but this is a common habit of the Aboriginal people. There is a lookout here which gives terrific views over the Arnhemland escarpment. You can view Nourlangie Rock from **Nawulandja Lookout**. Down below is the Anbangbang Billabong, which you may recognise from *Crocodile Dundee*.

Also in the Nourlangie Rock area is **Nanguluwur**, another art site 1.5 km away. It is very well signposted.

Ubirr is 43 km north of the park headquarters and has amazing Aboriginal rock art. From the lookout here you can see across the East Alligator River to the rocky outcrops of Arnhemland.

BUSH WALKING IN KAKADU

There are very few marked long-distance bush walks within the park, although this is being remedied. If you are venturing on a serious expedition you must register with the park rangers before you leave.

You can take the **Guluyambi Cruise** along the East Alligator River from Ubirr which lasts for about 1½ hrs.

KAKADU WILDLIFE

The varied habitats of the park results in an incredible diversity of plants, birds and animals. There are probably over 1,300 different plants – the number keeps increasing as biologists discover new varieties – more than 10,000 species of insect, about a quarter of the varieties of Australia's freshwater fish and over 120 different reptiles. One-third of all Australia's birds are represented in Kakadu (300 species), including the Jabiru stork, and among the 50 native mammals are kangaroos, wallabies, walleroos, 26 bat species, and dingoes. There is also the water buffalo, which was brought in from Indonesia early in the 19th century and went feral. It became so prevalent that it was damaging the environment, but an eradication programme found that some weeds increased as a result, creating a life-choking mat over the water. Keeping the ecology in fine balance is no easy task in a place like Kakadu.

Yellow Water is an inland lagoon formed by Jim Jim Creek, some 50 km south-west of Jabiru, near the Cooinda resort. There are five daily cruises but it is best to take the very first of the day, when the air is cooler and the wildlife at its best. For bookings tel: (08) 8979 0145.

The 12-km corrugated track from the Kakadu Hwy to **Barramundie Gorge**, 57 km south-west of Cooinda, is perfectly negotiable in an ordinary vehicle in the Dry. From the car park there is a path to a swimming hole and waterfall.

Gunlom, also known as Waterfall Creek, is on an unsealed road 36 km off the Kakadu Hwy near the south-western exit of the park. In the Dry you will probably not see any falls at all but there is a most pleasant swimming hole.

Jim Jim Falls and **Twin Falls** are 100 km south of the park headquarters and can only be reached with a 4-wheel drive vehicle. Jim Jim Falls drop 215 m over the edge of the escarpment. Seeing them requires some neat timing — in much of the Wet the road is closed, but in the middle of the Dry the falls dwindle to almost nothing. The ideal time is just as the Wet is ending and the road is passable – by someone else, not you.

It is almost impossible to comprehend the size and emptiness of Western Australia. The state covers one-third of Australia but only contains about a tenth of the population. It considers itself a state apart. Indeed, there has been a movement for secession on and off for many years. In 1933 there was a referendum on the subject and the vote for secession was passed by almost two to one. No one in the federal government took much notice but the idea pops up every now and again.

Western Australia has 5000 km of coastline and at its longest point the state stretches nearly 2400 km. Within this vast area – 2.5 million sq km – more than two-thirds of the population lives in Perth, the capital, or its immediate area. The number of people spread out among the rest of the state is therefore very thin indeed. Much of the state is simply not inhabited in any significant way: the Great Gibson Desert, the Great Sandy Desert, the Great Victoria Desert and the Nullarbor Plain are, to all intents and purposes empty, and the roads running across are unsealed. True, they have romantic names, such as the Canning Stock Route and the Gunbarrel Hwy, but driving them is not a task for the ill-equipped or the faint-hearted.

Perth is the civilised centre of this vast expanse of nothing, and can claim to be the most isolated city on earth. It is as near to another capital city as, say, Athens is to Copenhagen. In Europe between those two cities lie countries, people, cities, towns, villages without number. In Western Australia there is almost nothing. Empty space.

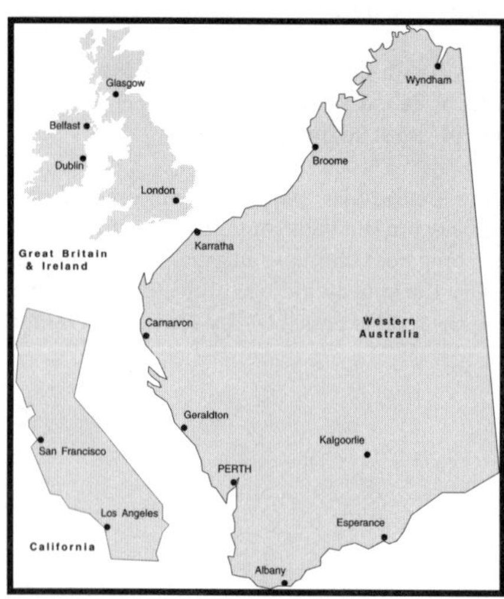

Think of Western Australia as the Great Plateau. Hanging on to the edge by their fingernails are the coastal plains, separated from the emptiness of the Great Plateau by scarplands. This is forbidding country – so forbidding that early explorers warned against it. It is very probable, but by no means certain, that the first European to sight the place was Willem de Vlamingh aboard the *Geelvinck*. In 1696 he found Rottnest Island off the mouth of the Swan River. It is not a very solid claim because there are records which show other sightings from earlier that century. This is called the 'official sighting', although how and why that official sanction is arrived at is not clear. But de Vlamingh sailed back to the Dutch colony in Indonesia and told the Dutch government in Batavia - now Jakarta - that it was not worth further effort.

Well over a century was to elapse before there was another serious effort, when the British came to deny the French, who were sniffing around the area, the chance of forming a new colony. Major Edmund Lockyer, with a party of 44 convicts and soldiers, landed in December 1826 at what is now Albany and took possession of Western Australia in the name of the Crown. The following year Captain James Stirling explored the Swan River, selected a town site and the colonists came out to this new land. The place nearly collapsed because of its isolation and the aridity of the region: what saved it was gold. The gold discovered in the early 1890s in Coolgardie and Kalgoorlie brought with it some measure of prosperity, but Western Australia was not seen as a viable entity. It was still run directly by the British government until 1890, only 11 years before the Oz states formed into a federation.

The Wildflower State

Western Australia calls itself the 'wildflower state'. This is a well-deserved title. Because it is isolated by the sea on three sides and an inhospitable desert on the fourth, Western Australia has developed a range of plants unique to the state. There are about 10,000 varieties of flowering plant to be found, most of them unique to Australia, some of them unique to the state. The jarrah forests in the southwest alone have over 3000 species

The Australian spring is the best time to see this amazing variety of wildflowers. The flower season is at its best between Aug and Nov, but at each end of the state the season is considerably extended, starting in late winter in the north and going strong well into the summer months down on the south coast.

There are tours to take you to view the wildflowers but, in truth, they are almost everywhere and the display in Kings Park in the heart of Perth itself is world class. Close to Perth they can be found profusion in the Nambung, John Forrest and Walyunga National Parks. Then there are wildflower routes through the Midlands, Geraldton and along the Brand and the Great Southern highways.

In the outback there are years when the ranges are carpeted for kilometre after kilometre with wildflowers – and other years when they are very scarce on the ground. The tourist office will have the latest news and there is a site on the Internet solely devoted to showing where the wildflowers of Western Australia are in bloom (www.casair.com.au/tourno19.html). Take only photographs, leave only footprints – the picking of wildflowers is prohibited.

Perth and its adjunct, Fremantle, are thought to enjoy the best weather in Australia, and the city is lush, green and verdant. Perth is thought by many Europeans, especially the British, to be the most attractive city in Australia. Probably as a result of this it has, as a percentage, more Britons than any other state, and the largest group of migrants still comes mainly from England. The attraction is obvious. Here is a city with the weather of the French Riviera during the Riviera's better months, where the language spoken is English and where the style of living is, in the best sense of the word, hedonistic. And the government tends to be to the right of the British Conservative party.

Perth extends over three parallel land strips. The first is a heavily eroded coastal reef and dune region about 6 km wide. Next comes a coastal plain, dunes, low sandhills and swamps extending about 16 km, and finally the lower slopes of the Darling Escarpment.

One aspect of Perth that has kept the city immensely attractive through all the phases of its development has been the Swan River. The foreshore south of the central business district has been reserved as park and recreational land and carefully cultivated and improved over the years.

The mean temperature in February, the hottest month, is 23°C, dropping to a mean of 13°C in the coldest month, July. There are occasional heatwaves in summer when the thermometer climbs over the 40°C mark, but these are rare. Despite an annual rainfall average of 900 mm, there is a pronounced dry season from November to March.

ARRIVAL AND DEPARTURE

Perth's international terminal is about 16 km east of the city, and the domestic terminal about 3 km to the west. There are shuttle buses from both into the city for about one-third the cost of a taxi.

Buses and Westrail country buses arrive at East Perth Rail and Interstate Bus Terminal in Wellington St.

INFORMATION

TOURIST OFFICE **Perth Tourist Information Office**, Ground Floor, Albert Facy House, Forrest Place, cnr Wellington St; tel: 1300 361 351.

INTERNET ACCESS **The Travellers Club Tour and Information Centre,** 499 Wellington St, is inexpensive and quick; tel: 9226 0660. **The Perth Tourist Lounge** has coin-operated access to the Internet and email at £2 per 15 minutes. It is on level 2 Carillon Arcade, 680 Hay St Mall; tel: 9481 8303. **The Lonely Planet Café**, corner of Lake and Newcastle Sts in Northbridge, also has coin-operated machines.

INTERNET SITES www.country-wide.com.au/ is an absolutely ace site put out by the publishers of the free magazine of the same title. A fund of information, it is an example of how it should be done, and rarely is.

TELEPHONE CODES

The code was changed recently and everyone appears to get it wrong. The area code for Western Australia is 08. If you are calling Western Australia from elsewhere in Australia you use 08. If you are calling from overseas you drop the 0 and just dial 8 as a prefix. So, from Britain you would dial 00 81 8 and then the 8-digit number you want.

MONEY There are **Thomas Cook foreign exchange bureaux** at Perth International Airport, Horrie-Miller Dr., New Burn; tel: 61 9 477 1477; Shop 2, Piccadilly Arcade, Hay St Mall; tel: 61 9 481 7900 and Ground Floor, 704 Hay St, tel: 61 9 481 7900.

ACCOMMODATION

Adelphi Hotel Apartments $$ 130a Mounts Bay Rd; tel: 9322 4666. 1-bedroom serviced apartments. Close to city, river and parks.

Airways City Hotel $$ 195 Adelaide Ter; tel: 323-7799.

City Holiday Apartments $$ 537 William St; tel: 9227 1112. Near city centre, fully self-contained.

Florina Lodge $$ 6 Kintail Rd, Applecross; tel: 9364 5322. 1-, 2- and 3-bedroomed self-contained apartments within five minutes of the city.

Hotel Regatta $ 560 Hay St; tel: 325 5155.

Inntown Hotel $$ Murray St, Cnr Pier St; tel: 325-2133.

Miss Maud Swedish Private Hotel $$ 97 Murray St; tel: 325 3900.

Mountway Holiday Units $$ 36 Mount St; tel: 9321 8307. Fully serviced apartments five minutes walk from the city.

Perth City Hotel $$ 200 Hay St; tel: 9220 7000. Within walking distance of the city shopping area.

Regency Motel $$ 61 Great Eastern Hwy, Rivervale; tel: 9362 3000. Restaurant, café, pool, spa, gym, tennis, videos, 24-hour room service, courtesy airport transfers.

Sullivans Hotel $$ 166 Mounts Bay Rd; tel: 321 8022.

Two Rivers Lodge $$ 1 North Rd; tel: 9449 5222. Restored Federation-style estate on the Swan River.

Wentworth Plaza Hotel $$ 300 Murray St; tel: 481 1000.

YHA of WA $ 253 William St; tel: 328 6121.

FOOD AND DRINK

Almost all restaurants are BYO – bring your own bottle – but only wine, not spirits and rarely beer. This applies to most licensed restaurants as well.

A-Shed Café Gallery at The Docks; tel: 9430 6542. Open 0900–1700 daily, late Fri–Sat.

Coco's Restaurant $$ The Esplanade, South Perth; tel: 9474 3030. Seafood and steak restaurant located on the South Perth foreshore. Please ring the restaurant for more information.

Doing Lunch $$ 44 King St. Serves, among other dishes, the King Street Plate, which is bits and pieces of savoury delicacies.

Emperor's Court $$ 66 Lake St, Northbridge; tel: 9328 8860. Claims to be Perth's most awarded Chinese restaurant.

Harry's Seafood Bar and Grill $$ 94 Aberdeen St, Northbridge; tel: 9328 2822. Indoor and outdoor dining in a vine-covered garden.

Hung Long Coffee House $ 344 William St, Northbridge. BYO. Vast range of Asian dishes, many of which are served up as a form of delicious, fragrant stew.

Indonesia Indah $$ 118–120 Barrack St; tel: 9221 3970. Genuine Indonesian restaurant with traditional dishes using Halal produce and no MSG. BYO. Open Tues–Sun.

Istanbul Restaurant $ 19b Essex St; tel: 9335 6068. Turkish cuisine at a small, friendly family restaurant.

Jessica's $$$ Hyatt Centre; tel: 9325 2511. Claims to be Perthís finest seafood restaurant, overlooks the Swan River.

Laguna Restaurant $$ 20 Roe St, Northbridge; tel: 9328 7888. Said to specialise in Japanese, Malaysian, Chinese, Thai,

Singaporean and Indonesian, which doesn't leave much out in Asian food. Open daily.

The Individual Thai Restaurant $$ 101 Edward St, East Perth; tel: 9227 6122. Award-winning top Thai tucker. Open daily.

The Tunnel $$ 291 William St, Northbridge; tel: 9325 3525. Italian restaurant. Wood-fired pizzas.

Viet Hoa $ 349 William St, Northbridge. BYO. Similar to Hung Long.

GETTING AROUND

For the most part you can walk around the centre easily, although cycling is very popular. Important: wearing a bicycle helmet is compulsory in Western Australia. For information on bicycle hire facilities, route maps or any other information, contact BikeWest on 9320 9320.

The Transperth train system provides a quick and easy way to get around. Travel is free on any Transperth bus or train as long as you board and alight within the Perth city centre, an area which covers all major shopping streets in Perth and Northbridge. You can travel from Perth to Fremantle (or the other way) in around 30 minutes, stopping at all the stops. All services originate from Perth station, starting at 0528 and finishing at 2328. Tickets are purchased on the platforms from ticket dispensers which take coins only but give change. There are note-changing machines at Perth station.

THE PERTH TRAM

This is not a true tram, but a bus made to look like one of the trams that operated in Perth in 1899. Visits Kings Park, the Casino, Old Perth Port at the Barrack St Jetty and the city shopping areas. A full tour takes 1½ hours, with an interesting commentary by knowledgeable drivers. You can break your journey at any point and rejoin later. Tickets are available on board. Tel: 9367 9404.

There is also a special free bus service, the Central Area Transit (CAT) system, which operates two routes around central Perth. Red buses travel in an east–west loop of the central business district, taking passengers between the WACA in the east and Outram St in the west. Blue CAT buses travel in a north–south loop, south to the Busport and north into Northbridge.

Westrail operates a daily rail service to Bunbury *The Australind* which also leaves from the city station. The Kalgoorlie train *The Prospector* runs every day and leaves from the East Perth terminal, West Parade, East Perth. For more information and bookings on these country trains, call 13 62 13.

Perth is well served by meter-operated taxi cabs. There are taxi ranks throughout the Perth central business district and Fremantle, or they can be ordered by telephoning the major operators: Swan Taxis (tel:131 388) or Black & White Taxis (tel: 9333 3333).

The Royal Automobile Club of WA (RAC) is at 228 Adelaide Ter, Perth (tel: 9421 4444) and other metropolitan and country branches. The RAC Breakdown Service operates at all hours (tel: 13 11 11). As a member of an affiliated interstate or overseas auto club, you will receive reciprocal membership - check with your own club before you leave.

HIGHLIGHTS

Perth is neatly marked out and therefore easy to explore. The Swan River sweeps through the city centre westwards towards the sea at Fremantle. The main shopping area is along the Hay St and Murray St malls and the arcades between. The northern boundary of the city centre is marked by the railway line and to the north is Northbridge, a popular restaurant and entertainment area. The western end of Perth slopes up to Kings Park, which overlooks the city and the Swan River. Further to the west, suburbs extend as far as Perth's superb Indian Ocean beaches.

The arts are well catered for in Perth. The **Art Gallery of Western Australia** is at the Perth Cultural Centre, James St, Northbridge. This is Western Australia's principal public art gallery and the collection of Aboriginal art is one of the finest in Australia. Open daily 1000–1700. Also in the Cultural Centre precinct is the **Perth Institute of Contemporary Arts**, in what was the old Perth Boys School. Entry is free. Open Tues–Sun 1100–1800.

Just around the corner, in Francis St, the **Western Australian Museum** is a complex rather that a single building. It is home to some of Perth's oldest buildings including the original Old Gaol and an early settler's cottage. It is Western Australia's largest and most comprehensive museum. Admission is free. Open Mon–Fri 1030–1700, Sat–Sun 1300–1700.

The **Craftwest Centre for Contemporary Craft** is located in the old Perth Railway Station in Wellington St and is a gallery and retail outlet for fine contemporary craft by leading Western Australian crafts people. A bit alternative lifestyle but very affordable and enjoyable. Open Mon–Fri 1000–1700, Sat 1000–1600, Sun 1400–1700.

London Court, which appears in all the tourist photographs, is an 18th-century-style arcade running between Hay St and St George's Terrace. It was actually built in 1936 and its fakery somehow jars. At one end of this shopping court St George and his dragon appear above the clock each quarter of an hour, while at the other end knights joust on horseback – useful if you want a backdrop for a photograph. Also in St George's Terrace is **St George's Cathedral**, in English Victorian Gothic Revival-style, and consecrated in 1888. You either like it or you don't.

Just off St George's Terrace, at the corner of Barrack St and on your way towards the river, is the Law Centre in Stirling Gardens. This contains the **Old Courthouse**, the oldest building in the city, dating from 1836. Guided tours and arrangements may also be made for groups to take part in mock trials and visit the Supreme Court to view court proceedings. Open Tues–Thur 1000–1400; tel: 9325 4787.

The **Perth Mint**, at 310 Hay St on the corner of Hill St, was very active during the gold rush. Daily demonstrations show pure gold bars being poured and moulded. There is an excellent viewing gallery and Perth Mint's bullion and proof issue coins are produced today. $ Open Mon–Fri 0900–1600, Sat–Sun 0900–1300; tel: 9421 7223.

Ten minutes' walk from the city centre is what was called the Barrack St Jetty but which is now Barrack Sq. This is a relatively new complex of cafés, shops and attractions known as **Old Perth Port**. The South Perth ferry, which will take you across the river and to the zoo, departs from here. There are also cruise boats which go downriver to Fremantle or on to Rottnest Island (see p. 374), or you can take a trip upstream to visit assorted wineries.

KINGS PARK

Kings Park covers 4 sq km on the western edge of the city and has been in existence since 1872, when 172 ha of native bushland on the summit of Mt Eliza was set aside as public open space. Two-thirds of the park still comprises natural bushland and is one of the most beautiful recreation areas in Australia. Much of it bursts into bloom during the WA spring wildflower season (Sept and Oct), when the display is superb.

There is a restaurant-café up there called Frasers – a splendid place to have breakfast and watch the city slowly come to life. This park is truly a magical spot and is certainly the most attractive inner city park in Australia.

ACROSS THE RIVER

One of the earliest buildings in the Swan River Colony was the **Old Mill** on Mill Point Rd, on the southern side of the Narrows Bridge. The foundation stone was laid by the first Governor, James Stirling, in 1835 for the designer-owner, William

Shenton. The mill, adjacent miller's cottage and grounds have all been restored and are furnished with relics of the pioneer days. Open daily 1000–1600.

Perth Zoo is at 20 Labouchere Rd, South Perth, which is only minutes from the city. On a per capita basis this is the most popular zoo in Australia. It is set in spectacular gardens with walkways, an Australian wildlife park and a Nocturnal House. Open daily 1000–1700.

BEYOND THE INNER CITY

In Whiteman Park is the **Motor Museum** (open Wed–Sat 1000–1600, Sun 1000–1700; tel: 9249 9457). There are normally about 85 historic cars and 25 motor bikes on show. They are privately owned and the display seems to change completely about four times a year.

The **Telecommunications Museum** at Almondbury Rd, Ardross, is in Wireless Hill Park, which has 40 hectares of natural bushland. The panoramas from the viewing towers are stunning. Open 1400–1700, but weekends only, which is a nuisance.

The **Scitech Discovery Centre**, on the corner of Railway Pde and Sutherland St, West Perth (tel: 9481 6295; open daily 1000–1700), has well over 160 exhibits which all promote the learning of scientific principles - and are as enjoyable as any funfair arcade.

And for something totally different there is the **Cameleer Park Camel Farm**, 300 Neaves Rd, Wanneroo, on the northern outskirts of the city and an easy drive from the centre. Take a short ride before booking anything more ambitious - some people get seasick on the ship of the desert. Tel: 9405 3558.

Western Australia's first marine park was **Marmion**, which extends along the northern metropolitan coastline from Trigg Island to Bums Rock and about 5 km offshore.

THE BEACHES

Perth residents claim that their home town has the best beaches and surf of any Australian city. There are 19 beaches in the city area, and there is truly a beach for everyone.

There are calm beaches on the Swan River at Crawley, Peppermint Grove and Como. And there are many patrolled surf beaches on the Indian Ocean coast, including the nude beach at Swanbourne. Some of the other surf beaches include Cottesloe, Port and Scarborough. Most metropolitan beaches are patrolled at weekends and public holidays during the summer season which runs Oct–Mar.

NIGHTLIFE

Perth has a most amazing music scene which is separate from, and different from that in the rest of Australia. One of the main band venues for mainstream entertainment is the **Perth Entertainment Center**, a building that, from a distance, resembles a giant hamburger. The main nightclub area in Perth is Northbridge, which boasts some 20 nightclubs, ten pubs, and a hundred or more restaurants.

The influences on the music scene are mainly European and Asian. The only way to see what is happening – the scene changes every day with new groups coming out of the woodwork – is to access the Nightlife Gig Guide which is at popstar.iinet.net.au/

DAY TRIPS

At Armadale, 27 km south-east of the city, **Pioneer World** has a working model of a 19th-century village, with shops, public buildings, goldfield operations and everything from newspaper printers to farriers.

The **Swan Valley vineyards** run along the river from Guildford right up to the Upper Swan. The valley may be overshadowed by the Margaret River when it comes to wine in WA (see p. 381), but it is only 16 km, or 20 minutes drive, east of the city, and the valley certainly rivals Margaret River for scenic beauty, particularly in the greener winter months.

Many vineyards are open for tastings and cellar sales, including two of WA's biggest producers – Sandalford and Houghton. The Houghton Winery produced the region's first commercial vintage – in 1842 – although Olive Farm Winery was established earlier. The wineries of the valley are well signposted once you get to Guildford, itself an easy one-road-all-the-way trip from Perth via Guildford Rd.

A good way to experience the valley is on one of the river cruises that ply the waters of the Swan River. Several companies offer trips with stops for lunch and tastings. These wine cruises are a great way to spend a day, but you do usually only get to see and taste at one of the larger vineyards. Contact: Oceanic Cruises (tel: 9325 1191), Captain Cook Cruises (tel: 9325 3341) and Boat Torque 2000 (tel: 9221 5844).

Then there's **Rottnest Island**, which has a lifestyle that attracts all of Perth during the annual holidays – avoid it, if you can, during Dec and Jan. In 1925, in a novel called *Black Swans*, Mollie Skinner wrote about Rottnest, 'It was the cleanest, sweetest, most delightful place in all the universe – the sandy, salt-like place where the air is indescribably exhilaratingly crisp and clear. Amongst that everlasting green shrub the wallaby abounded and over the lakes the ducks abounded, and off the rocks to seaward the fish abounded.' Mollie Skinner was not one of the great literary talents of Australia.

Rottnest is only 21 km north-north-west of Fremantle, opposite the mouth of the Swan River. It is about 11 km long, less than half that across, and is low-lying and mostly sand with five shallow salt lakes. The beaches and bays are mainly protected by offshore reefs that make them very safe. The waters and beaches are perfect for swimming, snorkelling, windsurfing, skin diving, sunbathing, surfing, boating and fishing.

There are no cars. Bring a bicycle across from the mainland or hire one on the island (and don't forget your helmet). There is also an island railway, called Rotto Rail – not a selling name – which is a light railway that once hauled guns and ammunition for the Army. Now it carries tourists. Tickets from the Visitors' Centre at the end of the jetty.

Getting to Rottnest is easy. Ferries leave from the Barrack St Jetty (old Perth Port, see p. 372) and from Northport in North Fremantle or Hillarys Boat Harbour. Flights leave from Perth Airport.

Penguin Island has other charms. It is not a rival to Rottnest for it is very different. It is situated in the Shoalwater Islands Marine Park, some 45 km from Perth, and boasts spectacular coastal scenery and diverse wildlife. It is home to the largest colony of little penguins on the west coast, as well as more than 30 species of birds, and is managed by the Department of Conservation and Land Management. The penguins are nocturnal on land, coming ashore in small flocks after sunset. Noisy courtship activities signal the start of the breeding season. Both parents will incubate the eggs, which are laid any time between mid-Apr and mid-Oct. Rescued and rehabilitated penguins are housed in a viewing enclosure in the Island Discovery Centre within the park.

Nearby **Seal Island**, another magic spot, is home to a group of protected rare Australian sea lions and often attracts groups of visiting dolphins. A range of ferry cruises is run by Penguin & Seal Island Cruises; tel: 9528 2004, or email rst@nettrek.com.au.

WHERE NEXT?

Fremantle, just downriver, is a delightful port town, and could be first stop on a tour of the south-western corner of WA (see p. 376). Strike east to the goldfields of Kalgoorlie (see p. 399), or follow the coastline north beside the Indian Ocean for Geraldton and Shark Bay (see p. 416).

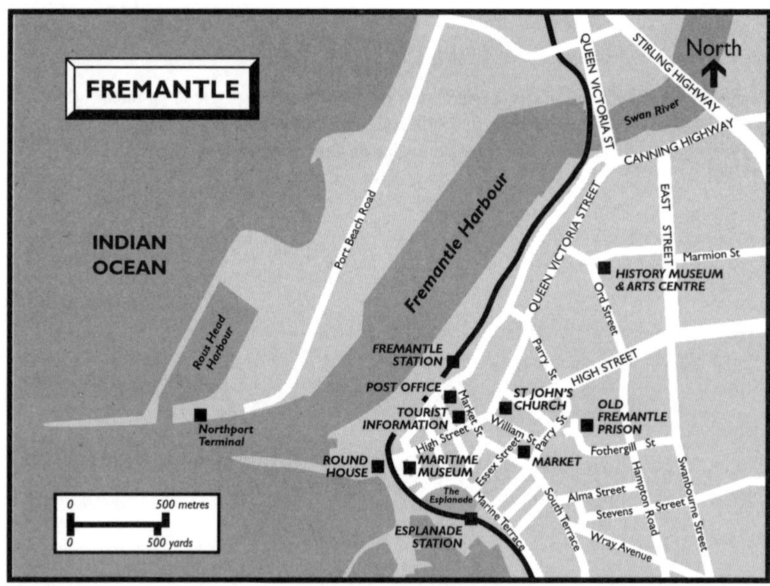

Although it is effectively a suburb of Perth, Fremantle has a style of its own. It is not a big place, with a population around 25,000, but it is very distinctive.

The name Fremantle comes from the captain of the *Challenger*, one of the trio of ships which, in 1829, brought the first European settlers to Western Australia. Captain Fremantle was 28 at the time and formally took possession of Western Australia in the name of Britain shortly after arriving. So Freo, as the town is called by locals who insist on using the Australian diminutive, was proclaimed by what, in Australian European colonisation terms, is very early indeed. The following year Advocate General George Fletcher Moore wrote: 'A bare, barren-looking district of sandy coast; the shrubs cut down for firewood, the herbage trodden bare, a few houses, many rugged-looking tents and contrivances for habitation ... a few cheerless, dissatisfied people with gloomy looks, plodding their way through the sand from hut to hut.' And, yet, within two years the port was enjoying considerable prosperity and by 1832 it became the port for the colony in Western Australia. The designer and builder of the port was C. Y. O'Connor, one of the more amazing figures in West Australia, who is buried in the local cemetery.

When the gold rush came in 1890 the port and town boomed. Prosperity continued while Fremantle remained the first port of call in Australia for liners from the 'Mother Country', Britain, but with the advent of jet aircraft in the 1960s the town started to slip into a sort of tatty somnolence. Then came the America's Cup. It is difficult for anyone who is not Australian to understand the effect that winning the Auld Mug from the United States had on Australia. On that day in 1983, not an occasion any Australian will ever forget, wildly celebrating crowds poured champagne over the head of the prime minister, Bob Hawke, and he did not mind.

Fremantle is no longer a major port but there is a very busy sailing and fishing harbour which is surrounded by restaurants and cafés. And Fremantle is still a major fishing port, which means that the quality of the fish served in the restaurants is very high, even for Australia.

ARRIVAL AND DEPARTURE

Trains run several times an hour from Perth. There are also regular buses and daily ferries; the latter run from Barrch St jetty.

INFORMATION

Tourist Information Office, Fremantle Town Hall, Kings Square; tel: 9431 7878.

Internet Access

Aria Café 7 South Ter; tel: 9335 3215.
Net Trek Café 8 Bannister St Mall; tel: 9336 4446; www.café.nettrek.com.au/

Internet Sites

Freonet www.freonet.net.au/
Fremantle Tourist Bureau holiday-wa.net/freotour.htm

ACCOMMODATION

Barbara's Cottage $$$ 26 Holdsworth St; tel: 9430 8051; Internet: www.iinet.net.au/~barbaras/ An 1886 original Victorian cottage classified by The National Estate and The National Trust. Near old Fremantle Prison and the Fremantle Markets in the Fremantle Heritage District.

Cottage of Fremantle $$ 6 Tuckfield St; tel: 9430 8104.

On the Ghost Trail

Worth experiencing, if you are that way inclined, are the Arts Centre's ghosts walks, which take you on a lamp-lit tour through the darkened corridors of one of Australia's most haunted buildings.

Esplanade Hotel $$$ Essex St, cnr Marine Ter; tel: 9430 4000.

Fremantle Colonial Accommodation $$$ 215 High St. An 1897 terrace house about 200 m from the Town Hall. Also has three old two-bedroom, 1850 cottages located at the Historical Fremantle Prison. They have been totally renovated.

Fremantle Hotel $$ High St, cnr Cliff St; tel: 9430 4300.

Fremantle Village & Chalet Centre $$ Lot 1 Cockburn Rd; tel: 9430 4866; Internet: www.nw.com.au/~psanders/index.htm. Offers chalets, caravans, rooms.

Norfolk Hotel $$ 47 South Ter; tel: 9335 5405.

Ocean View Lodge $$ 100 Hampton Rd; tel: 9336 2962.

Painted Fish $$ 37 Hulbert St, South Fremantle; tel: 9335 4886: Internet: www.paintedfish.webjump.com/. Slightly alternative lifestyle feel. A one-minute stroll from South Beach. No TV. Free bikes for exploring the city. Claims that ecologically safe products are used in the house and garden.

FOOD AND DRINK

This has been a stylish experience in Fremantle since the earliest days. In 1841 Edward Wilson Landor arrived and, as he recounted in *The Bushman: Or Life in a New Country*, 'We dined and slept at Francisco's Hotel, where we were served with French dishes in first-rate style, and drank good luck to ourselves in excellent claret.' Francisco's has, alas, gone but you can still eat in first-rate style and drink excellent claret. Here are some suggestions.

Prickles Café

Prickles Café serves a variety of unusual dishes. Items on offer include:

Crocodile meat – tastes like a cross between chicken and pork with the richness of crayfish.

Lilli-Pill – known as 'Chinese Apple', these berries taste like water-

Alfonso's Restaurant $ 47 South Ter; tel: 9335 3095.

Apicius Restaurant $ 2 Wray Ave; tel: 9335 9892.

Bridges Seafood Garden $$ 22 Tydeman Rd, North Fremantle; tel: 9430 4433. Fresh fish daily in a temperate garden all year around.

Gino's Café $ 1-5 South Ter; tel: 9336 1464: Internet: www.ginoscafe.com.au/. Claims the best coffee in Australia. Supports local artists with a wide range of paintings on the wall for sale. Some of them stunning. Open from 0600 until late.

Hai Palace Chinese Restaurant $ 404 South Ter; tel: 9335 2481.

Il Vicolo $ 95 Market St; tel: 9430 6126.

Prickles Café cont

melon. Riberries belong to the same family.

Kangaroo meat – rich in flavour, very lean, best eaten rare.

Emu meat – belonging to same family as ostriches, emus are a source of many products including meat, leather and oil. The meat is very red and rich in gamey flavour.

Possum – from Tasmania, possum has a taste similar to rabbit.

Bunya bunya nuts – large Australian pine nuts, taste is similar to macadamia nuts.

Camel – robust meat, mild in flavour, very juicy. And the list goes on and on.

Kailis Fish Market Café $$ Fishing Boat Harbour, Mews Rd; tel: 9335 7755. Multi-award winning seafood restaurant.

Maya Indian Restaurant $$ 75 Market St; tel: 9335 2796.

Mexican Kitchen $ 19 South Ter; tel: 9335 1394.

Nha Trang Vietnamese Restaurant $ 22 Norfolk St; tel: 93361061.

Overseas Chinese Restaurant $$ 62 High St; tel: 9430 4032.

Oyster Beds River Restaurant $$ 26 Riverside Rd; tel: 9339 1611.

Peranakan Place $ 9 Fleet St; tel: 9430 7351. Authentic Indonesian food.

Possums Restaurant $$ 15 Bannister St; tel: 9335 6545.

Prickles Café $$$ cnr South Ter and Douro Rd, South Fremantle; tel: tel: 9336 2194; Internet: www.fremantle.com/prickles/. Unique restaurant, unique dishes, unique flavours. Open lunch and dinner Mon–Sat.

Renaissance Café Restaurant $$ 29 South Ter Piazza; tel: 9335 9472.

Sail & Anchor $$ 64 South Ter; tel: 9335 8433. Has its own brewery.

Sails Seafood Restaurant $$$ 1st Floor, 47 Mews Rd; tel: 9430 5050. Very upmarket. For people who own yachts, but worth the money. Open daily.

Singapore Corner Chinese Restaurant $ Manning Arcade; tel: 9430 8098.

Song Tam Vietnamese Restaurant $ 211 South Ter; tel: 9335 2659.

HIGHLIGHTS

In a few square kilometres, it would be hard to find a greater variety of sights, sounds and experiences. It can be argued that Fremantle is one of the best-preserved 19th-century seaports in the world and it has over 150 buildings classified by the National Trust. Since the restoration for the America's Cup challenge, it has become a visual delight.

Exploring Fremantle is easy. You can walk most places, or even better, hire a bicycle – Fremantle is a great place for cycling. Perhaps a tour should begin, mid-morning, with a coffee or a locally brewed beer on South Terrace, sometimes called Cappuccino Strip for its outdoor-café atmosphere. On Fridays, Saturdays and

Sundays (and public holidays), a stroll through the venerable **Fremantle Markets**, also on South Terrace, will give you a strong feeling for the place and produce anything from potted shrimp to a 78 record or a busker wearing a boater. The buildings where the market are held (from about 1000 to late) are classified by the National Trust.

With its maritime tradition, Fremantle is a good place for pubs. The beautifully restored **Norfolk Hotel**, on the corner of South Terrace and Norfolk St, has a congenial courtyard area. Opposite the markets on the other side of the Henderson St mall, the **Sail & Anchor** brews its own beers on the premises. The most famous of these is Dogbolter which is powerfully alcoholic and flavourful and should be sipped as if it were wine. Never drink a second glass – instead, have one of the wood-fired pizzas which are available in the pub's garden.

The port area is rich in maritime history. The **Western Australia Maritime Museum** in Cliff St was built in the 1860s and is Gothic Revival architecture at its best. This area of Australia has a frightening record of shipwrecks and general maritime mayhem and much of this is reflected in the displays in the museum. You can see here a section of the *Batavia*, wrecked off the storm-blown west coast in 1629, and there are relics from three other early Dutch ships. Open Mon–Thur 1030–1700, Sat–Sun 1300–1700.

Fremantle Arts Centre, at 1 Finnerty St, is housed in a picturesque colonial Gothic revival building built by convicts. This is perhaps the port's most distinguished building. It was mentioned by Anthony Trollope on his visit in March 1872 (he plainly did not like the town, for he described it as 'a hot, white, ugly town with a very large prison, a lunatic asylum and a hospital for ancient worn-out convicts.') The Arts Centre is in the old asylum, and now mainly holds works by Western Australian artists. There is free live music in the courtyard on Sunday afternoons from September to April. Open Thur–Sun 1300–1700.

Another building of consequence is the **Round House**, at 10 Arthur Head. Completed in 1831 as a prison, it is the State's oldest public building and arguably the oldest building in Western Australia. The grounds are still attractive and the building itself is interesting. There is a tunnel that runs from the grounds which is where the whalers carried their supplies down to Bathers Beach. Open daily 1000–1700.

WHERE NEXT?

If Fremantle has been your first port of call in Western Australia, then Perth is the obvious next stop (see p. 366). South lies the beautiful Margaret River region and the south coast (see p. 381). See pp. 405 and 407 for routes into the sparser regions of WA.

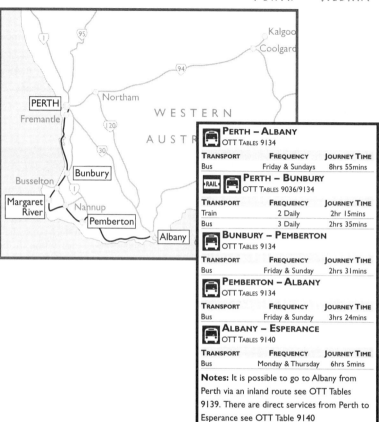

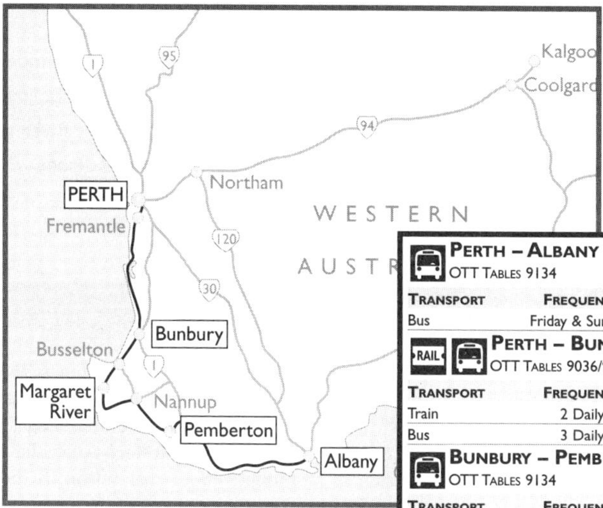

PERTH – ALBANY
OTT TABLES 9134

TRANSPORT	FREQUENCY	JOURNEY TIME
Bus	Friday & Sundays	8hrs 55mins

PERTH – BUNBURY
RAIL

OTT TABLES 9036/9134

TRANSPORT	FREQUENCY	JOURNEY TIME
Train	2 Daily	2hr 15mins
Bus	3 Daily	2hrs 35mins

BUNBURY – PEMBERTON
OTT TABLES 9134

TRANSPORT	FREQUENCY	JOURNEY TIME
Bus	Friday & Sunday	2hrs 31mins

PEMBERTON – ALBANY
OTT TABLES 9134

TRANSPORT	FREQUENCY	JOURNEY TIME
Bus	Friday & Sunday	3hrs 24mins

ALBANY – ESPERANCE
OTT TABLES 9140

TRANSPORT	FREQUENCY	JOURNEY TIME
Bus	Monday & Thursday	6hrs 5mins

Notes: It is possible to go to Albany from Perth via an inland route see OTT Tables 9139. There are direct services from Perth to Esperance see OTT Table 9140

ROUTE DETAIL

Take the coast road, Hwy 1, south to Bunbury (198 km). Continue on Hwy 10 (called the Bussell Hwy) through Busselton to Margaret River (108 km). Take Hwy 10 inland to Nannup and Pemberton (182 km). Rejoin Hwy 1 at Pemberton through Shannon National Park and along the south coast to Denmark and Albany (244 km). Total: 732 km.

EXPLORING THE SOUTHWEST

The drive around the coast south from Perth to Albany will show you one of the most favoured parts of the country. Bunbury is a large town noted for its cosmopolitan attractions as well as its beaches, while the beautiful valley of the Margaret River is famed for its wines. The country along the southern coast is very different from further north, with karri forests of some of the tallest trees in the world, amazing wildflowers, and the opportunity to go whale watching.

BUNBURY

Bunbury is the second-largest town (in area) in Western Australia and lies on the junction of the Collie and Preston rivers. It was not named after a character in *The Importance of Being Ernest,* despite all rumours to the contrary; it was named after Lt. H. W. St Pierre Bunbury, which is the sort of name that would have appealed to Oscar Wilde, so perhaps the reverse is true. Governor Stirling, Western Australia's first governor, requested Lieutenant Bunbury to pioneer land exploration in the south-west in 1836. Bunbury was favourably impressed with the area on his overland trek from Pinjarra to the Vasse River. In his journal, *Early Days in Western Australia* he wrote:'A township has been formed, or at least laid down on the maps, comprising the southern promontory and part of the north beach of Port Leschenault Inlet which the Governor named "Bunbury"in compliment of me.'

In 1841, Louisa Clifton, the wife of the Commissioner, wrote, 'Friends in England should be made acquainted with the dangers of this Australian coast in this season. A fatal grievance prevails on the point and I feel horrified to think of people coming out at any time of the year, to be exposed to such awful weather as this.' She did not last long in Australia and would plainly never have found a job with the tourist board.

In contrast to Mrs Clifton's experience, CSIRO - the Australian government scientific research body - has identified Bunbury as the centre of an area with the most comfortable climatic environment for human existence. And there is much to see. Bunbury can be thought of as the cultural capital of the south-west. It is only two hours from Perth and is famous for its white sandy beaches, great fishing and cosmopolitan lifestyle.

EN ROUTE

Australind, just north of Bunbury, gets its strange name from an amalgamation of 'Australia' and 'India' The idea was that the Western Australian Land Company, which purchased land in the area, would breed horses for sale to the British Army in India. Before that happened, however, the company went bust and most of the original settlers, who had arrived in 1841, left. The town is on the edge of an estuary which provides sheltered waters for sailing.

Bunbury Tourist Bureau, Old Railway Station, Carmody Place; tel: 9721 7922.
Old Station Coffee Lounge (in the old station next to the Tourist Bureau): users.highway1.com.au/~station/index.html
Port of Bunbury www.bunburytourism.org.au/

Admiral Motor Inn $$ 56 Spencer St; tel: 9721 7322.
Bunbury Backpackers $ 16 Clifton St; tel: 9721 3242. Double rooms available.
Bunbury Caravan & Chalet Villa $ Bussell Hy; tel: 9795 7100.
Bunbury Glade Caravan Park $ Timperley Rd; tel: 9721 3800; email wal@bunbury.iap.net.au
Burlington Hotel Motel $$ 51 Victoria St; tel: 9721 2075.
Bussell Motor Hotel $$ Bussell Hy; tel: 9721 1022.
Lighthouse Beach Resort $$ Carey St; tel: 9721 1311. Situated at one of the highest points in Bunbury with great views.
Ocean Drive Motel $$ 121 Ocean Dr; tel: 9721 2033.
Wander Inn $$ 16 Clifton St; tel: 9721 3242.
Welcome Inn $$ Ocean D.; tel: 9721 3100.
YHA of WA $ Moore St; cnr Stirling St; tel: 9791 2621.

A Lump Of Rump Steakhouse $$ 119 Beach Rd; tel: 9721 8691.
Barons Restaurant $$ Symmons St; tel: 9721 9966.
China City Garden Restaurant $$ 47 Victoria St; tel: 9721 1711.
Eagle Towers Restaurant $$ 192 Spencer St; tel: 9721 2762.
Jacaranda Diner $ 123 Victoria St; tel: 9791 2104.
Kebab Company $ 92 Symmons St; tel: 9791 1523.
La Roma Café & Pizza Restaurant $$ 52 Victoria St; tel: 9721 8557.
Louisa's Restaurant $$ 15 Clifton St; tel: 9721 9959.
Mancini's Café Restaurant $$ 66 Victoria St; tel: 9721 9944.
Ming Village Chinese Restaurant $$ 38 Victoria St; tel: 9721 6522.
Pasta Vino Italian Restaurant $$ 113 Spencer St; tel: 9721 7247.
Piccolino Pizza $ 5 Spencer St; tel: 9721 8282.
Ricardo's Restaurant $$ 183 Spencer St; tel: 9721 8241.

The Vinery $$ Bourke St; tel: 9721 9855.
Top Of The Town Garden Restaurant 91 Victoria St; tel: 9721 2202.

HIGHLIGHTS

The fastest way to orient yourself in Bunbury – not a simple town to navigate – is to go first to the **Old Railway Station**, which was the terminus for the railway line from Perth until the service was discontinued in 1985. Now it is the local bus depot and Tourist Bureau. The Tourist Bureau has *Walk About* and *Browse Around* brochures which give you self-guided tours to the town. The most important of these is the Heritage Trail which combines driving and walking and takes you to some 50 sites of interest.

The city has several attractive heritage buildings dating from around the 18th century and many have been totally restored. **The Bunbury Arts Complex** is housed in what was the Convent of Mercy, blessed and opened in 1897, which in turn stands on the site of the original Catholic Chapel, built in the late 1860s. Within the arts complex, the **Bunbury City and Regional Galleries** are open daily, except Tues.

St Patrick's Cathedral dominates several of the views, being positioned at the top of Bury Hill on Parkfield St. It was supposedly completed in 1921, except that there was not enough money for the steeple. That 18.3 m addition came along 46 years later but it all looks very integrated. It's worth viewing the interior to see what can be done with the local wood, jarrah, when you have an inspired carpenter.

One of the easiest ways to get a feel for Bunbury is to go with Rosemarie from **Bunbury Walking Tours**. Tours start from the tourist office and Rosemarie knows all about the history of the place – such as the time in the 1940s when 300 horses stampeded through the streets of Bunbury. You can choose from either a 45- or 90-minute walk; Wed and Sat at 1000, but you can arrange any other time by appointment. Tel: 9795 9261.

Boulters's Height is the town's most popular lookout. The view is of the city, the port, the north shore and the Leschenault Estuary. Reach it on foot from the junction of Wittenoom and Stirling Sts, at the base of the 26-m waterfall constructed in Mar 1966 to tie in with a visit by the Queen Mother. When it is switched on, the water tumbles down the eastern face of the heights.

King Cottage Museum, at 77 Forest Ave, was built around 1870 – there is some debate about the exact date. The owner, Henry King, and his four sons built it with bricks made from clay found on the property. The Bunbury Historical Society opened it as a museum in 1968 and has furnished it with items from the 1870–1920 period. Like so many small town museums run by amateur societies, the interior can only be seen on weekends:

Sat and Sun, school holidays and public holidays 1400–1600, $. Incidentally, the Kings are buried in the grounds of St Mark's.

THE STORY OF ST MARK'S

St Mark's Anglican church in the nearby hamlet of Picton is claimed to be the oldest church in the state. The church is testament to one man's faith. In 1840, the *Samuel Wright*, an American whaling ship, was wrecked in Koombana Bay. Captain Coffin, the sadly named master of the ship, turned adversity to his own ends and used salvaged timber from the wreck to build a cottage in Picton. Two years later he sold the cottage to the Rev. John Ramsden Wollaston, who had come there to be chaplain of Australind and arrived to find the place collapsing under debt. Wollaston decided that God was testing his faith. Enlisting the help of some of the locals he built his own very primitive church. In 1942 the building was extensively restored, but you can still get a feeling of the effort that went into building it from scratch with no money and very little support from the Anglican church. The church is on the corner of Flynn and Charterhouse Close – it's not easy to find so ask for a map and directions at the tourist office.

The Leschenault Inlet abounds with birdlife – pelicans, ducks, black swans, magpies, wagtails, parrots and many others. In the area are also kangaroos, wallabies and possums, but its true wealth lies, perhaps, in the abundance of flora – the wildflowers which have made Western Australia famous.

The **Bunbury Entertainment Centre**, on the shores of the inlet, was opened in 1990 and contains the largest entertainment venue in regional Western Australia. A state-of-the-art, multifunctional complex, it can cater for straight theatre, concerts, films, conferences and exhibitions. Tel: 9721 3413.

Koombana Bay has a **Dolphin Education Centre** $ and if you arrive early in the morning on most days you will be greeted by dolphins. They apparently enjoy swimming with humans, but it is advised that you do not touch them.

Big Swamp Wetlands and Boardwalk has a 100-m elevated boardwalk from which you can look for some 70 different kinds of birds as well as the long-necked turtle. The Wildlife Park features kangaroos, wallabies, snakes, fruit bats, koalas and a large walk-in aviary containing a variety of birds. Open daily except Tue, 1000–1700. The Park is on Prince Phillip Dr, 3 km from the city centre.

MARGARET RIVER

Margaret River was originally a dairy town – it still is to a certain extent – but over the past few years it has been gaining fame as the centre of a major wine-growing region and as a tourist destination in its own right. The town and its name now appear to have a built-in magical appeal. The town, 10 km inland from where the river flows into the Indian Ocean, developed slowly between 1910 and 1920. The railway arrived in 1927, closed 30 years later. Then, in the early 1970s, wine growing was successfully attempted and since then the district has boomed.

EN ROUTE

Busselton is in a beautiful site. John Garett Bussell, after whom the town was named, certainly thought so when he first saw the place in about 1830: 'Here was a spot that the creative fancy of a Greek would have peopled with Dryad and Naiad and all the beautiful phantoms and wild imagery of his sylvan mythology. Wide waving lawns were sloping down to the water's edge. Trees thick and tangled were stopping to the banks.' Yes, it is purple prose, but the area around Busselton is still like that and inspires writers today. **St Mary's Church** in Busselton, on Geographe Bay, is the oldest stone church in the state. (St Mark's in Picton is said to be the oldest church in Western Australia; see p. 385.)

Tourist Information Bureau, cnr Tunbridge Rd and Bussell Hwy; tel: 9757 2911.

Adamsons Riverside Accommodation $$ 71 Bussell Hwy;tel: 9757 2013.
Boodjidup Lodge & Units $$ 212 Railway Ter; tel: 9757 2720.
Colonial Motel $$ Wallcliffe Rd; tel: 9757 2633.
Edge of the Forest $$ Bush surroundings near to Margaret River township; tel: 9757 2351.
Prevelly Park Beach Resort $$ 99 Mitchell Dr, tel: 9757 2374.
Captain Freycinet Inn $$ Tunbridge St, cnr Bussell Hwy; tel: 9757 2033. Despite the name, a modern motel.

1885 Inn & Restaurant $$$ Farrelly St, next to St Thomas More Church; tel: 9757 3177. Built as a country house in 1888 this is the ideal place to sample one of the 150-odd Margaret River wines in the cellar.
Basil Bush Restaurant $$ Wallcliffe Rd; tel: 9757 3735.
Country Kitchen Delights $$ 99 Bussell Hwy; tel: 9757 2611.
Harry's Mexican Wave $ 157 Bussell Hwy; tel: 9757 2703.
Mama's Oriental $ Bussell Hwy; tel: 9757 2622.
Shell Roadhouse Restaurant $ 91 Bussell Hwy; tel: 9757 2327.

HIGHLIGHTS

As you come into the town from the north you first see **Rotary Park**, where a steam engine is on display. The engine was built in England in 1889, shipped to Margaret River the following year and used for log hauling until 1909. After working elsewhere it came back to Margaret River in 1964 to stand as a memorial.

The **Old Settlement Historical Museum** is privately owned and is well worth visiting, for it is light years better than most of the amateur efforts around Australia. It is a living museum and you can happily spend an afternoon exploring the site. Open daily 0900–1700.

Ellensbrook House is the Bussell family homestead. It was built in the 1850s with what was available, a tough way to construct a house. The ridge beam is a mast found as driftwood. A framework of bush poles and paper bark, gathered from the banks of the Margaret River with the help of the local Aboriginal people, has been sealed with plaster made by burning limestone from nearby dunes. Hand-hewn slabs were used for later weather-board additions. The house has changed little over the years, but is now a National Trust listed property and has recently had a major refurbishment and restoration. $ Open Mon–Fri 1000–1500 (daily in school hols). The house is a longish walk from the road – vehicle access is promised – but it is well worth the effort.

THE BUSSELL FAMILY

Bussell is a recurrent name in the history of the area. In 1834 the family settled along the Vasse valley; their homestead, Ellensbrook, was named by Alfred Bussell after his wife. Their name was given, against their wishes, to Busselton, and Margaret River was named after Margaret Wicher, a family friend. At Margaret River, Alfred tried to emulate a grand English country house by building Wallcliffe in 1865.

In 1876, 16-year-old Grace Bussell and Sam Isaacs, an Aboriginal, rode 12 km on horseback to go to the rescue of survivors from the *Georgette*, shipwrecked on a reef off Calgardup Beach. They ferried survivors to shore and a monument at Calgardup Beach commemorates their bravery.

About 500 m away from the house is the **Meekadarribee waterfall** – the moon's bathing place. It is surrounded by tall peppermint trees which arch over a limestone cave behind the falls.

One of the most remarkable attractions in this remarkably attractive town is **Eagles Heritage**. It opened in January 1988 to care for birds of prey that were taken there injured, orphaned or displaced. The centre now boasts the largest collection of raptors in Australia, including eagles, hawks, falcons and owls. You can see 21 of the 24 diurnal species and 5 of the 8 species of owl here.

The centre is situated on 12 ha of bushland and visitors can enjoy a 1-km walk which takes approximately 30–40 minutes and features an abundance of wildflowers and orchids (in season). All the aviaries are built of natural bushpoles and nylon netting which saves the birds from injury. A major feature is the enormous free-fly cage where the injured birds can learn to fly again before being released back into their own environment. The centre is a few minutes drive south of Margaret River along Boodjidup Rd. $ Open daily 1000–1700, with free-flight displays at 1100 and 1330.

Four spectacular **caves** are within easy reach of Margaret River – Lake, Mammoth,

EN ROUTE

Beedelup National Park, off Vasse Hwy, contains the Underwood Tree which is 400 years old and has a 3 by 4 m hole cut into it, hacked out using a chai saw. This took ten hours. You can stand in the hole with over 151 tonnes of tree above you. Also in the park are Beedelup Cascades and Falls, which drop over a steep gorge 107 m high in two sections. They are set in beautiful forest surroundings and feature a short walk crossing Beedelup Brook on a footbridge built from a karri log.

Jewel and Moondyne. All have conducted tours and are well lit so that you can see the stalactites and stalagmites.

Bellview Shell Museum at Whitchcliffe, 6 km south of Margaret River, has one of the best shell collections in Australia.

Of the many **wineries** you can visit in the area, try:
Cape Mentelle, Wallcliffe Rd; tel: 9757 3266; open daily 1000–1630.
Chateau Xanadu, Terry Rd; tel: 9757 2581; open daily 1000–1630.
Devil's Lair, Rocky Rd, Forest Grove via Margaret River; tel: 9336 3262; email: allison@devils-lair.com. Open for cellar sales by appointment.
Leeuwin Estate, Stevens Rd; tel: 9757 6253; open daily for lunch. Saturday evenings for dinner. Wine tasting and winery tours daily.
Redgate Wines, Boodjidup Rd; tel: 9757 6208; open daily 1000–1700.
Rosa Brook Estate, Rosa Brook Rd; tel: 9157 2286; open Thur–Sun 1100–1600.

PEMBERTON

Pemberton is a successful logging town surrounded by vast areas of national park and state forest, mainly karri trees. Some of the tallest hardwood trees in the world grow in this area. The tallest tree felled here was 104 m high.

The first European to settle in the area was Edward Brockman, son of Perth's first mayor, who arrived here in 1861. He bred horses for the Indian market and established a homestead, Warren House, in 1863. It still stands where the Pemberton–Northcliffe road crosses the Warren River. Pemberton Walcott, the man who gave the town its name, arrived in 1862 but his farming enterprise failed and he left the district just two years later. A road linking Vasse (now Busselton) to Pemberton was built – by convicts – in 1866.

The town is only 25 km from the Southern Ocean and even in summer the nights can be cool, while winters are cool and wet with heavy dews and forest mists. As a result, most accommodation in the area has wood fires.

EN ROUTE

On a detour to the coast, there are sandy beaches and good fishing at Windy Harbour. The road to Albany is along the splendidly named Pacific Hwy Rte 1 that circumnavigates mainland Australia. Sadly, the name is all that is splendid about the highway.

Pemberton Tourist Centre, Brockman St; tel: 9776 1133.
Pemberton Telecentre, Kennedy St; tel: 9776 1745; email smcbride@karriweb.net.au. Open 1000–1600 daily.
The Pemberton HomePage
www.gwb.com.au/gwb/pemberton/index.html

Forest Lodge and Motel $$ Vasse Hwy; tel: 9776 1113
Gloucester Motel $$ Ellis St; tel: 9776 1266. Beautiful views of the forest. Restaurant.
Karri Valley Resort $$ Vasse Hwy; tel: 9776 2020. Self-contained chalets with secluded forest views, and lakeside motel units.
Kookaburra Cottage $$ Kennedy St; tel: 9776 1246. A beautiful rammed earth home in the heart of karri country offering bed and breakfast.
Pemberton Caravan Park $ Pumphill Rd; tel: 9776 1300. Next to the Pemberton Pool.

Chloe's Kitchen $ 5 Pem-bee Ct; tel: 9776 1433.
Gryphons Restaurant $$ 246 Dickinson St; tel: 9776 1159.
Pemberton Chinese Restaurant $ 3 Dean St; tel: 9776 1514.
Shamrock Restaurant $$ Brockman St; tel: 9776 1186.
Silver Birch Restaurant $$ Widdeson St; tel: 9776 1019.

HIGHLIGHTS

This is a timber town, and all else is secondary. In 1913, Pemberton mills supplied half a million sleepers for the rail line across the Nullarbor Plain. The World Forestry Commission visited the district in 1928 and judged karri second only to Californian redwood as a timber tree; the Pemberton National Parks Board was formed two years later to administer Pemberton, Warren and Beedelup national parks.

For an idea of working life in the forest before the turn of the century, the **Brockman sawpit** on the Pemberton–Northcliffe road has been restored to its original state of around 1865. In those days, lengths of timber were cut by hand with a cross-saw. The sawmill is no longer in use, but can be viewed.

The **Gloucester Tree** is 2.4 km east of the town, named after a visit by the Duke of Gloucester. This great karri tree houses the world's highest fire lookout, built in 1946. It is possible to climb it up 153 rungs of alternate wooden karri pegs and steel spikes for 61 m. This is only for the very fit and should not be attempted if there is any sort of a wind. The whole thing sways and can make a climber feel seasick.

On the **Pemberton Tramway** you can ride in a 1907 replica tram through towering karri and marri forests along one of the most scenic rail lines in Australia, crossing rivers and streams on rustic wooden bridges to enjoy the quiet beauty of the forest. Departs daily at 1045 and 1400 – the trip takes 1¼ hours and the turn-around point is the Warren River. On Tues, Thur and Sat there is a 5-hour trip – this includes 1½ hours in Northcliffe – which leaves at 1015. Tel: 9776 1322.

For those to whom steam trains provide the ultimate thrill, a **steam train service** operates May–Nov between Pemberton and Lyall (10 km south of Manjimup). This historic section of railway was originally a State Saw Mills line, completed in early 1914. Everything imaginable was transported on this railway. There was even a payroll robbery in 1925 between Collins Siding and Barrenhurst. The return trip takes just under 3 hours and travels through beautiful forest and pasture. Departs Pemberton railway station Sat 1030 and 1415, Sun 1030.
For the true enthusiast, there are also driving courses, so you get a chance to drive a diesel or a steam locomotive. The diesel locomotive courses are available all year round, the steam locomotive courses from May to October. The locomotives currently available are:
Steam Locomotive V1213: a 135-tonne, British-built 2-8-2, one of 24 operated by Westrail in the days of steam.
Diesel Locomotive Class Y: a 40-tonne, British-built Bo-Bo Diesel Electric, 18 of which were operated by Westrail.
For more information contact Ian Willis 9761 322.

The **Pemberton swimming pool** is a mountain pool formed by the damming of the Lefroy Brook in 1929. You can catch your own rainbow trout at the **Pemberton Trout and Marron Hatchery** just 2 km out of town. It supplies brown and rainbow trout fingerlings (little fish, a finger long) to stock dams and rivers all over Western Australia. Open 0930–1730 daily. Tel: 9776 1400.

Other attractions include the **Big Brook Arboretum**, with 32 different species of tree, and the **One-Hundred-Year Forest**, which consists of trees of roughly the same age. It is so named because it was cleared for wheat-growing in the early days. When the area was abandoned, natural regeneration from a fire induced seed fall from the surrounding areas and the karri forest was started. It was recognised and dedicated as a state forest 31 years later.

Warren National Park has some of the very little virgin karri forest remaining in Western Australia, with trees over 80 m high. The 18 km Rainbow Trail recalls where, in the 1920s, the steam locomotives used to haul giant karri logs along a bush tramway to the Pemberton sawmill.

Pemberton is a new wine-growing region. The main varieties planted are Pinot Noir, Chardonnay and Cabernet Sauvignon. Several wines have already won major awards. Most of the **wineries** offer cellar sales and some also have a café or restaurant. Bus tours of the wineries are available. These are a few that welcome visitors.

Gloucester Ridge, 100 m from the Gloucester Tree. Open daily 1000–1600.

Salitage Winery, on the Vasse Hwy, uses only estate grown fruit.

Warren Vineyard, on Conte Rd, 3 km west of the post office, was established in 1985 and produces mainly fine reds.

ALBANY

Albany has been called both the Gem of the Southern Ocean and Queen of the Southlands. One suspects these names came from the fertile imaginations of the tourist office, but a view from the top of Mt Clarence (and a steep but safe drive) offers panoramic views which shows that the names may be only slightly over the top.

The name Albany is very English but it could have been different – this was the proposed site for a French settlement. There are many such places around the coasts of Australia and New Zealand, but in every case the British got there first or came with more people.

You could consider Albany the capital for the Great Southern Region. The area has a Mediterranean-type climate; the rain tends to be concentrated in the winter months but there is no truly dry season. The most popular time to visit is from Aug–Oct where the wildflowers are in bloom and the whales pass during their annual migration.

Tourist Information Bureau, Old Railway Station, Proudlove Parade; tel 9841 1088.

Motels line the highway coming into town. You can sort one out with the Vacancy sign showing but try and get the furthest unit from the road.
Ace Motor Inn $ 314 Albany Hwy; tel: 9841 2911.

Not all visitors to the town have had a happy time. Anthony Trollope was outraged that he had to take a signed certificate from a policeman in Albany to prove to other Australian states that he had 'not been a lag.' Visitors are no longer required to do this.

Albany Backpackers $ Stirling Terrace and Spencer St; tel: 9841 8848: Internet: www.albanybackpackers.com.au/. Opposite the tourist bureau.
Albany Happy Days Caravan Park $ 21 Millbrook Rd; tel: 9844 3267.
Balneaire Seaside Resort $$ 27 Adelaide Crest, 3.5 km from the centre of town; tel: 9842 2877; Internet: www.balneaire.com.au/
Brackenhurst Bed & Breakfast $$ 68–70 Brunswick Rd; tel: 9842 3158. Historic guest house circa 1880s, close to town.
Discovery Inn $$ 9 Middleton Rd, 3.5 km out of town, one street back from Middleton Beach; tel: 9842 5535; Internet: www.fullcomp.com.au/~jokenira/
Dog Rock Motel $$ 303 Middleton Rd; tel: 9841 4422.
Dolphin Lodge Albany $$ 32 Adelaide Cres; tel: 9841 6600.
Flinders Park Lodge cnr Lower King and Harbour Rd; tel: 9844 7062; Internet: www.parklodge.com.au/. Eight guest rooms, most overlooking acres of land with views to Oyster Harbour, the hills beyond and the lights of Emu Point.
Middleton Beach Bed & Breakfast $$ 7 Griffiths St; tel: 9844 1135; Internet: www.homestayonline.com.au/example.html. 100 m from the beach. Not for smokers.
Ryan's Premier Hotel/Motel $ 208 York St; tel: 9841 1544.
YHA of WA Inc $ 49 Duke St; tel: 9841 3949.

Adelaides Restaurant Princess $ Royal Fortress; tel: 9842 1090.
Al Fornetto Ristorante & Pizzeria $ 132 York St; tel: 9842 1060.
Auntie Browns Restaurant $ 280 York St; tel: 9841 6177.
Beachside Middleton Beach $ 1 Flinders Pde; tel: 9841 7733.
Café Bizarre $ 42 Stirling Ter; tel: 9841 6003.
Café On The Terrace $ 134 Stirling Ter; tel: 9842 1012.
Food Station $ 112 Lower York St; tel: 9842 2366.
Kooka's Restaurant $ 204 Stirling Ter; tel: 9841 5889.
Three Plenties Palace $ 148 York St; tel: 9841 4121.
Tuscano's Café Restaurant $ 63 Frederick St; tel: 9842 2454.
Whalers Galley $ Whaling Station; tel: 9844 4347.

HIGHLIGHTS

The first recorded European sighting of this area was probably in 1627, by Francois Thyssen and Peter Noyts (it was outlined on a Dutch East India chart of 1628). The huge natural harbour of King George Sound, on which Albany is sited, was discovered, charted and named in 1792 by Captain George Vancouver, who served with Captain Cook and after whom Vancouver, in Canada, is named. In a second voyage to the area, Vancouver sent a party ashore, which climbed Mt Clarence and sighted Princess Royal Harbour to the north. The French explorer Bruny d'Entrecasteaux came by the same year and Matthew Flinders landed here in 1801. Within a few years King George Sound was a regular stopping place for ships, including sealers and whalers.

In late 1826, Major Edmund Lockyer arrived in the brig *Amity* with troops and convicts to establish a penal colony, but this lasted only until 1831. In 1976, for the town's 150th anniversary, the people of Albany decided to reconstruct the ***Amity***; it is moored only 200 m from the landing place of the original vessel.

Lockyer, unaware of Vancouver's previous visit, had named the village Frederickstown in honour of Frederick, Duke of Albany. The name was never popular and in 1832 it was formally changed to Albany. With one of the greatest natural harbours in the world, it became a major port of call for warships in the Indian Ocean and mail steamers on the Australian run. However, when Fremantle was established as a port in 1900 Albany declined. It regained some popularity when it was discovered as a tourist resort.

Albany was an important whaling station, and since the international ban on whaling, the whales are starting to come back. If you can't be there when they migrate you can still visit what is claimed to be the world's largest whale museum and Australia's last whaling station. **Whaleworld** (Frenchman's Bay Rd) may be the only whaling museum in the world. Created from an operational whaling station, until 1978 it was the Cheynes Beach Whaling Company. In its time the station's chasers took up to 850 whales per season. Today, the restored Cheynes IV whale chaser is the centrepiece of Whaleworld. Open daily 0900–1700, with 40-minute tours starting every hour.

WHALE WATCHING

Southern right whales can be seen from July–Nov calving in the calm waters of sheltered bays in the Bremer Bay area. They can be observed from many vantage points along the coastline, at times as close as only 6 m from shore. Occasionally humpback whales can be seen from a distance, as well as other marine mammals such as dolphins and seals.

Albany has a number of interesting old buildings reflecting its early history. **St John's Church of England**, in Church St, dates from 1846. It was the first church consecrated in Western Australia and has beautiful stained-glass windows and an imposing tower.

The **Old Gaol**, just back from the harbour, was built in 1851 as the convict hiring department and became the district gaol in 1872. After it had stood empty for many years, the Albany Historical Society began its restoration in 1968. The museum contains a fascinating collection of social and historical artefacts. Visitors can shut themselves in the black hole – not recommended for the claustrophobic – or ramble through the numerous small rooms and cells. There is an audio-visual display of its history.

The **Albany Residency**, nearby, was built in the early 1850s, and in 1975 it became the first branch of the Western Australian Museum outside the Perth area. It is a focal point for both the social and natural history of the Albany region.

Another museum is at the Old Post Office, now the **Inter Colonial Communications Museum**. The building, with its roof of she-oak shingles, was planned in 1866 and opened in 1870. The ground floor was the customs and bond store, the middle level for mail sorting and post office, and the third level (Stirling Terrace) was the court, magistrate's and jury rooms and holding cells for prisoners. Open daily 1000–1600.

Dog Rock in Middleton Rd is Albany's unofficial mascot and, after Gundagai, the most photographed 'dog' in Australia. It is, in fact, a granite outcrop that looks like the enormous head of a bloodhound sniffing the breeze.

Patrick Taylor Cottage, on the corner of Stirling Terrace and Parade St, was built in 1832 of wattle and daub. It has been restored as much as possible to its former state and is now a museum containing clothes of the period, household goods, old clocks and silverware.

The Old Farm, off Middleton Rd, Strawberry Hill, was the site of the government farm for the settlement of Albany. It was developed from 1827 to 1830 and then bought by Sir Richard Spencer for 15 guineas. The two-storey stone building was built for him in 1836 and is one of the oldest in Western Australia. It has been maintained by the National Trust since 1964 and has splendid gardens.

Torndirrup National Park is on the coast south of Albany and Princess Royal Harbour and includes some of the most spectacular scenery in Australia. The Gap is a 24-m drop to the sea. When a heavy swell is running, the thunder of the ocean and the drifting spray are an awesome experience. The Natural Bridge, like a huge, granite suspension bridge, is an awe-inspiring sight in rough seas. Visitors are asked to be wary of king waves that have been known to surge up 9 m and have taken lives.

Nearby is the 4,639-ha Two Peoples Bay Nature Reserve, the sanctuary of the noisy scrub bird, thought for many years to be extinct. The bird is a brilliant mimic and several pairs are thought still to exist.

WILDFLOWER TOURS

More than 3,500 varieties of wildflower have been listed within a 48-km radius of Albany. For botanists this is paradise. The botanical illustrator wrote in 1893: 'In one place I sat down and without moving I could pick twenty five different flowers within the reach of my hand. The banksias were quite marvellous, their huge bushy flowers a foot in length, and so full of honey that the natives were said to get tipsy sucking them.' (This idea that you can get tipsy from banksia is incorrect – I have tested it!)

The two favourite places to visit for wildflowers are the nearby national parks. The flowers can change quite rapidly and the tourist office will be able to advise you. It's well worth making the effort.

Stirling Range National Park was named after the first governor of Western Australia. The park covers 115,671 ha and there are many tracks providing easy access to wildlife and flowers. The western access via Tourist Drive No 253 from Cranbrook takes travellers along the Salt River Rd, Red Gum Springs Rd and into the heart of the park. Picnic areas with barbecue facilities are located throughout the park. The ecology is delicately balanced and to ensure the flora and fauna are preserved, camping and fires are permitted only where facilities are provided. Five of the peaks within the park rise to over 1,000 m and are often shrouded in mist.

Porongurup National Park has some of the oldest rock in the world and covers 2,401 ha. Easy walking tracks lead to most of the peaks giving spectacular views. In the Porongurups 'climbing' is a bit of a misnomer. The walks are all relatively easy and not over-long.

Both of these national parks are about 40 km from Albany and offer magnificent climbs, spectacular views and beautiful wildflowers. There are said to be almost 1,000 species of wildflowers in these ranges, more than 100 unique to the area.

WHERE NEXT?

Hwy 30 will take you back to Perth along a direct inland route (450 km). About the same distance east along Hwy 1 will bring you to the beaches and clear waters of Esperance and the Bay of Isles (see p. 396).

Esperance

Although Esperance is a small town with a population of something under 7,000, it has some considerable importance in the area. It is a service centre for the surrounding agricultural area – this is one of the oldest apple-growing areas in Western Australia and is now starting to be seen as a holiday destination of high potential. It has everything that a holidaymaker needs although, like so many places in Western Australia, it suffers from the tyranny of distance – it's a long way from major centres of population (Perth, for example is over 900 km away).

Information

Esperance Tourist Bureau, Museum Village, Dempster St; tel: 8971 2330.

Accommodation

Most of the motels - standard Australian model - are along The Esplanade. If you have not booked, drive along it looking for Vacancies signs and then choose the one you like.

A Small Claim to Fame

In 1979, Esperance town council, totally unintimidated by the potential wrath of the United States, served the crashdown team at NASA with an infringement notice for littering.

Bay of Isles Motel $$ 32 The Esplanade; tel: 8971 3999.

Captain Huon Motel $$ 5 The Esplanade; tel: 8971 2383.

Esperance Bayview Motel $$ 31 Dempster St; tel: 8971 1533.

Esperance Motor Hotel $$ 14 Andrew St; tel: 8971 1555.

Esperance Seafront Caravan Park $ Goldfields Rd; tel: 8971 1251. Caravan and tent sites, grassy, shady, camp kitchen.

Esperance Travellers Inn $$ Goldfields Rd; tel: 8971 1677.

Jetty Motel $$ 1 The Esplanade; tel: 8971 5978.

Old Hospital Motel $$ 1a William St; tel: 8971 3587. Nine self-contained units, central, TV, video, microwave.

Pier Hotel $$ The Esplanade; tel: 8971 1777.

YHA of WA $ Goldfields Rd; tel: 8971 1040.

FOOD AND DRINK

You do not come to Esperance for a great culinary experience, but there are plenty of restaurants that cater to the economy-minded traveller. The main restaurant thoroughfare is Dempster St.

Beachfront Café $ 19 The Esplanade; tel: 8971 7107. Open daily 0700–2000.

Emperor's Garden Chinese Restaurant $ 123 Dempster St; tel: 8907 12866.

Golden Orient Chinese Restaurant $ 49 Dempster St; tel: 8907 13744.

Gray Starling Restaurant $ 126 Dempster St; tel: 8907 15880.

Pizza Kitchen Esperance $ 85 Dempster St; tel: 8907 14666.

HIGHLIGHTS

The beaches and waters around Esperance have been described as some of the finest and clearest in the world. The Esperance archipelago contains over 100 islands and has a wealth of maritime life, including seals, sea lions and dolphins. And, like all of the other towns along this coast, it is an ideal spot to watch the migrations of the whales – the southern right whales come here July–Nov to calve in the warm and sheltered waters. Known as the Bay of Isles, this is another of the fisherman's paradises on the Western Australia coastline – virtually any point off the Esperance coast will produce a good catch.

One of the biggest attractions is a cruise out around some of the islands. These cruises have full commentaries and last for 3½ hours. Visitors can see sea eagles being hand fed, dolphins at play and colonies of sea lions and seals, plus a host of other marine life and sea birds. **Esperance Diving and Fishing** has a purpose-built cruise vessel which can carry up to ten passengers and offers whale watching, fishing and scuba-diving. It is at 72 The Esplanade, directly opposite the Taylor St Jetty. Tel: 89907 15111; www.gei.net.au/~espdive/

The history of Esperance is recorded in the **Esperance Municipal Museum** (open daily 1330–1630, cnr James and Dempster St).

DAY TRIPS

As a town from which to explore national parks, Esperance has few equals: there are four national parks within striking distance. Most importantly, all are accessible by sealed road.

Only 56 km from Esperance, **Cape Le Grand National Park** is probably the most spectacular and beautiful area on the west coast. It has a wide range of bays with white sand and clear water, among them Hellfire Bay, Thistle Cove and Lucky Bay. The view across the bay and the national park from Frenchman's Peak is worth the journey alone. About 6 km east of Cape Le Grand is Mississippi Hill and Rossiter Bay. It was here in 1841 that English explorers Eyre and Wylie met Captain Rossiter of the French whaler *Mississippi* at the end of their long and arduous expedition from Adelaide. There is camping (in designated areas only) here; take your own water and supplies.

Further east along the coast, 120 km from Esperance and just past Duke of Orleans Bay, comes **Cape Arid National Park**. The park stretches over nearly 20,000 ha of sandplains and heathlands, but is better known for its sweeping beaches, clear blue seas and Precambrian granite headlands.

On the coast to the west of Esperance is **Stokes National Park**, which covers an area of 10,667 ha and has the historic Moir Homestead. The coastal scenery is beautiful and there is ocean fishing and sandy beaches good for swimming. You will see copious birdlife (over 40 species have been recorded), grey kangaroos and probably the occasional seal. Access to the park is on good gravel roads from the main highway to camping bays close to the inlet. There are caravan pads and borehole toilets at the sites, but no water. Other roads wthin the park are 4-wheel drive tracks only (caravans are restricted to the gravel roads).

About halfway between Esperance and Albany (see p. 392) is the huge **Fitzgerald River National Park**. Like all these national parks, it has almost deserted beaches and clear blue waters and an over-abundance of maritime life.

Kalgoorlie has always had a certain reputation in Australia. When the country was more strictly run by wowsers –- meaning anyone who disapproves of sex – Kalgoorlie was the only city in Australia that had brothels which operated under both city and police tolerance. And it was the only city in Australia where the pubs stayed open night and day – this at a time when all of the pubs in the rest of the country had to close at 0600 (thus creating that awful spectacle, the Six O'clock Swill).

Today, licensing hours throughout Australia are relaxed, and Melbourne, of all places, boasts in the Daily Planet the largest and most luxurious 'house of excellent repute' in the country. But original sin started with Kalgoorlie, and there is still a sort of hint of a leer associated with it. The name Kalgoorlie comes from an Aboriginal word said to mean 'silky pear'. On the other hand a British magazine described it as the 'mad bastard capital of Australia', which is unkind but accurate enough to sting.

The reason Kalgoorlie attracted so much attention from ladies of the night is because for a long time it was the richest square mile in the world. And the source of that wealth was gold.

Kalgoorlie is unusual in that it is a gold mining town that has avoided becoming a ghost town. The surrounding countryside, stripped of its vegetation by the early miners, is forbiddingly ugly and the summers are extremely hot. Don't go there in Dec or Jan because the heat will be a foretaste of hell and you will find that the local population have rather smartly gone elsewhere for their holidays. During the rest of the year, however, the town is a major tourist attraction that has its charms and where there is much to see.

GETTING THERE AND GETTING AROUND

There are several flights a day from Perth to Kalgoorlie airport, south of the town.

Kalgoorlie is 595 km east of Perth, along the long, straight road of Hwy 94. By bus the journey takes 5½–8 hours and several companies cover the route (it is included on Greyhound Pioneer's Perth–Sydney route).

INFORMATION

Kalgoorlie-Boulder Tourist Centre, 250 Hannan St; tel: 9021 1966.

INTERNET SITE **Kalgoorlie-Boulder Virtual Tourism** www.kalbldtc.com.au/

ACCOMMODATION

Old Australian Hotel $ 138 Hannan St; tel: 9457 7766.

Hannan's View Motel $$ 430 Hannan St; tel: 9091 3333.

Hospitality Inn $$ Hannan St; tel: 9021 2888.

Midas Motel $$ 409 Hannan St; tel: 9021 3088.

Palace Hotel $$ Hannan St, cnr Maritana St; tel: 9021 2788.

Quality Kalgoorlie Plaza $$$ 45 Egan St; tel: 9021 4544.

Star & Garter Hotel/Motel $ 497 Hannan St; tel: 9021 3004.

Tower Hotel $$ Maritana St; tel: 9021 3211.

FOOD AND DRINK

Amy's Restaurant $ 1 Macdonald; tel: 9021 1749. Open Tues–Sat 1800–late. Continental and Australian.

Basil's on Hannan $$ 268 Hannan St; tel: 9021 7832. Open Mon–Tues 0800–1700, Wed–Sat 0800–late, Sun 0900–1630. Pasta, Italian and Continental.

Fu Wah Chinese Restaurant $ 6 Hannan St; tel: 9021 6242.

Kadees Bistro $ 6 Maritana St; tel: 9021 7235. Open Tues–Sun 1830–late. Continental, Italian.

Kalgoorlie Café $ 277 Hannan St; tel: 9021 3002.

Mediterranean Lebanese Food $ 3 Woolworths Plaza; tel: 9091 3491.

New Hong Kong Chinese Restaurant $ 248 St Barbara Sq, Hannan St; tel: 9021 1336. Open daily. Lunch and dinner.

Pizza Cantina $ 211 Hannan St; tel: 9021 4870.

Top End Thai Restaurant $ 71 Hannan St; tel: 90914027; Internet: www.thai.net.au/. Open Mon–Sat 1800–2100. BYO.

HIGHLIGHTS

Technically, the town is Kalgoorlie-Boulder, for in 1989 the two towns amalgamated. The main street of Boulder, Burt St, lies 5 km from the main street of Kalgoorlie, Hannan St. Boulder was named after The Great Boulder Mine, the first mine to be established on the Golden Mile.

The Top End Thai Restaurant is almost a tourist destination in its own right. It is in one of the town's oldest buildings (1897) which originally housed one of Kalgoorlie's numerous pubs – Tattersal's Hotel, and later The Savoy. The name Top End comes from its situation at the eastern end of Hannan St, in what is referred to as the Top End Block (Hannan St has a noticeable slope), near the Mt Charlotte gold mine. The food is very authentic, and its sister restaurant in Perth has won a swag of awards for the same cuisine.

Kalgoorlie was originally known as Hannans, after the prospector Paddy Hannan. Gold had been found in Coolgardie (see p 403) and in 1893, Patrick Hannan, Tom Flanagan and Daniel Shea were prospecting to the east. One of the horses cast a shoe near Mt Charlotte and the group had to camp for the night. They were lying on a fortune – in a few days they collected 100 oz of nuggets. **Paddy Hannan's Tree**, which marks the site where Hannan, Flanagan and Shea struck lucky, is in Outridge Terrace.

The easily won alluvial gold was worked out in a year or so but when the seam was found under the Golden Mile the bigger companies moved in. The town was surveyed and proclaimed in 1895 and the first local newspaper, the *Western Argus*, established the same year. Many buildings from those early boom years survive. After that, the goldfield's prosperity came and went in cycles. In disputes in 1897 over the distinction between alluvial and other mining claims, an effigy of the minister for mines was hanged and burned.

Gold production peaked in 1903 but the mines started up again in 1931 when gold increased in price. Other declines followed in 1942, the 1950s and then 1963, when many mines on the eastern goldfields were closed. Gold was replaced in importance by a nickel boom in the 1970s. Nickel was first discoverd in 1966 and two years later Kalgoorlie had the only commercial nickel smelter in Australia and the second of its kind in the world. But the Kalgoorlie Goldfields are the largest in Western Australia and the Golden Mile still managed to produce 632,034 oz of gold as recently as 1995/96.

At the turn of the last century when more than 8,000 people were riding bicycles in the district, the machine was known locally as 'the ship of the desert'.

The town is still all about gold mining. From early on it was seen that the way to get the gold was reef, open-cut and deep-shaft mining, which is the way it has been mined to this day. The open-cut mine, which is currently at a depth of 260 m, is expected to increase to a depth of 575 m, 2 km in width and almost 5 km in length. **Hannans North** in Broadarrow Rd allows you to go underground, under the care of an experienced guide, to the original mine workings and witness the life of miners at the turn of the 20th century. For safety reasons you will need to wear proper shoes when you are underground. Once you are back on the surface you can ride the railway around the 7-ha site with its restored historic buildings and mining machinery. There is also a regular gold pouring demonstration. Open daily 0900–1700, with tours on demand (allow 3 hrs). Tel: (08) 914 074.

In the **School of Mines Museum** in Cassidy St (open Mon–Fri 1000–1600, except Dec–Jan when it's too hot) there are replicas of the giant nuggets found in the region. The **Museum of the Goldfields**, at the end of Hannan St, has a 400-oz gold bar on display in the underground vault, along with the Western Australian State Gold Collection. It also houses many other exhibits relating to life in the goldfields since the beginning of the 20th century.

You can also ride the **Loopline Railway**, which carried ore from the mine to the stamper for crushing, and was once the busiest in Western Australia. A train departs daily from the terminus in Burt St at 1000, with an extra tour at 1045 at weekends and holidays. The Historical Society has a display at the station, open daily 0900–1200.

In Sutherland St is the **Mt Charlotte Reservoir** and Lookout. The reservoir, one of the greatest hydraulic engineering works in the world, is the remarkable design of Charles Yelverton O'Connor, the state's water engineer. Water was scarcer than gold in Kalgoorlie in the early 20th century, and O'Connor's brilliant but seemingly impossible plan was to pipe water across the desert from Mundaring, near Perth, where the Helena River had been dammed. Despite ongoing criticism, enormous obstacles and five years of construction, on 22 Jan, 1903, water gushed from pipes on Mt Charlotte to fill the reservoir. The water had travelled for ten days through eight pumping stations and a 340-m climb – a journey of 560 km. Water has flowed ever since. Distressed by the criticism of the experts who said it would never work, however, O'Connor committed suicide only days before his amazing scheme was put into operation.

You can't go to Kalgoorlie without at least seeing a game of two-up (coin-tossing). It is illegal almost everywhere else except in casinos and on The One Day of the Year (Anzac Day). In Kalgoorlie the law is more liberally interpreted and there is a permanent floating Bus Two-Up School. This is held in a corrugated iron ring in the bush every afternoon from 1600. The tourist office will give you the current details.

TOURS

To the north of Kalgoorlie lies a series of **ghost towns** such as Bonnievale, Grants Patch, Broad Arrow and Ora Banda. If you would like to try your own luck, there is a **self-prospecting for gold** package tour out at the Boorara Fossicking Area, 18 km from Kalgoorlie. You can hire a metal detector from the Visitor Centre to increase your chances of striking gold, and there is even a gold prospecting package which can be bought from the tourist centre so that you can camp on the lease.

DAY TRIPS

In the bush around Kalgoorlie there are over 60 species of eucalyptus to be found, including many flowering varieties. The wildflowers are outstanding July–Oct. **Goongarrie National Park** covers nearly 50,000 ha, including large areas of mulga, an arid habitat of rough, sparse grassland. The park can be reached by travelling north towards Menzies and turning east on the signed gravel road (reasonable standard). Spring is the best time to visit.

Tourist brochures like to refer to **Coolgardie** as the best-known ghost town in Australia, but a town with 690 inhabitants can hardly be said to have given up the ghost. Mark you, the town is not what it was at its peak in 1896, when the gold rush meant there were 23 hotels, eight newspapers, two stock exchanges and six banks to service a population of some 20,000 within the town and probably half as many again in the surrounding area. At the time it was the third-largest town in Western Australia and regarded as civilisation, while Kalgoorlie, then known as Hannans, was the wild frontier.

Everything you go to see in Coolgardie revolves around gold. Discoveries started in 1892 when Arthur Bayley and William Ford found alluvial gold on Fly Flat. Then Paddy Hannan registered the Kalgoorlie claim and the gold rush was on. It was relatively short-lived; by 1902 the gold was starting to run out. The wild days were over and the town started to slide into oblivion, as did the prospectors. Arthur Bayley may have struck it rich, but he died by the time he was 31.

The most imposing building in town, solid Victorian architecture at its best, is the **Warden's Court** in Bayley St, built in 1898 using local stone. It contains the tourist office, the Mining Registrar's office and the courthouse. One good way of getting an understanding of the town is by way of Goldfields Exhibition, staged here by the Tourist Bureau. It is open 0900–1700 daily and it is much better than most efforts of this kind. Among the fascinating photographs is one showing Herbert Hoover, who spent time out here before going back to the United States and becoming president.

The **railway station** in Woodward St was built in 1876 and closed in 1971 when the standard-gauge railway was relocated north of the town. It is now a museum, open daily 0900–1700, and has a dramatic account of the Modesto Varischetti rescue from a flooded gold mine in 1907.

Another memento of early goldfields' life is **Warden Finnerty's residence** in Hunt St. This dates from 1894 and it was here that John Michael Finnerty, warden and resident magistrate of the Coolgardie goldfields, lived and meted out justice. The house has now been restored by the National Trust, but as it is only open in the hottest part of the day (Mon–Thur, Sat 1300–1600 and Sun 1000–1600), when sightseeing is not to be recommended, you may have to be satisfied with admiring it from the outside. Next door is the **gaol tree** to which prisoners who were awaiting trial were chained – it makes for a good photograph.

The broad main street is still wide enough to turn a camel train. The early gold fields were supplied by camels and you can repeat that experience at the Camel Farm, 3 km to the west and open daily 0900–1700.

Coolgardie Tourist Bureau, Bayley St; tel: 9026 6090.

Coolgardie Caltex Motel $ 110 Bayley St; tel: 9026 6049.
Coolgardie Caravan Park $ 99 Bayley St; tel: 9026 6009.
Coolgardie Motel $$ Bayley St; tel: 9026 6080. Also has an à la carte restaurant.
Coolgardie Motor Inn $$ 10 Bayley St; tel: 9026 6002.
Gold Rush Lodge $ 75 Bayley St; tel: 9026 6446.

WHERE NEXT?

South lies the Southern Ocean, Esperance and the coastal national parks (see pp. 381–389). Westwards is the state capital, Perth (p. 366) and its neighbour Fremantle (p. 376).

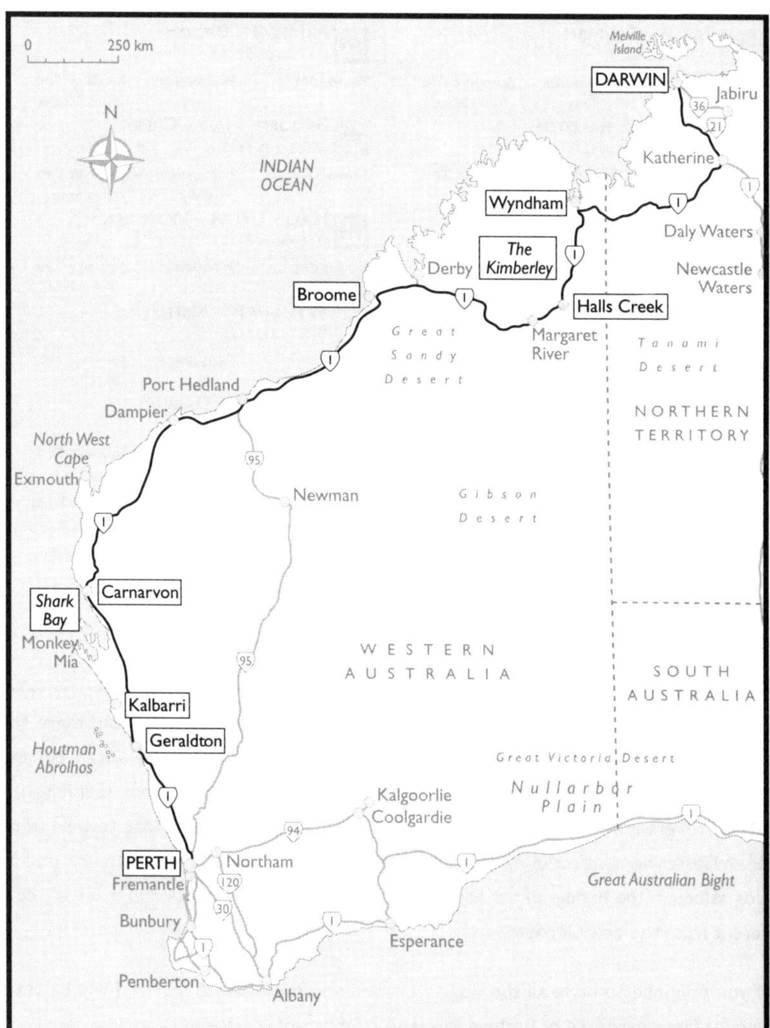

In discussing the journey from Perth to Darwin you need to consider the distance involved. On the quickest route it is over 4000 km. Yes, it can be done, but it is time intensive and it is definitely not recommended if you are on a time budget.

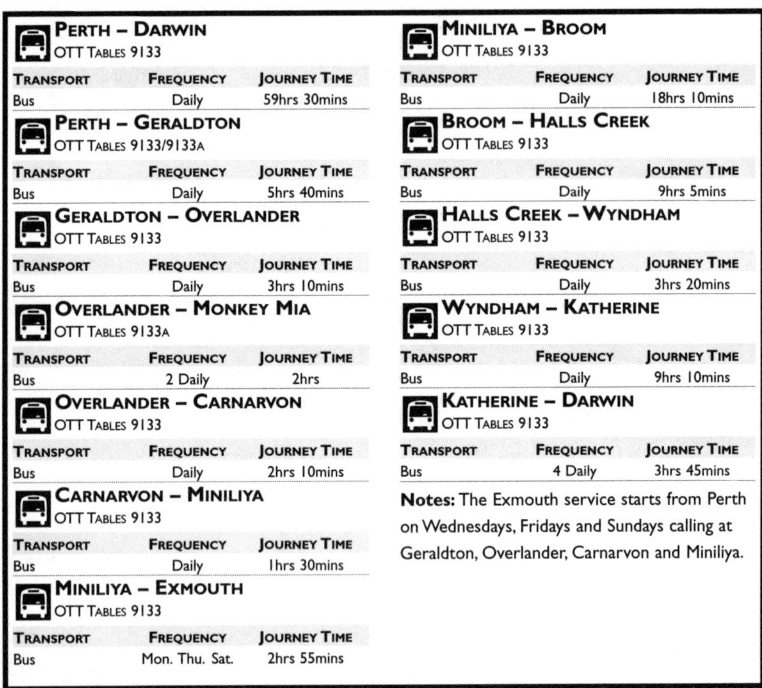

PERTH – DARWIN
OTT TABLES 9133

TRANSPORT	FREQUENCY	JOURNEY TIME
Bus	Daily	59hrs 30mins

PERTH – GERALDTON
OTT TABLES 9133/9133A

TRANSPORT	FREQUENCY	JOURNEY TIME
Bus	Daily	5hrs 40mins

GERALDTON – OVERLANDER
OTT TABLES 9133

TRANSPORT	FREQUENCY	JOURNEY TIME
Bus	Daily	3hrs 10mins

OVERLANDER – MONKEY MIA
OTT TABLES 9133A

TRANSPORT	FREQUENCY	JOURNEY TIME
Bus	2 Daily	2hrs

OVERLANDER – CARNARVON
OTT TABLES 9133

TRANSPORT	FREQUENCY	JOURNEY TIME
Bus	Daily	2hrs 10mins

CARNARVON – MINILIYA
OTT TABLES 9133

TRANSPORT	FREQUENCY	JOURNEY TIME
Bus	Daily	1hrs 30mins

MINILIYA – EXMOUTH
OTT TABLES 9133

TRANSPORT	FREQUENCY	JOURNEY TIME
Bus	Mon. Thu. Sat.	2hrs 55mins

MINILIYA – BROOM
OTT TABLES 9133

TRANSPORT	FREQUENCY	JOURNEY TIME
Bus	Daily	18hrs 10mins

BROOM – HALLS CREEK
OTT TABLES 9133

TRANSPORT	FREQUENCY	JOURNEY TIME
Bus	Daily	9hrs 5mins

HALLS CREEK – WYNDHAM
OTT TABLES 9133

TRANSPORT	FREQUENCY	JOURNEY TIME
Bus	Daily	3hrs 20mins

WYNDHAM – KATHERINE
OTT TABLES 9133

TRANSPORT	FREQUENCY	JOURNEY TIME
Bus	Daily	9hrs 10mins

KATHERINE – DARWIN
OTT TABLES 9133

TRANSPORT	FREQUENCY	JOURNEY TIME
Bus	4 Daily	3hrs 45mins

Notes: The Exmouth service starts from Perth on Wednesdays, Fridays and Sundays calling at Geraldton, Overlander, Carnarvon and Miniliya.

You could drive as far north as Carnarvon (see p. 418), and then fly from there to Darwin. Or drive to Carnarvon and come back by the inland route which passes through Gascoyne, Meeberrie, Billabalong, Mullewa (just inland from Geraldton), Morawa, Perenjori, Wubin, Northam and then into Perth. None of those towns listed after Gascoyne consists of much more than two houses, a pub, a petrol station and a dog asleep in the middle of the road, but it is a taste of the outback and it is very different from the coastal route.

If you continue to drive all the way to Darwin you must realise that you will be traversing large expanses of nothing followed by much of the same. Along the way you will visit Broome (see p. 423) and Halls Creek, but it is, as they say, a long way between drinks. Combining driving with flying is the way to go.

PERTH – CARNARVON
OTT TABLES 9133

TRANSPORT	FREQUENCY	JOURNEY TIME
Bus	Daily	11hrs 55mins

PERTH – GERALDTON
OTT TABLES 9133/9133A

TRANSPORT	FREQUENCY	JOURNEY TIME
Bus	Daily	5hrs 40mins

GERALDTON – OVERLANDER
OTT TABLES 9133

TRANSPORT	FREQUENCY	JOURNEY TIME
Bus	Daily	3hrs 10mins

OVERLANDER – MONKEY MIA
OTT TABLES 9133A

TRANSPORT	FREQUENCY	JOURNEY TIME
Bus	2 Daily	2hrs

OVERLANDER – CARNARVON
OTT TABLES 9133

TRANSPORT	FREQUENCY	JOURNEY TIME
Bus	Daily	2hrs 10mins

Notes: The Perth to Exmouth service starts from Perth on Wednesdays, Fridays and Sundays calling at Geraldton, Overlander, Carnarvon and Miniliya.

ROUTE DETAIL

The main route simply follows Hwy 1 on this section of its route around Australia. From Perth to Geraldton is 423 km, and Carnarvon a further 481 km. Two highlights, however, are major detours from the highway: the turn-off to Kalbarri is 100 km north of Geraldton, while a further 179 km along Hwy 1 is Overlander Roadhouse and the turn-off for Denham and Monkey Mia (130 km from Hwy 1 to Denham). Total: approx 1,300 km, excluding local explorations.

Perth – Shark Bay

The Indian Ocean and Dolphins

The coastline north of Perth is barely known compared with its Queensland counterpart on the east coast, but it has some of the finest marine attractions in the world – from diving on old shipwrecks and excellent surfing to the thrill of feeding wild dolphins. The area around Geraldton is scenic and appealing, while Shark Bay is a World Heritage Site with some truly unique habitats.

GERALDTON

Geraldton, a popular holiday location, is 421 km north of Perth and 481 km south of Carnarvon, which in Western Australia are not considered formidable distances. It calls itself Sun City, and as it boasts an average of eight hours of sunshine a day, this is a fair claim. It also has good beaches, good fishing, splendid scenery, many restaurants and lots of accommodation.

In 1846, the Gregory brothers led an expedition to open up vast areas in the district. This was the start of a long period of determined Aboriginal resistance to European settlement, a conflict which, in truth, is not yet totally resolved.

The first official airmail service in Australia was established in 1921 between Geraldton and Derby.

The best way to get an idea of the town is to follow the **Geraldton Heritage Trail**, a 30-km driving tour of both the natural and cultural heritage of Geraldton. There are 30 points of interest included and by the time you have finished you will have a good overall feel for the place.

Geraldton has had a fairly exciting history. Three major vessels were wrecked on these coasts: the *Batavia* (1629), the *Zuydorp* (1712) and the Zeewijk (1727) from the Dutch East India Company mariners pioneering Indian Ocean sea routes. The **Geraldton Maritime Museum** on Marine Terrace has a fascinating display of material from these and other wrecks, and items recovered from the campsites set up by survivors. Open Mon–Sat 1000–1700, Sun 1300–1700.

Next door is the original old railway building, built to serve the Geraldton–Northampton railway in 1879. This was the first government railway building in Western Australia. Now it has been converted into **Geraldton Museum** and is one of the best museums of its kind in the country, with excellent natural and cultural displays. Open daily 1000–1700.

The **Residency** was built by convict labour in 1861 for the Government Resident of the town – a sort of governor appointed by direct authority of the British government. This residence, splendid in comparison to the rest of the town's buildings, became a hospital in 1924 and later a community centre.

Lobster Capital of the World

Geraldton is famous for cray fishing. It calls itself the lobster capital of the world and claims the largest lobster fleet on the west coast, but the crustaceans caught in the area in such numbers lack nippers, so technically 'lobster' is incorrect – these are crayfish. The market for them boomed in the 1970s, particularly due to American demand. They were renamed rock lobsters so that the American market would not confuse them with the crawfish, native to the rivers and bayous of the southern states.

Inland, along Cathedral Dr, is the truly wonderful **St Francis Xavier Cathedral**, probably the best example of the work of the architect-turned-priest, Monsignor John Hawes. He began the design before he came to Geraldton in 1915 and work started the following year. Progress was hampered by the sparseness of the population and religious politics, and the cathedral was finally completed in 1938. It is most odd, yet charming, in that it seems to have borrowed its styles from other cathedrals with both a catholic and Catholic abandon. It is one of the most interesting religious buildings in Australia and is just as fascinating on the inside as it is on the outside. There is a John Hawes Heritage Trail where you can trace his other works, and the tourist office will provide you with a map.

Famous Names in Geraldton

Edith Cowan was born in Geraldton in 1861 and was, in 1921, elected to the Western Australia Legislative Assembly as Australia's first woman member of parliament.

The **Rev. C. G. Nicolay**, who arrived as Anglican chaplain in 1870, was an English eccentric in the grand manner. He tried, but failed, to establish a coffee plantation and then became editor of the *Western Australian Times* in Perth. He wrote The *Handbook of Western Australia* in 1876 and was responsible for the creation of an Aboriginal reserve of 20,235 ha in the Upper Murchison district in 1878. He also founded Western Australia's first public museum.

Novelist **Randolph Stow** was born in Geraldton in 1935 and his novel The *Merry-Go-Round in the Sea* is set in the town.

Out to the west of the town, the **Port Moore Lighthouse** was built in 1878 and stands 34 m high (an earlier lighthouse – Bluff Point – was destroyed by fire in 1952). The **Lighthouse Keeper's Cottage** in Chapman Rd was built in 1876 and is now the headquarters of the Geraldton Historical Society. Open Thur only.

Geraldton has some excellent surfing. In the summer it needs a strong breeze to build up the waves, but in winter the waves are up to 2–3 m at spots such as Flat Rocks, Greenough, Coronation, PipeLine and Back Beach.

Tourist Bureau, Bill Sewell Complex, Chapman Rd; tel: 9921 3999. Sited in what was the Old Victoria District Hospital, built in 1884.
Geraldton Tourist www.wn.com.au/tourism/
Geraldton Historical Society bilby.wn.com.au/gol/Services/GHS/ghs_home.htm

Abrolhos Reef Lodge $$ 126 Brand Highway; tel: 9921 3811.
Batavia Motor Inn $$ 54 Fitzgerald St; tel: 9921 3500.
Club Sun City Resort $$ 137 Cathedral Ave; tel: 9921 6111.
Drummond Cove Holiday Park $$ NW Coastal Highway; tel: 9938 2524; Internet: www.wn.com.au/dcovehp/. 10 minutes north of the town. Set in the bush facing the beach.
Geraldton Goodwood Lodge $$ Tel: 9921 5666. 18 self-catering suites with ocean views.
Hacienda Motel $$ Durlacher St; tel: 9921 2155.
Mariner Hotel Motel $$ 298 Chapman Rd; tel: 9921 2544.
Queens Hotel $$ 97 Durlacher St; tel: 9921 1064.
Wintersun Hotel $$ 441 Chapman Rd; tel: 9923 1211.

Beach Break Bar & Grill $ 166 Chapman Rd; tel: 9964 3382.
Belvedere Café & Restaurant $ 149 Marine Ter; tel: 9921 7266.
Boatshed Seafood Restaurant $$ 357 Marine Ter; tel: 9921 5500. Seven nights a week. Not lunch. Licensed.
Cruisers Restaurant $$ 6 Armstrong St; tel: 9964 1666.
Cuisine Connection $ 56 Durlacher St; tel: 9964 2289.
Fiddlers Restaurant $$ 103 Marine Ter; tel: 9921 6644.
Golden Coins Chinese Restaurant $$ 198 Marine Ter; tel: 9921 7878.
Huckleberry's Bar & Grill $$ 298 Chapman Rd; tel: 9921 2544.
Jade House Chinese Restaurant $ 57 Marine Ter; tel: 9964 1222.
Lemon Grass Restaurant $ 18 Snowdon St; tel: 9964 1172.
Los Amigos Mexican Restaurant $$ 105 Durlacher St; tel: 9964 1900.

Reflection Restaurant $$ Foreshore Dr; tel: 992 12921.
Rose Chinese Restaurant $ 9 Forrest St; tel: 9921 5645.
Skeetas Garden Restaurant $$ 9 George Rd; tel: 9964 1619.
Tanti's Restaurant $$ 174 Marine Ter; tel: 9964 2311.

DAY TRIPS

Geraldton is in the centre of one of the richest native flora regions in the world, which makes it a perfect base for **wildflower walking** or **driving tours** throughout the year, although July and Oct are the favourite months. The Tourist Bureau has maps, information, brochures and booklets on all wildflower sites and can provide last-minute information.

Surrounding the town to the north, east and south is the **Shire of Greenough**, named after the scenic river which winds through it. Its next-door neighbour is the equally beautiful Chapman Valley. The areas known as the Front and Back Flats were once vast lagoons that were gradually cut off from the sea and then filled with alluvial soil brought down by the meandering and frequently flooding river, resulting in an extremely fertile land.

Greenough is famous for its leaning trees (Eucalyptus camaldulensis) which bend themselves into fascinating shapes to escape the salt blown in from the sea. Their shape comes not from constant wind but their sensitivity to the salt content of the wind.

The **Greenough Hamlet**, with its 11 original buildings, including the police station and courthouse, store, cottage, churches, presbytery, convent and schoolhouses, is the only such collection of original buildings to be found in Australia.

The **Greenough Walkway Heritage Trail**, a distance of 57 km, begins at the Pioneer Museum and ends at the picturesque Ellendale Pool, a favourite picnic spot for locals and travellers alike.

The **Houtman Abrolhos Islands**, 80 km west of Geraldton, is an extraordinary series of about 100 small islands on the edge of the continental shelf. They run from North Island to the Pelsaert group. None of the islands rises more than 14 m above sea-level and their treacherous reefs have wrecked many ships.

The Abrolhos is where survivors of the wreck of the *Batavia* came ashore – some of them managed to get to Jakarta by ship's boat, a most remarkable achievement – and thus it is probably the site of the first White settlement in Australia. Sadly, it was also the scene of murder most foul when some of the survivors turned on the others. Later, a Dutch expedition returned and hung some of those remaining and marooned two of the mutineers, Wouter Loos and Jan Pelgrom, on the mainland at Kalbarri. Although no one knows exactly what became of them, there is genetic evidence that they integrated with the local Aboriginal people.

The islands boast sea eagles, turtles, a myriad fish, bronze whaler sharks, dolphins and lots of crayfish. In the crystal-clear water around the islands there is clear visibility down to 92 m (50 fathoms).

No visitor is allowed to stay the night on the islands, but there are day tours for skin diving, fishing, surfing or just sightseeing – the tourist office has details.

KALBARRI

Kalbarri is on the coast, 66 km from the turn-off on Hwy 1 and the setting-off point for **Kalbarri National Park**. This park covers 186,000 ha and is divided by the 100-km-long Murchison River which has cut spectacular gorges through the rock – The Loop, Z Bend, Ross Graham Lookout and Hawks Head. All these gorges are well signposted and access is via well-maintained gravel roads and well-marked trails. During the wildflower season the park puts on an amazing display – more than 850 varieties have been discovered here.

To the south of the town the road is fine to Wittecarra Gully – there is a cairn there to mark the site of the first permanent landing of Europeans – but after that it is unsealed and uneven, and care should be taken.

In Kalbarri itself, the pelicans are fed on the river bank along Grey St every morning at 0845. Local volunteers give a brief account of these birds as they feed them fish. Another species of bird is to be found along Red Bluff Rd. **Rainbow Jungle** (open Tues–Sat 0900–1700, Sun 1000–1530) is a parrot breeding centre and has a successful programme for breeding Australia's endangered species.

Cruise up the Murchison River on the **Kalbarri River Queen** (tel: 9937 1104) or propel yourself in a hired canoe from **Kalbarri Canoe Safaris** (tel: 9937 1245).

i *Tourist Information Office*, Allen Community Centre, Grey St; tel: **9937 1104.**

SHARK BAY

Shark Bay is a series of islands and semi-enclosed gulfs divided by the Peron Peninsula. With 1,500 km of coastline and covering 30,000 sq km, it is half land and half sea, and has been declared a World Heritage Site.

Aboriginal people inhabited the bay area for thousands of years and evidence of their presence can still be seen in numerous cave shelters and shell middens around the peninsula. They were probably among the first Australian Aboriginals who had contact with Europeans. The first Europeans came here in Oct 1616, when Dutchman Captain Dirk Hartog landed at Cape Inscription and left behind an inscribed pewter plate to record the fact. Then, in 1627, the Dutch ship *Gulden Zeepaard*, en route to Indonesia, ran too far south and travelled along 1,700 km of Australia's coastline. That was an accident, but the discovery was carefully recorded on Dutch maps of the day. Dirk Hartog was followed 81 years later by another Dutch explorer, Captain William de Vlamingh, who replaced the original pewter plate with one of his own. (The Hartog pewter plate is in the Rikjsmuseum in Amsterdam, while that of de Vlamingh is on show at Fremantle Maritime Museum, see p. 380) Shark Bay was given its name by English navigator William Dampier in 1699 after he caught a 3.4-m shark there.

The nomenclature in this area gets a little complicated. It is generally known as the Gascoyne area and extends up the coast past Carnarvon to the Ningaloo Reef. But this is not enough for those trying to market tourism and now we are told this is the Outback Coast. The problem is, none of the locals know what you are talking about when you mention the name.

As Shark Bay is at the northern extreme of the southern wildflower varieties and at the southern extreme of the northern varieties it has the longest wildflower season of any part of Western Australia, with over 700 species of flowering plants, of which many are exclusive to the World Heritage Site.

Denham, on the west side of the Peron Peninsula, is the westernmost town in Australia. It is a good base from which to explore the area, including the miracle of Monkey Mia. To reach Denham, and thus Shark Bay, turn off Hwy 1 opposite the Overlander Roadhouse: this brings you to two peninsulas that run parallel to the coast. The first, Peron, runs out past the Hamelin Pool and Shell Beach to Denham, Monkey Mia and finally the lighthouse. The seaward peninsula is somewhat longer and eventually ends up as Dirk Hartog Island.

i **Denham Shark Bay Tourist Centre**, 53 Knight Ter; tel: 9948 1253.

An alternative to driving is to take the Dolphin Express hovercraft from Carnarvon, which runs every day. Or you can fly: Western Airlines and Skywest Airlines offer regular air services to Denham-Shark Bay from Perth.

Department of Conservation and Land Management (CALM), 67 Knight Ter, Denham; tel: 9948 1208. CALM is responsible for managing François Peron National Park, Hamelin Pool Marine Nature Reserve, Shark Bay Marine Park and the numerous island nature reserves in the bay. Contact them for information before you visit.
Shark Bay Tourist Association www.sharkbay.asn.au/. An excellent site and an example of how it should be done.
Monkey Mia Dolphin Resort
www.monkeymia.com.au/resort/index.html

Bay Lodge $$ 95 Knight Ter, Denham: tel: 9948 1278; Internet: www.baylodge.com.au. Beachfront accommodation made from shell brick constructed from shells from the famous Shell Beach.
Blue Dolphin Caravan Park $ 5 Hamelin Rd, Denham; tel: 9948 1385. On-site vans, many with en suite, some with air-conditioning.
Denham Seaside Caravan Park $ Knight Ter, Denham beachfront; tel: 9948 1242.
Denham Villas $$ 4 Durlacher St, Denham; tel: 9948 1264. Each villa is fully self-contained, including kitchen, bathroom and laundry.
Heritage Resort Hotel Shark Bay $$ Durlacher St, cnr Knight Ter, Denham; tel: 9948 1133; Internet: www.sharkbay.asn.au/members/heritage/
Monkey Mia Dolphin Resort $$$ Monkey Mia; tel: 9948 1320.
Shark Bay Caravan Park $ 4 Spaven Way, Denham; tel: 9948 1387.
Shark Bay Holiday Cottages $ Knight Ter, Denham; tel: (08) 9948 1206.
Tradewinds Holiday Village $$ 3 Knight Ter, Denham; tel: 9948 1222. New waterfront apartments.
YHA of WA $ Monkey Mia Bay Lodge; tel: 9948 1278.

Bay Café and Takeaway $ 69 Knight Ter, Denham; tel: 9948 1308. Locally caught snapper and whiting and great ocean views from a shady pergola.
Bough Shed $$ The Monkey Mia Dolphin Resort; tel: 9948 1171. Open daily, breakfast, lunch and dinner. Licensed.
Old Pearlers Restaurant Knight Ter; tel: 9948 1373. The

only restaurant in the world built entirely from coquina shells carved from Shell Beach. Fresh local seafood with crabs and crayfish in season.

HIGHLIGHTS

About 30 km after turning off Hwy 1 is the Hamelin Pool Telegraph Station, originally built in 1884 and now a visitor's centre for **Hamelin Pool Marine Nature Reserve**. Evidence of the beginnings of life on earth can be found in these saline waters. Hamelin Pool is one of only two places in the world where living marine stromatolites are known to occur, and it is the only place where they can easily be seen from shore.

Microscopic organisms – invisible to the human eye – concentrate and recycle nutrients which combine with sedimentary grains to form domes of rock-like materials known as stromatolites. Stromatolites first colonised the shallow waters of Hamelin Pool only 2,000–3,000 years ago, but the organisms that built them were the earliest forms of life on earth, with a lineage dating back 3,500 million years. A wooden boardwalk with informative panels lets you view the stromatolites without damaging them. They may be the first expression of life on earth but they are not enthralling to look at.

Shell Beach, on the Hamelin–Denham road, has been formed by countless tiny white shells of the burrowing bivalve Fragum erugafum. Some of the shell deposits are up to 10 m deep and the beach, depending how you measure it, runs for nearly 100 km.

Nanga Station, 50 km before Denham, was built from shell blocks cut from a nearby quarry. The half- million-acre sheep station also has a bottle-shop licence and restaurant. **Nanga Wildlife Park** offers a glimpse of Australia's native fauna, including kangaroos, dingoes, emus and even crocodiles. Station tours are available and catamarans, sailboards and dinghies can be hired on the beach.

Denham was once a thriving pearling town, boasting the only street in the world to be paved in pearl shell. Several buildings, including St Andrews Church and the Old Pearler Restaurant on Knight Terrace, have been built of local shell blocks. Denham has become the centre of Shark Bay's tourism and fishing industries.

Manta rays, turtles and other aquatic life are all easy to view in Shark Bay because of the clarity of the waters. The bay is home to some of the world's near-extinct or endangered marine life, including over 10,000 dugong, the most secure colony of these ungainly but endearing mammals left on earth. The dugong (a Malay name)

THE DOLPHINS OF MONKEY MIA

For almost 30 years wild bottle-nosed dolphins have made a ritual of visiting Monkey Mia, which has become one of the most important dolphin research centres in the world. It started back in the 1960s when a visitor out fishing began feeding one of the dolphins from a boat. Other dolphins soon joined in and over three generations have become so adapted that they now swim right into the beach to be fed. They truly appear to enjoy and understand this relationship with humans.

Most mornings, small groups of dolphins visit the beach to interact with visitors, who can walk among them in the shallows and feed them under the supervision of the park rangers. They are fed only freshly caught local fish and never more than one-third of their daily requirement, to ensure that they do not become dependent on human hand-outs. Dolphins quite often offer visitors fish which they themselves have caught in return. Many have developed a technique of carrying a sponge on their beak; this is thought to be used as a tool for fossicking among the sea-grass beds for food.

A separate section of the beach is set aside where visitors can swim with the dolphins and observe their antics. The dolphins show a marked attraction towards heavily pregnant women.

It is important to remember that Monkey Mia's dolphins are wild animals and must support themselves in an environment that can be hostile and dangerous. The young calves must learn natural behaviour from their mother, to ensure that they know how to survive in the wild. Too much feeding and long periods at the beach would significantly reduce these vital lessons.

Since 1984, over a dozen scientists from Australia, North America and Europe have been involved in research here. Most of the research focuses on the offshore population of over 400 animals, but with particular emphasis on the 100-plus dolphins who frequent the beach. Researchers investigate different aspects of dolphin ecology, reproduction and behaviour, including male and mother–calf relationships, juvenile social development, ranging patterns, community structure, habitat and diet. A catalogue of fin pictures helps identify each animal.

Monkey Mia is 27 km north-east of Denham. There is a small entrance charge, and the place to start is at the Dolphin Information Centre on the beach (run by the National Park and Wildlife Service and not a commercial organisation). A leaflet outlines the way in which you should approach and feed these most attractive of animals. There are problems looming with the massive increase of visitors and it is likely that some sort of rationing control and booking system will be introduced. Check before you go.

is one of two surviving sirenians, or sea cows, the other being the manatee. They live for 70 years, measure about 2.7 m and weigh up to 400 kg. It is possible the dugong is the origin of the mermaid myth.

Dugongs spend much of their time grazing on the soft and delicate sea grasses. Females do not calf until they are at least 10 years old, then they bear a single calf every 3 to 7 years after a gestation of 13 months. Mothers are attentive and care for their young for up to 2 years, communicating with them through bird-like chirps and high pitched squeaks and squeals. Calves never venture far from their mothers and frequently ride on their back, particularly when danger threatens. At Monkey Mia there is the rare chance to go on a dugong-watching cruise, travelling aboard a specially equipped sailing catamaran that brings you close to dugongs in the wild. This cruise operates every day from the Monkey Mia Dolphin Resort jetty.

Between Denham and Monkey Mia is the **François Peron National Park**, for which you need a 4-wheel-drive vehicle if you wish to explore it properly. Several tours operate out of Denham, which is the way to see the park with the least fuss. The park is 52,500 ha of true wilderness, with salt lakes and arid scenery.

WHERE NEXT?

Carnarvon is the base from which to set off for two of Australia's most incredible, yet least-known natural wonders: Ningaloo Reef and Mt Augustus (p. 421).

CARNARVON

Carnarvon is pretty much a long way from anywhere. The Tourist Board tries its best by referring to the town as 'the sun's winter home' which is romantic but not inaccurate.

The Dutch navigator Dirk Hartog was probably the first European to examine the coast, in 1686. William Dampier, explorer and part-time pirate – not an uncommon combination of trades – followed in 1699 and reported that the country seemed barren and useless. He was the first whingeing Pom and thus set a tradition which persists to this day.

No settlers came until sheep stations were established in the 1870s, and in 1883 the township of Carvarvon was named after Lord Carnarvon, Secretary of State for the Colonies from 1866 to 1874.

Today, Carnarvon is the centre of a high-tech area; it is the satellite tracking station of the Overseas Telecommunications Commission, the base of Radio Australia and was a space vehicle tracking station operated by NASA for ten years until 1974. These are located in the Brown Range, 12 km behind the town. The huge satellite tracking station – locally called the Big Dish (it is 29.6 m across) – dominates the skyline and is in the process of becoming something of a historical monument because it was here that Australia received its first satellite broadcast.

Carnarvon is a prosperous town partly due to the influx of technicians, partly to the prawning industry and partly to the success of the irrigated fruit and vegetable farms near the mouth of the Gascoyne River. It does attract visitors but that is not a primary source of revenue. A whaling station continued operations until 1962, by which time the disappearance of the whales had made it uneconomic. However, now the whales are coming back, and Carnarvon has made a small industry out of watching them as they make their annual stately progression to and from their breeding grounds.

INFORMATION

Carnarvon Tourist Bureau, 90 Robinson St; tel: (08) 9941 1446.

INTERNET SITES Virtual tour of plantations along Gascoyne River. Part of Carnarvon Horticulture web site for fruit and vegetable growers on www.carnarvonhorticulture.org.au/virtual_tour.htm

ACCOMMODATION

Carnarvon Backpackers $ 50 Olivia Ter; tel: 9941 1095.

Carnarvon Caravan Park $ Robinson St; tel: 9941 8101.

Carnarvon Gateway Motel $$ 309 Robinson St; tel: 9941 1532.

Carnarvon Hotel Motel $$ 28 Olivia Ter; tel: 9941 1181.

Carnarvon Tourist Centre Caravan Park $ 90 Robinson St; tel: 9941 1438. Self-contained park cabins.

Fascine Lodge $$ David Brand Dr.; tel: 9941 2411. Swimming-pool.

Gascoyne Hotel Motel $$ 88 Olivia Ter; tel: 9941 1412.

Gateway Motel $$ 309 Robinson St; tel: 9941 1532.

Hospitality Inn $$ West St; tel: 9941 1600.

FOOD

This is not a gourmet destination. But there is more fresh fruit on sale than you would believe.

Dragon Pearl Chinese Restaurant $$ 17 Francis St; tel: 9941 1941.

Kingsford Restaurant $$ David Brand Dr.; tel: 9941 2411. Licensed; à la carte.

Schnappers $$ 309 Robinson Rd; tel: 9941 1532. Licensed; à la carte.

HIGHLIGHTS

Carnarvon's grassy waterfront goes by the strange name of The Fascine. Fascine is a Latin word meaning a bundle of sticks and in the early days these were used along the foreshore to stop erosion when the Gascoyne River was in full spate. Now it flows gently and is lined with palms, and in the evening is the most pleasant place in town.

CARNARVON

The original port of Carnarvon is part of the Carnarvon Heritage Precinct, which consists of One-Mile Jetty, Lighthouse Keeper's Cottage Museum, the Carnarvon Tramway and a memorial to Australia's worst naval disaster, the sinking of *HMAS Sydney*. The precinct is a continuing project run by amateurs who give up immense amounts of time to it; you can check progress on www.wn.com.au/cheritageg/news.htm.

One-Mile Jetty – almost 1500 m long – has a toy train running its length, giving a rather bumpy ride. The idea is that eventually – Real Soon Now – you will be able to take the train all the way from town to the jetty, which is on Babbage Island, 3.5 km out of town (take the turning at the Caltex petrol station and on past the lighthouse). The jetty was built in 1897, lengthened in 1904 and widened in 1912. It stopped being used by ships in 1966, fell into disrepair and was burnt by vandals in 1985. However, the locals set up a fund and rebuilt the jetty.

THE BIG BANANA

Carnarvon's Big Banana is what many might consider a visitor-repellent. The tourist board says: 'There is an exclusive list of Australian rural towns that feature a landmark "Big Something", whether it be the Big Pineapple, Big Crocodile, or Giant Ram. Carnarvon is among them with its vertically positioned Big Banana ... You won't miss it!' If you have any sort of luck, you will. Avert the gaze

The lighthouse on Babbage Island, named after English mathematician Charles Babbage, the father of computing, is a modern replacement of an original erected in 1897. **Lighthouse Keeper's Cottage** was built around 1900 and was used by the keeper and his family until the lighthouse was electrified in the 1970s. Community effort has seen to the preservation of the cottage, which is open daily 1000–1200 and 1400–1600 (tel: 9941 4309 to check times).

At **Westoby Banana Plantation** there are tours of a fully operational banana plantation, presented by an experienced guide. After the tour you can enjoy light lunches in a tropical garden setting. The plantation is on the left side of Robinson St as you enter town. Open daily 1000–1600, except Tues.

Pelican Point, 5km southwest, is a popular swimming and picnic spot. To get there follow the Babbage Island road and ignore the turn-off to the jetty near the lighthouse.

DAY TRIPS

The **Blowholes** were discovered in 1911 and are some 70 km north of Carnarvon.

Powerful jets of water are forced up with enormous pressure through the holes in the rock sometimes to a height of 20m. These can be immensely dangerous and people can get killed when a rogue wave hits - you must observe all the warning signs and act with prudence. You get there by way of the North West Coastal Hwy, or the Bibbawura Bore tracks. About 1 km south of the Blowholes lies a small reef adjacent to the island which contains tropical fish and shells.

Red Bluff is 71 km north of the Blowholes via a limestone coastal road. It has become a popular surfing spot, with waves ranging from 1 m to 6 m depending on the time of year.

There are two breathtaking natural phenomena in this corner of Western Australia, each very different but equally remarkable. They are not a casual day-trip but well worth the effort.

Mount Augustus is 480 km east of Carnarvon and an incredible sight. It's the world's largest monad rock, twice the size of Ayers Rock, yet it is almost unknown to tourists. There are several tours to Mount Augustus, both from Perth - a trip of several days - and from Carnarvon. If you are driving there yourself head first to Gascoyne Junction (173 km). Gascoyne Junction has one small pub which is genuine outback Australia and is also the general store. Not to be missed, as this is the last place you can get a cold beer. There is a 47-km track around Mount Augustus; it is an unsealed track but fine with a 2-wheel-drive vehicle provided the insurance covers you.

The North West Cape extends into the Indian Ocean to the north of Carnarvon, and running for 260 km off its western side is the **Ningaloo Reef**. If the Great Barrier Reef didn't exist this would be considered one of the great natural wonders of Australia. This reef, which the majority of tourists know nothing about, is not only the largest fringing coral reef in Australia, but also the largest reef in the world to be found so close to a continental landmass. It is about 20 m offshore at its nearest point and less than 7 km at its furthest. There are lots of safe deserted swimming beaches of white sand.

Take Hwy 1 (the North West Coastal Hwy) for 118 km until you get to the Minilya Road House. Turn left along Learmonth Minilya Road to the small resort of Coral Bay - 78 km - and then about the same distance on to Exmouth. These two towns give access to the reef.

Ningaloo is home to approximately 250 species of coral and 520 species of fish, and is an amazing place to see dugongs, greenback turtles and whale sharks. Whale sharks, the world's largest fish, visit the reef Mar–late May to feed on the spawn the spawn released by the coral. This is the only place in the world where they are known to appear regularly in any numbers, far enough inshore to be easily accessible to observers. In June–July and Oct–Nov you can watch the humpback whales as they make their stately progression to and from their breeding grounds. One of the companies that offers cruises and diving on the reef is **Exmouth Ningaloo Deep**, PO Box 757, Exmouth; tel: Heather on 9949 1663; e-mail: ningaloodeep@nwc.net.au

Where Next?

This is another point where the decision should be made whether to fly, drive on or turn back. To drive even to Broome (see p. 423) will take three days minimum and perhaps a week depending on how you push along. Unless you have time and enough to spare then you should consider flying.

Broome, at the southern tip in the Kimberley region, and once the pearling capital of the world, is both a very up-market resort and, in a sense, an alternative destination. It is also a long way from anywhere: 2230 km north of Perth and 1885 km south of Darwin.

The first inhabitants of the Broome area was a tribe of Aborigines called the Djugan and it is also very probable that the area was visited by Asian seafarers. In 1644, Dutch navigator Abel Tasman sighted the Australian coast near Broome, and in 1699, English navigator William Dampier landed somewhere near the town. His report on the area was so damning that other sailors stayed well clear of the area until the beginning of the 19th century.

Then came the discovery of rich pearling grounds off the coast. Despite the fact that it was dangerous and that cyclones ravaged the area, by 1925, the peak of the trade, some 350 luggers with 3000 men were working out of Broome. Often the divers went down to more than 27 m and there was an appalling death rate. Most of the good divers were Japanese and the number of Japanese graves in the cemeteries show how the divers suffered.

Plastics and artificial pearls almost totally killed the trade – by the late 1950s it was pretty much all over and Broome was almost deserted. The industry never quite died out, however; there are still some luggers fishing for young pearl oysters to supply stock for the cultured pearl farms at Kuri Bay and Cygnet, where a Japanese-Australian consortium has been operating since 1954.

You can see reminders of Broome's pearling past all over the town: in the houses built for the pearlers, in Chinatown, which was once home to 3000 Asians and is now the small commercial centre of the town; and in the Japanese cemetery.

ARRIVAL AND DEPARTURE

The airport handles scheduled domestic flights by Ansett and Qantas. **Broome Aviation** provides scheduled regular public transport services between Broome and Fitzroy Crossing, Halls Creek and Kununurra. **Skippers Aviation** provides scheduled regular public transport services between Broome and Derby, connecting with mainline services into and out of Broome.

Broome is trying to upgrade itself by having an international airport. So far it has the name, and complete customs, immigration and quarantine facilities in place. It has its own website at www.broomeair.com.au/html/flight.htm. International flights are still in the negotiation stage but are expected Real Soon Now.

INFORMATION

TOURIST OFFICE **Broome Tourist Bureau**, Cnr Bagot St and Broome Rd; tel: 922 222.

INTERNET SITE **Broome** ebroome.com/index2.htm

ACCOMMODATION

Broome Apartments $$ Park Court, Haas St; tel:1800 801 225; email:parkcourt@bigpond.com. Fully self-contained, air-conditioned 1-, 2- and 3-bedroom units. at moderate rates. Quiet central location opposite parklands. Weekly and off-season rates.

Broome Bird Observatory $$ Roebuck Bay, 18km from Broome; tel: 9193 5600. An active bird research facility with camping, chalet and budget accommodation. Opportunities for guest participation, plus regular interpretative tours.

Broome Motel $$ Frederick St; tel: 1800 683 867.

Broometime Lodge $ Forrest St; tel: 1800 804 322.

Kimberley Klub $ Frederick St; tel: 9192 3233. Shared and private rooms available. Prize-winning establishment.

Mangrove Hotel $$$ Carnarvon St; tel: 1800 094 818. Overlooking Roebuck Bay. Restaurant.

Ocean Lodge $$ Cable Beach Rd; .tel: 9193 7700. Opposite the Broome Aquatic Centre, between Chinatown and Cable Beach

Palms Resort $$$ Broome Town Beach; tel: 9192 1898. Set in a hectare of tropical gardens.

Roebuck Bay Hotel $ Carnarvon St; tel: 1800 098 824. In Chinatown on Roebuck Bay. Superior, standard and backpacker's accommodation.

Food

Beer & Satay Hut $$ Palms Resort, Walcott Street. Burgers, seafood, pizza in outdoor garden setting.

Bloom's Café $ Carnarvon, Chinatown; tel: 9193 6366. Open daily for breakfast, lunch and dinner.

Charters Restaurant $$ Mangrove Hotel, Carnarvon St; tel: 9192 1303. Magnificent view of Roebuck Bay.

Kimberley Kitchen $$ Nippon Inn, Dampier Ter, Chinatown. Open Tue–Sat.

Matso's Gallery & Coffee House $$ Hamersley St. Licensed.

Noodlefish $ Hamersley St. Thai food. Open 7 nights a week.

Tea House Thai Garden Dora and Saville Sts. Thai cuisine in a garden.

The Old Zoo Café Challenor Dr. Breakfast and lunch daily. In the old Pearl Coast Zoological Gardens.

Town Beach Café $$ Town Beach, Robinson St. Lunch and dinner in open air.

Highlights

Broome is a multicultural town because of the Japanese, Filipino and Malay pearl divers who were an essential part of its history. Chinatown, with its unique mixture of occidental and oriental buildings, has been restored and even the street signs are in five languages. The tourist office has a guide to a **Heritage Trail** through the town.

The **Broome Historical Society Museum** is housed in the old Customs House in Saville St. It is very small but extremely well done, without the over-ordered structure which is so off-putting in some museums - a real highlight of the town. Features include a display of pearling and many old photographs and files which piece together the town's fascinating history. Open Mon–Fri 1000–1600 (Apr–Nov) and sporadically Nov–Apr.

Movies with a Difference

Nightlife in Broome is not great but what there is, is unique. *Sun Pictures* in Chinatown is not a picture theatre – it is a picture garden. Opened in 1916, it claims to be the world's oldest theatre of its type. As it was the only entertainment in the area it was immensely popular and often enjoyed Saturday night crowds of over 600. You can still see movies under the stars and even bring a picnic dinner with you.

Captain Gregory's House was built in 1917 for the man

who operated one of Broomeís most successful pearling businesses. This fine example of early Broome architecture has now been converted to an art gallery. It is on the corner of Hamersley and Carnarvon Sts in the same grounds as Matso's Gallery and Broome Brewery.

Flying boat wrecks sunk by the Japanese air raid on Broome during World War II are about 1 km offshore from Town Beach and visible only on very low tides. Check with the Tourist Bureau for tide times and viewing information.

The **court house** in Hamersley St was originally a cable station, the terminus of the cable across the Timor Sea from Java, opened in 1889. Its presence in the town, however, is a complete accident: the teak building had been shipped from England the year before, but was intended for Kimberley, South Africa, not the Kimberleys, Australia!

Cable Beach, where the cable terminated, has talc white sand and runs for 22 km. The beach is unusual in that the sea will recede as much as 500 m at low tide. About 6 km from Broome rise the craggy red cliffs of **Gantheaume Point**. At low spring tide you can examine the dinosaurs' tracks embedded in the sandstone at the base of the cliffs – they are believed to date back about 130 million years. Near by is **Anastasia's Pool**, a small pool blasted from the sandstone by a pearler named Patrick Percy, who decided to make a safe bathing place for his arthritic wife.

During the 1980s, the 624-km of road from Port Hedland across the fringes of the Great Sandy Desert was sealed, sparking a minor tourist boom and occasioning the creation of the **Cable Beach Club** (tel: (091) 922 505) by Lord MacAlpine. A few kilometres outside Broome, this 5-star resort offers tropical rustic life with service to international standards. Lord MacAlpine eventually sold all his Australian interests, but the style and the ambience remain.

Broome is popular with bird-watchers, with the **Broome Bird Observatory** on Roebuck Bay rating as one of Australia's top non-breeding grounds for migrant Arctic waders from Siberia. Nearly 250 different types of birds are to be found in the area, and there are self-interpretative walks.

If you want to see how pearls are harvested the **Willie Creek Pearl Farm** in Lullfitz Dr., 35 km from Broome, has demonstrations of how it produces south-sea cultured pearls from the silver-lipped oyster. Shell displays and curios may be seen in several places around the town, including Shell House in Guy Street and Paspaley Pearling Company in Short St.

DAY TRIPS

Broome is the gateway to the vast Kimberley Region (see p. 428). Exploring it by car is almost always beyond the scope of most visitors, but there are plenty of easier trips.

To the south of Broome is **Eighty Mile Beach**. Unique among features named in this way, it is indeed 80 miles long (137 km, to be precise). This is where the Great Sandy Desert meets the Indian Ocean.

Beagle Bay is 118 km north of Broome – considered a short step in this part of the country. Beagle Bay church was built by Pallotine monks with raw materials from the area and completed in 1918. Its altar is beautifully decorated with shell pearl.

Beyond the Beagle Bay Reserve, the **Dampier Peninsula** has red pindan cliffs, azure waters and a wonderful variety of flora and fauna. Several Aboriginal communities offer bush-tucker walks and mud-crabbing tours. Access is by 4-wheel-drive only but there are a variety of day tours available from Broome. The Tourist Bureau has details.

Rowley Shoals, 260 km offshore, is on the edge of the continental shelf. This is one of the best diving areas in the world with magnificent coral gardens, where giant clams and large reef fish astound visitors. The Broome Tourist Bureau has a list of operators.

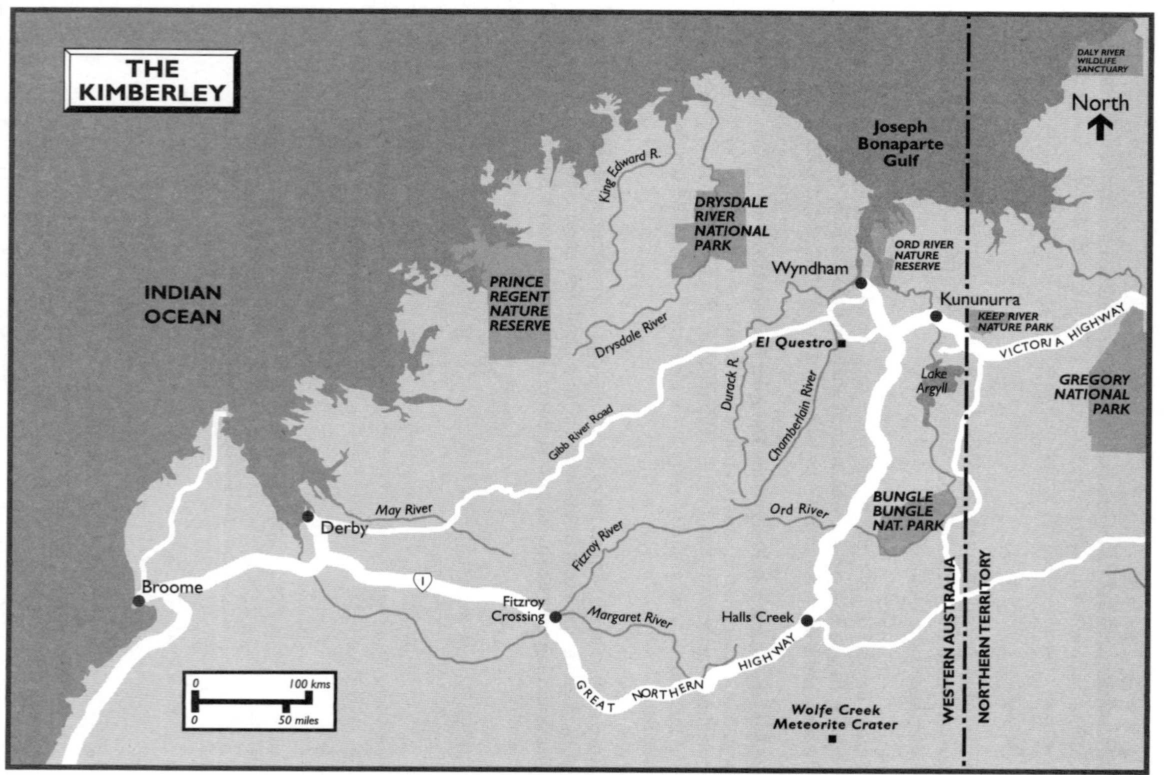
THE KIMBERLEY
DALY RIVER WILDLIFE SANCTUARY
North
Joseph Bonaparte Gulf
King Edward R.
DRYSDALE RIVER NATIONAL PARK
ORD RIVER NATURE RESERVE
Wyndham
Kununurra
KEEP RIVER NATURE PARK
VICTORIA HIGHWAY
INDIAN OCEAN
PRINCE REGENT NATURE RESERVE
Drysdale River
El Questro
Durack R.
Chamberlain River
Lake Argyll
GREGORY NATIONAL PARK
Gibb River Road
BUNGLE BUNGLE NAT. PARK
May River
Ord River
Derby
Fitzroy River
WESTERN AUSTRALIA
NORTHERN TERRITORY
Broome
1
Fitzroy Crossing
Margaret River
Halls Creek
GREAT NORTHERN HIGHWAY
0
100 kms
0
50 miles
Wolfe Creek Meteorite Crater

The Kimberley is unimaginably large, almost unknown to tourists and contains some of the best cattle country (and some of the biggest cattle stations) in the world. There are diamonds near Lake Argyle and gold at Halls Creek, rugged ranges, broad tidal flats, rainforest pockets, gorges and waterfalls. The Kimberley has them all. Yes, it is a tough trip to make. Yes, it is only for the truly adventurous. Yes, it is well worth the effort.

If you are going to this remote area, the best time is Apr–Sept, in the Dry. Temperatures are mild and the humidity low, you can almost guarantee there will be no rain and the skies are a bright clear blue much of the time. The night skies are superb for stargazing and offer great viewing of any comets or other objects that may be passing. The area is at its busiest during the coolest months of June and July, but there are those who believe that the Kimberley is at its very best just after The Big Wet: in early Mar it can be a green and verdant land. In the summer, outside temperatures can reach 52°C. If you have never experienced that sort of heat, and very few people have, breathing becomes difficult and anything but very lethargic movement utterly impossible. Dec–Feb is also the Wet and this is not a time to go exploring. Most of the rain comes thundering down over a period of 25 days in Jan–Feb, the roads are flooded and impassable and the main town, Halls Creek, is totally cut off.

GETTING THERE

Ansett offers regular daily flights to Halls Creek from Perth, Broome and Darwin. Driving yourself is the other option, but there is a daily bus service between Darwin and Broome along Hwy 1, (OTT table 9133) which is known on this remote stretch as the Great Northern Highway.

HALLS CREEK

Halls Creek lies on the northern edge of the Tanami Desert. It is roughly 2,800 km from Perth and 1,200 km from Darwin, and the closest large regional centre is Kununurra, 360 km to the north-east. It is indeed in the Never Never. As one of the most isolated towns in Western Australia, if you can say you have explored Halls Creek you are not only rare among tourists but rare among all Australians. Although the town is on Hwy 1 it is used mainly as an overnight stop by travellers, rarely as a destination in itself.

GOLD FEVER

Halls Creek came about, of course, because of gold. In 1872, the state government offered a reward of £5,000 to anyone finding gold which produced 10,000 oz within two years of the discovery.

There were several expeditions and one led by Charles Hall found payable gold near the head of the Elvire River in July 1885. The first gold rush in Western Australia was on in earnest. The reward was, of course, never paid: Halls Creek produced enough gold to satisfy the reward requirements but much of it was taken across the border to avoid paying tax at the customs stations on the coast. In the end Charles Hall received £500 and this only after a bitter legal battle.

As with so many towns in this area there is an old town and a new town. The new town was established in 1955, 15 km from the old site. The old town no longer exists except for a few mud foundations and a lot of empty bottles.

Halls Creek has a frontier atmosphere and it is a real part of the wild west – attending a rodeo here is another experience altogether. Although it is basically a Kimberley cattle town, Halls Creek is a base from which to see some rare distinctions and attractions. Nearest is **China Wall** which looks as though it was constructed like the Great Wall of China but is, in fact, a freak of nature. The weathered white quartz is set in the stone as if it were mortar, with the appearance of a wall running for many kilometres across country. It is 5 km east of the town and then about 1.5 km off the road.

Halls Creek Information Centre, Memorial Centre, Great Northern Hwy; tel: 9168 6262. NB: only open Apr–Sept, 0800–1600. Also has information on trips into the Kimberley to sights such as Wolf Creek Crater and the Bungle Bungles.
Internet Access: Halls Creek Telecentre tel: 9168 6658; email hctc@bigpond.com
Internet Site: Halls Creek
www.users.bigpond.com/hctc/default.htm

Halls Creek Caravan Park $ Roberta Ave; tel: 9168 6169. The only caravan park in Halls Creek.
Halls Creek Lodge $$ Cummins St, off Duncan Rd; tel: 9168 8999. At the site of Old Halls Creek, 15 km from town on Duncan Rd. The Lodge includes a restaurant and you can swim in a nearby dam.
Halls Creek Motel $$ 194 Great Northern Hwy; tel: 9168 6001.
Kimberley Hotel Motel $$ Tel: 9168 6101. Budget and backpacker accommodation is also available. Swimming pool and a restaurant.

Halls Creek Lodge $$ 15 km from town on Duncan Rd; tel: 9168 8999.
Kimberley Hotel Motel $$ Tel: 9168 6101.

WOLF CREEK CRATER

Wolf Creek Crater is claimed to be the second-largest meteorite crater on earth, having a diameter of 853 m and a depth of 61 m. It was probably formed about 2 million years ago, but Europeans did not 'discover' it until 1947.

The crater is located 151 km due south of Halls Creek. Access is along a dirt road and you will need a 4-wheel drive vehicle, so it is best to go on one of the many tours available (enquire at Halls Creek Information Centre). The road is normally only open May–Nov.

PURNULULU (BUNGLE BUNGLE) NATIONAL PARK

Known to Europeans only since 1983, the Bungle Bungles are mind-blowing, one of the finest natural sights in Australia. They are a series of massive rock towers in a sort of beehive shape, with tiger stripes in the form of horizontal banding produced by black lichens and orange silica. There is Aboriginal art here, too, and dramatic gorges and caves, within a park covering 280,000 ha.

The Bungle Bungles are pretty inaccessible. The first part of the journey is fine, 109 km north from Halls Creek, but then you have to turn east on the Spring Creek Track. This track is one of the worst in Australia - a country that specialises in desperate tracks - and although it is only 55 km long, it takes well over two hours to navigate it safely. You can only make it Apr–Oct. It is best to go on a guided tour with someone who knows the area very well (ask for information in Halls Creek). The Bungle Bungles make the trip well worth while.

EL QUESTRO AND EMMA GORGE

El Questro was developed in 1991 as a truly Australian holiday destination, designed to show visitors one of the world's last unspoilt frontiers. It is on the

ATTRACTIONS BETWEEN EL QUESTRO AND WYNDHAM

There are many **Aboriginal rock paintings** in the area. There is also a **prison tree**, a hollow tree in which Aboriginal prisoners were locked up en route to court. The **Grotto**, a rock-edged water hole near Wyndham, is a shaded, cool oasis.

eastern perimeter of the Kimberley and runs for approximately 80 km into the heart of the region. In old measurements the property covers a million acres.

The prices charged at El Questro are astronomical and intended for the jet set who will undoubted fly in. But there is affordable accommodation at El Questro's Emma Gorge Resort. The resort entrance is about 1 km off the Great Northern Hwy, 52 m before Wyndham.

Accommodation consists of tented cabins set in a landscaped area. The cabins each have two single beds and their raised roofs allow the tropical sounds and scents to filter through. They all have 240v power and fans for the warmer nights. This is a way of exploring part of the Kimberley without desperately, seriously, roughing it. Tel: 9169 1777.

WYNDHAM

Wyndham, on the Cambridge Gulf that runs into the Timor Sea, is the most northerly town and port in Western Australia. It is the terminus of the Great Northern Hwy, the end of the line.

Wyndham started as a port to service the Kimberley goldfields. It was also the point through which the telegraph line from Perth passed, and the Flying Doctor base for the region was established here in 1935. (Wyndham was attacked by Japanese aircraft in 1942, but there were no casualties.)

The summer climate is excessively hot and humid, and locals boast the highest per capita beer consumption in Australia. But Wyndham has its elusive charms. Arthur Upfield got it right when, in *Cake in the Hatbox* (1955), he wrote: 'For ten miles the track was almost level as it crossed the flats south of Wyndham, a ship sailing on a sea of grass and yellow and as tall as ripe wheat. Thereafter it proceeded up an ever narrowing valley between flat-topped ranges sparsely covered with stunted scrub and armoured with red and grey granite.'

The original town is now known as Wyndham Port, while a new town opened up 3 km away on the road to Kununurra. This second town is sometimes known as Wyndham Three Mile and sometimes as Wyndham East. The population of both towns together is well under 2,000.

Until 1985 the meatworks was Wyndham's main industry. Since this closed down the town has operated as a service centre for the pastoral industry, mining and tourism. The port also serves some large mango and banana plantations. It's a very quiet town. There is a **Heritage Walk** around the buildings in the old port area and the tourist office can provide a printed guide.

Isolated though it is from the mainstream, Wyndham has still fallen for the 'Big' syndrome which so afflicts Australian tourism. Near the entrance to the new town is the 20-m-long Big Crocodile. It's better to visit **Wyndham Crocodile Farm**, established to breed estuarine and salt water crocodiles commercially for their hides and meat. Set in scenic grounds, the farm is open to visitors and there are daily feedings.

Near the farm is the **Afghan cemetery**. This area was once totally dependent for supplies on camel trains operated by what were called Afghans. They were, in fact, nothing of the sort, coming mainly from Pakistan, but it is woven permanently into Australian folklore that they were Afghans and nothing is going to change it.

The **Five Rivers Lookout** to the east of the town is clearly signposted. It offers staggering views of the Kimberley over the five rivers (the Durack, King, Pentecost, Forrest and Ord) and the vast mudflats which run forever as far as the eye can see.

Wyndham Tourist Information Centre, Old Port Post Office, O'Donnell St; tel: 9161 1054.

K-Aus Accommodation $ 6 O'Donnell St; tel: 9161 1401.
Wyndham Caravan Park $ Baker St; tel: 91611064.
Wyndham Town Hotel $$ O'Donnell St; tel: 9161 1202.

Wyndham Community Club Hotel Great Northern Hwy; tel: 9161 1130.

WHERE NEXT?

The nearest points of civilisation either side of the Kimberley are Broome to the west (see p. 423) and Darwin to the north-east (see p. 348). About 600 km east along Hwy 1 is Katherine. From here it is 300 km north to Darwin or a mere 1,175 km south to Alice Springs (for the Alice–Darwin route, see p. 340).

Tasmania

Tasmania is Australia's smallest and most southerly state. But size is relative: including its 20 or so offshore islands, it is not far off the size of the Republic of Ireland or West Virginia, is on a par with Sri Lanka and is twice the size of the Netherlands. Nearly half a million people live on the island, mostly in Hobart, the capital, and Launceston in the north, the only other city. It has better preserved historical monuments than any other states and nowhere is more than 115 km from the sea, which makes it a most delightful place to visit. It is extremely easy to explore by car.

Tasmania is shaped like a triangle with two dots at the top, one on each side. These dots, which are King Island and the Furneaux Group, lie in the Bass Strait which separates Tasmania from the rest of Australia. Until something like 12,000 years ago they were part of a land bridge that connected mainland Australia and Tasmania. At the pointed end of the triangle which faces south, halfway between Tasmania and the Antarctic continent, is Macquarie Island which has, among other things, elephant seals and four million penguins.

Tasmania is named after the Dutch navigator Abel Janszoon Tasman, but he himself named it Van Diemen's Land, a name it kept until 1856. As commander of the ships *Heemskirk* and *Zeehan*, Tasman had been sent to discover the mysterious Southern Land by Antony Van Diemen, Governor-General of the Dutch East Indies Company. In Nov 1642 Tasman sighted the island's west coast. He landed on the Forestier Peninsula, near Blackmans Bay on the western bank of the Derwent River. One hundred and fifty years later the British came to make this a convict settlement and one of the furthest reaches of the British Empire.

At the time of the establishment of the first white settlement there were reckoned to be about 5,000 Aboriginal people in Tasmania. Flocks were set to graze on prime Aboriginal hunting land, and when hunting parties began to take sheep, whites indiscriminately killed Aborigines in retaliation. In about 1826 a group of Aboriginal men, seeking revenge for the rape of their women, speared a shepherd and killed 100 sheep. In return, a group of 30 unarmed Aborigines was killed by shepherds, and their bodies thrown over a cliff which is now misleadingly called Suicide Cove. In 1828 Governor Arthur declared martial law, expelling all Aboriginal people from the settled districts and, in practice, giving settlers a licence to shoot on sight. The British government,

TIGERS AND DEVILS

Because of its millennia of separation, Tasmania has a wildlife and flora uniquely its own. As well as its own indigenous kangaroo, it has the fearsome Tasmanian devil and that mystery animal, the marsupial Tasmanian tiger.

Tasmanian tigers were still common at the beginning of the 20th century but were hunted extensively because they were alleged to have threatened sheep. They have been extinct since 1933 when the last one died in the Hobart Zoo. That is the official story but the number of sightings since have rivalled sightings of flying saucers.

The tiger, or thylacine, was about 1.5 m long, and had light brown fur with dark stripes across its lower back and what are thought to be the widest opening jaws of any mammal. In Jan 1995, an officer of the Parks and Wildlife Service, normally a most phlegmatic and cool-headed bunch, observed a tiger in the eastern Pyengana region. The government launched an investigation to confirm its existence. It is rare to meet a Tasmanian who truly believes the tiger is extinct – that it is not still out there in impenetrable bush. Tiger skins and a preserved tiger can be seen in Hobart Museum.

The Tasmanian devil is appropriately named. It is an ugly, mostly black, dog-like animal with large jaws and strong teeth. It has a ferocious nature, and is not the sort of animal you can pick up for a cuddle.

alarmed by these events, planned to round up the remaining Aborigines and confine them to Bruny Island. In 1830, a militia of 3,000 settlers formed an armed human barrier, the Black Line, to sweep across the island, clearing Aborigines before them in preparation for 'resettlement'. The line failed, and in the end only 135 Aboriginal people were found to be moved to a makeshift settlement on Flinders Island. Within four years, most had died: a dreadful record.

A word should, perhaps, be said about the relationship between Tasmanians — called Taswegians by most other Australians — and those other Australians. On both sides there is the suggestion, not much more than that, that they are a nation apart. Somerset Maugham, who ever had a poisonous pen, wrote in *The Bread-Winner*, 'You know, of course, that the Tasmanians, who never committed adultery, are now extinct.' There is, indeed, a feeling in Australia that Taswegians are more moral than the average Australian and are perhaps more temperate, more sober, even slightly dull and settled in their ways.

TASMANIA

It is not generally realised that the most impenetrable jungle in the world is in Tasmania, nor that parts of the state are still unexplored – it is too difficult to hack your way in. More than 20 per cent of Tasmania is covered by national parks or reserved areas, and although these have been the subject of enormous and heartfelt antagonisms, still not fully resolved (see p. 446), they give Tasmania unrivalled regions of wild beauty. Tasmania's central plateau has an average height above sea level of 1000 m in the south and is scattered with some 3,000 lakes of assorted sizes.

Tasmania escapes the excesses of Australia's summer heat. Winter evenings can be a bit nippy and warmer clothes are useful no matter what the season. But Tasmania is not, despite what many Australians would have you believe, a cold-climate country. It is closer to the equator than Rome and is warmer, on average, than Madrid.

Getting there is very easy because there are frequent daily flights from every other Australian state (see Hobart, p. 437). You can also take the car ferry across the Bass Strait to Devonport (see p. 462). It may appear to be stating the obvious but Tasmania is a state of Australia. Australians sometimes get this wrong and, more understandably, so do visitors. There is no duty-free allowance when you fly into Tasmania.

The island has four major towns. Hobart, the capital, in the south and Launceston in the north are rated as cities although Hobart has a population of roughly 200,000 and Launceston less than 100,000. The port towns of Burnie and Devonport are on the north coast. All the towns are joined by what are grandly called National Highways and what would be called country roads in other countries. The highways are sealed and are of good quality although they are, like most Australian roads, fairly narrow. In wilderness areas there are unsealed roads which can quite often be navigated by a normal car, but care must be taken (see conditions for car hire, p. 24). Four-wheel drive vehicles must stay on marked tracks and roads. Unlike roads in most parts of the rest of Australia, the roads of Tasmania twist and turn their way through the landscape, so the average journey time tends to be longer by a margin of say 25 per cent than it would be in other states. Despite claims by the locals, traffic jams do not exist in Tasmania.

Hobart has always had a singular advantage because of its siting. The city is on the west bank of the Derwent River estuary with, rising behind it, the forest-clad slopes of Mt Wellington, which is snow-capped for several months of the year. In such a beautiful setting it would be difficult for a city to be ugly. But Hobart is also one of the most beautiful cities in Australia, possibly because for a long time it escaped the ravages of developers.

In 1803 the governor of New South Wales dispatched a Lieutenant Bowen to found a village at Risdon Cove, on the Derwent estuary. At the same time he sent Captain David Collins to occupy a site on Port Phillip Bay on the south coast of the mainland (see p. 189). Collins reported that the place was unsatisfactory for settlement and received permission to transfer to Tasmania. In Feb 1804 Collins took over from Bowen at Risdon and a few days later decamped to the present site of Hobart. The village of tents and wattle-and-daub huts that soon grew up was named after Robert Hobart, Fourth Earl of Buckinghamshire and Secretary of State for the colonies. When Governor Lachlan Macquarie visited in 1811, the straggle of makeshift huts offended his Scots sense of order and good discipline, so he ordered a survey and had building regulations instituted. The town started to grow: in 1813 it became the administrative centre for all of Van Diemen's Land and in 1825 the colonial capital of Van Diemanís Land. It was by now a solid, well-to-do town hardly less important than Sydney, with a population of 5000.

Today Hobart explodes at its once-a-year party that is the Sydney to Hobart Yacht Race (see p. 441), but throughout the year the city operates with an immense amount of style.

GETTING THERE AND GETTING AROUND

Hobart airport is 26 km east of the city. A shuttle service, run by Redline, is much cheaper than a taxi.

Ferries from the mainland arrive, not in Hobart, but in Devonport, on the north side of the island (see p. 462).

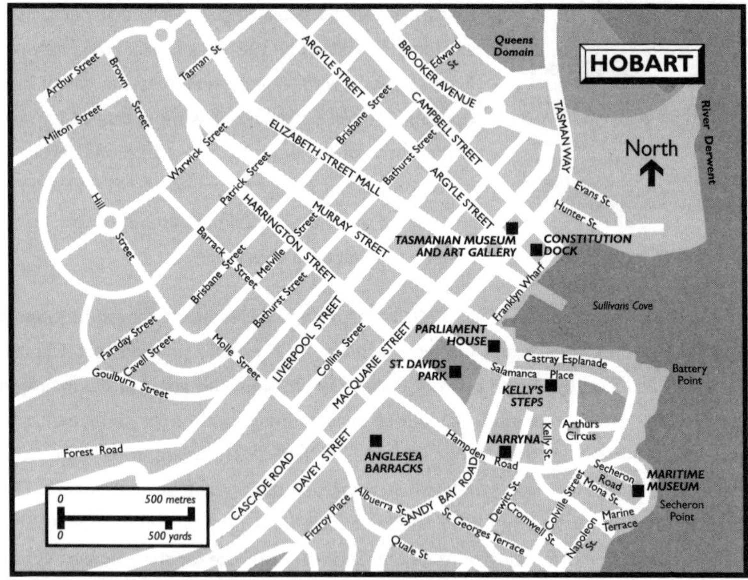

Hobart is quite compact and the easiest way to see it is to walk. Alternatively you can buy multiple tickets for the excellent public transport system, called the Hobart Metro. The eastern bank of the Derwent is connected to the rest of the city by the Tasman Bridge (rebuilt after being rammed by a ship in 1975) and Bowen Bridge, and also a ferry service from Brooke St Pier, but this only operates on weekdays.

For exploring further afield, the best way is by hired car. All the major car hire companies are there but also some which are less expensive. Worth checking are Advance Car Rentals (call toll-free 1800 030 118); Bargain Cars, 173 Harrington St; tel: 6234 6959; or Rent A Bug in Hobart; tel: 6231 0300.

INFORMATION

Tasmanian Travel and Information Centre, 20 Davey St; tel: 6230 8233.

INTERNET SITES **Hobart City Council** http://www.hcc.tas.gov.au/start.htm

If you log on to www.tco.asn.au you can get an up-to-the-minute list of online access centres around Tasmania.

POST AND PHONES The main post office is in Elizabeth St. The phone code for Tasmania is 03 (confusingly, the same as Victoria).

ACCOMMODATION

The amount of accommodation available in Hobart is quite remarkable given the size of the town. Tasmania, more than any other Australian state, offers a wide range of bed and -breakfast establishments. If you intend staying for any length of time they are worth checking out with the tourist office.

Alabama Hotel $ 72 Liverpool St; tel: 6234 3737.

Brunswick Hotel $ 67 Liverpool St; tel: 6234 4981.

Country Comfort $$ 34 Murray St; tel: 6223 4355.

Fountainside Motor Inn $$ Liverpool St, cnr Brooker Ave; tel: 6234 2911.

Hillpark House $$ 344 Park St; tel: 6228 7094. English cooked breakfast. 5 mins from city.

Hobart Macquarie Motor Inn $$ 167 Macquarie St; tel: 6234 4422.

Hobart Midcity Motor Inn $$ 96 Bathurst St; tel: 6234 6333.

Lodge on Elizabeth $$ 249 Elizabeth St; tel: 6231 3830.

National Park Hotel $$ National Park; tel: 6288 1103.

Westside Hotel $$$ 156 Bathurst St; tel: 6232 6255.

Woolstore $$ Macquarie St; tel: 6235 5355. Big apartments and hotel rooms.

FOOD AND DRINK

The Tasmania tourist office hate this being mentioned but eating out in Tasmania tends to be noticeably more expensive than in the rest of Australia. There is no particular reason why this should be so. Much of the dining action in Hobart takes place within strolling distance of Salamanca Place.

Amigo's $$ 329 Elizabeth St; tel: 6236 6115. Mexican, BYO. Open daily.

Berties Pasta Restaurant $ 115 Collins St; tel: 6223 3595. Fresh pasta made on the premises. Open Mon–Sat 0900–2300.

Chinese Lantern Restaurant $ 186 Collins St; tel: 6234 9595. Cantonese. Open Mon–Sat, lunch and dinner. Licensed.

Drunken Admiral $$ 17–19 Hunter St; tel: 6234 1903. In an early waterfront warehouse. Seafood, licensed.

Fortuna Restaurant $$ 275 Elizabeth St; tel: 6234 3731. Vegetarian Chinese, BYO, licensed. Open seven days.

Le Provencal $$ 417 Macquarie St; tel: 6224 2526. Open dinner Tues–Sat. French provincial cooking.

Meehan's Restaurant $$ 1 Davey St; tel: 6235 4535. Lunch Mon–Fri, dinner Mon–Sat. Wonderful views of the waterfront with the food nearly as good. Tries very hard for a unique Tasmanian cuisine. Non-smoking.

Mikaku Japanese Restaurant $$$ Salamanca Pl; tel: 6224 0882. Japanese, licensed. Open daily. Be warned, they have karaoke parties upstairs.

Mure's Upper Deck Restaurant $$$ Victoria Dock; tel: 6231 2121. Seafood, licensed. Open daily for lunch and dinner.

Panache Café Restaurant $$ 89 Salamanca Pl; tel: 6224 2929. Seafood and Tasmanian wines with outdoor dining. Open daily.

Paris $$ 356 Macquarie St; tel: 6224 2200. Classic French cooking. BYO.

Prego $$ 196 Macquarie St; tel: 6223 2362. Italian nouvelle cuisine which is something of a contradiction in terms, licensed, BYO. Open daily for dinner, Tues–Fri for lunch.

Salamanca's Food Fair & Café $ 55 Salamanca Pl; tel: 6224 3667. Licensed café. Open seven days. Good for light snacks and a glass of wine.

Seoul Restaurant $$ 149b Collins St; tel: 6234 7090. Korean, Licensed. Open Mon–Sat for dinner.

Sisco's Restaurant $$ Murray St Pier; tel: 6223 2059. Spanish, licensed, BYO. Open Mon–Sat.

Zanskar Café $ 39 Barrack St; tel: 6231 3983. Vegetarian, no alcohol. Open Mon–Fri. Don't even think about smoking.

HIGHLIGHTS

It is easy to find your way around Hobart. In the centre the streets are arranged around the Elizabeth St Mall, which runs down to the waterfront wharfs. Salamanca Place runs along the south side of the waterfront towards the well-preserved early colonial district of Battery Point. Follow the river around from Battery Point and you come to Sandy Bay. Here stands Hobart's university and Wrest Point Casino, one of Hobart's landmarks. To the north of the centre is the Domain, a recreation area that

THE SYDNEY TO HOBART YACHT RACE

One of the world's great sailing events began shortly after World War II as a suggested post-Christmas cruise out from Sydney; it escalated into a race to Hobart. Of the nine yachts competing only one completed it — Rani, skippered by Captain John Illingworth RN, a guest of the Sydney Cruising Yacht Club. The race, which takes place between Christmas and the New Year, is unremittingly tough — in 1993, for example, only 38 of the 104 yachts finished. At the end awaits Constitution Dock and the celebration of The Little Drink, a party where the quantity of beer drunk per head of crew is not printable lest it cast a doubt on all the other statistics. It defies belief.

includes the Royal Botanic Gardens and abuts the Derwent River.

Hobart is defined by its position on the Derwent estuary and its deep water port – one of the ten deepest city ports in the world. The waterfront has strenuously resisted modernisation and still shows its rich historical associations and unique, picturesque charm. The central Franklin Wharf bounds **Constitution Dock**, where the annual Sydney to Hobart Yacht Race ends, and nearby is Hunter St, which has a row of fine Georgian warehouses that have not been tarted up.

A warehouse behind Constitution Dock, built in 1808 and so probably the oldest building in central Hobart, now contains the **Tasmanian Museum and Art Gallery**. It includes the commissariat store (1808) which issued the supplies for the people and the new colony; the bond store (1824); and the Cottage, built originally as a private store or stable before 1810 and converted into a residence for the Governor's secretary in 1828. Among the exhibits are some splendid photographs of the allegedly extinct Tasmanian tiger. 40 Macquarie St; open daily 1000–1700.

The **Allport Library and Museum of Fine Arts** at 91 Murray St is one of the four collections of the State Library Service. The Allport family settled in Van Diemen's Land in 1831. Henry Allport, a Hobart solicitor, died in 1965 and gave to the people of Tasmania his collection of 18th- and 19th-century furniture, colonial paintings, silver, objets d'art, fine china and rare and antique books. It is housed on the ground floor of the State Library. Open Mon–Fri 0930–1700.

SALAMANCA MARKET

The market began in 1972 with ten stalls occupying a small section of Salamanca Place; it has now become something of an institution. The 'Winter' market operates 0830–1400 and the 'Summer' market 0830–1500. There are some 300 stalls and the place has a tremendous buzz and a rather alternative feel. As you shop you are serenaded by a harpist who is a classical musician of repute. A cassette of his music makes a marvellous souvenir of Tasmania.

The heart of the old city is **Salamanca Place**, one of the more elegant courtyards of Australia. The square is surrounded by sandstone warehouses constructed in the early 1830s, a prime example of Australian colonial architecture. They were the centre of Hobart Town's trade and commerce, catering in large part for the whaling trade. Today they contain galleries, restaurants, nightspots and shops. Every Sat morning a popular open-air craft market is held here.

Parliament House is at the north end of Salamanca Place with the law courts directly opposite. Parliament House was built by convicts between 1835 and 1840, initially as Hobart's first customs house and bond store: it was converted to parliamentary use when the colony became self-governing in 1856. Now the lower ground floor has become a museum of historical archives and is open to the public on weekdays. The oak plantation that you see as you approach was planted while the building was under construction.

Alongside is **St David's Park**, which was built on the site of the first cemetery. Some of the tombstones have been moved and set into sandstone walls as a reminder of the early days of Hobart and of the difficulties the earliest settlers faced.

From Salamanca Place it is only a short walk – up Kelly's steps at the end of the square and follow the signs – to **Battery Point**. This was named after the battery of guns placed here when the British government was seriously concerned that the Russian fleet would invade outposts of the British Empire. That this was a total nonsense was shown a little later when the Russian fleet was effectively destroyed by the Japanese. But, at the time, it was believed that the Russians might invade Australia and New Zealand, and you will find such batteries all around the coastlines. The battery still has the **Anglesea Barracks** which date from 1814, making them the oldest military establishment in Australia.

Battery Point's pubs, churches, houses and narrow winding streets have all been preserved and the National Trust has listed many of the buildings. To see its full charm walk to **Arthur Circus** where a group of Georgian cottages built in 1847–52 forms one of the most charming urban landscapes in Australia.

Cutting through this area is Hampden Rd, which has antique shops, coffee houses and colonial cottages. One of them, No. 103, is **Narryna**, a mansion which now houses the **Van Diemen's Land Folk Museum**. The furnishings are in keeping with its age and in the grounds there is a smithy and a collection of horse-drawn vehicles. Open Mon–Fri 1000–1700, Sat–Sun 1400–1700.

At the top of the hill, close to St George's Anglican Church on Secheron St is the **Maritime Museum**. One of the landmarks of Hobart, the museum is housed in a former colonial mansion, Secheron House, which was built in 1831 for the Surveyor-General of the colony, George Frankland. It is considered one of the best examples of Georgian architecture in Hobart and has a wide veranda added in the 1840s, overlooking the Derwent River. The museum was set up in 1974 as a community museum run by volunteers, and has an extensive collection of models, artefacts, artworks and photographs showing Tasmania's shipping history since 1804. Open daily 1000–1630.

On the sloping banks of the Derwent just north of the city centre is the Queen's Domain. At the base of the hill are Hobart's **Royal Botanical Gardens** (open daily 0800–1645), which have some superb formal gardens. One interesting piece of early scientific endeavour here is a wall built in 1829 by convicts. It is connected to Government House and could be heated by means of internal fireplaces to provide an appropriate environment for exotic plants.

Many Australians are willing to swear that the **Cascade Brewery** produces Australia's finest drop. There are tours of the brewery in Woodstock Gdns, south-west of the city centre, at 0930 and 1300 Mon–Fri. You have to book (tel: 6221 8300) and there is a small charge ($$) for the tour. But you get to sample the product.

BEYOND THE CENTRE

Mt Wellington (1,270 m) provides a wonderful backdrop for the city and is only a 22 km drive away, with an observation and information centre on the summit. On a clear day you can see, if not forever, about 100 km inland. The road to the summit is somewhat tortuous and is sometimes closed due to snow in the winter, when the strength of the wind up there could blow a dog off its chain – have a care getting out of the car. Luckily, there is a sheltered lookout.

The **Taroona Shot Tower** is 10 km south of Hobart, along the shores of the Derwent. The tower, which is open to visitors (0900—1730; $), was in use until just before World War II. From the top there are wonderful views of the Derwent estuary. From here you can stroll down to Taroona Beach and then wander the 3 km to Kingston Beach, admiring the scenery as you go.

Just south of Kingston is the **Australian Antarctic Headquarters** — tel: 6229 0209 – which has an exhibition, open weekdays 0900–1700. Kingston is the gateway to the Tinderbox Peninsula. A blowhole at **Blackmans Bay** gives spectacular displays in stormy weather and from **Pierson Point** at the tip of the peninsula are tremendous views of Bruny Island.

DAY TRIPS

Tasmania is often referred to within Australia as the Apple Isle and **Huonville** is the centre of the largest apple-producing area in the state. Although it is only 37 km south-west of Hobart it has a very different style and pace. In Hobart people walk more briskly than they do in Huonville. You can take a jet boat ride on the Huon River or hire pedal boats and aqua-bikes.

Enclosing the eastern side of Storm Bay is the **Tasman Peninsula**, which has superb scenery, many bush walks and a most beautiful and complicated coastline. **Tasman Arch** is a natural arch between two cliffs cut by wave action. At the **Devil's Kitchen** the waves roar onto the rocks hundreds of feet below. The sea rushes in under the rock and shoots into the air at the **Blowhole**. These are all near Eaglehawk Neck, site of the notorious dog barrier that guarded the entrance to the peninsula and to **Port Arthur**, Australia's most infamous convict prison. Nowadays it is one of Tasmaniaís most visited sites..

HUON PINE

The name of the town comes from the huon pine, whose wood is prized for being clean, relatively free of knots and slow to rot. The trees, which are unique to Tasmania, favour swampy conditions and are the second-oldest living things on earth after the bristlecone pines of North America. The timber was used extensively in shipbuilding and also in the construction of some of the pioneer aircraft. Demand was such that the forests were eventually commercially exhausted, and what is left is protected. You will find many craftspeople offering small objects in huon, carved from sunken logs that have been hauled from the rivers. Although it would not be tactful to mention this to Tasmanians, for decorative purposes the wood is pretty boring as it has little figuring and an almost plastic finish.

PORT ARTHUR

A sad and emotional place, Port Arthur is still well worth visiting. From 1830 until 1877 this was the most infamous convict settlement of Australia. Over 12,000 convicts were sentenced to spend time there – it has been suggested that the figure may have been as high as 30,000. Many of them never left.

In 1830 Lieutenant-Governor George Arthur chose the Tasman Peninsula as the place to confine those he termed the 'worst of the worst'. This meant convicts who, while in custody, had committed further crimes. The reason this awful, and awesome, place was chosen was that it offered only one land escape route, at Eaglehawk Neck – and the Neck, only 100 m across, was manned by guards who ran a chain from one side to the other with, tethered to it, between 9 and 18 savage dogs. In *The*

Escape of the Notorious Sir William Heans (1919), William Gosse Hay saw the Tasman Peninsula as a pear and Eaglehawk Neck its stalk. He wrote: 'A few celebrated escapes were accomplished along the Hobart Road from the flower to the stalk, the prisoner swimming over, braving the dogs, soldiers and sharks which watched it. Except by the stalk, how could anyone escape from the pear?'

One of the most astounding facts about Port Arthur is that flogging was not widely used as a punishment. Instead, offenders were sentenced to solitary confinement. This meant, for example, they were allowed to go to church but sat in individual pews so that no contact was possible and the only thing in view was the prison chaplain. When they exercised they wore masks to prevent them speaking to anyone. After a spell of this treatment many convicts went mad; and the madness often led to death.

It would be wrong to think of Port Arthur as just a penal settlement. It had many industries, such as timber milling, shipbuilding, coal mining and brick-manufacturing. In the 1830s a primitive railway running for 7 km was laid between Taranna and Deep Bay. But there were no steam engines involved – convicts pushed the trains.

The penal settlement lasted 37 years, and continued for 14 years after transportation ceased. In recent times a terrible footnote was added to the bitter memories of this place. In April 1996 Port Arthur hit the world's headlines when a gun-crazed lunatic massacred 35 innocent visitors here.

In 1979 Port Arthur's national significance as a historic site was recognised when the Tasmanian and Federal governments committed $9 million to a seven-year conservation and development programme. Now, despite its harrowing history, Port Arthur is a beautiful and tranquil site with green lawns and huge English trees, and it feels more like parkland than prison.

i **Visitor Information Office**, Historic Site, Arthur Hwy; tel: 6250 2363.

Port Arthur and the Tasman Peninsula
http://www.tassie.net.au/portarthur/

Port Arthur http://www.portarthur.org.

WHERE NEXT?

The quaint oast houses of New Norfolk (see p. 449) and the moonscape around Queenstown (see p. 425) are an introduction to some of the contrasting faces of Tasmania, while the island's 'northern capital', Launceston, is just 200 km away (see p. 452).

National Parks of Tasmania

There have been protected natural areas in Tasmania in one form or another for well over a century. In 1863, land was first set aside as 'reserves for scenic purposes'. These reservations were made under the Waste Lands Act of 1863 and subsequently under the Crown Lands Act. By 1899 Tasmania had 12 reserves. In 1915 the government established the Scenery Preservation Board and in 1971 the National Parks and Wildlife Service started in Tasmania.

National parks now cover over 20 per cent of the island, but have been the subject of a series of long and bitter struggles between the Tasmanian government, supported by the majority of the population of the states on the one side, and the conservationists on the other. Towns, families and friends were split in their support, and it would be fair to say that the struggle has not ended to this day.

The government of Tasmania has not always been conservation conscious, as can be judged by the devastated landscape of Queenstown (see p. 462). Then, in 1972, the government flooded Lake Pedder for a hydroelectric scheme. In response the Wilderness Society was formed, which started a war — campaign is too soft a term — against the Hydro-Electricity Commission's next plan, the damming of the Franklin. This was Tasmania's last wild river. The protests ran for nearly ten years. In 1981 the whole south-west area was proposed as a World Heritage Area, but the government ignored this and continued with its plans. The Franklin Blockade, organised by the Wilderness Society, began on 14 Dec 1982 and continued for two months, with protesters lying down in front of the bulldozers. In all 1,200 protesters made the journey upriver from Strahan. Eventually the Labor government of Bob Hawke was voted in and in March 1983 the Federal government forbade further work on the hydroelectric scheme. This created immense bitterness among Tasmanians who supported the dam. They believed that they were being denied employment by mainlanders who rarely visited the state.

The Wilderness Society still exists, and still campaigns, but some of the tensions are starting to ease as Tasmanians find that the wealth of national parks is attracting more and more tourists and that tourism is now a substantial industry.

THE EASTERN PARKS

On the far north-eastern coast, above St Helens, is the **Mt William National Park** which is a native animal sanctuary. Tasmania's only native kangaroo, the Forester, Bennett's wallaby and the Tasmanian devil all live here. **Ben Lomond National Park** is 50 km east of Launceston and is also a major winter ski resort. Closer to the sea is **Douglas Apsley**, created in 1989, which can be traversed north to south in a three-day hike. The peninsula of the **Freycinet National Park**, which lies further south, has white sands, black swans and granite peaks. Within this park is Schouten Island, 1 km offshore. Further down the coast still is **Maria Island**, where no vehicles are allowed, but there is an unspoiled landscape and a wealth of wildlife, including a marine reserve. Access is by ferry from Louisville, near Triabunna.

OTHER PROTECTED AREAS

Tasmania has numerous other regions designated as conservation areas, protected areas, state reserves etc. The first **marine reserves** were established at Governor Island, Maria Island, Tinderbox and Ninepins Point, and much of the north-west shore is covered by **coastal reserves**.

THE NORTH COAST PARKS

To the east of Burnie (see p. 459) is **Rocky Cape National Park** and to the east of Devonport the similarly sized **Asbestos Range** (see p. 459). Offshore, the southern end of Flinders Island, in the Furneaux Group, is protected by **Strzelecki National Park**, which has campsites and walking trails.

THE WESTERN PARKS

Due south of Devonport is the latest addition to Tasmania's national parks system: the karst caves of **Mole Creek**. From here a grand sweep of parks starts in the north with **Cradle Mountain-Lake St Clair**, with its Overland Track and Tasmania's highest mountain, Mt Ossa (1,617 m). The mountain that gives the park its name is probably one of Tasmania's most recognised natural features. Abutting it is the **Walls of Jerusalem National Park**, which has forests of pencil pines and many lakes and tarns. Access is by foot only.

EXPLORING THE PARKS

Daily or holiday passes are available. $. For information, tel: (03) 6233 6191 or www.parks.tas.gov.au

Adjoining Cradle Mountain to the south is the **Franklin-Lower Gordon Wild Rivers National Park** –the park, created in 1980, that resulted from the Franklin Blockade protests. This park is virtually inaccessible. You can fly over it, or explore the edges by cruising the Gordon River (see p. 466) or, if you are adventurous, you can go on a raft down the Franklin – but only between Dec and Mar and not always then, for this is by far the most dangerous rafting river in Australia. The full trip takes 8–14 days. By and large the area remains unvisited.

South again, the **South-west National Park** is equally remote and half as large again as Franklin-Gordon. Almost, but not quite adjoining its eastern border is **Mt Field National Park** (see p. 451). Finally, on the south-eastern fringes and only 80 km from Hobart, is the **Hartz Mountain National Park**. This is a rugged but accessible region, with hiking rewarded by tremendous views.

In 1982 this great mass of contiguous parks, together with other adjoining protected areas, was declared a World Heritage Area covering 1.38 million ha.

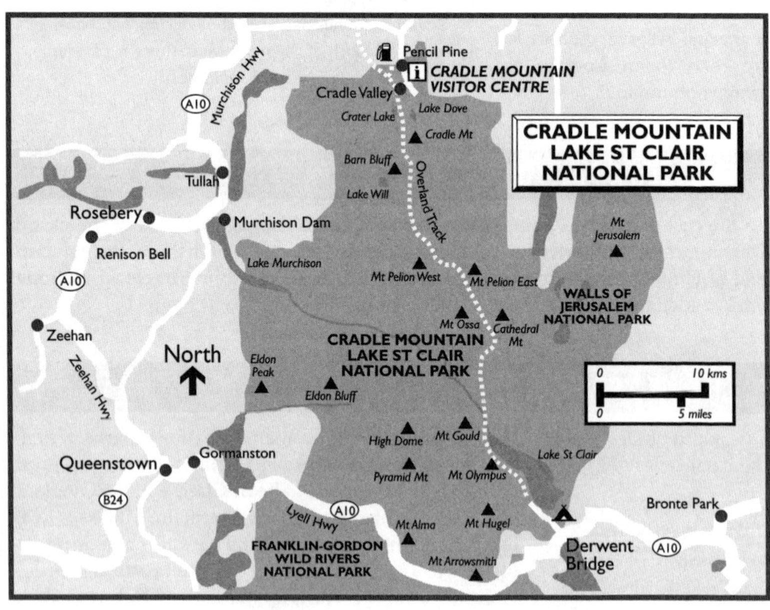

New Norfolk, upriver from Hobart, is at the heart of what was Tasmania's hop-growing country. Although it would be an exaggeration to say that Australia ran on beer for a hundred years, the first experimental crops in the mid-19th century grew into the largest hop farm in the southern hemisphere. Styles in beer have changed and hops are no longer the important agricultural crop they once were, but the area is full of the conical oast houses in which the hops were dried.

The first European to sight the area was probably Lt John Hayes, who first sailed up the Derwent in 1793. The first serious group of settlers to arrive were from the abandoned colony of Norfolk Island. A vanguard of 34 islanders arrived in 1807 and within a year 544 Norfolk Islanders – convicts and free settlers — had been transplanted. They were guaranteed free rations for a year and each was given 4 acres of land to cultivate.

The young town, which Governor Lachlan Macquarie named Elizabeth Town in honour of his wife, thrived so well that the executive council of Van Diemen's Land (effectively the colony's government) recommended in 1825 that it should become the capital of Tasmania instead of Hobart. Nothing came of the plan because of the expense of shifting civil servants from Hobart. Two years later the town was renamed New Norfolk, in honour of its early settlers. The whole town is registered with the National Trust.

Getting There and Getting Around

New Norfolk is 37 km north-west of Hobart, and connected to the capital by the Lyell Hwy (A10). Buses run regularly between the two towns during the week, but infrequently at weekends.

Information

Council Offices, Circle St; tel: 6261 2777.

Accommodation

Amaroo Motel $$ Lyell Hwy, cnr Pioneer Ave; tel: 6261 2000.

Bush Inn $ Montagu St; tel: 6261 2011.

Glen Derwent Cottages $$ Lyell Hwy; tel: 6261 3244. Non-smoking.

New Norfolk Esplanade Caravan $ Esplanade St; tel: 6261 1268. Holiday cabins.

New Norfolk Hotel $$ 79 High St; tel: 6261 2166.

Rosies Inn $$ 5 Oast St; tel: 6261 1171. Non-smoking.

FOOD AND DRINK

Martin Cash Pizza Restaurant $ 15 Stephen St; tel: 6261 2150. Italian, BYO. Closed Mon. Dinner only.

Ponds Restaurant $$ Salmon Ponds Rd, Plenty; tel: 6261 1614. What else but fish? Licensed.

Shanghai Restaurant $$ 50 High St; tel: 6261 2866. Chinese. Licensed. Open daily.

Tynwald $$ Tynwald Park, Lyell Hwy; tel: 6261 2667. Specialises in game. The mansion, named after the parliament on the Isle of Man, is 150 years old and you can dine on local produce in a candle-lit dining room. Open daily for dinner.

Lucki's Takeaway & Restaurant $ 19 High St; tel: 6261 1856.

HIGHLIGHTS

St Matthew's Church of England, facing Arthur Sq, was built in 1823 and is Tasmania's oldest existing church, although only the original walls and the flagged floor of the nave remain. The modifications to the church were almost a continuous process: it was substantially extended in 1833; in 1870 a tower was added; and in 1994 the church was given a chancel and a makeover of the windows, roof and transepts. It is well worth viewing to see if you can spot the original bits and to view the splendid stained-glass windows.

The **Bush Inn** at 49 Montagu St is claimed to be the oldest continuously licensed hotel in Australia, the licence having been given to Mrs Ann Bridger in Sept 1825. Many other pubs have made the same claim but it is very probable that the Bush Inn does hold the record. It has been considerably extended and altered from the original and, in the process, lost much of its original charm. There is a story, which may well be true, that in the 1920s Dame Nellie Melba stood on the balcony and sang opera selections to the assembled populace. As her motto was 'Give 'em muck' this may not have been quite as enthralling an experience as it sounds.

The **Old Colony Inn** further down Montagu St was built in 1835 and contains fine antiques and a collection of items dating back to the penal era. It also has a restaurant attached.

Willow Court is now part of the Royal Derwent Hospital and is the only, and reputedly the oldest, mental hospital in Tasmania. It was originally designed and built in 1830 as a military hospital. The name comes from a willow in the courtyard and the building has much style and presence.

From Convict to Constable

One of New Norfolk's most remarkable inhabitants was Denis McCarty, a Fenian rebel who had been transported. He became the town's constable and built the first house in the district. He also built the road between Hobart and New Norfolk.

Just off the Lyell Hwy is the **Oast House**, which is both a unique museum devoted to the history of the hop industry and a tearoom. The building has been classified by the National Trust. It was built in the 1820s and converted into a kiln for drying hops in 1867. $ Open daily 1000–1700.

Other industries have grown up to take the place of hops. Chief among them is paper manufacture, but trout farming is also important and long-established. At **Salmon Ponds** in Plenty, only 9 km away, the first rainbow and brown trout in the southern hemisphere were bred in 1864. This site is now run by the Inland Fisheries Commission as a historic site and you can visit the farm on Lower Bushy Park Rd any day of the week; tel: 6261 1076. How did they get the trout here back in 1864? The eggs were carried in an ice chest on the clipper *Norfolk* to Melbourne, from there to Hobart on a steamship, then by river-steamer, horses and finally messengers to the farm, where their descendants, some of them over half a metre long, live to this day.

Day Trips

Only an hour's drive away is **Mt Field National Park**. Mt Field was one of Tasmania's first national parks and the area within the park around Russell Falls, near the entrance, was made into a reserve in 1885. This is one of the major refuges for the Tasmanian devil. Some of the eucalypt trees in the park are over 400 years old, 90 m high and 20 m around the base.

Launceston

Launceston is named after the English town in Cornwall, and sits on the Tamar River, another Cornish echo. Indeed, there are many British reminders in this attractive town. A great description came from Elspeth Huxley, when she wrote in *Their Shining Eldorado*: 'Victoriana is everywhere. Buildings in alternate layers of cream and liver-red like a Neapolitan ice, their waywardly pitched roofs flounced with ornament and filled with scrolls; balconies also full of scroll-work; tortured brick, unexpected turrets, multi-coloured tiles, heavy colonnades, thick vaulted doorways, potted palms in dark lobbies; an overgrown English country town. The narrowish streets are packed with people, the women mostly wearing gloves.' They have stopped wearing gloves but the rest remains true.

The first European to explore the Tamar up to the site of present-day Launceston was William Collins who made the journey in 1804. The following year Lieutenant-Colonel William Paterson arrived with a group of settlers and almost immediately the township became the headquarters for northern Tasmania. The town originally rejoiced under the name of Patersonia, but was renamed in honour of the birthplace of Governor King.

The town hall was built in 1864, just in time to take care of the expansion that followed a mining boom in norteastern Tasmania in the 1870s and 1880s. It was this mining boom that prompted the railway connection to Hobart in 1876.

Launceston is bounded by the North Esk and South Esk rivers as they meet to form the Tamar, and one of its most famous attractions is the breathtaking gorge on the South Esk.

GETTING THERE AND GETTING AROUND

Launceston is 200 km along the Midland Hwy (Rte 1) from Hobart, and 100 km from Devonport where the car ferry docks (see p. 457). Buses travel the routes regularly. You can also fly into Launceston from the mainland, principally Melbourne, and Redline provides a shuttle service for less than half the taxi fare.

Getting around Launceston is easy. Everything is within walking distance, and the centre is arranged in a grid pattern, so you should never get lost.

INFORMATION

Tasmanian Travel Centre, cnr St John and Paterson St; tel: 6336 3133.

Despite having been in existence since 1824, the *Launceston Examiner* has shown other country papers how to embrace the Internet. Its website is exemplary. www.examiner.com.au.

ACCOMMODATION

Balmoral Motor Inn $$ 19 York St; tel: 6331 8000.

Batman Fawkner Inn $ 35 Cameron St; tel: 6331 7222.

Centennial Hotel $ Balfour St; tel: 6331 4957.

Hotel Tasmania $ 191 Charles St; tel: 6331 7355.

Launceston Holiday Village Resort $$ 10 Casino Rise; tel: 6343 1744.

Mews Motel $ 89 Margaret St; tel: 6331 2861.

Motel Maldon $$ 32 Brisbane St; tel: 6331 3211.

Parklane Motel $$ 9 Brisbane St; tel: 6331 4233.

Parkside Motor Inns $$ 3 Brisbane St; tel: 6331 2055.

Tamar River Villas $$ 23–7 Elouera St; tel: 6327 1022.

FOOD AND DRINK

Arpar's Thai Restaurant $ cnr Charles and Paterson Sts; tel: 6331 2786. Open daily for dinner, lunch Fri. Licensed. BYO.

Bailey's Restaurant $$ 150 George St; tel: 6334 2343. Holds murder mystery nights. Open Tues–Sat for dinner.

Calabrisella $$ 56 Wellington St; tel: 6331 1958. Italian. Dinner only. Closed Tues.

Franco's Restaurant $$ 197 Charles St; tel: 6331 8648. Italian. Closed Mon.

Golden Sea Dragon $$ cnr Bathurst & Canning Sts; tel: 6331 7728. Cantonese.

Gorge Restaurant $$ Cataract Gorge; tel: 6431 3330. Game. Closed Mon.

Jade Garden $$ 64 George St; tel: 6331 2535. Cantonese. Open daily.

La Cantina $$ 63 George St; tel: 6331 7835. Italian. Open daily, licensed.

Montezuma's $$ 63 Brisbane St; tel: 6331 8999. Open for

LAUNCESTON

lunch Mon–Fri, dinner daily. Mexican food.

Olde Basin Shoppe $ 346 Upper York St; tel: 6331 7118. Baked potatoes and Cornish pasties. For the family. No alcohol. Open daily. Eat in or take away.

Original Pizza Pub $ 111 Wellington St; tel: 6331 4280. Pizza, licensed. Open daily.

Pierre's Coffee House & Restaurant $$ 88 George St; tel: 6331 6835. Open Mon–Sat. Casual dining. Tasmanian wines by the glass.

Quigleys $$ 96 Balfour St; tel: 6331 6971. Specialises in game and seafood. Open for lunch Tues–Fri, dinner Mon–Fri.

Ritchies Mill Arts Centre $ Paterson St; tel: 6331 4153. Casual dining in the old mill. Open daily.

Satay House $$ Innocent St, Kings Meadows; tel: 6344 5955. Tasmania's first and very authentic Indonesian restaurant. Dinner Mon–Sat from 1830. BYO.

Shrimps Restaurant $$ 72 George St; tel: 6334 0584. Seafood, licensed. Open for lunch and dinner Mon–Sat.

Tairyo Japanese Restaurant and Sushi Bar $$ Shop 25, Yorktown Sq; tel: 6334 2620. BYO; open every day for lunch, Tues–Fri dinner. If you knew sushi, as they know sushi!

Victoria's Tassie Fare Restaurant $$ cnr Cimitiere and Tamar St; tel: 6331 7433. A la carte, licensed. Speciality seafood dishes. Open daily.

Woofies $$ Macquarie House, Civic Sq.; tel: 6334 0695. A la carte, Licensed. Closed Sun.

HIGHLIGHTS

Central to the city is Brisbane St Mall, between Charles and St John Sts. To the east is Yorktown Square, a charming area of restored buildings.

The **Community History Museum**, on the corner of Cimitiere and St John Sts, is in the old Johnstone and Wilmot store which was built in 1842 and is still maintained in its original condition. Open Mon–Sat 1000–1600, Sun 1400–1600. **Macquarie House** in Civic Square was built in 1830 and is now part of the Queen Victoria Museum (see below).

The **Old Umbrella Shop**, classified by the National Trust, was built in the 1860s and was owned by three generations of the Shott family. The interior is lined with Tasmanian blackwood timber. It is at 60 George St and open Mon–Fri 0900–1700, Sat 0900–1200.

Launceston has many beautiful public squares, parks and reserves. The **City Park** has an elegant fountain and a bandstand, and **Princes Square** has a bronze fountain bought at the 1858 Paris Exhibition.

In **Royal Park**, near the junction of the Esk and Tamar rivers, is the **Queen Victoria Museum and Art Gallery**. Built in the Victorian era, it displays its imperial splendour both inside and out. It has a unique collection of Tasmanian artefacts, relics and colonial paintings. It also has a Chinese joss house built in the 1870s by Chinese labourers who were brought to work the tin mines. Open Mon–Sat 1000–1700, Sun 1400–1700. Launceston Planetarium is housed in the museum and has shows Tues–Fri 1500, Sat 1400 and 1500 ($). It is one of only four in Australia.

A gentle 10-min walk from the city centre is the nature reserve of **Cataract Gorge**. The South Esk River cuts a deep canyon through the hills near its junction with the Tamar, and as it enters and becomes the Tamar the rivers are constricted into a gorge by almost vertical cliffs. When there has been heavy rain in the highlands this can result in spectacular rapids.

There are two walking tracks, one on either side of the gorge. These lead up to First Basin, filled with water from the South Esk River. There is a chairlift ride - at something just short of 500 m the longest single span chairlift in the world — across the basin to the reserve on the other side, which takes about 6 mins. It operates daily 0900–1630, but weekends only mid-June to first week of Aug. If you are of a nervous disposition you can cross by the suspension bridge, although this is called 'the Swinging Bridge' by the locals and does feel rather less than solid. Either route takes you to the **Cliff Grounds** which are elegant gardens with a rotunda.

Penny Royal World ($$$), near the bottom of the gorge, claims to take you back to a 'world of yesteryear'. It started as a collection of buildings situated at Barton, which was moved stone by stone to Launceston. Exhibits include working 19th-century watermills and windmills, gunpowder mills and model boats. You can take a ride on a barge or cruise up the gorge on the PS *Lady Stelfox*. The mill complex is linked by a restored tramway to the Penny Royal Gunpowder Mill at the old Cataract Quarry site. It also includes modern accommodation, restaurants and a tavern.

TROUT FISHING

Launceston Lakes is a private company that has the fishing rights to five lakes with 5 km of shoreline, all within 20 mins of the city. You do not need a licence and lessons are given on fly-fishing if required. 1166 Ecclestone Rd; tel: 6396 6100.

Further upstream along the South Esk is the **Trevallyn Dam** and hydroelectric power station. The station is close to Duck Reach, the site of Australia's first, and one of the world's earliest, hydroelectric projects. In 1895 Launceston became the first city in the southern hemisphere to be lit by electricity generated by water power and the plant was in continuous operation for 60 years. The original buildings and suspension bridge across the river are still standing.

One of Launcestonís major historic attractions is **Franklin House**, 6 km south of the city at 413 Hobart Rd. It is a fine example of a Georgian-style house and was built by convicts in 1838 for Britton Jones, an early Launceston brewer and innkeeper. By 1842 it had changed hands and, for the next 40 years, it was the W. K. Hawkes School for Boys. It now belongs to the National Trust, which first opened it to the public in 1961 – in fact the National Trust was established in Tasmania in 1960 specifically to purchase the building. Open daily 0900–1700.

DAY TRIPS

North of Launceston, the **Tamar Valley** is Tasmania's premier winemaking region, where most of the vineyards are small and family-run. The tourist office has a brochure detailing a well-signed Wine Route, which will lead you deep into the valley and to the vineyards.

WHERE NEXT?

The northeastern corner of Tasmania is rich farming and forest country. The main town is ***Scottsdale****, 65 km northeast of Launceston. West of the mouth of the Tamar, on the Bass Strait, lie the north coast towns of Devonport and Burnie* *(see p. 457)**.*

Devonport and the North Coast

This is where the ferries from the mainland arrive, and Devonport is often labelled 'the gateway to Tasmania'. It is an ideal base for exploring the northern part of the island, and the chief attractions in the town itself are the Aboriginal carvings and the restored railway.

The first European settler arrived in 1826, but was killed by local Aborigines three years later which had a discouraging effect on settlement. Devonport developed as a shipping port, but a major boost came in 1959, when the ferry terminal for Bass Strait vehicular ferries from Melbourne was established. Although Devonport was named after the English coastal town in Devon, it stands at the mouth of the River Mersey, and visitors from Merseyside will find it fitting that one of the two townships amalgamated to form Devonport was called Formby.

The industrial port of Burnie is also worth a short visit for its links to Tasmania's historically important commerce in timber and copper, and for the rugged country that lies beyond.

Getting there and getting around

The passenger and vehicle ferry, *Spirit of Tasmania*, sails between Devonport and the mainland, docking at Melbourne. The ferry departs Melbourne each Mon, Wed and Fri at 1800 and returns to Melbourne on Tues, Thur and Sat at the same time; tel: 13 2010. This is the most inexpensive way of getting to Tasmania if you are starting from Melbourne. The 240 km crossing takes about 14 hrs, crossing what can be one of the roughest stretches of water in the world. If you are not a good sailor check the weather forecast, stock up on suitable tablets and consider flying. The ferry docks at the Esplanade, on the eastern side of the Mersey, and a Redline bus runs to the town centre.

You can also fly from Melbourne and Hobart, and Devonport is linked to most Tasmanian towns by bus.

Information

Tasmanian Travel and Information, Devonport Showcase, 5 Best St; tel: 6424 4466.

Internet Access **Devonport Online Access Centre**, Devonport Library Building, 21 Oldaker St; tel: 6424 9413; email devonport@tco.asn.au

Internet Sites **Devonport** http://www.tasvacations.com.au/devonport.htm
Guide to Devonport http://www.devonport.tco.asn.au/devonport/

Accommodation

Abel Tasman Tourist Park $ 6 Wright St; tel: 6427 8794.

Argosy Motor Inn $$ 221 Tarleton St; tel: 6427 8872.

Bay View Holiday Village $$ 2 Caroline St; tel: 6427 0499.

Edgewater Motor Inn $ 2 Thomas St; tel: 6427 8441.

Elimatta Motor Inn $ 15 Victoria Pde; tel: 6424 6555.

Gateway Inn $$ 16 Fenton St; tel: 6424 4922.

Hotel Formby $ 82 Formby Rd; tel: 6424 1601.

Food and Drink

Accents $$ 140 North Fenton St; tel: 6424 8411. BYO. European with good vegetarian dishes. Open Mon–Sat.

Autographs on the Beach $$ Mersey Bluff; tel: 6424 2204. Seafood. Open daily.

Chinese Chef $ 4b Kempling St; tel: 6424 7306. Cantonese. BYO. Open daily.

New Mandarin Inn $$156 Williams St; tel: 6424 4398. Cantonese. BYO. Open daily for dinner, lunch except Sun.

Old Rectory $$ 71 Wright St; tel: 6427 8037. BYO. Dinner only. Non-smoking.

Rialto Gallery Restaurant $$ 159 Rooke St; tel: 6424 6793. Italian. BYO. Dinner Tues–Sat.

Spurs Cantina Restaurant $$ 18 King St; tel: 6424 7851. Dinner only Wed–Sun. Licensed. Steaks.

Taco Villa $ Kempling St; tel: 6424 6762. Mexican. Closed Mon. BYO.

Highlights

The **Tasmanian Maritime and Folk Museum** is on Victoria Pde and tells graphically of the rich history of passenger and cargo shipping, whalers, sealers, and fishing fleets dating back to the first white settlement. $ Open daily (except Mon) 1300–1630 summer, 1400–1600 winter.

The former home of Sir Joseph Lyons, the only premier of Tasmania to become prime minister of Australia (in the 1930s) is at **Home Hill**, 77 Middle Rd. It has been made a National Trust property and is open Tues, Thur, Sat and Sun 1400–1600. $.

In 1929 Aboriginal rock carvings were discovered on Mersey Bluff, on the northern edge of town. The site was declared protected, and the **Tiagarra Tasmanian Aboriginal Culture and Art Centre** was established there in 1972. You can see the carvings themselves just outside the centre, and inside are dioramas showing the lifestyle of the Aboriginal people of the region. $ Open daily 0900–1630; closed July. The lighthouse on the bluff was built in 1889 and is said to be visible 27 km out at sea.

A 7-km cycle and walking track extends around the picturesque foreshore from the city past the Olympic swimming pool to the historic Don River Railway. The railway from Launceston arrived in 1885 and the port grew rapidly in the 1890s; then in 1916 a railway was installed to haul limestone from the Broken Hill Proprietary quarries. This was closed in 1963, but local enthusiasts have restored 3.5 km of the original track as the **Don River Tourist Railway**. It starts at Don Recreation Ground, 4 km out of town on the Bass Hwy, and runs along the Don River to Coles Beach, hourly 1100–1600; $$. On Sun and public holidays steam locomotives are used; the diesel used the rest of the time may offend purists but is perfectly acceptable to everyone else. Associated with the railway is a museum which has the largest collection of locomotive carriages and traction engines in Australia.

Nearby **Braddons Lookout**, close to Forth, has a panoramic view of the coastline. Forth's spring of pure water is claimed to have medicinal qualities.

At Port Sorell, 20 km east of Devonport, the wildlife reserve of the **Asbestos Range National Park** stretches out along the coast. It has several marked trails, a variety of animals and no asbestos.

The Bass Hwy runs along the northern shore, dipping inland only to terminate at the remote north-western coastal township of Marrawah. The principal town along the way is Burnie, 50 km west on Emu Bay.

BURNIE

Burnie grew to service the enormously rich tin mine at Mt Bischoff, inland near

Waratah, which came into production in the early 1870s. In 1890 the breakwater was built to improve the safety of the harbour, and the Emu Bay Railway, the only privately owned rail company in the state, was extended ten years later so that it could serve mines in the Zeehan-Rosebery area.

When Associated Pulp and Paper Mills opened a factory in 1938 it quickly became the biggest paper producer in Australia, owning private forest and cutting rights over all land within 24 km of the Emu Bay Railway. This was a cartel monopoly on a grand scale and the company still effectively controls the production of almost all paper in Australia.

Despite being primarily an industrial port, Burnie has tremendous natural charm. Being in a major timber area, most of the houses are made of wood and rise in tiers up the hillsides with views out over the beach and the bay. It also has some excellent gardens and reserves, including **Emu Valley Rhododendron Gardens**, which has one of Australia's finest displays of wild and hybrid rhododendrons around its lakes.

Since Burnie is older than, say, Melbourne it is appropriate that it has a **Pioneer Village Museum**. This is a reconstruction of Burnie's small shops at the turn of the century and is housed in the Civic Centre in Little Alexander St. $ Open Mon–Fri 0900–1700, Sat, Sun 1330–1630.

Burnie Inn, the oldest remaining building, is a single-storey timber cottage built in the late 1840s by shipwright John Wiseman and has been re-erected in Burnie Park. The most impressive building in the town is the **police station** in Wilson St which was built in 1907 as a house and surgery for a dentist. It is Federation finery at its finest.

THE BURNIE FOOTRACE

Once a year the boardwalk is jammed with competitors in the **Burnie Ten Footrace**, one of the richest in Australia. The race draws hundreds of athletes and crowds of spectators every autumn.

The art of the region is well displayed at the **Burnie Regional Art Gallery** in Wilmot St. It has a permanent collection of regional art but also has touring and local exhibitions. Open Tues–Fri 1030–1700, Sat, Sun 1330–1630.

Burnie's busy shopping district leads directly to a boardwalk on the beach.

Round Hill, just outside the town, has panoramic views of the district. **Ridgley**, 11 km south, has picnic grounds and views of five waterfalls, the largest of which is the Guide Falls. There are well-marked and interesting bush walks.

WHERE NEXT?

Devonport is 1½ hrs away from Tasmania's most famous natural sight: Cradle Mountain (see p. 448). A regular bus service operates from the Devonport Visitor Centre and there are several Cradle Mountain day tours. Burnie is the gateway to Tasmania's scenic and historic northwest.

Burnie Tourist Information Office, Civic Square Precinct, off Little Alexander St; tel: 6434 6111.
15 Webnet, 230 Mount St (next door to Carolyn's Café).
Burnie http://www.view.com.au/overviews/burnie.htm

Burnie Town House $$ 139 Wilson St; tel: 6431 4455.
Duck House $$ 26 Queen St; tel: 6431 1712.
Glen Osborne House $$ 9 Aileen Cres; tel: 6431 9866.
Top of the Town Hotel-Motel $$ 195 Mount St; tel: 6431 4444.
Weller's Inn $ 36 Queen St; tel: 6431 1088.

Burnleigh $$ 8 Alexander St; tel: 6431 3947. A la carte. Licensed. Open daily for lunch and dinner.
Carolyn's $ Shop 2, 230 Mount St. Sheila, who runs it, claims the best cappuccino in Burnie. Open Mon–Fri 0830–1700, Sat 1000–1200.
Fortuna Garden $$ 66 Wilson St; tel: 6431 9035. Cantonese and Szechuan dishes; open daily. BYO and licensed.
Francis Flannery $$ 104 Wilson St; tel: 6431 9393; email: flannery@tas.webnet.com.au. Seafood specialities. Licensed.
Li Yin Chinese Restaurant $ 28 Ladbrooke St; tel: 6431 5413. All you can eat specials. Open daily, BYO.
Mandarin Palace $ 63 Wilson St; tel: 6431 5413. Cantonese. BYO.
Moods Restaurant and Glopots $$ 139 Wilson St; tel: 6431 4455.
Partners Restaurant $$ 104 Wilson St; tel: 6431 9393.
Rialto Gallery Restaurant $$ 46 Wilmot St; tel: 6431 7718. Venetian cuisine – Italian with frills. Licensed and BYO. Open daily for lunch and dinner.
Roses On The Park $$ Burnie Park; tel: 6431 9463. In the Burnie Inn which dates from 1847. Speciality is pancakes. Open daily for lunch, dinner Fri and Sat. Non-smoking.

Queenstown and Strahan

Do you go to visit a place where the local flora and fauna have been destroyed by mining and the countryside has been left looking like the landscape of the moon? This is something for the individual to decide.

Queenstown, the major town on the west coast, was established as a result of the discovery of gold and other minerals at nearby Mt Lyell, and mining has been continuous in this area since 1888. The gold ran out in 1891 and its place was taken by copper. The copper smelters started in 1895 and all the timber in the area was used to fire the furnaces. This process, until relatively recently, gave off sulphur fumes which prevented regeneration of the vegetation. To add to this heavy rain washed away the exposed topsoil and the minerals stained the skeletal rocks purple, grey and pink — the town is surrounded and overshadowed by brightly stained, naked hills.

In 1922 a change in processing eliminated many of the fumes and, little by little, there has been a very slow regeneration of plant cover. There are now two schools of thought. One is that the colours of this industrially created wasteland are, in themselves, a tourist attraction. The other is that the landscape should be restored as quickly as possible to some semblance of normality. As it stands there are impressive – or depressive — mountain views from the town centre and the first 3 km of the Lyell Hwy as it climbs steeply out of Queenstown is spectacular.

Strahan, the one-time port for Queenstown, has its own memorials to the heyday of mining, and is the access point for Tasmania's great south-western wilderness.

GETTING THERE AND GETTING AROUND

Queenstown is 270 km from Hobart along the Lyell Hwy. Buses run between the two towns, but not every day.

INFORMATION

Royal Automobile Club of Tasmania, Orr St; tel: 6471 1974.

Internet Site **Queenstown Tourism** http://www.queenstown.tco.asn.au/

ACCOMMODATION

Commercial Hotel $ Driffield St; tel: 6471 1826.

Gold Rush Motor Inn $$ Batchelor St; tel: 6471 1005.

Mountain View Holiday Lodge $$ Penghana Rd; tel: 6471 1163.

Mt Lyell Motor Inn $$ 1 Orr St; tel: 6471 1888. In 1898 this used to be the stock exchange.

Penghana $ 32 Esplanade; tel: 6471 2650. Community-owned: four rooms available and run as a bed and breakfast.

Queenstown Cabin $ 19 Grafton St; tel: 6471 1332.

Queenstown Motor Lodge Motel $ 54–8 Orr St; tel: 6471 1866.

Silver Hills Motel $$ Penghana Rd; tel: 6471 1755. Formerly single men's quarters for employees of the mine.

Westcoaster Motor Inn $$ Batchelor St; tel: 6471 1033.

FOOD AND DRINK

This is not a gourmet town but you will not starve. Stick to the seafood, which will be freshly caught – and choose to have it served as simply as possible.

Franklin Manor $$ The Esplanade; tel: 6471 7311. Open daily for dinner. Seafood.

Hamers Craypot Inn $$ The Esplanade; tel: 6471 7191. Open daily for dinner. Seafood.

Milan's Pizza Bar Restaurant $ 109 Port Rd; tel: 6447 2102.

Vic's Bistro Restaurant $$ 1 Penghana Rd; tel: 6471 1163. BYO.

HIGHLIGHTS

Despite the ugliness of the surrounding countryside Queenstown is listed as a historic town. You can see some of the reasons in the **Eric Thomas Galley Museum**. This was the Imperial Hotel, the first brick hotel in the town, and now 21 of its rooms house a photographic collection of mining life in the area. $ Corner of Driffield and Stitch Sts; open Mon–Fri 1000–1630, Sat, Sun 1300–1630.

The refinery closed in 1964, the smelters in 1969 and the West Lyell mine in 1972, but

MINING GHOST TOWNS

A 30-min drive from Queenstown is **Zeehan**. A century ago this was Tasmania's third largest town, with 26 hotels and a population of 10,000. One tin mine still operates and many of the townís historic buildings have survived including the Gaiety Theatre, at one time the largest theatre in Australia.

Gormanston, near Mt Lyell, was set up in 1881 as the original mining settlement with the discovery of Iron Blow. At the beginning of the 20th century it was quite a prosperous mining town but, now home to less than a dozen families, its glory days are well past – as they are also for **Linda**, 8 km from Queenstown, which is a ghost town in more than one sense. In 1912 Linda was the site of the area's last major mining disaster, when a fire killed 42 miners.

mining, albeit on a much smaller scale, still continues. There are daily tours of the **Mount Lyell Mine** (departures from the Western Arts and Crafts Centre at 1 Driffield St). Surface tours last an hour, beginning at 0915 and 1600, and an underground tour lasts 3½ hours or eternity depending on your endurance. In the holiday months you should book ahead: tel: 6471 2388.

Because of a decided absence of grass Queenstown has the only gravel sports oval in Australia – football and cricket are played on it regularly.

One way of getting an overall view of the area is to ride the **chairlift**, which rises to 150 m. The ropeway was originally constructed in 1895 and is run by Queenstown Ropeways (tel: 6471 2338) from Penghana Rd, on the north side of the town. The chairlift runs seven days a week, no matter what the weather, and the views from the top are extensive if not sublime. The return journey takes about 15 mins.

North of Queenstown, in the Yolande River Valley, is the **Lake Margaret Power Station** which is Australia's second oldest working hydroelectricity station. It was completed in 1914 and much of the original machinery is still working.

DAY TRIPS

There are extensive nature walks on the **Mullens and Franklin River Nature Trail**, and one of the great attractions of the Franklin River is white-water rafting. To the west is the old port of **Strahan** and access to part of the **Franklin-Lower Gordon Wild Rivers National Park**.

STRAHAN

Strahan is the only town on the somewhat bleak and surf-swept west coast of

Tasmania. In 1899, the Mount Lyell Mining Company constructed 35 km of railway to bring copper and passengers here. It crossed difficult country and needed 48 bridges, and in some sections was so steep that rack and pinion were needed to help the two steam engines haul the train up the slopes. The effort was worthwhile for access to **Macquarie Harbour**, the second largest in the southern hemisphere after Sydney. But it was never a port, where ships could easily and safely enter. The mouth of the harbour is only 80 m across and rightly called Hell's Gates. A formidable bar limits the port to ships of shallow draft and they have a very tough time in the rough weather which is prevalent in the area. The first recorded entry into the landlocked harbour was made in 1815 by explorer James Kelly.

SALUTE TO THE MINERS

The men who mined the ore are well remembered at **Miners Siding**. First, there is the splendid **Mount Lyell No. 3 Abt Locomotive**. Built and commissioned in Queenstown in 1898, it travelled almost one million miles during its working life. From 1896 to 1932, the railway was the only transport link between Queenstown and the outside world. This engine, one of a fleet of five, made its last journey in 1963.

Also at Miners Siding is **Miners Sunday**, a tableau in bronze and huon pine by sculptor Stephen Walker. It shows an early miner with his family on his day of rest, and was commissioned by the Mount Lyell Mining and Railway Co. Ltd and donated to the town to commemorate the centenary of the Lyell District.

Finally, 11 bronze historical plaques, entitled **Ten Decades of Man and Mining**, depict 21 facets of the evolution of the Lyell district and, again, are the work of the sculptor Stephen Walker.

In 1821 two ships with 74 convicts were sent to establish a penal colony. It was a tough post. The prison settlement on **Sarah Island** hardly lasted a decade because it was far too difficult to keep supplied with the necessities of life; it became known as the worst prison for convicts in Australia. The convicts lived in appalling conditions and worked upriver for 12 hours a day, often wearing leg-irons. Sarah Island inmates were subsequently moved to Port Arthur (see p. 446).

The arrival of the timber men turned the town into a milling centre for huon pine, which grows well in this wet region (see p. 445). Then, during the mining boom, Strahan became a busy port shipping the copper out. Now the harbour caters mainly to abalone and cray fishermen.

Buildings such as the post office and the Union Steamship Company building are reminders of past prosperity. The Customs House, next door to the post office, houses the tourist office and has details of the **Strahan Historic Foreshore Walkway** that links West Strahan Beach, the town centre and the old Regatta Point railway station.

Strahan's 30-km long **Ocean Beach** is the longest in Tasmania, but visitors mainly come to Strahan for the **Gordon River** and a taste of true wilderness.

This is the wettest part of Australia after the tropical lowlands of north Queensland. It has rugged coastlines, wild rivers, open plains, thick rainforest and spectacular peaks. Tough and unforgiving country, it is virtually inaccessible to all but very experienced and well-equipped bush walkers. It is also precious and has been declared a World Heritage Site, in the teeth of bitter opposition (see p. 446).

The easiest way to see at least some of this wild country is by cruising up-river. A number of companies (enquire at the tourist office) will take you by launch, cutting through spectacular mountain country covered by rainforest. The riverís deep brown colour is caused by the tannin from the buttongrass plains and does not mean it is polluted in any way; it is perfectly drinkable. At Heritage Landing there is a boardwalk that takes you above the rainforest floor.

i **Strahan Tourist Information Office,** Wharf Centre, The Esplanade; tel: 6471 7488.

WHERE NEXT?

To follow the route taken by the mined ores, take the Murchison Hwy to Burnie on the north coast (see p. 460).

CUSTOMS

Immigration and customs services at Australian airports among the quickest and most courteous in the world. But they are very serious about certain things. They are not that worried about whether you bring in two bottles of the demon grog or one, or if you have 250 cigarettes or 300. By and large you can bring most articles into the country duty free, provided they are for your personal use. In fact, you can make your duty-free purchases at the airport where you land, before you go through immigration.

However, customs are tigers when it comes to drugs, animal products, foodstuffs, plants and plant products. They must be declared and if you flout the rules you are taking a serious risk. There are quarantine bins at every airport where you can dump food and other prohibited products. As for illicit drugs, sniffer dogs are used at all airports and jail sentences are almost mandatory. You can bring in reasonable quantities of prescribed medications – it helps to bring your prescription with you.

Despite all rumours to the contrary, you do not go through customs when you fly from mainland Australia to Tasmania (although some Australians aver that this is the case).

ELECTRICITY

The electrical current in Australia is 220–240 volts, AC 50Hz. The Australian three-pin power outlet is different from that in other countries, so you will need an adaptor – most hotels can supply converters and electrical stores stock suitable equipment. Note that this does not apply to laptop computers, which are already set up to take different currents and cycles. If the extension cord to your charger will not fit, and you are staying in a hotel or motel, you will find that the lead for the electric kettle – supplied in every room – will do as an emergency stop-gap. If your appliances are 110V, check if there is a 110/240V switch. If not, you will need a voltage converter. Universal outlets for 240V or 110V shavers are usually found in leading hotels.

EMERGENCIES

To call the ambulance, fire and police services, dial 000. In cities the response will be almost instantaneous; in the country it will depend on the distance to the nearest town.

Emergency clinics are open 24 hours a day in all the major towns and the standard of service is excellent. There is one anomaly: a separate charge is made to everyone for using an ambulance. This is not covered by the health service.

To report loss or theft of Thomas Cook MasterCard Travellers Cheques, tel: (1 800) 127 495; for loss of MasterCard cards, tel: (1 800) 120 113 (both numbers are toll free). Emergency assistance in both cases is also available from branches of Thomas Cook in Australia.

FESTIVALS

The following events are not to be missed if you are in the vicinity (further details will be found in the relevant chapters).

JANUARY	Late January sees the Australian Tennis Open tournament in Melbourne.
FEBRUARY/MARCH	Adelaide has two major festivals: the Adelaide Arts Festival, in even-numbered years; and the Barossa Valley Vintage Festival in odd-numbered years. The Australian Formula One Grand Prix car race takes place in Melbourne at Albert Park (mid-March).
MARCH/APRIL	Bells Beach surf classic, every Easter near Torquay in south-west Victoria.
JUNE	A major event in Cape York (northern Queensland) is the Laura Aboriginal Dance and Cultural Festival, held in odd-numbered years on the last weekend of June.
AUGUST	(first weekend): Mt Isa Rodeo.
SEPTEMBER	Australian Football League (or Aussie Rules): grand final on the last Saturday of the month in Melbourne.
NOVEMBER	Melbourne Cup (horse race): first Tuesday in November at Flemington racecourse.
DECEMBER	The gruelling Sydney to Hobart Yacht Race leaves on Boxing Day. Its arrival on New Year's Eve on the Hobart waterfront is cause for much liquid celebration with the sailors.

OPENING TIMES

It is impossible to generalise about opening hours in Australia as there are major differences between the big cities, tourist centres and small towns. Banks are open Mon–Fri 0930–1600; post offices 0900–1700. Traditionally, all shops and services closed on Saturday afternoons and Sundays – a situation that still prevails in many sleepy country towns – but most major cities now have shopping and business activity at weekends too.

Shopping hours vary from state to state, but generally big department stores open

0900–1730 Mon–Fri with late night shopping either on Thur or Fri until 2100; and 0900–1700 on Sat. Some states have Sunday trading and major stores open 1000–1600. The biggest supermarket chains are moving towards 24-hr, 7-day trading in the large cities, and the trend is catching on elsewhere. Air-conditioned shopping at 0300 in the heat of the summer has distinct advantages.

POST AND TELEPHONE SERVICES

Australia Post provides a domestic letter service and a range of associated postal services, handling more than 4 billion items of mail a year. Most small towns as well as city centres and suburbs have their own post offices. A standard letter within Australia costs 45 cents to mail, and will usually be delivered within two to three days. The international mail service is reliable and quick for both letters and packages - many letters from Australia make it to their destinations within the UK and the USA less than five days after posting.

Australia has an extensive network of public telephones throughout the country, with most telephones accepting coins and prepaid telephone cards — although the move to prepaid telephone calls only is very noticeable. You can buy phonecards in values of $2, $5, $10, $20 and $50 at most newsagencies. Interstate calls are quite expensive during business hours, cheaper in the evening and at weekends.

If you are phoning Australia from overseas, dial 00 for international, followed by 61 for Australia, the area code without the first zero, then the number you want. If, for example, you were calling Sydney from Britain, you would dial 00 61 2 XXXX XXXX. Within Australia but outside Sydney you would dial (02) XXXX XXXX.

Most digital mobile (cellular) telephones will work in Australia. There is total coverage in the built-up areas and fair coverage on every main road. In the wide open spaces you will need a satellite phone to communicate.

SOME INTERNATIONAL DIALLING CODES:

Australia	61
New Zealand	64
Republic of Ireland	353
South Africa	27
UK	44
USA and Canada	1

PUBLIC HOLIDAYS

The major public holidays in Australia are national ones:

1 January:	New Year's Day
26 January:	Australia Day

Easter	(Good Friday, Easter Sunday, Easter Monday): some time in March/April
25 April:	Anzac Day
8 June:	Queen's Birthday
25 December:	Christmas Day
26 December:	Boxing Day

There are other holidays that vary between states, such as Melbourne Cup day in Victoria, the annual agricultural show days in most major cities and towns, and Labour Day. On public holidays, all banks will be closed, most shops shut, and public transport services scaled down to their normal Sunday schedules. Check local newspapers for details of services, facilities and tourist activities that remain open on public holidays.

TOILETS

Public toilets do exist, but they are few in number and not noted for their scrupulous cleanliness. However, all petrol stations have clean toilets and, although these are supposedly reserved for customers, there is no problem if you ask politely. All hotels and pubs also have clean toilets which are accessible to the public. In national parks, those supervised by the National Parks and Wildlife Service tend to be clean and usable. The slang for a toilet is 'dunny', although this is regarded as common and is gradually disappearing from use.

TOURIST OFFICES

Like most other countries, Australia in theory invests heavily in its overseas tourist offices and is represented in many countries.

AUSTRALIAN TOURIST COMMISSION

GREAT BRITAIN	Gemini House, 10–18 Putney Hill, London SW15 6AA, Tel (brochure line): (090) 68 63 32 35 (Calls cost 60p per minute, which is offputting.)
USA AND CANADA	27911 Franklin Parkway, Valencia, CA, Tel (freephone): (800) 333 4305 (appears to be a continuous recording).

STATE OFFICES:

NEW SOUTH WALES	Tourism House, 55 Harrington Street, The Rocks, Sydney, NSW 2000, Australia, Tel (2) 99 31 11 11
	2nd Floor, Australian Centre, The Strand , London, WC2B 4LC, Tel (0171) 887 5003/ (0891) 070 707
NORTHERN TERRITORY	GPO Box 1155, Darwin, NT 0801, Australia , Tel (8) 89 99 39 00

	1st Floor, Beaumont House, Lambton Road, London, SW20 OLW, Tel (0181) 944 2992
QUEENSLAND	Level 36, Riverside Centre, 123 Eagle Street, Brisbane, QLD 4001, Australia., Tel (7) 34 06 54 00
	Queensland House, 392–393 The Strand, London, WC2R OLZ, Tel (0171) 240 0525
SOUTH AUSTRALIA	Terrace Towers, 178 North terrace, Adelaide, SA 5000, Australia, Tel: (8) 83 03 22 22
	1st Floor , Beaumont House,, Lambton Road, London, SW20 OLW, Tel (0181) 944 5375
TASMANIA	GPO Box 399, Trafalgar Centre, 110 Collins Street, Hobart, TAS 7000, Australia, (03) 62 30 81 69
VICTORIA	GPO Box 2219T, 55 Collins Street, Melbourne , VIC 3001, Tel (3) 96 53 97 77
	Australia Centre, Victoria House, Melbourne Place , The Strand, London, WC2B 4LG, Tel (0171) 240 7176
WESTERN AUSTRALIA	GPO Box X2261, 6th Floor , 16 George's Terrace, Perth, WA6000, Australia, Tel (8) 92 20 17 00
	Australia Centre, The Strand, London, WC2B 4LG, Tel (0171) 240 2881

It is difficult to reach these offices by telephone – plainly, if large numbers of visitors want to visit a country it is difficult to handle all the telephone queries. (The British Tourist Authority in Sydney started charging by the minute for its calls but abandoned the idea under a storm of protest.) The number of tourists coming to Australia zoomed past 4 million back in 1997 and is now nearer 5 million per year. On the other hand, inbound tourism contributes over $18 billion in export earnings to the Australian economy a year, which puts it among the top ranks as an export earner. It directly employs 7 per cent of the workforce. So you would think a solution to the problem of providing telephone information would be well within financial reach.

In the meantime, phoning for information is not a real option. And donít hold your breath waiting for a reply to a letter or fax unless you are a travel agent. Your best bet is to go straight to the Internet: the Australian Tourist Commissionís official site, http:/www.australia.com, is a massive and comprehensive site, or you might find it easier to try one of the sites listed below.

INTERNET INFORMATION

There is more information available on the Internet about Australia then you would believe possible. Some sites, however, are infinitely better than others.

http://www.walkabout.fairfax.com.au is run by the Sydney Morning Herald. Almost all the information on the site is produced by Bruce Elder, who has been writing about Australia since forever. Nearly every town in Australia is covered and where there is not full coverage you are invited to email your questions, which he will answer straight away. The site has its biases but overall it is an absolute treasure.

http://travel.roughguides.com/content/2818/cities.htm. At one time Rough Guide put every word it published on the Internet; it then stopped, and now it has started again. It is full of good information which is regularly updated. Again, it covers most of the towns in Australia, although not quite as many as Walkabout. On the other hand, it offers opinions about restaurants and accommodation which is missing from Walkabout.

http://www.cowleys.com.au/public/acsp.htm. Cowleyís is a guide to pretty well everything. Type in the name of a town and click on accommodation and you will get a list of what is available and, very important, in most cases gives the price of a single room. This is one of the definitive databases of Australia that is just being upgraded.

http://www/csu.edu.au/australia/ozguide.html. Charles Sturt University has put together this site of links to other sites which will give you information. It works very well but it is not a primary source of information. Use it if Walkabout and Rough Guide do not have the answers.

The search engine Yahoo lists literally thousands of sites but you will find that many of them have gone walkabout or are broken links, and many of the others provide very limited information — normally limited to who is willing to pay. Use Rough Guide, Walkabout, Cowleyís and this book and you will not go far wrong.

WEIGHTS AND MEASURES

Australia has converted to the metric system. For conversion tables, see

EMBASSIES AND CONSULATES

Most countries are represented with an embassy or consulate in Canberra, ACT.

Austria: 12 Talbot St, Forrest ACT 2603. Tel: 6295 1533

Belgium: 19 Arkana St, Yarralumla, ACT 2600; Tel: 6273 2501

Canada: Commonwealth Ave, Yarralumla, ACT 2600; Tel: 6273 3844

China: 15 Coronation Dr., Yarralumla ACT 2600; Tel: 6273 4471

Finland: 10 Darwin Ave, Yarralumla ACT 2600; Tel: 6273 3800

Germany: 119 Empire Circuit, Yarralumla ACT 2600; tel: 6270 1911

Greece: 9 Turrana St, Yarralumla ACT 2600; tel: 6273 3011

Netherlands: 120 Empire Circuit, Yarralumla ACT 2600; tel: 6273 3111

New Zealand: High Commission, Commonwealth Avenue, Yarralumla ACT 2600; tel: 6270 4211

Norway: 17 Humter St, Yarralumla ACT 2600; tel: 6273 3444

Republic of Ireland: 20 Arkana St, Yarralumla ACT 2600; tel: 6273 3022

South Africa: High Commission, Rhodes Pl., State Circle Yarralumla ACT 2600; tel: 6273 2424

Singapore: High Commission, 12 Forster Cres., Yarralumla; ACT 2600; tel: 6273 3944

Spain: 15 Arkana St, Yarralumla ACT 2600; tel: 6273 3555

Sweden: Turrana St, Yarralumla ACT 2600; tel: 6273 3033

Switzerland: 7 Melbourne Ave, Forrest ACT 2603; tel: 6273 3977

UK: British High Commission, Commonwealth Ave, Yarralumla ACT 2600; tel: 6270 6666

Consulate, BP House, 193 North Quay, Brisbane QLD, tel: 236 2575

Consulate, c/o- Hassell Pty Ltd, Level 5, 70 Hindmarsh Square, Adelaide SA; tel: 224 0363

Consulate, 17th Floor, 90 Collins Street, Melbourne VIC; tel: 650 2990

Consulate, Level 26, Allendale Square, 77 St George Terrace, Perth WA; tel: 221 2344

USA: 21 Moonah Pl., Yarralumla ACT 2600; tel: 6270 5000

Consulate General, Level 59, MLC Centre, 19-29 Martin Pl., Sydney NSW; tel: 373 9200

Consulate, 383 Wickham Terrace, Brisbane QLD; tel: 405 5555

Consulate, 553 St Kilda Road, Melbourne VIC; tel: 526 5900

Consulate, 13th Floor, St George's Court, 16 St George's Terrace, Perth WA; tel: 231 9444

DISTANCES (approx. conversions)

1 kilometre (km) = 1000 metres (m) 1 metre = 100 centimetres (cm)

Metric	Imperial/US	Metric	Imperial/US	Metric	Imperial/US
1 cm	3/8 in.	10 m	33 ft (11 yd)	3 km	2 miles
50 cm	20 in.	20 m	66 ft (22 yd)	4 km	2½ miles
1 m	3 ft 3 in.	50 m	164 ft (54 yd)	5 km	3 miles
2 m	6 ft 6 in.	100 m	330 ft (110 yd)	10 km	6 miles
3 m	10 ft	200 m	660 ft (220 yd)	20 km	12½ miles
4 m	13 ft	250 m	820 ft (275 yd)	25 km	15½ miles
5 m	16 ft 6 in.	300 m	984 ft (330 yd)	30 km	18½ miles
6 m	19 ft 6 in.	500 m	1640 ft (550 yd)	40 km	25 miles
7 m	23 ft	750 m	½ mile	50 km	31 miles
8 m	26 ft	1 km	5/8 mile	75 km	46 miles
9 m	29 ft (10 yd)	2 km	1½ miles	100 km	62 miles

24-HOUR CLOCK

(examples)

0000 = Midnight	1200 = Noon	1800 = 6 pm
0600 = 6 am	1300 = 1 pm	2000 = 8 pm
0715 = 7.15 am	1415 = 2.15 pm	2110 = 9.10 pm
0930 = 9.30 am	1645 = 4.45 pm	2345 = 11.45 pm

TEMPERATURE

Conversion Formula: °C ˇ 9 ÷ 5 + 32 = °F

°C	°F	°C	°F	°C	°F	°C	°F
-20	-4	-5	23	10	50	25	77
-15	5	0	32	15	59	30	86
-10	14	5	41	20	68	35	95

WEIGHT

1kg = 1000g 100 g = 3fi oz

Kg	Lbs	Kg	Lbs	Kg	Lbs
1	2¼	5	11	25	55
2	4½	10	22	50	110
3	6½	15	33	75	165
4	9	20	45	100	220

FLUID MEASURES

1 ltr.(l) = 0.88 Imp. quarts = 1.06 US quarts

Ltrs.	Imp. gal.	US gal.	Ltrs.	Imp. gal.	US gal.
5	1.1	1.3	30	6.6	7.8
10	2.2	2.6	35	7.7	9.1
15	3.3	3.9	40	8.8	10.4
20	4.4	5.2	45	9.9	11.7
25	5.5	6.5	50	11.0	13.0

MEN'S SHIRTS

Aus/UK	Europe	US
14	36	14
15	38	15
15½	39	15½
16	41	16
16½	42	16½
17	43	17

MEN'S CLOTHES

Aus/UK	Europe	US
36	46	36
38	48	38
40	50	40
42	52	42
44	54	44
46	56	46

LADIES' CLOTHES

Aus/UK	France	Italy	Rest of Europe	US
10	36	38	34	8
12	38	40	36	10
14	40	42	38	12
16	42	44	40	14
18	44	46	42	16
20	46	48	44	18

AREAS

1 hectare = 2.471 acres

1 hectare = 10,000 sq meters

1 acre = 0.4 hectares

This index lists places and topics in alphabetical sequence. All references are to page numbers. To find routes between cities, see pp. 14–15

If you enjoyed using this book, or even if you didn't, please help us improve future editions by taking part in our reader survey. Every returned form will be acknowledged, and to show our appreciation we will give you £1 off your next purchase of a Thomas Cook guidebook. Just take a few minutes to complete and return this form to us.

When did you buy this book? ______________________________

Where did you buy it? (Please give town/city and if possible name of retailer)

____

____

When did you/do you intend to travel in Australia? ______________

For how long (approx.)? ______________

How many people in your party? ______________

Which towns, cities and other locations did you/do you intend mainly to visit?

____

____

____

How will you travel around Australia? By Rail ☐ By Car ☐ By Bus ☐ By Air ☐

____

Did you/will you:

☐ Make all your travel arrangements independently?

☐ Travel on an Airpass? ☐ Travel on a Rail Pass?

☐ If you purchased a rail or bus pass, where did you buy it? ______________

☐ Use other passes or tickets, please give brief details: ______________

____

Did you/do you intend to use this book:

☐ For planning your trip?

☐ During the trip itself?

☐ Both?

Did you/do you intend also to purchase any of the following travel publications for your trip?

☐ *Thomas Cook Overseas Timetable*

☐ *Thomas Cook World Timetable Independent Traveller's Edition*

☐ Other guidebooks or maps, please specify

____

____

Have you used any other Thomas Cook guidebooks in the past? If so, which?

____

____

Please rate the following features within this guide for their value to you (Circle vu for 'very useful', u for 'useful', nu for 'little or no use'):

The 'Reaching Australia' section on pages 16–20	vu	u	nu
The 'Travelling around Australia' section on pages 21–29	vu	u	nu
The 'Travel Basics' section on pages 32–46	vu	u	nu
The 'Travel Directory' section on pages 467–473	vu	u	nu
The recommended routes throughout the book	vu	u	nu
Information on towns and cities	vu	u	nu
The maps of towns and cities	vu	u	nu

This book will be updated annually, which allows us to amend and enhance the information we include within it, but we need our readers to tell us what they would like to see changed and improved. Please use this space to make any comments you have concerning this book.

Your age category: under 21 21–30 31–40 41–50 over 50

Your name: Mr/Mrs/Miss/Ms
(First name or initials)
(Last name)

Your full address: (Please include postal or zip code)

Your daytime telephone number:

Please detach this page and send it to: **The Editor, Independent Traveller's Australia, Thomas Cook Publishing, PO Box 227, Peterborough PE3 6PU, United Kingdom.**

We will be pleased to send you details of how to claim your discount upon receipt of this questionnaire.

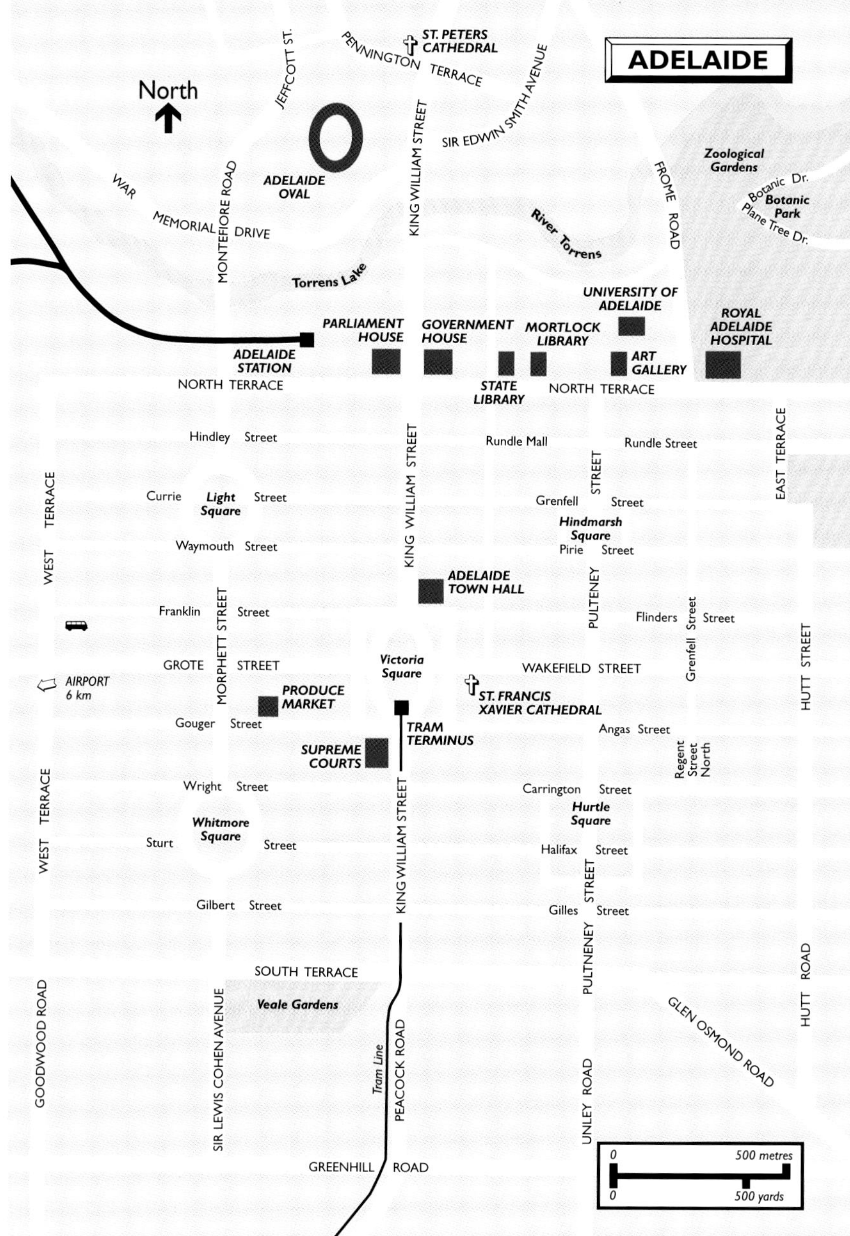
ADELAIDE
North
JEFFCOTT ST.
PENNINGTON TERRACE
ST. PETERS CATHEDRAL
SIR EDWIN SMITH AVENUE
KING WILLIAM STREET
ADELAIDE OVAL
WAR MEMORIAL DRIVE
MONTEFIORE ROAD
Torrens Lake
River Torrens
FROME ROAD
Zoological Gardens
Botanic Dr.
Botanic Park
Plane Tree Dr.
UNIVERSITY OF ADELAIDE
PARLIAMENT HOUSE
GOVERNMENT HOUSE
MORTLOCK LIBRARY
ROYAL ADELAIDE HOSPITAL
ADELAIDE STATION
ART GALLERY
STATE LIBRARY
NORTH TERRACE
NORTH TERRACE
Hindley Street
Rundle Mall
Rundle Street
EAST TERRACE
Currie Street
Light Square
Grenfell Street
Hindmarsh Square
Waymouth Street
Pirie Street
WEST TERRACE
ADELAIDE TOWN HALL
PULTENEY STREET
Franklin Street
MORPHETT STREET
Flinders Street
Grenfell Street
GROTE STREET
Victoria Square
WAKEFIELD STREET
HUTT STREET
AIRPORT 6 km
PRODUCE MARKET
ST. FRANCIS XAVIER CATHEDRAL
Gouger Street
TRAM TERMINUS
Angas Street
SUPREME COURTS
Regent Street North
Wright Street
Carrington Street
Hurtle Square
WEST TERRACE
Whitmore Square
Sturt Street
Halifax Street
Gilbert Street
Gilles Street
PULTNENEY STREET
SOUTH TERRACE
Veale Gardens
GOODWOOD ROAD
SIR LEWIS COHEN AVENUE
Tram Line
PEACOCK ROAD
UNLEY ROAD
GLEN OSMOND ROAD
HUTT ROAD
GREENHILL ROAD
0
500 metres
0
500 yards

MELBOURNE

North

Carlton Gardens

Melbourne Airport 24 kms

LATROBE STREET

MUSEUM STATION LIBRARY

MUSEUM OF VICTORIA

Little Lonsdale Street

LONSDALE STREET

HER MAJESTY'S THEATRE

Little Bourke Street

CHINATOWN

Russell Street

BOURKE STREET

MAIN SHOPPING MALL DISTRICT

ELIZABETH STREET

SWANSTON STREET

EXHIBITION STREET

SPRING STREET

Little Collins Street

TOWN HALL

COLLINS STREET

Flinders Lane

FLINDERS STREET STATION

FLINDERS STREET

NICHOLSON ST.

VICTORIA STREET

ALBERT STREET

Gisbourne Street

PARLIAMENT HOUSE

Cathedral Pl.

MacArthur Street

Parliament Pl.

Landsdowne Street

Treasury Place

Treasury Gardens

Fitzroy Gardens

CAPTAIN COOK'S COTTAGE